Computer Concepts II

Portland Community College

CIS 121

Author: George W. Reynolds, Mark Ciampa, Sasha Vodnik, Joyce Farrell, Carlos Coronel, Steven Morris, Mark Shellman, Alfred Basta, Dustin A. Finamore,

CENGAGE
Learning·

Australia • Brazil • Japan • Korea • Mexico • Singapore • Spain • United Kingdom • United States

Computer Concepts II: Portland Community College , CIS 121

Ethics in Information Technology
George W. Reynolds

©2015 Cengage Learning. All rights reserved.

Security Awareness: Applying Practical Security In Your World
Mark Ciampa

©2017 Cengage Learning. All rights reserved.

HTML5 and CSS3—Illustrated Introductory
Sasha Vodnik

©2016 Cengage Learning. All rights reserved.

Programming Logic and Design, Comprehensive
Joyce Farrell

©2015 Cengage Learning. All rights reserved.

Database Systems,12e: Design, Implementation, & Management
Carlos Coronel, Steven Morris

©2017 Cengage Learning. All rights reserved.

New Perspectives Microsoft® Office 365™ & Access® 2016
Mark Shellman, Sasha Vodnik

©2017 Cengage Learning. All rights reserved.

please see 'acknowledgements' page for full list

For product information and technology assistance, contact us at
Cengage Learning Customer & Sales Support, 1-800-354-9706
For permission to use material from this text or product,
submit all requests online at **cengage.com/permissions**
Further permissions questions can be emailed to
permissionrequest@cengage.com

This book contains select works from existing Cengage Learning resources and was produced by Cengage Learning Custom Solutions for collegiate use. As such, those adopting and/or contributing to this work are responsible for editorial content accuracy, continuity and completeness.

Compilation © 2017 Cengage Learning

ISBN:978-1-337-44565-8

Cengage Learning

Cengage Learning is a leading provider of customized learning solutions with office locations around the globe, including Singapore, the United Kingdom, Australia, Mexico, Brazil, and Japan. Locate your local office at:
www.international.cengage.com/region.

Cengage Learning products are represented in Canada by Nelson Education, Ltd.

For your lifelong learning solutions, visit **www.cengage.com/custom.**

Visit our corporate website at **www.cengage.com.**

Acknowledgements

The content of this text has been adapted from the following product(s):

Title: Ethics in Information Technology, Edition: First, ISBN: 9781285197159, Copyright: 2015, Author: George W. Reynolds
Content used: ch3

Title: Security Awareness: Applying Practical Security In Your World, Edition: First, ISBN: 9781305500372, Copyright: 2017, Author: Mark Ciampa
Content used: ch3

Title: HTML5 and CSS3—Illustrated Introductory, Edition: First, ISBN: 9781305394056, Copyright: 2016, Author: Sasha Vodnik
Content used: ch4, ch8

Title: Programming Logic and Design, Comprehensive, Edition: First, ISBN: 9781285776712, Copyright: 2015, Author: Joyce Farrell
Content used: ch2, ch3

Title: Database Systems,12e: Design, Implementation, & Management, Edition: First, ISBN: 9781305627482, Copyright: 2017, Author: Carlos Coronel, Steven Morris
Content used: ch4

Title: New Perspectives Microsoft® Office 365™ & Access® 2016, Edition: First, ISBN: 9781305880290, Copyright: 2017, Author: Mark Shellman, Sasha Vodnik
Content used: ch3

Title: Linux Operations and Administration, Edition: First, ISBN: 9781111035303, Copyright: 2013, Author: Alfred Basta, Dustin A. Finamore, Nadine Basta, Serge Palladino
Content used: ch3

Title: Data Communications and Computer Networks, Edition: First, ISBN: 9781305116634, Copyright: 2016, Author: Curt M. White
Content used: ch1

Acknowledgements

The content of this text has been adapted from the following product(s):

Title: Ethics in Information Technology, Edition: First, ISBN: 9781285197159, Copyright: 2015,
Author: George W. Reynolds
Content used: ch3

Title: Security Awareness: Applying Practical Security in Your World, Edition: First, ISBN:
9781305500372, Copyright: 2017, Author: Mark Ciampa
Content used: ch3

Title: HTML5 and CSS3--Illustrated Introductory, Edition: First, ISBN: 9781305394056, Copyright:
2016, Author: Sasha Vodnik
Content used: ch4, ch8

Title: Programming Logic and Design, Comprehensive, Edition: First, ISBN: 9781285776712,
Copyright: 2016, Author: Joyce Farrell
Content used: ch2, ch3

Title: Database Systems 12e--Design, Implementation, & Management, Edition: First, ISBN:
9781305627482, Copyright: 2017, Author: Carlos Coronel, Steven Morris
Content used: ch4

Title: New Perspectives Microsoft® Office 365™ & Access® 2016, Edition: First, ISBN:
9781305880283, Copyright: 2017, Author: Mark Shellman, Sasha Vodnik
Content used: ch2

Title: Linux Operations and Administration, Edition: First, ISBN: 9781111035303, Copyright: 2013,
Author: Alfred Basta, Dustin A. Finamore, Nadine Basta, Serge Palladino
Content used: ch3

Title: Data Communications and Computer Networks, Edition: First, ISBN: 9781305116634,
Copyright: 2016, Author: Curt M. White
Content used: ch1

Brief Contents

Chapter 1 Ethics for IT Workers and IT Users 1

Chapter 2 Computer Security 41

Chapter 3 Laying Out Elements With CSS 81

Chapter 4 Organizing Content with Lists and Tables 107

Chapter 5 Elements of High-Quality Programs 139

Chapter 6 Understanding Structure 189

Chapter 7 Entity Relationship (ER) Modeling 227

Chapter 8 Module 2: Building a Database and Defining Table Relationships 279

Chapter 9 Managing Files and Directories in Linux 343

Chapter 10 Introduction to Computer Networks and Data Communications 373

Index 398

CHAPTER

ETHICS FOR IT WORKERS AND IT USERS

QUOTE
This above all: to thine own self be true.   —William Shakespeare, playwright

VIGNETTE

New York City Payroll Project Riddled with Fraud

The CityTime project was meant to replace a largely manual, paper-based payroll system for the city of New York (NYC). The goal was to provide a tool that would help city administrators manage a workforce of over 100,000 employees spread across 63 departments. It was also intended to simplify the employee time-reporting process, which was complicated by numerous union timekeeping rules, and to identify employees who tried to fraudulently inflate their paychecks. The project was initiated in 1998 when the city awarded the contract to a subsidiary of MCI, a telecommunications company that later ran into financial scandals and, ultimately, filed for bankruptcy.[1]

In 2001, the CityTime contract was reassigned to Science International Applications Incorporated (SAIC), a defense company. In an unusual move, the handoff to SAIC occurred without the contract going through the normal competitive bidding process required for contracts of this size. Around the same time, Spherion Atlantic Enterprises was hired as a subcontractor to provide quality assurance on the CityTime project, with an initial contract of $3.4 million. The city's contract with Spherion was eventually revised 11 times, with a resulting cost of $48 million.[2]

Richard Valcich, the NYC payroll office executive director during the initial years of the project, accused SAIC of dragging its feet on the project and was skeptical of the company's ability to deliver a quality product. However, Valcich retired in 2004 and was replaced by Joel Bondy, a staunch advocate of the project.[3] In this role, Bondy was responsible for overseeing and re-awarding Spherion's contract. It was later discovered that Bondy worked for Spherion for two years prior to joining the city.

In another questionable move, the CityTime contract was switched from a fixed-price contract to a "time and materials" contract, and the project costs spiraled out of control—from $224 million in 2006 to $628 million by 2009. This switch in the terms of the contract plus lack of project oversight made it even easier for those involved with the project to commit fraud.[4]

At a city hearing in December 2010, Bondy revealed that Spherion employees were billing the city at a rate of $236.25 per hour and that a number of former city employees had become Spherion employees.[5] Mr. Bondy resigned shortly after this meeting.[6]

That same month, federal prosecutors charged several consultants for the CityTime project with a multimillion dollar fraud scheme, which allegedly started in 2005. The consultants were accused of manipulating the city into paying for contracts to businesses that the consultants controlled, and then redirecting part of the money to enrich themselves personally.[7]

In May 2011, federal investigators arrested Gerald Denault, the senior project manager at SAIC, for allegedly receiving over $5 million in kickbacks and for committing wire fraud and money laundering. Denault had convinced his employer to hire TechnoDyne LLC as the main subcontractor for the project. TechnoDyne eventually received $450 million out of the $600 million paid to SAIC and siphoned off millions to a bogus India-based consulting firm owned by Denault.[8] The two owners of TechnoDyne are now fugitives and their whereabouts are unknown. Six other defendants are scheduled to go to trial in 2013.[9]

In March 2012, SAIC agreed to pay $500 million to avoid prosecution for its role in the CityTime scandal; most of that money was to go back to the city of New York. By this time, it was estimated that NYC had paid out $652 million—with an outstanding bill of $41 million—owed on the project, which was originally estimated to cost $63 million and to be completed in 2003.[10]

Questions to Consider

1. What were some early warning signs that signaled things were not going well with the City-Time project?
2. What steps should city managers and SAIC have taken at an early stage of the project to identify and prevent fraud?

LEARNING OBJECTIVES

As you read this chapter, consider the following questions:

1. What key characteristics distinguish a professional from other kinds of workers, and is an IT worker considered a professional?
2. What factors are transforming the professional services industry?
3. What relationships must an IT worker manage, and what key ethical issues can arise in each?
4. How do codes of ethics, professional organizations, certification, and licensing affect the ethical behavior of IT professionals?
5. What is meant by compliance, and how does it help promote the right behaviors and discourage undesirable ones?

IT PROFESSIONALS

A **profession** is a calling that requires specialized knowledge and often long and intensive academic preparation. Over the years, the United States government adopted labor laws and regulations that required a more precise definition of what is meant by a *professional* employee. The United States Code of federal regulations defines a "professional employee" as one who is engaged in the performance of work:

> "(i) requiring knowledge of an advanced type in a field of science or learning customarily acquired by a prolonged course of specialized intellectual instruction and study in an institution of higher learning or a hospital (as distinguished from knowledge acquired by a general academic education, or from an apprenticeship, or from training in the performance of routine mental, manual, mechanical, or physical activities);
> (ii) requiring the consistent exercise of discretion and judgment in its performance;
> (iii) which is predominantly intellectual and varied in character (as distinguished from routine mental, manual, mechanical, or physical work); and
> (iv) which is of such character that the output produced or the result accomplished by such work cannot be standardized in relation to a given period of time."[11]

In other words, professionals such as doctors, lawyers, and accountants require advanced training and experience; they must exercise discretion and judgment in the course of their work; and their work cannot be standardized. Many people would also expect professionals to contribute to society, to participate in a lifelong training program (both formal and informal), to keep abreast of developments in their field, and to assist other professionals in their development. In addition, many professional roles carry special rights and responsibilities. Doctors, for example, prescribe drugs, perform surgery, and request confidential patient information while maintaining doctor–patient confidentiality.

Are IT Workers Professionals?

Many business workers have duties, backgrounds, and training that qualify them to be classified as professionals, including marketing analysts, financial consultants, and IT specialists such as mobile application developers, software engineers, systems analysts, and network administrators. One could argue, however, that not every IT role requires "knowledge of an advanced type in a field of science or learning customarily acquired by a prolonged course of specialized intellectual instruction and study," to quote again from the United States Code. From a *legal* perspective, IT workers are not recognized as professionals because they are not licensed by the state or federal government. This distinction is important, for example, in malpractice lawsuits, as many courts have ruled that IT workers are not liable for malpractice because they do not meet the legal definition of a professional.

Professional Relationships That Must Be Managed

IT workers typically become involved in many different relationships, including those with employers, clients, suppliers, other professionals, IT users, and society at large—as illustrated in Figure 2-1. In each relationship, an ethical IT worker acts honestly and appropriately. These various relationships are discussed in the following sections.

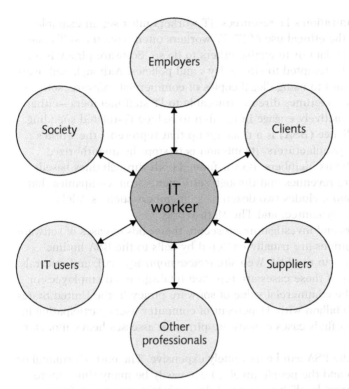

FIGURE 2-1 Professional relationships IT workers must manage
Credit: Course Technology/Cengage Learning.

Relationships Between IT Workers and Employers

IT workers and employers have a critical, multifaceted relationship that requires ongoing effort by both parties to keep it strong. An IT worker and an employer typically agree on fundamental aspects of this relationship before the worker accepts an employment offer. These issues may include job title, general performance expectations, specific work responsibilities, drug-testing requirements, dress code, location of employment, salary, work hours, and company benefits. Many other aspects of this relationship may be addressed in a company's policy and procedures manual or in the company's code of conduct, if one exists. These issues may include protection of company secrets; vacation policy; time off for a funeral or an illness in the family; tuition reimbursement; and use of company resources, including computers and networks.

Other aspects of this relationship develop over time as the need arises (for example, whether the employee can leave early one day if the time is made up another day). Some aspects are addressed by law—for example, an employee cannot be required to do anything illegal, such as falsify the results of a quality assurance test. Some aspects are specific to the role of the IT worker and are established based on the nature of the work or project—for example, the programming language to be used, the type and amount of documentation to be produced, and the extent of testing to be conducted.

As the stewards of an organization's IT resources, IT workers must set an example and enforce policies regarding the ethical use of IT. IT workers often have the skills and knowledge to abuse systems and data or to enable others to do so. Software piracy is an area in which IT workers may be tempted to violate laws and policies. Although end users often get the blame when it comes to using illegal copies of commercial software, software piracy in a corporate setting is sometimes directly traceable to IT staff members—either they allow it to happen or they actively engage in it, often to reduce IT-related spending.

The **Business Software Alliance (BSA)** is a trade group that represents the world's largest software and hardware manufacturers. Its mission is to stop the unauthorized copying of software produced by its members. BSA is funded both through dues based on member companies' software revenues and through settlements from companies that commit piracy. BSA membership includes two dozen or so members such as Adobe, Apple, Intel, McAfee, Microsoft, Symantec, and The Math Works.

More than 100 BSA lawyers and investigators prosecute thousands of cases of software piracy each year. BSA investigations are usually triggered by calls to the BSA hotline (1-888-NO-PIRACY), reports sent to the BSA Web site (*www.nopiracy.org*), and referrals from member companies. Many of these cases are reported by disgruntled employees or former employees. For 2011, the commercial value of software piracy in the United States was estimated to be nearly $10 billion with 31 percent of computer users participating in this illegal activity.[12] When BSA finds cases of software piracy, it assesses heavy monetary penalties.

Failure to cooperate with the BSA can be extremely expensive. The cost of criminal or civil penalties to a corporation and the people involved can easily be many times more expensive than the cost of "getting legal" by acquiring the correct number of software licenses. Software manufacturers can file a civil suit against software pirates with penalties of up to $150,000 per copyrighted work. Furthermore, the government can criminally prosecute violators and fine them up to $250,000, incarcerate them for up to five years, or both.

In 2012, the Alexander Automotive Group paid $325,000 to settle claims that it was using unlicensed Microsoft software on its computers. As part of the settlement agreement with BSA, the firm deleted all unlicensed copies of software from its computers, purchased the licenses required to become compliant, and agreed to implement more effective software management procedures. BSA was alerted to this situation by a report sent to its Web site.[13]

Trade secrecy is another area that can present challenges for IT workers and their employers. A **trade secret** is information, generally unknown to the public, that a company has taken strong measures to keep confidential. It represents something of economic value that has required effort or cost to develop and that has some degree of uniqueness or novelty. Trade secrets can include the design of new software code, hardware designs, business plans, the design of a user interface to a computer program, and manufacturing processes. Examples include the Colonel's secret recipe of 11 herbs and spices used to make the original KFC chicken, the formula for Coke, and Intel's manufacturing process for the i7 quad core processing chip. Employers worry that employees may reveal these secrets to competitors, especially if they leave the company. As a result, companies often require employees to sign confidentiality agreements and promise not to reveal the company's trade secrets.

Zynga is a provider of online social games such as ChefVille, CityVille, FarmVille, FrontierVille, and Zynga Poker that boast over 300 million active monthly users.[14] After just over a year with Zynga, the firm's general manager of CityVille left to become a vice president at Kixeye, a competitor. Zynga claimed that the employee stole files with data critical to the business—including financial projections, marketing plans, and game designs.[15] Zynga filed a request for a temporary restraining order barring its former employee from sharing or copying the information or from engaging in any actions using the information to develop online games employing these trade secrets.

Another issue that can create friction between employers and IT workers is whistle-blowing. **Whistle-blowing** is an effort by an employee to attract attention to a negligent, illegal, unethical, abusive, or dangerous act by a company that threatens the public interest. Whistle-blowers often have special information based on their expertise or position within the offending organization. For example, an employee of a chip manufacturing company may know that the chemical process used to make the chips is dangerous to employees and the general public. A conscientious employee would call the problem to management's attention and try to correct it by working with appropriate resources within the company. But what if the employee's attempt to correct the problem through internal channels was thwarted or ignored? The employee might then consider becoming a whistle-blower and reporting the problem to people outside the company, including state or federal agencies that have jurisdiction. Obviously, such actions could have negative consequences on the employee's job, perhaps resulting in retaliation and firing.

The H-1B visa is a work visa that allows foreigners to come to the United States and work full-time in specialty occupations that require at least a four-year bachelor's degree in a specific field. A U.S. consultant for India-based outsourcing firm Infosys filed a whistle-blower lawsuit against the firm for abusing H-1B program rules. The lawsuit alleged that at a management meeting in Bangalore, Infosys officials discussed the need to "creatively" circumvent the H-1B visa restrictions. The lawsuit further alleged that Infosys brought workers to the United States on B-1 visas (which are intended for workers coming to the United States for short-term work assignments only), but that these workers were assigned full-time jobs. It also claimed that Infosys was not paying the B-1 workers the prevailing wage and was not withholding federal and state income taxes.[16] The whistle-blower filed a separate lawsuit in which he claimed that Infosys retaliated against him for the filing of the visa-related lawsuit by lowering his bonuses, harassing him, and giving him no meaningful work to do.[17]

Relationships Between IT Workers and Clients

IT workers provide services to clients; sometimes those "clients" are coworkers who are part of the same organization as the IT worker. In other cases, the client is part of a different organization. In relationships between IT workers and clients, each party agrees to provide something of value to the other. Generally speaking, the IT worker provides hardware, software, or services at a certain cost and within a given time frame. For example, an IT worker might agree to implement a new accounts payable software package that meets a client's requirements. The client provides compensation, access to key contacts, and perhaps a work space. This relationship is usually documented in contractual terms—who does what, when the work begins, how long it will take, how much the client pays, and so on. Although there is often a vast disparity in technical expertise between IT workers and their clients, the two parties must work together to be successful.

Typically, the client makes decisions about a project on the basis of information, alternatives, and recommendations provided by the IT worker. The client trusts the IT worker to use his or her expertise and to act in the client's best interests. The IT worker must trust that the client will provide relevant information, listen to and understand what the IT worker says, ask questions to understand the impact of key decisions, and use the information to make wise choices among various alternatives. Thus, the responsibility for decision making is shared between client and IT worker.

One potential ethical problem that can interfere with the relationship between IT workers and their clients involves IT consultants or auditors who recommend their own products and services or those of an affiliated vendor to remedy a problem they have detected. Such a situation has the potential to undermine the objectivity of an IT worker due to a **conflict of interest**—a conflict between the IT worker's (or the IT firm's) self-interest and the interests of the client. For example, an IT consulting firm might be hired to assess a firm's IT strategic plan. After a few weeks of analysis, the consulting firm might provide a poor rating for the existing strategy and insist that its proprietary products and services are required to develop a new strategic plan. Such findings would raise questions about the vendor's objectivity and whether its recommendations can be trusted.

Problems can also arise during a project if IT workers find themselves unable to provide full and accurate reporting of the project's status due to a lack of information, tools, or experience needed to perform an accurate assessment. The project manager may want to keep resources flowing into the project and hope that problems can be corrected before anyone notices. The project manager may also be reluctant to share status information because of contractual penalties for failure to meet the schedule or to develop certain system functions. In such a situation, the client may not be informed about a problem until it has become a crisis. After the truth comes out, finger-pointing and heated discussions about cost overruns, missed schedules, and technical incompetence can lead to charges of fraud, misrepresentation, and breach of contract.

Fraud is the crime of obtaining goods, services, or property through deception or trickery. Fraudulent misrepresentation occurs when a person consciously decides to induce another person to rely and act on a misrepresentation. To prove fraud in a court of law, prosecutors must demonstrate the following elements:

- The wrongdoer made a false representation of material fact.
- The wrongdoer intended to deceive the innocent party.
- The innocent party justifiably relied on the misrepresentation.
- The innocent party was injured.

As an example of alleged fraud, consider the case of Paul Ceglia, who in 2010 sued Facebook claiming to own a majority of the company. Ceglia claimed that he signed a contract with Mark Zuckerberg in 2003 to design and develop the Web site that eventually became Facebook. He alleged that he paid Zuckerberg $1,000 for the programming work and also invested an additional $1,000 in Zuckerberg's Facebook project in exchange for a 50 percent interest in Facebook.[18] Facebook lawyers have asserted that the lawsuit is an outright fraud and have depositions alleging that "Ceglia manufactured evidence, including purported emails with Zuckerberg, to support his false claim to an interest in Facebook" and that "Ceglia destroyed evidence that was inconsistent with his false claim." Facebook's attorneys pointed out that Zuckerberg did not even conceive of Facebook until eight months after Zuckerberg did the contract work (which, they say, was completely unrelated to Facebook) for Ceglia. They further alleged that Ceglia's emails to Zuckerberg were manufactured to support his claims. Eventually, Ceglia was arrested on federal mail and wire fraud charges.[19]

Misrepresentation is the misstatement or incomplete statement of a material fact. If the misrepresentation causes the other party to enter into a contract, that party may have the legal right to cancel the contract or seek reimbursement for damages.

Siri, the voice-activated software that comes with the Apple iPhone, has delighted many iPhone users; however, not everyone has had a positive experience. Shortly after one user in New York purchased an iPhone 4S, he realized that Siri was not performing as expected. When he asked Siri for directions, it did not understand the question or after a long delay gave incorrect directions. As a result, the user filed a lawsuit against Apple claiming that advertising for the Siri amounted to "intentional misrepresentation" and that Apple's claims about the Siri software were "misleading and deceptive." Attorneys for this user are considering turning the case into a class action against Apple.[20]

Breach of contract occurs when one party fails to meet the terms of a contract. Further, a **material breach of contract** occurs when a party fails to perform certain express or implied obligations, which impairs or destroys the essence of the contract. Because there is no clear line between a minor breach and a material breach, determination is made on a case-by-case basis. "When there has been a material breach of contract, the nonbreaching party can either: (1) rescind the contract, seek restitution of any compensation paid under the contract to the breaching party, and be discharged from any further performance under the contract; or (2) treat the contract as being in effect and sue the breaching party to recover damages."[21]

In an out-of-court settlement of a breach of contract lawsuit brought by the General Services Administration (GSA), Oracle Corporation agreed to pay the federal agency $200 million. Oracle entered into a contract with the GSA for the sale of software and technical support to various departments of the federal government. The contract required Oracle to provide the government with its pricing policies. The lawsuit arose when the GSA claimed that Oracle "knowingly failed to meet its contractual obligations to provide GSA with current, accurate, and complete information about its commercial sales practices, including discounts offered to other customers, and that Oracle knowingly made false statements to GSA about its sales practices and discounts." The GSA further claimed that Oracle failed to disclose that other customers received greater discounts than the GSA and that, based on its contract with Oracle, those discounts should have been passed on to the GSA.[22]

When IT projects go wrong because of cost overruns, schedule slippage, lack of system functionality, and so on, aggrieved parties might charge fraud, fraudulent misrepresentation, and/or breach of contract. Trials can take years to settle, generate substantial legal fees, and create bad publicity for both parties. As a result, the vast majority of such disputes are settled out of court, and the proceedings and outcomes are concealed from the public. In addition, IT vendors have become more careful about protecting themselves from major legal losses by requiring that contracts place a limit on potential damages.

Most IT projects are joint efforts in which vendors and customers work together to develop a system. Assigning fault when such projects go wrong can be difficult; one side might be partially at fault, while the other side is mostly at fault. Clients and vendors often disagree about who is to blame in such circumstances. Consider the following frequent causes of problems in IT projects:

- The customer changes the scope of the project or the system requirements.
- Poor communication between customer and vendor leads to performance that does not meet expectations.
- The vendor delivers a system that meets customer requirements, but a competitor comes out with a system that offers more advanced and useful features.
- The customer fails to reveal information about legacy systems or databases that make the new system extremely difficult to implement.

Relationships Between IT Workers and Suppliers

IT workers deal with many different hardware, software, and service providers. Most IT workers understand that building a good working relationship with suppliers encourages the flow of useful communication as well as the sharing of ideas. Such information can lead to innovative and cost-effective ways of using the supplier's products and services that the IT worker may never have considered.

IT workers can develop good relationships with suppliers by dealing fairly with them and not making unreasonable demands. Threatening to replace a supplier who can't deliver needed equipment tomorrow, when the normal industry lead time is one week, is aggressive behavior that does not help build a good working relationship.

Suppliers strive to maintain positive relationships with their customers in order to make and increase sales. To achieve this goal, they may sometimes engage in unethical actions—for example, offering an IT worker a gift that is actually intended as a bribe. Clearly, IT workers should not accept a bribe from a vendor, and they must be careful when considering what constitutes a bribe. For example, accepting invitations to expensive dinners or payment of entry fees for a golf tournament may seem innocent to the recipient, but it may be perceived as bribery by an auditor.

Bribery is the act of providing money, property, or favors to someone in business or government in order to obtain a business advantage. An obvious example is a software supplier sales representative who offers money to another company's employee to get its business. This type of bribe is often referred to as a kickback or a payoff. The person who offers a bribe commits a crime when the offer is made, and the recipient is guilty of a crime if he or she accepts the bribe. Various states have enacted bribery laws, which have sometimes been used to invalidate contracts involving bribes but have seldom been used to make criminal convictions.

A former midlevel supply chain manager at Apple pled guilty in 2011 to taking over $1 million in payments from certain iPhone, iPad, and iPod suppliers in China, Singapore, South Korea, and Taiwan. The kickbacks took place over several years and were in exchange for the employer providing confidential information about Apple's production plans, enabling the suppliers to negotiate more favorable deals with Apple. He now faces 20 years in prison on charges of money laundering, receiving kickbacks, and wire fraud.[23]

The **Foreign Corrupt Practices Act (FCPA)** makes it a crime to bribe a foreign official, a foreign political party official, or a candidate for foreign political office. The act applies to any U.S. citizen or company and to any company with shares listed on any U.S. stock exchange. However, a bribe is not a crime if the payment was lawful under the laws of the foreign country in which it was paid. Penalties for violating the FCPA are severe—corporations face a fine of up to $2 million per violation, and individual violators may be fined up to $100,000 and imprisoned for up to five years.

The FCPA also requires corporations whose securities are listed in the United States to meet U.S. accounting standards by having an adequate system of internal controls, including maintaining books and records that accurately and fairly reflect their transactions. The goal of these standards is to prevent companies from using slush funds or other means to disguise payments to foreign officials. A firm's business practices and its accounting information systems must be frequently audited by both internal and outside auditors to ensure that they meet these standards.

The FCPA permits facilitating payments that are made for "routine government actions," such as obtaining permits or licenses; processing visas; providing police protection; providing phone services, power, or water supplies; or facilitating actions of a similar nature. Thus, it is permissible under the FCPA to pay an official to perform some official function faster (for example, to speed customs clearance) but not to make a different substantive decision (for example, to award business to one's firm).[24]

There is growing global recognition of the need to prevent corruption. The United Nations Convention Against Corruption is a legally binding global treaty designed to fight bribery and corruption. During its November 2010 meeting, Finance Ministers and Central Bank Ministers of members of the Group of 20 (G20), which includes Argentina, China, India, Japan, Russia, the United Kingdom, the United States, and 13 other countries, pledged to implement this treaty effectively. In particular, the countries pledged to put in place mechanisms for the recovery of property from corrupt officials through international cooperation in tracing, freezing, and confiscating assets. Members also pledged to adopt and enforce laws against international bribery and put in place rules to protect whistle-blowers.[25]

In some countries, gifts are an essential part of doing business. In fact, in some countries, it would be considered rude not to bring a present to an initial business meeting. In the United States, a gift might take the form of free tickets to a sporting event from a personnel agency that wants to get on your company's list of preferred suppliers. But, at what point does a gift become a bribe, and who decides?

The key distinguishing factor is that no gift should be hidden. A gift may be considered a bribe if it is not declared. As a result, most companies require that all gifts be declared and that everything but token gifts be declined. Some companies have a policy of pooling the gifts received by their employees, auctioning them off, and giving the proceeds to charity.

When it comes to distinguishing between bribes and gifts, the perceptions of the donor and the recipient can differ. The recipient may believe he received a gift that in no way obligates him to the donor, particularly if the gift was not cash. The donor's intentions, however, might be very different. Table 2-1 shows some distinctions between bribes and gifts.

TABLE 2-1 Distinguishing between bribes and gifts

Bribes	Gifts
Are made in secret, as they are neither legally nor morally acceptable	Are made openly and publicly, as a gesture of friendship or goodwill
Are often made indirectly through a third party	Are made directly from donor to recipient
Encourage an obligation for the recipient to act favorably toward the donor	Come with no expectation of a future favor for the donor

Source Line: Course Technology/Cengage Learning.

Relationships Between IT Workers and Other Professionals

Professionals often feel a degree of loyalty to the other members of their profession. As a result, they are often quick to help each other obtain new positions but slow to criticize each other in public. Professionals also have an interest in their profession as a whole, because how it is perceived affects how individual members are viewed and treated. (For example, politicians are not generally thought to be very trustworthy, but teachers are.) Hence, professionals owe each other an adherence to the profession's code of conduct. Experienced professionals can also serve as mentors and help develop new members of the profession.

A number of ethical problems can arise among members of the IT profession. One of the most common is **résumé inflation**, which involves lying on a résumé by, for example, claiming competence in an IT skill that is in high demand. Even though an IT worker might benefit in the short term from exaggerating his or her qualifications, such an action can hurt the profession and the individual in the long run. Many employers consider lying on a résumé as grounds for immediate dismissal.

Yahoo! hired Scott Thompson, the president of eBay's PayPal electronic payments unit, as its new CEO in January 2012.[26] Just four months later, Thompson left the company, due, at least in part, to revelations that his résumé falsely claimed that he had earned a bachelor's degree in computer science.[27]

Some studies have shown that around 30 percent of all U.S. job applicants exaggerate their accomplishments, while roughly 10 percent "seriously misrepresent" their backgrounds.[28] Résumé inflation is an even bigger problem in Asia. According to a recent survey conducted by the University of Hong Kong and a Hong Kong–based company specializing in preemployment screening, over 62 percent of respondents confessed to exaggerating their years of experience, previous positions held, and job responsibilities; 33 percent confessed to having exaggerated even more.[29] Table 2-2 lists the areas of a résumé that are most prone to exaggeration.

TABLE 2-2 Most frequent areas of résumé falsehood or exaggeration

Area of exaggeration	How to uncover the truth
Dates of employment	Thorough reference check
Job title	Thorough reference check
Criminal record	Criminal background check
Inflated salary	Thorough reference check
Education	Verification of education claims with universities and other training organizations
Professional licenses	Verification of license with accrediting agency
Working for fictitious company	Thorough background check

Source Line: Lisa Vaas, "Most Common Resume Lies," The Ladders, July 17, 2009, www.theladders.com/career-advice/most-common-resume-lies.

Another ethical issue that can arise in relationships between IT workers and other professionals is the inappropriate sharing of corporate information. Because of their roles, IT workers may have access to corporate databases of private and confidential information about employees, customers, suppliers, new product plans, promotions, budgets, and so on. It might be sold to other organizations or shared informally during work conversations with others who have no need to know.

Relationships Between IT Workers and IT Users

The term **IT user** refers to a person who uses a hardware or software product; the term distinguishes end users from the IT workers who develop, install, service, and support the product. IT users need the product to deliver organizational benefits or to increase their productivity.

IT workers have a duty to understand a user's needs and capabilities and to deliver products and services that best meet those needs—subject, of course, to budget and time constraints. IT workers also have a key responsibility to establish an environment that supports ethical behavior by users. Such an environment discourages software piracy, minimizes the inappropriate use of corporate computing resources, and avoids the inappropriate sharing of information.

Relationships Between IT Workers and Society

Regulatory laws establish safety standards for products and services to protect the public. However, these laws are less than perfect, and they cannot safeguard against all negative side effects of a product or process. Often, professionals can clearly see the effect their work will have and can take action to eliminate potential public risks. Thus, society expects members of a profession to provide significant benefits and to not cause harm through their actions. One approach to meeting this expectation is to establish and maintain professional standards that protect the public.

Clearly, the actions of an IT worker can affect society. For example, a systems analyst may design a computer-based control system to monitor a chemical manufacturing process. A failure or an error in the system may put workers or residents near the plant at risk. As a result, IT workers have a relationship with members of society who may be affected by their actions. There is currently no single, formal organization of IT workers that takes responsibility for establishing and maintaining standards that protect the public. However, as discussed in the following sections, there are a number of professional organizations that provide useful professional codes of ethics to guide actions that support the ethical behavior of IT workers.

Professional Codes of Ethics

A **professional code of ethics** states the principles and core values that are essential to the work of a particular occupational group. Practitioners in many professions subscribe to a code of ethics that governs their behavior. For example, doctors adhere to varying versions of the 2,000-year-old Hippocratic oath, which medical schools offer as an affirmation to their graduating classes. Most codes of ethics created by professional organizations have two main parts: The first outlines what the organization aspires to become, and the second typically lists rules and principles by which members of the organization are expected to abide. Many codes also include a commitment to continuing education for those who practice the profession.

Laws do not provide a complete guide to ethical behavior. Just because an activity is not defined as illegal does not mean it is ethical. Nor can a professional code of ethics be expected to provide an answer to every ethical dilemma—no code can be a definitive collection of behavioral standards. However, following a professional code of ethics can produce many benefits for the individual, the profession, and society as a whole:

- *Ethical decision making*—Adherence to a professional code of ethics means that practitioners use a common set of core values and beliefs as a guideline for ethical decision making.
- *High standards of practice and ethical behavior*—Adherence to a code of ethics reminds professionals of the responsibilities and duties that they may be tempted to compromise to meet the pressures of day-to-day business. The code also defines acceptable and unacceptable behaviors to guide professionals in their interactions with others. Strong codes of ethics have procedures for censuring professionals for serious violations, with penalties that can include the loss of the right to practice. Such codes are the exception, however, and few exist in the IT arena.
- *Trust and respect from the general public*—Public trust is built on the expectation that a professional will behave ethically. People must often depend on the integrity and good judgment of a professional to tell the truth, abstain from giving self-serving advice, and offer warnings about the potential negative side effects of their actions. Thus, adherence to a code of ethics enhances trust and respect for professionals and their profession.
- *Evaluation benchmark*—A code of ethics provides an evaluation benchmark that a professional can use as a means of self-assessment. Peers of the professional can also use the code for recognition or censure.

Professional Organizations

No one IT professional organization has emerged as preeminent, so there is no universal code of ethics for IT workers. However, the existence of such organizations is useful in a field that is rapidly growing and changing. In order to stay on top of the many new developments in their field, IT workers need to network with others, seek out new ideas, and continually build on their personal skills and expertise. Whether you are a freelance programmer or the CIO of a *Fortune* 500 company, membership in an organization of IT workers enables you to associate with others of similar work experience, develop working relationships, and exchange ideas. These organizations disseminate information through email, periodicals, Web sites, meetings, and conferences. Furthermore, in recognition of the need for professional standards of competency and conduct, many of these organizations have developed codes of ethics. Four of the most prominent IT-related professional organizations are highlighted in the following sections.

Association for Computing Machinery (ACM)

The Association for Computing Machinery (ACM) is a computing society founded in 1947 with over 97,000 student and professional members in more than 100 countries. It is international in scope—with an ACM Europe, ACM India, and ACM China organization. ACM currently publishes over 50 journals and magazines and 30 newsletters—including *Communications of the ACM* (ACM's primary publication), *ACM Tech News* (coverage of timely topics for IT professionals), *XRDS* (for both graduate and undergraduate students considering computing careers), *RISKS Forum* (a moderated dialogue on risks to the public from computers and related systems), and *eLearn* (an online magazine about online education and training). The organization also offers a substantial digital library of bibliographic information, citations, articles, and journals. The ACM sponsors 37 special-interest groups (SIGs) representing major areas of computing. Each group provides publications, workshops, and conferences for information exchange.[30]

Institute of Electrical and Electronics Engineers Computer Society (IEEE-CS)

The Institute of Electrical and Electronics Engineers (IEEE) covers the broad fields of electrical, electronic, and information technologies and sciences. The IEEE-CS is one of the oldest and largest IT professional associations, with about 85,000 members. Founded in 1946, the IEEE-CS is the largest of the 38 societies of the IEEE. The IEEE-CS helps meet the information and career development needs of computing researchers and practitioners with technical journals, magazines, books, conferences, conference publications, and online courses. It also offers a Certified Software Development Professional (CSDP) program for experienced professionals and a Certified Software Development Associate (CSDA) credential for recent college graduates. The society sponsors many conferences, applications-related and research-oriented journals, local and student chapters, technical committees, and standards working groups.[31]

In 1993, the ACM and IEEE-CS formed a Joint Steering Committee for the Establishment of Software Engineering as a Profession. The initial recommendations of the committee were to define ethical standards, to define the required body of knowledge and recommended practices in software engineering, and to define appropriate curricula to acquire knowledge. The "Software Engineering Code of Ethics and Professional Practice" documents the ethical and professional responsibilities and obligations of software engineers. After a thorough review process, version 5.2 of the Software Engineering Code of Ethics was adopted by both the ACM and IEEE-CS in 1999.[32]

Association of Information Technology Professionals (AITP)

The Association of Information Technology Professionals (AITP) started in Chicago in 1951, when a group of machine accountants got together and decided that the future was bright for the IBM punched-card tabulating machines they were operating—a precursor of the modern electronic computer. They were members of a local group called the Machine Accountants Association (MAA), which first evolved into the Data Processing Management Association in 1962 and finally the AITP in 1996.[33]

The AITP provides IT-related seminars and conferences, information on IT issues, and forums for networking with other IT workers. Its mission is to provide superior leadership and education in information technology, and one of its goals is to help members make themselves more marketable within their industry. The AITP also has a code of ethics and standards of conduct. The standards of conduct are considered to be rules that no true IT professional should violate.

SysAdmin, Audit, Network, Security (SANS) Institute

The SysAdmin, Audit, Network, Security (SANS) Institute provides information security training and certification for a wide range of individuals, such as auditors, network administrators, and security managers. Each year, its programs train some 12,000 people, and a total of more than 165,000 security professionals around the world have taken one or more of its courses. SANS publishes a semiweekly news digest (NewsBites), a weekly security vulnerability digest (@Risk), and flash security alerts.[34]

At no cost, SANS makes available a collection of some 1,200 research documents about various topics of information security. SANS also operates Internet Storm Center—a program that monitors malicious Internet activity and provides a free early warning service to Internet users—and works with Internet service providers to thwart malicious attackers.

Table 2-3 provides the URL for the codes of ethics for the above IT professional organizations.

TABLE 2-3 Code of ethics for popular IT professional organizations

Organization	URL for code of ethics
Association for Computing Machinery	www.acm.org/about/code-of-ethics
Institute of Electrical and Electronics Engineers Computer Society (IEEE-CS)	http://seeri.etsu.edu/Codes/TheSECode.htm
Association of Information Technology Professionals (AITP)	www.aitp.org/?page=Ethics
SysAdmin, Audit, Network, Security (SANS) Institute	www.sans.org/security-resources/ethics.php

Source Line: Course Technology/Cengage Learning.

Certification

Certification indicates that a professional possesses a particular set of skills, knowledge, or abilities, in the opinion of the certifying organization. Unlike licensing, which applies only to people and is required by law, certification can also apply to products (e.g., the Wi-Fi CERTIFIED logo assures that the product has met rigorous interoperability testing to ensure that it will work with other Wi-Fi-certified products) and is generally voluntary. IT-related certifications may or may not include a requirement to adhere to a code of ethics, whereas such a requirement is standard with licensing.

Numerous companies and professional organizations offer certifications, and opinions are divided on their value. Many employers view them as a benchmark that indicates mastery of a defined set of basic knowledge. On the other hand, because certification is no substitute for experience and doesn't guarantee that a person will perform well on the job, some hiring managers are rather cynical about the value of certifications. Most IT employees are motivated to learn new skills, and certification provides a structured way of doing so. For such people, completing a certification provides clear recognition and correlates with a plan to help them continue to grow and advance in their careers. Others view certification as just another means for product vendors to generate additional revenue with little merit attached.

Deciding on the best IT certification—and even whether to seek a certification—depends on the individual's career aspirations, existing skill level, and accessibility to training. Is certification relevant to your current job or the one to which you aspire? Does the company offering the certification have a good reputation? What is the current and potential future demand for skills in this area of certification?

Vendor Certifications

Many IT vendors—such as Cisco, IBM, Microsoft, SAP, and Oracle—offer certification programs for those who use their products. Workers who successfully complete a program can represent themselves as certified users of a manufacturer's product. Depending on the job market and the demand for skilled workers, some certifications might substantially improve an IT worker's salary and career prospects. Certifications that are tied to a vendor's product are relevant for job roles with very specific requirements or certain aspects of broader roles. Sometimes, however, vendor certifications are too narrowly focused on the technical details of the vendor's technology and do not address more general concepts.

To become certified, one must pass a written exam. Because of legal concerns about whether other types of exams can be graded objectively, most exams are presented in a multiple-choice format. A few certifications, such as the Cisco Certified Internetwork Expert (CCIE) certification, also require a hands-on lab exam that demonstrates skills and knowledge. It can take years to obtain the necessary experience required for some certifications. Courses and training material are available to help speed up the preparation process, but such support can be expensive. Depending on the certification, study materials can cost $1,000 or more, and in-class formal training courses often cost more than $10,000.

Industry Association Certifications

There are many available industry certifications in a variety of IT-related subject areas. Their value varies greatly depending on where people are in their career path, what other certifications they possess, and the nature of the IT job market. Table 2-4 lists several of the certifications most in demand by employers.

TABLE 2-4 Certifications in high demand

Certification	Subject matter
Microsoft Certified Technology Specialist	Designing and optimizing solutions based on Microsoft products and technologies
Cisco Certified Internetwork Expert	Managing and troubleshooting large networks
Cisco Certified Network Professional Security	Configuring and designing firewalls and the security settings on routers and switches
CompTIA A+	Performing computer and network maintenance, troubleshooting, and installation—including addressing security issues
Project Management Institute's Project Management Professional (PMP)	Leading and directing projects

Source Line: Course Technology/Cengage Learning.

Certification requirements generally oblige an individual to have the prerequisite education and experience, and to sit for and pass an exam. In order to remain certified, the individual must typically pay an annual certification fee, earn continuing education credits, and—in some cases—pass a periodic renewal test.

Certifications from industry associations generally require a higher level of experience and a broader perspective than vendor certifications; however, industry associations often lag in developing tests that cover new technologies. The trend in IT certification is to move from purely technical content to a broader mix of technical, business, and behavioral competencies, which are required in today's demanding IT roles. This trend is evident in industry association certifications that address broader roles, such as project management and network security.

Government Licensing

In the United States, a **government license** is government-issued permission to engage in an activity or to operate a business. It is generally administered at the state level and often requires that the recipient pass a test of some kind. Some professionals must be licensed, including certified public accountants (CPAs), lawyers, doctors, various types of medical and daycare providers, and some engineers.

States have enacted legislation to establish licensing requirements and protect public safety in a variety of fields. For example, Texas passed the Engineering Registration Act after a tragic school explosion at New London, Texas, in 1937. Under the act and subsequent revisions, only duly licensed people may legally perform engineering services for the public, and public works must be designed and constructed under the direct supervision of a licensed professional engineer. People cannot call themselves engineers or professional engineers unless they are licensed, and violators are subject to legal penalties. Most states have similar laws.

The Case for Licensing IT Workers

The days of simple, stand-alone information systems are over. Modern systems are highly complex, interconnected, and critically dependent on one another. Highly integrated enterprise resource planning (ERP) systems help multibillion-dollar companies control all of their business functions, including forecasting, production planning, purchasing, inventory control, manufacturing, and distribution. Complex computers and information systems manage and control the nuclear reactors of power plants that generate electricity. Medical information systems monitor the vital statistics of hospital patients on critical life support. Every year, local, state, and federal government information systems are entrusted with generating and distributing millions of checks worth billions of dollars to the public.

As a result of the increasing importance of IT in our everyday lives, the development of reliable, effective information systems has become an area of mounting public concern. This concern has led to a debate about whether the licensing of IT workers would improve information systems. Proponents argue that licensing would strongly encourage IT workers to follow the highest standards of the profession and practice a code of ethics. Licensing would also allow for violators to be punished. Without licensing, there are no clear, well-defined requirements for heightened care and no concept of professional malpractice.

Issues Associated with Government Licensing of IT Workers

Australia, Great Britain, and the Canadian provinces of Ontario and British Columbia have adopted licensing for software engineers. In the United States, the National Council of Examiners for Engineering and Surveying (NCEES) has developed a professional exam for electrical engineers and computer engineers. However, there are many reasons why there are few international or national licensing programs for IT workers in the United States:

- *There is no universally accepted core body of knowledge.* The core **body of knowledge** for any profession outlines agreed-upon sets of skills and abilities that all licensed professionals must possess. At present, however, there are no universally accepted standards for licensing programmers, software engineers, and other IT workers. Instead, various professional societies, state agencies, and federal governments have developed their own standards.
- *It is unclear who should manage the content and administration of licensing exams.* How would licensing exams be constructed, and who would be responsible for designing and administering them? Would someone who passes a license exam in one state or country be accepted in another state or country? In a field as rapidly changing as IT, workers must commit to ongoing, continuous education. If an IT worker's license were to expire every few years (like a driver's license), how often would practitioners be required to prove competence in new practices in order to renew their license? Such

questions would normally be answered by the state agency that licenses other professionals.

- *There is no administrative body to accredit professional education programs*. Unlike the American Medical Association for medical schools or the American Bar Association for law schools, no single body accredits professional education programs for IT. Furthermore, there is no well-defined, step-by-step process to train IT workers, even for specific jobs such as programming. There is not even broad agreement on what skills a good programmer must possess; it is highly situational, depending on the computing environment.

- *There is no administrative body to assess and ensure competence of individual workers*. Lawyers, doctors, and other licensed professionals are held accountable to high ethical standards and can lose their license for failing to meet those standards or for demonstrating incompetence. The AITP standards of conduct state that professionals should "take appropriate action in regard to any illegal or unethical practices that come to [their] attention. However, [they should] bring charges against any person only when [they] have reasonable basis for believing in the truth of the allegations and without any regard to personal interest." The AITP code addresses the censure issue much more forcefully than other IT codes of ethics, although it has seldom, if ever, been used to censure practicing IT workers.

IT Professional Malpractice

Negligence has been defined as not doing something that a reasonable person would do, or doing something that a reasonable person would not do. **Duty of care** refers to the obligation to protect people against any unreasonable harm or risk. For example, people have a duty to keep their pets from attacking others and to operate their cars safely. Similarly, businesses must keep dangerous pollutants out of the air and water, make safe products, and maintain safe operating conditions for employees.

The courts decide whether parties owe a duty of care by applying a **reasonable person standard** to evaluate how an objective, careful, and conscientious person would have acted in the same circumstances. Likewise, defendants who have particular expertise or competence are measured against a **reasonable professional standard**. For example, in a medical malpractice suit based on improper treatment of a broken bone, the standard of measure would be higher if the defendant were an orthopedic surgeon rather than a general practitioner. In the IT arena, consider a hypothetical negligence case in which an employee inadvertently destroyed millions of customer records in an Oracle database. The standard of measure would be higher if the defendant were a licensed, Oracle-certified database administrator (DBA) with 10 years of experience rather than an unlicensed systems analyst with no DBA experience or specific knowledge of the Oracle software.

If a court finds that a defendant actually owed a duty of care, it must then determine whether the duty was breached. A **breach of the duty of care** is the failure to act as a reasonable person would act. A breach of duty might consist of an action, such as throwing a lit cigarette into a fireworks factory and causing an explosion, or a failure to act when there is a duty to do so—for example, a police officer not protecting a citizen from an attacker.

Professionals who breach the duty of care are liable for injuries that their negligence causes. This liability is commonly referred to as **professional malpractice**. For example, a CPA who fails to use reasonable care, knowledge, skill, and judgment when auditing a client's books is liable for accounting malpractice. Professionals who breach this duty are liable to their patients or clients, and possibly to some third parties.

Courts have consistently rejected attempts to sue individual parties for computer-related malpractice. Professional negligence can only occur when people fail to perform within the standards of their profession, and software engineering is not a uniformly licensed profession in the United States. Because there are no uniform standards against which to compare a software engineer's professional behavior, he or she cannot be subject to malpractice lawsuits.

IT USERS

Chapter 1 outlined the general topic of how corporations are addressing the increasing risks of unethical behavior. This section focuses on encouraging employees' ethical use of IT, which is an area of growing concern as more companies provide employees with PCs, tablets, cellphones, and other devices to access to corporate information systems, data, and the Internet.

Common Ethical Issues for IT Users

This section discusses a few common ethical issues for IT users. Additional ethical issues will be discussed in future chapters.

Software Piracy

As mentioned earlier in this chapter, software piracy in a corporate setting can sometimes be directly traceable to IT professionals—they might allow it to happen, or they might actively engage in it. Corporate IT usage policies and management should encourage users to report instances of piracy and to challenge its practice. For example, the software piracy rate in China exceeds 80 percent, so it is clear that the business managers and IT professionals in that country do not take a strong stand against the practice.

Sometimes IT users are the ones who commit software piracy. A common violation occurs when employees copy software from their work computers for use at home. When confronted, the IT user's argument might be: "I bought a home computer partly so I could take work home and be more productive; therefore, I need the same software on my home computer as I have at work." However, if no one has paid for an additional license to use the software on the home computer, this is still piracy.

The increasing popularity of the Android smartphone operating system has created a serious software piracy problem. Some IT end users have figured out how to download applications from the Android Market Web site without paying for them, and then use the software or sell it to others. One legitimate Android application developer complained that his first application was pirated within a month and that the number of downloads from the pirate's site were greater than his own. Professional developers become discouraged as they watch their sales sink while pirates' sales rocket.[35]

Inappropriate Use of Computing Resources

Some employees use their computers to surf popular Web sites that have nothing to do with their jobs, participate in chat rooms, view pornographic sites, and play computer games. These activities eat away at worker productivity and waste time. Furthermore, activities such as viewing sexually explicit material, sharing lewd jokes, and sending hate email could lead to lawsuits and allegations that a company allowed a work environment conducive to racial or sexual harassment. A survey by the Fawcett Society found that one in five men admit to viewing porn at work, while a separate study found that 30 percent of mobile workers are viewing porn on their Web-enabled phones.[36,37] Organizations typically fire frequent pornography offenders and take disciplinary action against less egregious offenders.

Recently, the executive director of the Pentagon's Missile Defense Agency issued a memo to its 8,000 employees warning them to stop using their work computers to access Internet porn sites. One concern of government officials is that many pornography sites are infected with computer viruses and other malware; criminals and foreign intelligence agencies often use such sites as a means to gain access to government and corporate computer networks. For example, a foreign agent can embed malware capable of stealing data or opening computer communications ports whenever certain photos or videos are downloaded to a computer.[38]

Inappropriate Sharing of Information

Every organization stores vast amounts of information that can be classified as either private or confidential. Private data describes individual employees—for example, their salary information, attendance data, health records, and performance ratings. Private data also includes information about customers—credit card information, telephone number, home address, and so on. Confidential information describes a company and its operations, including sales and promotion plans, staffing projections, manufacturing processes, product formulas, tactical and strategic plans, and research and development. An IT user who shares this information with an unauthorized party, even inadvertently, has violated someone's privacy or created the potential that company information could fall into the hands of competitors. For example, if an employee accessed a coworker's payroll records via a human resources computer system and then discussed them with a friend, it would be a clear violation of the coworker's privacy.

In late 2010, hundreds of thousands of leaked State Department documents were posted on the WikiLeaks Web site. As of this writing, it appears that the source of the leaks was a low-level IT user (an Army private) with access to confidential documents. The documents revealed details of behind-the-scenes international diplomacy, often divulging candid comments from world leaders and providing particulars of U.S. tactics in Afghanistan, Iran, and North Korea.[39] The leaked documents strained relations between the United States and some of its allies. It is also possible that the incident will lead to less sharing of sensitive information with the United States because of concerns over further disclosures.

Supporting the Ethical Practices of IT Users

The growing use of IT has increased the potential for new ethical issues and problems; thus, many organizations have recognized the need to develop policies that protect against abuses. Although no policy can stop wrongdoers, it can set forth the general rights and responsibilities of all IT users, establish boundaries of acceptable and unacceptable behavior, and enable management to punish violators. Adherence to a policy can improve services to users, increase productivity, and reduce costs. Companies can take several of the following actions when creating an IT usage policy.

Establishing Guidelines for Use of Company Software

Company IT managers must provide clear rules that govern the use of home computers and associated software. Some companies negotiate contracts with software manufacturers and provide PCs and software so that IT users can work at home. Other companies help employees buy hardware and software at corporate discount rates. The goal should be to ensure that employees have legal copies of all the software they need to be effective, regardless of whether they work in an office, on the road, or at home.

Defining the Appropriate Use of IT Resources

Companies must develop, communicate, and enforce written guidelines that encourage employees to respect corporate IT resources and use them to enhance their job performance. Effective guidelines allow some level of personal use while prohibiting employees from visiting objectionable Internet sites or using company email to send offensive or harassing messages.

Structuring Information Systems to Protect Data and Information

Organizations must implement systems and procedures that limit data access to just those employees who need it. For example, sales managers may have total access to sales and promotion databases through a company network, but their access should be limited to products for which they are responsible. Furthermore, they should be prohibited from accessing data about research and development results, product formulas, and staffing projections if they don't need it to do their jobs.

Installing and Maintaining a Corporate Firewall

A **firewall** is hardware or software that serves as a barrier between an organization's network and the Internet; a firewall also limits access to the company's network based on the organization's Internet-usage policy. A firewall can be configured to serve as an effective deterrent to unauthorized Web surfing by blocking access to specific objectionable Web sites. (Unfortunately, the number of such sites is continually growing, so it is difficult to block them all.) A firewall can also serve as an effective barrier to incoming email from certain Web sites, companies, or users. It can even be programmed to block email with certain kinds of attachments (for example, Microsoft Word documents), which reduces the risk of harmful computer viruses.

Table 2-5 provides a manager's checklist for establishing an IT usage policy. The preferred answer to each questions is yes.

TABLE 2-5 Manager's checklist for establishing an IT usage policy

Question	Yes	No
Is there a statement that explains the need for an IT usage policy?		
Does the policy provide a clear set of guiding principles for ethical decision making?		
Is it clear how the policy applies to the following types of workers?		
• Employees		
• Part-time workers		
• Temps		
• Contractors		
Does the policy address the following issues?		
• Protection of the data privacy rights of employees, customers, suppliers, and others		
• Control of access to proprietary company data and information		
• Use of unauthorized or pirated software		
• Employee monitoring, including email, wiretapping and eavesdropping on phone conversations, computer monitoring, and surveillance by video		
• Respect of the intellectual rights of others, including trade secrets, copyrights, patents, and trademarks		
• Inappropriate use of IT resources, such as Web surfing, blogging, personal emailing, and other use of computers for purposes other than business		
• The need to protect the security of IT resources through adherence to good security practices, such as not sharing user IDs and passwords, using hard-to-guess passwords, and frequently changing passwords		
• The use of the computer to intimidate, harass, or insult others through abusive language in emails and by other means		
Are disciplinary actions defined for IT-related abuses?		
Is there a process for communicating the policy to employees?		
Is there a plan to provide effective, ongoing training relative to the policy?		
Has a corporate firewall been implemented?		
Is the corporate firewall maintained and kept up to date?		

Source Line: Course Technology/Cengage Learning.

Compliance

Compliance means to be in accordance with established policies, guidelines, specifications, or legislation. Records management software, for example, may be developed in compliance with the U.S. Department of Defense's Design Criteria Standard for Electronic Management Software applications (known as *DoD 5015*) that defines mandatory functional requirements for records management software used within the Department of Defense. Commercial software used within an organization should be distributed in compliance with the vendor's licensing agreement.

In the legal system, compliance usually refers to behavior in accordance with legislation—such as the Sarbanes–Oxley Act of 2002, which established requirements for internal controls to govern the creation and documentation of accurate and complete financial statements, or the U.S. Health Insurance Portability and Accountability Act of 1996 (HIPAA), which requires employers to ensure the security and privacy of employee healthcare data. Failure to be in compliance to specific pieces of legislation can lead to criminal or civil penalties specified in that legislation.

Failure to be in compliance with legislation can also lead to lawsuits or government fines. For instance, the California Online Privacy Protection Act of 2003 requires "commercial operators of online services, including mobile and social apps, which collect personally identifiable information from Californians, to conspicuously post a privacy policy," according to the California Attorney General's office. Such a policy must outline what data is gathered, for what purposes the data is being collected, and with whom the data may be shared. Developers of mobile applications face fines of up to $2,500 for every noncompliant application that is downloaded. Several organizations, including Delta, United Airlines, and Open Table, were notified by the Attorney General's office in late 2012 that they were not in compliance and were given 30 days to provide specific plans and a timeline for becoming compliant with the law.[40]

Demonstrating compliance with multiple government and industry regulations, many with similar but sometimes conflicting requirements, can be a major challenge. As a result, many organizations have implemented specialized software to track and record compliance actions, hired management consultants to provide advice and training, and even created a new position, the chief compliance officer (CCO), to deal with the issues.

In 1972, the Securities and Exchange Commission (SEC) recommended that publicly held organizations establish audit committees.[41] The **audit committee** of a board of directors provides assistance to the board in fulfilling its responsibilities with respect to the oversight of the following areas of activity:

- The quality and integrity of the organization's accounting and reporting practices and controls, including the financial statements and reports
- The organization's compliance with legal and regulatory requirements
- The qualifications, independence, and performance of the company's independent auditor (a certified public accountant who provides a company with an accountant's opinion but who is not otherwise associated with the company)
- The performance of the company's internal audit team

In some cases, audit committees have uncovered violations of law and reported their findings to appropriate law enforcement agencies. For example, the audit committee of Sensata Technology (which designs, manufactures, and distributes electronic sensors and controls) conducted an investigation into whether certain company officials had violated foreign bribery laws in connection with a business deal in China. As a result of that investigation, the audit committee reported possible Foreign Corrupt Practices Act violations to the SEC and the Department of Justice.[42]

In addition to an audit committee, most organizations also have an internal audit department whose primary responsibilities are to

- Determine that internal systems and controls are adequate and effective
- Verify the existence of company assets and maintain proper safeguards over their protection
- Measure the organization's compliance with its own policies and procedures
- Ensure that institutional policies and procedures, appropriate laws, and good practices are followed
- Evaluate the adequacy and reliability of information available for management decision making

Although the members of the internal audit team are not typically experts in detecting and investigating financial statement fraud, they can offer advice on how to develop and test policies and procedures that result in transactions being recorded in accordance with generally accepted accounting principles (GAAP). This can go a long way toward deterring fraud related to an organization's financial statements. Quite often in cases of financial statement fraud, senior management (including members of the audit committee) ignored or tried to suppress the recommendations of the internal audit team, especially when red flags were raised.

The audit committee and members of the internal audit team have a major role in ensuring that both the IT organization and IT users are in compliance with the various organizational guidelines and policies as well as various legal and regulatory practices.

Summary

- The key characteristics that distinguish professionals from other kinds of workers are as follows: (1) They require advanced training and experience; (2) they must exercise discretion and judgment in the course of their work; and (3) their work cannot be standardized.

- A professional is expected to contribute to society, to participate in a lifelong training program, to keep abreast of developments in the field, and to help develop other professionals.

- From a legal standpoint, a professional has passed the state licensing requirements (if they exist) and earned the right to practice there.

- From a legal perspective, IT workers are not recognized as professionals because they are not licensed by the state or federal government. As a result, IT workers are not liable for malpractice.

- IT professionals typically become involved in many different relationships, each with its own set of ethical issues and potential problems.

- In relationships between IT professionals and employers, important issues include setting and enforcing policies regarding the ethical use of IT, the potential for whistle-blowing, and the safeguarding of trade secrets.

- In relationships between IT professionals and clients, key issues revolve around defining, sharing, and fulfilling each party's responsibilities for successfully completing an IT project.

- A major goal for IT professionals and suppliers is to develop good working relationships in which no action can be perceived as unethical.

- In relationships between IT workers, the priority is to improve the profession through activities such as mentoring inexperienced colleagues and demonstrating professional loyalty.

- Résumé inflation and the inappropriate sharing of corporate information are potential problems in relationships between IT workers.

- In relationships between IT professionals and IT users, important issues include software piracy, inappropriate use of IT resources, and inappropriate sharing of information.

- When it comes to the relationship between IT workers and society at large, the main challenge for IT workers is to practice the profession in ways that cause no harm to society and provide significant benefits.

- A professional code of ethics states the principles and core values that are essential to the work of an occupational group.

- A code of ethics serves as a guideline for ethical decision making, promotes high standards of practice and ethical behavior, enhances trust and respect from the general public, and provides an evaluation benchmark.

- Several IT-related professional organizations have developed a code of ethics, including ACM, IEEE-CS, AITP, and SANS.

- Codes of ethics usually have two main parts—the first outlines what the organization aspires to become, and the second typically lists rules and principles that members are expected to live by. The codes also typically include a commitment to continuing education for those who practice the profession.

- Many people believe that the licensing and certification of IT workers would increase the reliability and effectiveness of information systems.

- Licensing and certification raise many issues, including the following: (1) There is no universally accepted core body of knowledge on which to test people; (2) it is unclear who should manage the content and administration of licensing exams; (3) there is no administrative body to accredit professional education programs; and (4) there is no administrative body to assess and ensure competence of individual professionals.

- The audit committee and members of the internal audit team have a major role in ensuring that both the IT organization and IT users are in compliance with organizational guidelines and policies as well as various legal and regulatory practices.

Key Terms

audit committee	government license
body of knowledge	IT user
breach of contract	material breach of contract
breach of duty of care	misrepresentation
bribery	negligence
Business Software Alliance (BSA)	profession
certification	professional code of ethics
compliance	professional malpractice
conflict of interest	reasonable person standard
duty of care	reasonable professional standard
firewall	résumé inflation
Foreign Corrupt Practices Act (FCPA)	trade secret
fraud	whistle-blowing

Self-Assessment Questions

The answers to the Self-Assessment Questions can be found in Appendix B.

1. A professional is someone who:
   a. requires advanced training and experience
   b. must exercise discretion and judgment in the course of his or her work
   c. does work that cannot be standardized
   d. all of the above

2. Although end users often get the blame when it comes to using illegal copies of commercial software, software piracy in a corporate setting is sometimes directly traceable to members of the _____ organization.

3. The mission of the Business Software Alliance is to _____.

4. Whistle-blowing is an effort by an employee to attract attention to a negligent, illegal, unethical, abusive, or dangerous act by a company that threatens the public interest. True or False?

5. _____ is the crime of obtaining goods, services, or property through deception or trickery.

6. _____ means to be in accordance with established policies, guidelines, specifications, or legislation.

7. Society expects professionals to act in a way that:
   a. causes no harm to society
   b. provides significant benefits
   c. establishes and maintains professional standards that protect the public
   d. all of the above

8. Most organizations have a(n) _____ team with primary responsibilities to determine that internal systems and controls are adequate and effective.

9. _____ is a process that one undertakes voluntarily to prove competency in a set of skills.
   a. Licensing
   b. Certification
   c. Registration
   d. all of the above

10. Senior management (including members of the audit committee) has the option of ignoring or suppressing recommendations of the internal audit committee. True or False?

11. _____ has been defined as not doing something that a reasonable person would do, or doing something that a reasonable person would not do.

12. A(n) _____ states the principles and core values that are essential to the work of a particular occupational group.

Discussion Questions

1. Would you rather be known as a person of modest means with an impeccable ethical character or as an unscrupulous person of wealth? Why?

2. How do you distinguish between misrepresentation and embellishment of one's professional accomplishments on a résumé? Provide an example of an embellishment that would not be considered misrepresentation.

3. Do laws provide a complete guide to ethical behavior? Can an activity be legal but not ethical?

4. In filling an open position in a U.S.-based IT organization, do you think that preference should be shown for qualified candidates from the United States over qualified candidates from foreign countries? Why or why not?

5. Does charging by the hour encourage unethical behavior on the part of contract workers and consultants?

6. Describe a situation in which there could be a conflict of interest between an IT worker's self-interest and the interests of a client. How should this potential conflict be addressed?

7. Should all IT workers be either licensed or certified? Why or why not?

8. Go to two or more of the Web sites identified in Table 2-3, and read the code of ethics found there. What commonalities do you find among the IT professional codes of ethics that you read? What differences are there? Do you think there are any important issues not addressed by these codes of ethics?

9. You are caught in the middle of a dilemma. You have been subpoenaed to be a witness in a work-related sexual harassment case involving your boss and a coworker. On many occasions, you heard your boss make statements to this employee that could be interpreted as sexual advancements. Your boss has made it clear that he will make things difficult for you at work if you testify in favor of the employee. You could choose to testify in a manner that would make it appear that your boss was not serious and that the employee was overreacting. On the other hand, it was clear to you that your boss was not joking with the employee and that he was harassing her. What kind of repercussions could there be if you testify in favor of your coworker? Would you be willing to risk those repercussions? Does it really matter if the case is dismissed because of your testimony?

10. What is the difference between breach of contract and material breach of contract? In a breach of contract dispute, what recourse can the nonbreaching party take?

11. Under the Foreign Corrupt Practices Act, under what conditions is a bribe not unlawful? Explain, and provide an example.

What Would You Do?

Use the five-step decision-making process discussed in Chapter 1 to analyze the following situations and recommend a course of action.

1. You are a new salesperson at a large software manufacturing firm. It is three weeks from the end of the sales quarter and you and your sales manager are sitting pretty—you have both already met your sales quota for the quarter. In addition, you just closed another deal with a new customer for $100,000 of software and customer service. This order would put you way over your sales quota for the current quarter. Your manager suggests that you hold this new order so it gets recorded against next quarter. She explains that because sales during the next three months tend to slow down, salespeople frequently miss their quotas and associated sales bonuses for that quarter. Holding this large order to next quarter would help you get an excellent start and almost guarantee that you meet your quota. What would you do?

2. You work part-time evenings and weekends as a real estate salesperson. You also work full-time for an IT consulting group. When ordering business cards for your real estate business, you decided to include your full-time work email address. As a result, you frequently find yourself receiving and sending emails related to your real estate work from your computer at your IT consulting job. You try to limit this activity to your lunch hour, but

there are often urgent messages that require an immediate reply. Lately the number of such emails is increasing. Sometimes you worry what would happen if your manager found out about this activity, but cutting off the flow of emails from your clients could have a serious impact on your ability to serve them and earn commissions. What should you do?

3. Your old roommate from college was recently let go from his firm during a wave of employee terminations to reduce costs. You two have kept in touch over the six years since school, and he has asked you to help him get a position in the IT organization where you work. You offered to review his résumé, make sure that it gets to the "right person," and even put in a good word for him. However, as you read the résumé, it is obvious that your friend has greatly exaggerated his accomplishments at his former place of work and even added some IT-related certifications you are sure he never earned. What would you do?

4. The daughter of the firm's CEO is scheduled to participate in a job interview for an entry-level position in the IT organization next week. You are a second-year employee in your firm's IT organization who will participate in the interview process. You will be one of three people who will interview her to form an assessment and make a group decision about whether or not she will be offered the position. How do you handle this situation?

5. You are in charge of awarding all computer hardware service contracts (valued at over $2 million per year) for your employer. In recent emails with the company's current service contractor, you casually exchanged ideas about family vacations. You mentioned that your family is planning on vacationing in the Scottsdale, Arizona, area. You are surprised when the contractor emails you an offer to use his company's condominium at a plush Scottsdale resort, complete with golf and health club privileges. He assures you that the condo would normally be empty that time of year and that other customers frequently use the condo. The resort is one you are familiar with but have never used because the rental is well over $5,000 per week. You would really like for your family to experience staying at a five-star resort but you worry about the potential consequences of accepting the offer. If your manager saw a copy of the emails exchanged with the contractor, could it appear that you were soliciting a bribe? Could this offer be considered a bribe? What would you do?

6. Your organization is preparing to submit a bid for a multimillion-dollar contract in South America. The contract is extremely important to your firm and would represent its first contract in South America. While meeting with your South American contacts, you are introduced to a consultant who offers to help your firm prepare and submit its bid, as well as to negotiate with the prospective customer company. The consultant is quite impressive in his knowledge of local government officials and managers and executives at the customer's company. The fee requested is only 1 percent of the potential value of the contract, but it is unclear exactly what the consultant will do. Later that day, your local contacts tell you that the use of such consultants is common. They say that they are familiar with this particular consultant and that he has a good reputation for getting results. Your company has never worked with such consultants in the past, and you are uncertain on how to proceed. What would you do?

7. You are a new human resources manager assigned to your firm's IT organization. One of your responsibilities is to screen résumés for job openings in the organization. You are in

the process of reviewing more than 100 résumés you received for a position as a Cisco network specialist. Your goal is to trim the group down to the top five candidates to invite to an in-house interview. About half the résumés are from IT workers with less than three years of experience who claim to have one or more Cisco certifications. There are also a few candidates with over five years of impressive experience but no Cisco certifications listed on their résumés. You were instructed to include only candidates with a Cisco certification in the list of finalists. However, you are concerned about possible résumé inflation and the heavy emphasis on certification versus experience. What would you do?

Cases

1. Whistle-Blower Claims Accounting Shenanigans at SuccessFactors

SuccessFactors is a U.S. multinational company that provides cloud-based human resources-related software applications. Under its "software-as-a-service" business model, the company provides software resources to subscribers who access them via the Internet for a fee. Annual revenue for the firm was $206 million in 2010.[43]

SuccessFactors spreads its costs over a large number of subscribers to keep its subscription rates low and generate income. Subscribers, in turn, rely on SuccessFactors to manage their data and software in a secure and reliable manner. Subscribers avoid large capital outlays for computing equipment and eliminate the costs associated with the purchase of hardware and software and the hiring of numerous computer operations and support people.

SuccessFactors has not been profitable—incurring losses in each fiscal period since its inception in 2001, with a loss of $12.5 million for 2010 and an accumulated deficit of $231.3 million.[44] Nevertheless, SAP paid $3.4 billion (over 10 times its 2011 revenue of $327 million) to acquire SuccessFactors in early 2012. (This number compares very unfavorably with the median price—three times revenue—paid in the 32 software mergers that occurred in North America in the five years prior to SAP's purchase of SuccessFactors.)[45] SAP was willing to pay such a premium to gain significant market share and expertise in the rapidly growing human resources software-as-a-service arena. At the time, SuccessFactors had a customer base of some 15 million subscription seat licenses spread across 3,500 customers.[46]

As with many companies, SuccessFactors supplemented the financial results that it reported in accordance with GAAP (generally accepted accounting principles that form the basis for financial reporting), with non-GAAP financial measures. The manner in which such non-GAAP measures are defined and calculated differ from company to company.[47] One of these non-GAAP financial measures was a measure called "backlog." SuccessFactors, and many other cloud computing service firms, invoice subscribers on an annual basis even if the term of the subscription agreement is longer than one year. Amounts that have been invoiced, but that have not yet been recognized as revenue, are recorded as deferred revenue. SuccessFactors reported the portion of the total contract value not yet invoiced as backlog.[48] SuccessFactors had a backlog of about $90 million at the end of 2007 compared with a backlog of $43 million at the end of 2006—an increase the company attributed to an upsurge in new contracts and customers.[49] In 2009, SuccessFactors stopped reporting this backlog figure, and the omission caught the eye of the SEC. When the agency inquired about why the company was no longer reporting this figure, SuccessFactors responded that it felt investors did not consider this figure useful.[50]

In the third quarter of 2010, Success Factors stated that it had adopted a 2009 SEC rule that limited the manner in which revenue could be reported on multiyear contracts.[51] However, in its 2011 annual report, filed just after SAP announced its intent to acquire the firm, but before the deal was finalized, SuccessFactors admitted that its accounting controls suffered from "a material weakness" and that its "internal control over financial reporting was not effective as of December 31, 2011."[52] Indeed, a SuccessFactors salesperson turned whistle-blower claimed that from 2009 to 2011, accounting controls at SuccessFactors were so weak that salespeople were able to improperly rewrite existing multiyear contracts as new contracts to earn additional commissions. If true, this would also accelerate revenue, making the company look more financially sound, while also reducing the backlog number. SAP investigated these claims with an examination conducted by an outside law firm and found no merit to the claims.[53]

Discussion Questions

1. In the end, SuccessFactors investors were not hurt by this alleged improper accounting because SAP paid such a high premium to acquire the firm, which helped SAP jump-start its cloud computing business. Was anyone hurt by this alleged improper accounting and, if so, who and how?

2. Should management encourage the reporting of non-GAAP financial measures that may be useful to investors? Why or why not?

3. What sort of measures should the management teams of service companies put in place to ensure that there is no improper accounting of multiyear contracts?

2. IBM and the State of Indiana Involved in a Breach of Contract Dispute

In December 2006, IBM and the Indiana Family and Social Services Administration (FSSA) entered into a 10-year, $1.16 billion contract to modernize the state's processes and systems for determining welfare eligibility. The state expected to generate $500 million in administrative costs savings over the life of the contract.[54]

FSSA claims it began to notice problems in the new system as early as the project's initial rollout to 10 northern Indiana counties in October 2007. As a result, further expansion was delayed. The state's lawyers wrote: "IBM assured FSSA that if the Region 2 rollout was implemented, IBM would recognize some efficiencies and economies of scale that would improve performance." Accordingly, FSSA agreed to roll out the system to the next region.[55]

By May 2008, the system had expanded into 59 of Indiana's 92 counties. In January 2009, a new FSSA secretary Anne Murphy took over and halted any further expansion until IBM submitted a corrective action plan. She set a deadline of July 2009, and her request included the stipulation that the contract be canceled if IBM failed to improve the situation by September 2009.[56] IBM estimated that addressing the issues would cost $180 million. In October 2009, the state announced it had canceled the deal because IBM failed to make the proposed improvements to the satisfaction of the state.[57]

In May 2010, the state of Indiana sued IBM for $1.3 billion, claiming breach of contract. The Indiana FSSA claimed that system-processing errors resulted in incorrect denials of benefits and delays in processing claims bringing harm to in-need citizens. The claims mishandling rate had climbed from 4 percent to 18 percent under the new system.[58] FSSA spokesman Marcus Barlow stated that "there was more staff working on eligibility during IBM's tenure than before IBM came, yet the results show that once IBM put their system in place, timeliness got worse, error rates went higher. Backlogs got larger."[59]

When the FSSA defined the project in 2006, they told IBM that, for staffing flexibility and efficiency, they wanted a system that would not assign one citizen to a single caseworker. Thus, IBM designed a task-based process that involved outsourcing 1,500 former FSSA employees to IBM. These workers interacted with welfare applicants to gather the necessary data to apply for welfare. Once these workers completed their tasks, the application was turned over to some 700 FSSA state workers who used the accumulated data to determine benefits eligibility.[60]

An IBM spokesman asserted that while there were delays in the system, it was because there were an insufficient number of workers to handle the number of claims. In addition, IBM pointed out that during contract negotiations with IBM, FSSA specified that the system be able to handle up to 4,200 applications per month. However, during the severe recession of 2008–2010, the number of applications frequently exceeded 10,000 per month.[61] The IBM spokesman made it clear that changing from the assigned caseworker approach was Indiana's idea, and was not proposed by IBM.[62] FSSA has since implemented a hybrid system that incorporates the "successful elements of the old welfare delivery system" and a "modernized system." This system assigns caseworkers to welfare recipients and allows for more face-to-face contact.

In its lawsuit, Indiana is demanding that IBM refund the $437 million the state already paid to IBM. Indiana also wants reimbursement of all overtime pay state employees earned working longer hours due to problems with the system. In addition, Indiana insists that IBM be liable for any federal penalties or damages from any lawsuits filed by others because of delays in payments to citizens. IBM countersued Indiana to keep the $400 million it was already paid and for an additional $53 million for the equipment it left in place, which FSSA workers are now using.[63]

In a press release issued at the time the lawsuit was filed, IBM claimed that Indiana had acknowledged that the new system had reduced fraud that was estimated to cost over $100 million per year, led to creation of 1,000 new jobs, and reduced Indiana's operating expenses by $40 million per year for 2008 and 2009 with projected savings of hundreds of millions in upcoming years.[64]

In a 2012 court ruling, the judge ruled that IBM is not entitled to the more than $400 million it sought from Indiana. In the same ruling, the judge denied IBM's claim for damages, while ordering Indiana to pay $12 million for equipment provided by IBM.[65]

Discussion Questions

1. Experienced observers point out that the development of a state social services system is always exceedingly difficult. Multiagency interaction and interdependence often leads to delays and complications in getting requirements finalized and agreed upon. And even if that is accomplished, changes in welfare policies by the state or federal government can render those requirements invalid and require considerable rework. Given the problems that IBM encountered on this contract, should it decline the future opportunities it may have to propose a new solution for a state social services system?

2. Present a strong argument that the state of Indiana is entitled to reimbursement of all funds paid to IBM as well as reimbursement of all overtime employees were paid due to fixing problems associated with the new system. Now present a strong argument that IBM should be allowed to keep all funds it has received so far for this new system.

3. Read about the judge's recent ruling in this case (*www.govtech.com/health/Nobody-Wins-in-Indiana-vs-IBM-Lawsuit-Judge-Says.html*). Do you agree or disagree with the ruling? Provide three reasons to support your opinion.

3. When Certification Is Justified

When Don Tennant, former editor-in-chief of *Computerworld*, published an editorial in favor of IT certification, he was promptly hit with a barrage of angry responses from IT workers.[66] They argued that testable IT knowledge does not necessarily translate into quality IT work. A worker needs good communication and problem-solving skills as well as perseverance to get the job done well. Respondents explained that hardworking IT workers focus on skills and knowledge that are related to their current projects and don't have time for certifications that will quickly become obsolete. Many readers indicated they suspected that vendors offer certification simply as a marketing ploy and a source of revenue. They accused managers without technical backgrounds of using certification as "a crutch, a poor but politically defensible substitute for knowing what and how well one's subordinates are doing."[67]

Any manager would certainly do well to review these insightful points, yet they beg the question: What useful purposes *can* certification serve within an organization?

Some CIOs and vice presidents of technology assert that many employers use certification as a means of training employees and increasing skill levels within the company. Some companies are even using certification as a perk to attract and keep good employees. Such companies may also enhance their employee training programs by offering a job-rotation program through which workers can acquire certification and experience.

Employers are also making good use of certification as a hiring gate both for entry-level positions and for jobs that require specific core knowledge. For example, a company with a Windows Server network might run an ad for a systems integration engineer and require a Microsoft Certified Systems Engineer (MCSE) certification. A company that uses Siebel customer relationship management software might require a new hire to have a certification in the latest version of Siebel.

In addition, specific IT fields, such as project management and security, have a greater need for certification. As the speed and complexity of production increase within the global marketplace, workers in a variety of industries are showing an increasing interest in project management certification. With mottos like "Do It, Do It Right, Do It Right Now," the Project Management Institute has already certified more than 400,000 people. IT industry employers are beginning to encourage and sometimes require project management certification.

Calls for training in the field of security management go beyond certification. The demand for security workers is expected to continue to grow rapidly in the next few years in the face of growing threats. Spam, computer viruses, spyware, botnets, and identity theft have businesses and government organizations worried. They want to make sure that their security managers can protect their data, systems, and resources.

One of the best-recognized security certifications is the CISSP, awarded by the International Information Systems Security Certification Consortium. Yet the CISSP examination, like so many other IT certification examinations, is multiple choice. Employers and IT workers alike have begun to recognize the limitations of these types of examinations. They want to ensure that examinees not only have core knowledge but also know how to use that knowledge—and a multiple-choice exam, even a six-hour, 250-question exam like the CISSP, can't provide that assurance.

Other organizations are catching on. Sun Microsystems requires the completion of programming or design assignments for some of its certifications. So, while there is no universal call for certification or a uniform examination procedure that answers all needs within the IT profession, certifying bodies are beginning to adapt their programs to better fulfill the evolving needs for certification in IT.

Discussion Questions

1. How can organizations and vendors change their certification programs to test for skills as well as core knowledge? What issues might this introduce?

2. What are the primary arguments against certification, and how can certifying bodies change their programs to overcome these shortcomings?

3. What are the benefits of certification? How might certification programs need to change in the future to better serve the needs of the IT community?

End Notes

1 "CityTime," *New York Times*, March 14, 2012, http://topics.nytimes.com/top/reference/timestopics/organizations/o/office_of_payroll_administration_nyc/citytime/index.html.

2 "CityTime," *New York Times*, March 14, 2012, http://topics.nytimes.com/top/reference/timestopics/organizations/o/office_of_payroll_administration_nyc/citytime/index.html.

3 "CityTime," *New York Times*, March 14, 2012, http://topics.nytimes.com/top/reference/timestopics/organizations/o/office_of_payroll_administration_nyc/citytime/index.html.

4 "CityTime," *New York Times*, March 14, 2012, http://topics.nytimes.com/top/reference/timestopics/organizations/o/office_of_payroll_administration_nyc/citytime/index.html.

5 Ali Winston, "Comptroller Moves to Rein in CityTime," *CityLimits*, February 26, 2012, www.citylimits.org/news/articles/3896/comptroller-moves.

6 Serge F. Kovaleski and John Eligon, "New York City Payroll Chief Resigns," *New York Times*, December 23, 2010, www.nytimes.com/2010/12/24/nyregion/24citytime.html.

7 Serge F. Kovaleski and John Eligon, "New York City Payroll Chief Resigns," *New York Times*, December 23, 2010, www.nytimes.com/2010/12/24/nyregion/24citytime.html.

8 David W. Chen and William K. Rashbaum, "With Arrest, Criticism for Payroll Project Grows," *New York Times*, May 27, 2011, www.nytimes.com/2011/05/28/nyregion/criticism-for-citytime-project-grows-as-a-manager-is-arrested.html.

9 Colin Moynihan, "Early Trial Planned for Defendants in CityTime Case," *New York Times*, March 15, 2012, http://cityroom.blogs.nytimes.com/2012/03/15/early-2013-trial-planned-for-defendants-in-citytime-case.

10 "CityTime," *New York Times*, March 14, 2012, http://topics.nytimes.com/top/reference/timestopics/organizations/o/office_of_payroll_administration_nyc/citytime/index.html.

11 U.S. Code, Title 5, Part III, Subpart F, Chapter 71, Subchapter 1, Section 7103, http://law.justia.com/us/codes/title5/5usc7103.html (accessed December 27, 2012).

12 BSA | The Software Alliance, "Record Period of Settlements Underscores Persistent Software Piracy Problem in the US," August 21, 2012, www.bsa.org/country/News%20and%20Events/News%20Archives/en/2012/en-08212012-US.aspx.

13 BSA | The Software Alliance, "Tennessee Automotive Dealer Pays Heavy Fines," March 7, 2012, www.bsa.org/country/News%20and%20Events/News%20Archives/en/2012/en-03072012-TN.aspx.

14 Anthony Ha, "Zynga Falls Short of Analysts Estimate for Q2: $332 Million in Revenue, Bookings Decline From Last Quarter, Lowered Outlook," *Tech Crunch*, July 25, 2012, http://techcrunch.com/2012/07/25/zynga-earnings-q2.

15 Tricia Duryee, "Zynga Files Suit Against Former Staffer, Claiming Theft of Trade Secrets," *AllThingsD.com*, October 14, 2012, http://allthingsd.com/20121014/zynga-files-suit-against-former-staffer-claiming-theft-of-trade-secrets.

16 Paul McDougall, "Indian Outsourcer Infosys Eyed for Visa Fraud," *InformationWeek*, August 18, 2011, www.informationweek.com/services/outsourcing/indian-outsourcer-infosys-eyed-for-visa/231500239.

17 Paul McDougall, "Infosys Wins Court Battle, But Visa Troubles Continue," *InformationWeek*, August 21, 2012, www.informationweek.com/global-cio/outsourcing/infosys-wins-court-battle-but-visa-troub/240005939.

18 Steven Musil, "Man Suing for Half of Facebook Loses Lawyer," *CNET*, June 28, 2011, http://news.cnet.com/8301-1023_3-20075244-93/man-suing-for-half-of-facebook-loses-lawyer.

19 Thomas Claburn, "Ceglia To Face Facebook Fraud Charges," *InformationWeek*, October 27, 2012, www.informationweek.com/internet/social-network/ceglia-to-face-facebook-fraud-charges/240010623.

20 "Misleading and Deceptive: Apple Sued Over Siri," *Sydney Morning Herald*, March 14, 2012, www.smh.com.au/digital-life/mobiles/misleading-and-deceptive-apple-sued-over-siri-20120314-1uz3d.html.

21 Henry R. Cheeseman, *"Contemporary Business Law,"* 3rd ed. (Upper Saddle River, NJ: Prentice Hall, 2000), 292.

22 Eli Segall, "Oracle to Pay $200M in Settlement," *Silicon Valley/San Jose Business Journal*, October 6, 2011, www.bizjournals.com/sanjose/news/2011/10/06/oracle-to-pay-200m-in-settlement.html?page=all.

[23] Paul McDougall, "Ex-Apple Manager Guilty In Kickback Scheme," *InformationWeek*, March 1, 2011, www.informationweek.com/hardware/apple-macintosh/ex-apple-manager-guilty-in-kickback-sche/229219586.

[24] United States Department of Justice, "Foreign Corrupt Practices Act: Antibribery Provisions," www.justice.gov/criminal/fraud/fcpa/docs/lay-persons-guide.pdf (accessed November 9, 2012).

[25] "G20 Throws Weight Behind Global Anti-Corruption Treaty," *TrustLaw*, November 12, 2010, www.trust.org/trustlaw/news/g20-throws-weight-behind-global-anti-corruption-treaty.

[26] Stu Woo, "New Chief Brings Affable Manner and A Boston Accent," *Wall Street Journal*, January 5, 2012, http://online.wsj.com/article/SB10001424052970203513604577140762129761548.html.

[27] Julianne Pepitone, "Yahoo Confirms CEO Is Out After Resume Scandal," *CNN Money*, May 14, 2002, http://money.cnn.com/2012/05/13/technology/yahoo-ceo-out/index.htm.

[28] Ropella, "Hiring Smart: How to Avoid the Top Ten Mistakes," www.ropella.com/index.php/knowledge/recruitingProcessArticles/hiring_smart, © 2012 Ropella Group Inc.

[29] Leo Ma, "Resume Exaggeration in Asia Pacific," *Ezine Articles*, http://ezinearticles.com/?Resume-Exaggeration-in-Asia-Pacific&id=4788569, August 6, 2010.

[30] Association for Computing Machinery, "Welcome," www.acm.org (accessed November 11, 2012).

[31] IEEE Computer Society, "About Us—About the Computer Society," www.computer.org/portal/web/about (accessed November 11, 2012).

[32] IEEE Computer Society, "Computer Society and ACM Approve Software Engineering Code of Ethics," *Computer Society Connection*, October 1999, www.computer.org/cms/Computer.org/Publications/code-of-ethics.pdf (accessed December 28, 2012).

[33] Association of Information Technology Professionals, "About AITP: History," www.aitp.org/organization/about/history/history.jsp (accessed November 11, 2012).

[34] SysAdmin, Audit, Network, Security (SANS) Institute, "Information Security Training, Certification & Research," www.sans.org/about/sans.php (accessed November 11, 2012).

[35] John Cox, "Android Software Piracy Rampant Despite Google's Efforts to Curb," *Network World*, September 29, 2010, www.networkworld.com/news/2010/092910-google-android-piracy.html.

[36] Andres Millington, "Porn in the Workplace is Now a Major Board-Level Concern for Business," *Business Computing World*, April 23, 2010, www.businesscomputingworld.co.uk/porn-in-the-workplace-is-now-a-major-board-level-concern-for-business.

[37] Dean Wilson, "Third of Mobile Workers Distracted by Porn, Report Finds," *TechEYE.net*, June 14, 2010, www.techeye.net/mobile/third-of-mobile-workers-distracted-by-porn-report-finds.

[38] Tony Capaccio, "Missile Defense Staff Warned to Stop Surfing Porn Sites," *Bloomberg*, August 2, 2012, www.bloomberg.com/news/2012-08-01/missile-defense-staff-warned-to-stop-surfing-porn-sites.html.

39 Associated Press, "WikiLeaks Reveals Sensitive Diplomacy," *Cincinnati Enquirer*, November 28, 2010.

40 Matthew J. Schwartz, "California Targets Mobile Apps for Missing Privacy Policies," *InformationWeek*, October 31, 2012, www.informationweek.com/government/mobile/california-targets-mobile-apps-for-missi/240012603.

41 Annemarie K. Keinath and Judith C. Walo, "Audit Committees Responsibilities," *The CPA Journal Online*, www.nysscpa.org/cpajournal/2004/1104/essentials/p22.htm (accessed November 11, 2012).

42 Shareholders Foundation, Inc. "Press Release: Sensata Technologies Holding N.V. Under Investor Investigation Over Possible Foreign Bribery," *PRLog*, October 26, 2010, www.prlog.org/11024869-sensata-technologies-holding-nv-under-investor-investigation-over-possible-foreign-bribery.html.

43 SuccessFactors, "SuccessFactors 2010 Annual Report," http://phx.corporate-ir.net/phoenix.zhtml?c=214238&p=irol-reportsAnnual (accessed January 13, 2013).

44 SuccessFactors, "SuccessFactors 2011 Annual Report," www.sap.com/corporate-en/investors/reports/pdf/SFSF-2011-Annual-Report.pdf (accessed January 13, 2013).

45 The Linesch Firm, "Whistleblower Sheds Light on Fraud," November 2, 2012, http://lineschfirm.com/wp/whistleblower-sheds-light-on-fraud.

46 Larry Dignan, "SAP Acquires SuccessFactors for $3.4 Billion: Cloud Consolidation Accelerates," *ZDNet*, December 3, 2011, www.zdnet.com/blog/btl/sap-acquires-successfactors-for-3-4-billion-cloud-consolidation-accelerates/64627.

47 "Press Release: SuccessFactors Announces Preliminary Fourth Quarter Fiscal 2011 Results," *PRNewswire*, February 2, 2012, www.bizjournals.com/prnewswire/press_releases/2012/02/02/SF46931.

48 SuccessFactors, "Annual Report 2008," http://media.corporate-ir.net/media_files/irol/21/214238/LetterAnnual08.pdf (accessed January 28, 2013).

49 SuccessFactors, "Annual Report 2008," http://media.corporate-ir.net/media_files/irol/21/214238/LetterAnnual08.pdf (accessed January 28, 2013).

50 Scott Priest, "Today in SAP: Allegations Build Over SuccessFactors' Accounting," *SAPexperts*, October 26, 2012, http://sapexperts.wispubs.com/IT/IT-Blog/2012/October/Today-in-SAP-10262012.

51 Francine McKenna, "Is the SEC's Ponzi Crusade Enabling Companies to Cook the Books, Enron-Style?," *Forbes*, October 18, 2012, www.forbes.com/sites/francinemckenna/2012/10/18/is-the-secs-ponzi-crusade-enabling-companies-to-cook-the-books-enron-style.

52 Julia Bort, "Whistleblower Explains One Way Cloud Companies Can Cook Their Books," *BusinessInsider,* October 25, 2012, www.businessinsider.com/successfactors-accounting-whistleblower-speaks-2012-10.

53 Francine McKenna, "Is the SEC's Ponzi Crusade Enabling Companies to Cook the Books, Enron-Style?," *Forbes*, October 18, 2012.

54 "IBM Closes In on $1.16bn Indiana Deal," *Computer Business Review*, November 29, 2006, www.cbronline.com/news/ibm_closes_in_on_116bn_indiana_deal (accessed November 12, 2010).

55 Associated Press, "Indiana: IBM Welfare Intake Work Flawed from Start," *Indianapolis Business Journal*, July 21, 2010, www.ibj.com/indiana-ibm-welfare-intake-work-flawed-from-start/PARAMS/article/21227.

56 Ken Kusmer, Associated Press, "IBM on Notice over Indiana Welfare Deal, *FortWayne.com*, www.newssentinel.com/apps/pbcs.dll/article?AID=/20090708/NEWS/907080335 (accessed December 19, 2010).

57 Audrey B., "IBM vs. Indiana: Big Blue Makes Indiana See Red," *Seeking Alpha* (blog), May 18, 2010, http://seekingalpha.com/article/205668-ibm-vs-indiana-big-blue-makes-indiana-see-red.

58 Robert Charette, "Indiana and IBM Sue Each Other Over Failed Outsourcing Contract," *IEEE Spectrum Risk Factor* (blog), May 14, 2010, http://spectrum.ieee.org/riskfactor/computing/it/indiana-and-ibm-sue-each-other-over-failed-outsourcing-contract.

59 Andy Opsahl, "IBM and Indiana Suing Each Other Over Canceled Outsourcing Deal," *Government Technology*, May 13, 2010, www.govtech.com/health/IBM-and-Indiana-Suing-Each-Other.html.

60 Andy Opsahl, "IBM and Indiana Suing Each Other Over Canceled Outsourcing Deal," *Government Technology*, May 13, 2010, www.govtech.com/health/IBM-and-Indiana-Suing-Each-Other.html.

61 Andy Opsahl, "IBM and Indiana Suing Each Other Over Canceled Outsourcing Deal," *Government Technology*, May 13, 2010, www.govtech.com/health/IBM-and-Indiana-Suing-Each-Other.html.

62 Andy Opsahl, "IBM and Indiana Suing Each Other Over Canceled Outsourcing Deal," *Government Technology*, May 13, 2010, www.govtech.com/health/IBM-and-Indiana-Suing-Each-Other.html.

63 Andy Opsahl, "IBM and Indiana Suing Each Other Over Cancelled Outsourcing Deal," *Government Technology*, May 13, 2010, www.govtech.com/health/IBM-and-Indiana-Suing-Each-Other.html.

64 IBM, "Press Release: IBM Seeks Enforcement of Indiana Welfare Contract," May 13, 2010, www-03.ibm.com/press/us/en/pressrelease/31641.wss.

65 Colin Wood, "Nobody Wins in Indiana vs. IBM Lawsuit, Judge Says," *Government Technology*, July 19, 2012, www.govtech.com/health/Nobody-Wins-in-Indiana-vs-IBM-Lawsuit-Judge-Says.html.

66 Don Tennant, "Certifiably Concerned," *Computerworld*, June 13, 2005, www.computerworld.com/s/article/102394/Certifiably_Concerned.

67 Don Tennant, "Certifiably Mad?," *Computerworld*, June 20, 2005, www.computerworld.com/s/article/102564/Certifiably_Mad.

ANSWERS TO SELF-ASSESSMENT QUESTIONS

1. d.; 2. IT; 3. stop the unauthorized copying of software produced
by its members; 4. True; 5. Fraud; 6. Compliance; 7. d.; 8. Internal audit; 9. b.; 10. True;
11. Negligence; 12. code of ethics

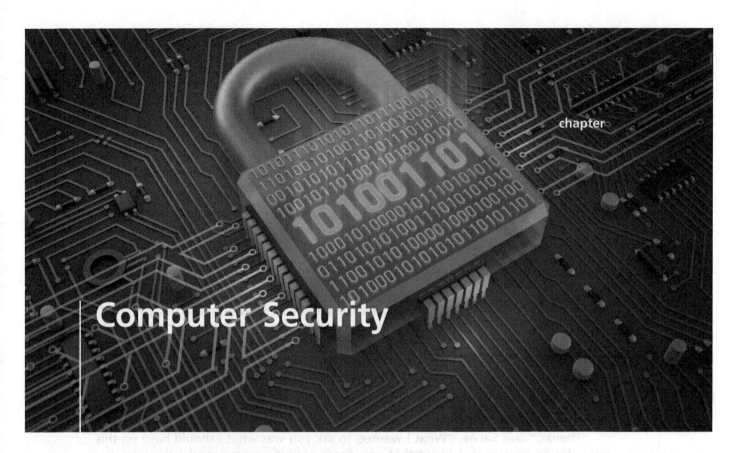

chapter

Computer Security

After completing this chapter you should be able to do the following:

- Define malware
- List the different types of malware
- Identify payloads of malware
- Describe the steps for securing software
- Explain how to create data backups

Security in Your World

"Excuse me, Dr. Antonelli. Do you have a minute?" Dr. Antonelli looked up from his computer. "Hi, Sanne. Yes, please come in." Sanne was taking an Introduction to Modern Technology course taught by Dr. Antonelli at the college, who also taught upper-level security courses. "I wanted to get your advice on something, and I knew you were the one to talk with," she said. Dr. Antonelli cleared off some papers from a chair. "Have a seat. What can I help you with? Something about our class?"

Sanne sat down in the chair and opened her backpack. "No, our class is going fine. At least until next week's exam!" Dr. Antonelli laughed. "You are doing just fine in this class. I just wish some of your classmates were as dedicated as you are!" Sanne grinned. "Thank you. Anyway, my Uncle Brian has been overseas on a consulting job for the past year and just got back home. Since he missed my birthday he had told me that he wanted to give me a nice gift when he got back. He just brought it over yesterday. It's a new computer. See?" Sanne handed the device to her teacher. "This is really nice, Sanne. It's one of those convertible models that you can use as either a laptop or as a tablet device. And it's so light. You will really enjoy this," said Dr. Antonelli.

"Thanks," said Sanne. "What I wanted to ask you was what I should have on this computer to protect it. I know that you teach security courses and I thought you could tell me what I needed to keep it from getting infected. My mother and brother both say that all I need is antivirus software. But after our class last week I don't think so. What would you do to protect it?" she asked.

Dr. Antonelli handed the device back to Sanne. "It's interesting that you should ask. I just read an article that asked over 200 security experts what they did to protect their computers and compared that with what non-experts said. The results were very different between the two groups," he said as he pulled a copy of the article out of his backpack. "Look. It says that 42 percent of the non-experts responded that antivirus software was one of the top three protections you should have. But among the security experts, installing antivirus software did not even make the list. And only 7 percent of all the experts even said that antivirus software was important."

Sanne looked at the paper Dr. Antonelli was holding. "Wow, that's a huge difference. So security experts say that antivirus is not that important but most users think that it is. Why do they think that?" she asked. Dr. Antonelli leaned back. "The authors of this journal article speculated that antivirus software offers a convenient install-and-forget type of solution that's very easy for users to manage. That's probably true. I also think that most users consider all attacks as coming from 'viruses' so they believe 'antivirus' then repels everything. But there are many different types of attacks against computers today besides viruses."

Sanne looked at Dr. Antonelli and asked, "So what are these other attacks?"

Protecting your personal technology device—be it a desktop, laptop, or tablet—is a challenge, even for the most advanced computer users. This is because many different types of attacks are launched against personal technology devices, and attackers are constantly modifying these attacks as well as creating new ones daily. According to a major security vendor, malicious software "events" directed at a business enterprise occur on average once every three minutes.[1]

Although virtually every computer user wishes for a single defensive program or one configuration setting that would fully protect their equipment, none exists. Just as a house must be protected against different types of threats—burglary, arson, vandalism, hurricanes, mold, and termites—so too must a computer be protected from a variety of attacks. And just as protecting against termites is much different than protecting against a hurricane, there are several different defenses that must be in place for a computer to remain safe.

In this chapter, you will learn about computer security. You will start by looking at the types of computer attacks that occur today. And then you will find out what defenses must be in place to keep our computers and the information stored on them secure.

Attacks Using Malware

Malware is software that enters a computer system without the user's knowledge or consent and then performs an unwanted and usually harmful action. Strictly speaking, malware uses a threat vector to deliver a malicious "payload" that performs a harmful function once it is invoked. However, *malware* is most often used as a general term that refers to a wide variety of damaging software programs.

Different types of malware have emerged over time as a result of security defenses becoming more sophisticated and the corresponding attacks becoming progressively more complex. However, there has been no standard established for the classification of the different types of malware. As a result, the definitions of the different types of malware are often confusing and may overlap. One method of classifying the various types of malware is by using the primary trait that the malware possesses. These traits are circulation, infection, concealment, and payload capabilities.

In order to detect malware on an infected computer, a software scanning tool can search for the malware, looking to match it against a known pattern of malicious software. To circumvent this detection of their software, attackers have become very sophisticated at masking the presence of their malware by having it "mutate" or change.

Circulation/Infection

Some malware has as its primary trait spreading rapidly to other systems in order to impact a large number of users. Malware can circulate through a variety of means: by using the network to which all the devices are connected, through USB flash drives that are shared among users, or by sending the malware as an email attachment. Some malware attaches itself to a benign program while other malware functions as a stand-alone process. Once the malware reaches a system through circulation, it must "infect" or embed itself into that system. Three types of malware have the primary traits of circulation and/or infection. These are viruses, worms, and Trojans.

Viruses A biological virus is an agent that reproduces inside a cell. When a cell is infected by a virus, the virus takes over the operation of that cell, converting it into a virtual factory to make more copies of it. The cell is forced to produce thousands or hundreds of thousands of identical copies of the original virus very rapidly (the polio virus can make more than *one million* copies of itself inside one single infected human cell). Biologists often say that viruses exist only to make more viruses. A **computer virus** (**virus**) is malicious computer code that, like its biological counterpart, reproduces itself on the same computer. Strictly speaking, a computer virus replicates itself (or an evolved copy of itself) without any human intervention.

Sometimes the terms *virus* and *malware* are used synonymously, especially by the general news media when reporting on a security incident. However, this is incorrect: a virus is only one type of malware.

Almost all viruses "infect" by inserting themselves into a computer file. A large number of different file types can contain a virus; for example, over 70 different Microsoft Windows file types can be infected. A virus that infects an executable program file is simply called a *program virus*. When the program is launched the virus is activated. A virus can also infect a data file like a Microsoft Office document or spreadsheet. One of the most common data file viruses is a *macro virus* that is written in a script known as a macro. A *macro* is a series of instructions that can be grouped together as a single command. Often macros are used to automate a complex set of tasks or a repeated series of tasks and are stored within the user document (such as in an Excel .XLSX worksheet or Word .DOCX file). Once the document is opened the macro instructions then execute whether those instructions are benign or a macro virus.

One of the first viruses found on a personal computer was written for the Apple II in 1982. Rich Skrenta, a ninth-grade student in Pittsburgh, wrote "Elk Cloner," which displayed his poem on the screen after every 50th use of the infected floppy disk. Unfortunately, the virus leaked out and found its way onto the computer used by Skrenta's math teacher.[2] In 1984, the mathematician Dr. Frederick Cohen introduced the term *virus* based on a recommendation from his advisor, who came up with the name from reading science fiction novels.

Early viruses were relatively straightforward in how they infected files. One basic type of infection is the *appender infection*. The virus first attaches or appends itself to the end of the infected file. It then inserts at the beginning of the file a "jump" instruction that points to the end of the file, which is the beginning of the virus code. When the program is launched, the jump instruction redirects control to the virus. Figure 3-1 shows how an appender infection works.

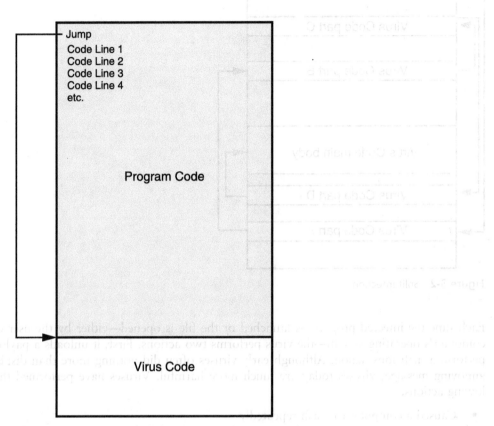

Figure 3-1 Appender infection

However, these types of viruses could easily by detected by software scanning for a virus. Most viruses today go to great lengths to avoid detection. One of the more sophisticated types of virus uses a *split infection*, which divides the malicious code itself into several parts (along with one main body of code), and then these parts are placed at random positions throughout the program code. To make detection even more difficult, these parts may contain unnecessary "garbage" code to mask their true purpose. A split infection virus is shown in Figure 3-2.

NOTE   Some viruses even scan for the presence of files that security researchers typically use. If those files are present, then it is assumed that the virus is being examined for weaknesses. The virus will then automatically self-destruct by deleting itself or cripple the computer so that it can no longer be used.

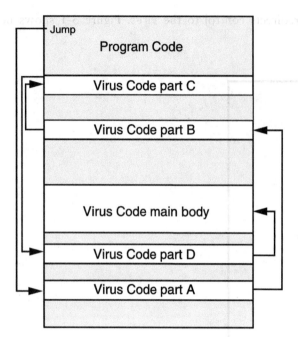

Figure 3-2 Split infection

Each time the infected program is launched or the file is opened—either by the user or the computer's operating system—the virus performs two actions. First, it unloads a payload to perform a malicious action. Although early viruses often did nothing more than display an annoying message, viruses today are much more harmful. Viruses have performed the following actions:

- Caused a computer to crash repeatedly
- Erased files from a hard drive
- Turned off the computer's security settings
- Reformatted the hard disk drive

 Sometimes a virus will remain dormant for a period of time before unleashing its payload.

The second action a virus takes when executed is to reproduce by inserting its code into another file on the same computer. A virus can only replicate on the host computer on which it is located; it cannot automatically spread to another computer by itself. Instead, it must rely on the actions of users to spread to other computers. Because viruses are generally attached to files, viruses are spread by a user transferring those files to other devices. For example, a user may send an infected file as an email attachment or copy an infected file to a USB flash drive and give the drive to another user. Once the virus reaches a new computer it begins to infect it. This means that a virus must have two "carriers": a file to which it attaches and a human to email or transport it to other computers.

Several similarities between biological and computer viruses exist: both must enter their host passively (by relying on the action of an outside agent), both must be on the correct host (a horse virus cannot make a human sick, just as an Apple Mac virus cannot infect a Windows computer), both can only replicate when inside the host, both may remain dormant for a period of time, and both types of viruses replicate at the expense of the host.

Worms A second type of malware that has as its primary purpose to spread is a worm. A **worm** is a malicious program that uses a computer network to replicate (worms are sometimes called *network viruses*). A worm is designed to enter a computer through the network and then take advantage of a vulnerability in an application or an operating system on the host computer. Once the worm has exploited the vulnerability on one system, it immediately searches for another computer on the network that has the same vulnerability.

One of the first wide-scale worms occurred in 1988. This worm exploited a misconfiguration in a program that allowed commands emailed to a remote system to be executed on that system, and it also carried a payload that contained a program that attempted to determine user passwords. Almost 10 percent of the devices connected to the Internet at that time were affected. The author of the worm was later convicted of federal crimes in connection with this incident.

Early worms were relatively harmless and designed simply to spread quickly and not corrupt the systems they infected. These worms slowed down the network through which they were transmitted by replicating so quickly that they consumed all network resources. Today's worms can leave behind a payload on the systems they infect and cause harm, much like a virus. Actions that worms have performed include:

- Deleting files on the computer
- Allowing the computer to be remotely controlled by an attacker.

Although viruses and worms are said to be automatically self-replicating, *where* they replicate is different. A virus will self-replicate *on* the host computer but not to other computers. A worm will self-replicate *between* computers (from one computer to another).

Trojans According to ancient legend, the Greeks won the Trojan War by hiding soldiers in a large hollow wooden horse that was presented as a gift to the city of Troy. Once the horse was wheeled into the fortified city, the soldiers crept out of the horse during the night and attacked the unsuspecting defenders.

A computer **Trojan horse** (or just **Trojan**) is an executable program that masquerades as performing a benign activity but also does something malicious. For example, a user may download what is advertised as a calendar program, yet when it is installed, in addition to installing the calendar it installs malware that scans the system for credit card numbers and passwords, connects through the network to a remote system, and then transmits that information to the attacker.

Unlike a virus that infects a system without the user's knowledge or consent, a Trojan program is installed on the computer system with the user's knowledge. What the Trojan conceals is its malicious payload.

Table 3-1 lists the differences between viruses, worms, and Trojans.

Action	Virus	Worm	Trojan
What does it do?	Inserts malicious code into a program or data file	Exploits a vulnerability in an application or operating system	Masquerades as performing a benign action but also does something malicious
How does it spread to other computers?	User transfers infected files to other devices	Uses a network to travel from one computer to another	User transfers Trojan file to other computers
Does it infect a file?	Yes	No	It can
Does it require user action to spread?	Yes	No	Yes

Table 3-1 Difference between viruses, worms, and Trojans

Concealment

Some types of malware have avoiding detection as a primary trait. A **rootkit** is a set of software tools used to hide the actions or presence of other types of software, such as Trojans, viruses, or worms. Rootkits do this by changing the operating system to force it to ignore their malicious files or activity. Rootkits also hide or remove all traces of evidence that may reveal the malware, such as log entries.

One approach used by rootkits is to alter or replace operating system files with modified versions that are specifically designed to ignore malicious evidence. For example, antimalware scanning software may be instructed to examine all files in a specific directory. In order to do this, the scanning software receives a list of those files from the operating system. A rootkit replaces the operating system's program that creates an accurate list of files with the rootkit's own routine that creates a list of files but omits any malicious files from the list. This is illustrated in Figure 3-3. The scanning software assumes that the operating system will willingly carry out those instructions and retrieve all files; it does not know that the computer is providing only files that the rootkit has approved. In essence, users can no longer trust their computer that contains a rootkit: the rootkit is in charge and hides what is occurring on the computer.

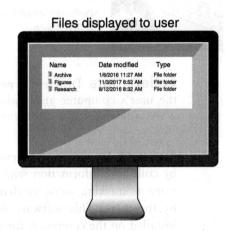

Figure 3-3   Computer infected with rootkit

Because a rootkit often substitutes its own malicious files and routines for legitimate operating system files, it can be very difficult to detect the presence of a rootkit; the operating system cannot be trusted to provide accurate information. In addition, these files and routines typically operate at a very low level in the operating system and cannot easily be repaired. Ultimately, the only safe and foolproof way to handle a rootkit infection is to reformat the hard drive and reinstall the operating system.

Payload Capabilities

When payload capabilities are the primary emphasis of malware, the focus is on what nefarious action(s) the malware performs. Does it allow the attacker to execute commands on the remote computer or to steal passwords and other valuable data from the user's system? Does it delete programs so the computer can no longer function properly? Or does the malware modify the system's security settings? And in some cases the purpose of this malware is to use the infected system to launch attacks against other computers. The primary payload capabilities are to execute commands, collect data, delete data, modify system security settings, and launch attacks.

Execute Commands When the payload allows an attacker to execute virtually any command on the victim's computer this is called **arbitrary code execution**. Most often arbitrary code execution takes advantage of a vulnerability in the operating system software or an application program. The attacker uses a relatively small piece of computer code called *shellcode* as the payload. The shellcode launches ("spawns") a command shell from which instructions can then be issued to the computer. When malware can trigger arbitrary code execution on Computer A remotely from Computer B over a network or the Internet, this is called **remote code execution**.

Many shellcode snippets are freely available for download. A small portion of shellcode would appear as \xda\xde\xd9\x74\x24\xf4\xb8\x22\xd2\x27\x7a\x29 \xc9\xb1\x4b.

Collect Data Different types of malware are designed to collect important data from the user's computer and make it available at the attacker. This malware includes spyware, adware, and ransomware.

Spyware **Spyware** is a general term used to describe software that secretly spies on users by collecting information without their consent. The Anti-Spyware Coalition defines spyware as tracking software that is deployed without adequate notice, consent, or control by the user.[3] This software uses the computer's resources, including programs already installed on the computer, for the purpose of collecting and distributing personal or sensitive information. Table 3-2 lists different technologies used by spyware.

Technology	Description	Impact
Automatic download software	Used to download and install software without the user's interaction	May be used to install unauthorized applications
Passive tracking technologies	Used to gather information about user activities without installing any software	May collect private information such as websites a user has visited
System modifying software	Modifies or changes user configurations, such as the web browser home page or search page, default media player, or lower-level system functions	Changes configurations to settings that the user did not approve
Tracking software	Used to monitor user behavior or gather information about the user, sometimes including personally identifiable or other sensitive information	May collect personal information that can be shared widely or stolen, resulting in fraud or identity theft

Table 3-2   Technologies used by spyware

Not all spyware is necessarily malicious. For example, spyware monitoring tools can help parents keep track of the online activities of their children while the children are surfing the web.

One type of nefarious spyware is a **keylogger** that silently captures and stores each keystroke that a user types on the computer's keyboard. The attacker then searches the captured text for any useful information such as passwords, credit card numbers, or personal information.

A keylogger can be a small hardware device or a software program. As a hardware device, the keylogger is inserted between the computer keyboard connection and USB port, as shown in Figure 3-4. Because the device resembles an ordinary keyboard plug and the computer keyboard USB port is often on the back of the computer, a hardware keylogger can easily go undetected. In addition, the device is beyond the reach of the computer's antimalware scanning software and thus raises no alarms. The attacker who installed the hardware keylogger returns at a later time and physically removes the device in order to access the information it has gathered.

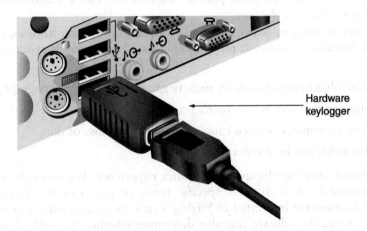

Hardware
keylogger

Figure 3-4   Hardware keylogger

NOTE   Today's hardware keyloggers have several advanced features. Some keyloggers will wirelessly transmit the captured information so that the user does not have to return and physically remove the device. Other keyloggers can be embedded into the keyboard itself and are completely invisible. The storage capacities of the hardware keyloggers can reach into the millions of keystrokes, thus capturing up to an entire year's worth of information.

Software keyloggers are programs installed on the computer that silently capture keystrokes. These programs act like rootkits and conceal themselves so that they cannot be easily detected by the user. An advantage of software keyloggers is that they do not require physical access to the user's computer as with a hardware keylogger. The software, often installed as a Trojan or by a virus, can routinely send captured information back to the attacker through the computer's Internet connection. Yet today's software keyloggers go far beyond just capturing a user's keystrokes: these programs can also make screen captures of everything that is on the user's screen and silently turn on the computer's web camera to record images of the user.

Keyloggers are often installed on public access computers, such as those in a school's open computer lab or a public library. If a sensitive password must be entered on one of these computers, almost all operating systems offer an on-screen "virtual" keyboard through which the keys are clicked with a mouse or touch screen, thus defeating a keylogger. For Windows computers it is found by clicking Accessories and then Ease of Use.

Adware **Adware** collects user information and then delivers advertising content in a manner that is unexpected and unwanted by the user. This is because adware programs essentially perform a tracking function, which monitors and tracks a user's online activities. It then sends a log of these activities to third parties—without the user's authorization or knowledge—who deliver their ads to the user.

Once the adware malware becomes installed, it typically displays advertising banners, popup ads, or opens new web browser windows at random intervals. Users generally reject adware because:

- Adware may display objectionable content, such as gambling sites or pornography.

- Frequent popup ads can interfere with a user's productivity.

- Popup ads can slow a computer or even cause crashes and the loss of data.

- Unwanted advertisements can be a nuisance.

Some adware goes beyond affecting the user's computer experience. For example, a user who visits online automobile sites to view specific types of cars can be tracked by adware and classified as someone interested in buying a new car. Based on the sequence and type of websites visited, the adware can also determine whether the surfers' behavior suggests they are close to making a purchase or are also looking at competitors' cars. This information is gathered by adware and then sold to automobile advertisers, who send the users regular mail advertisements about their cars or even call the user on the telephone.

Ransomware One of the fastest-growing types of malware is ransomware. **Ransomware** prevents a user's device from properly operating until a fee is paid. One type of ransomware locks up a user's computer and then displays a message that purports to come from a law enforcement agency. This message, using official-looking imagery, states that the user has performed an illegal action such as downloading pornography and must immediately pay a fine online by entering a credit card number. The computer remains "held hostage" and locked until the ransom payment is made by entering a numeric credit card number (the ransomware does not lock the numeric keys on the keyboard). Figure 3-5 shows a ransomware message from the Symantec website in its Security Response Center.

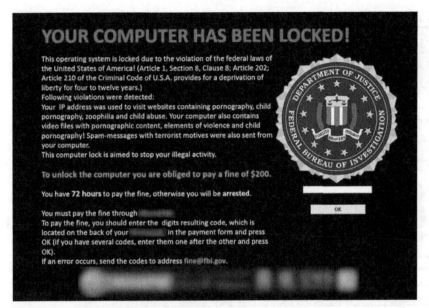

YOUR COMPUTER HAS BEEN LOCKED!

This operating system is locked due to the violation of the federal laws of the United States of America! (Article 1, Section 8, Clause 8; Article 202; Article 210 of the Criminal Code of U.S.A. provides for a deprivation of liberty for four to twelve years.)
Following violations were detected:
Your IP address was used to visit websites containing pornography, child pornography, zoophilia and child abuse. Your computer also contains video files with pornographic content, elements of violence and child pornography! Spam-messages with terrorist motives were also sent from your computer.
This computer lock is aimed to stop your illegal activity.

To unlock the computer you are obliged to pay a fine of $200.

You have **72 hours** to pay the fine, otherwise you will be **arrested**.

You must pay the fine through
To pay the fine, you should enter the digits resulting code, which is located on the back of your in the payment form and press OK (if you have several codes, enter them one after the other and press OK).
If an error occurs, send the codes to address fine@fbi.gov.

OK

Figure 3-5 Ransomware message

Source: Symantec Security Response

The ransom demanded is seldom exorbitant, and usually a payment of $300–$500 is required. The reason for the relatively modest fee is that attackers have determined the ideal price point. The ransom is not set so high that a user cannot or will not pay it or be motivated to contact law enforcement agencies. Instead, the lower ransom is usually seen by the user as more of a "nuisance fee" that is within the ability of most users to pay.

Another variation displays a fictitious warning that there is a problem with the computer such as (in a touch of irony) a malware infection or imminent hard drive failure. No matter what the condition of the computer, the ransomware always reports that there is a problem. This ransomware variation tells users that they must immediately purchase additional software online to fix the problem that in fact does not exist. The warning appears to be legitimate because it mimics the appearance of genuine software and—unlawfully—uses legitimate trademarks or icons. The ransomware example in Figure 3-6 uses color schemes and icons similar to those found on legitimate Windows software. Users who provide their credit card number to make the purchase find that the attackers simply capture that information and then use the card number for their own purposes.

In most instances, the ransomware embeds itself into the computer so that the message cannot be closed and rebooting the computer has no effect. In addition, most ransomware is part of a "package" in which other malware is also installed on the computer. This makes it very difficult to completely disinfect an infected computer.

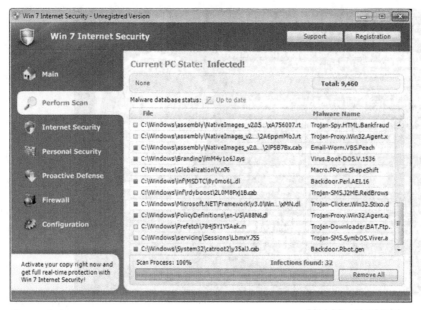

Figure 3-6 Ransomware computer infection

Source: Microsoft Security Intelligence Report

Delete Data The payload of other types of malware deletes data on the computer. This may involve deleting important user data files, such as documents or photos, or erasing vital operating system files so that the computer will no longer properly function.

One type of malware that is frequently used to delete data is a logic bomb. A **logic bomb** is computer code that is typically added to a legitimate program but lies dormant until it is triggered by a specific logical event. Once it is triggered, the program then deletes data or performs other malicious activities.

There have been several high-profile incidents in businesses regarding logic bombs. In one example, a Maryland government employee tried to destroy the contents of more than 4,000 servers by planting a logic bomb script that was scheduled to activate 90 days after his employment was terminated.[4] In another incident a temporary contract employee inserted a logic bomb that would delete data stored on computers regarding the project on which he was working after his contract expired; his plan was to have the company hire him back as a consultant—at a large fee—in order to fix the problem.[5] Logic bombs are difficult to detect before they are triggered. This is because logic bombs are often embedded in very large computer programs, some containing tens of thousands of lines of code, and a trusted employee can easily insert a few lines of computer code into a long program without anyone detecting it. In addition, these programs are not routinely scanned for malicious content.

Logic bombs have sometimes been used by legitimate software companies to ensure payment for their software. If a payment is not made by the due date, the logic bomb activates and prevents the software from being used again. In some instances, logic bombs even erase the software and the accompanying payroll or customer files from the computer.

For home computers most often a logic bomb is based on a specific time or date. When the computer system's internal clock reaches that time or date then the bomb detonates.

Logic bombs should not be confused with an *Easter egg*, which refers to an undocumented, yet benign hidden feature that launches by entering a set of special commands, key combinations, or mouse clicks. In an earlier version of Microsoft Excel there was actually an entire game called "The Hall of Tortured Souls" that was embedded as an Easter egg. Recent versions of the Google Chrome web browser running on Android devices also have an embedded game.

Modify System Security The payload of some types of malware attempts to modify the system's security settings so that more insidious attacks can be made. One type of malware in this category is called a backdoor. A **backdoor** gives access to a computer, program, or service that circumvents any normal security protections. Backdoors that are installed on a computer allow the attacker to return at a later time and bypass security settings.

Creating a legitimate backdoor is common practice by developers, who may need to access a program or device on a regular basis, yet do not want to be hindered by continual requests for passwords or other security approvals. The intent is for the backdoor to be removed once the application is finalized. However, in some instances backdoors have been left installed, and attackers have used them to bypass security.

Launch Attacks One of the common payloads of malware today is software that will allow the infected computer to be placed under the remote control of an attacker. This infected robot (*bot*) computer is known as a **zombie**. When hundreds, thousands, or even hundreds of thousands of zombie computers are gathered into a logical computer network, they create a **botnet** under the control of the attacker (**bot herder**).

Due to the multitasking capabilities of modern computers, a computer can act as a zombie while at the same time carrying out the tasks of its regular user. The user is completely unaware that his or her computer is being used for malicious activities.

Infected zombie computers wait for instructions through a *command and control* (C&C or C2) structure from the bot herders regarding which computers to attack and how.

A common botnet C&C mechanism used today is the Hypertext Transport Protocol (HTTP), which is the standard protocol for Internet usage, thus making it difficult to detect and block. For example, a zombie can receive its instructions by automatically signing in to a website that the bot herder operates or to a third-party website on which information has been placed that the zombie knows how to interpret as commands (this latter technique has an advantage in that the bot herder does not need to have an affiliation with that website). Other botnets use blogs or send specially coded attack commands through posts on the Twitter social networking service or notes posted in Facebook.

Some bot herders use a "dead drop" C&C mechanism. First a bogus Google Gmail email account is set up and the zombie malware has the account username and password coded into it. The bot herder then creates a draft email message in Gmail but never sends it. At set times the zombie logs in to Gmail and reads the draft to receive its instructions. The benefits of this dead drop are that the email message is never sent so there is no record of it and all Gmail transmissions are protected so that they cannot be viewed by outsiders.

Table 3-3 lists some of the attacks that can be generated through botnets.

Type of attack	Description
Spamming	Botnets are widely recognized as the primary source of spam email. A botnet consisting of thousands of zombies enables an attacker to send massive amounts of spam.
Spreading malware	Botnets can be used to spread malware and create new zombies and botnets. Zombies have the ability to download and execute a file sent by the attacker.
Manipulating online polls	Because each zombie has a unique Internet Protocol (IP) address, each "vote" by a zombie will have the same credibility as a vote cast by a real person. Online games can be manipulated in a similar way.
Denying services	Botnets can flood a web server with thousands of requests and overwhelm it to the point that it cannot respond to legitimate requests.

Table 3-3   Uses of botnets

In many ways a botnet is the ideal base of operations for attackers. Zombies are designed to operate in the background, often without any visible evidence of their existence. By keeping a low profile, botnets are sometimes able to remain active and operational for years.

The ubiquitous always-on Internet service provided by residential broadband ensures that a large percentage of zombies in a botnet are accessible at any given time. This has resulted in a staggering number of botnets. One botnet may have contained more than 50 million zombies, and another botnet was responsible for sending 60 percent of all worldwide spam (or over 60 billion emails daily).[6]

Security in Your World

Dr. Antonelli had just finished describing to Sanne the different types of attacks that a computer faces today. "I had no idea there were that many!" she said. "OK, so what do I do now? If antivirus software can't stop everything, do I need an anti-something for each one?"

Dr. Antonelli set down his coffee cup. "No, not really. There are some different protections that you'll want to install on your computer. But there are two things that I would consider to be critically important. The first is to make sure your new computer will automatically install software patches." Sanne pulled out a piece of paper from her backpack. "I remember that we talked about patches last week. These are software updates that fix software security problems on your computer." Dr. Antonelli smiled. "Yes, that's right. You will want your computer to automatically install them, so you don't have to do anything."

"That sounds good," said Sanne. "Now what's the second thing?" Dr. Antonelli said, "The second thing is something that everybody knows that they should do, but still very few people do it as regularly as they should. It's one of the most important protections you have against these attackers. Can you guess what it is?" Sanne thought for a moment and said, "I'm afraid you've got me stumped. What is it?" Dr. Antonelli opened up a desk drawer and pulled out a portable hard drive. "It's backing up everything on your computer on a device like this," he said. "With all the new attacks that come out each day, the overwhelming odds are that your new computer could get infected. Having a good backup will protect you so you won't lose anything that's on your computer."

Sanne smiled. "That's what I need. How do we get started?"

Computer Defenses

Because of the large number and different types of attacks and the fact that new attacks are being continually introduced, there are several security protections that a computer should have installed and configured to resist attacks. The defenses include managing patches, configuring personal firewalls, installing antimalware software, monitoring User Account Control, creating data backups, and knowing how to recover from an attack.

Managing Patches

Early operating systems were simply program loaders whose job was to launch applications. As more features and graphical user interfaces (GUIs) were added, they became more complex. Due to the increased complexity of operating systems, unintentional vulnerabilities were introduced that could be exploited by attackers. In addition, new attack tools made what were once considered secure functions and services on operating systems now vulnerable.

Microsoft's first operating system, MS-DOS v1.0, had 4,000 lines of code, while Windows 10 is estimated to have up to 80 million lines.

To address the vulnerabilities in operating systems that are uncovered after the software has been released, software vendors usually deploy a software "fix." A fix can come in a variety of formats. A security **patch** is a publicly released software security update intended to repair a vulnerability. **Feature updates** are enhancements to the software to provide new or expanded functionality, but do not address a security vulnerability. A **service pack** is software that is a cumulative package of all patches and feature updates.

Microsoft releases what it calls "service bulletins" that typically contain a set of patches for a group of software products, such as all the supported versions of Windows. These bulletins include a severity rating system that rates the impact of the vulnerability that the patch is fixing (Critical, Important, Moderate, or Low) and an Exploitability Index, which is the likelihood of an attack based on the vulnerability. This Exploitability Index is "1: Consistent Exploit Code Likely" (an attack could consistently exploit the vulnerability), "2: Inconsistent Exploit Code Likely" (an attack could be created but it would not function consistently in each case), and "3: Functioning Exploit Code Unlikely" (attacks based on the vulnerability are unlikely to be released).

Modern operating systems have the ability to perform automatic patch updates to their software so that the user's computer interacts with the vendor's online update service to receive the patches. Prior to Windows 10, Microsoft users had several options regarding accepting or even rejecting patches. These options included *Install updates automatically*, *Download updates but let me choose whether to install them*, *Check for updates but let me choose whether to download and install them*, and *Never check for updates*. However, with the release of Windows 10 Microsoft significantly changed its security update procedures and user options. These changes include:

- *Forced updates*. Users cannot refuse or delay security updates. All updates will be downloaded and installed automatically. Windows 10 Home edition users will also automatically receive feature updates, although Windows 10 Professional edition users can postpone feature updates for several months.

- *No selective updates*. Unlike in previous versions of Windows, users cannot select individual Windows updates to download and install. However, users can select if they wish to receive updates for other installed Microsoft products (such as Office).

- *Continual updates*. Microsoft traditionally has released its patches on the second Tuesday of each month, called "Patch Tuesday," unless the patch addresses a particularly serious vulnerability, and it is then released immediately. However, with Windows 10

Microsoft has said that patches will be distributed whenever they become available and are needed.

- *Choose when to reboot.* Some updates require that the computer must be rebooted in order for the updates to take effect. Now users can choose either the default "Automatic" (in which the computer will reboot whenever the computer is not being used) or "Notify to schedule restart" (the computer will not automatically reboot but the user will first be notified to schedule a reboot).

- *More efficient distribution.* If there are multiple Windows 10 devices connected to a network, then each device does not have to download the updates over the Internet individually. Instead, once one device has downloaded the updates these can then be distributed to the other devices across the local network. In addition, Windows will not download updates on mobile devices unless that device is connected to an unrestricted Wi-Fi network (so that it does not use the cellular data connections that users pay for).

- *Up-to-date resets.* With previous versions of Microsoft Windows, if a computer needed to be reset to its original configuration then all of the subsequent patches had to be reinstalled, a process that often would take hours of time and require the user to be at the computer in order to manage multiple reboots. With Windows 10, a "PC Reset" will install the current up-to-date Windows software.

The patch update options for Microsoft Windows 10 are seen in Figure 3-7.

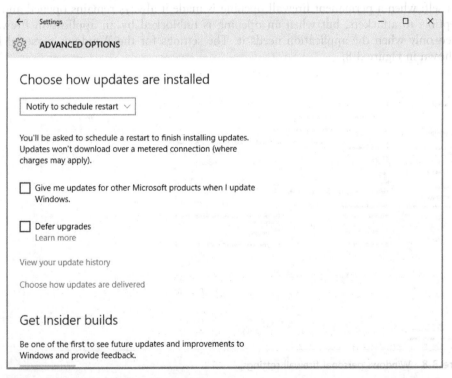

Figure 3-7   Windows 10 update options

Microsoft is following the trend among software vendors to automatically down-load and install patches without any user intervention or options. The Google Chrome web browser is automatically updated whenever it is necessary without even telling the user—and there are no user configuration settings to opt out of the updates.

Examining Firewalls

Both national and local building codes require commercial buildings, apartments, and other similar structures to have a *firewall*. In building construction, a firewall is usually a brick, concrete, or masonry unit positioned vertically through all stories of the building. Its purpose is to contain a fire and prevent it from spreading.

A computer **firewall**, technically called a *packet filter*, serves a similar purpose: it is designed to limit the spread of malware. There are two types of firewalls. A software-based **personal firewall** runs as a program on the local computer to block or filter traffic coming into and out of the computer. All modern operating systems include a *host-based application firewall*. As the name suggests these firewalls are *application-based*. That is, an application or program running on a computer may need to communicate with another computer on the local network or an Internet server to send and receive information. These transmissions normally would be blocked by the firewall. With an application firewall, an opening in the firewall just for that program can be created by the user simply approving the application to transmit (called *unblocking*). This is more secure than permanently opening an entry point on the firewall itself: when a permanent firewall opening is made it always remains opened and is then susceptible to attackers, but when an opening is unblocked by an application firewall it is opened only when the application needs it. The settings for the Windows personal firewall are shown in Figure 3-8.

Figure 3-8 Windows personal firewall settings

Application firewalls can limit the spread of malware into the computer as well as prevent a user's infected computer from attacking other computers. For most application firewalls, inbound connections (data coming in from another source) are blocked unless there is a specific firewall rule setting that allows them in. Outbound connections (data going out to another source) are allowed unless there is a rule that blocks them and the outbound rules are turned on.

The second type of firewall is a hardware-based **network firewall**. Although a personal host-based application software firewall that runs as a program on one computer is different in many respects from a network firewall designed to protected an entire network, their functions are essentially the same: to inspect network traffic and either accept or deny entry. Table 3-4 compares these two types of firewalls. Hardware firewalls are usually located at the "edge" of the network as the first line of defense defending the network and devices connected to it. Most home users have a network firewall as part of their networking equipment that provides Wi-Fi access or connects computers and devices such as printers together.

Even home networking devices that do not have a specific firewall can still perform functions that limit entry into the network by unauthorized outsiders.

Function	Personal firewall	Network firewall
Location	Runs on a single computer	Located on edge of the network
Scope of protection	Protects only computer on which it is installed	Protects all devices connected to the network
Type	Software that runs on computer	Separate hardware device
Filtering	Based on programs running on the computer	Provides sophisticated range of filtering mechanisms

Table 3-4   Personal and network firewalls

Personal and hardware firewalls overlap in some ways, but each provides unique benefits. A hardware firewall is isolated from the computer so that an infection on the computer that could compromise the personal firewall will not impact the hardware firewall. However, a hardware firewall knows very little about what program on the computer is making an outgoing connection. For this reason you should have both a personal and hardware firewall.

Users should periodically examine both their personal firewalls and network firewalls. These checks should include determining that the firewalls are functioning (many types of malware attempt to turn off firewalls), performing an external test on the firewall, and making sure that unnecessary entry points have not been made through the firewall.

The steps for examining a Windows 10 personal firewall are covered in Hands-On Project 2-1.

Installing Antimalware Software

At one time installing antimalware software was considered to be the primary defense against attackers. One of the first antimalware software security applications was **antivirus (AV)** software. This software can examine a computer for any infections as well as monitor computer activity and scan new documents that might contain a virus (this scanning is typically performed when files are opened, created, or closed). If a virus is detected, options generally include cleaning the file of the virus, quarantining the infected file, or deleting the file. Figure 3-9 shows the settings of a typical AV program.

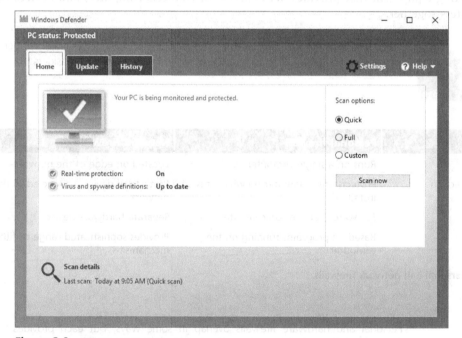

Figure 3-9 AV program settings

However, today AV is considered only part of a protection plan. Viruses are only one type of attack: worms, Trojans, spyware, ransomware, and many other types of malware all require different protections. And even if AV could offer comprehensive protection, AV vendors cannot keep up with the sheer number of new attacks. This is because many AV products scan files by attempting to match known virus patterns against potentially infected files, called *static analysis*. The host AV software contains a virus scanning engine and a database of known virus signatures, which are created by extracting a sequence of characters—a string—found in the virus that then serves as a virus's unique "signature." This database is called the **signature file**. By comparing the virus signatures against a potentially infected file (called *string scanning*), a match may indicate an infected file. The weakness of static analysis is that the AV vendor must constantly be searching for new viruses, extracting virus signatures, and distributing those updated databases to all users. Any out-of-date signature file could result in an infection.

A recent study examined how long it took the four major AV vendors to distribute their updates to protect against the latest viruses. After looking at "tens of thousands" of instances of malware and the average time it took the AV vendors to distribute their updates, the study found that after one week the AV software still was not able to detect 28 percent of the malware, and it took almost six months for the AV software to protect against all of the malware.[7]

This is not to say that AV software is completely unnecessary. A newer approach to AV is *dynamic heuristic detection*, which uses a variety of techniques to spot the characteristics of a virus instead of attempting to make matches using a signature file. One technique used is *code emulation* in which a "virtual" environment is created that simulates the central processing unit (CPU) and memory of the computer. Any questionable program code is executed in the virtual environment (no actual virus code is executed by the real computer) to determine if it is a virus. Dynamic heuristic detection helps improve the capabilities of AV software.

The difference between static analysis and dynamic heuristic detection is similar to how airport security personnel in some nations screen for terrorists. A known terrorist attempting to go through security can be identified by comparing his face against photographs of known terrorists (static analysis). But what about a new terrorist for whom there is no photograph? Security personnel can look at the person's characteristics—holding a one-way ticket, not checking any luggage, showing extreme nervousness—as possible indicators that the individual may need to be questioned (dynamic heuristic detection).

Another type of antimalware software is **antispyware** that helps prevent computers from becoming infected by different types of spyware. One example of antispyware is a **popup blocker**, which is a separate program or a feature incorporated within a browser that stops popup advertisements from appearing. A browser popup blocker allows the user to limit or block most popups. Users can select the level of blocking, ranging from blocking all popups to allowing specific popups. When a popup is detected, an alert can be displayed in the browser such as: *Popup blocked; to see this popup or additional options click here.*

Despite that fact that antimalware software like AV provides only limited protection it is nevertheless recommended that users install AV software to take advantage of the protection that it does provide. However, antimalware software should be considered as only one tool in a large arsenal of weapons that must be employed to defend against attackers.

Monitoring User Account Control (UAC)

A *user account* indicates the privilege level of a user; that is, it tells the computer which files and folders can be accessed and what configuration changes can be made to the computer.

Microsoft Windows users can be assigned one of three different types of user accounts, each giving a different level of control over the computer:

- *Guest accounts.* Guest accounts are intended for users who need temporary use of a computer. There are very few settings that can be changed from a guest account.

- *Standard accounts.* A standard account is designed for everyday computing activities and allows some settings to be modified.

- *Administrator accounts.* The highest level of user account is an administrator account. This provides the most control over a computer.

Modern operating systems contain a function that alerts the user to an event that the operating system is about to perform and may also ask explicit permission from the user to perform this task. This helps prevent a Trojan or other malware from secretly making changes or installing new software. In Microsoft Windows this security function is called **User Account Control (UAC)**. UAC provides information to users and obtains their approval before a program can make a change to the computer's settings.

When requesting approval from the user the UAC can perform two actions. First, it can temporarily switch to *secure desktop mode* in which the entire screen is dimmed. Desktop mode prevents an attacker from manipulating any UAC messages that appear on the screen. Second, a UAC dialog box appears. If the user has an administrator account, the user must click *Continue* or *Yes* before UAC will allow any changes to be made or software installed. Figure 3-10 shows UAC settings. If the user's level is Standard or Guest, then the administrator password must be entered by another person before any changes are permitted.

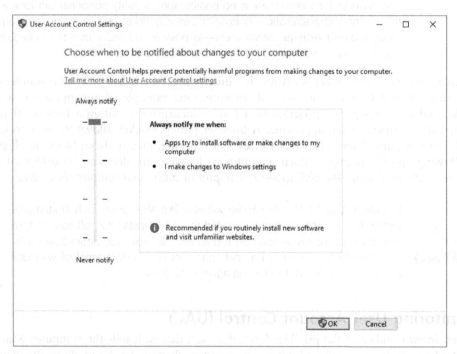

Figure 3-10   User Account Control settings

The Windows UAC interface also provides extended information. A shield icon warns users if they attempt to access any feature that requires UAC permission. In addition, the UAC prompt includes a description of the requested action. The UAC prompts are color-coded to indicate the level of risk, from red (highest risk) to yellow (lowest risk).

There are four levels of UAC that can be adjusted to the user's preference. These are *Always notify, Notify me only when programs try to make changes to my computer, Notify me only when programs try to make changes to my computer (do not dim my desktop)*, and *Never notify*. It is recommended that the highest protection level of *Always notify* should be set.

You should always pause when a UAC dialog box appears instead of just giving immediate approval. What were you doing when the box appeared? For example, if you were starting a software installation, then the UAC warning reflects your actions and you may approve it. However, if you were visiting a website or performing a software download and the UAC box appears, then you should deny the request.

Creating Data Backups

One of the most important defenses against attacks is frequently overlooked: it is to regularly create **data backups**. Creating a data backup means copying files from a computer's hard drive onto other digital media that is stored in a secure location. Data backups protect against computer attacks because they can restore infected computers to their properly functioning state. Data backups can also protect against hardware malfunctions, user error, software corruption, and natural disasters.

There are several ways to easily create backups. These may be divided into scheduled backups and continuous backups.

Scheduled Backups A *scheduled backup* is performed intentionally by the user. It could be performed every morning at 3:00 (automated) or whenever the user remembers that a backup is needed (on demand). When performing scheduled backups several questions must be asked in advance to ensure the backup meets the users' needs.

The first question is *what* data should be backed up. All user-created files that cannot be easily or quickly recreated should be backed up. These include any personal files, such as documents created with a word processor, digital photos, personal financial data, and other similar information. However, should programs installed on the computer, such as the operating system or a word processor program, also be backed up? If these programs are readily available elsewhere or can be retrieved easily, such as from a DVD or downloaded online, there is little need to back them up along with the data files.

The main reason to back up programs along with user data files is that it allows an infected computer to be completely restored more quickly from the backup instead of installing all of the programs individually from DVDs or online before restoring the user data files.

The second question is *what media* should be used. Optical disc storage like a DVD, although compact and inexpensive, nevertheless requires the user to be present during the backup process to continually "feed" discs into the drive if multiple discs are required. A more viable option is to use a portable external hard drive. These devices connect to the USB port of a computer and provide backup capabilities; they are fast, portable, and can store large amounts of data.

The third question is *where to store* the backup. Consider a user who installs a second hard drive in his computer to back up the data from primary hard drive each night. This would allow for the primary hard drive to be restored quickly in the event of an infection or primary hard drive failure. However, what about a theft, fire, tornado, or lightning strike? These events could destroy both the primary hard drive and the backup hard drive. It is recommended that a copy of the data backup be stored at an off-site location, such as at a work location, a friend's house, or on the Internet.

Home users should consider using the 3-2-1 backup plan. This plan says that you should always maintain *three* different copies of your backups (that does not count the original data itself) by using at least *two* different types of media on which to store these backups (a separate hard drive, an external hard drive, a USB device, online storage, etc.) and store *one* of the backups offsite.

The final question is *how frequently* the backup should be performed. It is recommended that backups be performed once per day on computers that are being used frequently. If that is not possible then a regular schedule (such as every Tuesday and Friday) should be implemented.

Modern operating systems can perform automated backups, and third-party software is also available that provides additional functionality.

Continuous Backups A *continuous backup* is one that is performed continually without any intervention by the user. Software monitors what files have changed and automatically updates the backed up files with the most recent versions. The first continuous backups were performed locally: changes to files on a user's hard drive were automatically updated to an attached USB hard drive. Today continuous backups can be performed online. There are several Internet services available that provide features similar to these:

- *Automatic continuous backup.* Once the initial backup is completed, any new or modified files are also backed up. Usually the backup software will "sleep" while the computer is being used and perform backups only when there is no user activity. This helps to lessen any impact on the computer's performance or Internet speed.

- *Universal access.* Files backed up through online services can be made available to another computer.

- *Optional program file backup*. In addition to user data files these services can as an option also back up all program and operating system files.

- *Delayed deletion*. Files that are copied to the online server will remain accessible for up to 30 days before they are deleted. This allows a user to have a longer window of opportunity to restore a deleted file.

- *Online or disc-based restore*. If a file or the entire computer must be restored this can be done online. Some services also provide the option of shipping to the user the backup files on DVDs.

The advantage of online continuous backups is they are performed automatically and stored at a remote location. These may provide the highest degree of protection today to users.

There are several services, some of which are free, that automatically back up any files that are placed in a designated folder on your computer. Although not as full-featured as online backup services, they do allow for backups of important data files.

Recovering from Attacks

Just as a homeowner cannot be absolutely certain that her house will never be broken into even if she has installed strong door locks, the same is true with computer security.

Preparation is the key to recovering from an attack. For Microsoft Windows users it is important to create a *recovery drive* (that can run from a USB flash drive) or *system repair disc* (that runs from a DVD disc) that can help repair Windows in the event of a serious error, such as errors caused by malware. In addition, there are several software vendors online that offer free downloadable *rescue discs*. These are downloadable images that can be used to create a bootable DVD or USB flash drive. When the computer is restarted it will bypass the infected hard drive and boot from the DVD or flash drive, which will then automatically scan and disinfect the computer.

Exceptional Security

MANAGING PATCHES—If necessary, set your computer's operating system to always install the most recent security patches automatically. Monitor the downloads and if the computer must be rebooted, select "Restart Now" as soon as the patches are installed; do not wait until later or select a restart time for a later date because the patches do not take effect until the computer is rebooted. Permit updates for other software products to also be installed. Pay attention to current security news and watch for information about patches that are available for other software, such as

(continues)

Adobe Flash and Oracle Java. Download and install these patches immediately. Switch to software products that perform automatic patch downloads and installations, such as Google Chrome.

MONITOR FIREWALLS—Periodically check the settings of the host-based application firewall to monitor which applications have permission to go through the firewall. Consider deleting those applications that are rarely used but still have permission to go through the firewall. Although all application firewalls have outbound rules they are not always turned on by default, essentially defeating their purpose. Be sure that outbound rules are turned on. Check the firewall on your wireless router or similar network device and be sure that it is turned on. Disable Universal Plug and Play (UPnP) on network firewalls. If you must absolutely use UPnP, look for a router that offers detailed status information about the state of forwarded ports, such as the app that made the UPnP request and details on the currently active port forwarding rules.

DATA BACKUPS—Implement a strong backup strategy. Have an image of your computer's hard drive automatically backed up every day. Every few days copy this image to an external USB hard drive that is stored in another room. Once per week copy the image to another external USB hard drive and keep this drive stored at a remote location. Periodically test a backup by installing it on another computer. Or consider an online continuous backup service.

OTHER—Set UAC to "Always notify." Make it a habit to pause when the UAC prompt appears and think about what you are doing before approving the request. Install AV software and run a complete scan at least once per week. Create a recovery disk of your operating system and store it at a remote location. Identify websites that have software that can be downloaded to boot and scan a computer for malware. Download the software and use it to scan your computer to check it for malware and to become familiar with the process. Save the name of the website with your recovery disk (do not save the scanning software since it can become quickly out of date).

Chapter Summary

- Malware is malicious software that enters a computer system without the owner's knowledge or consent and includes a wide variety of damaging actions. One method of classifying the various types of malware is by using the primary trait that the malware possesses. These traits are circulation, infection, concealment, and payload capabilities.

- One of the types of malware that has the primary trait of circulation is a computer virus. A virus is malicious computer code that reproduces itself on the same computer. A virus inserts itself into a computer file (a data file or program) and then tries to reproduce on the same computer as well as unload its malicious payload. Another type of such malware is a worm, which travels through a network and is designed to take advantage of a vulnerability in an application or an operating system in order to enter a user's computer. Once the worm has exploited the vulnerability on one system, it immediately searches for another computer that has the same vulnerability. A Trojan is a program advertised as performing one activity but in addition does something malicious. Some malware has as its primary trait avoiding detection. A rootkit is a set of software tools used to hide the actions or presence of other types of software.

- The destructive power of malware is to be found in its payload capabilities. When the payload allows an attacker to execute virtually any command on the victim's computer, this is called arbitrary code execution. Most often arbitrary code execution takes advantage of a vulnerability in the operating system software or an application program. Different types of malware are designed to collect important data from the user's computer and make it available to the attacker. Spyware is a general term used to describe software that secretly spies on users by collecting information without their consent. One type of spyware is a keylogger, which silently captures and stores each keystroke that a user types on the computer's keyboard. Adware is a software program that delivers advertising content in a manner that is unexpected and unwanted by the user. Ransomware locks up a user's computer and then displays a message that purports to come from a law enforcement agency or security software company and demands payment of a fine online before the computer is released.

- The payload of other types of malware deletes data on the computer. A logic bomb is computer code that is typically added to a legitimate program but lies dormant until it is triggered by a specific logical event. The payload of some types of malware attempts to modify the system's security settings so that more insidious attacks can be made. One type of malware in this category is called a backdoor. A backdoor gives access to a computer, program, or service that circumvents any normal security protections. One of the most common payloads of malware today is software that will allow the infected computer to be placed under the remote control of an attacker. This infected computer is known as a zombie. When zombie computers are gathered into a logical computer network, they create a botnet.

- Due to the increased complexity of software, unintentional vulnerabilities were introduced that could be exploited by attackers. In addition, new attack tools made what were once considered secure functions and services on operating systems now vulnerable. A security patch is a publicly released software security update intended to repair a vulnerability. Modern operating systems have the ability to perform automatic patch updates so that the user's computer interacts with the vendor's online update service to receive the patches.

- A computer firewall is designed to limit the spread of malware. There are two types of firewalls. A software-based personal firewall runs as a program on the local computer to block or filter traffic coming into and out of the computer. A hardware-based network firewall is usually located at the "edge" of the network as the first line of defense defending the network and devices connected to it.

- One of the first antimalware software security applications was antivirus (AV) software that can examine a computer for any infections as well as monitor computer activity and scan new documents that might contain a virus. Many AV products scan files by attempting to match known virus patterns against potentially infected files. The host AV software contains a virus scanning engine and a database of known virus signatures called the signature file. Due to delays in updating signature files AV software is no longer considered as the premier means of providing protection.

Another type of antimalware software is antispyware. One example of antispyware is a popup blocker, which is a separate program or a feature incorporated within a browser that stops popup advertisements from appearing.

■ Modern operating systems contain a function that alerts the user to an event that the operating system is about to perform and may also ask explicit permission from the user to perform this task. In Microsoft Windows this security function is called User Account Control (UAC).

■ One of the most important defenses against attacks is to create data backups on a regular basis. Creating a data backup means copying files from a computer's hard drive onto other digital media that is stored in a secure location. Data backups protect against computer attacks because they can restore infected computers to their properly functioning state. A scheduled backup is one that is performed intentionally by the user, whereas a continuous backup is one that is performed continually without any intervention by the user.

■ In spite of the best defenses, sooner or later an attack on a computer may be successful. System repair discs can be created from the operating system to help repair the software in the event of a successful attack. In addition, there are several software vendors online that offer free downloadable rescue discs.

Key Terms

Definitions for key terms can be found in the Glossary for this text.

adware	firewall	rootkit
antispyware	keylogger	service pack
antivirus (AV)	logic bomb	signature file
arbitrary code execution	malware	spyware
backdoor	network firewall	Trojan horse (Trojan)
bot herder	patch	User Account Control (UAC)
botnet	personal firewall	worm
computer virus (virus)	popup blocker	zombie
data backup	ransomware	
feature update	remote code execution	

Review Questions

1. A(n) _____ requires a user to transport it from one computer to another.
   a. adware
   b. worm
   c. rootkit
   d. virus

2. Which of these is NOT an action that a virus can take?

   a. transport itself through the network to another device

   b. reformat the hard disk drive

   c. cause a computer to crash

   d. erase files from a hard drive

3. Which malware locks up a user's computer and then displays a message that purports to come from a law enforcement agency?

   a. virus

   b. ransomware

   c. worm

   d. Trojan

4. Which of the following is not a type of malware that has as its primary trait circulation and/or infection?

   a. Trojan

   b. virus

   c. worm

   d. botnet

5. A user who installs a program that prints out coupons but in the background silently collects her passwords has installed a _____.

   a. virus

   b. worm

   c. Trojan

   d. logic bomb

6. Malware payload allows an attacker to execute virtually any command on the victim's computer; this is called _____.

   a. arbitrary code execution

   b. remote configuration

   c. master control

   d. extension reach code

7. Which of these could NOT be defined as a logic bomb?

   a. Erase all data if John Smith's name is removed from the list of employees.

   b. Reformat the hard drive three months after Susan Jones left the company.

   c. Send spam email to all users in the company.

   d. If the company's stock price drops below $10, then credit Jeff Brown with 10 additional years of retirement credit.

8. What is access a computer, program, or service that circumvents any normal security protections called?

    a. hole

    b. backdoor

    c. trapdoor

    d. honey pit

9. Which of these is a general term used for describing software that gathers information without the user's consent?

    a. pullware

    b. adware

    c. spyware

    d. scrapeware

10. Which statement regarding a keylogger is NOT true?

    a. Software keyloggers are easy to detect.

    b. Keyloggers can be used to capture passwords, credit card numbers, or personal information.

    c. Hardware keyloggers are installed between the keyboard connector and computer keyboard USB port.

    d. Software keyloggers can be designed to send captured information automatically back to the attacker through the Internet.

11. Botnets are composed of _____ .

    a. Internet Relay Chat (IRC) instruments

    b. zombies

    c. herders

    d. spam

12. Each of the following is the reason why adware is scorned, except _____ .

    a. it displays the attackers programming skills

    b. it can interfere with a user's productivity

    c. it displays objectionable content

    d. it can cause a computer to crash or slow down

13. Each of the following is a typical feature of a fee-based Internet backup service except _____ .

    a. backup to an external hard drive

    b. universal access

    c. file feedback information

    d. delayed deletion

14. How many carriers must a virus have to replicate and attack?

    a. one

    b. two

    c. three

    d. four

15. Which level of UAC provides the lowest level of security?

    a. Universal notify

    b. Always notify

    c. Never notify

    d. Notify on demand

16. Which of the following enhancements to software provides new or expanded functionality but does not address security vulnerabilities?

    a. feature update

    b. patch

    c. service pack

    d. resource package

17. Which type of firewall is an external hardware device?

    a. personal firewall

    b. remote firewall

    c. network firewall

    d. application resource firewall

18. The database that contains the sequence of characters of a virus is called the _____.

    a. string file

    b. malware DB

    c. virus resource file

    d. signature file

19. Each of the following is a question that the user should ask regarding data backups except _____.

    a. What content should be backed up?

    b. Who should do the backup?

    c. Where should the backup be stored?

    d. How frequently should be backup be performed?

20. A _____ is a downloadable image that can be used to scan a computer for malware.

    a. system repair disc

    b. rescue disc

    c. resource disc

    d. clean disc

Hands-On Projects

Project 3-1: Configure Microsoft Windows Security

It is important that security settings be properly configured on a computer in order to protect it. In this project, you will examine several security settings on a Microsoft Windows 10 computer.

This project shows how to configure Windows security for a personal computer. If this computer is part of a computer lab or office, these settings should not be changed without the proper permissions.

1. Click **Start** and **Settings**.

2. Click **Update and security**.

3. If necessary click **Windows Update** in the left pane.

4. Click **Advanced options,** then under **Choose how updates are installed** change to **Automatic (recommended).**

Remember that the safest approach is to restart the device as soon as any updates have been installed.

5. Click **Give me updates for other Microsoft products when I update Windows.** This will allow for updates for Microsoft software such as Office to also be updated.

6. Click **View your update history** to see the updates that have been installed on your computer.

7. Click the **back arrow.**

8. Click the **back arrow** to return to **Update & Security.**

9. Click **Windows Defender.** This is the Microsoft AV product that is part of Windows 10.

10. Be sure that all the settings are set to On.

11. Click **Use Windows Defender.** The Windows Defender dialog box appears.

12. Under **Scan options:** be sure that **Quick** is selected.

13. Now perform a Quick scan of the most essential files. Click **Scan now**. Depending upon your system it may take several minutes to complete. What was the result of the scan?

14. Click the **History** tab. Be sure that **Quarantined items** is selected and click **View details**. Has Defender already identified suspicious files on this computer and placed them in quarantine? When you are finished, close Windows Defender.

15. In the **Find a setting** search box enter **UAC** and press **Enter**.

16. Click **Change User Account Control Settings**. The **User Account Control Settings** dialog box opens.

17. Move the slider through all of the choices and notice the description of each.

18. Position the slider to **Always notify**. Why is this the best security setting? Click **OK** and then **Yes**.

19. Now check your personal firewall. Return to the **Settings** window. Click **Network and Internet**.

20. Click **Ethernet**.

21. Click **Windows Firewall** to view the firewall settings.

22. Click **Allow an app or feature through Windows Firewall** to display the **Allowed apps** dialog box as seen in Figure 3-11. Scroll through the list of apps that can transmit through the firewall. Are there apps that you are not using that should be removed from this list?

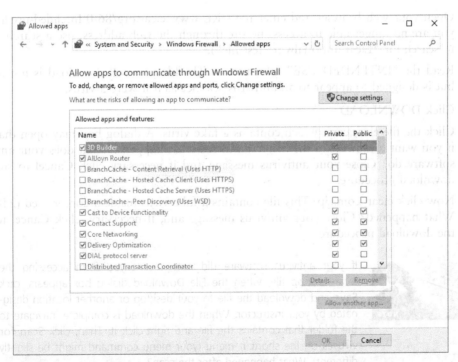

Figure 3-11   Allowed apps dialog box

23. Close the **Allowed apps** dialog box.

24. Close the **Settings** dialog box.

25. Finally, create a recovery drive for this computer. First insert a blank USB flash drive.

26. In the Windows search box enter **recoverydrive.exe** and press **Enter**. Click **Yes** in the UAC.

27. The Recovery Drive dialog box appears. Click **Next**.

28. The system gathers the appropriate files. In the **Select the USB flash drive** dialog box select the appropriate drive. Click **Next**.

29. Click **Create** to complete the process.

30. After the drive has been created close all windows.

Project 3-2: Test Antivirus Software

What happens when antivirus software detects a virus? In this project you download a virus test file to determine how your AV software reacts. The file downloaded is not a virus but is designed to appear to an antivirus scanner as if it were a virus.

You need to have antivirus software installed and running on your computer to perform this project.

1. Open your web browser and enter the URL **www.eicar.org/86-0-Intended-use.html** (if you are no longer able to access the site through the web address, use a search engine to search for "Eicar anti-malware test file").

2. Read the "INTENDED USE" information. The file you will download is not a virus but is designed to appear to an antivirus scanner as if it were a virus.

3. Click **DOWNLOAD**.

4. Click the file **eicar.com**, which contains a fake virus. A dialog box may open that asks if you want to download the file. Wait to see what happens. What does your antivirus software do? Close your antivirus message and if necessary click **Cancel** to stop the download procedure.

5. Now click **eicar_com.zip**. This file contains a fake virus inside a compressed (ZIP) file. What happened? Close your antivirus message and, if necessary, click **Cancel** to stop the download procedure.

If your antivirus software did not prevent you from accessing the eicar_com.zip file, when the File Download dialog box appears, click **Save** and download the file to your desktop or another location designated by your instructor. When the download is complete, navigate to the folder that contains the file and right-click it. Then, click **Scan for viruses** on the shortcut menu (your menu command might be slightly different). What happened after the scan?

6. Click **eicarcom2.zip**. This file has a double-compressed ZIP file with a fake virus. What happened? Close your antivirus message and, if necessary, click **Cancel** to stop the download procedure.

7. If necessary erase any files that were saved to your computer.

8. Close all windows.

Project 3-3: Analyze Files and URLs for Viruses Using VirusTotal

VirusTotal, a subsidiary of Google, is a free online service that analyzes files and URLs in order to identify potential malware. VirusTotal scans and detects any type of binary content, including a Windows executable program, Android, PDFs, and images. VirusTotal is designed to provide a "second opinion" on a file or URL that may have been flagged as suspicious by other AV software. In this project, you will use VirusTotal to scan a file and a URL.

1. Use Microsoft Word to create a document that contains the above paragraph about VirusTotal. Save the document as **VirusTotal.docx**.

2. Now save this document as a PDF. Click **File** and **Save As**.

3. Under **Save as type:** select **PDF (*.pdf)**.

4. Save this file as **YourName-VirusTotal.pdf**.

5. Exit Word.

6. Open your web browser and enter the URL **www.virustotal.com** (if you are no longer able to access the site through the web address, use a search engine to search for "Virus Total").

7. If necessary click the **File** tab.

8. Click **Choose File**.

9. Navigate to the location of **YourName-VirusTotal.pdf** and click **Open**.

10. Click **Scan it!**

11. If the **File already analysed** dialog box opens, click **Reanalyse**.

12. Wait until the analysis is completed.

13. Scroll through the list of AV vendors that have been polled regarding this file. A green checkmark means no malware was detected.

14. Click the **File detail** tab and read through the analysis.

15. Use your browser's back button to return to the VirusTotal home page.

16. Click **URL**.

17. Enter the URL of your school, place of employment, or other site with which you are familiar.

18. Click **Scan it!** If the **URL already analysed** dialog box opens, click **Reanalyse**.

19. Wait until the analysis is completed.

20. Scroll through the list of vendor analysis. Do any of these sites indicate **Unrate site** or **Malware site?**

21. Click **Additional information.**

22. How could VirusTotal be useful to users? How could it be useful to security researchers? However, could it also be used by attackers to test their own malware before distributing it to ensure that it does not trigger an AV alert? What should be the protections against this?

23. Close all windows.

Project 3-4: Creating a Disk Image Backup

To back up programs and operating system files in addition to user files, one solution is to create a disk image. A disk image file is created by performing a complete sector-by-sector copy of the hard drive instead of backing up using the drive's file system. In this project, you download Macrium Reflect to create an image backup.

1. Use your web browser to go to **www.macrium.com**.

2. Under **Download Trial** click **Home**.

3. Click **DOWNLOAD**.

4. Save the file to the desired location and then launch the program.

5. In the Macrium Reflect Download Agent click **Trial software**

6. Click **Download**.

7. Install this program onto your computer by accepting the default settings.

8. Launch Macrium Reflect.

9. If you are asked **Do you want to create Rescue Media Now?** Click **No**.

10. In the left pane click **Create an image of the partition(s) required to backup and restore Windows**.

11. The **Disk Image** dialog box appears. Select the location to store the backup. You cannot store the backup on the same hard drive that you are creating the image on; you must store it on another hard drive in that computer or on an external USB hard drive. Under **Destination** select the appropriate location. Click **Next**.

12. Do not edit the plan for the backup. Click **Next**.

13. Click **Finish**.

14. If necessary, click **Run this backup now** and then click **OK** to begin the backup. Note that, depending on the size of the data to be backed up and the speed of the computer, it will take several minutes to perform the backup.

15. Close all windows.

Case Projects

Case Project 3-1: Online Backup Services

There are several good continuous online backup services that can help make data backup easy for the user. Use a search engine to search for *online backup service reviews*, and select three different services. Research these services and note their features. Create a table that lists each service and compare their features. Be sure to also include costs. Which would you recommend? Why?

Case Project 3-2: Information Security Community Site Activity

The Information Security Community Site is an online companion to this textbook. It contains a wide variety of tools, information, discussion boards, and other features to assist learners. Go to *community.cengage.com/infosec*. Sign in with the login name and password that you created in Chapter 1.

What should be the penalty for those who create viruses, worms, and other destructive malware? Prison time? Monetary fines? How should it be enforced? And would this deter attackers? Record your responses on the Community Site discussion board.

Additional Case Projects for this chapter are available through the MindTap online learning environment.

References

1. "FireEye Advanced Threat Report–2H 2012," *FireEye*, Apr. 3, 2013, accessed Jan. 3, 2014, www2.fireeye.com/rs/fireye/images/fireeye-advanced-threat-report-2h2012.pdf.

2. "The First Computer Virus," accessed Mar. 3, 2011, www.worldhistorysite.com/virus.html.

3. "Anti-Spyware Coalition Definitions Document," *Anti-Spyware Coalition*, Nov. 19, 2007, accessed Aug. 13, 2015, www.antispywarecoalition.org/documents/definitions.htm.

4. Cluley, Graham, "Fannie Mae Worker Accused of Planting Malware Timebomb," *Naked Security Sophos Blog*, accessed Mar. 3, 2011, http://nakedsecurity.sophos.com/2009/01/29/fannie-mae-worker-accused-planting-malware-timebomb/.

5. DaBoss, "Logic Bombs," *Computer Knowledge*, Mar. 1, 2013, accessed Aug. 13, 2015, http://www.cknow.com/cms/vtutor/logic-bombs.html.

6. Thomas, Karl, "Nine bad botnets and the damage they did," *We Live Security*, Feb. 25, 2015, accessed Aug. 13, 2015, http://www.welivesecurity.com/2015/02/25/nine-bad-botnets-damage/.

7. "2015: Time to fix broken malware strategies," *Damballa Day before Zero Blog*, Feb. 12, 2015, accessed Aug. 24, 2015, https://www.damballa.com/time-to-fix-malware-strategies/.

Chapter 3

HTML5 & CSS3

Laying Out Elements With CSS

> **CASE** — As you continue building a website for Lakeland Reeds Bed & Breakfast, you want to more precisely influence where elements are positioned in a browser window and in relation to each other. In this unit, you practice using CSS properties that give you control over web page layout.

Unit Objectives

After completing this unit, you will be able to:

- Assess the CSS box model
- Set element width and borders
- Set margins and padding
- Align elements with `float`
- Control page flow with `clear`

- Implement fixed positioning
- Implement relative positioning
- Control stacking order
- Implement absolute positioning

Files You Will Need

 L   4 files   IC3   3 files

 SR   3 files   IC4   3 files

 IC1   3 files   VW   3 files

 IC2   3 files

For specific filenames, see Filenames_D.pdf in the Unit D Data Files folder.

Assess the CSS Box Model

Learning
Outcomes
•Describe the
components of the
CSS box model

CSS represents the characteristics of every web page element using the **box model**, which treats each element as a rectangular box having several global properties. The properties most significant to the box model are described in TABLE D-1. **CASE** ➤ *Before you enhance the layout of the Lakeland Reeds About Us page, you familiarize yourself with the CSS box model.*

DETAILS

A few concepts are important for using box model properties effectively:

QUICK TIP

A declaration of
border: 0; means
that the border for
the affected element
is not visible and takes
up no space.

- **Distinguishing between padding, border, and margin**

    The padding, border, and margin properties all create space around the contents of a web page element; it's important to understand the relationship of these components to each other in order to create the results you want. Of these three aspects of the box model, **border**, which represents a line around an element formatted with the width, style, and color that you specify, is the only one that can be seen in a web browser. A border serves as a reference point for the other two properties, as illustrated in FIGURE D-1. **Padding** is the space inside a border between the border and the element content, while **margin** is the space outside the border between the border and adjacent or parent elements.

QUICK TIP

Relative units are
useful when you want
to calculate the size of
document content
based on other
elements, while
absolute units are
best for elements that
need to keep specific
dimensions.

- **Understanding CSS units of measure**

    You specify a number as the value of the padding, margin, and width properties. In addition, the border property takes a number as one of the three components of its value. All of these numbers must be accompanied by the abbreviation for a unit of measure. CSS supports many units of measure, but the four most commonly used are ems (em), percent (%), pixels (px), and rems (rem), which are described in TABLE D-2. Ems, percent, and rems are **relative units**, meaning that they are calculated based on the sizes of other elements on a web page. Pixels are **absolute units**, meaning that they represent a specific length or height that doesn't change.

QUICK TIP

To calculate an
element's total vertical
space, you add the
height value to the
padding, border,
and margin values.

- **Calculating box size**

    Positive values for padding, border, and margin all increase the amount of space on a web page that an element occupies. However, an element's width and height values (and their min- and max- variants) do not include these properties. When you specify an element's width value or height value, it applies only to the element content. Any values you specify for padding, border, or margin are added to the width value or height value when a browser calculates the space occupied by an element. To determine how much horizontal room an element will occupy, you add the width value to the padding, border, and margin values, as FIGURE D-2 illustrates. There is one exception to this rule: when the bottom margin of one element is adjacent to the top margin of another element, the margins combine, or **collapse**, into a single margin equal to the greater of the two values.

TABLE D-1: Box model properties

property	description	example*
border	a visible border around an element specified with a thickness value, a style keyword, and a color name or value	border: 1px solid black;
padding	the space inside a border between the border and the element content	padding: 5%;
margin	the space outside a border between the border and adjacent or parent elements	margin: 10px;
width	the horizontal size of an element's content, excluding border, padding, and margin	width: 25%;
min-width	the minimum horizontal size of an element's content, excluding border, padding, and margin	min-width: 320px;
max-width	the maximum horizontal size of an element's content, excluding border, padding, and margin	max-width: 1000px;
height	the vertical size of an element's content, excluding border, padding, and margin	height: 5rem;
min-height	the minimum vertical size of an element's content, excluding border, padding, and margin	min-height: 2em;
max-height	the maximum vertical size of an element's content, excluding border, padding, and margin	max-height: 5em;

* Values in CSS units, with a % value based on width of parent element

FIGURE D-1: The CSS box model

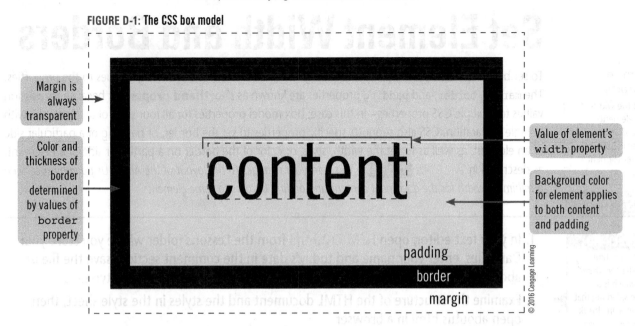

Margin is always transparent

Color and thickness of border determined by values of `border` property

Value of element's `width` property

Background color for element applies to both content and padding

content

padding

border

margin

© 2016 Cengage Learning

FIGURE D-2: Calculating web page space occupied by an element

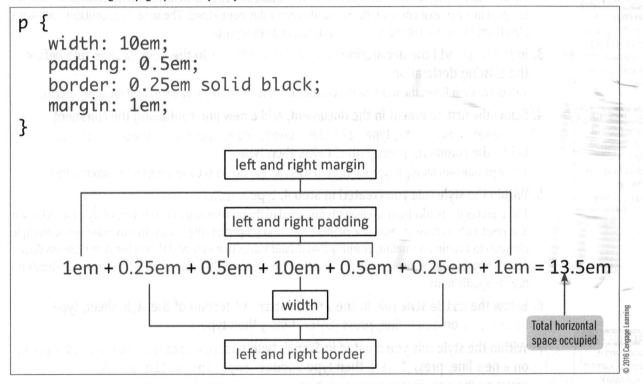

```
p {
    width: 10em;
    padding: 0.5em;
    border: 0.25em solid black;
    margin: 1em;
}
```

left and right margin

left and right padding

1em + 0.25em + 0.5em + 10em + 0.5em + 0.25em + 1em = 13.5em

width

left and right border

Total horizontal space occupied

© 2016 Cengage Learning

TABLE D-2: Commonly used CSS units of measure

abbreviation	unit	description	example
em	em	A multiple of the computed font size for the current element, where 1em represents 100% of this size	`padding: 1.4em;`
%	percent	A percentage of another value for the current element or an ancestor element; each CSS property that takes a value in % specifies what value the % calculation is based on	`margin: 10%;`
px	pixel	A unit equal to approximately 1/96 inch or 0.26 millimeter	`padding: 10px;`
rem	rem	A multiple of the computed font size for the html element, where 1rem represents 100% of this size	`margin: 0.25rem;`

© 2016 Cengage Learning

Set Element Width and Borders

To set box properties for web page elements, you create declarations that assign values to the properties. The `margin`, `border`, and `padding` properties are known as **shorthand properties** because they assign values to multiple CSS properties—in this case, box model properties for all four sides of an element—with a single declaration. CSS also supports specific properties to set the border, or padding of a particular side of an element, as well as to set the width, style, or color of the border on a particular side of an element, as described in **TABLE D-3**. **CASE** *You start your changes to the layout of the About Us page by specifying a minimum width for the document content and adding borders to some elements.*

STEPS

1. **In your text editor, open HTM_D-1.html from the Lessons folder where you store your Data Files, enter your name and today's date in the comment section, save the file as aboutus.html, then repeat for the file HTM_D-2.css, saving the file as styles.css**

2. **Examine the structure of the HTML document and the styles in the style sheet, then open aboutus.html in a browser**

   The content is grouped within `header`, `article`, `aside`, and `footer` elements. All the content sections are enclosed in a `div` element with the `class` attribute value `container`. The style sheet contains comments identifying the section of the page that each rule or rules apply to.

3. **In styles.css, add the declaration `max-width: 640px;` in the `.container` rule before the existing declaration**

   This declaration limits the width of the document content, making it easier to read on larger screens.

4. **Below the first comment in the document, add a new line containing the comment `/* reset styles */`, type `article, body, div, footer, header, h1, h2, p {` below the comment, press [Enter] twice, then type `}`**

   This style rule uses multiple type selectors to select all the elements containing text in aboutus.html.

5. **Within the style rule you created in Step 4, type `border: 0;`**

   This removes the border from all elements displayed in the browser window. This type of style rule is known as a **reset rule** because it resets one or more common properties (the border, in this example) of multiple elements to a common baseline, ensuring that default values that may be different between browsers do not cause a web page to be displayed inconsistently. When you set the value of a CSS property to 0, there's no need to specify units.

6. **Below the `aside` style rule in the `/* sidebar */` section of the style sheet, type `aside p {` on a new line, press [Enter] twice, then type `}`**

7. **Within the style rule you created in Step 6, type `border-bottom: 1px solid black;` on a new line, press [Enter], then type `border-top: 1px solid black;`**

   FIGURE D-3 shows the changes to the style sheet.

8. **Save your work, then reload aboutus.html in your browser**

   The document content is now exactly 640px wide and surrounded by a border. In addition, each paragraph in the `aside` element has a horizontal border above and below it.

9. **Right-click the text What a weekend!, click Inspect Element, then in the developer tools, click Computed (Chrome), Box Model (Firefox), or Layout (IE)**

   The developer tools illustrate the box model values for the selected p element, as shown in **FIGURE D-4**.

10. **Open aboutus.html on a handheld device such as a smartphone**

    The page is displayed at a narrower width to fit the device. This is because you set the width using `max-width`, allowing browsers to display the page at a narrower width when appropriate.

FIGURE D-3: width and border declarations added to style sheet

```
10    /* reset styles */
11    article, body, div, footer, header, h1, h2, p {
12        border: 0;
13    }
14
15    /* body and page container */
16    .container {
17        max-width: 640px;
18        background-color: beige;
19    }
```

Using max-width allows content to be displayed at a narrower width on smaller screens; note that declarations for box model properties are listed first within a style rule by convention

```
30    /* sidebar */
31    aside {
32        background-color: goldenrod;
33    }
34    aside p {
35        border-bottom: 1px solid black;
36        border-top: 1px solid black;
37    }
```

Declarations add top and bottom borders to aside p element without adding left or right borders

FIGURE D-4: Width and border properties applied to About Us page

Maximum width of element with container class value set to 640px

br element adds a line break within the h1 element, splitting the content into two lines

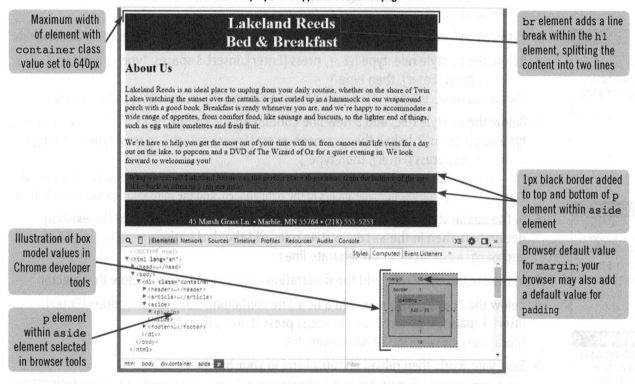

1px black border added to top and bottom of p element within aside element

Illustration of box model values in Chrome developer tools

Browser default value for margin; your browser may also add a default value for padding

p element within aside element selected in browser tools

TABLE D-3: Specific properties for components of box model

component	properties	description	values
border	border-width-side	thickness of a visible border	a border thickness, such as 1px
	border-style-side	style of a visible border	dashed, solid, or another keyword
	border-color-side	color of a visible border	a color name or value, such as black
padding	padding-side	space between border and content	a value in a CSS unit, such as 5%
margin	margin-side	space between border and adjacent elements	a value in a CSS unit, such as 1.2em

© 2016 Cengage Learning

Set Margins and Padding

You can assign different margin and padding values to different sides of an element by providing multiple values for the `margin` and `padding` shorthand properties, with a space separating each value, as described in **TABLE D-4**. In addition to numbers, the `margin` property supports the value `auto`. If you assign the value `auto` to the left and right margins of an element, the element is centered horizontally within its parent element. **CASE** *You continue your changes to the layout of the About Us page by specifying margins and padding.*

STEPS

1. **Return to styles.css in your editor, within the style rule below the `/* reset styles */` comment, add the declarations `padding: 0;` and `margin: 0;` on separate lines**

   These declarations expand your reset style rule to set the margin and padding to 0 on all sides of all elements.

2. **In the `.container` style rule, add the declaration `margin: 0 auto;` below the `max-width` declaration**

   The declaration sets the left and right margins to `auto`, centering the element horizontally within the browser window.

3. **In the `h1` style rule, add the declaration `padding: 0.4em;` before the existing declarations**

4. **Below the `h1` style rule, type `h2 {`, press [Enter], insert 3 spaces, type `padding: 0.4em 0.6em;`, press [Enter], then type `}`**

   The declaration sets the top and bottom padding to 0.4em and the left and right padding to 0.6em.

5. **Below the `h2` style rule, add a new line containing the comment `/* main content */`, type `article p {` below the comment, press [Enter], insert 3 spaces, type `padding: 0 1em 1em;`, press [Enter], then type `}`**

   This style rule uses 3 values to set padding for all p elements within the `article` element. The first value applies to the top, the second value applies to the right and left, and the third value applies to the bottom.

6. **In the `aside` style rule, add the declaration `padding: 1em 0;` before the existing declaration, then in the `aside p` style rule, add the declarations `padding: 0.4em 0;` and `margin: 0 0.6em;` on separate lines**

7. **In the `footer` style rule, add the declaration `padding: 0.6em;` below the selector**

8. **Below the `footer` style rule, add a new line containing `footer p {`, press [Enter], insert 3 spaces, type `margin: 0.4em;`, press [Enter], then type `}`**

   Your updated style sheet should match **FIGURE D-5**.

9. **Save your work, then reload aboutus.html in your browser**

   The document layout is updated to include the margins and padding you specified as shown in **FIGURE D-6**.

10. **Right-click the text What a weekend!, click Inspect Element, then in the developer tools, click Computed (Chrome), Box Model (Firefox), or Layout (IE)**

    The box model illustration in the developer tools is updated to include the margin and padding you specified for p elements within the `aside` element.

FIGURE D-5: padding and margin declarations added to style sheet

```
10    /* reset styles */
11    article, body, div, footer, header, h1, h2, p {
12        border: 0;
13        padding: 0;
14        margin: 0;
15    }
16
17    /* body and page container */
18    .container {
19        max-width: 640px;
20        margin: 0 auto;
21        background-color: beige;
22    }
23
24    /* headings */
25    header {
26        background-color: darkgreen;
27    }
28    h1 {
29        padding: 0.4em;
30        color: white;
31        text-align: center;
32    }
33    h2 {
34        padding: 0.4em 0.6em;
35    }
36
37    /* main content */
38    article p {
39        padding: 0 1em 1em;
40    }
41
```

```
42    /* sidebar */
43    aside {
44        padding: 1em 0;
45        background-color: goldenrod;
46    }
47    aside p {
48        border-bottom: 1px solid black;
49        border-top: 1px solid black;
50        padding: 0.4em 0;
51        margin: 0 0.6em;
52    }
53
54    /* footer section */
55    footer {
56        padding: 0.6em;
57        color: white;
58        background-color: darkgreen;
59        text-align: center;
60    }
61    footer p {
62        margin: 0.4em;
63    }
64    footer p.accent {
65        color: goldenrod;
66    }
```

Code continued with line 42 in figure to the right   Code continued from figure on the left

FIGURE D-6: padding and margin properties applied to About Us page

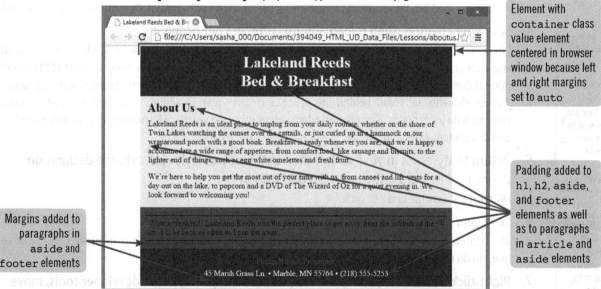

Element with container class value element centered in browser window because left and right margins set to auto

Padding added to h1, h2, aside, and footer elements as well as to paragraphs in article and aside elements

Margins added to paragraphs in aside and footer elements

TABLE D-4: Interpretation of different numbers of values for the margin and padding shorthand properties

# of values	values apply to	example
four	top, right, bottom, left	margin: 0 5% 5% 0;
three	top, left/right, bottom	padding: 0 2em 1em;
two	top/bottom, left/right	margin: 0 10px;
one (shorthand property)	top/left/bottom/right	padding: 5%;

Align Elements with float

Learning
Outcomes
•Float elements on
a web page

By default, a browser renders elements in a web document in the order they appear, with most elements displayed below the element that precedes them. This default arrangement of elements is known as **normal flow**. In some cases, though, you want the elements that follow an element to wrap around it, rather than being stacked below it. To do so, you use the CSS float property. The left and right values of the float property align the element horizontally with the left or right edge of the parent element, respectively, and allow elements that follow to fill in the remaining horizontal space. **FIGURE D-7** illustrates the effect of the float property on web page elements. **CASE** *The design of the About Us page calls for the aside element to be displayed as a sidebar along the right edge of the page, and the main content to be displayed to its left. You resize the aside and article elements so they fit side-by-side within the container element, and you use the float property to display them next to each other.*

STEPS

1. **Return to styles.css in your editor, enter** article { **on a new line below the** /* main content */ **comment, press [Enter] twice, then type** }

2. **In the** article **style rule, add the declaration** width: 70%;
   A percentage value for width is calculated based on the width of the parent element, which in this case is the element with the class value container. Using a percentage value for the article width allows it to scale if the document is displayed at a narrower width on a small screen. Setting the width to 70% leaves the remaining 30% of the parent width for the content of the aside element.

3. **In the** article **style rule, add the declaration** float: right;
   The article element comes before the aside element in the HTML document. Assigning it a float value of right aligns it with the right edge of the parent element, which is the element with the class value container, and lets the remaining elements, including the aside element, flow around it on the left side.

4. **Save your changes, then reload aboutus.html in your browser**
   The article element is narrower and displayed on the right side of the browser window, and the aside and footer elements are displayed to its left. However, because the article element is removed from the normal flow and has no background color specified, the background colors and borders of the aside and footer elements are visible behind the article element text. In addition, the content of the article element is no longer taken into account when determining the length of its parent element, so the article element content extends below the bottom border of the parent element.

QUICK TIP
Because the article and aside elements have no padding, borders, or margins, setting their widths to 70% and 30% makes them fit exactly within their parent element.

5. **Return to styles.css in your editor, then in the** aside **style rule, add the declaration** width: 30%; **before the** padding **declaration**
   FIGURE D-8 shows the updated code.

QUICK TIP
You'll adjust the appearance of the footer element in the next lesson to prevent it from overlapping the article content.

6. **Save your changes, then reload aboutus.html in your browser**
   The narrower aside element fits next to the article element content and its background color and margins do not extend across the page.

7. **Right-click the text About Us, click Inspect Element, then in the developer tools, move the mouse pointer over the opening** <article> **tag**
   The element is highlighted. Notice that it is only as wide as the area it occupies in the browser window, which is 70% of the width of its parent element, as shown in **FIGURE D-9**.

8. **Move the mouse pointer over the tags for the aside, footer, and header elements in the developer tools**
   Each element is highlighted in the browser window. The dimensions of the aside element reflect the width value you specified, while the header and footer elements extend the full width available within the parent element.

FIGURE D-7: Using the `float` property

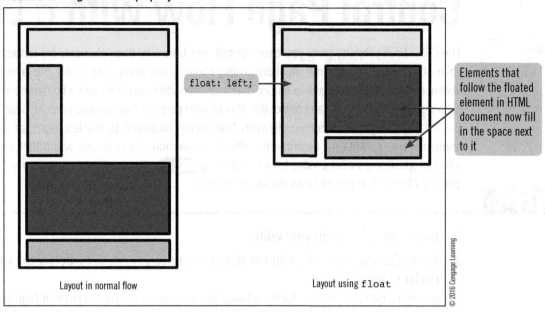

Layout in normal flow

float: left;

Layout using `float`

Elements that follow the floated element in HTML document now fill in the space next to it

© 2016 Cengage Learning

FIGURE D-8: Updated code for floating main content

```
37    /* main content */
38    article {
39        width: 70%;
40        float: right;
41    }
42    article p {
43        padding: 0 1em 1em;
44    }
45
46    /* sidebar */
47    aside {
48        width: 30%;
49        padding: 1em 0;
50        background-color: goldenrod;
51    }
```

FIGURE D-9: About Us page with floated `article` element

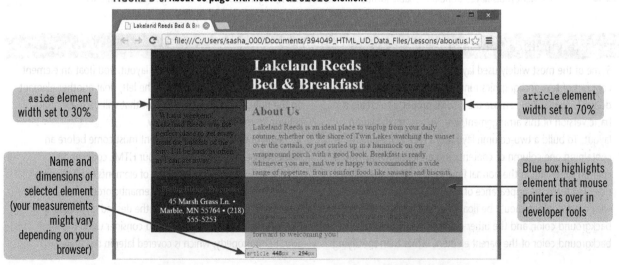

aside element width set to 30%

article element width set to 70%

Name and dimensions of selected element (your measurements might vary depending on your browser)

Blue box highlights element that mouse pointer is over in developer tools

Control Page Flow with `clear`

The CSS `float` property gives you basic control over how web page elements are rendered in relation to each other. However, in some situations, using `float` is not enough to create the layout you want. For instance, sometimes you want to ensure that text or another object follows a floated element, rather than running alongside it. You can control the flow of web page elements more precisely with the CSS `clear` property, which prevents floated elements from being displayed to the left, right, or on either side of another element. **TABLE D-5** describes the effects of common `clear` values, and **FIGURE D-10** illustrates the effect of specifying a `clear` value for an element. **CASE** *You use the* `clear` *property to ensure that the* `footer` *element is displayed below the* `aside` *element.*

STEPS

1. **Return to styles.css in your editor**

2. **In the `footer` style rule, add the declaration `clear: right;` below the existing declarations**

   Specifying the value `right` for the `clear` property prevents a floated element from being displayed to the right of the current element. **FIGURE D-11** shows the `clear` property inserted in the style sheet.

3. **Save your work**

4. **Reload aboutus.html in your browser**

   As **FIGURE D-12** shows, the `footer` element is now displayed below the `aside` element.

TABLE D-5: Values of the clear property

value	description
left	element is displayed at next location in the document where no element is floated to the left
right	element is displayed at next location in the document where no element is floated to the right
both	element is displayed at next location in the document where no element is floated either to the left or to the right
none	element is displayed at next available location in the document, regardless of surrounding floated elements

© 2016 Cengage Learning

Creating multicolumn layouts with `float`

Some of the most widely used layouts in print media involve columns of text and graphics running parallel to each other down the page. You can use the `float` property to create a basic version of this arrangement, known as a multicolumn layout. To build a two-column layout, you float an element containing one column of content, and either allow the other column to remain in the normal flow, or float it on the other side. To create the appearance of even columns, the column with more content should be floated and assigned a distinct background color, and the other column should use the background color of the parent element rather than specifying

its own. To create a three-column layout, you float an element that will serve as one column on the left, float another element on the right, and allow the element that will be the middle column to remain in the normal flow.

Remember that a floated element must come before an element that runs alongside it in your HTML code, and it's important not to change the order of elements in HTML simply for presentational purposes. If the semantic order of your HTML code doesn't lend itself to creating the desired layout using the `float` property, you should instead consider using the `position` property, which is covered later in this unit.

FIGURE D-10: Using the clear property

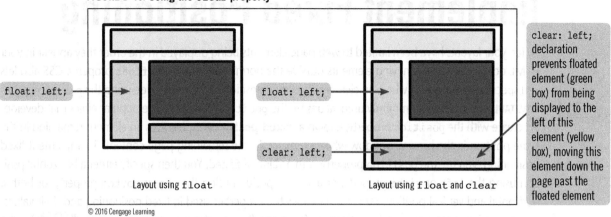

float: left;

float: left;

clear: left;

clear: left; declaration prevents floated element (green box) from being displayed to the left of this element (yellow box), moving this element down the page past the floated element

Layout using float

Layout using float and clear

© 2016 Cengage Learning

FIGURE D-11: Updated code including clear property

```
26    /* headings */
27    header {
28        width: 100%;
29        max-width: 640px;
30        position: fixed;
31        background-color: darkgreen;
32        z-index: -1;
33    }
```

FIGURE D-12: About Us page with footer using clear property

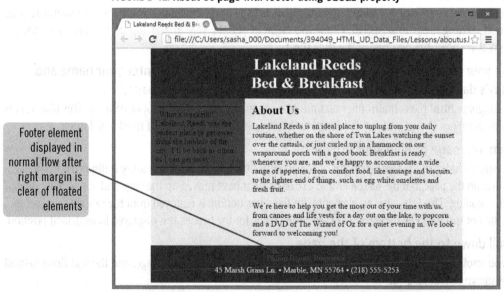

Footer element displayed in normal flow after right margin is clear of floated elements

Dealing with floated content that's longer than its parent element

An element's content can extend below the bottom of its container element, especially when the content of a floated element is longer than other elements on a page. When a floated element is followed by another element in the normal flow, the clear property can be useful in extending the formatting of the parent element to all the content within it. However, in some cases the order of elements in HTML code does not lend itself to this layout. In these cases, you can add the declaration overflow: auto; to the parent element

to extend it horizontally to give the appearance of the floated element still being in the normal flow.

In some browsers, this declaration results in a scroll bar being displayed on the right side of the parent element, which some designers find unsightly. Other approaches to solving this same problem that use more advanced CSS tools are in wide use. One popular method, known as a clearfix, is detailed at http://css-tricks.com/snippets/css/clear-fix/.

Implement Fixed Positioning

So far, your layouts have been limited to web page elements being displayed in the order they appear in your HTML documents, or by moving elements outside the normal flow using the `float` property. CSS also lets you specify more precisely where an element should be positioned on a web page using the `position` property. **TABLE D-6** describes commonly used values for the `position` property. One popular effect that developers create with the `position` property, known as **fixed positioning**, involves an element remaining in the same position in the browser window while a user scrolls the remaining page content. To implement fixed positioning, you use the `position` property with a value of `fixed`. You then specify either a horizontal position using the `left` or `right` property, or a vertical position using the `top` or `bottom` property, or both a horizontal and vertical position. **TABLE D-7** describes the properties used in fixed positioning and their values. **FIGURE D-13** illustrates how fixed positioning affects the flow of elements in a web page. **CASE** *You anticipate other pages in the Lakeland Reeds website will include so much information that users will need to scroll; you'd like the main heading to stay on the page as they do so. You use fixed positioning to do this.*

STEPS

1. **Return to styles.css in your text editor**

2. **Below the `/* headings */` comment and in the `header` style rule, add the declarations `width: 100%;`, `max-width: 640px;`, and `position: fixed;`**

   Fixed positioning removes the element from the normal flow, and it is sized relative to the browser window. Setting the `width` to 100% ensures that the `header` width is not limited to the width of its content, and setting the `max-width` to 640px gives the element the same maximum width as the remaining page content. Setting `top` to 0 specifies that the element should stay at the top of the browser window. **FIGURE D-14** shows the new rule in the style sheet.

QUICK TIP
You can generate lorem ipsum text using many free online services such as lipsum.com.

3. **Save your work, open HTM_D-3.html from the Lessons folder, enter your name and today's date in the comment section, then save the file as longpage.html**

   The longpage.html file contains filler text meant to simulate a page with a lot of content. This filler text is known as **lorem ipsum**. A long document makes it easier to see the effect of fixed positioning.

4. **Open longpage.html in your browser**

   The page includes all the same elements as the aboutus.html file. The main heading is displayed in the same location on the page, but the `aside` and `article` content have moved up the page and are partially hidden by the heading. This is because an element with fixed positioning is removed from the normal flow. Because you did not specify a `top`, `bottom`, `left`, or `right` value for the header, it is displayed in its default position.

5. **Scroll down to the bottom of the page**

   As you scroll, the main header remains in the same place at the top of the page, and the text flows behind it, as shown in **FIGURE D-15**.

TABLE D-6: Commonly used values of the `position` property

value	description
`absolute`	element is removed from the normal flow and positioned relative to the nearest ancestor element that has a position value other than `static`
`fixed`	element is removed from the normal flow and positioned relative to the browser window, and remains in this position even as a user scrolls through the document
`relative`	element remains in the normal flow and is positioned relative to its default position
`static` (default)	element is displayed in its default position in the normal flow

FIGURE D-13: Implementing fixed positioning

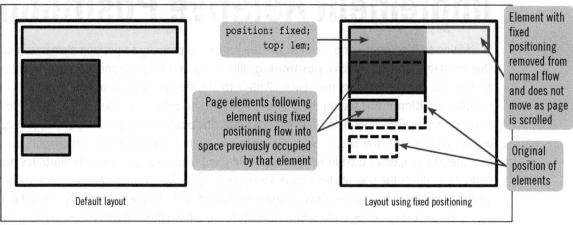

Page elements following element using fixed positioning flow into space previously occupied by that element

Element with fixed positioning removed from normal flow and does not move as page is scrolled

Original position of elements

© 2016 Cengage Learning

FIGURE D-14: header style rule added to style sheet

```
24    /* headings */
25    header {
26        width: 100%;
27        max-width: 640px;
28        position: fixed;
29        background-color: darkgreen;
30    }
```

FIGURE D-15: Test page showing header element using fixed positioning

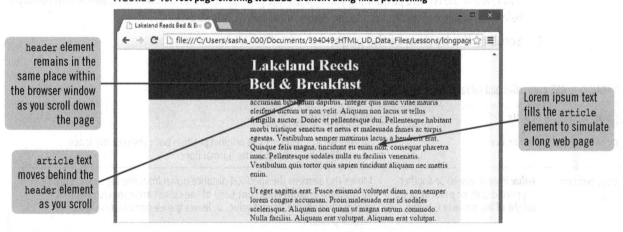

header element remains in the same place within the browser window as you scroll down the page

article text moves behind the header element as you scroll

Lorem ipsum text fills the article element to simulate a long web page

TABLE D-7: CSS properties and values used in fixed positioning

property	value	description
position	fixed	Removes element from normal flow, positions it relative to the browser window, and keeps it in this position even as a user scrolls through the document
top, bottom	*value* in ems, pixels, or another supported unit, or *percent* of the height of the browser window	Moves the element the specified distance down from the top edge (top) or up from the bottom edge (bottom) of the browser window; the default value, 0, leaves the element in its original vertical position
left, right	*value* in ems, pixels, or another supported unit, or *percent* of the width of the browser window	Moves the element the specified distance right from the left edge (left) or left from the right edge (right) of the browser window; the default value, 0, leaves the element in its original horizontal position

© 2016 Cengage Learning

Implement Relative Positioning

In addition to fixed positioning, you can use the position property to position elements in other ways. One of these, known as **relative positioning**, allows you to make adjustments to the default position of an element while preserving the space allotted to the element in the normal flow. You implement **relative positioning** by setting the position property to relative. You specify how far to move the element from its default location using either a horizontal position with the left or right property, or a vertical position with the top or bottom property, or both a horizontal and vertical position. **TABLE D-8** describes the properties used in relative positioning and their values. **FIGURE D-16** illustrates how relative positioning affects the flow of elements in a web page. **CASE** *With the header removed from the page flow, the remaining page content flows up and is overlapped by the* header *element. You use relative positioning on the* article, aside, *and* footer *elements to move them down to recreate the previous layout of the page, while preserving the fixed positioning of the header.*

STEPS

1. **Return to styles.css in your editor**

2. **In the .container rule, add the declarations position: relative; and top: 6.2em; after the existing declarations**

   The value of 6.2em for the element's top value moves it down from the top of the parent element exactly the height of the header element. **FIGURE D-17** shows the updated code.

3. **Save your work, refresh longpage.html in your browser, then scroll to the top of the page if necessary**

   As a result of the relative positioning you applied, the page content that follows the header is now displayed below the header element as it was previously, as shown in **FIGURE D-18**.

4. **Scroll to the bottom of the page.**

TABLE D-8: CSS properties and values used in relative positioning

property	value	description
position	relative	Moves element relative to its original position but preserves the space reserved for the element in the normal flow
top, bottom	**value** in ems, pixels, or another supported unit, or **percent** of the height of the browser window	Moves the element the specified distance down from the top edge (top) or up from the bottom edge (bottom) of the closest ancestor element that is also positioned; the default value, 0, leaves the element in its original vertical position
left, right	**value** in ems, pixels, or another supported unit, or **percent** of the width of the browser window	Moves the element the specified distance from the left edge (left) or from the right edge (right) of the closest ancestor element that is also positioned; the default value, 0, leaves the element in its original horizontal position

© 2016 Cengage Learning

Maintaining accessibility with positioning

When you alter the layout of your web pages using positioning, it's important to plan for non-visual user agents, as well as devices with smaller screens, to make sure your page content still flows logically. User agents that don't process positioning continue to render all content from top to bottom in the document. Thus, your HTML code should contain elements in the order users will encounter them. In addition, you can help all user agents understand the content of your pages and present it appropriately by using semantic elements to indicate the content of different columns; for instance, aside for a sidebar, article for main page content, and footer for the page footer.

FIGURE D-16: Implementing relative positioning

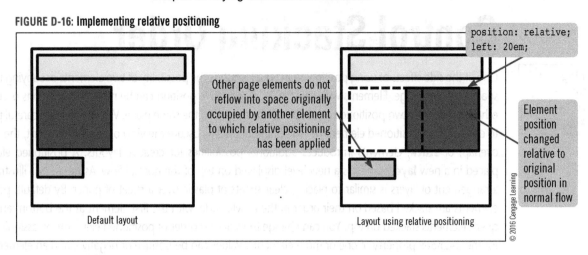

```
position: relative;
left: 20em;
```

Other page elements do not reflow into space originally occupied by another element to which relative positioning has been applied

Element position changed relative to original position in normal flow

Default layout

Layout using relative positioning

© 2016 Cengage Learning

FIGURE D-17: Styles for relative positioning added to style sheet

```
17   /* body and page container */
18   .container {
19       max-width: 640px;
20       margin: 0 auto;
21       background-color: beige;
22       position: relative;
23       top: 6.2em;
24   }
```

FIGURE D-18: Test page with relatively positioned element

Top of container element is below header element as a result of relative positioning

Control Stacking Order

Learning
Outcomes
• Set an element's
  stacking order

One of the side effects of using positioning in your layouts is the possibility of two elements occupying the same space on a web page. Elements with either a fixed or relative position can be moved to positions occupied by other elements, or two positioned elements can be moved to the same place. While it requires careful planning to ensure that a positioned element doesn't unintentionally obscure the view of another element, the ability to overlap, or **stack**, elements introduces additional possibilities for creative layouts. A positioned element is placed in a new **layer**, which is a new level displayed on top of the normal flow. As **FIGURE D-19** illustrates, the arrangement of layers is similar to placing clear sheets of plastic over a sheet of paper. By default, positioned elements are stacked based on their order in the HTML code, with the first element at the bottom and subsequent elements stacked on top. You can change the stacking order of positioned elements by assigning values for the z-index property of one or more elements. Values can be positive or negative, and an element with a larger z-index value is displayed on top of an element with a smaller value. **CASE** *You explore the effect of stacking order on the* header *element and the container using the* z-index *property.*

STEPS

QUICK TIP
Values for the
z-index property
can be any number,
including a negative
number. Stacking
order is based solely
on which element
has a larger
z-index value.

1. **Return to styles.css in your editor**

2. **In the header style rule, add the declaration z-index: -1; below the existing declarations**
   FIGURE D-20 shows the declaration inserted in the style sheet.

3. **Save your changes to styles.css**

4. **Reload longpage.html in your browser, scroll to the top of the page if necessary, then scroll down the page**
   The header element, which includes the main heading text, is now covered by the aside and article content in the stacking order, as shown in FIGURE D-21.

5. **Return to styles.css in your editor**

6. **In the header style rule, add /* before the declaration z-index: -1; , then add */ after the declaration**
   You do not want the container element to be displayed above the header element, so you remove the z-index declaration. Formatting the declaration as a comment preserves it in your code while ensuring that user agents ignore it when rendering documents.

7. **Save your changes to styles.css**

8. **Reload longpage.html in your browser, scroll to the top of the page if necessary, then scroll down the page**
   The header element once again remains above the aside and article content in the stacking order.

Understanding stacking context

Controlling stacking order with the z-index property is straightforward in many cases. However, in some situations, it's important to understand some of the finer details of the property in order to achieve the results you want. The z-index property determines stacking order based on a **stacking context**, which is the element containing elements to be stacked. When stacking sections of a page, stacking order works pretty predictably, as all elements share a stacking context—the html element. However, when both a parent and child element are positioned, you cannot use the z-index property to stack the child element above another element on the page. This is because the stacking context for this child element is its parent element, rather than the html element containing all page contents. You can learn more about the details of stacking context and strategies for working with it at developer.mozilla.org/en-US/docs/Web/Guide/CSS/Understanding_z_index.

FIGURE D-19: Stacking elements

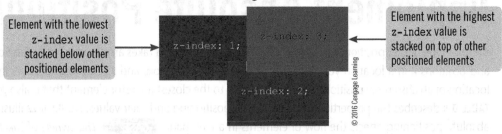

FIGURE D-20: `z-index` declaration added to `header` style rule

```
26   /* headings */
27   header {
28       width: 100%;
29       max-width: 640px;
30       position: fixed;
31       background-color: darkgreen;
32       z-index: -1;
33   }
```

FIGURE D-21: Test page with `z-index` value added to `header` element

container element displayed on top of header element because `header` has lower `z-index` value

Evaluating website layout types

By default, web page content occupies the entire width of a user's browser window. When most users accessed the web with a desktop computer, designers often used a **static layout**, which specifies a fixed width for the web page content. However, a static layout that's sized appropriately for a desktop computer often doesn't fit on the screen of a smaller device such as a smartphone. Designers for some websites find that setting a fixed width and expecting users to scroll and/or zoom to view the entire page is still their best option. However, many other sites have replaced static layouts with **fluid layouts**—also known as **liquid layouts**—in which the content size is constrained with the `min-width` and `max-width` properties and the columns are sized using percentages. A liquid layout fills the width of whatever window it's displayed in, up to the maximum width limit. This allows designers to take advantage of larger screens on desktop computers while still making the entire width of the site viewable on a handheld device.

Implement Absolute Positioning

Learning Outcomes
• Position elements using absolute positioning

Another type of CSS positioning is **absolute positioning**, which takes an element out of the normal flow and positions it in a location you specify. The `top`, `right`, `bottom`, and `left` properties specify the new location of an absolutely positioned element relative to the closest ancestor element that is also positioned. **TABLE D-9** describes the properties used in absolute positioning and their values. **FIGURE D-22** illustrates how absolute positioning affects the flow of elements in a web page. **CASE** ▶ *The owners of Lakeland Reeds would like you to add and position a text placeholder for a logo. You add a new p element for the logo text and use absolute positioning to position it next to the existing main heading text.*

STEPS

1. **Return to longpage.html in your text editor, then below the h1 element and before the closing </header> tag, enter the following code on a new line:**
   `<p class="logo">&#8466;&#8475;</p>`
   This code creates a new p element with the class attribute value `logo`, as shown in **FIGURE D-23**.

2. **Save your changes to longpage.html, then reload longpage.html in your browser**
   The cursive characters L and R are displayed in the bottom left corner of the header element, increasing the height of the header element so it overlaps some of the content below it.

3. **Return to styles.css in your editor, then enter the following style rule below the /* headings */ comment and below the h2 style rule:**
   ```
   p.logo {
       padding: 0.2em;
       border: 2px solid beige;
       color: goldenrod;
   }
   ```
   This style rule sets the padding, border, and color for the element with the `logo` class.

QUICK TIP
If you want to position an element in relation to an ancestor element that is not positioned, you can add the declaration `position: relative;` to the ancestor element. Without `top`, `right`, `bottom`, and `left` values, the ancestor element remains in its original position but serves as the reference point for absolutely positioning its descendant element.

4. **Within the p.logo style rule, insert the declarations** `position: absolute;`, `top: 2em;`, **and** `left: 2em;` **below the existing declarations, as shown in FIGURE D-24**
   These declarations set the position of the element to `absolute`, and position it 2em from the top and left of the nearest positioned ancestor element. Because the parent element, which is the `header` element, has a `position` value of `fixed`, the `top` and `left` values are calculated in relation to the `header` element.

5. **Save your changes to styles.css, reload longpage.html in your browser, then scroll up to the top of the page if necessary**
   The logo placeholder text is displayed next to the main heading and the space reserved for it in the normal flow is removed, as shown in **FIGURE D-25**.

6. **Load longpage.html on a smartphone, then scroll the page and verify that the layout is displayed as expected.**

7. **Validate your HTML and CSS code**

Creating a Cohesive Website

All the pages on a website should be visually similar enough that users can tell that they're on the same site. Visual design, including a color scheme and logo, plays an important role. In addition, page elements, such as headings and sidebars, should appear in a consistent place on every page. Your website designs should also make use of elements that are standard on most other websites, making your website instantly familiar to even first-time visitors. Thus, an important part of creating a new web design is exploring other websites sharing similar audiences or topics to get a clear understanding of the standard elements that users may expect to see.

FIGURE D-22: Implementing absolute positioning

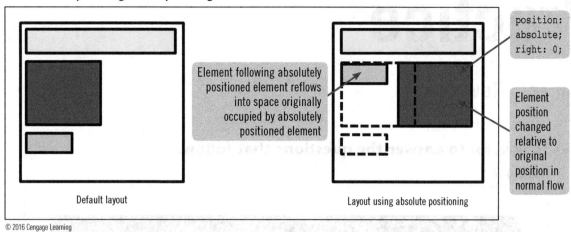

Element following absolutely positioned element reflows into space originally occupied by absolutely positioned element

Default layout

Layout using absolute positioning

position: absolute; right: 0;

Element position changed relative to original position in normal flow

© 2016 Cengage Learning

FIGURE D-23: Logo placeholder element added to longpage.html

```
20          <header>
21              <h1>Lakeland Reeds<br>Bed &amp; Breakfast</h1>
22              <p class="logo">&#8466;&#8475;</p>
23          </header>
```

code for cursive capital L

code for cursive capital R

FIGURE D-24: Style rule to absolutely position element with `logo` class value

```
39  h2 {
40      padding: 0.4em 0.6em;
41  }
42  p.logo {
43      padding: 0.2em;
44      border: 2px solid beige;
45      color: goldenrod;
46      position: absolute;
47      top: 2em;
48      left: 2em;
49  }
```

FIGURE D-25: Logo placeholder absolutely positioned

Logo placeholder text placed next to main heading using absolute positioning

TABLE D-9: CSS properties and values used in absolute positioning

property	value	description
position	absolute	Removes element from normal flow and positions it relative to the closest ancestor element that is also positioned
top, bottom	*value* in ems, pixels, or another supported unit, or *percent* of the height of the browser window	Moves the element the specified distance down from the top edge (top) or up from the bottom edge (bottom) of the closest ancestor element that is also positioned; the default value, 0, leaves the element in its original vertical position
left, right	*value* in ems, pixels, or another supported unit, or *percent* of the width of the browser window	Moves the element the specified distance right from the left edge (left) or left from the right edge (right) of the closest ancestor element that is also positioned; the default value, 0, leaves the element in its original horizontal position

© 2016 Cengage Learning

Practice

Concepts Review

Refer to FIGURE D-26 **to answer the questions that follow.**

FIGURE D-26

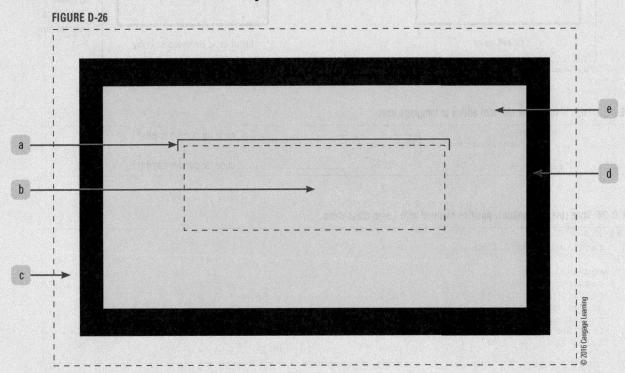

© 2016 Cengage Learning

1. **Which item represents the element border?**
2. **Which item represents the element content?**
3. **Which item represents the element width?**
4. **Which item represents the element padding?**
5. **Which item represents the element margin?**

Match each term with the statement that best describes it.

6. **relative positioning**
7. **absolute positioning**
8. **fixed positioning**
9. **lorem ipsum**
10. **layer**

a. a new level of content displayed on top of the normal flow
b. effect in which an element remains in the same position in the browser window while a user scrolls the remaining page content
c. standard filler text used for print layouts
d. lets you make adjustments to the default position of an element while preserving the space allotted to the element in the normal flow
e. takes an element out of the normal flow and allows other elements to flow into the space it would have occupied

Select the best answer from the list of choices.

11. **Which property do you use to align an element horizontally with the left or right edge of its parent element?**
    - **a.** `position`
    - **b.** `z-index`
    - **c.** `float`
    - **d.** `clear`

12. **Which property do you use to precisely specify the location of an element on a web page?**
    - **a.** `position`
    - **b.** `z-index`
    - **c.** `float`
    - **d.** `clear`

13. **Which property do you use to control the stacking order of positioned elements?**
    - **a.** `position`
    - **b.** `z-index`
    - **c.** `float`
    - **d.** `clear`

14. **Which property creates space that is unaffected by an element's background color?**
    - **a.** `width`
    - **b.** `padding`
    - **c.** `margin`
    - **d.** `border`

15. **Which declaration sets an element's padding to 0 on top, 1em on the right and left, and 2.5em on the bottom?**
    - **a.** `padding: 0 1em 1em 2.5em;`
    - **b.** `padding: 1em 2.5em;`
    - **c.** `padding: 0 2.5em 1em;`
    - **d.** `padding: 0 1em 2.5em;`

Skills Review

1. **Set element width and borders.**
   a. In your editor, open HTM_D-4.html from the SR folder where you store your Data Files for this unit, enter your first and last name and today's date in the comment section, save the file as **index.html**, then repeat for HTM_D-5.css, saving it as **styles.css**.
   b. Below the first comment section in styles.css, add a comment containing the text **reset styles**, then create a style rule that applies to the `article`, `body`, `div`, `footer`, `header`, `h1`, `h2`, `h3`, and `p` elements and sets all border widths to 0.
   c. Set the maximum width of the element with the `class` value `container` to 640px.
   d. Set the width of the `div` element within the `header` element to 70% and set 3px solid red borders on all sides.
   e. Add 3px solid black borders to all sides of `p` elements within the `header` element.
   f. Create a style rule that selects the `p` element nested in the `header` element with the `class` value `established`, set its width to 25%, then repeat for the `p` element nested in the `header` element with the `class` value `award` and for the `p` element nested in the `header` element with the `class` value `options`.
   g. Set the width of the `p` element nested in the `header` element with the `class` value `phone` to 50%, then set 3px solid red borders on all sides.
   h. Set the width of the `article` element to 65%.
   i. Add 3px solid black borders on all sides of the `footer` element.
   j. Save your changes, preview index.html in a browser, then verify that all the properties you set were applied successfully.

2. **Set margins and padding.**
   a. Return to styles.css in your editor, then in the style rule below the `reset styles` comment, add declarations that set padding and margins to 0.
   b. Set the top and bottom margins of the element with the `class` value `container` to 0 and the left and right margins to auto, then repeat for the `p` element within the `header` element with the `class` value `options` and for the `article` element. (*Hint*: You can set all four values with a single declaration.)
   c. For the `div` element within the `header` element, set the top margin to 0, the bottom margin to 0.6em, and the left and right margins to auto.
   d. Set padding for all `p` elements nested in the `header` element to 6px on all sides.

Skills Review (continued)

e. For the p element within the header element with the class value phone, set the top and bottom margins to 0.4em and the left and right margins to auto.

f. Set the padding for the article element to 5em on top and 1em on all other sides, and for the footer element to 0.5em on all sides.

g. Set margins for the h3 element to 1em on top, 0 on the right and left sides, and 0.4em on the bottom.

h. Create a style rule for p elements nested in the article element, then set the bottom margin of these elements to 0.5em.

i. Create a style rule for p elements with the class value myo nested within the article element, then set the left margin of these elements to 1em.

j. Create a style rule for p elements with the class value list nested within the article element, then set the left margin of these elements to 2em.

k. Save your changes, refresh or reload index.html in your browser, then verify that all the properties you set were applied successfully. Refer to **FIGURE D-27** as needed to compare your results to the completed document.

FIGURE D-27

3. **Align elements with float and control page flow with clear.**

a. Return to styles.css in your editor, float the p element with the class value established nested within the header element to the left, then float the p element with the class value award nested within the header element to the right.

b. Set the p element with the class value phone nested within the header element to clear floats on both margins.

c. Save your changes, refresh or reload index.html in your browser, then verify that all the properties you set were applied successfully.

4. **Implement fixed positioning.**

a. Return to styles.css in your editor, set the width of the header element to 100% and set its maximum width to 640px.

b. Give the header element a fixed position at the top of the browser window. (*Hint:* Set the top property to 0.)

c. Save your changes, refresh or reload index.html in your browser, scroll down the page, then verify that the properties you set were applied successfully. (*Hint:* Reduce the height of your browser window if necessary to check the scrolling behavior of the document.)

5. **Implement relative positioning.**

a. Return to styles.css in your editor, then relatively position the element with the class value container, setting its position to be 11em lower than its starting position.

b. Save your changes, refresh or reload index.html in your browser, then verify that all the properties you set were applied successfully.

6. **Control stacking order.**

a. Return to styles.css in your editor, then stack the header element below the container element. (*Hint:* Use -1 as the stacking value.)

b. Save your changes, refresh or reload index.html in your browser, scroll down to the bottom of the page, then verify that the header is displayed behind the scrolling content.

Skills Review (continued)

   c. Return to styles.css in your editor, then mark the declaration you added in Step a as a comment.

   d. Save your changes, refresh or reload index.html in your browser, scroll down to the bottom of the page, then verify that the header content remains on top of the scrolling content.

7. Implement absolute positioning.

   a. Return to index.html in your editor, add a p element with the class value pointright containing the character code ☛ just before the closing </header> tag, then add another p element below it with the class value pointleft and containing the character code ☚.

   b. Save your changes to index.html, then in styles.css, create style rules for the two elements you created in the previous step, setting the character color to red and the background color to black.

   c. Absolutely position the two elements you created in Step a, setting the element with the class value pointright 0.4em from the top of the parent element and 0.4em from its left side, and setting the element with the class value pointleft 0.4em from the top of the parent element and 0.4em from its right side.

   d. Save your changes, reload index.html in your browser, then verify that pointing finger icons are shown in the top left and right corners of the header. Your completed document should match **FIGURE D-27**.

   e. Open index.html on a smartphone and verify that the layout is displayed as expected.

   f. Validate your HTML and CSS code.

Independent Challenge 1

Sarah Nguyen, the owner of the Spotted Wren Garden Center, has asked you to enhance the layout of the website you created for the store. You start by implementing the new layout on the main page.

   a. In your editor, open HTM_D-6.html from the IC1 folder where you store your Data Files for this unit, enter your first and last name and today's date in the comment section, save the file as **index.html**, then repeat for HTM_D-7.css, saving it as **styles.css**.

   b. In styles.css, create a reset styles comment, then add a style rule under the comment that sets border, margin, and padding to 0 for the article, body, div, footer, header, h1, h2, h3, and p elements.

   c. Below the reset styles style rule, create a global styles section, set the bottom margin of h2 and h3 elements to 0.4em, then set the top and bottom margins of p elements to 0.4em.

   d. Set a bottom border on the header element of 3px solid red, then use the same settings for the top border of the footer element and the left border of the article element.

   e. Set the maximum width of the element with the class value container to 640px, then set the width of the article element to 52% and create a style rule to set the aside element to 38%.

   f. Float the aside element to the left and the article element to the right, then set the footer element to be displayed only when the left and right margins are clear of floated elements.

   g. Set the left and right margins of the element with the class value container to auto.

   h. Add 0.5em padding to the header and footer elements, and 2% padding to the article and aside elements.

FIGURE D-28

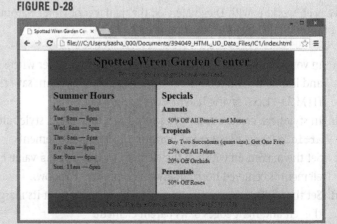

   i. Create a style rule for p elements within the article element, then set the left margin of these elements to 1em.

   j. Save your changes to styles.css, open index.html in a browser, then compare your document to **FIGURE D-28**.

   k. Open index.html on a smartphone and verify that the layout is displayed as expected.

   l. Validate your HTML and CSS code.

Independent Challenge 2

As you continue your volunteer work creating a website for the Murfreesboro Regional Soccer League, you incorporate some of the layout properties and techniques you've learned to enhance the appearance of the organization's main web page.

a. In your editor, open HTM_D-8.html from the IC2 folder where you store your Data Files for this unit, enter your first and last name and today's date in the comment section, save the file as **index.html**, then repeat for HTM_D-9.css, saving it as **styles.css**.

b. In styles.css, create a reset styles comment, then add a style rule that sets border, margin, and padding to 0 for the article, aside, body, div, footer, header, h1, h2, and p elements.

c. Create a body and page container comment, add a style rule for the element with the class value container below the comment, then set the maximum width of the element to 640px.

d. Create a main content comment, create a style rule for the article element, then set the width of the element to 55%

e. Set the width of the aside element to 35%.

f. Float the aside element to the left and the article element to the right, then set the footer element to be displayed only when the left and right margins are clear of floated elements.

g. Set the margins of the element with the class value container so the element is centered horizontally in the browser window.

h. Add 0.5em padding to the header and footer elements, 2% padding to the aside element, and 3% padding to the article element.

i. Create a style rule for the h2 element within the aside element, then set the bottom margin to 0.4em.

j. Create a style rule for p elements within the aside element, then set the top and bottom margins to 0.4em.

FIGURE D-29

k. Create a style rule for p elements with the class value description within the aside element, then set the left margin to 1em.

l. Add a 3px solid black border around the element with the class value container.

m. Save your changes to styles.css, open index.html in a browser, then compare your document to **FIGURE D-29**.

n. Open index.html on a smartphone and verify that the layout is displayed as expected.

o. Validate your HTML and CSS code.

Independent Challenge 3

You've been working with Diego Merckx, the manager of Hotel Natoma, to develop a new layout for the website. You style a page of museum listings with the new layout.

a. In your editor, open HTM_D-10.html from the IC3 folder where you store your Data Files for this unit, enter your first and last name and today's date in the comment section, save the file as **museums.html**, then repeat for HTM_D-11.css, saving it as **styles.css**.

b. In styles.css, create a reset styles comment, then add a style rule that sets border, margin, and padding to 0 for the article, body, div, footer, header, h1, h2, and p elements.

c. Set the maximum width of the element with the class value container to 800px, then set its margins so the element is centered horizontally in the browser window.

d. Set the width of the article element to 60%, then set its margins so its content is horizontally centered between the left and right edges of its parent element.

Independent Challenge 3 (continued)

e. Add 3px solid black borders to the left and right sides of the element with the `class` value `container`, and to the top and bottom of the `header` and `footer` elements.

f. Add 10px padding to the header and footer elements and 15px padding to the article element.

g. Apply fixed positioning to the `header` element 0 px from the top of the browser window, then specify a maximum width of 780px and a width of 100%.

h. Apply 4em of padding to the top of the element with the `class` value `container`, then save styles.css.

i. In museums.html, add 2 p elements as children of the `header` element, each containing the character code `&#9728;`, one with the `class` value `logoleft`, and the other with the `class` value `logoright`, then save museums.html.

j. In styles.css, create a style rule for the p elements nested in the `header` element, then set the text color for the elements to `linen`.

k. Create a style rule for the p element with the `class` value `logoleft` nested in the `header` element, absolutely position the element, then set the element 1em from the top and 3em from the left of the positioned ancestor element.

l. Create a style rule for the p element with the `class` value `logoright` nested in the `header` element, absolutely position the element, then set the element 1em from the top and 3em from the right of the positioned ancestor element.

m. Save your changes to styles.css, open museums.html in a browser, then compare your document to **FIGURE D-30**.

n. Reduce the height of your browser window if necessary so not all page contents are visible, scroll down the page, then verify that the `header` element remains fixed at the top of the window and the remaining text scrolls under it.

o. Open museums.html on a smartphone and verify that the layout is displayed as expected.

p. Validate your HTML and CSS code.

FIGURE D-30

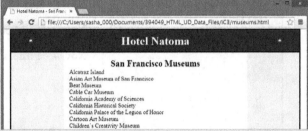

Independent Challenge 4—Explore

As you continue your work building the website for your client Eating Well in Season, you've developed a new visual layout for the site. You'll use positioning to apply the new layout to the main page of the site.

a. In your editor, open HTM_D-12.html from the IC4 folder where you store your Data Files for this unit, enter your first and last name and today's date in the comment section, save the file as **index.html**, then repeat for HTM_D-13.css, saving it as **styles.css**.

b. Add reset styles that set margins, padding, and border to 0 for all elements in use on the page.

c. Create a style rule for the element with the `class` value `container`, set the maximum width of the element to 800px, then center it in the browser window.

d. Set the width of the `article` element to 62.5%, create a style rule for the `aside` element, set its width to 37.5%, then use absolute positioning to display it against the top and right of the element with the `class` value `positioncontainer`. (*Hint*: You can use a `position` value of `relative` to make the parent element the positioning context without changing its location in the layout.)

FIGURE D-31

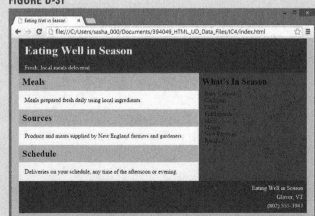

e. Set margins and padding for page elements until your document matches **FIGURE D-31** in a browser.

f. Open index.html on a smartphone and verify that the layout is displayed as expected.

g. Validate your HTML and CSS code.

Visual Workshop

In your editor, open the file HTM_D-14.html from the VW folder where you store your Data Files for this unit, enter your first and last name and today's date in the comment section, save the file as **index.html**, then repeat for HTM_D-15.css, saving it as **styles.css**. Edit styles.css to create the layout shown in **FIGURE D-32**. When you are finished, open index.html in a browser and on a smartphone and verify that the layout is displayed as expected, then validate your HTML and CSS code.

FIGURE D-32

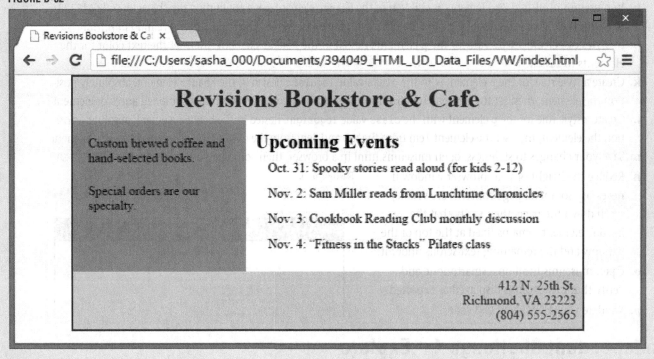

Chapter 4

HTML5 & CSS3

Organizing Content with Lists and Tables

CASE As you continue your work on the website for the Lakeland Reeds Bed & Breakfast, you format content using lists and tables.

Unit Objectives

After completing this unit, you will be able to:

- Create an ordered list
- Create an unordered list
- Create a description list
- Create a nav bar using a list
- Insert a table
- Debug tables
- Span columns and rows
- Format a table with CSS
- Apply a table-like structure to other elements

Files You Will Need

 L 10 files   IC3 12 files

 SR 10 files   IC4 9 files

 IC1 10 files   VW 7 files

 IC2 9 files

For specific filenames, see Filenames_H.pdf in the Unit H Data Files folder.

Create an Ordered List

You use the HTML ol element to create a list in which items are numbered or lettered sequentially. This type of list is known as an **ordered list** because the order in which the items are listed is important. You create each item in an ordered list with the li element. All the li elements for a list are nested within the opening and closing ol tags. The default marker for each list item is determined by the user agent rendering the web page but it is most often an Arabic numeral (1, 2, 3, . . .). You can use the values of the CSS list-style-type property shown in TABLE H-1 to change the markers to letters or to a different numbering style. **CASE** *Phillip Blaine, the owner of Lakeland Reeds Bed & Breakfast, has provided additional information that he'd like you to incorporate into the Reservations web page. You start by adding a list of the most popular weekends at Lakeland Reeds.*

STEPS

1. **In your editor, open HTM_H-1.html from the Lessons folder where you store your Data Files for this unit, save it as reserve.html, then repeat to save HTM_H-2.css as styles.css**

2. **In the comment at the top of each file, enter your name and today's date where indicated, then save the files**

3. **Return to reserve.html, insert a blank line beneath the paragraph** *Our most sought-after weekends,* **indent to the same level as the paragraph, type <ol>, press [Enter], indent to the same level, then type </ol>**
   All items in an ordered list are contained between the opening and closing tags for the ol element.

4. **Insert a blank line beneath <ol>, indent 3 additional spaces, then type** `<li>Independence Day (Jul. 4)</li>`
   The content of each list item is contained between the opening and closing tags for the li element.

5. **Press [Enter], indent as needed to the same level, then type** `<li>Memorial Day (last Monday in May)</li>`

6. **Press [Enter], indent as needed to the same level, type** `<li>Labor Day (first Monday in Sep.)</li>`, **then save your changes**
   FIGURE H-1 shows the completed HTML code for the ordered list.

7. **Return to styles.css in your editor, create a new style rule for the ol element at the end of the reset styles section, then add the declaration** `list-style-type: none;`
   This declaration removes the default numbering assigned by browsers from ol elements you create. Because you removed the default numbering, you are required to specify the list-style-type for each ordered list in your document.

8. **In the style rule that sets border, padding, and margin to 0 in the reset styles section, add the ol and li selectors to the list of selectors**

9. **Scroll down to the /* footer section */ comment and, above this comment, add the comment /* main content lists */, then, below this comment, create a style rule with the article ol selector and the declarations** `margin: 1em 0 1em 2em;`, `font-size: 1.3em;`, **and** `list-style-type: decimal;`
   FIGURE H-2 shows the changes to the style sheet.

10. **Save your changes, then open reserve.html in a browser**
    As **FIGURE H-3** shows, the list is displayed with each list item numbered sequentially starting at the number 1. Note that the list markers for an ordered list are always displayed outside the content box and on the left. If the list has left padding or margin (as in this example), the markers are displayed within the padding or margin area. If not, the markers are displayed outside the element on the left side.

FIGURE H-1: HTML code for ordered list

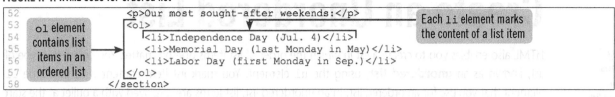

```
52        <p>Our most sought-after weekends:</p>
53        <ol>
54            <li>Independence Day (Jul. 4)</li>
55            <li>Memorial Day (last Monday in May)</li>
56            <li>Labor Day (first Monday in Sep.)</li>
57        </ol>
58    </section>
```

ol element contains list items in an ordered list

Each li element marks the content of a list item

FIGURE H-2: CSS code for ordered list

```
10    /* reset styles */
11    html {
12        font-size: 16px;
13    }
14    a, article, body, div, figcaption, figure, footer, header, h1,
15    h2, h3, img, li, nav, ol, p, section {
16        border: 0;
17        padding: 0;
18        margin: 0;
19    }
20    img {
21        max-width: 100%;
22        height: auto;
23        width: auto;
24    }
25    ol {
26        list-style-type: none;
27    }
```

li and ol selectors added to rule for border, padding, and margin in the reset styles section

list-style-type of none removes the default numbering assigned by browsers to ordered lists

```
137    /* main content lists */
138    article ol {
139        margin: 1em 0 1em 2em;
140        font-size: 1.3em;
141        list-style-type: decimal;
142    }
143
144    /* footer section */
```

list-style-type of decimal uses sequential numbers starting at 1

FIGURE H-3: Ordered list in Reservations web page

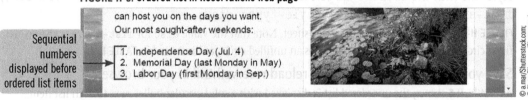

can host you on the days you want.
Our most sought-after weekends:

1. Independence Day (Jul. 4)
2. Memorial Day (last Monday in May)
3. Labor Day (first Monday in Sep.)

Sequential numbers displayed before ordered list items

© a.mar/Shutterstock.com;
© Elena Elisseeva/Shutterstock.com

TABLE H-1: Widely supported values for the CSS list-style-type property for the ol element

value	result	value	result
decimal	1. first item 2. second item	lower-latin lower-roman	i. first item ii. second item
decimal-leading-zero	01. first item 02. second item ... 10. tenth item 11. eleventh item	none	first item second item
		upper-alpha	A. first item B. second item
lower-alpha	a. first item b. second item	upper-latin upper-roman	I. first item II. second item

© 2016 Cengage Learning

Create an Unordered List

HTML also enables you to create a list in which the order of list items doesn't matter. You create this type of list, known as an **unordered list**, using the ul element. You mark list item content with the same li element that you use for an ordered list. In an unordered list, list items are displayed with a bullet at the start of each line. The default bullet character is a solid circle, but you can use the CSS list-style-type property with one of the values shown in TABLE H-2 to specify a different bullet shape. **CASE** ➤ *Visitors sometimes reserve the entire facility for special events. You add Phillip's list of special events to the Reservations web page as an unordered list.*

STEPS

1. **Return to reserve.html in your editor, insert a blank line beneath the paragraph that begins *Lakeland Reeds is also available*, indent to the same level as the paragraph, type <ul>, press [Enter], indent to the same level, then type </ul>**
   All items in an unordered list are contained between the opening and closing tags for the ul element.

2. **Insert a blank line beneath <ul>, indent 3 additional spaces, then type <li>Weddings</li>**
   While the containing element is specific to the type of list you're creating, you use the li element for list items when creating either ordered or unordered lists.

3. **Press [Enter], indent as needed to the same level, type <li>Birthdays</li>, then repeat to enter the code <li>Family Reunions</li>**
   FIGURE H-4 shows the completed HTML code for the unordered list.

4. **Save your changes, then return to styles.css in your editor**

5. **In the style rule that sets border, padding, and margin to 0 in the reset styles section, add the ul selector to the list of selectors, then add the ul selector to the ol style rule in the reset styles section**

6. **Scroll down to the main content lists section, then, below the article ol rule, add a new style rule with the article ul selector and the declarations margin: 1em 0 1em 2em;, font-size: 1.3em;, and list-style-type: disc;**
   FIGURE H-5 shows the changes to the style sheet. Note that the value disc for list-style-type creates a filled circle, while the value circle creates an unfilled circle, as illustrated in TABLE H-2.

7. **Save your changes, then refresh or reload reserve.html in your browser**
   As FIGURE H-6 shows, the unordered list is displayed with a solid circular bullet next to each list item.

TABLE H-2: Values for the CSS list-style-type property for the ul element

value	description	example
circle	unfilled circle	○ list item
disc	filled circle (default)	• list item
square	filled square	■ list item
none	no character	list item

© 2016 Cengage Learning

FIGURE H-4: HTML code for unordered list

```
60              <section>
61                  <h3>Special Events</h3>
62                  <figure class="alternate">
63                      <img src="images/frolic.jpg" width="350" height="209" alt="people
64                      swimming with a raft in the lake">
65                  </figure>
66                  <p>Lakeland Reeds is also available for booking group special events,
67                  including</p>
68                  <ul>
69                      <li>Weddings</li>
70                      <li>Birthdays</li>
71                      <li>Family Reunions</li>
72                  </ul>
73                  <p><a href="weddings.pdf">Guidelines and reservation form for a special
74                  event at Lakeland Reeds.</a> (PDF)</p>
75              </section>
```

ul element contains list items in an unordered list

Each li element marks the content of a list item

FIGURE H-5: CSS code for unordered list

```
10      /* reset styles */
11      html {
12          font-size: 16px;
13      }
14      a, article, body, div, figcaption, figure, footer, header, h1,
15      h2, h3, img, li, nav, ol, p, section, ul {
16          border: 0;
17          padding: 0;
18          margin: 0;
19      }
20      img {
21          max-width: 100%;
22          height: auto;
23          width: auto;
24      }
25      ol, ul {
26          list-style-type: none;
27      }
```

ul selector added to two rules in the reset styles section

```
137     /* main content lists */
138     article ol {
139         margin: 1em 0 1em 2em;
140         font-size: 1.3em;
141         list-style-type: decimal;
142     }
143     article ul {
144         margin: 1em 0 1em 2em;
145         font-size: 1.3em;
146         list-style-type: disc;
147     }
```

list-style-type of disc uses a filled circle

FIGURE H-6: Unordered list in Reservations web page

Filled circles displayed before unordered list items

Create a Description List

The dl element creates a **description list**, which enables you to specify a set of items and descriptions. A description list was known in previous versions of HTML as a **definition list**. Unlike ol and ul, dl does not use the li element to specify list items. Instead, a list item uses two elements: dt marks the term or item being described, and dd marks the description. **CASE** ▶ *The contact information for Phillip Blaine on the Reservations page is a set of items and their descriptions. You change the markup for this section to a definition list.*

STEPS

1. **Return to reserve.html in your editor, locate the div element with the class value contact, then in the opening and closing tags, replace div with dl**
   This changes the div element to a description list element.

2. **In the next line, replace the code <p><span> with <dt>, replace the code </span> with </dt>, move the insertion point after the closing </dt> tag, then press [Enter]**

3. **Indent to match the previous line, type <dd>, then replace the closing </p> tag with </dd>**
   Your changes in Steps 2 and 3 have marked the Proprietor label as a dt element and the name Phillip Blaine as a dd element.

4. **Repeat Steps 2 and 3 to convert each of the remaining 3 p elements to a dt and a dd element**
   FIGURE H-7 shows the completed HTML code for the description list.

5. **Save your changes, then return to styles.css in your editor**

6. **In the style rule that sets border, padding, and margin to 0 in the reset styles section, add the dd, dl, and dt selectors to the list of selectors**

7. **Scroll down to the main content lists section, then below the article ul rule, add a new style rule with the article dl selector and the declarations margin: 1em 0; and font-size: 1.3em;**

8. **Below the rule you created in the previous step, add a new style rule with the article dt selector and the declaration font-weight: bold;, then create a new style rule with the article dd selector and the declaration margin-left: 2em;**
   FIGURE H-8 shows the changes. The article dt style rule bolds the item in each set, and the article dd selector indents its description.

9. **Save your changes, then refresh or reload reserve.html in your browser**
   As **FIGURE H-9** shows, each dt element is displayed in bold and each dd element is indented.

Specifying custom bullets

In addition to choosing from the standard selection of bullet characters using the list-style-type property, you can instead choose to specify an image to display as the bullet character using the list-style-image property. The syntax is the same as that for specifying a background image: the text url followed by the path and filename of the image file, enclosed in quotes and parentheses. For instance, the code

```
ul {
    list-style-image:url("images/browntri.gif");
}
```

specifies the file browntri.gif, located in the images folder, as the bullet character for unordered lists.

FIGURE H-7: HTML code for description list

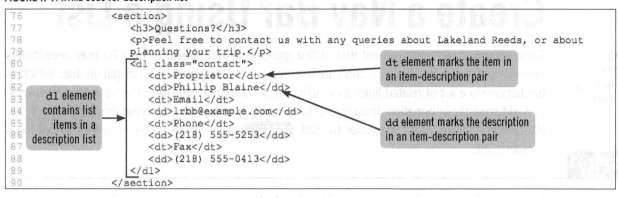

```
76      <section>
77          <h3>Questions?</h3>
78          <p>Feel free to contact us with any queries about Lakeland Reeds, or about
79          planning your trip.</p>
80          <dl class="contact">
81              <dt>Proprietor</dt>
82              <dd>Phillip Blaine</dd>
83              <dt>Email</dt>
84              <dd>lrbb@example.com</dd>
85              <dt>Phone</dt>
86              <dd>(218) 555-5253</dd>
87              <dt>Fax</dt>
88              <dd>(218) 555-0413</dd>
89          </dl>
90      </section>
```

- dl element contains list items in a description list
- dt element marks the item in an item-description pair
- dd element marks the description in an item-description pair

FIGURE H-8: CSS code for description list

```
10      /* reset styles */
11      html {
12          font-size: 16px;
13      }
14      a, article, body, dd, div, dl, dt, figcaption, figure, footer, header, h1,
15      h2, h3, img, li, nav, ol, p, section, ul {
16          border: 0;
17          padding: 0;
18          margin: 0;
19      }
```

- dd, dl, and dt selectors added to rule for border, padding, and margin in the reset styles section

```
142     article ul {
143         margin: 1em 0 1em 2em;
144         font-size: 1.3em;
145         list-style-type: disc;
146     }
147     article dl {
148         margin: 1em 0;
149         font-size: 1.3em;
150     }
151     article dt {
152         font-weight: bold;
153     }
154     article dd {
155         margin-left: 2em;
156     }
```

- Style rule bolds the item in each item-description pair
- Style rule indents the description in each item-description pair

FIGURE H-9: Description list in Reservations web page

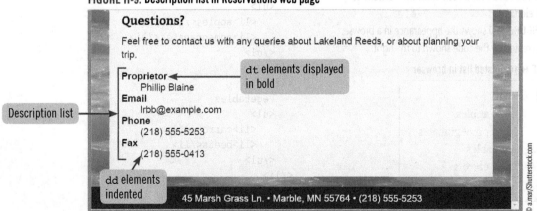

- dt elements displayed in bold
- Description list
- dd elements indented

Create a Nav Bar Using a List

Learning Outcomes
• Mark a nav bar as an unordered list

Some common web page content that at first glance may not appear to be a list may nevertheless benefit from being marked up using list elements. One example is a navigation bar, which is fundamentally a list of related links. By marking up a navigation bar using the ul and li elements, you add semantic information. In addition, list elements give you greater layout flexibility using fewer HTML tags, making your code easier to read. **CASE** *You convert the main navigation bar to an unordered list.*

STEPS

1. Return to reserve.html in your editor, locate the opening <nav> tag with the class value sitenavigation, add a new line below it, indent an additional 3 spaces, then type <ul>

2. Add a new line above the closing </nav> tag for the main nav bar, indent an additional 3 spaces, then type </ul>

TROUBLE
This is the <ul> tag you entered in step 1.

3. In the line below the opening <ul> tag, indent an additional 3 spaces, replace the opening <p> tag with <li>, then replace the closing </p> tag with </li>

4. Repeat Step 3 to convert the remaining p elements in the nav bar to li elements
   Your code should match **FIGURE H-11**.

5. Save your changes, return to styles.css in your editor, then scroll up to the site navigation bar section

6. In the nav.sitenavigation p style rule, change the selector to nav.sitenavigation li, then add the declarations font-size: 1.3em; and line-height: 1.4em;, as shown in **FIGURE H-12**

7. Save your work, then reload reserve.html in your browser
   As **FIGURE H-13** shows, there is no change in the appearance of the nav bar.

8. Move the mouse pointer over the Weather link and verify that it still changes color, click the Weather link and verify that a weather page opens, then click your browser's Back button to return to reserve.html

Creating nested lists

Sometimes nesting a list within another list is the clearest way to present information. It's easy to nest lists in HTML: you simply insert valid code for a list within the content of an li, dt, or dd element.

For instance, **FIGURE H-10** shows the appearance in a browser of the nested lists created by the code shown to the right:

FIGURE H-10: Nested list in browser

```
1. Fruits
     o apples
     o pomegranates
2. Vegetables
     o carrots
     o beets
```

```
<ol>
   <li>
      Fruits
      <ul>
         <li>apples</li>
         <li>pomegranates</li>
      </ul>
   </li>
   <li>
      Vegetables
      <ul>
         <li>carrots</li>
         <li>beets</li>
      </ul>
   </li>
</ol>
```

FIGURE H-11: HTML code for nav bar using `ul` and `li` elements

```
29          <nav class="sitenavigation">
30              <ul>
31                  <li><a href="index.html">Home</a></li>
                    <li><a href="aboutus.html">About Us</a></li>
                    <li><a href="reserve.html">Reservations</a></li>
                    <li><a href="events.html">Events</a></li>
                    <li><a href="http://wxug.us/lhn14">Weather</a></li>
                    <li><a href="https://goo.gl/maps/bwf5R">Directions</a></li>
37              </ul>
38          </nav>
```

Nav bar links nested within a ul element

Each li element marks a nav bar link

FIGURE H-12: Updated CSS code for nav bar

```
69      /* site navigation bar */
70      nav.sitenavigation {
71          color: #34180f;
72          text-align: center;
73          background-color: #B8944D;
74      }
75      nav.sitenavigation li {
76          margin: 0.3em 0.5em;
77          display: inline-block;
78          font-size: 1.3em;
79          line-height: 1.4em;
80      }
```

nav.sitenavigation li replaces nav.sitenavigation p selector

FIGURE H-13: Modified nav bar in browser

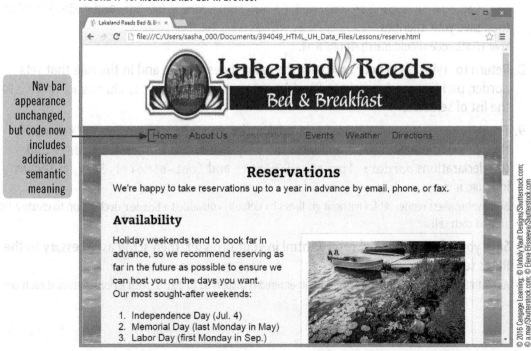

Nav bar appearance unchanged, but code now includes additional semantic meaning

Insert a Table

Learning Outcomes
• Create a table

In addition to a simple list of items or items and descriptions, HTML enables you to present a larger set of information as a table, which organizes data in horizontal **rows** and vertical **columns**. Each item in a table is displayed in a **cell**, which is the intersection of a row and a column. To create a table in HTML, you use the elements described in TABLE H-3. **CASE** ▶ *Phillip would like a table showing a breakdown of room rates. You add this table on the Reservations page.*

STEPS

QUICK TIP
Table content is placed between opening and closing table tags.

1. Return to reserve.html in your editor, insert a blank line below the h3 element containing the text *Rates*, indent to match the `<h3>` tag, type `<table>`, press [Enter], indent as needed, then type `</table>`

2. Insert a blank line beneath the opening `<table>` tag, indent 3 spaces more than the previous line, type `<thead>`, press [Enter], indent to match the previous line, then type `</thead>`

QUICK TIP
The thead and tbody elements group table rows into sections.

3. Press [Enter], indent to match the previous line, type `<tbody>`, press [Enter], indent as needed, then type `</tbody>`

4. Insert a blank line below the `<thead>` tag, indent 3 spaces more than the previous line, type `<tr>`, press [Enter], type `</tr>`, then repeat twice to add two more tr elements in the tbody section

QUICK TIP
The number of cells in each row is sufficient for a browser to calculate the number of columns; therefore, no element is required to specify the number or arrangement of columns.

5. Insert a blank line below the first `<tr>` tag in the thead section, indent 3 spaces more than the previous line, type `<th>Period</th>`, then enter the following additional th elements on separate lines: `<th>Sun Room</th>`, `<th>Reed Room</th>`, and `<th>Treehouse</th>`

6. Within the first tr element in the tbody section, enter the following td elements: `<td>May 1 - Sep. 15</td>`, `<td>$110</td>`, `<td>$125</td>`, and `<td>$150</td>`

7. Within the second tr element in the tbody section, enter the td elements `<td>Sep. 16 - Apr. 30</td>`, `<td>$100</td>`, `<td>$110</td>`, and `<td>$150</td>`, then save your changes

   Your HTML code should match FIGURE H-14.

8. Return to styles.css in your editor, in the reset styles section and in the rule that sets border, padding, and margin to 0, add `table`, `tbody`, `td`, `tfoot`, `th`, `thead`, and `tr` to the list of selectors

QUICK TIP
Specifying a border for the table element creates a border around the outside of a table, but not around individual cells within it.

9. Type `/* main content tables */` above the `/* footer section */` comment, then below the new comment create a new style rule with the selectors `td`, `th` and the declarations `border: 1px solid black;` and `font-size: 1.3em;`, as shown in FIGURE H-15

   Because browsers render tables without gridlines by default, you added a border declaration to create a line around each cell.

10. Save your changes, reload reserve.html in your browser, then scroll as necessary to the Rates section

    As FIGURE H-16 shows, the table content you entered is displayed in a grid, with a border around each cell.

FIGURE H-14: HTML code for table

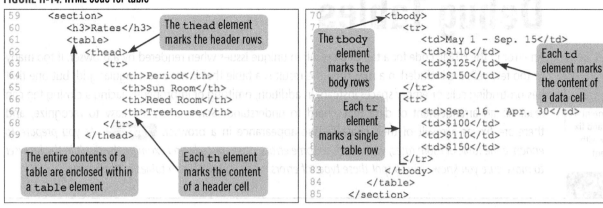

```
59     <section>
60        <h3>Rates</h3>              The thead element
61        <table>                    marks the header rows
62           <thead>
63              <tr>
64                 <th>Period</th>
65                 <th>Sun Room</th>
66                 <th>Reed Room</th>
67                 <th>Treehouse</th>
68              </tr>
69           </thead>
```

The entire contents of a table are enclosed within a table element

Each th element marks the content of a header cell

```
70           <tbody>
71              <tr>
72                 <td>May 1 - Sep. 15</td>
73                 <td>$110</td>
74                 <td>$125</td>
75                 <td>$150</td>
76              </tr>
77              <tr>
78                 <td>Sep. 16 - Apr. 30</td>
79                 <td>$100</td>
80                 <td>$110</td>
81                 <td>$150</td>
82              </tr>
83           </tbody>
84        </table>
85     </section>
```

The tbody element marks the body rows

Each tr element marks a single table row

Each td element marks the content of a data cell

Code continued with line 70 in figure to the right   Code continued from figure on the left

FIGURE H-15: CSS code for table

```
14    a, article, body, div, dd, dl, dt, figcaption, figure, footer, header, h1,
15    h2, h3, img, nav, ol, p, section, table, tbody, td, tfoot, th, thead, tr, ul {
16       border: 0;
17       padding: 0;
18       margin: 0;
19    }
```

Selectors added to rule for border, padding, and margin in the reset styles section

```
160   /* main content tables */
161   td, th {
162      border: 1px solid black;
163      font-size: 1.3em;
164   }
165
166   /* footer section */
```

border property for td and th elements adds a line around each cell

FIGURE H-16: Table in Reservations web page

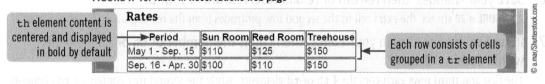

th element content is centered and displayed in bold by default

Rates			
Period	Sun Room	Reed Room	Treehouse
May 1 - Sep. 15	$110	$125	$150
Sep. 16 - Apr. 30	$100	$110	$150

Each row consists of cells grouped in a tr element

© a.mar/Shutterstock.com

TABLE H-3 HTML Table Structuring Elements

element	content	description
table	entire table	start and end of table content
thead		group of one or more rows that contain column headers; when printed, this content is displayed at the top of each page
tbody	group of rows	group of one or more rows that contain the main body of the table
tfoot		group of one or more rows that contain column footers; when printed, this content is displayed at the bottom of each page
tr	row	start and end of a row
th		content of a table header cell
td	cell	content of a standard table cell

© 2016 Cengage Learning

Debug Tables

Learning Outcomes
- Recognize and fix a table row with missing content
- Recognize and fix a table row with extra content

An error in the HTML code for a table can result in unique issues when rendered by a browser. If too many or too few cells are included in a row, then the result is a table that is not a rectangular grid, but one that has protruding cells or empty spaces instead. In addition, omitting or improperly placing a closing tag can result in an arrangement of data that's hard to understand. Some errors are easy to recognize, and therefore fix, as a result of their characteristic appearance in a browser. **CASE** *As you prepare to enhance the table of room rates, you introduce some errors into your code and examine the result in the browser to make sure you know how to spot these types of errors when you work with tables in the future.*

STEPS

1. **Return to reserve.html in your editor, locate the code `<td>$150</td>` within the second `tr` element, type `<!--` before the `<td>` tag, then type `-->` after the `</td>` tag**

   In order for a table to appear as a rectangular grid, each row must have the same amount of content. By commenting out this td element, you create a row that is missing a cell. **FIGURE H-17** shows the edited code.

   QUICK TIP
   You can visualize the role of each element in a table by opening your browser's developer tools, then mousing over each element to highlight it on the page.

2. **Save your changes, then refresh or reload reserve.html in your browser**

   As **FIGURE H-18** shows, the missing cell in the second row is reflected as an empty spot in the table.

3. **Return to reserve.html in your editor, then count the number of `th` or `td` elements that are not commented out within each `tr` element**

   The first and third rows each contain 4 th or td elements, while the second row contains only 3 td elements that are not commented out. This difference in the number of cells in each row results in the gap displayed in the browser.

4. **Remove the `<!--` and `-->` tags you added in Step 1**

5. **Below the final `td` element and within the second `tr` element, add a new line, indent to match the previous line, then type `<td>$150</td>`**

   QUICK TIP
   The extra cell is narrower than the other cells because by default, browsers set width to fit the content in the widest cell of a column.

   When entering the code for a table manually, it's also possible to enter too much content in a single row. Adding an extra cell to this row creates such a row. **FIGURE H-19** shows the edited code.

6. **Save your changes, then refresh or reload reserve.html in your browser**

   As **FIGURE H-20** shows, the extra cell in the second row protrudes from the rectangular shape of the table.

   TROUBLE
   If your table does not appear as expected, use **FIGURE H-14**, which shows the completed code for the table, to correct any errors.

7. **Return to reserve.html in your editor, then count the number of `th` or `td` elements within each `tr` element**

   The first and third rows each contain 4 th or td elements, while the second row contains 5 td elements. This difference in the number of cells in each row results in the protruding cell displayed in the browser.

8. **Remove the `td` element you added in Step 5, save your changes, then refresh or reload reserve.html in your browser**

   Your table once again appears as a rectangle with no protruding or missing cells.

FIGURE H-17: Table code to remove a cell

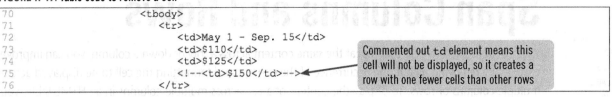

```
70              <tbody>
71                  <tr>
72                      <td>May 1 - Sep. 15</td>
73                      <td>$110</td>
74                      <td>$125</td>
75                      <!--<td>$150</td>-->
76                  </tr>
```

> Commented out td element means this cell will not be displayed, so it creates a row with one fewer cells than other rows

FIGURE H-18: Table with a missing cell in a browser

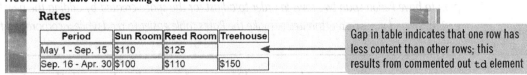

Rates

Period	Sun Room	Reed Room	Treehouse
May 1 - Sep. 15	$110	$125	
Sep. 16 - Apr. 30	$100	$110	$150

© a.mar/Shutterstock.com

> Gap in table indicates that one row has less content than other rows; this results from commented out td element

FIGURE H-19: Table code to create a row with an extra cell

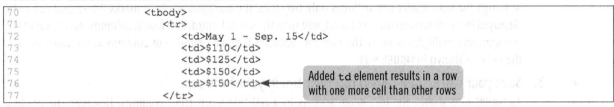

```
70              <tbody>
71                  <tr>
72                      <td>May 1 - Sep. 15</td>
73                      <td>$110</td>
74                      <td>$125</td>
75                      <td>$150</td>
76                      <td>$150</td>
77                  </tr>
```

> Added td element results in a row with one more cell than other rows

FIGURE H-20: Table with an extra cell in a browser

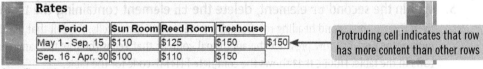

Rates

Period	Sun Room	Reed Room	Treehouse	
May 1 - Sep. 15	$110	$125	$150	$150
Sep. 16 - Apr. 30	$100	$110	$150	

© a.mar/Shutterstock.com

> Protruding cell indicates that row has more content than other rows

Resisting the temptation to use tables for layout

You can style table borders with all the properties that are available for other web page elements, including removing borders completely. In the early days of the web, many developers combined spanned rows and columns with invisible borders to enable the positioning of text, images, and other elements side by side, and in specific areas of a web page. However, as CSS grew and user agent support for it matured, the CSS position and float properties became the preferred method for creating visual layouts. While you can place elements in arbitrary locations by manipulating the number and sizes of rows and columns in a table, doing so erroneously assigns semantic meaning to your web page content; this suggests that user agents should attempt to understand it as a table of related data. In addition, this use of a table creates particularly strong challenges for non-visual user agents such as screen readers in conveying the relationships between web page elements. For these reasons, you should restrict your use of tables only to data whose meaning can be best understood in a grid layout.

Span Columns and Rows

Learning
Outcomes
• Display cell
  content in
  multiple columns
• Display cell
  content in
  multiple rows

When a table contains cells that repeat the same content across a row or down a column, you can improve usability by removing all but one occurrence of the content and formatting the cell to be displayed across multiple columns or rows. To display the content of a cell across multiple columns in an HTML table, you use the `colspan` attribute in the opening `th` or `td` tag for the cell in order to specify the number of columns in which the content should be displayed. Likewise, you use the `rowspan` attribute to specify the number of rows for cell content to span. **CASE** ▶ *Your plans for the Rates table include an additional row at the top labeling the room listings, as shown in the sketch in* **FIGURE H-21**. *Once the new row is added, you plan to have Period span two rows in order to adjust for the space created by adding the new top row. You add* `colspan` *and* `rowspan` *attributes to make the Rates table easier to read while incorporating this new content.*

STEPS

1. **Return to reserve.html in your editor, insert a new line beneath the `<thead>` tag, indent 3 additional spaces, type `<tr>`, press [Enter], indent as needed, then type `</tr>`**

2. **Between the opening and closing `tr` tags you just entered, indent two additional spaces, type `<th>Period</th>`, press [Enter], indent as needed, then type `<th colspan="3">Room</th>`**

   Although the new header row includes only two cells, the `colspan` attribute marks the second cell to be displayed in 3 columns, so the second cell will span the second, third, and fourth columns. As a result of the cell spanning multiple columns, the new row occupies the same number of columns as the other rows in the table, as shown in **FIGURE H-21**.

3. **Save your work, then reload reserve.html in your browser**

   As **FIGURE H-22** shows, the text *Room* appears in a cell that spans three columns. However, the heading *Period* is now duplicated in the two heading rows.

4. **Return to reserve.html in your editor, within the first `tr` element, click before the closing > in the opening tag for the `th` element containing the text *Period*, press [Spacebar], then type `rowspan="2"`**

5. **Within the second `tr` element, delete the `th` element containing the text *Period***

   Even though the second heading row contains code for only three cells, the cell that use the `rowspan` attribute in the previous row provides the additional content that keeps the row the same length as the other rows in the table. **FIGURE H-23** shows the completed HTML code for the table.

6. **Save your changes, then refresh reserve.html in your browser**

   As **FIGURE H-24** shows, the cell containing the text *Period* spans two rows.

FIGURE H-21: Sketch of table with cells spanning rows and columns

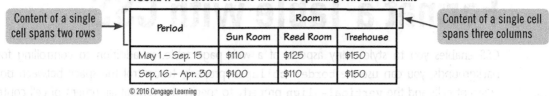

Content of a single cell spans two rows →

← Content of a single cell spans three columns

© 2016 Cengage Learning

FIGURE H-22: Table cell spanning multiple columns

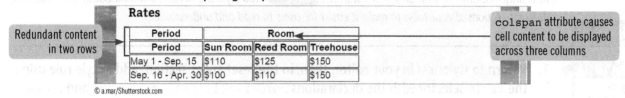

Redundant content in two rows

colspan attribute causes cell content to be displayed across three columns

© a.mar/Shutterstock.com

FIGURE H-23: Code containing `colspan` and `rowspan` attributes

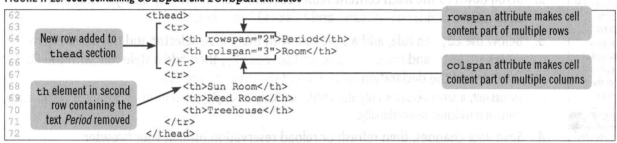

```
62          <thead>
63            <tr>
64              <th rowspan="2">Period</th>
65              <th colspan="3">Room</th>
66            </tr>
67            <tr>
68              <th>Sun Room</th>
69              <th>Reed Room</th>
70              <th>Treehouse</th>
71            </tr>
72          </thead>
```

New row added to thead section

th element in second row containing the text *Period* removed

rowspan attribute makes cell content part of multiple rows

colspan attribute makes cell content part of multiple columns

FIGURE H-24: Table cell spanning multiple rows

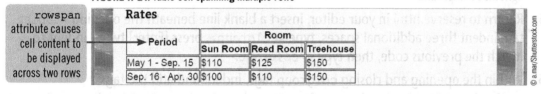

rowspan attribute causes cell content to be displayed across two rows

© a.mar/Shutterstock.com

Calculating the number of columns in a row

When you use `colspan` and `rowspan` attributes, you still need to confirm that your content fits the table dimensions. To do so, start by adding the values for all `colspan` attributes used in the row. Next, add the number of `th` or `td` elements in the row without `colspan` attributes. Finally, add the number of `th` or `td` cells in earlier rows whose content is part of the current row due to `rowspan` values. In short:

current row `colspan` total

+ cells in current row without `colspan`

+ cells spanning from previous rows with `rowspan`

= total columns

Running this calculation on any row of your table should produce

the same value as for any other row.

If one or more rows appear to be shorter or longer than the surrounding rows, it can be helpful to preview your web page in a browser and inspect the table to identify the cell where the content of one row no longer corresponds to the content above or below it. You may simply need to adjust a `rowspan` or `colspan` value, or add or remove a cell.

In a table that doesn't use colspan or rowspan attributes, you can verify that each row includes content for every column simply by ensuring that each row contains the same number of th or td elements.

Format a Table with CSS

Learning Outcomes
- Apply CSS properties to table columns

CSS enables you to style many aspects of a web page table. In addition to controlling fonts and backgrounds, you can use the `border-collapse` property to control the space between borders of adjacent cells and the `vertical-align` property to specify the vertical alignment of cell content. You can use these and other CSS properties to style an entire table, a table section (such as `thead` or `tbody`), or individual rows or cells. In addition, you can use the HTML `col` and `colgroup` elements to assign styles to a single column or to a group of columns. **CASE** *You style the borders and add background colors to different sections of your table to make it easier for users to read and understand.*

STEPS

QUICK TIP

The border-spacing property has no effect when border-collapse is set to collapse, but specifying a value of 0 ensures that browsers do not create extra space between the table's outermost cells and the border of the table element.

1. **Return to styles.css in your editor, then, in the reset styles section, add a style rule using the `table` selector with the declarations `border-collapse: collapse;` and `border-spacing: 0;`**

   Setting `border-collapse` to `collapse` eliminates the default space between the borders of adjacent cells.

2. **Scroll down to the main content tables section, then in the `td`, `th` style rule, add the declarations `padding: 0.4em;` and `text-align: center;`**

3. **Below the `td`, `th` rule, add a style rule with the `table` selector and the declarations `width: 100%;` and `border: 2px solid black;`, then add a style rule with the `th` selector and the declaration `background-color: #aecdf4;`**

   By default, a table occupies only the width necessary to display its content. At increased widths, each column is widened proportionally.

4. **Save your changes, then refresh or reload reservation.html in your browser**

   The content of all cells is centered and the cells have increased padding. The table occupies the entire width of the parent element and has a thicker outer border than the cell borders. In addition, the `th` cells have a light blue background.

QUICK TIP

Browsers render only the background (and related), border (and related), visibility, and width CSS properties applied to colgroup and col elements.

5. **Return to reserve.html in your editor, insert a blank line beneath the opening `<table>` tag, indent three additional spaces, type `<colgroup>`, press [Enter] twice, indent to match the previous code, then type `</colgroup>`**

QUICK TIP

Whenever you add col elements, they must cover all the columns in the table. Unless all columns are accounted for in col elements, your code won't validate.

6. **Within the opening and closing `colgroup` tags, indent and add the tags `<col class="table-heading-column">` and `<col class="table-data-columns" span="3">` on separate lines**

   FIGURE H-25 shows the HTML code. By default, each `col` element applies to a single column, starting from the left side of the table. However, you can group consecutive columns into a single `col` element by specifying the number of columns to include as the value of the `span` attribute. All `col` elements must be contained in a colgroup element.

7. **Save your work, return to styles.css in your editor, in the main content tables section, below the `th` rule, add a rule with the `.table-heading-column` selector and the declaration `background-color: #f1eace;`, then add a rule with the `.table-data-columns` selector and the declaration `background-color: white;`**

   Note that the second character in the color value is a number 1, not a letter l. **FIGURE H-26** shows the completed CSS code.

8. **Save your changes, then refresh or reload reserve.html in your browser**

   As **FIGURE H-27** shows, different background colors are applied to the columns based on the styling of the corresponding `col` elements. Styles specified for table cells, rows, or sections have a higher level of specificity than those applied to a `col` element; for this reason, the heading cells are rendered with the background color from the `th` rule rather than those specified for the `col` elements.

FIGURE H-25: col and colgroup elements added to HTML code for table

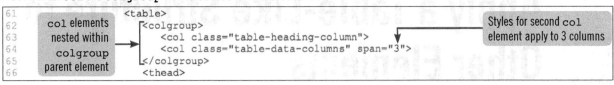

```
61
62    col elements         <table>
63    nested within         <colgroup>
64                            <col class="table-heading-column">                        Styles for second col
65      colgroup             <col class="table-data-columns" span="3">                 element apply to 3 columns
66    parent element        </colgroup>
                             <thead>
```

FIGURE H-26: Completed CSS code for table

```
28    table {
29        border-collapse: collapse;
30        border-spacing: 0;
31    }
32
33    /* document-wide styles */
```

```
164    /* main content tables */
165    td, th {
166        border: 1px solid black;
167        padding: 0.4em;
168        font-size: 1.3em;
169        text-align: center;
170    }
171    table {
172        width: 100%;                              Applies a background color to the first
173        border: 2px solid black;                 col element, which encompasses the
174    }                                            leftmost column of the table
175    th {
176        background-color: #aecdf4;
177    }
178    .table-heading-column {
179        background-color: #f1eace;               Applies a different background color
180    }                                            to the second col element, which
181    .table-data-columns {                        encompasses the remaining 3 columns
182        background-color: white;
183    }
```

FIGURE H-27: Table with background color and other styles applied

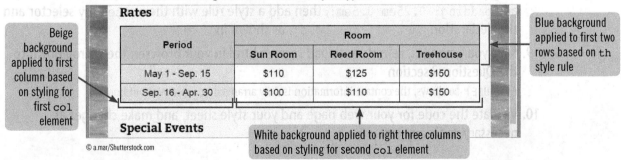

Beige background applied to first column based on styling for first col element

Blue background applied to first two rows based on th style rule

White background applied to right three columns based on styling for second col element

© a.mar/Shutterstock.com

Rates

Period	Room		
	Sun Room	Reed Room	Treehouse
May 1 - Sep. 15	$110	$125	$150
Sep. 16 - Apr. 30	$100	$110	$150

Special Events

Apply a Table-Like Structure to Other Elements

Sometimes you may want to arrange web page elements so they appear visually in a grid, even if these elements would not normally belong in a table. To implement this layout, you first use block-level elements, such as div elements, to create a structure that parallels the nesting of table, tr, th, and td elements in an HTML table. You then set the CSS display property to table-cell for the elements containing the table content, table-row for the container elements for each row, and table for the main parent element. **CASE** *You duplicate the description list containing contact information for making reservations and convert the copy to a table-like layout using CSS.*

STEPS

1. **Return to reserve.html in your editor, scroll down to the h3 element that contains the text *Questions?*, select the entire dl element including the opening and closing dl tags, then copy it to the Clipboard**

2. **Insert a new line before the opening <dl> tag, type <!--, insert a blank line after the closing </dl> tag, then type -->**

3. **Insert a new line before the opening <!-- tag, paste the content of the Clipboard, then in the opening and closing tags for the pasted description list, replace dl with div, preserving the class value in the opening tag**

4. **Insert a new line above the first dt element, indent to the same level as the dt element, type <div class="row">, insert a new line below the first dd element, indent to the same level as the dd element, then type </div>**

   The new div element serves the role of a tr element in a table.

5. **Indent the dt and dd elements within the new div element an additional 3 spaces, replace the opening <dt> tag with <div class="category">, replace the closing </dt> tag with </div>, then, in the opening and closing dd tags, replace dd with div**

6. **Repeat Steps 4 and 5 for the remaining three sets of dt and dd elements, then compare your code to FIGURE H-28**

7. **Save your changes, return to styles.css in your editor, add a new line above the /* footer section */ comment, then type /* main content CSS tables */**

8. **Below the new comment, add a style rule with the .contact selector and the declarations margin: 1em 0;, display: table;, and font-size: 1.3em;, add a style rule with the .row selector and the declaration display: table-row;, add a style rule with the .row div selector and the declarations display: table-cell; and padding: 0.25em 0.5em;, then add a style rule with the .category selector and the declaration font-weight: bold;, as shown in FIGURE H-29**

9. **Save your changes, refresh or reload reserve.html in your browser, then scroll down to the Questions? section**

   As FIGURE H-30 shows, the contact information is now arranged in a grid without borders.

10. **Validate the code for your web page and your style sheet, and make changes as necessary to fix any errors**

FIGURE H-28: Completed HTML code for displaying contact information in a table-like layout

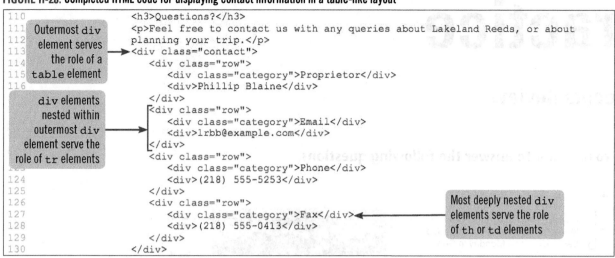

```
110          <h3>Questions?</h3>
111          <p>Feel free to contact us with any queries about Lakeland Reeds, or about
112          planning your trip.</p>
113      <div class="contact">
114          <div class="row">
115              <div class="category">Proprietor</div>
116              <div>Phillip Blaine</div>
             </div>
             <div class="row">
                 <div class="category">Email</div>
                 <div>lrbb@example.com</div>
             </div>
             <div class="row">
                 <div class="category">Phone</div>
124              <div>(218) 555-5253</div>
125          </div>
126          <div class="row">
127              <div class="category">Fax</div>
128              <div>(218) 555-0413</div>
129          </div>
130      </div>
```

Outermost `div` element serves the role of a `table` element

`div` elements nested within outermost `div` element serve the role of `tr` elements

Most deeply nested `div` elements serve the role of `th` or `td` elements

FIGURE H-29: Completed CSS code for displaying contact information in a table-like layout

```
185    /* main content CSS tables */
186    .contact {
187        margin: 1em 0;
188        display: table;
189        font-size: 1.3em;
190    }
191    .row {
192        display: table-row;
193    }
194    .row div {
195        display: table-cell;
196        padding: 0.25em 0.5em;
197    }
198    .category {
199        font-weight: bold;
200    }
201
202    /* footer section */
```

Element with the `table` value for the `display` property serves the role of a `table` element

Element with the `table-row` value for the `display` property serves the role of a `tr` element

Element with the `table-cell` value for the `display` property serves the role of a `th` or `td` element

FIGURE H-30: Contact information displayed in a table-like layout

Content displayed in a grid with two columns

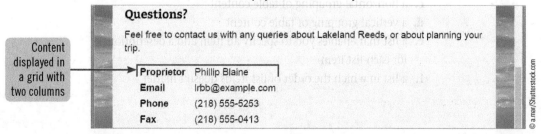

Questions?

Feel free to contact us with any queries about Lakeland Reeds, or about planning your trip.

Proprietor	Phillip Blaine
Email	lrbb@example.com
Phone	(218) 555-5253
Fax	(218) 555-0413

© a.mar/Shutterstock.com

Practice

Concepts Review

Refer to FIGURE H-31 **to answer the following questions.**

FIGURE H-31

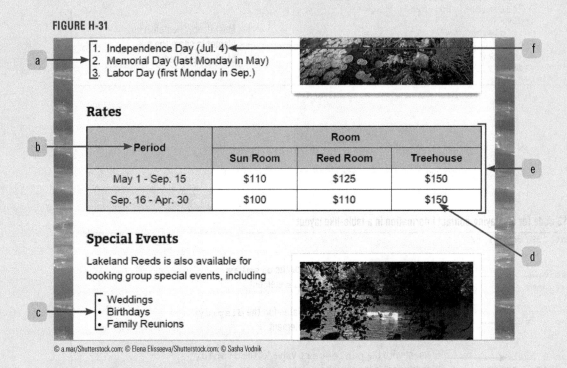

© a.mar/Shutterstock.com; © Elena Elisseeva/Shutterstock.com; © Sasha Vodnik

1. **Which item is created using the** td **element?**
2. **Which item is created using the** ul **element?**
3. **Which item is created using the** ol **element?**
4. **Which item is created using the** th **element?**
5. **Which item is created using the** table **element?**
6. **Which item is created using the** li **element?**

Match each term with the statement that best describes it.

7. **column**
8. **description list**
9. **ordered list**
10. **unordered list**
11. **row**
12. **cell**

a. a table component that displays a single item of data
b. a list in which items are numbered or lettered sequentially
c. a horizontal grouping of table content
d. a vertical grouping of table content
e. a list that enables you to specify an item and a description for each list item
f. a list in which the order of list items doesn't matter

Select the best answer from the list of choices.

13. **Which element do you use to create a list that is usually displayed with bullet characters?**
    - **a.** `dd`
    - **b.** `ul`
    - **c.** `dl`
    - **d.** `ol`

14. **What is a common cause of a protruding cell in a table?**
    - **a.** a missing `thead` element
    - **b.** a missing `tbody` element
    - **c.** a missing `th` or `td` element in one row
    - **d.** an extra `th` or `td` element in one row

15. **What is a common cause of an empty space in a table?**
    - **a.** a missing `thead` element
    - **b.** a missing `tbody` element
    - **c.** a missing `th` or `td` element in one row
    - **d.** an extra `th` or `td` element in one row

Skills Review

1. **Create an ordered list.**
   - **a.** In your editor, open the file HTM_H-3.html from the SR folder where you store your Data Files for this unit, save it as **index.html**, then repeat to save the file HTM_H_4.html as **history.html**, HTM_H_5.html as **location.html**, and HTM_H_6.css as **styles.css**.
   - **b.** Within the comment section at the top of each file, enter your first and last names and today's date, then save.
   - **c.** Return to index.html in your editor, then below the p element containing the text *Eat in, carry out, or call for delivery*, insert a p element with the `class` value `accent` containing the text **Enjoy award winning pizza in your home in just three steps:**.
   - **d.** Below the p element, insert starting and ending tags for an ordered list on separate lines at the same indent level.
   - **e.** On a new line and between the tags you just entered, indent three additional spaces, add a list item element containing the text **Call the location nearest you.**, then repeat to insert two additional list items containing the text **Place your order and listen for your doorbell.** and **Open the box and dig in!**
   - **f.** Save your changes, return to styles.css in your editor, then, in the reset styles section, add the `ol` and `li` selectors to the list of selectors in the style rule that sets border, padding, and margin to 0.
   - **g.** At the end of the reset styles section, add a rule for the `ol` element that sets `list-style-type` to `none`.
   - **h.** Scroll down as necessary to the `/* footer section */` comment, then above it add the text **main content lists** as a new comment.
   - **i.** Below the new comment you entered, create a style rule with the `article ol` selector that sets the width to 70%, the margin to `1em auto`, the padding to 1em, left-aligns text, precedes each list item with a decimal number, and sets the background color to **#ddd**.
   - **j.** Below the rule you created in the previous step, create a style rule with the `article ol li` selector that sets the left margin to 2em.
   - **k.** Save your changes, open index.html in your browser, then verify that the three list items you entered are displayed in a list numbered 1, 2, and 3.

2. **Create an unordered list.**
   - **a.** Return to history.html in your editor, locate the p element with the `class` value `contrastbox`, then edit the opening and closing tags for the element to make it an unordered list without a `class` value.
   - **b.** Edit the opening and closing tags for each p element within the unordered list to make each a list item.
   - **c.** Save your changes, return to styles.css in your editor, in the reset styles section add the `ul` selector to the list of selectors in the style rule that sets border, padding, and margin to 0, then add the `ul` selector to the style rule for `ol` elements that sets `list-style-type` to `none`.
   - **d.** Scroll down to the `/* main content lists */` comment, then in the two style rules above the comment, change the selector `article div.contrastbox` to `article ul` and change the selector `article div.contrastbox p` to `article ul li`.
   - **e.** Cut and paste the `/* main content lists */` comment so it is above the `article ul` style rule.

Skills Review (continued)

f. Save your changes, open history.html in your browser, then verify that the three words *flavor*, *aroma*, and *fresh* in the middle of the article are bold, centered, and displayed in a gray box and without bullet characters.

3. Create a description list.

a. Return to index.html in your editor, then within the `footer` element, add a blank line below the opening `<footer>` tag, indent an additional three spaces, enter the opening tag for a description list, add a blank line above the closing `</footer>` tag, indent an additional 3 spaces, then enter the closing tag for a description list.

b. For each p element within the `footer` element, increase the indent by three spaces, then remove the opening and closing p tags.

c. Mark the address *150 St. Joseph St.* as a description list term, move the `span` element and its content onto its own line at the same indent level, then mark the content of the new line as a description list description. (*Hint*: Include the `span` element within the code for the description item.) Repeat for the remaining two locations.

d. Save your changes, return to styles.css in your editor, then in the reset styles section add the `dl`, `dt`, and `dd` selectors to the list of selectors in the style rule that sets border, padding, and margin to 0.

e. Save your changes, reload index.html in your browser, then verify that each address and phone number is displayed on a separate line, and that each phone number is displayed in bold and indented in the contact information.

f. Return to index.html in your editor, copy the description list element to the Clipboard, including its opening and closing tags, return to history.html in your editor, replace the content of the `footer` element with the content of the Clipboard, save your changes, then repeat for location.html.

g. Reload history.html in your browser, verify that the footer content matches index.html, then repeat for location.html.

4. Create a navigation bar using a list.

a. Return to index.html in your editor, then within the `nav` element, add a blank line below the opening `<nav>` tag, indent an additional three spaces, enter the opening tag for an unordered list, add a blank line above the closing `</nav>` tag, indent an additional 3 spaces, then enter the closing tag for an unordered list.

b. For each p element within the `nav` element, increase the indent by three spaces, then replace the opening and closing p tags with tags that mark each element as a list item.

c. Save your changes, return to styles.css in your editor, scroll as necessary to the site navigation section, change the selector `nav.sitenavigation p` to `nav.sitenavigation li`, then change the selector `nav.sitenavigation p a` to `nav.sitenavigation li a`.

d. Save your changes, reload index.html in your browser, verify that the nav bar is displayed as shown in **FIGURE H-32**, click the History link, then verify that the History page is displayed. Note that the appearance of the nav bar on the History page will not match **FIGURE H-32**; you'll fix this in the following steps.

e. Return to index.html in your editor, then within the `nav` element, copy the unordered list tags and their content to the Clipboard.

f. Return to history.html in your editor, paste the content of the Clipboard to replace the content of the `nav` element, save your work, then repeat for location.html.

g. Refresh or reload history.html in your web browser, verify that the appearance of the nav bar matches that of index.html, click the Locations link, verify that the appearance of the nav bar matches the other pages, click the Home link, then verify that the index.html page is displayed.

FIGURE H-32

5. Insert a table.

a. Return to location.html in your editor, locate the h3 heading containing the text *Queen’s Park/UT*, insert a blank line beneath the p element containing the phone number, indent as needed to match the previous line, then insert opening and closing tags for a `table` element on separate lines at the same indent level.

b. Between the opening and closing tags you just entered, add opening and closing tags for table head and table body sections with each tag on its own line and indented three spaces more than the `table` tags.

Skills Review (continued)

   c. Within the table head tags, add opening and closing tags for a table row, with each tag on its own line and indented three spaces more than the table head tags. Repeat to add opening and closing tags for three table rows in the table body section.

   d. Within the table row element for the table head section, add table head cell elements containing the text **Day**, **Open**, and **Close** on separate lines, indented three spaces more than the opening table row tag. Repeat to add the following content to table data cell elements in the three table body rows:

      Row 1: **Mon-Thu, 11am, 10pm**   Row 2: **Fri-Sat, 11am, 11pm**   Row 3: **Sun, Noon, 10pm**

   e. Repeat Steps a–d to insert two more tables using the same content for the header row and the following content for the table body:

      h3 heading *St. Clair:*

      Row 1: **Mon-Thu, 11am, 9:30pm**   Row 2: **Fri-Sat, 11am, 11pm**   Row 3: **Sun, Noon, 9:30pm**

      h3 heading *Dundas:*

      Row 1: **Mon-Thu, 11am, 11pm**   Row 2: **Fri-Sat, 11am, Midnight**   Row 3: **Sun, Noon, 11pm**

   f. Save your changes, return to styles.css in your editor, then in the reset styles section add the `table`, `thead`, `tbody`, `th`, and `td` selectors to the list of selectors in the style rule that sets border, padding, and margin to 0.

   g. At the end of the reset styles section, create a style rule using the `table` selector that collapses borders and sets border spacing to 0.

   h. Scroll down as necessary to the `/* footer section */` comment, then above it add the text **main content tables** as a new comment.

   i. Below the new comment you entered, create a style rule with the `table` selector that sets the width to 50% and the margin to `0 auto`, create a rule with the `th` and `td` selectors that creates a 1px solid black border, create a rule with the `th` selector that sets padding to 0.1em 0.3em and background color to `#ffcc66`, then create a rule with the `td` selector that sets padding to 0.3em and left-aligns text.

   j. Save your changes, reload location.html in your browser, then verify that each table makes sense and contains all the information specified in the previous steps.

6. Debug tables.

   a. Return to location.html in your editor.

   b. In the table below the h3 heading *Queen’s Park/UT*, add a table data cell containing the text **10pm** below the code for the final cell in the first row of the table body section.

   c. Save your changes, refresh or reload location.html in your browser, then notice the effect of the extra cell.

   d. Return to location.html in your editor, then comment out the line of code you added in Step b.

   e. Comment out the code for the first table data cell in the second row of the table body section, save your changes, refresh or reload location.html in your browser, then notice the gap created by the missing cell.

   f. Return to location.html in your editor, remove the comment tags from the first table data cell in the second row of the table body section, save your changes, refresh or reload location.html in your browser, then verify that all tables are displayed without extra or missing cells.

7. Span columns and rows.

   a. Return to location.html in your editor, locate the table you inserted beneath the h3 heading *Queen’s Park/UT*, then insert opening and closing tags for a new row element just above the closing tag for the table head section.

   b. In the first table row, select the code for the cells containing the text *Open* and *Close*, cut the text to the Clipboard, then paste it within the table row element for the second row in the table head section.

   c. In the first table row, below the code for the table header cell containing the text *Day*, add code for a second table head element containing the text **Hours**.

   d. In the table header cell containing the text *Day* in the first row of the table header section, add an attribute that indicates that the cell content should span 2 rows.

Skills Review (continued)

e. In the table header cell containing the text *Hours* in the first row of the table header section, add an attribute that indicates that the cell content should span 2 columns.

f. Copy the table head section including the opening and closing tags to the Clipboard, then paste it to replace the table head section in each of the remaining 2 tables in the document.

g. Save your changes, reload location.html in your browser, then verify that the table structure matches that shown in **FIGURE H-33**. Note that the table formatting will not match the figure; you'll fix this in Step 8.

FIGURE H-33

8. **Format a table with CSS.**

a. Return to location.html in your editor, insert a blank line beneath the opening `<table>` tag for the first table you created, indent three additional spaces, then add a container element for column groups.

b. Within the container element, add an element that applies the `class` value `table-heading-column` to the first column, add another element that applies the `class` value `table-data-columns` and spans the last two columns. Repeat Steps a and b for the other two tables.

c. Save your changes, return to styles.css in your editor, scroll as necessary to the main content tables section, then at the bottom of the section add a style rule for the `class` value `table-heading-column` that sets the background color to `#ccc`.

d. Save your changes, open location.html in your browser, then verify that the days of the week in each table have a gray background, as shown in **FIGURE H-33**.

9. **Apply a table-like structure to other elements.**

a. Return to index.html in your editor, scroll down to the `footer` element, select the entire description list including the opening and closing tags, then copy it to the Clipboard.

b. Comment out the description list element, then above the comment out code, paste the Clipboard content.

c. In the opening and closing tags for the pasted description list, replace `dl` with `div`, specifying the `class` value `contact` in the opening tag.

d. Insert a new line above the first `dt` element, indent to the same level as the `dt` element, enter an opening `<div>` tag with the `class` value `row`, insert a new line below the first `dd` element, indent to the same level as the `dd` element, then insert a closing `</div>` tag.

e. Indent the `dt` and `dd` elements within the new `div` element an additional three spaces, in the opening and closing `dt` tags replace `dt` with `div`, then in the opening and closing `dd` tags, replace `dd` with `div`, specifying the `class` value `phone` in the opening tag.

f. Repeat Steps d and e for the remaining two sets of `dt` and `dd` elements.

g. Save your changes, copy the CSS table you created to the Clipboard, including its opening and closing tags, return to history.html in your editor, replace the content of the `footer` element with the content of the Clipboard, save your changes, then repeat for location.html.

h. Return to styles.css in your editor, add a new line above the `/* print styles */` comment, then add a comment containing the text **footer CSS table**.

i. Below the new comment, add a style rule with the `.contact` selector and declarations that set margins to `0 auto` and `display` to `table`, add a style rule with the `.row` selector and a declaration that sets `display` to `table-row`, add a style rule with the `.row div` selector and declarations that set `display` to `table-cell` and padding to `0.25em 0.5em;`, then add a style rule with the `.phone` selector and a declaration that bolds text.

j. Save your changes, refresh or reload location.html in your browser, verify that the contact information in the page footer uses a table-like structure.

k. Validate the code for your web pages and your style sheet, and make changes as necessary to fix any errors.

Independent Challenge 1

Sarah Nguyen, the owner of the Spotted Wren Garden Center, has given you additional content to add to the website you've been creating for her. You add this information using lists and tables.

a. In your editor, open HTM_H-7.html from the IC1 folder where you store your Data Files for this unit, save it as **hours.html**, then repeat to save HTM_H-8.html as **resource.html** and HTM_H-9.css as **styles.css**. In the comment at the top of each file, enter your name and today's date where indicated, then save the files.

b. Return to resource.html in your editor. Beneath the h3 heading *Omaha area plant hardiness zone information*, insert the following table. (*Hint*: Use `rowspan` attributes for the cells containing the text *Zone, Last frost, First frost, May 1,* and *Oct 15*. Use a `colspan` attribute for the cell containing the text *Average annual minimum temp*. The HTML character code for the degree symbol is `&deg;`).

TABLE H-4

Zone	Average annual minimum temp		Last frost	First frost
	Fahrenheit	**Celsius**		
4b	–25°F to –20°F	–28.9°C to –31.6°C		
5a	–20°F to –15°F	–26.2°C to –28.8°C	May 1	Oct 15
5b	–15°F to –10°F	–23.4°C to –26.1°C		

© 2016 Cengage Learning

c. Save your changes, return to styles.css in your editor, in the reset styles section add the `table`, `thead`, `tbody`, `th`, and `td` selectors to the list of selectors in the style rule that sets border, padding, and margin to 0. At the end of the reset styles section, create a style rule using the `table` selector that collapses borders and sets border spacing to 0.

d. Above the `/* footer section */` comment, add a comment containing the text **main content table**. Below the comment, add a style rule for `th` and `td` elements that creates a 1px solid black border and sets the padding to 0.5em, then add a rule for `th` elements that sets the background color to `yellow`. Save your changes.

e. Return to resource.html in your editor, then, in the code for the table, add a `colgroup` element that contains a child element with the `class` name `zone` for styling the first column, a child element with `class` name `temps` for styling the second and third columns, and a child element with the `class` name `frost` for styling the fourth and fifth columns. Save your changes, return to styles.css, in the main content table section add a style rule for the element with the `class` value `temps` that sets the background color to `#87f547`, then add a style rule for the element with the `class` value `frost` that sets the background color to `#f5a88c`. Save your changes, reload resource.html in your browser, then verify that the table appears as shown in **FIGURE H-34**.

FIGURE H-34

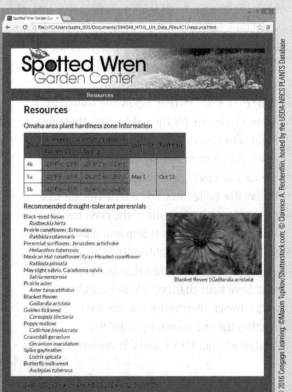

© 2016 Cengage Learning; ©Maxim Tupikov/Shutterstock.com; © Clarence A. Rechenthin, hosted by the USDA-NRCS PLANTS Database

Independent Challenge 1 (continued)

f. Return to resource.html in your editor. Below the h3 element containing the text *Recommended drought-tolerant perennials* and the figure that follows it, mark up the list of plant names as a description list with the common names as terms and the Latin names that follow as descriptions. Save your changes, return to styles.css in your editor, then, above the /* footer section */ comment, add a comment containing the text **main content description list.** Below the comment, create a style rule to style the content of all description elements in a description list in italic and with a 1em left margin. Scroll up as necessary to the reset styles section, then add the dd, dl, and dt selectors to the list of selectors in the style rule that sets border, padding, and margin to 0. Save your changes, reload resource.html in your browser, then verify that the definition list matches the one shown in FIGURE H-34.

g. Return to resource.html in your editor. Convert the code for the nav bar to an unordered list by changing the p element that encloses each link to an li element, then enclosing the code for all the links within a ul element. Repeat for hours.html, then save your changes to both documents. Return to styles.css in your editor, scroll as necessary to the site navigation section, then change the selector for the nav.sitenavigation p rule to nav.sitenavigation li. Scroll up as necessary to the reset styles section, then add the ul and li selectors to the list of selectors in the style rule that sets border, padding, and margin to 0. At the end of the reset styles section, create a style rule using the ul selector that sets list-style-type to none. Save your changes, refresh or reload resource.html in your browser, then verify that the appearance of the navigation bar is unchanged. Click the Hours link, verify that the Hours page opens, then verify that the nav bar on that page is unchanged.

h. Return to hours.html in your editor. Beneath the h2 heading, insert a new line containing a div element with the class value table at the same indent level as the previous line. Add a closing tag for the div element below the last line of store hours information. Enclose each line of code containing store hours information in a div element with the class value row, then delete the opening and closing p tags from each line. For each line, enclose the abbreviation of the day of the week within a div element, delete the colon (:) that follows it, move the remainder of the line onto a new line, then enclose the content of the new line in a div element. Save your changes.

i. Return to styles.css in your editor. Above the /* footer section */ comment, add a comment containing the text **main content CSS table.** Below the comment, create a style rule for the table class that sets margins to 1em 0, font size to 1.3em, and makes the element display like a table, create a rule for the row class that makes the elements display like table rows, add a style rule for div elements within elements of the class row that sets padding to 0.25em 0.5em and makes the elements display like table cells, then add a style rule for the day class that makes text bold. Save your changes, reload hours.html in your browser, then verify that the list of hours matches the one shown in FIGURE H-35.

FIGURE H-35

j. Validate all your HTML and CSS documents.

Independent Challenge 2

You add new information about the Murfreesboro Regional Soccer League to the website that you are creating. You mark up the new information using an unordered list and several tables. You also change the markup for the nav bar to an unordered list.

a. In your editor, open HTM_H-10.html from the IC2 folder where you store your Data Files for this unit, save it as **started.html**, then repeat to save HTM_H-11.html as **schedule.html** and HTM_H-12.css as **styles.css**. In the comment at the top of each file, enter your name and today's date where indicated, then save the files.

b. In started.html, locate the paragraph that begins *If you're interested in joining up*, then insert a blank line below it. Add an unordered list containing the following four list items: **Child/Teen (6–18): $50, Student (19–24): $50, Adult (25–59): $65**, and **Senior (60+): $40**. Save your changes, then return to styles.css in your editor. In the reset styles section, add the ul and li selectors to the list of selectors in the style rule that sets border, padding, and margin to 0. At the end of the reset styles section, create a style rule using the ul selector that sets list-style-type to none. Above the /* footer section */ comment, add a comment containing the text **main content unordered list**. Below the comment, create a style rule for unordered lists within the article element that sets margins to 0 0 1em 3em, adds 7% padding on the left side, uses filled circles for list item markers, and sets the font size to 1.2em. Save your changes, open started.html in a browser, then verify that the bulleted list you created matches FIGURE H-36.

c. Return to started.html in your editor. Convert the code for the nav bar to an unordered list by enclosing the p elements that mark nav bar items within an element that marks an unordered list, then changing each p element that encloses a nav bar item to a list item element. Repeat for schedule.html, then save your changes to both documents. Return to styles.css in your editor. In the site navigation section, below the nav.sitenavigation rule, create a style rule that applies only to list item elements within the nav element with the class value sitenavigation that sets the font size to 1.2em. Save your work, reload started.html in your browser, then verify that the appearance of the nav bar matches FIGURE H-36. Click the Schedules link, ensure that the Schedules page opens, then verify the appearance of the nav bar also matches FIGURE H-36.

FIGURE H-36

Independent Challenge 2 (continued)

d. Return to schedule.html in your editor, then convert the four lists of game dates and times into tables. Create a heading row for each table with heading cells containing the text **Date** and **Time**. Split the information for each game into two cells, the first containing the date and the second containing the start time. Set the `class` value for the first table to `red-team-schedule`, the second table to `blue-team-schedule`, the third table to `green-team-schedule`, and the fourth table to `yellow-team-schedule`. Save your changes, then return to styles.css in your editor. Above the comment `/* main content unordered list */`, add a comment containing the text **main content tables**, then below the new comment add a style rule for `table` elements that sets the width to 90% and sets margins to 0 auto. Add a style rule for table header cells and table data cells that creates 1px solid black borders and sets padding to 0.5em. Add a style rule for table header cell elements that sets the background color to `#ddd`. Create a rule for the element with the class value `red-team-schedule` that creates a 5px solid red border, then create a rule that adds a 5px solid red bottom border to header cells within this element Create a rule for the element with the class value `blue-team-schedule` that creates a 5px solid blue border, then create a rule that adds a 5px solid blue bottom border to header cells within this element and sets their text color to `blue`. Create a rule for the element with the class value `green-team-schedule` that creates a 5px solid green border, then create a rule that adds a 5px solid green bottom border to header cells within this element and sets their text color to `green`. Create a rule for the element with the class value `yellow-team-schedule` that creates a 5px solid border using the color `#e6da57`, then create a rule that adds a 5px solid bottom border using the color `#e6da57` to header cells within this element and sets their text color to `yellow`. Save your changes, refresh or reload schedule.html in your browser, then verify that all four tables are displayed correctly. Fix any missing or extra cells.

e. Using **FIGURE H-37** as a guide, add a third column to each table that displays the field letter where each game will be played. (*Hint*: To add a column, add a new cell at the end of each row element.) Save your work, refresh or reload schedule.html in your browser, then verify that your tables match those shown in **FIGURE H-37**.

f. Validate all your HTML and CSS documents.

FIGURE H-37

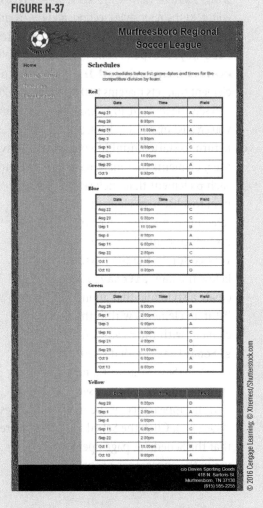

Independent Challenge 3

As you continue your work on the website for Hotel Natoma, you incorporate additional information about the hotel and local attractions using some of the techniques for organizing content that you learned in this unit.

FIGURE H-38

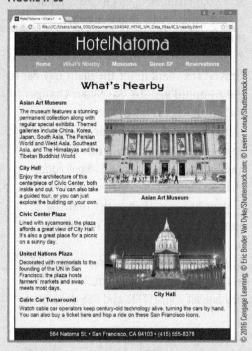

a. In your editor, open HTM_H-13.html from the IC3 folder where you store your Data Files for this unit, save it as **nearby.html**, then repeat to save HTM_H-14.html as **museums.html**, HTM_H-15.html as **greensf.html**, and HTM_H-16.css as **styles.css**. In the comment at the top of each file, enter your name and today's date where indicated, then save the files.

b. In nearby.html, mark the list of nearby locations and descriptions as a description list. Save your changes, then in styles.css, above the comment `/* footer section */`, create a comment containing the text **main content description list**. Add a style rule that bolds the text of description list term items, then add a rule that sets margins of 0.4em 0 1em for description list description items. In the reset styles section, add the `dd`, `dl`, and `dt` selectors to the list of selectors in the style rule that sets border, padding, and margin to 0. Save your changes, open nearby.html in a browser, then verify that it matches **FIGURE H-38**.

c. In museums.html, mark the list of museums as an unordered list. Save your changes, then in styles.css, above the comment `/* main content description list */`, create a comment containing the text **main content unordered lists**. Create a style rule for unordered lists that sets the left margin to 5%, displays a filled circle next to each list item, and sets the line height to 1.4em. In the reset styles section, add the `ul` and `li` selectors to the list of selectors in the style rule that sets border, padding, and margin to 0. At the end of the reset styles section, create a style rule using the `ul` selector that sets `list-style-type` to none. Save your changes, open museums.html in a browser, then verify that it matches **FIGURE H-39**.

FIGURE H-39

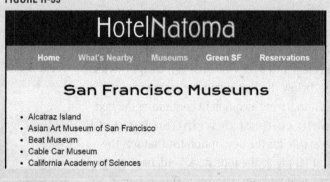

d. In greensf.html, mark the list of destinations as an ordered list. Save your changes, then in styles.css, above the comment `/* footer section */`, create a comment containing the text **main content ordered list**. Create a style rule for ordered lists that sets left and right margins to 5% and uses decimal numbering, then create a style rule for list items within an ordered list that creates 0.6em padding on the left. In the reset styles section, add the `ol` selector to the list of selectors in the style rule that sets border, padding, and margin to 0 and in the style rule that sets `list-style-type` to none.

Independent Challenge 3 (continued)

e. Save your changes, open greensf.html in a browser, then verify that it matches **FIGURE H-40**.

f. Return to greensf.html in your editor, then convert the markup for the main nav bar to use an unordered list. Save your changes, then in styles.css, in the site navigation section, change the selector for the `nav.sitenavigation p` rule to `nav.sitenavigation li`. Save your changes, refresh or reload greensf.html in your browser, then verify that the appearance of the nav bar remains unchanged.

g. Return to your editor, then repeat Step d for nearby.html and for museums.html.

h. Validate all your HTML and CSS documents.

FIGURE H-40

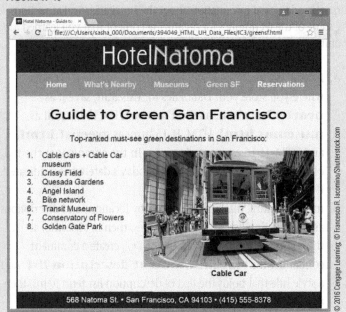

© 2016 Cengage Learning. © Francesco R. Iacomino/Shutterstock.com

Independent Challenge 4 – Explore

As you continue your work on the website for Eating Well In Season, a provider of locally-sourced, healthy meals, you mark existing information using lists and you incorporate new information in a table.

a. In your editor, open HTM_H-17.html from the IC3 folder where you store your Data Files for this unit, save it as **menus.html**, then repeat to save HTM_H-18.html as **pricing.html**, and HTM_H-19.css as **styles.css**. In the comment at the top of each file, enter your name and today's date where indicated, then save the files.

b. In menus.html, mark the list of meals and menu items under the *Sample Menus* h2 heading as a description list. (*Hint*: More than one dd element can follow each dt element.) Save your changes, then in styles.css, below the last rule in the main content section, create a comment containing the text **main content description list**. Add a style rule for the description list that sets the font family to the font stack Verdana, Geneva, sans-serif and sets margins to 0 1em 1em, then create a rule for description list term items that formats text in bold and sets a top margin of 1em. In the reset styles section, add the dd, dl, and dt selectors to the list of selectors in the style rule that sets border, padding, and margin to 0. Save your changes, open menus.html in a browser, then verify that the display of the description list matches the one in **FIGURE H-41**.

FIGURE H-41

© 2016 Cengage Learning

Independent Challenge 4 – Explore (continued)

c. In menus.html, mark the content of the sidebar below the h2 element as an unordered list. Save your changes, then in styles.css, below the last rule in the sidebar section, create a comment containing the text **sidebar unordered lists**. Create a style rule for unordered lists within aside elements that sets the left margin to 2em and uses the image bullet.png from the images folder as the item marker (*Hint:* Use the list-style-image property with the syntax url("*path/filename*")). In the reset styles section, add the ul and li selectors to the list of selectors in the style rule that sets border, padding, and margin to 0. At the end of the reset styles section, create a style rule using the ul selector that sets list-style-type to none. Save your changes, refresh or reload menus. html in your browser, then verify that it matches FIGURE H-41.

d. Return to menus.html in your editor, then convert the markup for the main nav bar to use an unordered list. Save your changes, then in styles.css, in the site navigation section, change the selector for the nav.sitenavigation p rule to nav.sitenavigation li. Save your changes, refresh or reload menus.html in your browser, then verify that the appearance of the nav bar remains unchanged.

e. Return to menus.html in your editor, copy the unordered list from the sidebar, switch to pricing.html in your editor, then paste the unordered list in the code for the sidebar, replacing the existing content below the h2 element. Repeat to copy the ordered list in the nav bar for menus.html and paste it in pricing.html.

f. In the article element in pricing.html, create the table shown in TABLE H-5. Specify the class value specific-headers for the second row of the header section. Save your changes.

g. Return to styles.css in your editor, above the main content description list section, create a comment containing the text **main content table**. Create a style rule for the table element that sets a width of 90% and margins to 1em auto. Create a rule for table header cells and table data cells that sets width to 33.3%, creates a 1px solid black border, sets padding to 0.3em 1em, and sets the font family to Verdana, Geneva, sans-serif. Create a rule for table header cells that sets the background color to #98c13d. Create a rule for table header cells nested in the element with the class value .specific-headers that sets the background color to rgb(246,224,65). Save your changes, open pricing.html in a browser, then verify that it matches FIGURE H-42.

h. Validate all of your HTML and CSS documents and make any edits necessary to address any issues.

TABLE H-5

Meal	Monthly Cost	
	once a week	daily
Lunch	$60	$390
Dinner	$80	$520
Both	$125	$800

© 2016 Cengage Learning

FIGURE H-42

© 2016 Cengage Learning

Visual Workshop

In your editor, open the file HTM_H-20.html from the VW folder where you store your Data Files for this unit and save it as **events.html**. Repeat to save HTM_H-21.css as **styles.css**. Add your first and last names and today's date to the comment section at the top of each file, then save your changes. Add the table shown in **FIGURE H-43**, within the `div` element nested in the `article` element. (*Hint*: Use the `title` class to italicize the book title, and use the color `rgb(253,245,230)` for the table header background.) Convert the code for the nav bar to an unordered list, changing and adding to the style sheet as necessary. Validate your HTML and CSS code.

FIGURE H-43

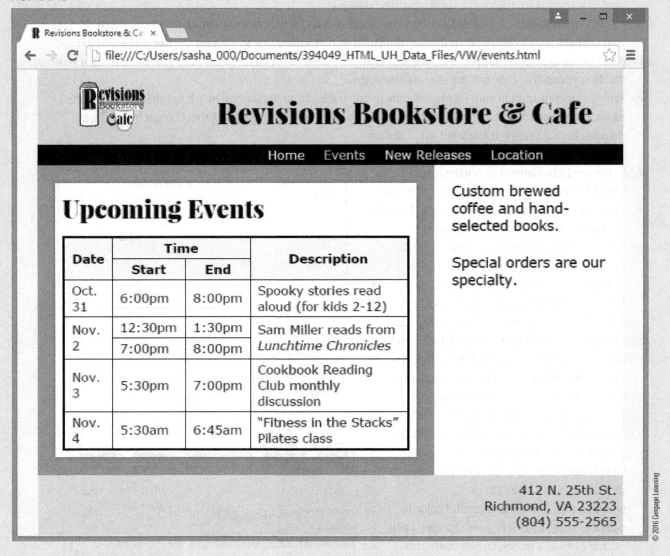

Elements of
High-Quality Programs

In this chapter, you will learn about:

- ◎ Declaring and using variables and constants
- ◎ Performing arithmetic operations
- ◎ The advantages of modularization
- ◎ Modularizing a program
- ◎ Hierarchy charts
- ◎ Features of good program design

Declaring and Using Variables and Constants

As you learned in Chapter 1, data items include all the text, numbers, and other information that are processed by a computer. When you input data items into a computer, they are stored in variables in memory where they can be processed and converted to information that is output.

When you write programs, you work with data in three different forms: literals (or unnamed constants), variables, and named constants.

Understanding Unnamed, Literal Constants and their Data Types

All programming languages support two broad data types; **numeric** describes data that consists of numbers and **string** describes data that is nonnumeric. Most programming languages support several additional data types, including multiple types for numeric values that are very large or very small and for those that do and do not have fractional decimal digits. Languages such as C++, C#, Visual Basic, and Java distinguish between **integer** (whole number) numeric variables and **floating-point** (fractional) numeric variables that contain a decimal point. (Floating-point numbers are also called **real numbers**.) Thus, in some languages, the values 4 and 4.3 would be stored in different types of numeric variables. Additionally, many languages allow you to distinguish between smaller and larger values that occupy different numbers of bytes in memory. You will learn a little more about these specialized data types later in this chapter, and even more when you study a programming language, but this book uses the two broadest types: numeric and string.

When you use a specific numeric value, such as 43, within a program, you write it using the digits and no quotation marks. A specific numeric value is often called a **numeric constant** (or **literal numeric constant**) because it does not change—a 43 always has the value 43. When you store a numeric value in computer memory, additional characters such as dollar signs and commas are not input or stored. Those characters can be added to output for readability, but they are not part of the number.

A specific text value, or string of characters, such as "Amanda", is a **string constant** (or **literal string constant**). String constants, unlike numeric constants, appear within quotation marks in computer programs. String values are also called **alphanumeric values** because they can contain alphabetic characters as well as numbers and other characters. For example, "$3,215.99 U.S.", including the dollar sign, comma, periods, letters, and numbers, is a string. Although strings can contain numbers, numeric values cannot contain alphabetic characters. The numeric constant 43 and the string constant "Amanda" are examples of **unnamed constants**—they do not have identifiers like variables do.

 Watch the video *Declaring Variables and Constants*.

Working with Variables

Variables are named memory locations whose contents can vary or differ over time. For example, in the number-doubling program in Figure 2-1, myNumber and myAnswer are variables. At any moment in time, a variable holds just one value. Sometimes, myNumber holds 2 and myAnswer holds 4; at other times, myNumber holds 6 and myAnswer holds 12. The ability of variables to change in value is what makes computers and programming worthwhile. Because one memory location can be used repeatedly with different values, you can write program instructions once and then use them for thousands of separate calculations. *One* set of payroll instructions at your company produces each employee paycheck, and *one* set of instructions at your electric company produces each household's bill.

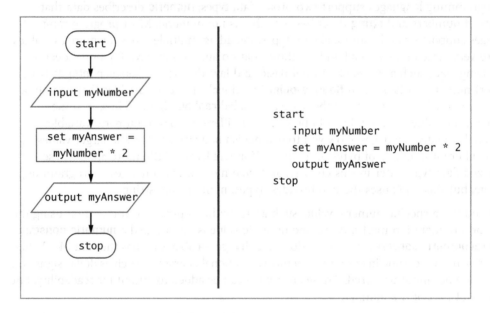

```
start
    input myNumber
    set myAnswer = myNumber * 2
    output myAnswer
stop
```

Figure 2-1   Flowchart and pseudocode for the number-doubling program
© 2015 Cengage Learning

In most programming languages, before you can use any variable, you must include a declaration for it. A **declaration** is a statement that provides a data type and an identifier for a variable. An **identifier** is a program component's name. A data item's **data type** is a classification that describes the following:

- What values can be held by the item

- How the item is stored in computer memory

- What operations can be performed on the item

As mentioned earlier, most programming languages support several data types, but in this book, only two data types will be used: num and string.

When you declare a variable, you provide both a data type and an identifier. Optionally, you can declare a starting value for any variable. Declaring a starting value is known as **initializing the variable**. For example, each of the following statements is a valid declaration. Two of the statements include initializations, and two do not:

```
num mySalary
num yourSalary = 14.55
string myName
string yourName = "Juanita"
```

Figure 2-2 shows the number-doubling program from Figure 2-1 with the added declarations shaded. Variables must be declared before they are used for the first time in a program. Some languages require all variables to be declared at the beginning of the program, others allow variables to be declared at the beginning of each module, and others allow variables to be declared anywhere at all as long as they are declared before their first use. This book will follow the convention of declaring all variables together.

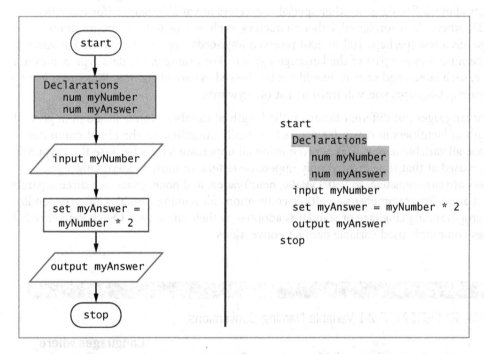

Figure 2-2 Flowchart and pseudocode of number-doubling program with variable declarations
© 2015 Cengage Learning

In many programming languages, if you declare a variable and do not initialize it, the variable contains an unknown value until it is assigned a value. A variable's unknown value commonly is called **garbage**. Although some languages use a default value for some variables (such as assigning 0 to any unassigned numeric variable), this book will assume that an unassigned variable holds garbage. In many languages it is illegal to use a garbage-holding variable in an arithmetic statement or to display it as output. Even if you work with a language that allows you to display garbage, it serves no purpose to do so and constitutes a logical error.

When you create a variable without assigning it an initial value (as with myNumber and myAnswer in Figure 2-2), your intention is to assign a value later—for example, by receiving one as input or placing the result of a calculation there.

Naming Variables

The number-doubling example in Figure 2-2 requires two variables: myNumber and myAnswer. Alternatively, these variables could be named userEntry and programSolution, or inputValue and twiceTheValue. As a programmer, you choose reasonable and descriptive names for your variables. The language translator (interpreter or compiler) then associates the names you choose with specific memory addresses.

Every computer programming language has its own set of rules for creating identifiers. Most languages allow letters and digits within identifiers. Some languages allow hyphens in variable names, such as hourly-wage, and some allow underscores, as in hourly_wage. Some languages allow dollar signs or other special characters in variable names (for example, hourly$); others allow foreign-alphabet characters, such as π or Ω. Each programming language has a few (perhaps 100 to 200) reserved **keywords** that are not allowed as variable names because they are part of the language's syntax. For example, the data type names in a language, such as num and string, would not be allowed as variable names. When you learn a programming language, you will learn its list of keywords.

Different languages put different limits on the length of variable names, although in general, the length of identifiers in newer languages is virtually unlimited. In the oldest computer languages, all variable names were written using all uppercase letters because the keypunch machines used at that time created only uppercase letters. In most modern languages, identifiers are case sensitive, so HoUrLyWaGe, hourlywage, and hourlyWage are three separate variable names. Programmers use multiple conventions for naming variables, often depending on the programming language or standards adopted by their employers. Quick Reference 2-1 describes commonly used variable naming conventions.

QUICK REFERENCE 2-1 Variable Naming Conventions

Convention for naming variables	Examples	Languages where commonly used
Camel casing is the convention in which the variable starts with a lowercase letter and any subsequent word begins with an uppercase letter. It is sometimes called **lower camel casing** to emphasize the difference from Pascal casing.	hourlyWage lastName	Java, C#

(continues)

(continues)

Convention for naming variables	Examples	Languages where commonly used
Pascal casing is a convention in which the first letter of a variable name is uppercase. It is sometimes called **upper camel casing** to distinguish it from lower camel casing.	`HourlyWage` `LastName`	Visual Basic
Hungarian notation is a form of camel casing in which a variable's data type is part of the identifier.	`numHourlyWage` `stringLastName`	C for Windows API programming
Snake casing is a convention in which parts of a variable name are separated by underscores.	`hourly_wage` `last_name`	C, C++, Python, Ruby
Mixed case with underscores is a variable naming convention similar to snake casing, but new words start with an uppercase letter.	`Hourly_Wage` `Last_Name`	Ada
Kebob case is sometimes used as the name for the style that uses dashes to separate parts of a variable name. The name derives from the fact that the words look like pieces of food on a skewer.	`hourly-wage` `last-name`	Lisp (with lowercase letters), COBOL (with uppercase letters)

Adopting a naming convention for variables and using it consistently will help make your programs easier to read and understand.

Even though every language has its own rules for naming variables, you should not concern yourself with the specific syntax of any particular computer language when designing the logic of a program. The logic, after all, works with any language. The variable names used throughout this book follow only three rules:

1. *Variable names must be one word.* The name can contain letters, digits, hyphens, or underscores. No language allows embedded spaces in variable names, and most do not allow punctuation such as periods, commas, or colons. This book uses only alphabetic letters, digits, and underscores in variable names. Therefore, r is a legal variable name, as are `rate` and `interestRate`. The variable name `interest rate` is not allowed because of the space.

2. *Variable names must start with a letter.* Some programming languages allow variable names to start with a nonalphabetic character such as an underscore. Almost all programming languages prohibit variable names that start with a digit. This book follows the most common convention of starting variable names with a letter.

When you write a program using an editor that is packaged with a compiler in an IDE, the compiler may display variable names in a different color from other program components. This visual aid helps your variable names stand out from words that are part of the programming language.

3. *Variable names should have some appropriate meaning.* This is not a formal rule of any programming language. When computing an interest rate in a program, the computer does not care if you call the variable g, u84, or fred. As long as the correct numeric result is placed in the variable, its actual name doesn't matter. However, it's much easier to follow the logic of a statement like set interestEarned = initialInvestment * interestRate than a statement like set f = i * r or set someBanana = j89 * myFriendLinda. When a program requires changes, which could be months or years after you write the original version, you and your fellow programmers will appreciate clear, descriptive variable names in place of cryptic identifiers. Later in this chapter, you will learn more about selecting good identifiers.

Notice that the flowchart in Figure 2-2 follows the preceding rules for variables: Both variable names, myNumber and myAnswer, are single words without embedded spaces, and they have appropriate meanings. Some programmers name variables after friends or create puns with them, but computer professionals consider such behavior unprofessional and amateurish.

Assigning Values to Variables

When you create a flowchart or pseudocode for a program that doubles numbers, you can include a statement such as the following:

```
set myAnswer = myNumber * 2
```

Such a statement is an **assignment statement**. This statement incorporates two actions. First, the computer calculates the arithmetic value of myNumber * 2. Second, the computed value is stored in the myAnswer memory location.

The equal sign is the **assignment operator**. The assignment operator is an example of a **binary operator**, meaning it requires two operands—one on each side. (An **operand** is simply a value used by an operator.) The assignment operator always operates from right to left, which means that it has **right-associativity** or **right-to-left associativity**. This means that the value of the expression to the right of the assignment operator is evaluated first, and then the result is assigned to the operand on the left. The operand to the right of an assignment operator must be a value—for example, a named or unnamed constant or an arithmetic expression. The operand to the left of an assignment operator must be a name that represents a memory address—the name of the location where the result will be stored.

For example, if you have declared two numeric variables named someNumber and someOtherNumber, then each of the following is a valid assignment statement:

```
set someNumber = 2
set someNumber = 3 + 7
set someOtherNumber = someNumber
set someOtherNumber = someNumber * 5
```

In each case, the expression to the right of the assignment operator is evaluated and stored at the location referenced on the left side. The result to the left of an assignment operator is called an **lvalue**. The *l* is for left. Lvalues are always memory address identifiers.

The following statements, however, are *not* valid:

```
set 2 + 4 = someNumber
set someOtherNumber * 10 = someNumber
set someNumber + someOtherNumber = 10
```

> **Don't Do It**
> The operand to the left of an assignment operator must represent a memory address.

In each of these cases, the value to the left of the assignment operator is not a memory address, so the statements are invalid.

When you write pseudocode or draw a flowchart, it might help you to use the word *set* in assignment statements, as shown in these examples, to emphasize that the left-side value is being set. However, in most programming languages, the word *set* is not used, and assignment statements take the following simpler form:

```
someNumber = 2
someOtherNumber = someNumber
```

Because the abbreviated form is how assignments appear in most languages, this convention is used for the rest of this book.

Understanding the Data Types of Variables

Computers handle string data differently from the way they handle numeric data. You may have experienced these differences if you have used application software such as spreadsheets or database programs. For example, in a spreadsheet, you cannot sum a column of words. Similarly, every programming language requires that you specify the correct type for each variable, and that you use each type appropriately.

- A **numeric variable** is one that can hold digits and have mathematical operations performed on it. In this book, all numeric variables can hold a decimal point and a sign indicating positive or negative; some programming languages provide specialized numeric types for these options. In the statement myAnswer = myNumber * 2, both myAnswer and myNumber are numeric variables; that is, their intended contents are numeric values, such as 6 and 3, 14.8 and 7.4, or −18 and −9.

- A **string variable** can hold text, such as letters of the alphabet, and other special characters, such as punctuation marks. If a working program contains the statement lastName = "Lincoln", then lastName is a string variable. A string variable also can hold digits either with or without other characters. For example, "235 Main Street" and "86" are both strings. A string like "86" is stored differently than the numeric value 86, and you cannot perform arithmetic with the string. Programmers frequently use strings to hold digits when they will never be used in arithmetic statements–for example, an account number or a zip code.

Type-safety is the feature of some programming languages that prevents assigning values of an incorrect data type. You can assign data to a variable only if it is the correct type. (Such languages are called *strongly typed*.) If you declare `taxRate` as a numeric variable and `inventoryItem` as a string, then the following statements are valid:

```
taxRate = 2.5
inventoryItem = "monitor"
```

The following are invalid because the type of data being assigned does not match the variable type:

```
taxRate = "2.5"
inventoryItem = 2.5
taxRate = inventoryItem
inventoryItem = taxRate
```

> **Don't Do It**
> If `taxRate` is numeric and `inventoryItem` is a string, then these assignments are invalid.

 Watch the video *Understanding Data Types*.

Declaring Named Constants

Besides variables, most programming languages allow you to create named constants. A **named constant** is similar to a variable, except it can be assigned a value only once. You use a named constant when you want to assign a useful name for a value that will never be changed during a program's execution. Using named constants makes your programs easier to understand by eliminating magic numbers. A **magic number** is an unnamed constant, like 0.06, whose purpose is not immediately apparent.

For example, if a program uses a sales tax rate of 6 percent, you might want to declare a named constant as follows:

```
num SALES_TAX_RATE = 0.06
```

After `SALES_TAX_RATE` is declared, the following statements have identical meaning:

```
taxAmount = price * 0.06
taxAmount = price * SALES_TAX_RATE
```

The way in which named constants are declared differs among programming languages. This book follows the convention of using all uppercase letters in constant identifiers, and using underscores to separate words for readability. Using these conventions makes named constants easier to recognize. In many languages a constant must be assigned its value when it is declared, but in some languages a constant can be assigned its value later. In both cases, however, a constant's value cannot be changed after the first assignment. This book follows the convention of initializing all constants when they are declared.

When you declare a named constant, program maintenance becomes easier. For example, if the value of the sales tax rate changes from 0.06 to 0.07 in the future, and you have declared a named constant `SALES_TAX_RATE`, you only need to change the value assigned to the named constant at the beginning of the program, then retranslate the program into machine language, and all references to `SALES_TAX_RATE` are automatically updated. If you used the unnamed literal 0.06 instead, you would have to search for every instance of the value and replace it with the new one. Additionally, if the literal 0.06 was used in other calculations within the program (for example, as a discount rate or price), you would have to carefully select which instances of the value to alter, and you would be likely to make a mistake.

 Sometimes, using unnamed literal constants is appropriate in a program, especially if their meaning is clear to most readers. For example, in a program that calculates half of a value by dividing by two, you might choose to use the unnamed literal 2 instead of incurring the extra time and memory costs of creating a named constant HALF and assigning 2 to it. Extra costs that result from adding variables or instructions to a program are known as **overhead**.

TWO TRUTHS & A LIE

Declaring and Using Variables and Constants

1. A variable's data type describes the kind of values the variable can hold and the types of operations that can be performed with it.

2. If name is a string variable, then the statement set name = "Ed" is valid.

3. The operand to the right of an assignment operator must be a name that represents a memory address.

The false statement is #3. The operand to the left of an assignment operator must be a name that represents a memory address—the name of the location where the result will be stored. The value to the right of an assignment operator might be a constant, arithmetic expression, or other value.

Performing Arithmetic Operations

Most programming languages use the following standard arithmetic operators:

+ (plus sign)—addition

− (minus sign)—subtraction

* (asterisk)—multiplication

/ (slash)—division

Many languages also support additional operators that calculate the remainder after division, raise a number to a power, manipulate individual bits stored within a value, and perform other operations.

Each of the standard arithmetic operators is a binary operator; that is, each requires an expression on both sides. For example, the following statement adds two test scores and assigns the sum to a variable named totalScore:

```
totalScore = test1 + test2
```

The following adds 10 to totalScore and stores the result in totalScore:

```
totalScore = totalScore + 10
```

In other words, this example increases the value of totalScore. This last example looks odd in algebra because it might appear that the value of totalScore and totalScore plus 10 are equivalent. You must remember that the equal sign is the assignment operator, and that the statement is actually taking the original value of totalScore, adding 10 to it, and assigning the result to the memory address on the left of the operator, which is totalScore.

In programming languages, you can combine arithmetic statements. When you do, every operator follows **rules of precedence** (also called the **order of operations**) that dictate the order in which operations in the same statement are carried out. The rules of precedence for the basic arithmetic statements are as follows:

- Expressions within parentheses are evaluated first. If there are multiple sets of parentheses, the expression within the innermost parentheses is evaluated first.

- Multiplication and division are evaluated next, from left to right.

- Addition and subtraction are evaluated next, from left to right.

The assignment operator has a very low precedence. Therefore, in a statement such as d = e * f + g, the operations on the right of the assignment operator are always performed before the final assignment to the variable on the left.

 When you learn a specific programming language, you will learn about all the operators that are used in that language. Many programming language books contain a table that specifies the relative precedence of every operator used in the language.

For example, consider the following two arithmetic statements:

```
firstAnswer = 2 + 3 * 4
secondAnswer = (2 + 3) * 4
```

After these statements execute, the value of firstAnswer is 14. According to the rules of precedence, multiplication is carried out before addition, so 3 is multiplied by 4, giving 12, and then 2 and 12 are added, and 14 is assigned to firstAnswer. The value of secondAnswer, however, is 20, because the parentheses force the contained addition operation to be performed first. The 2 and 3 are added, producing 5, and then 5 is multiplied by 4, producing 20.

Forgetting about the rules of arithmetic precedence, or forgetting to add parentheses when you need them, can cause logical errors that are difficult to find in programs. For example, the following statement might appear to average two test scores:

```
average = score1 + score2 / 2
```

However, it does not. Because division has a higher precedence than addition, the preceding statement takes half of score2, adds it to score1, and stores the result in average. The correct statement is:

```
average = (score1 + score2) / 2
```

You are free to add parentheses even when you don't need them to force a different order of operations; sometimes you use them just to make your intentions clearer. For example, the following statements operate identically:

```
totalPriceWithTax = price + price * TAX_RATE
totalPriceWithTax = price + (price * TAX_RATE)
```

In both cases, `price` is multiplied by `TAX_RATE` first, then it is added to `price`, and finally the result is stored in `totalPriceWithTax`. Because multiplication occurs before addition on the right side of the assignment operator, both statements are the same. However, if you feel that the statement with the parentheses makes your intentions clearer to someone reading your program, then you should use them.

All the arithmetic operators have **left-to-right associativity**. This means that operations with the same precedence take place from left to right. Consider the following statement:

```
answer = a + b + c * d / e - f
```

Multiplication and division have higher precedence than addition or subtraction, so the multiplication and division are carried out from left to right as follows:

c is multiplied by d, and the result is divided by e, giving a new result.

Therefore, the statement becomes:

```
answer = a + b + (temporary result just calculated) - f
```

Then, addition and subtraction are carried out from left to right as follows:

a and b are added, the temporary result is added, and then f is subtracted. The final result is then assigned to `answer`.

Another way to say this is that the following two statements are equivalent:

```
answer = a + b + c * d / e - f
answer = a + b + ((c * d) / e) - f
```

Quick Reference 2-2 summarizes the precedence and associativity of the five most frequently used operators.

QUICK REFERENCE 2-2 Precedence and Associativity of Five Common Operators

Operator symbol	Operator name	Precedence (compared to other operators in this table)	Associativity
=	Assignment	Lowest	Right-to-left
+	Addition	Medium	Left-to-right
−	Subtraction	Medium	Left-to-right
*	Multiplication	Highest	Left-to-right
/	Division	Highest	Left-to-right

Watch the video *Arithmetic Operator Precedence.*

The Integer Data Type

As mentioned earlier in this chapter, many modern programming languages allow programmers to make fine distinctions between numeric data types. In particular, many languages treat integer numeric values (whole numbers) and floating-point numeric values (numbers with decimal places) differently. In these languages, you can always assign an integer, such as 3, to a floating-point variable or named constant, and it will be converted to 3.0. However, you cannot assign a floating-point value (such as 3.0) directly to an integer variable, because the decimal position values will be lost, even when they are 0.

When you work with a language that makes distinctions between integer and floating-point values, you can combine the different types in arithmetic expressions. When you do, addition, subtraction, and multiplication work as expected. For example, the result of 2.3 + 5 is 7.3, and the result of 4.2 * 2 is 8.4. When you mix types, division works as expected as well. For example, the result of 9.3 / 3 is 3.1.

However, in many languages, dividing an integer by another integer is a special case. In languages such as Java, C++, and C#, dividing two integers results in an integer, and any fractional part of the result is lost. For example, in these languages, the result of 7 / 2 is 3, not 3.5 as you might expect. Programmers say that the decimal portion of the result is cut off, or *truncated.*

 When programming in a language that truncates the results of integer division, you must be particularly careful with numbers lower than 1. For example, if you write a program that halves a recipe, you might use an expression such as 1 / 2 * cupsSugar. No matter what the value of cupsSugar is, the result will always be 0 because 2 goes into 1 zero whole times.

Many programming languages also support a **remainder operator**, which is sometimes called the *modulo operator* or the *modulus operator*. When used with two integer operands, the remainder operator is the value that remains after division. For example, 24 Mod 10 is 4 because when 24 is divided by 10, 4 is the remainder. In Visual Basic, the remainder operator is the keyword Mod. In Java, C++, and C#, the operator is the percent sign (%).

The remainder operator can be useful in a variety of situations. For example, you can determine whether a number is even or odd by finding the remainder when the number is divided by 2. Any number that has a remainder of 0 is even, and any number with a remainder of 1 is odd.

Because the remainder operator differs among programming languages, and because the operation itself is handled differently when used with negative operands, the remainder operator will not be used in the rest of this language-independent book. Similarly, this book uses one data type, num, for all numeric values, and it is assumed that both integer and floating-point values can be stored in num variables and named constants.

TWO TRUTHS & A LIE

Performing Arithmetic Operations

1. Parentheses have higher precedence than any of the common arithmetic operators.

2. Operations in arithmetic statements occur from left to right in the order in which they appear.

3. The following adds 5 to a variable named points:

   points = points + 5

The false statement is #2. Operations of equal precedence in an arithmetic statement are carried out from left to right, but operations within parentheses are carried out first, multiplication and division are carried out next, and addition and subtraction take place last.

Understanding the Advantages of Modularization

Programmers seldom write programs as one long series of steps. Instead, they break down their programming problems into smaller units and tackle one cohesive task at a time. These smaller units are **modules**. Programmers also refer to them as **subroutines**, **procedures**, **functions**, or **methods**; the name usually reflects the programming language being used. For example, Visual Basic programmers use *procedure* (or *subprocedure*). C and C++ programmers call their modules *functions*, whereas C#, Java, and other object-oriented language programmers are more likely to use *method*. Programmers in COBOL, RPG, and BASIC (all older languages) are most likely to use *subroutine*.

 You can learn about modules that receive and return data in Chapter 9 of the comprehensive version of this book.

A main program executes a module by calling it. To **call a module** is to use its name to invoke the module, causing it to execute. When the module's tasks are complete, control returns to the spot from which the module was called in the main program. When you access a module, the action is similar to putting a DVD player on pause. You abandon your primary action (watching a video), take care of some other task (for example, making a sandwich), and then return to the main task exactly where you left off.

The process of breaking down a large program into modules is **modularization**; computer scientists also call it **functional decomposition**. You are never required to modularize a large program to make it run on a computer, but there are at least three reasons for doing so:

- Modularization provides abstraction.

- Modularization helps multiple programmers to work on a problem.

- Modularization allows you to reuse work more easily.

Modularization Provides Abstraction

One reason that modularized programs are easier to understand is that they enable a programmer to see the "big picture." **Abstraction** is the process of paying attention to important properties while ignoring nonessential details. Abstraction is selective ignorance. Life would be tedious without abstraction. For example, you can create a list of things to accomplish today:

```
Do laundry
Call Aunt Nan
Start term paper
```

Without abstraction, the list of chores would begin:

```
Pick up laundry basket
Put laundry basket in car
Drive to Laundromat
Get out of car with basket
Walk into Laundromat
Set basket down
Find quarters for washing machine
… and so on.
```

You might list a dozen more steps before you finish the laundry and move on to the second chore on your original list. If you had to consider every small, low-level detail of every task in your day, you would probably never make it out of bed in the morning. Using a higher-level, more abstract list makes your day manageable. Abstraction makes complex tasks look simple.

 Abstract artists create paintings in which they see only the big picture—color and form—and ignore the details. Abstraction has a similar meaning among programmers.

Likewise, some level of abstraction occurs in every computer program. Fifty years ago, a programmer had to understand the low-level circuitry instructions the computer used. But now, newer high-level programming languages allow you to use English-like vocabulary in which one broad statement corresponds to dozens of machine instructions. No matter which high-level programming language you use, if you display a message on the monitor, you are never required to understand how a monitor works to create each pixel on the screen. You write an instruction like `output message` and the details of the hardware operations are handled for you by the operating system.

Modules provide another way to achieve abstraction. For example, a payroll program can call a module named `computeFederalWithholdingTax()`. When you call this module from your program, you use one statement; the module itself might contain dozens of statements. You can write the mathematical details of the module later, someone else can write them, or you can purchase them from an outside source. When you plan your main payroll program, your only concern is that a federal withholding tax will have to be calculated; you save the details for later.

Modularization Helps Multiple Programmers to Work on a Problem

When you divide any large task into modules, you gain the ability to more easily divide the task among various people. Rarely does a single programmer write a commercial program that you buy. Consider any word-processing, spreadsheet, or database program you have used. Each program has so many options, and responds to user selections in so many possible ways, that it would take years for a single programmer to write all the instructions. Professional software developers can write new programs in weeks or months, instead of years, by dividing large programs into modules and assigning each module to an individual programmer or team.

Modularization Allows You to Reuse Work

If a module is useful and well written, you may want to use it more than once within a program or in other programs. For example, a routine that verifies the validity of dates is useful in many programs written for a business. (For example, a month value is valid if it is not lower than 1 or higher than 12, a day value is valid if it is not lower than 1 or higher than 31 if the month is 1, and so on.) If a computerized personnel file contains each employee's birth date, hire date, last promotion date, and termination date, the date-validation module can be used four times with each employee record. Other programs in an organization can also use the module; these programs might ship customer orders, plan employees' birthday parties, or calculate when loan payments should be made. If you write the date-checking instructions so they are entangled with other statements in a program, they are difficult to isolate and reuse. On the other hand, if you place the instructions in a separate module, the unit is easy to use and portable to other applications. The feature of modular programs that allows individual modules to be used in a variety of applications is **reusability**.

You can find many real-world examples of reusability. When you build a house, you don't invent plumbing and heating systems; you incorporate systems with proven designs. This certainly reduces the time and effort it takes to build a house. The systems you choose are in service in other houses, so they have been tested under a variety of circumstances, increasing their reliability. **Reliability** is the feature of programs that assures you a module has been proven to function correctly. Reliable software saves time and money. If you create the functional components of your programs as stand-alone modules and test them in your current programs, much of the work will already be done when you use the modules in future applications.

TWO TRUTHS & A LIE

Understanding the Advantages of Modularization

1. Modularization eliminates abstraction, a feature that makes programs more confusing.

2. Modularization makes it easier for multiple programmers to work on a problem.

3. Modularization allows you to reuse work more easily.

The false statement is #1. Modularization enables abstraction, which allows you to see the big picture.

Modularizing a Program

Most programs consist of a **main program**, which contains the basic steps, or the **mainline logic**, of the program. The main program then accesses modules that provide more refined details.

When you create a module, you include the following:

- A header—The **module header** includes the module identifier and possibly other necessary identifying information.

- A body—The **module body** contains all the statements in the module.

- A return statement—The **module return statement** marks the end of the module and identifies the point at which control returns to the program or module that called the module. In most programming languages, if you do not include a return statement at the end of a module, the logic will still return. However, this book follows the convention of explicitly including a return statement with every module.

Naming a module is similar to naming a variable. The rules and conventions for naming modules are slightly different in every programming language, but in this text, module names follow the same general rules used for variable identifiers:

- Module names must start with a letter and cannot contain spaces.

- Module names should have some meaning.

Although it is not a requirement of any programming language, it frequently makes sense to use a verb as all or part of a module's name, because modules perform some action. Typical module names begin with action words such as get, calculate, and display. When you program in visual languages that use screen components such as buttons and text boxes, the module names frequently contain verbs representing user actions, such as click or drag.

Additionally, in this text, module names are followed by a set of parentheses. This will help you distinguish module names from variable names. This style corresponds to the way modules are named in many programming languages, such as Java, C++, and C#.

As you learn more about modules in specific programming languages, you will find that you sometimes place variable names within the parentheses that follow module names. Any variables enclosed in the parentheses contain information you want to send to the module. For now, the parentheses at the end of module names will be empty in this book.

When a main program wants to use a module, it calls the module. A module can call another module, and the called module can call another. The number of chained calls is limited only by the amount of memory available on your computer. In this book, the flowchart symbol used to call a module is a rectangle with a bar across the top. You place the name of the module you are calling inside the rectangle.

Some programmers use a rectangle with stripes down each side to represent a module in a flowchart, and this book uses that convention if a module is external to a program. For example, prewritten, built-in modules that generate random numbers, compute standard trigonometric functions, and sort values often are external to your programs. However, if the module is being created as part of the program, the book uses a rectangle with a single stripe across the top.

In a flowchart, you draw each module separately with its own sentinel symbols. The beginning sentinel contains the name of the module. This name must be identical to the name used in the calling program or module. The ending sentinel contains return, which indicates that when the module ends, the logical progression of statements will exit the module and return to the calling program or module. Similarly, in pseudocode, you start each module with its name and end with a return statement; the module name and return statements are vertically aligned and all the module statements are indented between them.

For example, consider the program in Figure 2-3, which does not contain any modules. It accepts a customer's name and balance due as input and produces a bill. At the top of the bill, the company's name and address are displayed on three lines, which are followed by the customer's name and balance due. To display the company name and address, you can simply include three output statements in the mainline logic of a program, as shown in Figure 2-3, or you can modularize the program by creating both the mainline logic and a displayAddressInfo() module, as shown in Figure 2-4.

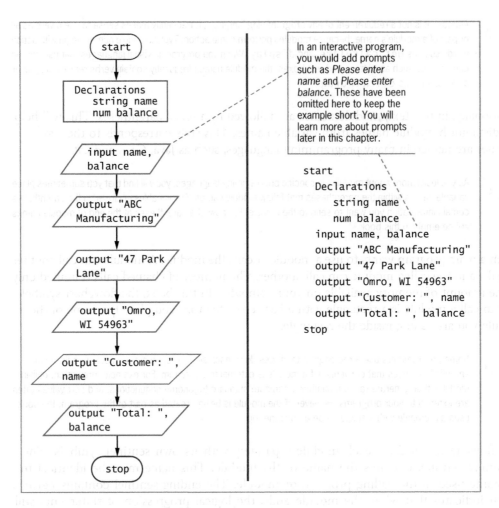

In an interactive program, you would add prompts such as *Please enter name* and *Please enter balance*. These have been omitted here to keep the example short. You will learn more about prompts later in this chapter.

```
start
    Declarations
        string name
        num balance
    input name, balance
    output "ABC Manufacturing"
    output "47 Park Lane"
    output "Omro, WI 54963"
    output "Customer: ", name
    output "Total: ", balance
stop
```

Figure 2-3 Program that produces a bill using only main program

© 2015 Cengage Learning

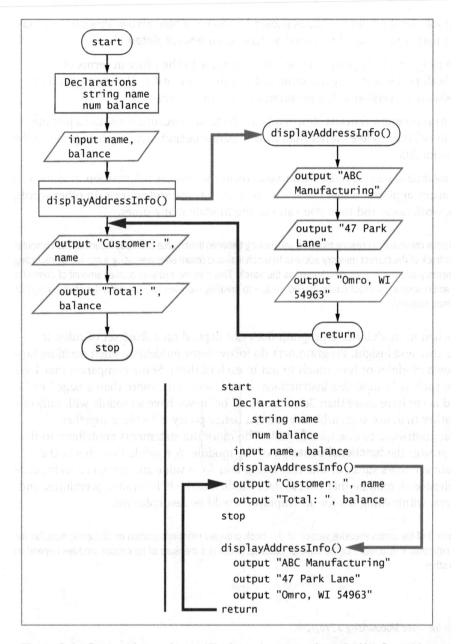

Figure 2-4 Program that produces a bill using main program that calls `displayAddressInfo()` module
© 2015 Cengage Learning

When the `displayAddressInfo()` module is called in Figure 2-4, logic transfers from the main program to the `displayAddressInfo()` module, as shown by the large red arrow in both the flowchart and the pseudocode. There, each module statement executes in turn before logical control is transferred back to the main program, where it continues with the statement that follows the module call, as shown by the large blue arrow. Programmers say the statements that are contained in a module have been **encapsulated**.

Neither of the programs in Figures 2-3 and 2-4 is superior to the other in terms of functionality; both perform exactly the same tasks in the same order. However, you may prefer the modularized version of the program for at least two reasons:

- First, the main program remains short and easy to follow because it contains just one statement to call the module, rather than three separate output statements to perform the work of the module.

- Second, a module is easy to reuse. After you create the address information module, you can use it in any application that needs the company's name and address. In other words, you do the work once, and then you can use the module many times.

 A potential drawback to creating modules and moving between them is the overhead incurred. The computer keeps track of the correct memory address to which it should return after executing a module by recording the memory address in a location known as the **stack**. This process requires a small amount of computer time and resources. In most cases, the advantage to creating modules far outweighs the small amount of overhead required.

Determining when to modularize a program does not depend on a fixed set of rules; it requires experience and insight. Programmers do follow some guidelines when deciding how far to break down modules or how much to put in each of them. Some companies may have arbitrary rules, such as "a module's instructions should never take more than a page," or "a module should never have more than 30 statements," or "never have a module with only one statement." Rather than use such arbitrary rules, a better policy is to place together statements that contribute to one specific task. The more the statements contribute to the same job, the greater the **functional cohesion** of the module. A module that checks the validity of a date variable's value, or one that asks a user for a value and accepts it as input, is considered cohesive. A module that checks date validity, deducts insurance premiums, and computes federal withholding tax for an employee would be less cohesive.

 Chapter 9 of the comprehensive version of this book provides more information on designing modules for high cohesion. It also explores the topic of *coupling*, which is a measure of how much modules depend on each other.

 Watch the video *Modularizing a Program*.

Declaring Variables and Constants within Modules

You can place any statements within modules, including input, processing, and output statements. You also can include variable and constant declarations within modules. For example, you might decide to modify the billing program in Figure 2-4 so it looks like the one in Figure 2-5. In this version of the program, three named constants that hold the three lines of company data are declared within the displayAddressInfo() module. (See shading.)

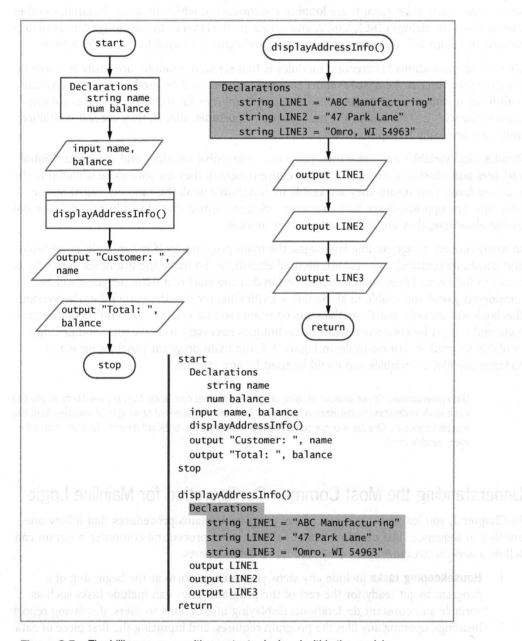

```
start
    Declarations
        string name
        num balance
    input name, balance
    displayAddressInfo()
    output "Customer: ", name
    output "Total: ", balance
stop

displayAddressInfo()
    Declarations
        string LINE1 = "ABC Manufacturing"
        string LINE2 = "47 Park Lane"
        string LINE3 = "Omro, WI 54963"
    output LINE1
    output LINE2
    output LINE3
return
```

Figure 2-5   The billing program with constants declared within the module
© 2015 Cengage Learning

Variables and constants are usable only in the module in which they are declared. Programmers say the data items are **visible** or **in scope** only within the module in which they are declared. That means the program only recognizes them there. Programmers also say that variables and constants are **local** to the module in which they are declared. In other words, when the strings LINE1, LINE2, and LINE3 are declared in the displayAddressInfo() module in Figure 2-5, they are not recognized and cannot be used by the main module.

One of the motivations for creating modules is that separate modules are easily reusable in multiple programs. If the displayAddressInfo() module will be used by several programs within the organization, it makes sense that the definitions for its variables and constants must come with it. This makes the modules more **portable**; that is, they are self-contained units that are easily transported.

Besides local variables and constants, you can create global variables and constants. **Global** variables and constants are known to the entire program; they are said to be declared at the *program level*. That means they are visible to and usable in all the modules called by the program. The opposite is not true—variables and constants declared within a module are not usable elsewhere; they are visible only to that module.

In many modern programming languages, the main program itself is a module, so variables and constants declared there cannot be used elsewhere. To make the examples in this book easier to follow, variables and constants declared at the start of a main program will be considered global and usable in all modules. Until Chapter 9 in the comprehensive version, this book will use only global variables and constants so that you can concentrate on the main logic and not yet be concerned with the techniques necessary to make one module's data available to another. For example, in Figure 2-5, the main program variables name and balance are global variables and could be used by any module.

Many programmers do not approve of using global variables and constants. They are used here so you can more easily understand modularization before you learn the techniques of sending local variables from one module to another. Chapter 9 of the comprehensive version of this book will describe how you can make every variable local.

Understanding the Most Common Configuration for Mainline Logic

In Chapter 1, you learned that a procedural program contains procedures that follow one another in sequence. The mainline logic of almost every procedural computer program can follow a general structure that consists of three distinct parts:

1. **Housekeeping tasks** include any steps you must perform at the beginning of a program to get ready for the rest of the program. They can include tasks such as variable and constant declarations, displaying instructions to users, displaying report headings, opening any files the program requires, and inputting the first piece of data.

Inputting the first data item is always part of the housekeeping module. You will learn the theory behind this practice in Chapter 3. Chapter 7 covers file handling, including what it means to open and close a file.

2. **Detail loop tasks** do the core work of the program. When a program processes many records, detail loop tasks execute repeatedly for each set of input data until there are no more. For example, in a payroll program, the same set of calculations is executed repeatedly until a check has been produced for each employee.

3. **End-of-job tasks** are the steps you take at the end of the program to finish the application. You can call these finish-up or clean-up tasks. They might include displaying totals or other final messages and closing any open files.

Figure 2-6 shows the relationship of these three typical program parts. Notice how the housekeeping() and endOfJob() tasks are executed just once, but the detailLoop() tasks repeat as long as the eof condition has not been met. The flowchart uses a flowline to show how the detailLoop() module repeats; the pseudocode uses the words while and endwhile to contain statements that execute in a loop. You will learn more about the while and endwhile terms in subsequent chapters; for now, understand that they are a way of expressing repeated actions.

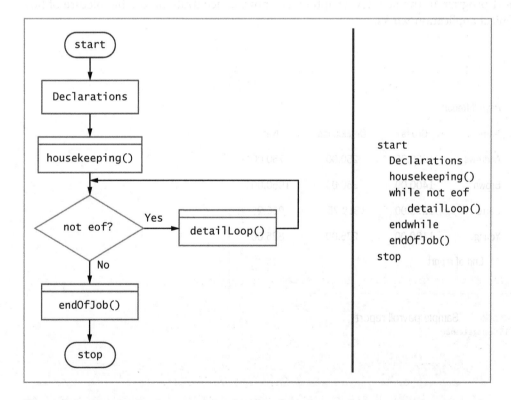

Figure 2-6 Flowchart and pseudocode of mainline logic for a typical procedural program
© 2015 Cengage Learning

Many everyday tasks follow the three-module format just described. For example, a candy factory opens in the morning, and the machines are started and filled with ingredients. These housekeeping tasks occur just once at the start of the day. Then, repeatedly during the day, candy is manufactured. This process might take many steps, each of which occurs many times. These are the steps in the detail loop. Then, at the end of the day, the machines are cleaned and shut down. These are the end-of-job tasks.

Not all programs take the format of the logic shown in Figure 2-6, but many do. Keep this general configuration in mind as you think about how you might organize many programs. For example, Figure 2-7 shows a sample payroll report for a small company. A user enters employee names until there are no more to enter, at which point the user enters *XXX*. As long as the entered name is not *XXX*, the user enters the employee's weekly gross pay. Deductions are computed as a flat 25 percent of the gross pay, and the statistics for each employee are output. The user enters another name, and as long as it is not *XXX*, the process continues. Examine the logic in Figure 2-8 to identify the components in the housekeeping, detail loop, and end-of-job tasks. You will learn more about the payroll report program in the next few chapters. For now, concentrate on the big picture of how a typical application works.

Payroll Report			
Name	Gross	Deductions	Net
Andrews	1000.00	250.00	750.00
Brown	1400.00	350.00	1050.00
Carter	1275.00	318.75	956.25
Young	1100.00	275.00	825.00
***End of report			

Figure 2-7 Sample payroll report
© 2015 Cengage Learning

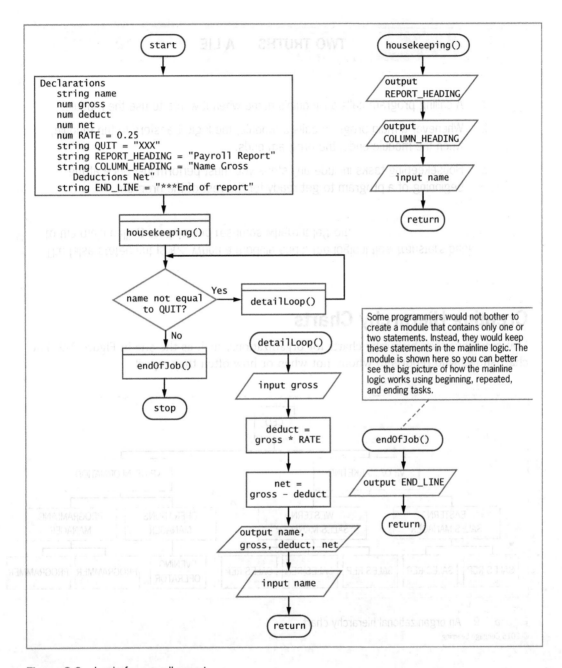

Figure 2-8 Logic for payroll report
© 2015 Cengage Learning

TWO TRUTHS & A LIE

Modularizing a Program

1. A calling program calls a module's name when it wants to use the module.

2. Whenever a main program calls a module, the logic transfers to the module; when the module ends, the program ends.

3. Housekeeping tasks include any steps you must perform just once at the beginning of a program to get ready for the rest of the program.

The false statement is #2. When a module ends, the logical flow transfers back to the main calling module and resumes where it left off.

Creating Hierarchy Charts

You may have seen hierarchy charts for organizations, such as the one in Figure 2-9. The chart shows who reports to whom, not when or how often they report.

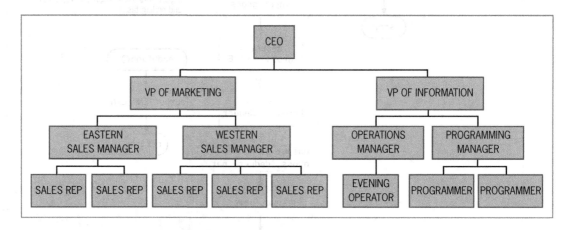

Figure 2-9   An organizational hierarchy chart
© 2015 Cengage Learning

When a program has several modules calling other modules, programmers often use a program **hierarchy chart** (sometimes called a *structure chart*) that operates in a similar manner to show the overall picture of how modules are related to one another. A hierarchy chart does not tell you what tasks are to be performed *within* a module, *when* the modules are called, *how* a module executes, or *why* they are called—that information is in the flowchart or pseudocode. A hierarchy chart tells you only *which* modules exist within a program and *which* modules call others. The hierarchy chart for the program in Figure 2-8 looks like Figure 2-10. It shows that the main module calls three others—housekeeping(), detailLoop(), and endOfJob().

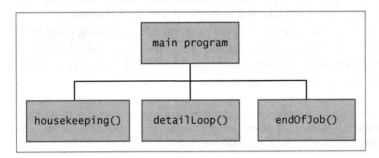

Figure 2-10 Hierarchy chart of payroll report program in Figure 2-8
© 2015 Cengage Learning

Figure 2-11 shows an example of a hierarchy chart for the billing program of a mail-order company. The hierarchy chart is for a more complicated program, but like the payroll report chart in Figure 2-10, it supplies module names and a general overview of the tasks to be performed, without specifying any details.

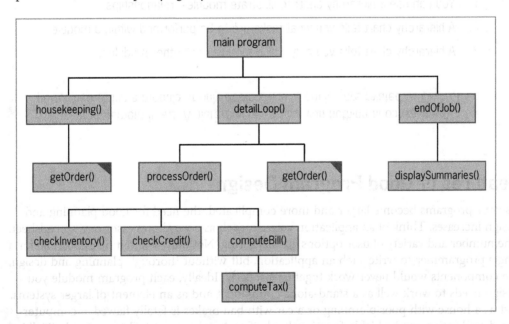

Figure 2-11 Billing program hierarchy chart
© 2015 Cengage Learning

Because program modules are reusable, a specific module may be called from several locations within a program. For example, in the billing program hierarchy chart in Figure 2-11, you can see that the getOrder() module is used twice. By convention, you blacken a corner of each box that represents a module used more than once. This action alerts readers that any change to this module could have consequences in multiple locations.

A hierarchy chart can be both a planning tool for developing the overall relationship of program modules before you write them and a documentation tool to help others see how modules are related after a program is written. For example, if a tax law changes, a programmer might be asked to rewrite the computeTax() module in the billing program diagrammed in Figure 2-11. As the programmer changes the computeTax() module, the hierarchy chart shows other dependent modules that might be affected. A hierarchy chart is useful for getting the big picture in a complex program.

Hierarchy charts are used in procedural programming, but other types of diagrams frequently are used in object-oriented environments. Chapter 13 of the comprehensive edition of this book describes the Unified Modeling Language, which uses a set of diagrams to describe a system.

TWO TRUTHS & A LIE

Creating Hierarchy Charts

1. You can use a hierarchy chart to illustrate modules' relationships.

2. A hierarchy chart tells you what tasks are to be performed within a module.

3. A hierarchy chart tells you only which modules call other modules.

The false statement is #2. A hierarchy chart tells you nothing about tasks performed within a module; it only depicts how modules are related to each other.

Features of Good Program Design

As your programs become larger and more complicated, the need for good planning and design increases. Think of an application you use, such as a word processor or a spreadsheet. The number and variety of user options are staggering. Not only would it be impossible for a single programmer to write such an application, but without thorough planning and design, the components would never work together properly. Ideally, each program module you design needs to work well as a stand-alone component and as an element of larger systems. Just as a house with poor plumbing or a car with bad brakes is fatally flawed, a computer-based application can be highly functional only if each component is designed well. Walking through your program's logic on paper (called desk-checking, as you learned in Chapter 1) is an important step to achieving superior programs. Additionally, you can implement several design features while creating programs that are easier to write and maintain. To create good programs, you should do the following:

- Provide program comments where appropriate.

- Choose identifiers thoughtfully.

- Strive to design clear statements within your programs and modules.

- Write clear prompts and echo input.

- Continue to maintain good programming habits as you develop your programming skills.

Using Program Comments

When you write programs, you often might want to insert program comments. **Program comments** are written explanations that are not part of the program logic but that serve as documentation for readers of the program. In other words, they are nonexecuting statements that help readers understand programming statements. Readers might include users who help you test the program and other programmers who might have to modify your programs in the future. Even you, as the program's author, will appreciate comments when you make future modifications and forget why you constructed a statement in a certain way.

The syntax used to create program comments differs among programming languages. This book starts comments in pseudocode with two forward slashes. For example, Figure 2-12 contains comments that explain the origins and purposes of variables in a real estate program.

 Program comments are a type of **internal documentation**. This term distinguishes them from supporting documents outside the program, which are called **external documentation**. Appendix C discusses other types of documentation.

```
Declarations
    num sqFeet
        // sqFeet is an estimate provided by the seller of the property
    num pricePerFoot
        // pricePerFoot is determined by current market conditions
    num lotPremium
        // lotPremium depends on amenities such as whether lot is waterfront
```

Figure 2-12 Pseudocode that declares variables and includes comments

© 2015 Cengage Learning

In a flowchart, you can use an annotation symbol to hold information that expands on what is stored within another flowchart symbol. An **annotation symbol** is most often represented by a three-sided box that is connected to the step it references by a dashed line. Annotation symbols are used to hold comments or sometimes statements that are too long to fit neatly into a flowchart symbol. For example, Figure 2-13 shows how a programmer might use some annotation symbols in a flowchart for a payroll program.

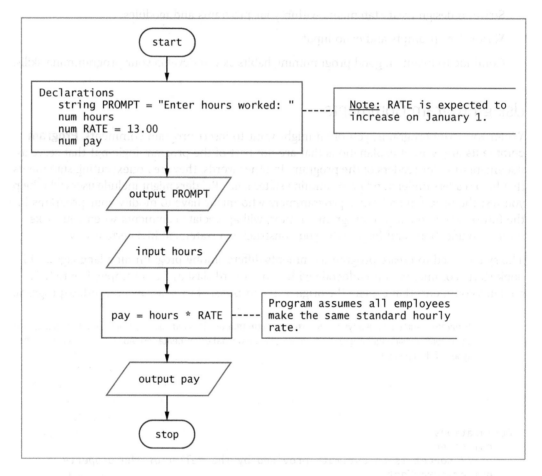

Figure 2-13   Flowchart that includes annotation symbols
© 2015 Cengage Learning

 You probably will use comments in your coded programs more frequently than you use them in pseudocode or flowcharts. For one thing, flowcharts and pseudocode are more English-like than the code in some languages, so your statements might be less cryptic. Also, your comments will remain in the program as part of the program documentation, but your planning tools are likely to be discarded once the program goes into production.

Including program comments is not necessary to create a working program, but comments can help you to remember the purpose of variables or to explain complicated calculations, especially when you come back to a program months or years after writing it. Some students do not like to include comments in their programs because it takes time to type them and they aren't part of the "real" program, but the programs you write in the future probably will require some comments. When you acquire your first programming job and modify a program written by another programmer, you will appreciate well-placed comments that explain complicated sections of the code.

An additional responsibility regarding comments is that they must be kept current as a program is modified. Outdated comments can provide misleading information about a program's status.

Choosing Identifiers

The selection of good identifiers is an often-overlooked element in program design. When you write programs, you choose identifiers for variables, constants, and modules. You learned the rules for naming variables and modules earlier in this chapter: Each must be a single word with no embedded spaces and must start with a letter. Those simple rules provide a lot of leeway in naming program elements, but not all identifiers are equally good. Choosing good identifiers simplifies your programming job and makes it easier for others to understand your work.

Some general guidelines include the following:

- Although not required in any programming language, it usually makes sense to give a variable or constant a name that is a noun (or a combination of an adjective and noun) because it represents a thing. Similarly, it makes sense to give a module an identifier that is a verb, or a combined verb and noun, because a module takes action.

- Use meaningful names. Creating a data item named someData or a module named firstModule() makes a program cryptic. Not only will others find it hard to read your programs, but you will forget the purpose of these identifiers even within your own programs. All programmers occasionally use short, nondescriptive names such as x or temp in a quick program; however, in most cases, data and module names should be meaningful. Programmers refer to programs that contain meaningful names as **self-documenting**. This means that even without further documentation, the program code explains itself to readers.

- Use pronounceable names. A variable name like pzf is neither pronounceable nor meaningful. A name that looks meaningful when you write it might not be as meaningful when someone else reads it; for instance, preparead() might mean "Prepare ad" to you, but "Prep a read" to others. Look at your names critically to make sure they can be pronounced. Very standard abbreviations do not have to be pronounceable. For example, most businesspeople would interpret ssn as a Social Security number.

- Don't forget that not all programmers share your culture. An abbreviation whose meaning seems obvious to you might be cryptic to someone in a different part of the world, or even a different part of your country. For example, you might name a variable roi to hold a value for *return on investment*, but a French-speaking person might interpret the meaning as *king*.

- Be judicious in your use of abbreviations. You can save a few keystrokes when creating a module called getStat(), but is the module's purpose to find the state in which a city is located, input some statistics, or determine the status of some variables? Similarly, is a variable named fn meant to hold a first name, file number, or something else? Abbreviations can also confuse people in different lines of work: AKA might suggest a sorority (Alpha Kappa Alpha) to a college administrator, a registry (American Kennel Association) to a dog breeder, or an alias (also known as) to a police detective.

To save typing time when you develop a program, you can use a short name like `efn`. After the program operates correctly, you can use a text editor's Search and Replace feature to replace your coded name with a more meaningful name such as `employeeFirstName`. When working in an integrated development environment, you can use the technique known as *refactoring* to rename every instance of an identifier.

Many IDEs support an automatic statement-completion feature that saves typing time. After the first time you use a name like `employeeFirstName`, you need to type only the first few letters before the compiler editor offers a list of available names from which to choose. The list is constructed from all the names you have used that begin with the same characters.

- Usually, avoid digits in a name. A zero can be confused with the letter *O*, and the lowercase letter *l* is misread as the numeral 1. Of course, use your judgment: `budgetFor2014` probably will not be misinterpreted.

- Use the rules your language allows to separate words in long, multiword variable names. For example, if the programming language you use allows hyphens or underscores, then use a module name like `initialize-data()` or `initialize_data()`, which is easier to read than `initializedata()`. Another option is to use camel casing to create an identifier such as `initializeData()`. If you use a language that is case sensitive, it is legal but confusing to use variable names that differ only in case. For example, if a single program contains `empName`, `EmpName`, and `Empname`, confusion is sure to follow.

- Consider including a form of the verb *to be*, such as *is* or *are*, in names for variables that are intended to hold a status. For example, use `isFinished` as a string variable that holds a *Y* or *N* to indicate whether a file is exhausted. The shorter name `finished` is more likely to be confused with a module that executes when a program is done. (Many languages support a Boolean data type, which you assign to variables meant to hold only true or false. Using a form of *to be* in identifiers for Boolean variables is appropriate.)

- Many programmers follow the convention of naming constants using all uppercase letters, inserting underscores between words for readability. In this chapter you saw examples such as `SALES_TAX_RATE`.

- Organizations sometimes enforce different rules for programmers to follow when naming program components. It is your responsibility to find out the conventions used in your organization and to adhere to them.

Programmers sometimes create a **data dictionary**, which is a list of every variable name used in a program, along with its type, size, and description. When a data dictionary is created, it becomes part of the program documentation.

When you begin to write programs, the process of determining what variables, constants, and modules you need and what to name them all might seem overwhelming. The design process is crucial, however. When you acquire your first professional programming assignment, the design process might very well be completed already. Most likely, your first assignment will be to write or modify one small member module of a much larger application. The more the original programmers adhered to naming guidelines, the better the original design was, and the easier your job of modification will be.

Designing Clear Statements

In addition to using program comments and selecting good identifiers, you can use the following tactics to contribute to the clarity of the statements within your programs:

- Avoid confusing line breaks.

- Use temporary variables to clarify long statements.

Avoiding Confusing Line Breaks

Some older programming languages require that program statements be placed in specific columns. Most modern programming languages are free-form; you can arrange your lines of code any way you see fit. As in real life, with freedom comes responsibility; when you have flexibility in arranging your lines of code, you must take care to make sure your meaning is clear. With free-form code, programmers are allowed to place two or three statements on a line, or, conversely, to spread a single statement across multiple lines. Both make programs harder to read. All the pseudocode examples in this book use appropriate, clear spacing and line breaks.

Using Temporary Variables to Clarify Long Statements

When you need several mathematical operations to determine a result, consider using a series of temporary variables to hold intermediate results. A **temporary variable** (or **work variable**) is not used for input or output, but instead is just a working variable that you use during a program's execution. For example, Figure 2-14 shows two ways to calculate a value for a real estate `salespersonCommission` variable. Each example achieves the same result—the salesperson's commission is based on the square feet multiplied by the price per square foot, plus any premium for a lot with special features, such as a wooded or waterfront lot. However, the second example uses two temporary variables: `basePropertyPrice` and `totalSalePrice`. When the computation is broken down into less complicated, individual steps, it is easier to see how the total price is calculated. In calculations with even more computation steps, performing the arithmetic in stages would become increasingly helpful.

```
// Using a single statement to compute commission
salespersonCommission = (sqFeet * pricePerFoot + lotPremium) * commissionRate

// Using multiple statements to compute commission
basePropertyPrice = sqFeet * pricePerFoot
totalSalePrice = basePropertyPrice + lotPremium
salespersonCommission = totalSalePrice * commissionRate
```

Figure 2-14 Two ways of achieving the same `salespersonCommission` result
© 2015 Cengage Learning

Programmers might say using temporary variables, like the second example in Figure 2-14, is *cheap*. When executing a lengthy arithmetic statement, even if you don't explicitly name temporary variables, the programming language compiler creates them behind the scenes (although without descriptive names), so declaring them yourself does not cost much in terms of program execution time.

Writing Clear Prompts and Echoing Input

When program input should be retrieved from a user, you almost always want to provide a prompt for the user. A **prompt** is a message that is displayed on a monitor to ask the user for a response and perhaps explain how that response should be formatted. Prompts are used both in command-line and GUI interactive programs.

For example, suppose a program asks a user to enter a catalog number for an item the user is ordering. The following prompt is not very helpful:

`Please enter a number.`

The following prompt is more helpful:

`Please enter a five-digit catalog order number.`

The following prompt is even more helpful:

`The five-digit catalog order number appears to the right of the item's picture in the catalog. Please enter it now.`

When program input comes from a stored file instead of a user, prompts are not needed. However, when a program expects a user response, prompts are valuable. For example, Figure 2-15 shows the flowchart and pseudocode for the beginning of the bill-producing program shown earlier in this chapter. If the input was coming from a data file, no prompt would be required, and the logic might look like the logic in Figure 2-15.

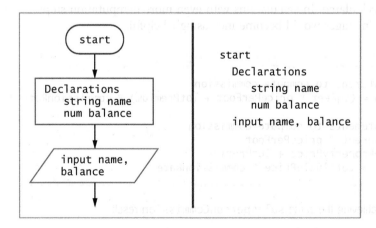

Figure 2-15 Beginning of a program that accepts a name and balance as input
© 2015 Cengage Learning

However, if the input was coming from a user, including prompts would be helpful. You could supply a single prompt such as *Please enter a customer's name and balance due*, but inserting more requests into a prompt generally makes it less likely that the user can remember to enter all the parts or enter them in the correct order. It is almost always best to include a separate prompt for each item to be entered. Figure 2-16 shows an example.

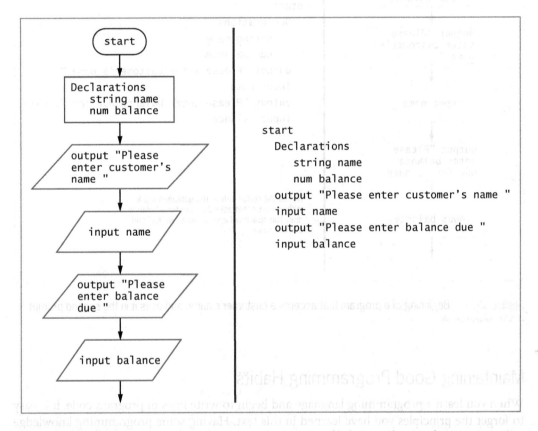

Figure 2-16 Beginning of a program that accepts a name and balance as input and uses a separate prompt for each item
© 2015 Cengage Learning

Users also find it helpful when you echo their input. **Echoing input** is the act of repeating input back to a user either in a subsequent prompt or in output. For example, Figure 2-17 shows how the second prompt in Figure 2-16 can be improved by echoing the user's first piece of input data in the second prompt. When a user runs the program that is started in Figure 2-17 and enters *Green* for the customer name, the second prompt will not be *Please enter balance due*. Instead, it will be *Please enter balance due for Green*. For example, if a clerk was about to enter the balance for the wrong customer, the mention of *Green* might be enough to alert the clerk to the potential error.

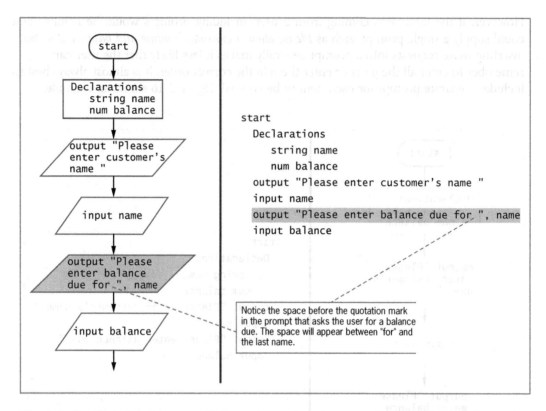

Figure 2-17 Beginning of a program that accepts a customer's name and uses it in the second prompt
© 2015 Cengage Learning

Maintaining Good Programming Habits

When you learn a programming language and begin to write lines of program code, it is easy to forget the principles you have learned in this text. Having some programming knowledge and a keyboard at your fingertips can lure you into typing lines of code before you think things through. But every program you write will be better if you plan before you code. Maintaining the habits of first drawing flowcharts or writing pseudocode, as you have learned here, will make your future programming projects go more smoothly. If you desk-check your program logic on paper before coding statements in a programming language, your programs will run correctly sooner. If you think carefully about the variable and module names you choose, and design program statements to be easy to read and use, your programs will be easier to develop and maintain.

TWO TRUTHS & A LIE

Features of Good Program Design

1. A program comment is a message that is displayed on a monitor to ask the user for a response and perhaps explain how that response should be formatted.

2. It usually makes sense to give each variable a name that contains a noun and to give each module a name that contains a verb.

3. Echoing input can help a user to confirm that a data item was entered correctly.

The false statement is #1. A program comment is a written explanation that is not part of the program logic but that serves as documentation for those reading the program. A prompt is a message that is displayed on a monitor to ask the user for a response and perhaps explain how that response should be formatted.

Chapter Summary

- Programs contain data in three different forms: literals (or unnamed constants), variables, and named constants. Each of these types of data can be numeric or string. Variables are named memory locations, the contents of which can vary. A variable declaration includes a data type and an identifier; optionally, it can include an initialization. Every computer programming language has its own set of rules for naming variables; however, all variable names must be written as one word without embedded spaces and should have appropriate meaning. A named constant is similar to a variable, except it can be assigned a value only once.

- Most programming languages use +, −, *, and / as the four standard arithmetic operators. Every operator follows rules of precedence that dictate the order in which operations in the same statement are carried out; multiplication and division always take precedence over addition and subtraction. The rules of precedence can be overridden using parentheses.

- Programmers break down programming problems into smaller, cohesive units called modules, subroutines, procedures, functions, or methods. To execute a module, you call it from another program or module. Any program can contain an unlimited number of modules, and each module can be called an unlimited number of times. Modularization provides abstraction, allows multiple programmers to work on a problem, and makes it easier for you to reuse work.

- When you create a module, you include a header, a body, and a `return` statement. A program or module calls a module's name to execute it. You can place any statements within modules, including declarations, which are local to the module. Global variables and constants are those that are known to the entire program. The mainline logic of almost every procedural computer program can follow a general structure that consists of three distinct parts: housekeeping tasks, detail loop tasks, and end-of-job tasks.

- A hierarchy chart illustrates modules and their relationships; it indicates which modules exist within a program and which modules call others.

- As programs become larger and more complicated, the need for good planning and design increases. You should use program comments where appropriate. Choose identifiers wisely, strive to design clear statements within your programs and modules, write clear prompts and echo input, and continue to maintain good programming habits as you develop your programming skills.

Key Terms

Numeric describes data that consists of numbers.

String describes data that is nonnumeric.

An **integer** is a whole number.

A **floating-point** number is a number with decimal places.

Real numbers are floating-point numbers.

A **numeric constant** (or **literal numeric constant**) is a specific numeric value.

A **string constant** (or **literal string constant**) is a specific group of characters enclosed within quotation marks.

Alphanumeric values can contain alphabetic characters, numbers, and punctuation.

An **unnamed constant** is a literal numeric or string value.

A **declaration** is a statement that provides a data type, an identifier, and, optionally, an initial value.

An **identifier** is a program component's name.

A data item's **data type** is a classification that describes what values can be assigned, how the item is stored, and what types of operations can be performed with the item.

Initializing a variable is the act of assigning its first value, often at the same time the variable is declared.

Garbage describes the unknown value stored in an unassigned variable.

Keywords comprise the limited word set that is reserved in a language.

Camel casing is a naming convention in which the initial letter is lowercase, multiple-word names are run together, and each new word within the name begins with an uppercase letter.

Lower camel casing is another name for the *camel casing* naming convention.

Pascal casing is a naming convention in which the initial letter is uppercase, multiple-word names are run together, and each new word within the name begins with an uppercase letter.

Upper camel casing is another name for the *Pascal casing* naming convention.

Hungarian notation is a naming convention in which a data type or other information is stored as part of a name.

Snake casing is a convention in which parts of a name are separated by underscores.

Mixed case with underscores is a naming convention similar to snake casing, but new words start with an uppercase letter.

Kebob case is sometimes used as the name for the style that uses dashes to separate parts of a name.

An **assignment statement** assigns a value from the right of an assignment operator to the variable or constant on the left of the assignment operator.

The **assignment operator** is the equal sign; it is used to assign a value to the variable or constant on its left.

A **binary operator** is an operator that requires two operands—one on each side.

An **operand** is a value used by an operator.

Right-associativity and **right-to-left associativity** describe operators that evaluate the expression to the right first.

An **lvalue** is the memory address identifier to the left of an assignment operator.

A **numeric variable** is one that can hold digits, have mathematical operations performed on it, and usually can hold a decimal point and a sign indicating positive or negative.

A **string variable** can hold text that includes letters, digits, and special characters such as punctuation marks.

Type-safety is the feature of some programming languages that prevents assigning values of an incorrect data type.

A **named constant** is similar to a variable, except that its value cannot change after the first assignment.

A **magic number** is an unnamed constant whose purpose is not immediately apparent.

Overhead describes the extra resources a task requires.

Rules of precedence dictate the order in which operations in the same statement are carried out.

The **order of operations** describes the rules of precedence.

Left-to-right associativity describes operators that evaluate the expression to the left first.

The **remainder operator** is an arithmetic operator used in some programming languages; when used with two integer operands, it results in the remainder after division.

Modules are small program units that you can use together to make a program. Programmers also refer to modules as **subroutines, procedures, functions,** or **methods**.

To **call a module** is to use the module's name to invoke it, causing it to execute.

Modularization is the process of breaking down a program into modules.

Functional decomposition is the act of reducing a large program into more manageable modules.

Abstraction is the process of paying attention to important properties while ignoring nonessential details.

Reusability is the feature of modular programs that allows individual modules to be used in a variety of applications.

Reliability is the feature of modular programs that assures you a module has been tested and proven to function correctly.

A **main program** runs from start to stop and calls other modules.

The **mainline logic** is the logic that appears in a program's main module; it calls other modules.

The **module header** includes the module identifier and possibly other necessary identifying information.

The **module body** contains all the statements in the module.

The **module return statement** marks the end of the module and identifies the point at which control returns to the program or module that called the module.

Encapsulation is the act of containing a task's instructions in a module.

A **stack** is a memory location in which the computer keeps track of the correct memory address to which it should return after executing a module.

The **functional cohesion** of a module is a measure of the degree to which all the module statements contribute to the same task.

Visible describes data items when a module can recognize them.

In scope describes data that is visible.

Local describes variables that are declared within the module that uses them.

A **portable** module is one that can more easily be reused in multiple programs.

Global describes variables that are known to an entire program.

Housekeeping tasks include steps you must perform at the beginning of a program to get ready for the rest of the program.

Detail loop tasks of a program include the steps that are repeated for each set of input data.

End-of-job tasks hold the steps you take at the end of the program to finish the application.

A **hierarchy chart** is a diagram that illustrates modules' relationships to each other.

Program comments are written explanations that are not part of the program logic but that serve as documentation for those reading the program.

Internal documentation is documentation within a coded program.

External documentation is documentation that is outside a coded program.

An **annotation symbol** contains information that expands on what appears in another flowchart symbol; it is most often represented by a three-sided box that is connected to the step it references by a dashed line.

Self-documenting programs are those that contain meaningful identifiers that describe their purpose.

A **data dictionary** is a list of every variable name used in a program, along with its type, size, and description.

A **temporary variable** (or **work variable**) is a variable that you use to hold intermediate results during a program's execution.

A **prompt** is a message that is displayed on a monitor to ask the user for a response and perhaps explain how that response should be formatted.

Echoing input is the act of repeating input back to a user either in a subsequent prompt or in output.

Exercises

 Review Questions

1. What does a declaration provide for a variable?

    a. a name

    b. a data type

    c. both of the above

    d. none of the above

2. A variable's data type describes all of the following *except* _____.

    a. what values the variable can hold

    b. how the variable is stored in memory

    c. what operations can be performed with the variable

    d. the scope of the variable

3. The value stored in an uninitialized variable is _____.

   a. garbage   c. compost
   b. null   d. its identifier

4. The value 3 is a _____.

   a. numeric variable   c. string variable
   b. numeric constant   d. string constant

5. The assignment operator _____.

   a. is a binary operator   c. is most often represented by a colon
   b. has left-to-right associativity   d. two of the above

6. Which of the following is true about arithmetic precedence?

   a. Multiplication has a higher precedence than division.
   b. Operators with the lowest precedence always have left-to-right associativity.
   c. Division has higher precedence than subtraction.
   d. all of the above

7. Which of the following is a term used as a synonym for *module* in some programming languages?

   a. method   c. both of these
   b. procedure   d. none of these

8. Which of the following is a reason to use modularization?

   a. Modularization avoids abstraction.
   b. Modularization reduces overhead.
   c. Modularization allows you to more easily reuse your work.
   d. Modularization eliminates the need for syntax.

9. What is the name for the process of paying attention to important properties while ignoring nonessential details?

   a. abstraction   c. extinction
   b. extraction   d. modularization

10. Every module has all of the following *except* _____.

    a. a header   c. a body
    b. local variables   d. a return statement

11. Programmers say that one module can _____ another, meaning that the first module causes the second module to execute.

    a. declare   c. enact
    b. define   d. call

12. The more that a module's statements contribute to the same job, the greater the _____ of the module.

    a. structure   c. functional cohesion

    b. modularity   d. size

13. In most modern programming languages, a variable or constant that is declared in a module is _____ in that module.

    a. global   c. in scope

    b. invisible   d. undefined

14. Which of the following is *not* a typical housekeeping task?

    a. displaying instructions   c. opening files

    b. printing summaries   d. displaying report headings

15. Which module in a typical program will execute the most times?

    a. the housekeeping module   c. the end-of-job module

    b. the detail loop   d. It is different in every program.

16. A hierarchy chart tells you _____.

    a. what tasks are to be performed within each program module

    b. when a module executes

    c. which routines call which other routines

    d. all of the above

17. What are nonexecuting statements that programmers place within code to explain program statements in English?

    a. comments   c. trivia

    b. pseudocode   d. user documentation

18. Program comments are _____.

    a. required to create a runnable program

    b. a form of external documentation

    c. both of the above

    d. none of the above

19. Which of the following is valid advice for naming variables?

    a. To save typing, make most variable names one or two letters.

    b. To avoid conflict with names that others are using, use unusual or unpronounceable names.

    c. To make names easier to read, separate long names by using underscores or capitalization for each new word.

    d. To maintain your independence, shun the conventions of your organization.

20. A message that asks a user for input is a(n) _____.

    a. comment   c. echo
    b. prompt   d. declaration

 Programming Exercises

1. Explain why each of the following names does or does not seem like a good variable name to you.

   a. d

   b. dsctamt

   c. discountAmount

   d. discount Amount

   e. discount

   f. discountAmountForEachNewCustomer

   g. discountYear2015

   h. 2015Discountyear

2. If productCost and productPrice are numeric variables, and productName is a string variable, which of the following statements are valid assignments? If a statement is not valid, explain why not.

   a. productCost = 100

   b. productPrice = productCost

   c. productPrice = productName

   d. productPrice = "24.95"

   e. 15.67 = productCost

   f. productCost = $1,345.52

   g. productCost = productPrice - 10

   h. productName = "mouse pad"

   i. productCost + 20 = productPrice

   j. productName = 3-inch nails

   k. productName = 43

   l. productName = "44"

   m. "99" = productName

   n. productName = brush

    o. `battery = productName`

    p. `productPrice = productPrice`

    q. `productName = productCost`

3.   Assume that `income = 8` and `expense = 6`. What is the value of each of the following expressions?

    a. `income + expense * 2`

    b. `income + 4 - expense / 2`

    c. `(income + expense) * 2`

    d. `income - 3 * 2 + expense`

    e. `4 * ((income - expense) + 2) + 10`

4.   Draw a typical hierarchy chart for a program that produces a monthly bill for a cell phone customer. Try to think of at least 10 separate modules that might be included. For example, one module might calculate the charge for daytime phone minutes used.

5.   a. Draw the hierarchy chart and then plan the logic for a program needed by the sales manager of The Henry Used Car Dealership. The program will determine the profit on any car sold. Input includes the sale price and actual purchase price for a car. The output is the profit, which is the sale price minus the purchase price. Use three modules. The main program declares global variables and calls housekeeping, detail, and end-of-job modules. The housekeeping module prompts for and accepts a sale price. The detail module prompts for and accepts the purchase price, computes the profit, and displays the result. The end-of-job module displays the message *Thanks for using this program.*

    b. Revise the profit-determining program so that it runs continuously for any number of cars. The detail loop executes continuously while the sale price is not 0; in addition to calculating the profit, it prompts the user for and gets the next sale price. The end-of-job module executes after 0 is entered for the sale price.

6.   a. Draw the hierarchy chart and then plan the logic for a program that calculates a person's body mass index (BMI). BMI is a statistical measure that compares a person's weight and height. The program uses three modules. The first prompts a user for and accepts the user's height in inches. The second module accepts the user's weight in pounds and converts the user's height to meters and weight to kilograms. Then, it calculates BMI as weight in kilograms divided by height in meters squared, and displays the results. There are 2.54 centimeters in an inch, 100 centimeters in a meter, 453.59 grams in a pound, and 1,000 grams in a kilogram. Use named constants whenever you think they are appropriate. The last module displays the message *End of job.*

    b. Revise the BMI-determining program to execute continuously until the user enters 0 for the height in inches.

7. Draw the hierarchy chart and design the logic for a program that calculates service charges for Hazel's Housecleaning service. The program contains housekeeping, detail loop, and end-of-job modules. The main program declares any needed global variables and constants and calls the other modules. The housekeeping module displays a prompt for and accepts a customer's last name. While the user does not enter *ZZZZ* for the name, the detail loop accepts the number of bathrooms and the number of other rooms to be cleaned. The service charge is computed as $40 plus $15 for each bathroom and $10 for each of the other rooms. The detail loop also displays the service charge and then prompts the user for the next customer's name. The end-of-job module, which executes after the user enters the sentinel value for the name, displays a message that indicates the program is complete.

8. Draw the hierarchy chart and design the logic for a program that calculates the projected cost of an automobile trip. Assume that the user's car travels 20 miles per gallon of gas. Design a program that prompts the user for a number of miles driven and a current cost per gallon. The program computes and displays the cost of the trip as well as the cost if gas prices rise by 10 percent. The program accepts data continuously until 0 is entered for the number of miles. Use appropriate modules, including one that displays *End of program* when the program is finished.

9. a. Draw the hierarchy chart and design the logic for a program needed by the manager of the Stengel County softball team, who wants to compute slugging percentages for his players. A slugging percentage is the total bases earned with base hits divided by the player's number of at-bats. Design a program that prompts the user for a player jersey number, the number of bases earned, and the number of at-bats, and then displays all the data, including the calculated slugging average. The program accepts players continuously until 0 is entered for the jersey number. Use appropriate modules, including one that displays *End of job* after the sentinel is entered for the jersey number.

   b. Modify the slugging percentage program to also calculate a player's on-base percentage. An on-base percentage is calculated by adding a player's hits and walks, and then dividing by the sum of at-bats, walks, and sacrifice flies. Prompt the user for all the additional data needed, and display all the data for each player.

   c. Modify the softball program so that it also computes a gross production average (GPA) for each player. A GPA is calculated by multiplying a player's on-base percentage by 1.8, then adding the player's slugging percentage, and then dividing by four.

10. Draw the hierarchy chart and design the logic for a program for the River Falls Homes Construction Company. Design a program that prompts the user for a lot number in the River Falls subdivision and data about the home to be built there, including number of bedrooms, number of bathrooms, and the number of cars the garage holds. Output is the price of the home, which is a $50,000 base price plus $17,000 for each bedroom, $12,500 for each bathroom, and $6,000 for

each car the garage holds. The program accepts lot numbers continuously until 0 is entered. Use named constants where appropriate. Also, use appropriate modules, including one that displays *End of job* after the sentinel is entered for the lot number.

11. Draw the hierarchy chart and design the logic for a program for Arnie's Appliances. Design a program that prompts the user for a refrigerator model name and the interior height, width, and depth in inches. Calculate the refrigerator capacity in cubic feet by first multiplying the height, width, and depth to get cubic inches, and then dividing by 1728 (the number of cubic inches in a cubic foot). The program accepts model names continuously until "XXX" is entered. Use named constants where appropriate. Also use modules, including one that displays *End of job* after the sentinel is entered for the model name.

Performing Maintenance

1. A file named MAINTENANCE02-01.txt is included with your downloadable student files. Assume that this program is a working program in your organization and that it needs modifications as described in the comments (lines that begin with two slashes) at the beginning of the file. Your job is to alter the program to meet the new specifications.

Find the Bugs

1. Your downloadable files for Chapter 2 include DEBUG02-01.txt, DEBUG02-02.txt, and DEBUG02-03.txt. Each file starts with some comments that describe the problem. Comments are lines that begin with two slashes (//). Following the comments, each file contains pseudocode that has one or more bugs you must find and correct.

2. Your downloadable files for Chapter 2 include a file named DEBUG02-04.jpg that contains a flowchart with syntax and/or logical errors. Examine the flowchart and then find and correct all the bugs.

Game Zone

1. For games to hold your interest, they almost always include some random, unpredictable behavior. For example, a game in which you shoot asteroids loses some of its fun if the asteroids follow the same, predictable path each time you play. Therefore, generating random values is a key component in creating most interesting computer games. Many programming languages come with a built-in

module you can use to generate random numbers. The syntax varies in each language, but it is usually something like the following:

```
myRandomNumber = random(10)
```

In this statement, myRandomNumber is a numeric variable you have declared and the expression random(10) means "call a method that generates and returns a random number between 1 and 10." By convention, in a flowchart, you would place a statement like this in a processing symbol with two vertical stripes at the edges, as shown below.

```
myRandomNumber =
random(10)
```

Create a flowchart or pseudocode that shows the logic for a program that generates a random number, then asks the user to think of a number between 1 and 10. Then display the randomly generated number so the user can see whether his or her guess was accurate. (In future chapters, you will improve this game so that the user can enter a guess and the program can determine whether the user was correct.)

Up for Discussion

1. Many programming style guides are published on the Web. These guides suggest good identifiers, explain standard indentation rules, and identify style issues in specific programming languages. Find style guides for at least two languages (for example, C++, Java, Visual Basic, or C#) and list any differences you notice.

2. What advantages are there to requiring variables to have a data type?

3. As this chapter mentions, some programming languages require that named constants are assigned a value when they are declared; other languages allow a constant's value to be assigned later in a program. Which requirement do you think is better? Why?

4. Many products use Pascal casing or camel casing in their names—for example, *MasterCard*. Name as many more as you can.

5. Distance measurement is one situation in which using integer division and the remainder operator might be useful. For example, if the programming language supports it, you can divide a measurement of 123 inches by 12 to get 10 feet, and then use the remainder operator to discover that the measurement is 3 inches over 10 feet. Think of several other situations in which you might find a remainder operator useful.

6. Would you prefer to write a large program by yourself, or to work on a team in which each programmer produces one or more modules? Why?

7. Extreme programming is a system for rapidly developing software. One of its tenets is that all production code is written by two programmers sitting at one machine. Is this a good idea? Does working this way as a programmer appeal to you? Why or why not?

Understanding Structure

In this chapter, you will learn about:

◎ The disadvantages of unstructured spaghetti code

◎ The three basic structures—sequence, selection, and loop

◎ Using a priming input to structure a program

◎ The need for structure

◎ Recognizing structure

◎ Structuring and modularizing unstructured logic

The Disadvantages of Unstructured Spaghetti Code

Professional business applications usually get far more complicated than the examples you have seen so far in Chapters 1 and 2. Imagine the number of instructions in the computer programs that guide an airplane's flight or audit an income tax return. Even the program that produces your paycheck at work contains many, many instructions. Designing the logic for such a program can be a time-consuming task. When you add hundreds or thousands of instructions to a program, it is easy to create a complicated mess. The descriptive name for logically snarled program statements is **spaghetti code**, because the logic is as hard to follow as one noodle through a plate of spaghetti. Not only is spaghetti code confusing, the programs that contain it are prone to error, difficult to reuse, and hard to use as building blocks for larger applications. Programs that use spaghetti code logic are **unstructured programs**; that is, they do not follow the rules of structured logic that you will learn in this chapter. **Structured programs** *do* follow those rules, and eliminate the problems caused by spaghetti code.

For example, suppose that you start a job as a dog washer and that you receive the instructions shown in Figure 3-1. This flowchart is an example of unstructured spaghetti code. A computer program that is organized similarly might "work"—that is, it might produce correct results—but it would be difficult to read and maintain, and its logic would be hard to follow.

You might be able to follow the logic of the dog-washing process in Figure 3-1 for two reasons:

- You might already know how to wash a dog.
- The flowchart contains a limited number of steps.

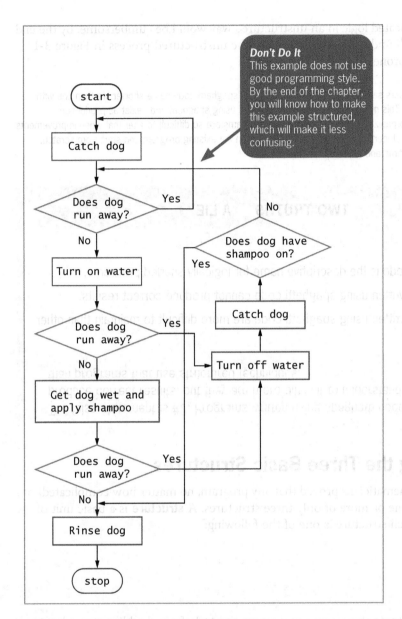

> **Don't Do It**
> This example does not use good programming style. By the end of the chapter, you will know how to make this example structured, which will make it less confusing.

Figure 3-1 Spaghetti code logic for washing a dog
© 2015 Cengage Learning

However, imagine that you were not familiar with dog washing, or that the process was far more complicated. (For example, imagine you must wash 100 dogs concurrently while applying flea and tick medication, giving them haircuts, and researching their genealogy.)

Depicting more complicated logic in an unstructured way would be cumbersome. By the end of this chapter, you will understand how to make the unstructured process in Figure 3-1 clearer and less error-prone.

 Software developers say that a program that contains spaghetti code has a shorter life than one with structured code. This means that programs developed using spaghetti code exist as production programs in an organization for less time. Such programs are so difficult to alter that when improvements are required, developers often find it easier to abandon the existing program and start from scratch. This takes extra time and costs more money.

TWO TRUTHS & A LIE

The Disadvantages of Unstructured Spaghetti Code

1. Spaghetti code is the descriptive name for logically snarled programs.

2. Programs written using spaghetti code cannot produce correct results.

3. Programs written using spaghetti code are more difficult to maintain than other programs.

The false statement is #2. Programs written using spaghetti code can produce correct results, but they are more difficult to understand and maintain than programs that use structured techniques.

Understanding the Three Basic Structures

In the mid-1960s, mathematicians proved that any program, no matter how complicated, can be constructed using one or more of only three structures. A **structure** is a basic unit of programming logic; each structure is one of the following:

- sequence
- selection
- loop

With these three structures alone, you can diagram any task, from doubling a number to performing brain surgery. You can diagram each structure with a specific configuration of flowchart symbols.

The Sequence Structure

The **sequence structure** is shown in Figure 3-2. It performs actions or tasks in order, one after the other. A sequence can contain any number of tasks, but there is no option to branch off and skip any of the tasks. Once you start a series of actions in a sequence, you must continue step by step until the sequence ends.

As an example, driving directions often are listed as a sequence. To tell a friend how to get to your house from school, you might provide the following sequence, in which one step follows the other and no steps can be skipped:

```
go north on First Avenue for 3 miles
turn left on Washington Boulevard
go west on Washington for 2 miles
stop at 634 Washington
```

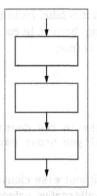

Figure 3-2 Sequence structure
© 2015 Cengage Learning

The Selection Structure

The **selection structure**, or **decision structure**, is shown in Figure 3-3. With this structure, one of two courses of action is taken based on the answer to a question. A flowchart that describes a selection structure begins with a decision symbol, and the branches of the decision must join at the bottom of the structure. Pseudocode that describes a selection structure starts with if. Pseudocode uses the **end-structure statement** endif to clearly show where the structure ends.

Some people call the selection structure an **if-then-else** because it fits the following statement:

```
if someCondition is true then
   do oneProcess
else
   do theOtherProcess
endif
```

Figure 3-3 Selection structure
© 2015 Cengage Learning

For example, you might provide part of the directions to your house as follows:

```
if traffic is backed up on Washington Boulevard then
   continue for 1 block on First Avenue and turn left on Adams Lane
else
   turn left on Washington Boulevard
endif
```

Similarly, a payroll program might include a statement such as:

```
if hoursWorked is more than 40 then
   calculate regularPay and overtimePay
else
   calculate regularPay
endif
```

These if-else examples can also be called **dual-alternative ifs** (or **dual-alternative selections**) because they contain two alternatives—the action taken when the tested condition is true and the action taken when it is false. Note that it is perfectly correct for one branch of the selection to be a "do nothing" branch. In each of the following examples, an action is taken only when the tested condition is true:

```
if it is raining then
    take an umbrella
endif
```

```
if employee participates in the dental plan then
    deduct $40 from employee gross pay
endif
```

The previous examples without `else` clauses are **single-alternative ifs** (or **single-alternative selections**); a diagram of their structure is shown in Figure 3-4. In these cases, you do not take any special action if it is not raining or if the employee does not belong to the dental plan. The branch in which no action is taken is called the **null case** or **null branch**.

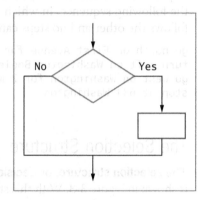

Figure 3-4   Single-alternative selection structure
© 2015 Cengage Learning

The Loop Structure

The **loop structure** is shown in Figure 3-5. A loop continues to repeat actions while a condition remains true. The action or actions that occur within the loop are the **loop body**. In the most common type of loop, a condition is evaluated; if the answer is true, you execute the loop body and evaluate the condition again. If the condition is still true, you execute the loop body again and then reevaluate the condition. This continues until the condition becomes false, and then you exit the loop structure. Programmers call this structure a **while loop**; pseudocode that describes this type of loop starts with

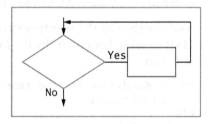

Figure 3-5   Loop structure
© 2015 Cengage Learning

`while` and ends with the end-structure statement `endwhile`. A flowchart that describes the `while` loop structure always begins with a decision symbol that has a branch that returns to a spot prior to the decision. You may hear programmers refer to looping as **repetition** or **iteration**.

The `while` loop tests a condition before executing the loop body even once. Another type of structured loop tests a condition after the first loop body execution. You will learn more about this alternate type of loop in Chapter 4 and in Appendix D. For the rest of this chapter, assume that all loops are `while` loops that ask the controlling question before the loop body ever executes. All logical problems can be solved using only the three structures—sequence, selection, and `while` loop.

Some programmers call a `while` loop a **while...do loop**, because it fits the following statement:

```
while testCondition continues to be true do
    someProcess
endwhile
```

When you provide directions to your house, part of the directions might be:

```
while the address of the house you are passing remains below 634
    travel forward to the next house
    look at the address on the house
endwhile
```

You encounter examples of looping every day, as in each of the following:

```
while you continue to be hungry
    take another bite of food
    determine whether you still feel hungry
endwhile
```

```
while unread pages remain in the reading assignment
    read another unread page
    determine whether there are more pages to read
endwhile
```

Combining Structures

All logic problems can be solved using only these three structures—sequence, selection, and loop. The structures can be combined in an infinite number of ways. For example, you can have a sequence of tasks followed by a selection, or a loop followed by a sequence. Attaching structures end to end is called **stacking structures**. For example, Figure 3-6 shows a structured flowchart achieved by stacking structures, and shows pseudocode that follows the flowchart logic.

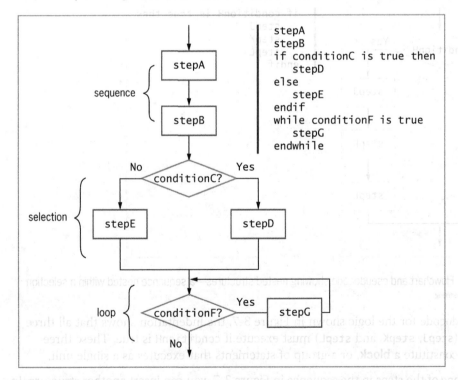

Figure 3-6   Structured flowchart and pseudocode with three stacked structures
© 2015 Cengage Learning

Whether you are drawing a flowchart or writing pseudocode, you can use any opposite, mutually exclusive words to represent decision outcomes—for example, *Yes* and *No* or *true* and *false*. This book follows the convention of using *Yes* and *No* in flowchart diagrams and *true* and *false* in pseudocode.

The pseudocode in Figure 3-6 shows a sequence, followed by a selection, followed by a loop. First stepA and stepB execute in sequence. Then a selection structure starts with the test of conditionC. The instruction that follows the if clause (stepD) executes when its tested condition (conditionC) is true, the instruction that follows else (stepE) executes when the tested condition is false, and any instructions that follow endif execute in either case. In other words, statements beyond the endif statement are "outside" the selection structure. Similarly, the endwhile statement shows where the loop structure ends. In Figure 3-6, while conditionF continues to be true, stepG continues to execute. If any statements followed the endwhile statement, they would be outside of, and not a part of, the loop.

Besides stacking structures, you can replace any individual steps in a structured flowchart diagram or pseudocode with additional structures. This means that any sequence, selection, or loop can contain other sequence, selection, or loop structures. For example, you can have a sequence of three tasks on one branch of a selection, as shown in Figure 3-7. Placing a structure within another structure is called **nesting structures**.

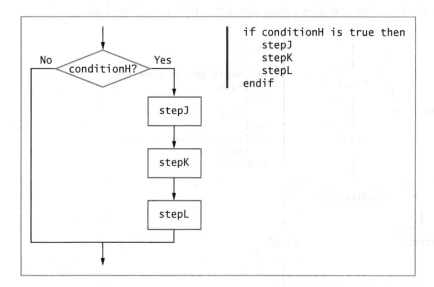

Figure 3-7 Flowchart and pseudocode showing nested structures—a sequence nested within a selection
© 2015 Cengage Learning

In the pseudocode for the logic shown in Figure 3-7, the indentation shows that all three statements (stepJ, stepK, and stepL) must execute if conditionH is true. These three statements constitute a **block**, or a group of statements that executes as a single unit.

In place of one of the steps in the sequence in Figure 3-7, you can insert another structure. In Figure 3-8, the process named stepK has been replaced with a loop structure that begins with a test of the condition named conditionM.

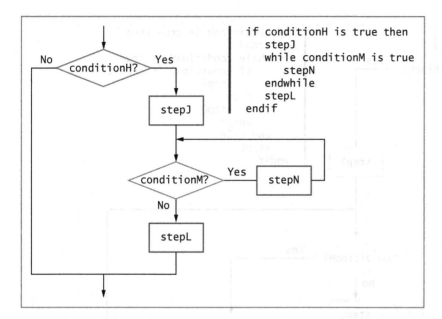

```
if conditionH is true then
    stepJ
    while conditionM is true
        stepN
    endwhile
    stepL
endif
```

Figure 3-8 Flowchart and pseudocode showing nested structures—a loop nested within a sequence, nested within a selection
© 2015 Cengage Learning

In the pseudocode shown in Figure 3-8, notice that `if` and `endif` are vertically aligned. This shows that they are "on the same level." Similarly, `stepJ`, `while`, `endwhile`, and `stepL` are aligned, and they are evenly indented. In the flowchart in Figure 3-8, you could draw a vertical line through the symbols containing `stepJ`, the entry and exit points of the `while` loop, and `stepL`. The flowchart and the pseudocode represent exactly the same logic.

When you nest structures, the statements that start and end a structure are always on the same level and are always in pairs. Structures cannot overlap. For example, if you have an `if` structure that contains a `while` structure, then the `endwhile` statement will come before the `endif`. On the other hand, if you have a `while` that contains an `if`, then the `endif` statement will come before the `endwhile`.

There is no limit to the number of levels you can create when you nest and stack structures. For example, Figure 3-9 shows logic that has been made more complicated by replacing `stepN` with a selection. The structure that performs `stepP` or `stepQ` based on the outcome of `conditionO` is nested within the loop that is controlled by `conditionM`. In the pseudocode in Figure 3-9, notice how the `if`, `else`, and `endif` that describe the condition selection are aligned with each other and within the `while` structure that is controlled by `conditionM`. As before, the indentation used in the pseudocode reflects the logic laid out graphically in the flowchart.

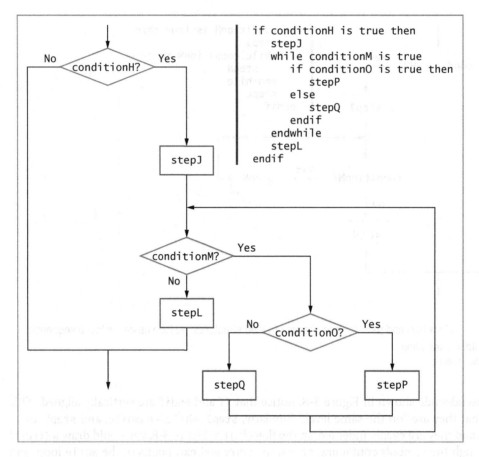

```
if conditionH is true then
    stepJ
    while conditionM is true
        if conditionO is true then
            stepP
        else
            stepQ
        endif
    endwhile
    stepL
endif
```

Figure 3-9 Flowchart and pseudocode for a selection within a loop within a sequence within a selection
© 2015 Cengage Learning

Many of the preceding examples are generic so that you can focus on the relationships of the symbols without worrying what they do. Keep in mind that generic instructions like stepA and generic conditions like conditionC can stand for anything. For example, Figure 3-10 shows the process of buying and planting flowers outdoors in the spring after the danger of frost is over. The flowchart and pseudocode structures are identical to those in Figure 3-9. In the exercises at the end of this chapter, you will be asked to develop more scenarios that fit the same pattern.

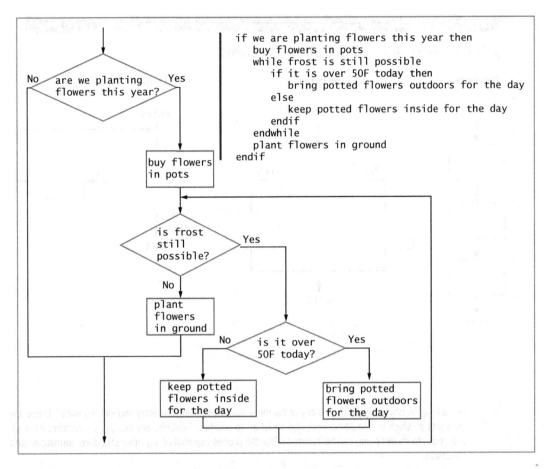

```
if we are planting flowers this year then
    buy flowers in pots
    while frost is still possible
        if it is over 50F today then
            bring potted flowers outdoors for the day
        else
            keep potted flowers inside for the day
        endif
    endwhile
    plant flowers in ground
endif
```

Figure 3-10   The process of buying and planting flowers in the spring
© 2015 Cengage Learning

The possible combinations of logical structures are endless, but each segment of a structured program is a sequence, a selection, or a loop. The three structures are shown together in Quick Reference 3-1. Notice that each structure has one entry point and one exit point. One structure can attach to another only at one of these points.

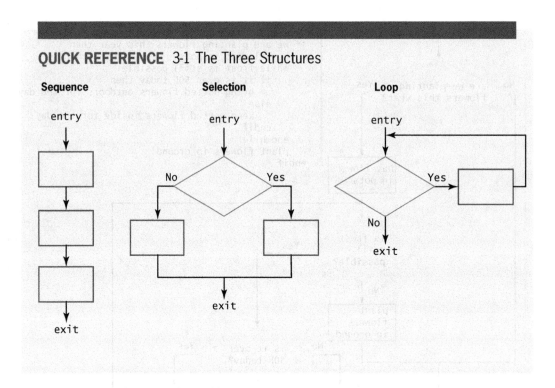

QUICK REFERENCE 3-1 The Three Structures

Try to imagine physically picking up any of the three structures using the entry and exit "handles." These are the spots at which you could connect one structure to another. Similarly, any complete structure, from its entry point to its exit point, can be inserted within the process symbol of any other structure, forming nested structures.

In summary, a structured program has the following characteristics:

- A structured program includes only combinations of the three basic structures— sequence, selection, and loop. Any structured program might contain one, two, or all three types of structures.

- Each of the structures has a single entry point and a single exit point.

- Structures can be stacked or connected to one another only at their entry or exit points.

- Any structure can be nested within another structure.

A structured program is never required to contain examples of all three structures. For example, many simple programs contain only a sequence of several tasks that execute from start to finish without any needed selections or loops. As another example, a program might display a series of numbers, looping to do so, but never making any decisions about the numbers.

Watch the video *Understanding Structure*.

TWO TRUTHS & A LIE

Understanding the Three Basic Structures

1. Each structure in structured programming is a sequence, selection, or loop.

2. All logic problems can be solved using only three structures—sequence, selection, and loop.

3. The three structures cannot be combined in a single program.

The false statement is #3. The three structures can be stacked or nested in an infinite number of ways.

Using a Priming Input to Structure a Program

Recall the number-doubling program discussed in Chapter 2; Figure 3-11 shows a similar program. The program accepts a number as input and checks for the end-of-data condition. If the condition is not met, then the number is doubled, the answer is displayed, and the next number is input.

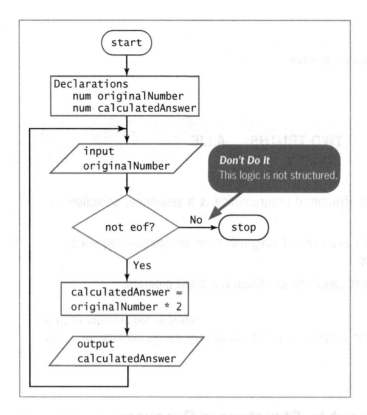

Figure 3-11 Unstructured flowchart of a number-doubling program
© 2015 Cengage Learning

 Recall from Chapter 1 that this book uses **eof** to represent a generic end-of-data condition when the exact tested parameters are not important to the discussion. In this example, the test is for **not eof** because processing will continue while the end of the data has not been reached.

Is the program represented by Figure 3-11 structured? At first, it might be hard to tell. The three allowed structures were illustrated in Quick Reference 3-1, and the flowchart in Figure 3-11 does not look exactly like any of those three shapes. However, because you may stack and nest structures while retaining overall structure, it might be difficult to determine whether a flowchart as a whole is structured. It is easiest to analyze the flowchart in Figure 3-11 one step at a time. The beginning of the flowchart looks like Figure 3-12. Is this portion of the flowchart structured? Yes, it is a sequence of two tasks—making declarations and inputting a value.

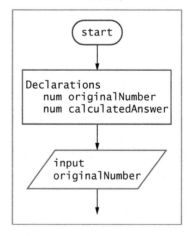

Figure 3-12 Beginning of a number-doubling flowchart
© 2015 Cengage Learning

Adding the next piece of the flowchart looks like Figure 3-13. After a value is input for `originalNumber`, the `not eof?` condition is tested. The sequence is finished; either a selection or a loop is starting. You might not know which one, but you do know that with a sequence, each task or step must follow without any opportunity to branch off. So, which type of structure starts with the question in Figure 3-13? Is it a selection or a loop?

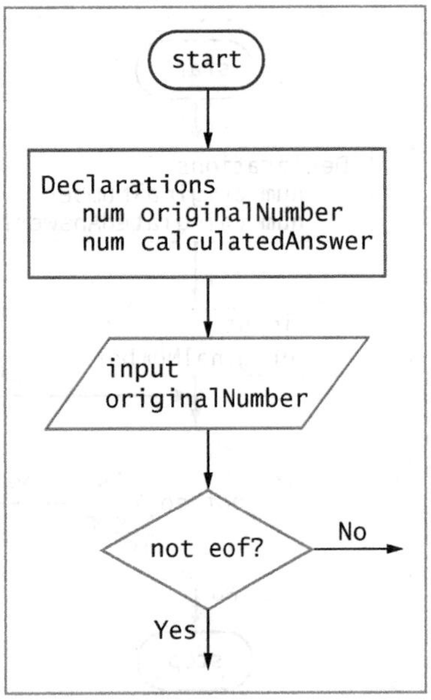

Selection and loop structures both start with a question, but they differ as follows:

- In a selection structure, the logic branches in one of two directions after the question, and then the flow comes back together; the question is not asked a second time within the selection structure.

- In a loop, each time the answer to the question results in the execution of the loop body, the flow of logic returns to the question that started the loop. When the body of a loop executes, the question that controls the loop is always asked again.

Figure 3-13 Number-doubling flowchart continued
© 2015 Cengage Learning

If the end-of-data condition is not met in the number-doubling problem in the original Figure 3-11, then the result is calculated and output, a new number is obtained, and the logic returns to the question that tests for the end of the file. In other words, while the answer to the `not eof?` question continues to be *Yes*, a body of two statements continues to execute. Therefore, the `not eof?` question starts a structure that is more likely to be a loop than a selection.

The number-doubling problem *does* contain a loop, but it is not a structured loop. In a structured `while` loop, the rules are:

1. You ask a question.

2. If the answer indicates you should execute the loop body, then you do so.

3. After you execute the loop body, then you must go right back to ask the question again—you can't go anywhere else!

The flowchart in Figure 3-11 asks a question. If the answer is *Yes* (that is, while `not eof?` is true), then the program performs two tasks in the loop body: It does the arithmetic and it displays the results. Doing two things is acceptable because two tasks with no possible branching constitute a sequence, and it is fine to nest one structure within another structure. However, when the sequence ends, the logic does not flow right back to the loop-controlling question. Instead, it goes *above* the question to get another number. For the loop in Figure 3-11 to be a structured loop, the logic must return to the `not eof?` question when the embedded sequence ends.

The flowchart in Figure 3-14 shows the program with the flow of logic returning to the `not eof?` question immediately after the nested two-step sequence. Figure 3-14 shows

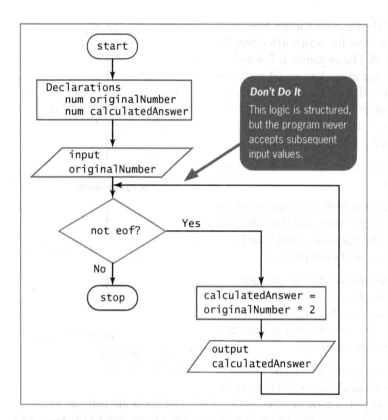

Figure 3-14 Structured, but nonfunctional, flowchart of number-doubling problem
© 2015 Cengage Learning

a structured flowchart, but it has one major flaw—the flowchart does not do the job of continuously doubling different numbers.

Follow the flowchart through a typical program run, assuming the eof condition is an input value of 0. Suppose that when the program starts, the user enters 9 for the value of originalNumber. That is not eof, so the number is multiplied by 2, and 18 is displayed as the value of calculatedAnswer. Then the question not eof? is asked again. The not eof? condition must still be true because a new value representing the sentinel (ending) value has not been entered and cannot be entered. The logic never returns to the input originalNumber task, so the value of originalNumber never changes. Therefore, 9 doubles again and the answer 18 is displayed again. The not eof? result is still true, so the same steps are repeated. This goes on *forever*, with the answer 18 being calculated and output repeatedly. The program logic shown in Figure 3-14 is structured, but it does not work as intended. Conversely, the program in Figure 3-15 works, but it is not structured because after the tasks execute within a structured loop, the flow of logic must return directly to the loop-controlling question. In Figure 3-15, the logic does not return to this question; instead, it goes "too high" outside the loop to repeat the input originalNumber task.

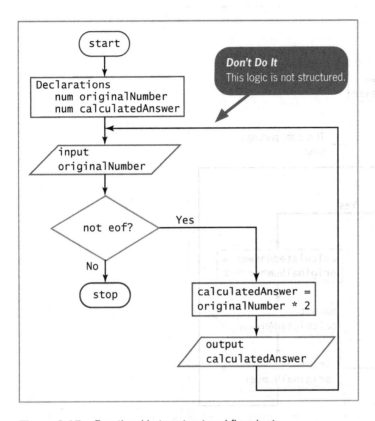

Figure 3-15 Functional but unstructured flowchart
© 2015 Cengage Learning

How can the number-doubling problem be both structured and work as intended? Often, for a program to be structured, you must add something extra. In this case, it is a priming input step. A **priming input** or **priming read** is an added statement that gets the first input value in a program. For example, if a program will receive 100 data values as input, you input the first value in a statement that is separate from the other 99. You must do this to keep the program structured.

Consider the solution in Figure 3-16; it is structured *and* it does what it is supposed to do. It contains a shaded, additional `input originalNumber` statement. The program logic contains a sequence and a loop. The loop contains another sequence.

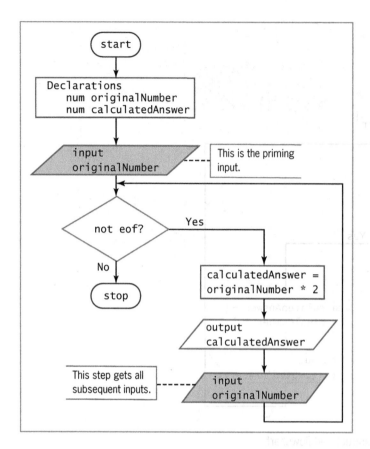

Figure 3-16 Functional, structured flowchart for the number-doubling problem
© 2015 Cengage Learning

The additional `input originalNumber` step shown in Figure 3-16 is typical in structured programs. The first of the two input steps is the priming input. The term *priming* comes from the fact that the input is first, or *primary* (it gets the process going, as in "priming the pump"). The purpose of the priming input step is to control the upcoming loop that begins with the `not eof?` question. The last element within the structured loop gets the next, and all subsequent, input values. This is also typical in structured loops—the last step executed within the loop body alters the condition tested in the question that begins the loop, which in this case is the `not eof?` question.

 In Chapter 2, you learned that the group of preliminary tasks that sets the stage for the main work of a program is called the housekeeping section. The priming input is an example of a housekeeping task.

Figure 3-17 shows another way you might attempt to draw the logic for the number-doubling program. At first glance, the figure might seem to show an acceptable solution to the problem—it is structured, it contains a sequence followed by a single loop with a sequence of three steps nested within it, and it appears to eliminate the need for the priming input statement. When the program starts, the declarations are made and the `not eof?` question is asked. If it is not the end of input data, then the program gets a number, doubles it, and displays it. Then, if the `not eof?` condition remains true, the program gets another number, doubles it, and displays it. The program might continue while many numbers are input. At some point, the input number will represent the `eof` condition; for example, the program might have been written to recognize the value *0* as the program-terminating value. After the `eof` value is entered, its condition is not immediately tested. Instead, a result is calculated and displayed one last time before the loop-controlling question is asked again. If the program was written to recognize `eof` when `originalNumber` is 0, then an extraneous answer of 0 will be displayed before the program ends. Depending on the language you are using and on the type of input being used, the results might be worse: The program might terminate by displaying an error message or the value output might be indecipherable garbage. In any case, this last output is superfluous—no value should be doubled and output after the `eof` condition is encountered.

As a general rule, a program-ending test should always come immediately after an input statement because that's the earliest point at which it can be evaluated. Therefore, the best solution to the number-doubling problem remains the one shown in Figure 3-16—the structured solution containing the priming input statement.

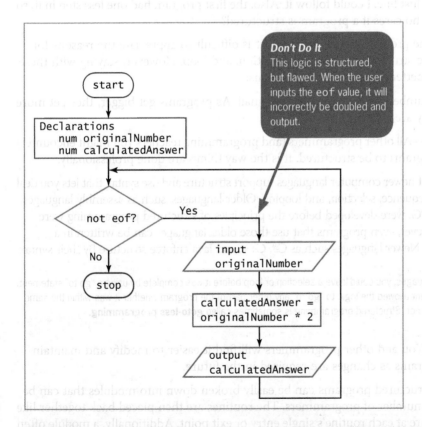

Figure 3-17   Structured but incorrect solution to the number-doubling problem
© 2015 Cengage Learning

TWO TRUTHS & A LIE

Using a Priming Input to Structure a Program

1. A priming input is the statement that repeatedly gets all the data that is input in a program.

2. A structured program might contain more instructions than an unstructured one.

3. A program can be structured yet still be incorrect.

The false statement is #1. A priming input gets the first input.

Understanding the Reasons for Structure

At this point, you may very well be saying, "I liked the original number-doubling program back in Figure 3-11 just fine. I could follow it. Also, the first program had one less step in it, so it was less work. Who cares if a program is structured?"

Until you have some programming experience, it is difficult to appreciate the reasons for using only the three structures—sequence, selection, and loop. However, staying with these three structures is better for the following reasons:

- *Clarity*—The number-doubling program is small. As programs get bigger, they get more confusing if they are not structured.

- *Professionalism*—All other programmers (and programming teachers you might encounter) expect your programs to be structured. It is the way things are done professionally.

- *Efficiency*—Most newer computer languages support structure and use syntax that lets you deal efficiently with sequence, selection, and looping. Older languages, such as assembly languages, COBOL, and RPG, were developed before the principles of structured programming were discovered. However, even programs that use those older languages can be written in a structured form. Newer languages such as C#, C++, and Java enforce structure by their syntax.

 In older languages, you could leave a selection or loop before it was complete by using a "go to" statement. The statement allowed the logic to "go to" any other part of the program whether it was within the same structure or not. Structured programming is sometimes called **goto-less programming**.

- *Maintenance*—You and other programmers will find it easier to modify and maintain structured programs as changes are required in the future.

- *Modularity*—Structured programs can be easily broken down into modules that can be assigned to any number of programmers. The routines are then pieced back together like modular furniture at each routine's single entry or exit point. Additionally, a module often can be used in multiple programs, saving development time in the new project.

Recognizing Structure

When you are beginning to learn about structured program design, it is difficult to detect whether a flowchart of a program's logic is structured. For example, is the flowchart segment in Figure 3-18 structured?

Yes, it is. It has a sequence and a selection structure.

Is the flowchart segment in Figure 3-19 structured?

Yes, it is. It has a loop and a selection within the loop.

Is the flowchart segment in the upper-left corner of Figure 3-20 structured?

No, it is not built from the three basic structures. One way to straighten out an unstructured flowchart segment is to use the "spaghetti bowl" method; that is, picture the flowchart as a bowl of spaghetti that you must untangle. Imagine you can grab one piece of pasta at the top of the bowl and start pulling. As you "pull" each symbol out of the tangled mess, you can untangle the separate paths until the entire segment is structured.

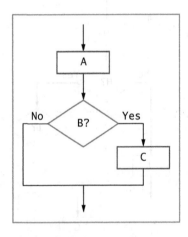

Figure 3-18 Example 1
© 2015 Cengage Learning

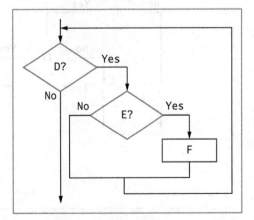

Figure 3-19 Example 2
© 2015 Cengage Learning

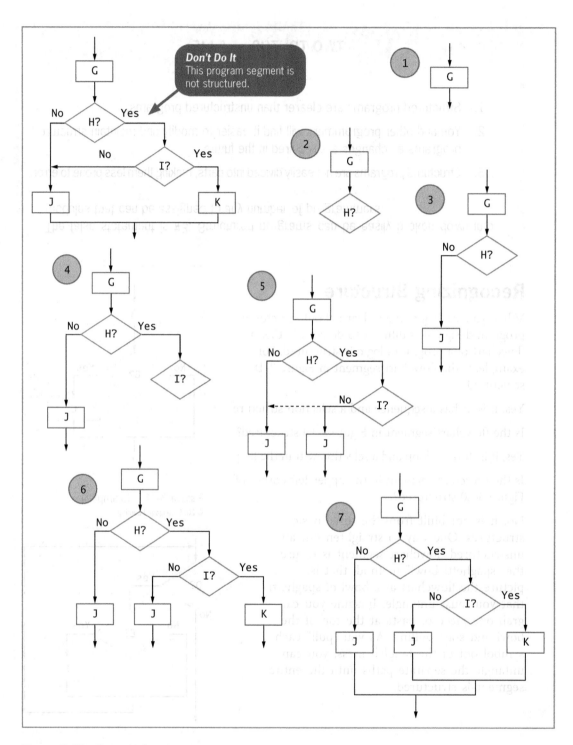

Figure 3-20 Example 3 and process to structure it
© 2015 Cengage Learning

Look at the diagram in the upper-left corner of Figure 3-20. If you could start pulling the arrow at the top, you would encounter a box labeled G. (See Figure 3-20, Step 1.) A single process like G is part of an acceptable structure—it constitutes at least the beginning of a sequence structure.

Imagine that you continue pulling symbols from the tangled segment. The next item in the flowchart is a question that tests a condition labeled H, as you can see in Figure 3-20, Step 2. At this point, you know the sequence that started with G has ended. Sequences never have questions in them, so the sequence is finished; either a selection or a loop is beginning with question H. A loop must return to the loop-controlling question at some later point. You can see from the original logic that whether the answer to H is *Yes* or *No*, the logic never returns to H. Therefore, H begins a selection structure, not a loop structure.

To continue detangling the logic, you would pull up on the flowline that emerges from the left side (the *No* side) of Question H. You encounter J, as shown in Step 3 of Figure 3-20. When you continue beyond J, you reach the end of the flowchart.

Now you can turn your attention to the *Yes* side (the right side) of the condition tested in H. When you pull up on the right side, you encounter Question I. (See Step 4 of Figure 3-20.)

In the original version of the flowchart in Figure 3-20, follow the line on the left side of Question I. The line emerging from the left side of selection I is attached to J, which is outside the selection structure. You might say the I-controlled selection is becoming entangled with the H-controlled selection, so you must untangle the structures by repeating the step that is causing the tangle. (In this example, you repeat Step J to untangle it from the other usage of J.) Continue pulling on the flowline that emerges from J until you reach the end of the program segment, as shown in Step 5 of Figure 3-20.

Now pull on the right side of Question I. Process K pops up, as shown in Step 6 of Figure 3-20; then you reach the end.

At this point, the untangled flowchart has three loose ends. The loose ends of Question I can be brought together to form a selection structure; then the loose ends of Question H can be brought together to form another selection structure. The result is the flowchart shown in Step 7 of Figure 3-20. The entire flowchart segment is structured—it has a sequence followed by a selection inside a selection.

 If you want to try structuring a more difficult example of an unstructured program, see Appendix B.

Structuring and Modularizing Unstructured Logic

Recall the dog-washing process illustrated in Figure 3-1 at the beginning of this chapter. When you look at it now, you should recognize it as an unstructured process. Can this process be reconfigured to perform precisely the same tasks in a structured way? Of course!

Figure 3-21 demonstrates how you might approach structuring the dog-washing logic. Part 1 of the figure shows the beginning of the process. The first step, *Catch dog*, is a simple sequence. This step is followed by a question. When a question is encountered, the sequence is over, and either a loop or a selection starts. In this case, after the dog runs away, you must catch the dog and determine whether he runs away again, so a loop begins. To create a structured loop like the ones you have seen earlier in this chapter, you can repeat the *Catch dog* process and return immediately to the *Does dog run away?* question.

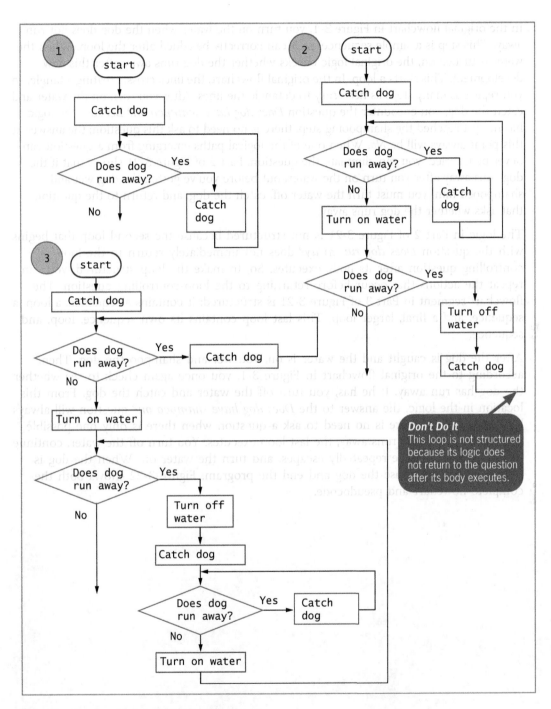

Figure 3-21   Steps to structure the dog-washing process

In the original flowchart in Figure 3-1, you turn on the water when the dog does not run away. This step is a simple sequence, so it can correctly be added after the loop. When the water is turned on, the original logic checks whether the dog runs away after this new development. This starts a loop. In the original flowchart, the lines cross, creating a tangle, so you repeat as many steps as necessary to detangle the lines. After you turn off the water and catch the dog, you encounter the question *Does dog have shampoo on?* Because the logic has not yet reached the shampooing step, there is no need to ask this question; the answer at this point always will be *No*. When one of the logical paths emerging from a question can never be traveled, you can eliminate the question. Part 2 of Figure 3-21 shows that if the dog runs away after you turn on the water, but before you've gotten the dog wet and shampooed him, you must turn the water off, catch the dog, and return to the question that asks whether the dog runs away.

The logic in Part 2 of Figure 3-21 is not structured because the second loop that begins with the question *Does dog run away?* does not immediately return to the loop-controlling question after its body executes. So, to make the loop structured, you can repeat the actions that occur before returning to the loop-controlling question. The flowchart segment in Part 3 of Figure 3-21 is structured; it contains a sequence, a loop, a sequence, and a final, larger loop. This last loop contains its own sequence, loop, and sequence.

After the dog is caught and the water is on, you wet and shampoo the dog. Then, according to the original flowchart in Figure 3-1, you once again check to see whether the dog has run away. If he has, you turn off the water and catch the dog. From this location in the logic, the answer to the *Does dog have shampoo on?* question will always be *Yes*; as before, there is no need to ask a question when there is only one possible answer. So, if the dog runs away, the last loop executes. You turn off the water, continue to catch the dog as he repeatedly escapes, and turn the water on. When the dog is caught at last, you rinse the dog and end the program. Figure 3-22 shows both the complete flowchart and pseudocode.

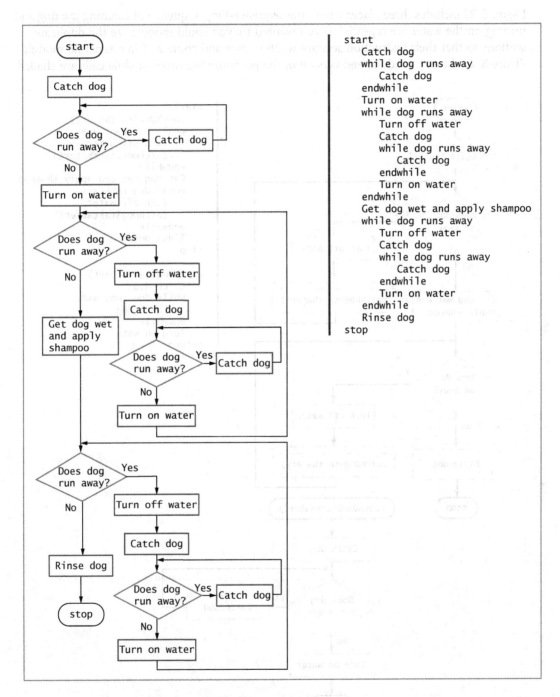

Figure 3-22 Structured dog-washing flowchart and pseudocode
© 2015 Cengage Learning

The flowchart in Figure 3-22 is complete and is structured. It contains alternating sequence and loop structures.

Figure 3-22 includes three places where the sequence-loop-sequence of catching the dog and turning on the water are repeated. If you wanted to, you could modularize the duplicate sections so that their instruction sets are written once and contained in a separate module. Figure 3-23 shows a modularized version of the program; the three module calls are shaded.

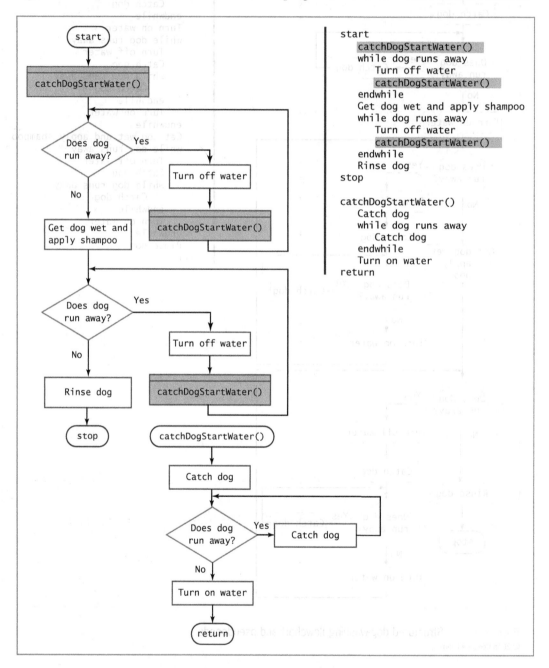

Figure 3-23 Modularized version of the dog-washing program
© 2015 Cengage Learning

One advantage to modularizing the steps needed to catch the dog and start the water is that the main program becomes shorter and easier to understand. Another advantage is that if this process needs to be modified, the changes can be made in just one location. For example, if you decided it was necessary to test the water temperature each time you turned on the water, you would add those instructions only once in the modularized version. In the original version in Figure 3-22, you would have to add those instructions in three places, causing more work and increasing the chance for errors.

No matter how complicated, any set of steps can always be reduced to combinations of the three basic sequence, selection, and loop structures. These structures can be nested and stacked in an infinite number of ways to describe the logic of any process and to create the logic for every computer program written in the past, present, or future.

For convenience, many programming languages allow two variations of the three basic structures. The case structure is a variation of the selection structure and the do loop is a variation of the while loop. You can learn about these two structures in Appendix D. Even though these extra structures can be used in most programming languages, all logical problems can be solved without them.

Watch the video *Structuring Unstructured Logic*.

TWO TRUTHS & A LIE

Structuring and Modularizing Unstructured Logic

1. When you encounter a question in a logical diagram, a sequence should be ending.

2. In a structured loop, the logic returns to the loop-controlling question after the loop body executes.

3. If a flowchart or pseudocode contains a question to which the answer never varies, you can eliminate the question.

The false statement is #1. When you encounter a question in a logical diagram, either a selection or a loop should start. However, any type of structure might end before the question is encountered.

Chapter Summary

- Spaghetti code is the descriptive name for unstructured program statements that do not follow the rules of structured logic.

- Clearer programs can be constructed using only three basic structures: sequence, selection, and loop. These three structures can be combined in an infinite number of ways by stacking and nesting them. Each structure has a single entry point and a single exit point; one structure can attach to another only at one of these points.

- A priming input is the statement that gets the first input value prior to starting a structured loop. Usually, the last step within the loop body gets the next and all subsequent input values.

- Programmers use structured techniques to promote clarity, professionalism, efficiency, and modularity.

- One way to order an unstructured flowchart segment is to imagine it as a bowl of spaghetti that you must untangle.

- Any set of logical steps can be rewritten to conform to the three structures: sequence, selection, and loop.

Key Terms

Spaghetti code is snarled, unstructured program logic.

Unstructured programs are programs that do *not* follow the rules of structured logic.

Structured programs are programs that do follow the rules of structured logic.

A **structure** is a basic unit of programming logic; each structure is a sequence, selection, or loop.

A **sequence structure** contains series of steps executed in order. A sequence can contain any number of tasks, but there is no option to branch off, skipping any of the tasks.

A **selection structure** or **decision structure** contains a question, and, depending on the answer, takes one of two courses of action before continuing with the next task.

An **end-structure statement** designates the end of a pseudocode structure.

An **if-then-else** is another name for a dual-alternative selection structure.

Dual-alternative ifs (or **dual-alternative selections**) define one action to be taken when the tested condition is true and another action to be taken when it is false.

Single-alternative ifs (or **single-alternative selections**) take action on just one branch of the decision.

The **null case** or **null branch** is the branch of a decision in which no action is taken.

A **loop structure** continues to repeat actions while a test condition remains true.

A **loop body** is the set of actions that occur within a loop.

A **while loop** is a structure that continues to repeat a process while some condition remains true.

Repetition and **iteration** are alternate names for a loop structure.

A **while…do loop** is an alternate name for a **while** loop.

Stacking structures is the act of attaching structures end to end.

Nesting structures is the act of placing a structure within another structure.

A **block** is a group of statements that executes as a single unit.

A **priming input** or **priming read** is the statement that reads the first input prior to starting a structured loop that uses the data.

Goto-less programming is a name to describe structured programming, because structured programmers do not use a "go to" statement.

Exercises

Review Questions

1. Snarled program logic is called _____ code.

   a. snake   c. spaghetti
   b. string   d. gnarly

2. The three structures of structured programming are _____.

   a. sequence, selection, and loop   c. sequence, order, and process
   b. selection, loop, and iteration   d. if, else, and then

3. A sequence structure can contain _____.

   a. only one task   c. no more than three tasks
   b. exactly three tasks   d. any number of tasks

4. Which of the following is *not* another term for a selection structure?

   a. decision structure   c. dual-alternative **if** structure
   b. loop structure   d. **if-then-else** structure

5. The structure that tests a condition, takes action if the result is true, and then tests the condition again can be called all of the following except a(n) _____.

   a. iteration   c. repetition
   b. loop   d. **if-then-else**

6. Placing a structure within another structure is called _____ the structures.

   a. stacking   c. building
   b. untangling   d. nesting

7. Attaching structures end to end is called _____ .

   a. stacking   c. building
   b. untangling   d. nesting

8. When an action is required if a condition is true, but no action is needed if it is false, you use a _____ .

   a. sequence   c. dual-alternative selection
   b. loop   d. single-alternative selection

9. To take action as long as a condition remains true, you use a _____ .

   a. sequence   c. dual-alternative selection
   b. loop   d. single-alternative selection

10. When you must perform one action when a condition is true and a different one when it is false, you use a _____ .

    a. sequence   c. dual-alternative selection
    b. loop   d. single-alternative selection

11. Which of the following attributes do all three basic structures share?

    a. Their flowcharts all contain exactly three processing symbols.
    b. They all have one entry and one exit point.
    c. They all contain a decision.
    d. They all begin with a process.

12. Which is true of stacking structures?

    a. Two incidences of the same structure cannot be stacked adjacently.
    b. When you stack structures, you cannot nest them in the same program.
    c. Each structure has only one point where it can be stacked on top of another.
    d. When you stack structures, the top structure must be a sequence.

13. When you input data in a loop within a program, the input statement that precedes the loop _____ .

    a. is the only part of the program allowed to be unstructured
    b. cannot result in eof
    c. is called a priming input
    d. executes hundreds or even thousands of times in most business programs

14. A group of statements that executes as a unit is a _____ .

    a. block
    b. family
    c. chunk
    d. cohort

15. Which of the following is acceptable in a structured program?

    a. placing a sequence within the true branch of a dual-alternative decision
    b. placing a decision within a loop
    c. placing a loop within one of the steps in a sequence
    d. All of these are acceptable.

16. In a selection structure, the structure-controlling question is _____ .

    a. asked once at the beginning of the structure
    b. asked once at the end of the structure
    c. asked repeatedly until it is false
    d. asked repeatedly until it is true

17. When a loop executes, the structure-controlling question is _____ .

    a. asked exactly once
    b. never asked more than once
    c. asked either before or after the loop body executes
    d. asked only if it is true, and not asked if it is false

18. Which of the following is *not* a reason for enforcing structure rules in computer programs?

    a. Structured programs are clearer to understand than unstructured ones.
    b. Other professional programmers will expect programs to be structured.
    c. Structured programs usually are shorter than unstructured ones.
    d. Structured programs can be broken down into modules easily.

19. Which of the following is *not* a benefit of modularizing programs?

    a. Modular programs are easier to read and understand than nonmodular ones.
    b. If you use modules, you can ignore the rules of structure.
    c. Modular components are reusable in other programs.
    d. Multiple programmers can work on different modules at the same time.

20. Which of the following is true of structured logic?

    a. You can use structured logic with newer programming languages, such as Java and C#, but not with older ones.
    b. Any task can be described using some combination of the three structures: sequence, selection, and loop.
    c. Structured programs require that you break the code into easy-to-handle modules that each contain no more than five actions.
    d. All of these are true.

Programming Exercises

1. In Figure 3-10, the process of buying and planting flowers in the spring was shown using the same structures as the generic example in Figure 3-9. Use the same logical structure as in Figure 3-9 to create a flowchart or pseudocode that describes some other process you know.

2. Each of the flowchart segments in Figure 3-24 is unstructured. Redraw each segment so that it does the same thing but is structured.

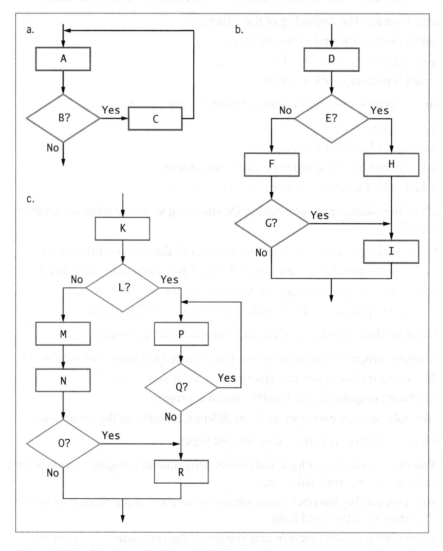

Figure 3-24 Flowcharts for Exercise 2 *(continues)*
© 2015 Cengage Learning

(continued)

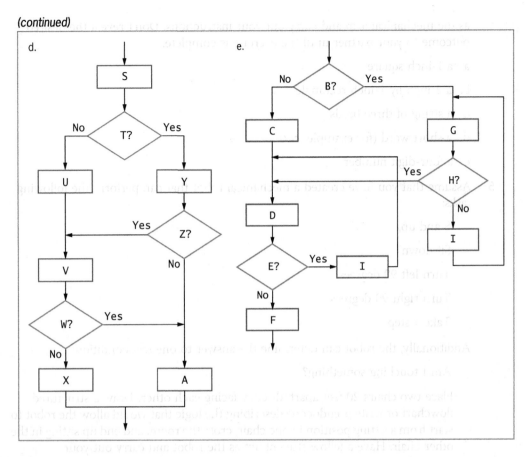

Figure 3-24 Flowcharts for Exercise 2
© 2015 Cengage Learning

3. Write pseudocode for each example (a through e) in Exercise 2, making sure your pseudocode is structured and accomplishes the same tasks as the flowchart segment.

4. Assume that you have created a mechanical arm that can hold a pen. The arm can perform the following tasks:

- Lower the pen to a piece of paper.

- Raise the pen from the paper.

- Move the pen 1 inch along a straight line. (If the pen is lowered, this action draws a 1-inch line from left to right; if the pen is raised, this action just repositions the pen 1 inch to the right.)

- Turn 90 degrees to the right.

- Draw a circle that is 1 inch in diameter.

Draw a structured flowchart or write structured pseudocode describing the logic that would cause the arm to draw or write the following. Have a fellow student act as the mechanical arm and carry out your instructions. Don't reveal the desired outcome to your partner until the exercise is complete.

a. a 1-inch square

b. a 2-inch by 1-inch rectangle

c. a string of three beads

d. a short word (for example, *cat*)

e. a four-digit number

5. Assume that you have created a mechanical robot that can perform the following tasks:

- Stand up.

- Sit down.

- Turn left 90 degrees.

- Turn right 90 degrees.

- Take a step.

Additionally, the robot can determine the answer to one test condition:

- Am I touching something?

a. Place two chairs 20 feet apart, directly facing each other. Draw a structured flowchart or write pseudocode describing the logic that would allow the robot to start from a sitting position in one chair, cross the room, and end up sitting in the other chair. Have a fellow student act as the robot and carry out your instructions.

b. Draw a structured flowchart or write pseudocode describing the logic that would allow the robot to start from a sitting position in one chair, stand up and circle the chair, cross the room, circle the other chair, return to the first chair, and sit. Have a fellow student act as the robot and carry out your instructions.

6. Draw a structured flowchart or write pseudocode that describes the process of guessing a number between 1 and 100. After each guess, the player is told that the guess is too high or too low. The process continues until the player guesses the correct number. Pick a number and have a fellow student try to guess it by following your instructions.

7. Looking up a word in a dictionary can be a complicated process. For example, assume that you want to look up *logic*. You might open the dictionary to a random page and see *juice*. You know this word comes alphabetically before *logic*, so you flip forward and see *lamb*. That is still not far enough, so you flip forward and see *monkey*. You have gone too far, so you flip back, and so on. Draw a structured flowchart or write pseudocode that describes the process of looking up a word in a dictionary. Pick a word at random and have a fellow student attempt to carry out your instructions.

8. Draw a structured flowchart or write structured pseudocode describing how to do a load of laundry. Include at least two decisions and two loops.

9. Draw a structured flowchart or write structured pseudocode describing how to study for an exam. Include at least two decisions and two loops.

10. Draw a structured flowchart or write structured pseudocode describing how to wrap a present. Include at least two decisions and two loops.

11. Draw a structured flowchart or write structured pseudocode describing the steps to prepare your favorite dish. Include at least two decisions and two loops.

Performing Maintenance

1. A file named MAINTENANCE03-01.txt is included with your downloadable student files. Assume that this program is a working program in your organization and that it needs modifications as described in the comments (lines that begin with two slashes) at the beginning of the file. Your job is to alter the program to meet the new specifications.

Find the Bugs

1. Your downloadable files for Chapter 3 include DEBUG03-01.txt, DEBUG03-02.txt, and DEBUG03-03.txt. Each file starts with some comments that describe the problem. Comments are lines that begin with two slashes (//). Following the comments, each file contains pseudocode that has one or more bugs you must find and correct.

2. Your downloadable files for Chapter 3 include a file named DEBUG03-04.jpg that contains a flowchart with syntax and/or logical errors. Examine the flowchart and then find and correct all the bugs.

Game Zone

1. Choose a simple children's game and describe its logic, using a structured flowchart or pseudocode. For example, you might try to explain Rock, Paper, Scissors; Musical Chairs; Duck, Duck, Goose; the card game War; or the elimination game Eenie, Meenie, Minie, Moe.

2. Choose a television game show such as *Wheel of Fortune* or *Jeopardy!* and describe its rules using a structured flowchart or pseudocode.

3. Choose a sport such as baseball or football and describe the actions in one limited play period (such as an at-bat in baseball or a possession in football) using a structured flowchart or pseudocode.

Up for Discussion

1. Find more information about one of the following people and explain why he or she is important to structured programming: Edsger Dijkstra, Corrado Bohm, Giuseppe Jacopini, and Grace Hopper.

2. Computer programs can contain structures within structures and stacked structures, creating very large programs. Computers also can perform millions of arithmetic calculations in an hour. How can we possibly know the results are correct?

3. Develop a checklist of rules you can use to help you determine whether a flowchart or pseudocode segment is structured.

Chapter

Entity Relationship (ER) Modeling

In this chapter, you will learn:
- The main characteristics of entity relationship components
- How relationships between entities are defined, refined, and incorporated into the database design process
- How ERD components affect database design and implementation
- That real-world database design often requires the reconciliation of conflicting goals

Preview

This chapter expands coverage of the data-modeling aspect of database design. Data modeling is the first step in the database design journey, serving as a bridge between real-world objects and the database model that is implemented in the computer. Therefore, the importance of data-modeling details, expressed graphically through entity relationship diagrams (ERDs), cannot be overstated.

Most of the basic concepts and definitions used in the entity relationship model (ERM) were introduced in Chapter 2, Data Models. For example, the basic components of entities and relationships and their representation should now be familiar to you. This chapter goes much deeper, analyzing the graphic depiction of relationships among the entities and showing how those depictions help you summarize the wealth of data required to implement a successful design.

Finally, the chapter illustrates how conflicting goals can be a challenge in database design and might require design compromises.

Data Files and Available Formats

	MS Access	Oracle	MS SQL	My SQL		MS Access	Oracle	MS SQL	My SQL
CH04_TinyCollege	✓	✓	✓	✓	CH04_Clinic	✓	✓	✓	✓
CH04_TinyCollege_Alt	✓	✓	✓	✓	CH04_PartCo	✓	✓	✓	✓
CH04_ShortCo	✓	✓	✓	✓	CH04_CollegeTry	✓	✓	✓	✓

Data Files Available on cengagebrain.com

Note

Because this book generally focuses on the relational model, you might be tempted to conclude that the ERM is exclusively a relational tool. Actually, conceptual models such as the ERM can be used to understand and design the data requirements of an organization. Therefore, the ERM is independent of the database type. Conceptual models are used in the conceptual design of databases, while relational models are used in the logical design of databases. However, because you are familiar with the relational model from the previous chapter, the relational model is used extensively in this chapter to explain ER constructs and the way they are used to develop database designs.

4-1 The Entity Relationship Model (ERM)

You should remember from Chapter 2, Data Models, and Chapter 3, The Relational Database Model, that the ERM forms the basis of an ERD. The ERD represents the conceptual database as viewed by the end user. ERDs depict the database's main components: entities, attributes, and relationships. Because an entity represents a real-world object, the words *entity* and *object* are often used interchangeably. Thus, the entities (objects) of the Tiny College database design developed in this chapter include students, classes, teachers, and classrooms. The order in which the ERD components are covered in the chapter is dictated by the way the modeling tools are used to develop ERDs that can form the basis for successful database design and implementation.

In Chapter 2, you also learned about the various notations used with ERDs—the original Chen notation and the newer Crow's Foot and UML notations. The first two notations are used at the beginning of this chapter to introduce some basic ER modeling concepts. Some conceptual database modeling concepts can be expressed only using the Chen notation. However, because the emphasis is on *design and implementation* of databases, the Crow's Foot and UML class diagram notations are used for the final Tiny College ER diagram example. Because of its emphasis on implementation, the Crow's Foot notation can represent only what could be implemented. In other words:

- The Chen notation favors conceptual modeling.

- The Crow's Foot notation favors a more implementation-oriented approach.

- The UML notation can be used for both conceptual and implementation modeling.

Online Content

To learn how to create ER diagrams with the help of Microsoft Visio, go to *www.cengagebrain.com*: Appendix A, Designing Databases with Visio Professional: A Tutorial, shows you how to create Crow's Foot ERDs. Appendix H, Unified Modeling Language (UML), shows you how to create UML class diagrams.

4-1a Entities

Recall that an entity is an object of interest to the end user. In Chapter 2, you learned that, at the ER modeling level, an entity actually refers to the *entity set* and not to a single entity occurrence. In other words, an *entity* in the ERM corresponds to a table—not to a row—in the relational environment. The ERM refers to a table row as an *entity instance* or *entity occurrence*. In the Chen, Crow's Foot, and UML notations, an entity is represented by a rectangle that contains the entity's name. The entity name, a noun, is usually written in all capital letters.

4-1b Attributes

Attributes are characteristics of entities. For example, the STUDENT entity includes the attributes STU_LNAME, STU_FNAME, and STU_INITIAL, among many others. In the original Chen notation, attributes are represented by ovals and are connected to the entity rectangle with a line. Each oval contains the name of the attribute it represents. In the Crow's Foot notation, the attributes are written in the attribute box below the entity rectangle. (See Figure 4.1.) Because the Chen representation consumes more space, software vendors have adopted the Crow's Foot attribute display.

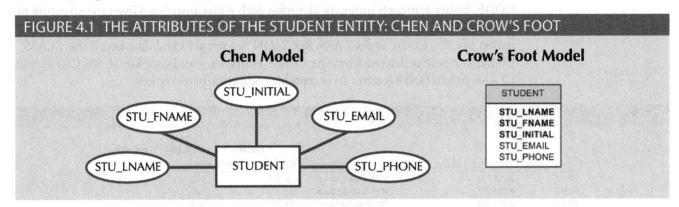

FIGURE 4.1 THE ATTRIBUTES OF THE STUDENT ENTITY: CHEN AND CROW'S FOOT

Required and Optional Attributes A **required attribute** is an attribute that must have a value; in other words, it cannot be left empty. As shown in Figure 4.1, the two boldfaced attributes in the Crow's Foot notation indicate that data entry will be required. STU_LNAME and STU_FNAME require data entries because all students are assumed to have a last name and a first name. However, students might not have a middle name, and perhaps they do not yet have a phone number and an email address. Therefore, those attributes are not presented in boldface in the entity box. An **optional attribute** is an attribute that does not require a value; therefore, it can be left empty.

Domains Attributes have a domain. As you learned in Chapter 3, a *domain* is the set of possible values for a given attribute. For example, the domain for a grade point average (GPA) attribute is written (0,4) because the lowest possible GPA value is 0 and the highest possible value is 4. The domain for a gender attribute consists of only two possibilities: M or F (or some other equivalent code). The domain for a company's date of hire attribute consists of all dates that fit in a range (for example, company startup date to current date).

Attributes may share a domain. For instance, a student address and a professor address share the same domain of all possible addresses. In fact, the data dictionary may let a newly declared attribute inherit the characteristics of an existing attribute if the same attribute name is used. For example, the PROFESSOR and STUDENT entities may each have an attribute named ADDRESS and could therefore share a domain.

Identifiers (Primary Keys) The ERM uses **identifiers**—one or more attributes that uniquely identify each entity instance. In the relational model, entities are mapped to tables, and the entity identifier is mapped as the table's primary key (PK). Identifiers are underlined in the ERD. Key attributes are also underlined in a frequently used shorthand notation for the table structure, called a **relational schema**, that uses the following format:

TABLE NAME (**KEY_ATTRIBUTE 1**, ATTRIBUTE 2, ATTRIBUTE 3, … ATTRIBUTE K)

For example, a CAR entity may be represented by:

CAR (**CAR_VIN**, MOD_CODE, CAR_YEAR, CAR_COLOR)

Each car is identified by a unique vehicle identification number, or CAR_VIN.

Composite Identifiers Ideally, an entity identifier is composed of only a single attribute. For example, the table in Figure 4.2 uses a single-attribute primary key named

required attribute
In ER modeling, an attribute that must have a value. In other words, it cannot be left empty.

optional attribute
In ER modeling, an attribute that does not require a value; therefore, it can be left empty.

identifiers
One or more attributes that uniquely identify each entity instance.

relational schema
The organization of a relational database as described by the database administrator.

CLASS_CODE. However, it is possible to use a **composite identifier**, a primary key composed of more than one attribute. For instance, the Tiny College database administrator may decide to identify each CLASS entity instance (occurrence) by using a composite primary key of CRS_CODE and CLASS_SECTION instead of using CLASS_CODE. Either approach uniquely identifies each entity instance. Given the structure of the CLASS table shown in Figure 4.2, CLASS_CODE is the primary key, and the combination of CRS_CODE and CLASS_SECTION is a proper candidate key. If the CLASS_CODE attribute is deleted from the CLASS entity, the candidate key (CRS_CODE and CLASS_SECTION) becomes an acceptable composite primary key.

FIGURE 4.2 THE CLASS TABLE (ENTITY) COMPONENTS AND CONTENTS

Database name: Ch04_TinyCollege

CLASS_CODE	CRS_CODE	CLASS_SECTION	CLASS_TIME	ROOM_CODE	PROF_NUM
10012	ACCT-211	1	MWF 8:00-8:50 a.m.	BUS311	105
10013	ACCT-211	2	MWF 9:00-9:50 a.m.	BUS200	105
10014	ACCT-211	3	TTh 2:30-3:45 p.m.	BUS252	342
10015	ACCT-212	1	MWF 10:00-10:50 a.m.	BUS311	301
10016	ACCT-212	2	Th 6:00-8:40 p.m.	BUS252	301
10017	CIS-220	1	MWF 9:00-9:50 a.m.	KLR209	228
10018	CIS-220	2	MWF 9:00-9:50 a.m.	KLR211	114
10019	CIS-220	3	MWF 10:00-10:50 a.m.	KLR209	228
10020	CIS-420	1	W 6:00-8:40 p.m.	KLR209	162
10021	QM-261	1	MWF 8:00-8:50 a.m.	KLR200	114
10022	QM-261	2	TTh 1:00-2:15 p.m.	KLR200	114
10023	QM-362	1	MWF 11:00-11:50 a.m.	KLR200	162
10024	QM-362	2	TTh 2:30-3:45 p.m.	KLR200	162
10025	MATH-243	1	Th 6:00-8:40 p.m.	DRE155	325

Note

Remember that Chapter 3 made a commonly accepted distinction between COURSE and CLASS. A CLASS constitutes a specific time and place of a COURSE offering. A class is defined by the course description and its time and place, or section. Consider a professor who teaches Database I, Section 2; Database I, Section 5; Database I, Section 8; and Spreadsheet II, Section 6. The professor teaches two courses (Database I and Spreadsheet II), but four classes. Typically, the COURSE offerings are printed in a course catalog, while the CLASS offerings are printed in a class schedule for each term.

composite identifier
In ER modeling, a key composed of more than one attribute.

composite attribute
An attribute that can be further subdivided to yield additional attributes. For example, a phone number such as 615-898-2368 may be divided into an area code (615), an exchange number (898), and a four-digit code (2368). Compare to *simple attribute*.

If the CLASS_CODE in Figure 4.2 is used as the primary key, the CLASS entity may be represented in shorthand form as follows:

CLASS (**CLASS_CODE**, CRS_CODE, CLASS_SECTION, CLASS_TIME, ROOM_CODE, PROF_NUM)

On the other hand, if CLASS_CODE is deleted, and the composite primary key is the combination of CRS_CODE and CLASS_SECTION, the CLASS entity may be represented as follows:

CLASS (**CRS_CODE**, **CLASS_SECTION**, CLASS_TIME, ROOM_CODE, PROF_NUM)

Note that *both* key attributes are underlined in the entity notation.

Composite and Simple Attributes Attributes are classified as simple or composite. A **composite attribute**, not to be confused with a composite key, is an attribute that can be further subdivided to yield additional attributes. For example, the attribute ADDRESS can be subdivided into street, city, state, and zip code. Similarly, the attribute PHONE_ NUMBER can be subdivided into area code and exchange number. A **simple attribute** is an attribute that cannot be subdivided. For example, age, sex, and marital status would be classified as simple attributes. To facilitate detailed queries, it is wise to change composite attributes into a series of simple attributes.

The database designer must always be on the lookout for composite attributes. It is common for business rules to use composite attributes to simplify policies, and users often describe entities in their environment using composite attributes. For example, a user at Tiny College might need to know a student's name, address, and phone number. The designer must recognize that these are composite attributes and determine the correct way to decompose the composite into simple attributes.

Single-Valued Attributes A **single-valued attribute** is an attribute that can have only a single value. For example, a person can have only one Social Security number, and a manufactured part can have only one serial number. *Keep in mind that a single-valued attribute is not necessarily a simple attribute.* For instance, a part's serial number (such as SE-08-02-189935) is single-valued, but it is a composite attribute because it can be subdivided into the region in which the part was produced (SE), the plant within that region (08), the shift within the plant (02), and the part number (189935).

Multivalued Attributes **Multivalued attributes** are attributes that can have many values. For instance, a person may have several college degrees, and a household may have several different phones, each with its own number. Similarly, a car's color may be subdivided into many colors for the roof, body, and trim. In the Chen ERM, multivalued attributes are shown by a double line connecting the attribute to the entity. The Crow's Foot notation does not identify multivalued attributes. The ERD in Figure 4.3 contains all of the components introduced thus far; note that CAR_VIN is the primary key, and CAR_COLOR is a multivalued attribute of the CAR entity.

> **simple attribute**
> An attribute that cannot be subdivided into meaningful components. Compare to *composite attribute*.
>
> **single-valued attribute**
> An attribute that can have only one value.
>
> **multivalued attribute**
> An attribute that can have many values for a single entity occurrence. For example, an EMP_ DEGREE attribute might store the string "BBA, MBA, PHD" to indicate three different degrees held.

FIGURE 4.3 A MULTIVALUED ATTRIBUTE IN AN ENTITY

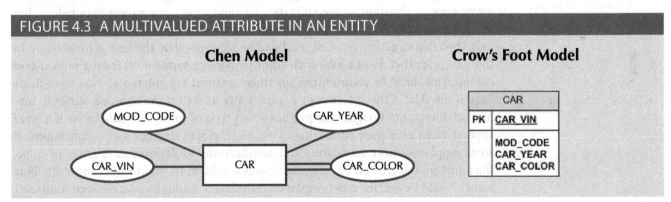

Note

In the ERD models in Figure 4.3, the CAR entity's foreign key (FK) has been typed as MOD_ CODE. This attribute was manually added to the entity. Actually, proper use of database modeling software will automatically produce the FK when the relationship is defined. In addition, the software will label the FK appropriately and write the FK's implementation details in a data dictionary. Therefore, when you use professional database modeling software, *never type the FK attribute yourself*; let the software handle that task when the relationship between the entities is defined. (You can see how this works in Appendix A, Designing Databases with Visio Professional: A Tutorial, at *www.cengagebrain.com*.)

Implementing Multivalued Attributes Although the conceptual model can handle M:N relationships and multivalued attributes, *you should not implement them in the RDBMS*. Remember from Chapter 3 that in the relational table, each column and row intersection represents a single data value. So, if multivalued attributes exist, the designer must decide on one of two possible courses of action:

1. Within the original entity, create several new attributes, one for each component of the original multivalued attribute. For example, the CAR entity's attribute CAR_COLOR can be split to create the new attributes CAR_TOPCOLOR, CAR_BODY-COLOR, and CAR_TRIMCOLOR, which are then assigned to the CAR entity. (See Figure 4.4.)

FIGURE 4.4 SPLITTING THE MULTIVALUED ATTRIBUTE INTO NEW ATTRIBUTES

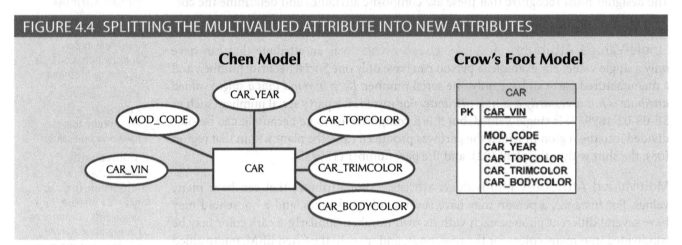

Although this solution seems to work, its adoption can lead to major structural problems in the table. It is only acceptable if every instance will have the same number of values for the multivalued attribute, and no instance will ever have more values. However, even in this case, it is a gamble that new changes in the environment will never create a situation where an instance would have more values than before. For example, if additional color components—such as a logo color—are added for some cars, the table structure must be modified to accommodate the new color section. In that case, cars that do not have such color sections generate nulls for the nonexistent components, or their color entries for those sections are entered as N/A to indicate "not applicable." (The solution in Figure 4.4 is to split a multivalued attribute into new attributes, but imagine the problems this type of solution would cause if it were applied to an employee entity that contains employee degrees and certifications. If some employees have 10 degrees and certifications while most have fewer or none, the number of degree/certification attributes would be 10, and most of those attribute values would be null for most employees.) In short, although you have seen solution 1 applied, it is not always acceptable.

2. Create a new entity composed of the original multivalued attribute's components. This new entity allows the designer to define color for different sections of the car. (See Table 4.1.) Then, this new CAR_COLOR entity is related to the original CAR entity in a 1:M relationship.

Using the approach illustrated in Table 4.1, you even get a fringe benefit: you can now assign as many colors as necessary without having to change the table structure. The ERM shown in Figure 4.5 reflects the components listed in Table 4.1. This is the preferred way to deal with multivalued attributes. Creating a new entity in a 1:M relationship with the original entity yields several benefits: it is a more flexible, expandable solution, and it is compatible with the relational model!

TABLE 4.1

COMPONENTS OF THE MULTIVALUED ATTRIBUTE

SECTION	COLOR
Top	White
Body	Blue
Trim	Gold
Interior	Blue

FIGURE 4.5 A NEW ENTITY SET COMPOSED OF A MULTIVALUED ATTRIBUTE'S COMPONENTS

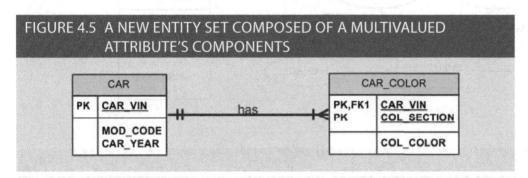

Note

If you are used to looking at relational diagrams such as the ones produced by Microsoft Access, you expect to see the relationship line *in the relational diagram* drawn from the PK to the FK. However, the relational diagram convention is not necessarily reflected in the ERD. In an ERD, the focus is on the entities and the relationships between them, rather than how those relationships are anchored graphically. In a complex ERD that includes both horizontally and vertically placed entities, the placement of the relationship lines is largely dictated by the designer's decision to improve the readability of the design. (Remember that the ERD is used for communication between designers and end users.)

Derived Attributes Finally, a **derived attribute** is an attribute whose value is calculated (derived) from other attributes. The derived attribute need not be physically stored within the database; instead, it can be derived by using an algorithm. For example, an employee's age, EMP_AGE, may be found by computing the integer value of the difference between the current date and the EMP_DOB. If you use Microsoft Access, you would use the formula INT((DATE() – EMP_DOB)/365). In Microsoft SQL Server, you would use SELECT DATEDIFF("YEAR", EMP_DOB, GETDATE()), where DATEDIFF is a function that computes the difference between dates. The first parameter indicates the measurement (in this case, years). If you use Oracle, you would use SYSDATE instead of DATE(). (You are assuming, of course, that EMP_DOB was stored in the Julian date format.)

Similarly, the total cost of an order can be derived by multiplying the quantity ordered by the unit price. Or, the estimated average speed can be derived by dividing trip distance by the time spent en route. A derived attribute is indicated in the Chen notation by a dashed line that connects the attribute and the entity. (See Figure 4.6.) The Crow's Foot notation does not have a method for distinguishing the derived attribute from other attributes.

Derived attributes are sometimes referred to as *computed attributes*. Computing a derived attribute can be as simple as adding two attribute values located on the same row, or it can be the result of aggregating the sum of values located on many table rows (from the same table or from a different table). The decision to store derived attributes in

derived attribute
An attribute that does not physically exist within the entity and is derived via an algorithm. For example, the Age attribute might be derived by subtracting the birth date from the current date.

database tables depends on the processing requirements and the constraints placed on a particular application. The designer should be able to balance the design in accordance with such constraints. Table 4.2 shows the advantages and disadvantages of storing (or not storing) derived attributes in the database.

FIGURE 4.6 DEPICTION OF A DERIVED ATTRIBUTE

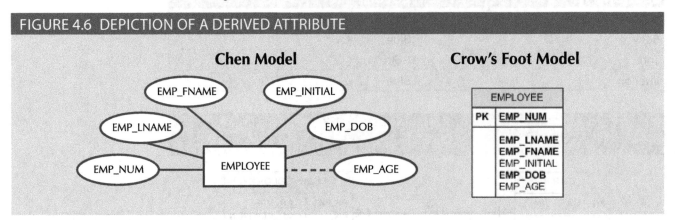

TABLE 4.2

ADVANTAGES AND DISADVANTAGES OF STORING DERIVED ATTRIBUTES

	DERIVED ATTRIBUTE	
	STORED	NOT STORED
Advantage	Saves CPU processing cycles Saves data access time Data value is readily available Can be used to keep track of historical data	Saves storage space Computation always yields current value
Disadvantage	Requires constant maintenance to ensure derived value is current, especially if any values used in the calculation change	Uses CPU processing cycles Increases data access time Adds coding complexity to queries

4-1c Relationships

Recall from Chapter 2 that a relationship is an association between entities. The entities that participate in a relationship are also known as **participants**, and each relationship is identified by a name that describes the relationship. The relationship name is an active or passive verb; for example, a STUDENT *takes* a CLASS, a PROFESSOR *teaches* a CLASS, a DEPARTMENT *employs* a PROFESSOR, a DIVISION *is managed by* an EMPLOYEE, and an AIRCRAFT *is flown by* a CREW.

Relationships between entities always operate in both directions. To define the relationship between the entities named CUSTOMER and INVOICE, you would specify that:

- A CUSTOMER may generate many INVOICEs.

- Each INVOICE is generated by one CUSTOMER.

Because you know both directions of the relationship between CUSTOMER and INVOICE, it is easy to see that this relationship can be classified as 1:M.

The relationship classification is difficult to establish if you know only one side of the relationship. For example, if you specify that:

A DIVISION is managed by one EMPLOYEE.

participants
An ER term for entities that participate in a relationship. For example, in the relationship "PROFESSOR teaches CLASS," the *teaches* relationship is based on the participants PROFESSOR and CLASS.

You don't know if the relationship is 1:1 or 1:M. Therefore, you should ask the question "Can an employee manage more than one division?" If the answer is yes, the relationship is 1:M, and the second part of the relationship is then written as:

An EMPLOYEE may manage many DIVISIONs.

If an employee cannot manage more than one division, the relationship is 1:1, and the second part of the relationship is then written as:

An EMPLOYEE may manage only one DIVISION.

4-1d Connectivity and Cardinality

You learned in Chapter 2 that entity relationships may be classified as one-to-one, one-to-many, or many-to-many. You also learned how such relationships were depicted in the Chen and Crow's Foot notations. The term **connectivity** is used to describe the relationship classification.

Cardinality expresses the minimum and maximum number of entity occurrences associated with one occurrence of the related entity. In the ERD, cardinality is indicated by placing the appropriate numbers beside the entities, using the format (x,y). The first value represents the minimum number of associated entities, while the second value represents the maximum number of associated entities. Many database designers who use Crow's Foot modeling notation do not depict the specific cardinalities on the ER diagram itself because the specific limits described by the cardinalities cannot be implemented directly through the database design. Correspondingly, some Crow's Foot ER modeling tools do not print the numeric cardinality range in the diagram; instead, you can add it as text if you want to have it shown. When the specific cardinalities are not included on the diagram in Crow's Foot notation, cardinality is implied by the use of the symbols shown in Figure 4.7, which describe the connectivity and participation (discussed next). The numeric cardinality range has been added using the Microsoft Visio text drawing tool.

FIGURE 4.7 CONNECTIVITY AND CARDINALITY IN AN ERD

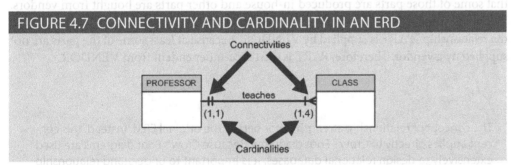

Knowing the minimum and maximum number of entity occurrences is very useful at the application software level. For example, Tiny College might want to ensure that a class is not taught unless it has at least 10 students enrolled. Similarly, if the classroom can hold only 30 students, the application software should use that cardinality to limit enrollment in the class. However, keep in mind that the DBMS cannot handle the implementation of the cardinalities at the table level—that capability is provided by the application software or by triggers. You will learn how to create and execute triggers in Chapter 8, Advanced SQL.

As you examine the Crow's Foot diagram in Figure 4.7, keep in mind that the cardinalities represent the number of occurrences in the *related* entity. For example, the cardinality (1,4) next to the CLASS entity in the "PROFESSOR teaches CLASS" relationship indicates that each professor teaches up to four classes, which means that the PROFESSOR table's primary key value occurs at least once and no more than four times as foreign key values in the CLASS table. If the cardinality had been written as (1,N), there would be no upper limit to the number of classes a professor might teach. Similarly, the cardinality (1,1) next to the PROFESSOR entity indicates that each class is taught by one and only one professor. That is, each CLASS entity occurrence is associated with one and only one entity occurrence in PROFESSOR.

connectivity
The classification of the relationship between entities. Classifications include 1:1, 1:M, and M:N.

cardinality
A property that assigns a specific value to connectivity and expresses the range of allowed entity occurrences associated with a single occurrence of the related entity.

Connectivities and cardinalities are established by concise statements known as business rules, which were introduced in Chapter 2. Such rules, derived from a precise and detailed description of an organization's data environment, also establish the ERM's entities, attributes, relationships, connectivities, cardinalities, and constraints. Because business rules define the ERM's components, making sure that all appropriate business rules are identified is an important part of a database designer's job.

Note

The placement of the cardinalities in the ER diagram is a matter of convention. The Chen notation places the cardinalities on the side of the related entity. The Crow's Foot and UML diagrams place the cardinalities next to the entity to which they apply.

Online Content

Because the careful definition of complete and accurate business rules is crucial to good database design, their derivation is examined in detail in Appendix B, The University Lab: Conceptual Design. The modeling skills you are learning in this chapter are applied in the development of a real database design in Appendix B. The initial design shown in Appendix B is then modified in Appendix C, The University Lab: Conceptual Design Verification, Logical Design, and Implementation. (Both appendixes are available at *www.cengagebrain.com*.)

existence-dependent
A property of an entity whose existence depends on one or more other entities. In such an environment, the existence-independent table must be created and loaded first because the existence-dependent key cannot reference a table that does not yet exist.

4-1e Existence Dependence

An entity is said to be **existence-dependent** if it can exist in the database only when it is associated with another related entity occurrence. In implementation terms, an entity is existence-dependent if it has a mandatory foreign key—that is, a foreign key attribute that cannot be null. For example, if an employee wants to claim one or more dependents for tax-withholding purposes, the relationship "EMPLOYEE claims DEPENDENT" would be appropriate. In that case, the DEPENDENT entity is clearly existence-dependent on the EMPLOYEE entity because it is impossible for the dependent to exist apart from the EMPLOYEE in the database.

If an entity can exist apart from all of its related entities, then it is **existence-independent**, and it is referred to as a **strong entity** or **regular entity**. For example, suppose that the XYZ Corporation uses parts to produce its products. Furthermore, suppose that some of those parts are produced in-house and other parts are bought from vendors. In that scenario, it is quite possible for a PART to exist independently from a VENDOR in the relationship "PART is supplied by VENDOR" because at least some of the parts are not supplied by a vendor. Therefore, PART is existence-independent from VENDOR.

Note

The concept of relationship strength is not part of the original ERM. Instead, this concept applies directly to Crow's Foot diagrams. Because Crow's Foot diagrams are used extensively to design relational databases, it is important to understand relationship strength as it affects database implementation. The Chen ERD notation is oriented toward conceptual modeling and therefore does not distinguish between weak and strong relationships.

4-1f Relationship Strength

The concept of relationship strength is based on how the primary key of a related entity is defined. To implement a relationship, the primary key of one entity (the parent entity, normally on the "one" side of the one-to-many relationship) appears as a foreign key in the related entity (the child entity, mostly the entity on the "many" side of the one-to-many relationship). Sometimes the foreign key also is a primary key component in the related entity. For example, in Figure 4.5, the CAR entity primary key (CAR_VIN) appears as both a primary key component and a foreign key in the CAR_COLOR entity. In this section, you will learn how various relationship strength decisions affect primary key arrangement in database design.

Weak (Non-Identifying) Relationships A **weak relationship**, also known as a **non-identifying relationship**, exists if the primary key of the related entity does not contain a primary key component of the parent entity. By default, relationships are established by having the primary key of the parent entity appear as a foreign key (FK) on the related entity (also known as the child entity). For example, suppose the 1:M relationship between COURSE and CLASS is defined as:

COURSE (**CRS_CODE**, DEPT_CODE, CRS_DESCRIPTION, CRS_CREDIT)

CLASS (**CLASS_CODE**, CRS_CODE, CLASS_SECTION, CLASS_TIME, ROOM_CODE, PROF_NUM)

In this case, a weak relationship exists between COURSE and CLASS because CRS_CODE (the primary key of the parent entity) is only a foreign key in the CLASS entity. In this example, the CLASS primary key did not inherit a primary key component from the COURSE entity.

Figure 4.8 shows how the Crow's Foot notation depicts a weak relationship by placing a dashed relationship line between the entities. The tables shown below the ERD illustrate how such a relationship is implemented.

FIGURE 4.8   A WEAK (NON-IDENTIFYING) RELATIONSHIP BETWEEN COURSE AND CLASS

Table name: COURSE   **Database name: Ch04_TinyCollege**

CRS_CODE	DEPT_CODE	CRS_DESCRIPTION	CRS_CREDIT
ACCT-211	ACCT	Accounting I	3
ACCT-212	ACCT	Accounting II	3
CIS-220	CIS	Intro. to Microcomputing	3
CIS-420	CIS	Database Design and Implementation	4
MATH-243	MATH	Mathematics for Managers	3
QM-261	CIS	Intro. to Statistics	3
QM-362	CIS	Statistical Applications	4

Table name: CLASS

CLASS_CODE	CRS_CODE	CLASS_SECTION	CLASS_TIME	ROOM_CODE	PROF_NUM
10012	ACCT-211	1	MWF 8:00-8:50 a.m.	BUS311	105
10013	ACCT-211	2	MWF 9:00-9:50 a.m.	BUS200	105
10014	ACCT-211	3	TTh 2:30-3:45 p.m.	BUS252	342
10015	ACCT-212	1	MWF 10:00-10:50 a.m.	BUS311	301
10016	ACCT-212	2	Th 6:00-8:40 p.m.	BUS252	301
10017	CIS-220	1	MWF 9:00-9:50 a.m.	KLR209	228
10018	CIS-220	2	MWF 9:00-9:50 a.m.	KLR211	114
10019	CIS-220	3	MWF 10:00-10:50 a.m.	KLR209	228
10020	CIS-420	1	W 6:00-8:40 p.m.	KLR209	162
10021	QM-261	1	MWF 8:00-8:50 a.m.	KLR200	114
10022	QM-261	2	TTh 1:00-2:15 p.m.	KLR200	114
10023	QM-362	1	MWF 11:00-11:50 a.m.	KLR200	162
10024	QM-362	2	TTh 2:30-3:45 p.m.	KLR200	162
10025	MATH-243	1	Th 6:00-8:40 p.m.	DRE155	325

existence-independent
A property of an entity that can exist apart from one or more related entities. Such a table must be created first when referencing an existence-dependent table.

strong entity
An entity that is existence-independent, that is, it can exist apart from all of its related entities. Also called a *regular entity*.

regular entity
See *strong entity*.

weak (non-identifying) relationship
A relationship in which the primary key of the related entity does not contain a primary key component of the parent entity.

Strong (Identifying) Relationships A **strong (identifying) relationship** exists when the primary key of the related entity contains a primary key component of the parent entity. For example, suppose the 1:M relationship between COURSE and CLASS is defined as:

COURSE (**CRS_CODE**, DEPT_CODE, CRS_DESCRIPTION, CRS_CREDIT)

CLASS (**CRS_CODE, CLASS_SECTION**, CLASS_TIME, ROOM_CODE, PROF_NUM)

In this case, the CLASS entity primary key is composed of CRS_CODE and CLASS_SECTION. Therefore, a strong relationship exists between COURSE and CLASS because CRS_CODE (the primary key of the parent entity) is a primary key component in the CLASS entity. In other words, the CLASS primary key did inherit a primary key component from the COURSE entity. (Note that the CRS_CODE in CLASS is *also* the FK to the COURSE entity.)

The Crow's Foot notation depicts the strong (identifying) relationship with a solid line between the entities, as shown in Figure 4.9.

FIGURE 4.9 A STRONG (IDENTIFYING) RELATIONSHIP BETWEEN COURSE AND CLASS

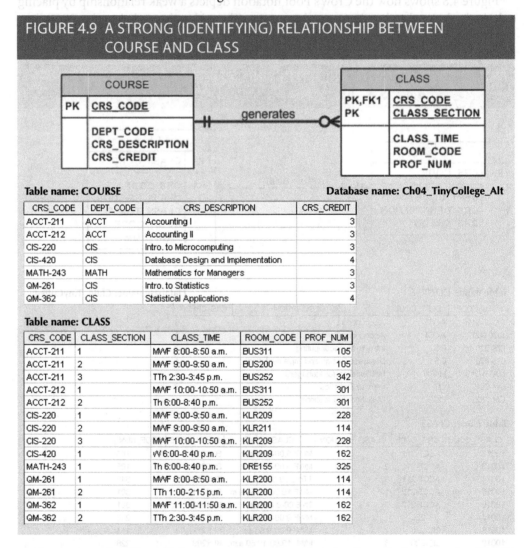

Table name: COURSE   **Database name: Ch04_TinyCollege_Alt**

CRS_CODE	DEPT_CODE	CRS_DESCRIPTION	CRS_CREDIT
ACCT-211	ACCT	Accounting I	3
ACCT-212	ACCT	Accounting II	3
CIS-220	CIS	Intro. to Microcomputing	3
CIS-420	CIS	Database Design and Implementation	4
MATH-243	MATH	Mathematics for Managers	3
QM-261	CIS	Intro. to Statistics	3
QM-362	CIS	Statistical Applications	4

Table name: CLASS

CRS_CODE	CLASS_SECTION	CLASS_TIME	ROOM_CODE	PROF_NUM
ACCT-211	1	MWF 8:00-8:50 a.m.	BUS311	105
ACCT-211	2	MWF 9:00-9:50 a.m.	BUS200	105
ACCT-211	3	TTh 2:30-3:45 p.m.	BUS252	342
ACCT-212	1	MWF 10:00-10:50 a.m.	BUS311	301
ACCT-212	2	Th 6:00-8:40 p.m.	BUS252	301
CIS-220	1	MWF 9:00-9:50 a.m.	KLR209	228
CIS-220	2	MWF 9:00-9:50 a.m.	KLR211	114
CIS-220	3	MWF 10:00-10:50 a.m.	KLR209	228
CIS-420	1	W 6:00-8:40 p.m.	KLR209	162
MATH-243	1	Th 6:00-8:40 p.m.	DRE155	325
QM-261	1	MWF 8:00-8:50 a.m.	KLR200	114
QM-261	2	TTh 1:00-2:15 p.m.	KLR200	114
QM-362	1	MWF 11:00-11:50 a.m.	KLR200	162
QM-362	2	TTh 2:30-3:45 p.m.	KLR200	162

strong (identifying) relationship
A relationship that occurs when two entities are existence-dependent; from a database design perspective, this relationship exists whenever the primary key of the related entity contains the primary key of the parent entity.

As you examine Figure 4.9, you might wonder what the O symbol next to the CLASS entity signifies. You will discover the meaning of this cardinality in Section 4-1h, Relationship Participation.

In summary, whether the relationship between COURSE and CLASS is strong or weak depends on how the CLASS entity's primary key is defined. Remember that the nature of the relationship is often determined by the database designer, who must use professional

Note

Keep in mind that the *order in which the tables are created and loaded is very important.* For example, in the "COURSE generates CLASS" relationship, the COURSE table must be created before the CLASS table. After all, it would not be acceptable to have the CLASS table's foreign key refer to a COURSE table that did not yet exist. In fact, *you must load the data of the "1" side first in a 1:M relationship to avoid the possibility of referential integrity errors*, regardless of whether the relationships are weak or strong.

judgment to determine which relationship type and strength best suit the database transaction, efficiency, and information requirements. That point will be emphasized in detail!

4-1g Weak Entities

In contrast to the strong or regular entity mentioned in Section 4-1f, a **weak entity** is one that meets two conditions:

1. The entity is existence-dependent; it cannot exist without the entity with which it has a relationship.

2. The entity has a primary key that is partially or totally derived from the parent entity in the relationship.

For example, a company insurance policy insures an employee and any dependents. For the purpose of describing an insurance policy, an EMPLOYEE might or might not have a DEPENDENT, but the DEPENDENT must be associated with an EMPLOYEE. Moreover, the DEPENDENT cannot exist without the EMPLOYEE; that is, a person cannot get insurance coverage as a dependent unless the person is a dependent of an employee. DEPENDENT is the weak entity in the relationship "EMPLOYEE has DEPENDENT." This relationship is shown in Figure 4.10.

FIGURE 4.10 A WEAK ENTITY IN AN ERD

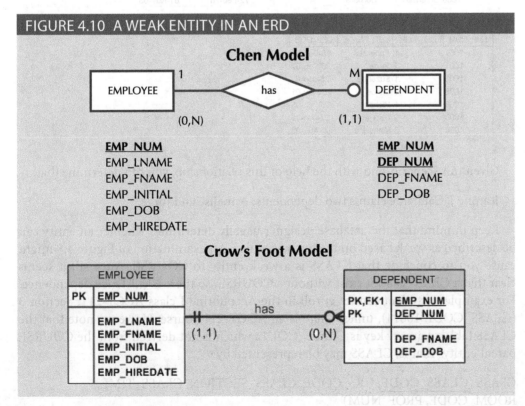

weak entity
An entity that displays existence dependence and inherits the primary key of its parent entity. For example, a DEPENDENT requires the existence of an EMPLOYEE.

Note that the Chen notation in Figure 4.10 identifies the weak entity by using a double-walled entity rectangle. The Crow's Foot notation generated by Visio Professional uses the relationship line and the PK/FK designation to indicate whether the related entity is weak. A strong (identifying) relationship indicates that the related entity is weak. Such a relationship means that both conditions have been met for the weak entity definition—the related entity is existence-dependent, and the PK of the related entity contains a PK component of the parent entity.

Remember that the weak entity inherits part of its primary key from its strong counterpart. For example, at least part of the DEPENDENT entity's key shown in Figure 4.10 was inherited from the EMPLOYEE entity:

EMPLOYEE (**EMP_NUM**, EMP_LNAME, EMP_FNAME, EMP_INITIAL, EMP_DOB, EMP_HIREDATE)

DEPENDENT (**EMP_NUM, DEP_NUM**, DEP_FNAME, DEP_DOB)

Figure 4.11 illustrates the implementation of the relationship between the weak entity (DEPENDENT) and its parent or strong counterpart (EMPLOYEE). Note that DEPENDENT's primary key is composed of two attributes, EMP_NUM and DEP_NUM, and that EMP_NUM was inherited from EMPLOYEE.

FIGURE 4.11 A WEAK ENTITY IN A STRONG RELATIONSHIP

Table name: EMPLOYEE   Database name: Ch04_ShortCo

EMP_NUM	EMP_LNAME	EMP_FNAME	EMP_INITIAL	EMP_DOB	EMP_HIREDATE
1001	Callifante	Jeanine	J	12-Mar-64	25-May-97
1002	Smithson	William	K	23-Nov-70	28-May-97
1003	Washington	Herman	H	15-Aug-68	28-May-97
1004	Chen	Lydia	B	23-Mar-74	15-Oct-98
1005	Johnson	Melanie		28-Sep-66	20-Dec-98
1006	Ortega	Jorge	G	12-Jul-79	05-Jan-02
1007	O'Donnell	Peter	D	10-Jun-71	23-Jun-02
1008	Brzenski	Barbara	A	12-Feb-70	01-Nov-03

Table name: DEPENDENT

EMP_NUM	DEP_NUM	DEP_FNAME	DEP_DOB
1001	1	Annelise	05-Dec-97
1001	2	Jorge	30-Sep-02
1003	1	Suzanne	25-Jan-04
1006	1	Carlos	25-May-01
1008	1	Michael	19-Feb-95
1008	2	George	27-Jun-98
1008	3	Katherine	18-Aug-03

Given this scenario, and with the help of this relationship, you can determine that:

Jeanine J. Callifante claims two dependents, Annelise and Jorge.

Keep in mind that the database designer usually determines whether an entity can be described as weak based on the business rules. An examination of Figure 4.8 might cause you to conclude that CLASS is a weak entity to COURSE. After all, it seems clear that a CLASS cannot exist without a COURSE, so there is existence dependence. For example, a student cannot enroll in the Accounting I class ACCT-211, Section 3 (CLASS_CODE 10014), unless there is an ACCT-211 course. However, note that the CLASS table's primary key is CLASS_CODE, which is not derived from the COURSE parent entity. That is, CLASS may be represented by:

CLASS (**CLASS_CODE**, CRS_CODE, CLASS_SECTION, CLASS_TIME, ROOM_CODE, PROF_NUM)

The second weak entity requirement has not been met; therefore, by definition, the CLASS entity in Figure 4.8 may not be classified as weak. On the other hand, if the CLASS entity's primary key had been defined as a composite key composed of the combination CRS_CODE and CLASS_SECTION, CLASS could be represented by:

CLASS (**CRS_CODE**, **CLASS_SECTION**, CLASS_TIME, ROOM_CODE, PROF_NUM)

In that case, as illustrated in Figure 4.9, the CLASS primary key is partially derived from COURSE because CRS_CODE is the COURSE table's primary key. Given this decision, CLASS is a weak entity by definition. (In Visio Professional Crow's Foot terms, the relationship between COURSE and CLASS is classified as strong, or identifying.) In any case, CLASS is always existence-dependent on COURSE, *whether or not it is defined as weak.*

4-1h Relationship Participation

Participation in an entity relationship is either optional or mandatory. Recall that relationships are bidirectional; that is, they operate in both directions. If COURSE is related to CLASS, then by definition, CLASS is related to COURSE. Because of the bidirectional nature of relationships, it is necessary to determine the connectivity of the relationship from COURSE to CLASS and the connectivity of the relationship from CLASS to COURSE. Similarly, the specific maximum and minimum cardinalities must be determined in each direction for the relationship. Once again, you must consider the bidirectional nature of the relationship when determining participation.

Optional participation means that one entity occurrence does not *require* a corresponding entity occurrence in a particular relationship. For example, in the "COURSE generates CLASS" relationship, you noted that at least some courses do not generate a class. In other words, an entity occurrence (row) in the COURSE table does not necessarily require the existence of a corresponding entity occurrence in the CLASS table. (Remember that each entity is implemented as a table.) Therefore, the CLASS entity is considered to be *optional* to the COURSE entity. In Crow's Foot notation, an optional relationship between entities is shown by drawing a small circle (O) on the side of the optional entity, as illustrated in Figure 4.9. The existence of an *optional entity* indicates that its minimum cardinality is 0. (The term *optionality* is used to label any condition in which one or more optional relationships exist.)

Note

Remember that the burden of establishing the relationship is always placed on the entity that contains the foreign key. In most cases, that entity is on the "many" side of the relationship.

Mandatory participation means that one entity occurrence *requires* a corresponding entity occurrence in a particular relationship. If no optionality symbol is depicted with the entity, the entity is assumed to exist in a mandatory relationship with the related entity. If the mandatory participation is depicted graphically, it is typically shown as a small hash mark across the relationship line, similar to the Crow's Foot depiction of a connectivity of 1. The existence of a mandatory relationship indicates that the minimum cardinality is at least 1 for the mandatory entity.

optional participation
In ER modeling, a condition in which one entity occurrence does not require a corresponding entity occurrence in a particular relationship.

mandatory participation
A relationship in which one entity occurrence must have a corresponding occurrence in another entity. For example, an EMPLOYEE works in a DIVISION. (A person cannot be an employee without being assigned to a company's division.)

Note

You might be tempted to conclude that relationships are weak when they occur between entities in an optional relationship and that relationships are strong when they occur between entities in a mandatory relationship. However, this conclusion is not warranted. Keep in mind that relationship participation and relationship strength do not describe the same thing. You are likely to encounter a strong relationship when one entity is optional to another. For example, the relationship between EMPLOYEE and DEPENDENT is clearly a strong one, but DEPENDENT is clearly optional to EMPLOYEE. After all, you cannot require employees to have dependents. Also, it is just as possible for a weak relationship to be established when one entity is mandatory to another. The relationship strength depends on how the PK of the related entity is formulated, while the relationship participation depends on how the business rule is written. For example, the business rules "Each part must be supplied by a vendor" and "A part may or may not be supplied by a vendor" create different optionalities for the same entities! Failure to understand this distinction may lead to poor design decisions that cause major problems when table rows are inserted or deleted.

When you create a relationship in Microsoft Visio, the default relationship will be mandatory on the "1" side and optional on the "many" side. Table 4.3 shows the various connectivity and participation combinations that are supported by the Crow's Foot notation. Recall that these combinations are often referred to as cardinality in Crow's Foot notation when specific cardinalities are not used.

TABLE 4.3

CROW'S FOOT SYMBOLS

SYMBOL	CARDINALITY	COMMENT
O⪤	(0,N)	Zero or many; the "many" side is optional.
I⪤	(1,N)	One or many; the "many" side is mandatory.
II	(1,1)	One and only one; the "1" side is mandatory.
OI	(0,1)	Zero or one; the "1" side is optional.

Because relationship participation is an important component of database design, you should examine a few more scenarios. Suppose that Tiny College employs some professors who conduct research without teaching classes. If you examine the "PROFESSOR teaches CLASS" relationship, it is quite possible for a PROFESSOR not to teach a CLASS. Therefore, CLASS is *optional* to PROFESSOR. On the other hand, a CLASS must be taught by a PROFESSOR. Therefore, PROFESSOR is *mandatory* to CLASS. Note that the ERD model in Figure 4.12 shows the cardinality next to CLASS to be (0,3), indicating that a professor may teach no classes or as many as three classes. Also, each CLASS table row references one and only one PROFESSOR row—assuming each class is taught by one and only one professor—represented by the (1,1) cardinality next to the PROFESSOR table.

FIGURE 4.12 AN OPTIONAL CLASS ENTITY IN THE RELATIONSHIP "PROFESSOR TEACHES CLASS"

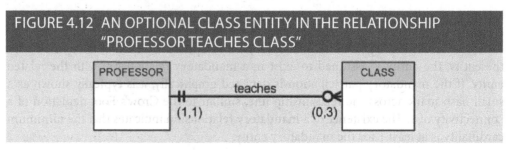

It is important that you clearly understand the distinction between mandatory and optional participation in relationships. Otherwise, you might develop designs in which awkward and unnecessary temporary rows (entity instances) must be created just to accommodate the creation of required entities.

It is also important to understand that the semantics of a problem might determine the type of participation in a relationship. For example, suppose that Tiny College offers several courses; each course has several classes. Note again the distinction between *class* and *course* in this discussion: a CLASS constitutes a specific offering (or section) of a COURSE. Typically, courses are listed in the university's course catalog, while classes are listed in the class schedules that students use to register for their classes.

By analyzing the CLASS entity's contribution to the "COURSE generates CLASS" relationship, it is easy to see that a CLASS cannot exist without a COURSE. Therefore, you can conclude that the COURSE entity is *mandatory* in the relationship. However, two scenarios for the CLASS entity may be written, as shown in Figures 4.13 and 4.14.

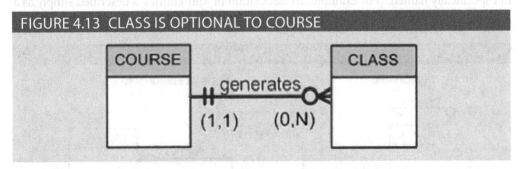

FIGURE 4.13 CLASS IS OPTIONAL TO COURSE

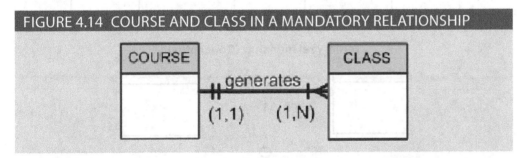

FIGURE 4.14 COURSE AND CLASS IN A MANDATORY RELATIONSHIP

The different scenarios are a function of the problem's semantics; that is, they depend on how the relationship is defined.

1. *CLASS is optional.* It is possible for the department to create the COURSE entity first and then create the CLASS entity after making the teaching assignments. In the real world, such a scenario is very likely; there may be courses for which sections (classes) have not yet been defined. In fact, some courses are taught only once a year and do not generate classes each semester.

2. *CLASS is mandatory.* This condition is created by the constraint imposed by the semantics of the statement "Each COURSE generates one or more CLASSes." In ER terms, each COURSE in the "generates" relationship must have at least one CLASS. Therefore, a CLASS must be created as the COURSE is created to comply with the semantics of the problem.

Keep in mind the practical aspects of the scenario presented in Figure 4.14. Given the semantics of this relationship, the system should not accept a course that is not associated with at least one class section. Is such a rigid environment desirable from an operational point of view? For example, when a new COURSE is created, the database first updates the COURSE table, thereby inserting a COURSE entity that does not yet have a CLASS associated with it.

Naturally, the apparent problem seems to be solved when CLASS entities are inserted into the corresponding CLASS table. However, because of the mandatory relationship, the system will temporarily violate the business rule constraint. For practical purposes, it would be desirable to classify the CLASS as optional to produce a more flexible design.

Finally, as you examine the scenarios in Figures 4.13 and 4.14, keep in mind the role of the DBMS. To maintain data integrity, the DBMS must ensure that the "many" side (CLASS) is associated with a COURSE through the foreign key rules.

4-1i Relationship Degree

A **relationship degree** indicates the number of entities or participants associated with a relationship. A **unary relationship** exists when an association is maintained within a single entity. A **binary relationship** exists when two entities are associated. A **ternary relationship** exists when three entities are associated. Although higher degrees exist, they are rare and are not specifically named. (For example, an association of four entities is described simply as a *four-degree relationship*.) Figure 4.15 shows these types of relationship degrees.

relationship degree
The number of entities or participants associated with a relationship. A relationship degree can be unary, binary, ternary, or higher.

unary relationship
An ER term used to describe an association *within* an entity. For example, an EMPLOYEE might manage another EMPLOYEE.

binary relationship
An ER term for an association (relationship) between two entities. For example, PROFESSOR teaches CLASS.

ternary relationship
An ER term used to describe an association (relationship) between three entities. For example, a DOCTOR prescribes a DRUG for a PATIENT.

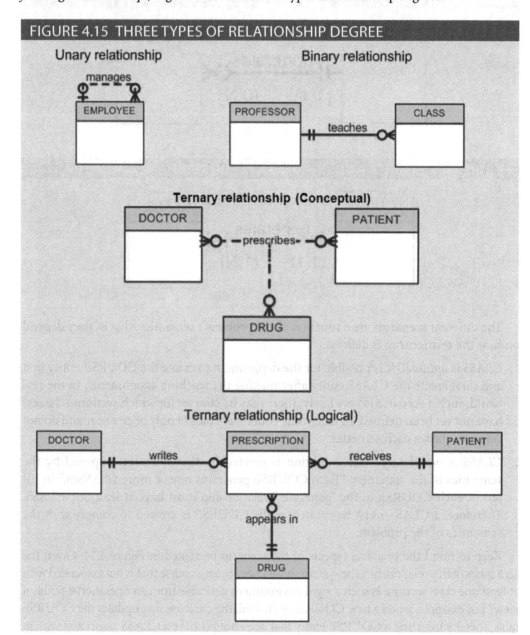

FIGURE 4.15 THREE TYPES OF RELATIONSHIP DEGREE

Unary Relationships In the case of the unary relationship shown in Figure 4.15, an employee within the EMPLOYEE entity is the manager for one or more employees within that entity. In this case, the existence of the "manages" relationship means that EMPLOYEE requires another EMPLOYEE to be the manager—that is, EMPLOYEE has a relationship with itself. Such a relationship is known as a **recursive relationship**. The various cases of recursive relationships are explained in Section 4-1j.

Binary Relationships A binary relationship exists when two entities are associated in a relationship. Binary relationships are the most common type of relationship. In fact, to simplify the conceptual design, most higher-order (ternary and higher) relationships are decomposed into appropriate equivalent binary relationships whenever possible. In Figure 4.15, "a PROFESSOR teaches one or more CLASSes" represents a binary relationship.

Ternary and Higher-Order Relationships Although most relationships are binary, the use of ternary and higher-order relationships does allow the designer some latitude regarding the semantics of a problem. A ternary relationship implies an association among three different entities. For example, in Figure 4.16, note the relationships and their consequences, which are represented by the following business rules:

- A DOCTOR writes one or more PRESCRIPTIONs.

- A PATIENT may receive one or more PRESCRIPTIONs.

- A DRUG may appear in one or more PRESCRIPTIONs. (To simplify this example, assume that the business rule states that each prescription contains only one drug. In short, if a doctor prescribes more than one drug, a separate prescription must be written for each drug.)

recursive relationship
A relationship found within a single entity type. For example, an EMPLOYEE is married to an EMPLOYEE or a PART is a component of another PART.

FIGURE 4.16 THE IMPLEMENTATION OF A TERNARY RELATIONSHIP

Database name: Ch04_Clinic

Table name: DRUG

DRUG_CODE	DRUG_NAME	DRUG_PRICE
AF15	Afgapan-15	25.00
AF25	Afgapan-25	35.00
DRO	Droalene Chloride	111.89
DRZ	Druzocholar Cryptolene	18.99
KO15	Koliabar Oxyhexalene	65.75
OLE	Oleander-Drizapan	123.95
TRYP	Tryptolac Heptadimetric	79.45

Table name: PATIENT

PAT_NUM	PAT_TITLE	PAT_LNAME	PAT_FNAME	PAT_INITIAL	PAT_DOB	PAT_AREACODE	PAT_PHONE
100	Mr.	Kolmycz	George	D	15-Jun-1942	615	324-5456
101	Ms.	Lewis	Rhonda	G	19-Mar-2005	615	324-4472
102	Mr.	Vandam	Rhett		14-Nov-1958	901	675-8993
103	Ms.	Jones	Anne	M	16-Oct-1974	615	898-3456
104	Mr.	Lange	John	P	08-Nov-1971	901	504-4430
105	Mr.	Williams	Robert	D	14-Mar-1975	615	890-3220
106	Mrs.	Smith	Jeanine	K	12-Feb-2003	615	324-7883
107	Mr.	Diante	Jorge	D	21-Aug-1974	615	890-4567
108	Mr.	Wiesenbach	Paul	R	14-Feb-1966	615	897-4358
109	Mr.	Smith	George	K	18-Jun-1961	901	504-3339
110	Mrs.	Genkazi	Leighla	W	19-May-1970	901	569-0093
111	Mr.	Washington	Rupert	E	03-Jan-1966	615	890-4925
112	Mr.	Johnson	Edward	E	14-May-1961	615	898-4387
113	Ms.	Smythe	Melanie	P	15-Sep-1970	615	324-9006
114	Ms.	Brandon	Marie	G	02-Nov-1932	901	882-0845
115	Mrs.	Saranda	Hermine	R	25-Jul-1972	615	324-5505
116	Mr.	Smith	George	A	08-Nov-1965	615	890-2984

Table name: DOCTOR

DOC_ID	DOC_LNAME	DOC_FNAME	DOC_INITIAL	DOC_SPECIALTY
29827	Sanchez	Julio	J	Dermatology
32445	Jorgensen	Annelise	G	Neurology
33456	Korenski	Anatoly	A	Urology
33989	LeGrande	George		Pediatrics
34409	Washington	Dennis	F	Orthopaedics
36221	McPherson	Katye	H	Dermatology
36712	Dreifag	Herman	G	Psychiatry
38995	Minh	Tran		Neurology
40004	Chin	Ming	D	Orthopaedics
40028	Feinstein	Denise	L	Gynecology

Table name: PRESCRIPTION

DOC_ID	PAT_NUM	DRUG_CODE	PRES_DOSAGE	PRES_DATE
32445	102	DRZ	2 tablets every four hours -- 50 tablets total	12-Nov-16
32445	113	OLE	1 teaspoon with each meal -- 250 ml total	14-Nov-16
34409	101	KO15	1 tablet every six hours -- 30 tablets total	14-Nov-16
36221	109	DRO	2 tablets with every meal -- 60 tablets total	14-Nov-16
38995	107	KO15	1 tablet every six hours -- 30 tablets total	14-Nov-16

As you examine the table contents in Figure 4.16, note that it is possible to track all transactions. For instance, you can tell that the first prescription was written by doctor 32445 for patient 102, using the drug DRZ.

4-1j Recursive Relationships

As you just learned, a *recursive relationship* is one in which a relationship can exist between occurrences of the same entity set. (Naturally, such a condition is found within a unary relationship.) For example, a 1:M unary relationship can be expressed by "an EMPLOYEE may manage many EMPLOYEEs, and each EMPLOYEE is managed by one EMPLOYEE." Also, as long as polygamy is not legal, a 1:1 unary relationship may be expressed by "an EMPLOYEE may be married to one and only one other EMPLOYEE." Finally, the M:N unary relationship may be expressed by "a COURSE may be a prerequisite to many other COURSEs, and each COURSE may have many other COURSEs as prerequisites." Those relationships are shown in Figure 4.17.

FIGURE 4.17 AN ER REPRESENTATION OF RECURSIVE RELATIONSHIPS

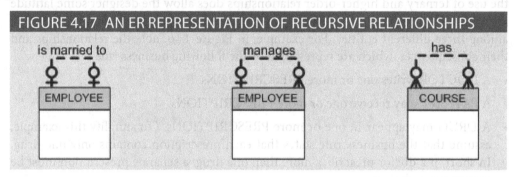

The 1:1 relationship shown in Figure 4.17 can be implemented in the single table shown in Figure 4.18. Note that you can determine that James Ramirez is married to Louise Ramirez, who is married to James Ramirez. Also, Anne Jones is married to Anton Shapiro, who is married to Anne Jones.

FIGURE 4.18 THE 1:1 RECURSIVE RELATIONSHIP "EMPLOYEE IS MARRIED TO EMPLOYEE"

Database name: Ch04_PartCo
Table name: EMPLOYEE_V1

EMP_NUM	EMP_LNAME	EMP_FNAME	EMP_SPOUSE
345	Ramirez	James	347
346	Jones	Anne	349
347	Ramirez	Louise	345
348	Delaney	Robert	
349	Shapiro	Anton	346

Unary relationships are common in manufacturing industries. For example, Figure 4.19 illustrates that a rotor assembly (C-130) is composed of many parts, but each part is used to create only one rotor assembly. Figure 4.19 indicates that a rotor assembly is composed of four 2.5-cm washers, two cotter pins, one 2.5-cm steel shank, four 10.25-cm rotor blades, and two 2.5-cm hex nuts. The relationship implemented in Figure 4.19 thus enables you to track each part within each rotor assembly.

If a part can be used to assemble several different kinds of other parts and is itself composed of many parts, two tables are required to implement the "PART contains PART" relationship. Figure 4.20 illustrates such an environment. Parts tracking is increasingly important as managers become more aware of the legal ramifications of producing more complex output. In many industries, especially those involving aviation, full parts tracking is required by law.

FIGURE 4.19 ANOTHER UNARY RELATIONSHIP:"PART CONTAINS PART"

Table name: PART_V1   **Database name: Ch04_PartCo**

PART_CODE	PART_DESCRIPTION	PART_IN_STOCK	PART_UNITS_NEEDED	PART_OF_PART
AA21-6	2.5 cm. washer, 1.0 mm. rim	432	4	C-130
AB-121	Cotter pin, copper	1034	2	C-130
C-130	Rotor assembly	36		
E129	2.5 cm. steel shank	128	1	C-130
X10	10.25 cm. rotor blade	345	4	C-130
X34AW	2.5 cm. hex nut	879	2	C-130

FIGURE 4.20 THE IMPLEMENTATION OF THE M:N RECURSIVE RELATIONSHIP "PART CONTAINS PART"

Table name: COMPONENT   **Database name: Ch04_PartCo**

COMP_CODE	PART_CODE	COMP_PARTS_NEEDED
C-130	AA21-6	4
C-130	AB-121	2
C-130	E129	1
C-131A2	E129	1
C-130	X10	4
C-131A2	X10	1
C-130	X34AW	2
C-131A2	X34AW	2

Table name: PART

PART_CODE	PART_DESCRIPTION	PART_IN_STOCK
AA21-6	2.5 cm. washer, 1.0 mm. rim	432
AB-121	Cotter pin, copper	1034
C-130	Rotor assembly	36
E129	2.5 cm. steel shank	128
X10	10.25 cm. rotor blade	345
X34AW	2.5 cm. hex nut	879

The M:N recursive relationship might be more familiar in a school environment. For instance, note how the M:N "COURSE requires COURSE" relationship illustrated in Figure 4.17 is implemented in Figure 4.21. In this example, MATH-243 is a prerequisite to QM-261 and QM-362, while both MATH-243 and QM-261 are prerequisites to QM-362.

FIGURE 4.21 IMPLEMENTATION OF THE M:N RECURSIVE RELATIONSHIP "COURSE REQUIRES COURSE"

Table name: COURSE   **Database name: Ch04_TinyCollege**

CRS_CODE	DEPT_CODE	CRS_DESCRIPTION	CRS_CREDIT
ACCT-211	ACCT	Accounting I	3
ACCT-212	ACCT	Accounting II	3
CIS-220	CIS	Intro. to Microcomputing	3
CIS-420	CIS	Database Design and Implementation	4
MATH-243	MATH	Mathematics for Managers	3
QM-261	CIS	Intro. to Statistics	3
QM-362	CIS	Statistical Applications	4

Table name: PREREQ

CRS_CODE	PRE_TAKE
CIS-420	CIS-220
QM-261	MATH-243
QM-362	MATH-243
QM-362	QM-261

Finally, the 1:M recursive relationship "EMPLOYEE manages EMPLOYEE," shown in Figure 4.17, is implemented in Figure 4.22.

One common pitfall when working with unary relationships is to confuse participation with referential integrity. In theory, participation and referential integrity are very different concepts and are normally easy to distinguish in binary relationships. In practical terms, conversely, participation and referential integrity are very similar because they are both implemented through constraints on the same set of attributes. This similarity often leads to confusion when the concepts are applied within the limited structure of a unary relationship. Consider the unary 1:1 spousal relationship between employees, which is described in Figure 4.18. Participation, as described previously, is bidirectional, meaning that it must be addressed in both directions along the relationship. Participation in Figure 4.18 addresses the following questions:

- Must every employee have a spouse who is an employee?

- Must every employee be a spouse to another employee?

FIGURE 4.22 IMPLEMENTATION OF THE 1:M RECURSIVE RELATIONSHIP "EMPLOYEE MANAGES EMPLOYEE"

Database name: Ch04_PartCo

Table name: EMPLOYEE_V2

EMP_CODE	EMP_LNAME	EMP_MANAGER
101	Waddell	102
102	Orincona	
103	Jones	102
104	Reballoh	102
105	Robertson	102
106	Deltona	102

For the data shown in Figure 4.18, the correct answer to both questions is "No." It is possible to be an employee and not have another employee as a spouse. Also, it is possible to be an employee and not be the spouse of another employee.

Referential integrity deals with the correspondence of values in the foreign key with values in the related primary key. Referential integrity is not bidirectional, and therefore answers only one question:

- Must every employee spouse be a valid employee?

For the data shown in Figure 4.18, the correct answer is "Yes." Another way to frame this question is to consider whether every value provided for the EMP_SPOUSE attribute must match some value in the EMP_NUM attribute.

In practical terms, both participation and referential integrity involve the values used as primary keys and foreign keys to implement the relationship. Referential integrity requires that the values in the foreign key correspond to values in the primary key. In one direction, participation considers whether the foreign key can contain a null. In Figure 4.18, for example, employee Robert Delaney is not required to have a value in EMP_SPOUSE. In the other direction, participation considers whether every value in the primary key must appear as a value in the foreign key. In Figure 4.18, for example, employee Robert Delaney's value for EMP_NUM (348) is not required to appear as a value in EMP_SPOUSE for any other employee.

4-1k Associative (Composite) Entities

M:N relationships are a valid construct at the conceptual level, and therefore are found frequently during the ER modeling process. However, implementing the M:N relationship, particularly in the relational model, requires the use of an additional entity, as you learned in Chapter 3. The ER model uses the associative entity to represent an M:N relationship between two or more entities. This associative entity, also called a *composite* or *bridge entity*, is in a 1:M relationship with the parent entities and is composed of the primary key attributes of each parent entity. Furthermore, the associative entity can have additional attributes of its own, as shown by the ENROLL associative entity in Figure 4.23. When using the Crow's Foot notation, the associative entity is identified as a strong (identifying) relationship, as indicated by the solid relationship lines between the parents and the associative entity.

FIGURE 4.23 CONVERTING THE M:N RELATIONSHIP INTO TWO 1:M RELATIONSHIPS

Table name: STUDENT

Database name: Ch04_CollegeTry

STU_NUM	STU_LNAME
321452	Bowser
324257	Smithson

Table name: ENROLL

CLASS_CODE	STU_NUM	ENROLL_GRADE
10014	321452	C
10014	324257	B
10018	321452	A
10018	324257	B
10021	321452	C
10021	324257	C

Table name: CLASS

CLASS_CODE	CRS_CODE	CLASS_SECTION	CLASS_TIME	ROOM_CODE	PROF_NUM
10014	ACCT-211	3	TTh 2:30-3:45 p.m.	BUS252	342
10018	CIS-220	2	MWF 9:00-9:50 a.m.	KLR211	114
10021	QM-261	1	MWF 8:00-8:50 a.m.	KLR200	114

Note that the composite ENROLL entity in Figure 4.23 is existence-dependent on the other two entities; the composition of the ENROLL entity is based on the primary keys of the entities that are connected by the composite entity. The composite entity may also contain additional attributes that play no role in the connective process. For example, although the entity must be composed of at least the STUDENT and CLASS primary keys, it may also include such additional attributes as grades, absences, and other data uniquely identified by the student's performance in a specific class.

Finally, keep in mind that the ENROLL table's key (CLASS_CODE and STU_NUM) is composed entirely of the primary keys of the CLASS and STUDENT tables. Therefore, no null entries are possible in the ENROLL table's key attributes.

Implementing the small database shown in Figure 4.23 requires that you define the relationships clearly. Specifically, you must know the "1" and the "M" sides of each relationship, and you must know whether the relationships are mandatory or optional. For example, note the following point:

- A class may exist (at least at the start of registration) even though it contains no students. Therefore, in Figure 4.24, an optional symbol should appear on the STUDENT side of the M:N relationship between STUDENT and CLASS.

You might argue that to be classified as a STUDENT, a person must be enrolled in at least one CLASS. Therefore, CLASS is mandatory to STUDENT from a purely conceptual point of view. However, when a student is admitted to college, that student has not yet signed up for any classes. Therefore, *at least initially*, CLASS is optional to STUDENT. Note that the practical considerations in the data environment help dictate the use of optionalities.

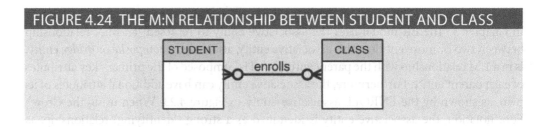

FIGURE 4.24 THE M:N RELATIONSHIP BETWEEN STUDENT AND CLASS

If CLASS is *not* optional to STUDENT from a database point of view, a class assignment must be made when the student is admitted. However, that's *not* how the process actually works, and the database design must reflect this. In short, the optionality reflects practice.

Because the M:N relationship between STUDENT and CLASS is decomposed into two 1:M relationships through ENROLL, the optionalities must be transferred to ENROLL. (See Figure 4.25.) In other words, it now becomes possible for a class not to occur in ENROLL if no student has signed up for that class. Because a class need not occur in ENROLL, the ENROLL entity becomes optional to CLASS. Also, because the ENROLL entity is created before any students have signed up for a class, the ENROLL entity is also optional to STUDENT, at least initially.

FIGURE 4.25 A COMPOSITE ENTITY IN AN ERD

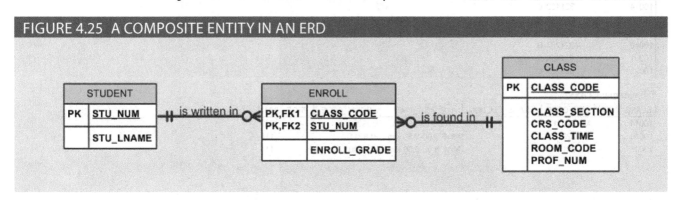

- As students begin to sign up for their classes, they will be entered into the ENROLL entity. Naturally, if a student takes more than one class, that student will occur more than once in ENROLL. For example, note that in the ENROLL table in Figure 4.23, STU_NUM = 321452 occurs three times. On the other hand, each student occurs only once in the STUDENT entity. (Note that the STUDENT table in Figure 4.23 has only one STU_NUM = 321452 entry.) Therefore, in Figure 4.25, the relationship between STUDENT and ENROLL is shown to be 1:M, with the "M" on the ENROLL side.

- As you can see in Figure 4.23, a class can occur more than once in the ENROLL table. For example, CLASS_CODE = 10014 occurs twice. However, CLASS_CODE = 10014 occurs only once in the CLASS table to reflect that the relationship between CLASS and ENROLL is 1:M. Note that in Figure 4.25, the "M" is located on the ENROLL side, while the "1" is located on the CLASS side.

4-2 Developing an ER Diagram

The process of database design is iterative rather than a linear or sequential process. The verb *iterate* means "to do again or repeatedly." Thus, an **iterative process** is based on repetition of processes and procedures. Building an ERD usually involves the following activities:

- Create a detailed narrative of the organization's description of operations.
- Identify the business rules based on the description of operations.

iterative process
A process based on repetition of steps and procedures.

- Identify the main entities and relationships from the business rules.
- Develop the initial ERD.
- Identify the attributes and primary keys that adequately describe the entities.
- Revise and review the ERD.

During the review process, additional objects, attributes, and relationships probably will be uncovered. Therefore, the basic ERM will be modified to incorporate the newly discovered ER components. Subsequently, another round of reviews might yield additional components or clarification of the existing diagram. The process is repeated until the end users and designers agree that the ERD is a fair representation of the organization's activities and functions.

During the design process, the database designer does not depend simply on interviews to help define entities, attributes, and relationships. A surprising amount of information can be gathered by examining the business forms and reports that an organization uses in its daily operations.

To illustrate the use of the iterative process that ultimately yields a workable ERD, start with an initial interview with the Tiny College administrators. The interview process yields the following business rules:

1. Tiny College (TC) is divided into several schools: business, arts and sciences, education, and applied sciences. Each school is administered by a dean who is a professor. Each professor can be the dean of only one school, and a professor is not required to be the dean of any school. Therefore, a 1:1 relationship exists between PROFESSOR and SCHOOL. Note that the cardinality can be expressed by writing (1,1) next to the entity PROFESSOR and (0,1) next to the entity SCHOOL.

2. Each school comprises several departments. For example, the school of business has an accounting department, a management/marketing department, an economics/finance department, and a computer information systems department. Note again the cardinality rules: The smallest number of departments operated by a school is one, and the largest number of departments is indeterminate (N). On the other hand, each department belongs to only a single school; thus, the cardinality is expressed by (1,1). That is, the minimum number of schools to which a department belongs is one, as is the maximum number. Figure 4.26 illustrates these first two business rules.

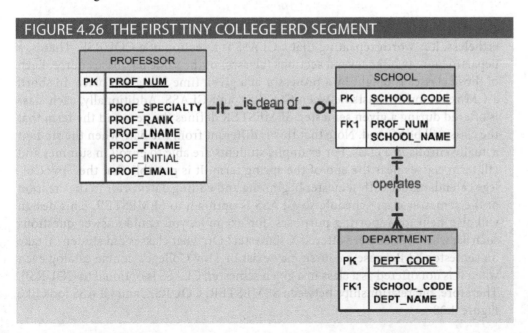

FIGURE 4.26 THE FIRST TINY COLLEGE ERD SEGMENT

Note

It is again appropriate to evaluate the reason for maintaining the 1:1 relationship between PROFESSOR and SCHOOL in the "PROFESSOR is dean of SCHOOL" relationship. It is worth repeating that the existence of 1:1 relationships often indicates a misidentification of attributes as entities. In this case, the 1:1 relationship could easily be eliminated by storing the dean's attributes in the SCHOOL entity. This solution would also make it easier to answer the queries "Who is the dean?" and "What are the dean's credentials?" The downside of this solution is that it requires the duplication of data that is already stored in the PROFESSOR table, thus setting the stage for anomalies. However, because each school is run by a single dean, the problem of data duplication is rather minor. The selection of one approach over another often depends on information requirements, transaction speed, and the database designer's professional judgment. In short, do not use 1:1 relationships lightly, and make sure that each 1:1 relationship within the database design is defensible.

3. Each department may offer courses. For example, the management/marketing department offers courses such as Introduction to Management, Principles of Marketing, and Production Management. The ERD segment for this condition is shown in Figure 4.27. Note that this relationship is based on the way Tiny College operates. For example, if Tiny College had some departments that were classified as "research only," they would not offer courses; therefore, the COURSE entity would be optional to the DEPARTMENT entity.

FIGURE 4.27 THE SECOND TINY COLLEGE ERD SEGMENT

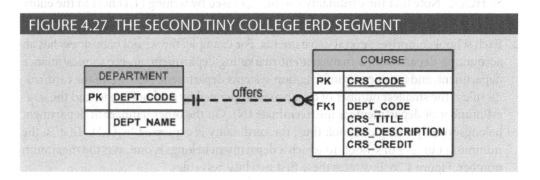

4. The relationship between COURSE and CLASS was illustrated in Figure 4.9. Nevertheless, it is worth repeating that a CLASS is a section of a COURSE. That is, a department may offer several sections (classes) of the same database course. Each of those classes is taught by a professor at a given time in a given place. In short, a 1:M relationship exists between COURSE and CLASS. Additionally, each class is offered during a given semester. SEMESTER defines the year and the term that the class will be offered. Note that this is different from the date when the student actually enrolls in a class. For example, students are able to enroll in summer and fall term classes near the end of the spring term. It is possible that the Tiny College calendar is set with semester beginning and ending dates prior to the creation of the semester class schedule so CLASS is optional to SEMESTER. This design will also help for reporting purposes, for example, you could answer questions such as: what classes were offered X semester? Or, what classes did student Y take on semester X? Because a course may exist in Tiny College's course catalog even when it is not offered as a class in a given semester, CLASS is optional to COURSE. Therefore, the relationships between SEMESTER, COURSE, and CLASS look like Figure 4.28.

FIGURE 4.28 THE THIRD TINY COLLEGE ERD SEGMENT

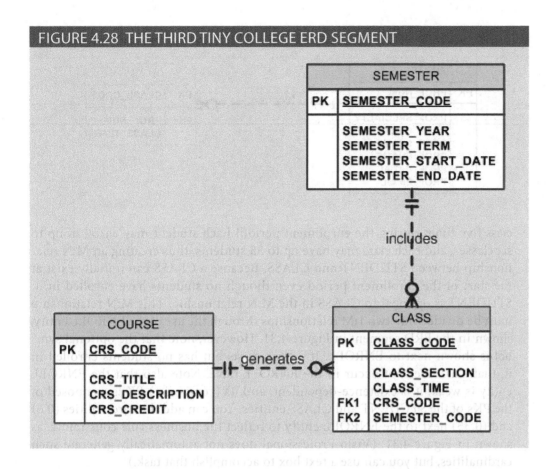

5. Each department should have one or more professors assigned to it. One and only one of those professors chairs the department, and no professor is required to accept the chair position. Therefore, DEPARTMENT is optional to PROFESSOR in the "chairs" relationship. Those relationships are summarized in the ER segment shown in Figure 4.29.

FIGURE 4.29 THE FOURTH TINY COLLEGE ERD SEGMENT

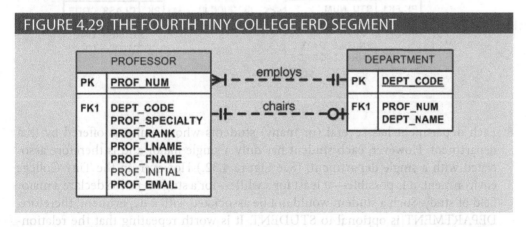

6. Each professor may teach up to four classes; each class is a section of a course. A professor may also be on a research contract and teach no classes at all. The ERD segment in Figure 4.30 depicts those conditions.

7. A student may enroll in several classes but take each class only once during any given enrollment period. For example, during the current enrollment period, a student may decide to take five classes—Statistics, Accounting, English, Database, and History—but that student would not be enrolled in the same Statistics

FIGURE 4.30 THE FIFTH TINY COLLEGE ERD SEGMENT

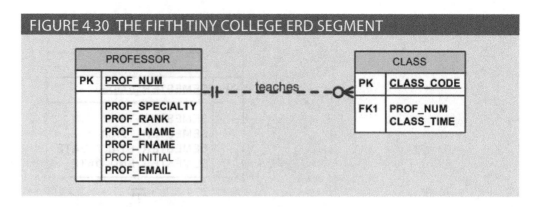

class five times during the enrollment period! Each student may enroll in up to six classes, and each class may have up to 35 students, thus creating an M:N relationship between STUDENT and CLASS. Because a CLASS can initially exist at the start of the enrollment period even though no students have enrolled in it, STUDENT is optional to CLASS in the M:N relationship. This M:N relationship must be divided into two 1:M relationships through the use of the ENROLL entity, shown in the ERD segment in Figure 4.31. However, note that the optional symbol is shown next to ENROLL. If a class exists but has no students enrolled in it, that class does not occur in the ENROLL table. Note also that the ENROLL entity is weak: it is existence-dependent, and its (composite) PK is composed of the PKs of the STUDENT and CLASS entities. You can add the cardinalities (0,6) and (0,35) next to the ENROLL entity to reflect the business rule constraints, as shown in Figure 4.31. (Visio Professional does not automatically generate such cardinalities, but you can use a text box to accomplish that task.)

FIGURE 4.31 THE SIXTH TINY COLLEGE ERD SEGMENT

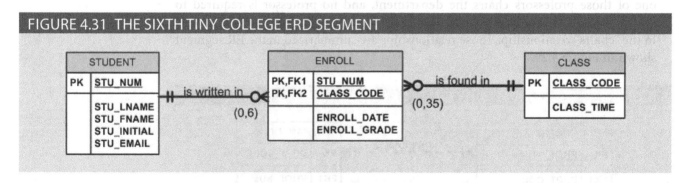

8. Each department has several (or many) students whose major is offered by that department. However, each student has only a single major and is therefore associated with a single department. (See Figure 4.32.) However, in the Tiny College environment, it is possible—at least for a while—for a student not to declare a major field of study. Such a student would not be associated with a department; therefore, DEPARTMENT is optional to STUDENT. It is worth repeating that the relationships between entities and the entities themselves reflect the organization's operating environment. That is, the business rules define the ERD components.

9. Each student has an advisor in his or her department; each advisor counsels several students. An advisor is also a professor, but not all professors advise students. Therefore, STUDENT is optional to PROFESSOR in the "PROFESSOR advises STUDENT" relationship. (See Figure 4.33.)

FIGURE 4.32 THE SEVENTH TINY COLLEGE ERD SEGMENT

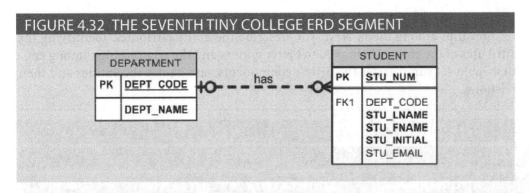

FIGURE 4.33 THE EIGHTH TINY COLLEGE ERD SEGMENT

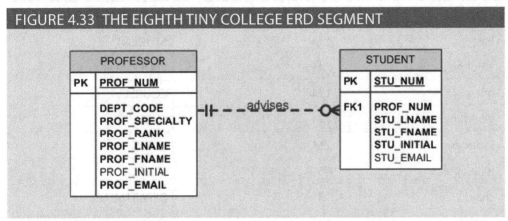

10. As you can see in Figure 4.34, the CLASS entity contains a ROOM_CODE attribute. Given the naming conventions, it is clear that ROOM_CODE is an FK to another entity. Clearly, because a class is taught in a room, it is reasonable to assume that the ROOM_CODE in CLASS is the FK to an entity named ROOM. In turn, each room is located in a building. So, the last Tiny College ERD is created by observing that a BUILDING can contain many ROOMs, but each ROOM is found in a single BUILDING. In this ERD segment, it is clear that some buildings do not contain (class) rooms. For example, a storage building might not contain any named rooms at all.

FIGURE 4.34 THE NINTH TINY COLLEGE ERD SEGMENT

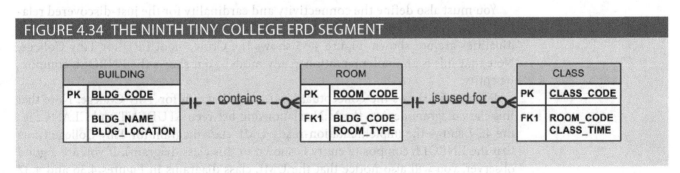

Using the preceding summary, you can identify the following entities:

PROFESSOR	SCHOOL	DEPARTMENT
COURSE	CLASS	SEMESTER
STUDENT	BUILDING	ROOM

ENROLL (the associative entity between STUDENT and CLASS)

Once you have discovered the relevant entities, you can define the initial set of relationships among them. Next, you describe the entity attributes. Identifying the attributes of the entities helps you to better understand the relationships among entities. Table 4.4 summarizes the ERM's components, and names the entities and their relations.

TABLE 4.4

COMPONENTS OF THE ERM

ENTITY	RELATIONSHIP	CONNECTIVITY	ENTITY
SCHOOL	operates	1:M	DEPARTMENT
DEPARTMENT	has	1:M	STUDENT
DEPARTMENT	employs	1:M	PROFESSOR
DEPARTMENT	offers	1:M	COURSE
COURSE	generates	1:M	CLASS
SEMESTER	includes	1:M	CLASS
PROFESSOR	is dean of	1:1	SCHOOL
PROFESSOR	chairs	1:1	DEPARTMENT
PROFESSOR	teaches	1:M	CLASS
PROFESSOR	advises	1:M	STUDENT
STUDENT	enrolls in	M:N	CLASS
BUILDING	contains	1:M	ROOM
ROOM	is used for	1:M	CLASS

Note: ENROLL is the composite entity that implements the M:N relationship "STUDENT enrolls in CLASS."

You must also define the connectivity and cardinality for the just-discovered relations based on the business rules. However, to avoid crowding the diagram, the cardinalities are not shown. Figure 4.35 shows the Crow's Foot ERD for Tiny College. Note that this is an implementation-ready model, so it shows the ENROLL composite entity.

Figure 4.36 shows the conceptual UML class diagram for Tiny College. Note that this class diagram depicts the M:N relationship between STUDENT and CLASS. Figure 4.37 shows the implementation-ready UML class diagram for Tiny College (note that the ENROLL composite entity is shown in this class diagram). If you are a good observer, you will also notice that the UML class diagrams in Figures 4.36 and 4.37 show the entity and attribute names but do not identify the primary key attributes. The reason goes back to UML's roots. UML class diagrams are an object-oriented modeling language, and therefore do not support the notion of "primary or foreign keys" found mainly in the relational world. Rather, in the object-oriented world, objects inherit a unique object identifier at creation time. For more information, see Appendix G, Object-Oriented Databases.

FIGURE 4.35 THE COMPLETED TINY COLLEGE ERD

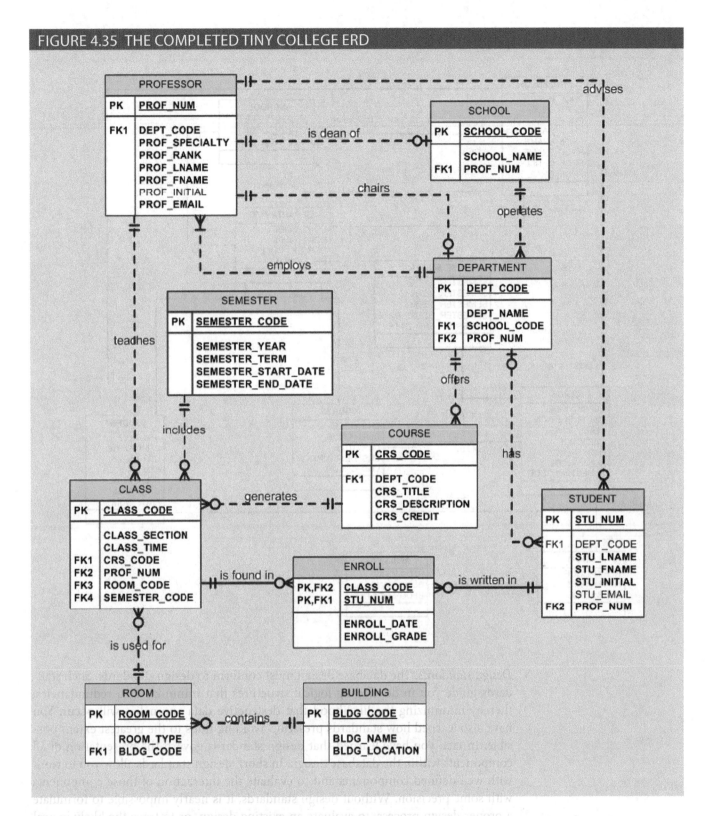

4-3 Database Design Challenges: Conflicting Goals

Database designers must often make design compromises that are triggered by conflicting goals, such as adherence to design standards (design elegance), processing speed, and information requirements.

FIGURE 4.36 THE CONCEPTUAL UML CLASS DIAGRAM FOR TINY COLLEGE

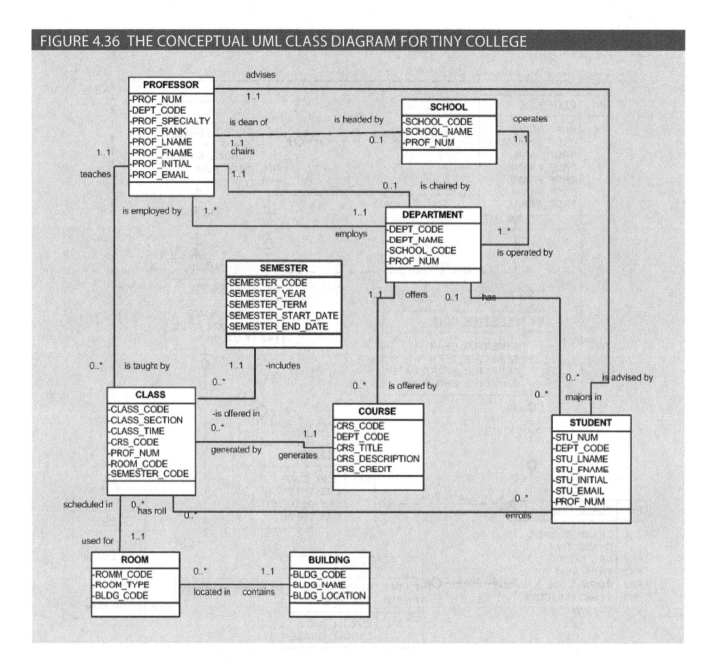

- *Design standards.* The database design must conform to design standards. Such standards guide you in developing logical structures that minimize data redundancies, thereby minimizing the likelihood that destructive data anomalies will occur. You have also learned how standards prescribe avoiding nulls to the greatest extent possible. In fact, you have learned that design standards govern the presentation of all components within the database design. In short, design standards allow you to work with well-defined components and to evaluate the interaction of those components with some precision. Without design standards, it is nearly impossible to formulate a proper design process, to evaluate an existing design, or to trace the likely logical impact of changes in design.

- *Processing speed.* In many organizations, particularly those that generate large numbers of transactions, high processing speeds are often a top priority in database design. High processing speed means minimal access time, which may be achieved by minimizing the number and complexity of logically desirable relationships.

FIGURE 4.37 THE IMPLEMENTATION-READY UML CLASS DIAGRAM FOR TINY COLLEGE

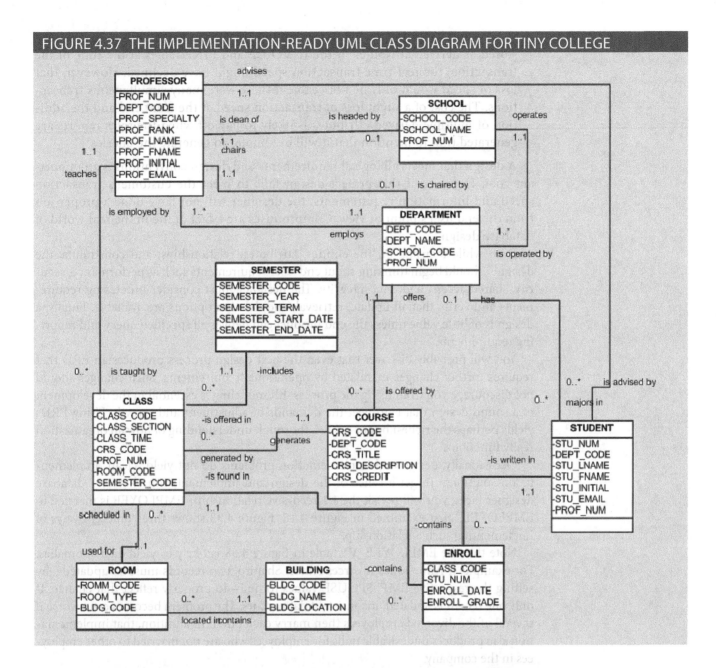

For example, a "perfect" design might use a 1:1 relationship to avoid nulls, while a design that emphasizes higher transaction speed might combine the two tables to avoid the use of an additional relationship, using dummy entries to avoid the nulls. If the focus is on data-retrieval speed, you might also be forced to include derived attributes in the design.

- *Information requirements.* The quest for timely information might be the focus of database design. Complex information requirements may dictate data transformations, and they may expand the number of entities and attributes within the design. Therefore, the database may have to sacrifice some of its "clean" design structures and high transaction speed to ensure maximum information generation. For example, suppose that a detailed sales report must be generated periodically. The sales report includes all invoice subtotals, taxes, and totals; even the invoice lines include subtotals. If the sales report includes hundreds of thousands (or even millions) of invoices, computing the totals, taxes, and subtotals is likely to take some time. If those computations had been made and the results had been stored as derived attributes in the INVOICE and LINE tables at the time of the transaction, the real-time transaction speed might have declined. However, that loss of speed would only be noticeable if there were many simultaneous transactions. The cost of a slight loss of transaction speed at the front end and the addition of multiple derived attributes is likely to pay off when the sales reports are generated (not to mention that it will be simpler to generate the queries).

A design that meets all logical requirements and design conventions is an important goal. However, if this perfect design fails to meet the customer's transaction speed and information requirements, the designer will not have done a proper job from the end user's point of view. Compromises are a fact of life in the real world of database design.

Even while focusing on the entities, attributes, relationships, and constraints, the designer should begin thinking about end-user requirements such as performance, security, shared access, and data integrity. The designer must consider processing requirements and verify that all update, retrieval, and deletion options are available. Finally, a design is of little value unless the end product can deliver all specified query and reporting requirements.

You will probably discover that even the best design process produces an ERD that requires further changes mandated by operational requirements. Such changes should not discourage you from using the process. ER modeling is essential in the development of a sound design that can meet the demands of adjustment and growth. Using ERDs yields perhaps the richest bonus of all: a thorough understanding of how an organization really functions.

Occasionally, design and implementation problems do not yield "clean" implementation solutions. To get a sense of the design and implementation choices a database designer faces, you will revisit the 1:1 recursive relationship "EMPLOYEE is married to EMPLOYEE," first examined in Figure 4.18. Figure 4.38 shows three different ways of implementing such a relationship.

Note that the EMPLOYEE_V1 table in Figure 4.38 is likely to yield data anomalies. For example, if Anne Jones divorces Anton Shapiro, two records must be updated—by setting the respective EMP_SPOUSE values to null—to properly reflect that change. If only one record is updated, inconsistent data occurs. The problem becomes even worse if several of the divorced employees then marry each other. In addition, that implementation also produces undesirable nulls for employees who are *not* married to other employees in the company.

Another approach would be to create a new entity shown as MARRIED_V1 in a 1:M relationship with EMPLOYEE. (See Figure 4.38.) This second implementation does eliminate the nulls for employees who are not married to other employees in the same company. (Such employees would not be entered in the MARRIED_V1 table.) However, this approach still yields possible duplicate values. For example, the marriage between employees 345 and 347 may still appear twice, once as 345,347 and once as 347,345. (Because each of those permutations is unique the first time it appears, the creation of a unique index will not solve the problem.)

As you can see, the first two implementations yield several problems:

- Both solutions use synonyms. The EMPLOYEE_V1 table uses EMP_NUM and EMP_SPOUSE to refer to an employee. The MARRIED_V1 table uses the same synonyms.

- Both solutions are likely to produce redundant data. For example, it is possible to enter employee 345 as married to employee 347 and to enter employee 347 as married to employee 345.

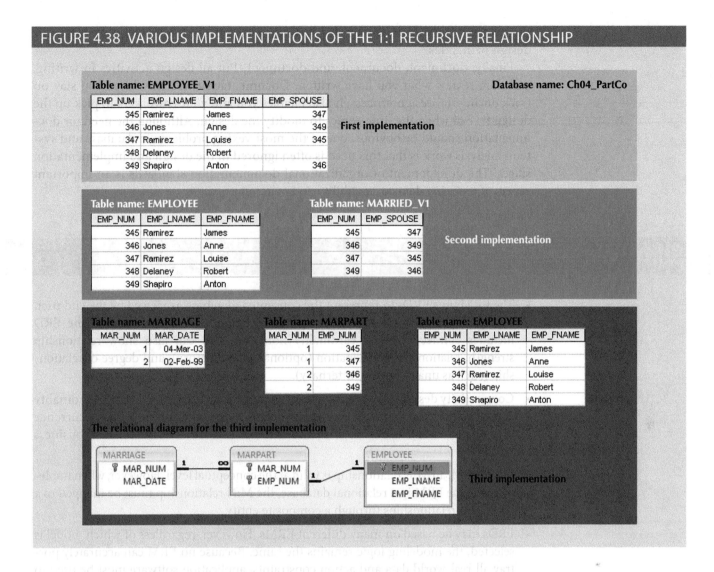

FIGURE 4.38 VARIOUS IMPLEMENTATIONS OF THE 1:1 RECURSIVE RELATIONSHIP

- Both solutions are likely to produce inconsistent data. For example, it is possible to have data pairs such as 345,347 and 348,345 and 347,349, none of which will violate entity integrity requirements because they are all unique. However, this solution would allow any one employee to be married to multiple employees.

A third approach would be to have two new entities, MARRIAGE and MARPART, in a 1:M relationship. MARPART contains the EMP_NUM foreign key to EMPLOYEE. (See the relational diagram in Figure 4.38.) However, even this approach has issues. It requires the collection of additional data regarding the employees' marriage—the marriage date. If the business users do not need this data, then requiring them to collect it would be inappropriate. To ensure that an employee occurs only once in any given marriage, you would have to create a unique index on the EMP_NUM attribute in the MARPART table. Another potential problem with this solution is that the database implementation would theoretically allow more than two employees to "participate" in the same marriage.

As you can see, a recursive 1:1 relationship yields many different solutions with varying degrees of effectiveness and adherence to basic design principles. Any of the preceding solutions would likely involve the creation of program code to help ensure the integrity and consistency of the data. In a later chapter, you will examine the creation of database triggers that can do exactly that. Your job as a database designer is to use your professional judgment to yield a solution that meets the requirements imposed by business rules, processing requirements, and basic design principles.

Finally, document, document, and document! Put all design activities in writing, and then review what you have written. Documentation not only helps you stay on track during the design process, it also enables you and your coworkers to pick up the design thread when the time comes to modify the design. Although the need for documentation should be obvious, one of the most vexing problems in database and systems analysis work is that this need is often ignored in the design and implementation stages. The development of organizational documentation standards is an important aspect of ensuring data compatibility and coherence.

Summary

- The ERM uses ERDs to represent the conceptual database as viewed by the end user. The ERM's main components are entities, relationships, and attributes. The ERD includes connectivity and cardinality notations, and can also show relationship strength, relationship participation (optional or mandatory), and degree of relationship (such as unary, binary, or ternary).

- Connectivity describes the relationship classification (1:1, 1:M, or M:N). Cardinality expresses the specific number of entity occurrences associated with an occurrence of a related entity. Connectivities and cardinalities are usually based on business rules.

- In the ERM, an M:N relationship is valid at the conceptual level. However, when implementing the ERM in a relational database, the M:N relationship must be mapped to a set of 1:M relationships through a composite entity.

- ERDs may be based on many different ERMs. However, regardless of which model is selected, the modeling logic remains the same. Because no ERM can accurately portray all real-world data and action constraints, application software must be used to augment the implementation of at least some of the business rules.

- Unified Modeling Language (UML) class diagrams are used to represent the static data structures in a data model. The symbols used in the UML class and ER diagrams are very similar. The UML class diagrams can be used to depict data models at the conceptual or implementation abstraction levels.

- Database designers, no matter how well they can produce designs that conform to all applicable modeling conventions, are often forced to make design compromises. Those compromises are required when end users have vital transaction-speed and information requirements that prevent the use of "perfect" modeling logic and adherence to all modeling conventions. Therefore, database designers must use their professional judgment to determine how and to what extent the modeling conventions are subject to modification. To ensure that their professional judgments are sound, database designers must have detailed and in-depth knowledge of data-modeling conventions. It is also important to document the design process from beginning to end, which helps keep the design process on track and allows for easy modifications in the future.

Key Terms

binary relationship
cardinality
composite attribute
composite identifier
connectivity
derived attribute
existence-dependent
existence-independent
identifier
iterative process

mandatory participation
multivalued attribute
optional attribute
optional participation
participants
recursive relationship
regular entity
relational schema
relationship degree
required attribute

simple attribute
single-valued attribute
strong entity
strong (identifying) relationship
ternary relationship
unary relationship
weak entity
weak (non-identifying) relationship

Online Content

Flashcards and crossword puzzles for key term practice are available at *www.cengagebrain.com*.

Review Questions

1. What two conditions must be met before an entity can be classified as a weak entity? Give an example of a weak entity.

2. What is a strong (or identifying) relationship, and how is it depicted in a Crow's Foot ERD?

3. Given the business rule "an employee may have many degrees," discuss its effect on attributes, entities, and relationships. (*Hint:* Remember what a multivalued attribute is and how it might be implemented.)

4. What is a composite entity, and when is it used?

5. Suppose you are working within the framework of the conceptual model in Figure Q4.5.

FIGURE Q4.5 THE CONCEPTUAL MODEL FOR QUESTION 5

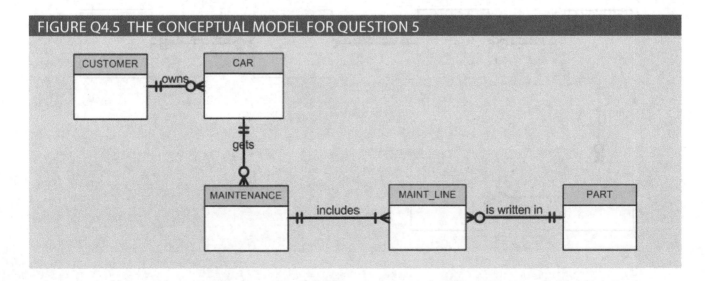

Given the conceptual model in Figure Q4.5:

   a. Write the business rules that are reflected in it.

   b. Identify all of the cardinalities.

6. What is a recursive relationship? Give an example.

7. How would you (graphically) identify each of the following ERM components in a Crow's Foot notation?

   a. an entity

   b. the cardinality (0,N)

   c. a weak relationship

   d. a strong relationship

8. Discuss the difference between a composite key and a composite attribute. How would each be indicated in an ERD?

9. What two courses of action are available to a designer who encounters a multivalued attribute?

10. What is a derived attribute? Give an example.

11. How is a relationship between entities indicated in an ERD? Give an example using the Crow's Foot notation.

12. Discuss two ways in which the 1:M relationship between COURSE and CLASS can be implemented. (*Hint:* Think about relationship strength.)

13. How is a composite entity represented in an ERD, and what is its function? Illustrate the Crow's Foot notation.

14. What three (often conflicting) database requirements must be addressed in database design?

15. Briefly, but precisely, explain the difference between single-valued attributes and simple attributes. Give an example of each.

16. What are multivalued attributes, and how can they be handled within the database design?

Questions 17–20 are based on the ERD in Figure Q4.17.

FIGURE Q4.17 THE ERD FOR QUESTIONS 17-20

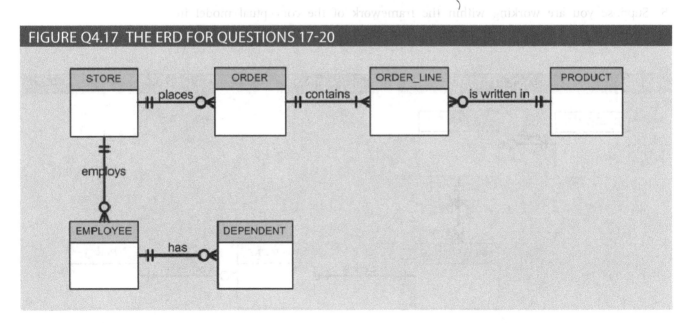

17. Write the 10 cardinalities that are appropriate for this ERD.

18. Write the business rules reflected in this ERD.

19. What two attributes must be contained in the composite entity between STORE and PRODUCT? Use proper terminology in your answer.

20. Describe precisely the composition of the DEPENDENT weak entity's primary key. Use proper terminology in your answer.

21. The local city youth league needs a database system to help track children who sign up to play soccer. Data needs to be kept on each team, the children who will play on each team, and their parents. Also, data needs to be kept on the coaches for each team.

    Draw a data model with the entities and attributes described here.

    Entities required: Team, Player, Coach, and Parent

    Attributes required:

    Team: Team ID number, Team name, and Team colors

    Player: Player ID number, Player first name, Player last name, and Player age

    Coach: Coach ID number, Coach first name, Coach last name, and Coach home phone number

    Parent: Parent ID number, Parent last name, Parent first name, Home phone number, and Home address (Street, City, State, and Zip code)

    The following relationships must be defined:

    - Team is related to Player.
    - Team is related to Coach.
    - Player is related to Parent.

    Connectivities and participations are defined as follows:

    - A Team may or may not have a Player.
    - A Player must have a Team.
    - A Team may have many Players.
    - A Player has only one Team.
    - A Team may or may not have a Coach.
    - A Coach must have a Team.
    - A Team may have many Coaches.
    - A Coach has only one Team.
    - A Player must have a Parent.
    - A Parent must have a Player.
    - A Player may have many Parents.
    - A Parent may have many Players.

Problems

1. Use the following business rules to create a Crow's Foot ERD. Write all appropriate connectivities and cardinalities in the ERD.
   - A department employs many employees, but each employee is employed by only one department.
   - Some employees, known as "rovers," are not assigned to any department.
   - A division operates many departments, but each department is operated by only one division.
   - An employee may be assigned many projects, and a project may have many employees assigned to it.
   - A project must have at least one employee assigned to it.
   - One of the employees manages each department, and each department is managed by only one employee.
   - One of the employees runs each division, and each division is run by only one employee.

2. Create a complete ERD in Crow's Foot notation that can be implemented in the relational model using the following description of operations. Hot Water (HW) is a small start-up company that sells spas. HW does not carry any stock. A few spas are set up in a simple warehouse so customers can see some of the models available, but any products sold must be ordered at the time of the sale.
   - HW can get spas from several different manufacturers.
   - Each manufacturer produces one or more different brands of spas.
   - Each and every brand is produced by only one manufacturer.
   - Every brand has one or more models.
   - Every model is produced as part of a brand. For example, Iguana Bay Spas is a manufacturer that produces Big Blue Iguana spas, a premium-level brand, and Lazy Lizard spas, an entry-level brand. The Big Blue Iguana brand offers several models, including the BBI-6, an 81-jet spa with two 6-hp motors, and the BBI-10, a 102-jet spa with three 6-hp motors.
   - Every manufacturer is identified by a manufacturer code. The company name, address, area code, phone number, and account number are kept in the system for every manufacturer.
   - For each brand, the brand name and brand level (premium, mid-level, or entry-level) are kept in the system.
   - For each model, the model number, number of jets, number of motors, number of horsepower per motor, suggested retail price, HW retail price, dry weight, water capacity, and seating capacity must be kept in the system.

3. The Jonesburgh County Basketball Conference (JCBC) is an amateur basketball association. Each city in the county has one team as its representative. Each team has a maximum of 12 players and a minimum of 9 players. Each team also has up to 3 coaches (offensive, defensive, and physical training coaches). During the season,

each team plays 2 games (home and visitor) against each of the other teams. Given those conditions, do the following:

- Identify the connectivity of each relationship.
- Identify the type of dependency that exists between CITY and TEAM.
- Identify the cardinality between teams and players and between teams and city.
- Identify the dependency between COACH and TEAM and between TEAM and PLAYER.
- Draw the Chen and Crow's Foot ERDs to represent the JCBC database.
- Draw the UML class diagram to depict the JCBC database.

4. Create an ERD based on the Crow's Foot notation using the following requirements:

- An INVOICE is written by a SALESREP. Each sales representative can write many invoices, but each invoice is written by a single sales representative.
- The INVOICE is written for a single CUSTOMER. However, each customer can have many invoices.
- An INVOICE can include many detail lines (LINE), each of which describes one product bought by the customer.
- The product information is stored in a PRODUCT entity.
- The product's vendor information is found in a VENDOR entity.

5. The Hudson Engineering Group (HEG) has contacted you to create a conceptual model whose application will meet the expected database requirements for the company's training program. The HEG administrator gives you the following description of the training group's operating environment. (*Hint:* Some of the following sentences identify the volume of data rather than cardinalities. Can you tell which ones?)

The HEG has 12 instructors and can handle up to 30 trainees per class. HEG offers 5 Advanced Technology courses, each of which may generate several classes. If a class has fewer than 10 trainees, it will be canceled. Therefore, it is possible for a course not to generate any classes. Each class is taught by one instructor. Each instructor may teach up to 2 classes or may be assigned to do research only. Each trainee may take up to 2 classes per year.

Given that information, do the following:

a. Define all of the entities and relationships. (Use Table 4.4 as your guide.)

b. Describe the relationship between instructor and class in terms of connectivity, cardinality, and existence dependence.

6. Automata, Inc., produces specialty vehicles by contract. The company operates several departments, each of which builds a particular vehicle, such as a limousine, truck, van, or RV.

- Before a new vehicle is built, the department places an order with the purchasing department to request specific components. Automata's purchasing department is interested in creating a database to keep track of orders and to accelerate the process of delivering materials.
- The order received by the purchasing department may contain several different items. An inventory is maintained so the most frequently requested items are delivered almost immediately. When an order comes in, it is checked to determine whether the requested item is in inventory. If an item is not in inventory, it must be ordered from a supplier. Each item may have several suppliers.

Given that functional description of the processes at Automata's purchasing department, do the following:

a. Identify all of the main entities.

b. Identify all of the relations and connectivities among entities.

c. Identify the type of existence dependence in all the relationships.

d. Give at least two examples of the types of reports that can be obtained from the database.

7. United Helpers is a nonprofit organization that provides aid to people after natural disasters. Based on the following brief description of operations, create the appropriate fully labeled Crow's Foot ERD.

- Volunteers carry out the tasks of the organization. The name, address, and telephone number are tracked for each volunteer. Each volunteer may be assigned to several tasks, and some tasks require many volunteers. A volunteer might be in the system without having been assigned a task yet. It is possible to have tasks that no one has been assigned. When a volunteer is assigned to a task, the system should track the start time and end time of that assignment.

- Each task has a task code, task description, task type, and task status. For example, there may be a task with task code "101," a description of "answer the telephone," a type of "recurring," and a status of "ongoing." Another task might have a code of "102," a description of "prepare 5,000 packages of basic medical supplies," a type of "packing," and a status of "open."

- For all tasks of type "packing," there is a packing list that specifies the contents of the packages. There are many packing lists to produce different packages, such as basic medical packages, child-care packages, and food packages. Each packing list has an ID number, a packing list name, and a packing list description, which describes the items that should make up the package. Every packing task is associated with only one packing list. A packing list may not be associated with any tasks, or it may be associated with many tasks. Tasks that are not packing tasks are not associated with any packing list.

- Packing tasks result in the creation of packages. Each individual package of supplies produced by the organization is tracked, and each package is assigned an ID number. The date the package was created and its total weight are recorded. A given package is associated with only one task. Some tasks (such as "answer the phones") will not produce any packages, while other tasks (such as "prepare 5,000 packages of basic medical supplies") will be associated with many packages.

- The packing list describes the *ideal* contents of each package, but it is not always possible to include the ideal number of each item. Therefore, the actual items included in each package should be tracked. A package can contain many different items, and a given item can be used in many different packages.

- Each item that the organization provides has an item ID number, item description, item value, and item quantity on hand stored in the system. Along with tracking the actual items that are placed in each package, the quantity of each item placed in the package must be tracked as well. For example, a packing list may state that basic medical packages should include 100 bandages, 4 bottles of iodine, and 4 bottles of hydrogen peroxide. However, because of the limited supply of items, a given package may include only 10 bandages, 1 bottle of iodine, and no hydrogen peroxide. The fact that the package includes bandages and iodine needs to be recorded along with the quantity of each item included. It is possible for the organization to have items that have not been included in any package yet, but every package will contain at least one item.

8. Using the Crow's Foot notation, create an ERD that can be implemented for a medical clinic using the following business rules:

- A patient can make many appointments with one or more doctors in the clinic, and a doctor can accept appointments with many patients. However, each appointment is made with only one doctor and one patient.

- Emergency cases do not require an appointment. However, for appointment management purposes, an emergency is entered in the appointment book as "unscheduled."

- If kept, an appointment yields a visit with the doctor specified in the appointment. The visit yields a diagnosis and, when appropriate, treatment.

- With each visit, the patient's records are updated to provide a medical history.

- Each patient visit creates a bill. Each patient visit is billed by one doctor, and each doctor can bill many patients.

- Each bill must be paid. However, a bill may be paid in many installments, and a payment may cover more than one bill.

- A patient may pay the bill directly, or the bill may be the basis for a claim submitted to an insurance company.

- If the bill is paid by an insurance company, the deductible is submitted to the patient for payment.

9. Create a Crow's Foot notation ERD to support the following business operations:

- A friend of yours has opened Professional Electronics and Repairs (PEAR) to repair smartphones, laptops, tablets, and MP3 players. She wants you to create a database to help her run her business.

- When a customer brings a device to PEAR for repair, data must be recorded about the customer, the device, and the repair. The customer's name, address, and a contact phone number must be recorded (if the customer has used the shop before, the information already in the system for the customer is verified as being current). For the device to be repaired, the type of device, model, and serial number are recorded (or verified if the device is already in the system). Only customers who have brought devices into PEAR for repair will be included in this system.

- Since a customer might sell an older device to someone else who then brings the device to PEAR for repair, it is possible for a device to be brought in for repair by more than one customer. However, each repair is associated with only one customer. When a customer brings in a device to be fixed, it is referred to as a repair request, or just "repair," for short. Each repair request is given a reference number, which is recorded in the system along with the date of the request, and a description of the problem(s) that the customer wants fixed. It is possible for a device to be brought to the shop for repair many different times, and only devices that are brought in for repair are recorded in the system. Each repair request is for the repair of one and only one device. If a customer needs multiple devices fixed, then each device will require its own repair request.

- There are a limited number of repair services that PEAR can perform. For each repair service, there is a service ID number, description, and charge. "Charge" is how much the customer is charged for the shop to perform the service, including any parts used. The actual repair of a device is the performance of the services necessary to address the problems described by the customer. Completing a repair request may require the performance of many services. Each service can be performed many different times during the repair of different devices, but each service will be performed only once during a given repair request.

- All repairs eventually require the performance of at least one service, but which services will be required may not be known at the time the repair request is made. It is possible for services to be available at PEAR but that have never been required in performing any repair.

- Some services involve only labor activities and no parts are required, but most services require the replacement of one or more parts. The quantity of each part required in the performance of each service should also be recorded. For each part, the part number, part description, quantity in stock, and cost is recorded in the system. The cost indicated is the amount that PEAR pays for the part. Some parts may be used in more than one service, but each part is required for at least one service.

10. Luxury-Oriented Scenic Tours (LOST) provides guided tours to groups of visitors to the Washington D.C. area. In recent years, LOST has grown quickly and is having difficulty keeping up with all of the various information needs of the company. The company's operations are as follows:

- LOST offers many different tours. For each tour, the tour name, approximate length (in hours), and fee charged is needed. Guides are identified by an employee ID, but the system should also record a guide's name, home address, and date of hire. Guides take a test to be qualified to lead specific tours. It is important to know which guides are qualified to lead which tours and the date that they completed the qualification test for each tour. A guide may be qualified to lead many different tours. A tour can have many different qualified guides. New guides may or may not be qualified to lead any tours, just as a new tour may or may not have any qualified guides.

- Every tour must be designed to visit at least three locations. For each location, a name, type, and official description are kept. Some locations (such as the White House) are visited by more than one tour, while others (such as Arlington Cemetery) are visited by a single tour. All locations are visited by at least one tour. The order in which the tour visits each location should be tracked as well.

- When a tour is actually given, that is referred to as an "outing." LOST schedules outings well in advance so they can be advertised and so employees can understand their upcoming work schedules. A tour can have many scheduled outings, although newly designed tours may not have any outings scheduled. Each outing is for a single tour and is scheduled for a particular date and time. All outings must be associated with a tour. All tours at LOST are guided tours, so a guide must be assigned to each outing. Each outing has one and only one guide. Guides are occasionally asked to lead an outing of a tour even if they are not officially qualified to lead that tour. Newly hired guides may not have ever been scheduled to lead any outings. Tourists, called "clients" by LOST, pay to join a scheduled outing. For each client, the name and telephone number are recorded. Clients may sign up to join many different outings, and each outing can have many clients. Information is kept only on clients who have signed up for at least one outing, although newly scheduled outings may not have any clients signed up yet.

a. Create a Crow's Foot notation ERD to support LOST operations.

b. The operations provided state that it is possible for a guide to lead an outing of a tour even if the guide is not officially qualified to lead outings of that tour. Imagine that the business rules instead specified that a guide is never, under any circumstance, allowed to lead an outing unless he or she is qualified to lead outings of that tour. How could the data model in Part a. be modified to enforce this new constraint?

Note

You can use the following cases and additional problems from the Instructor Online Companion as the basis for class projects. These problems illustrate the challenge of translating a description of operations into a set of business rules that will define the components for an ERD you can implement successfully. These problems can also be used as the basis for discussions about the components and contents of a proper description of operations. If you want to create databases that can be successfully implemented, you must learn to separate the generic background material from the details that directly affect database design. You must also keep in mind that many constraints cannot be incorporated into the database design; instead, such constraints are handled by the application software.

Cases

11. The administrators of Tiny College are so pleased with your design and implementation of their student registration and tracking system that they want you to expand the design to include the database for their motor vehicle pool. A brief description of operations follows:

- Faculty members may use the vehicles owned by Tiny College for officially sanctioned travel. For example, the vehicles may be used by faculty members to travel to off-campus learning centers, to travel to locations at which research papers are presented, to transport students to officially sanctioned locations, and to travel for public service purposes. The vehicles used for such purposes are managed by Tiny College's Travel Far But Slowly (TFBS) Center.

- Using reservation forms, each department can reserve vehicles for its faculty, who are responsible for filling out the appropriate trip completion form at the end of a trip. The reservation form includes the expected departure date, vehicle type required, destination, and name of the authorized faculty member. The faculty member who picks up a vehicle must sign a checkout form to log out the vehicle and pick up a trip completion form. (The TFBS employee who releases the vehicle for use also signs the checkout form.) The faculty member's trip completion form includes the faculty member's identification code, the vehicle's identification, the odometer readings at the start and end of the trip, maintenance complaints (if any), gallons of fuel purchased (if any), and the Tiny College credit card number used to pay for the fuel. If fuel is purchased, the credit card receipt must be stapled to the trip completion form. Upon receipt of the trip completion form, the faculty member's department is billed at a mileage rate based on the vehicle type used: sedan, station wagon, panel truck, minivan, or minibus. (*Hint:* Do *not* use more entities than are necessary. Remember the difference between attributes and entities!)

- All vehicle maintenance is performed by TFBS. Each time a vehicle requires maintenance, a maintenance log entry is completed on a prenumbered maintenance log form. The maintenance log form includes the vehicle identification, brief description of the type of maintenance required, initial log entry date, date the maintenance was completed, and name of the mechanic who released the vehicle back into service. (Only mechanics who have an inspection authorization may release a vehicle back into service.)

- As soon as the log form has been initiated, the log form's number is transferred to a maintenance detail form; the log form's number is also forwarded to the parts department manager, who fills out a parts usage form on which the maintenance log number is recorded. The maintenance detail form contains separate lines for each maintenance item performed, for the parts used, and for identification of the mechanic who performed the maintenance. When all maintenance items have been completed, the maintenance detail form is stapled to the maintenance log form, the maintenance log form's completion date is filled out, and the mechanic who releases the vehicle back into service signs the form. The stapled forms are then filed, to be used later as the source for various maintenance reports.

- TFBS maintains a parts inventory, including oil, oil filters, air filters, and belts of various types. The parts inventory is checked daily to monitor parts usage and to reorder parts that reach the "minimum quantity on hand" level. To track parts usage, the parts manager requires each mechanic to sign out the parts that are used to perform each vehicle's maintenance; the parts manager records the maintenance log number under which the part is used.

- Each month TFBS issues a set of reports. The reports include the mileage driven by vehicle, by department, and by faculty members within a department. In addition, various revenue reports are generated by vehicle and department. A detailed parts usage report is also filed each month. Finally, a vehicle maintenance summary is created each month.

Given that brief summary of operations, draw the appropriate (and fully labeled) ERD. Use the Crow's foot methodology to indicate entities, relationships, connectivities, and participations.

12. During peak periods, Temporary Employment Corporation (TEC) places temporary workers in companies. TEC's manager gives you the following description of the business:

- TEC has a file of candidates who are willing to work.

- Any candidate who has worked before has a specific job history. (Naturally, no job history exists if the candidate has never worked.) Each time the candidate works, one additional job history record is created.

- Each candidate has earned several qualifications. Each qualification may be earned by more than one candidate. (For example, more than one candidate may have earned a Bachelor of Business Administration degree or a Microsoft Network Certification, and clearly a candidate may have earned both a BBA and a Microsoft Network Certification.)

- TEC offers courses to help candidates improve their qualifications.

- Every course develops one specific qualification; however, TEC does not offer a course for every qualification. Some qualifications are developed through multiple courses.

- Some courses cover advanced topics that require specific qualifications as prerequisites. Some courses cover basic topics that do not require any prerequisite qualifications. A course can have several prerequisites. A qualification can be a prerequisite for more than one course.

- Courses are taught during training sessions. A training session is the presentation of a single course. Over time, TEC will offer many training sessions for each course; however, new courses may not have any training sessions scheduled right away.

- Candidates can pay a fee to attend a training session. A training session can accommodate several candidates, although new training sessions will not have any candidates registered at first.

- TEC also has a list of companies that request temporaries.

- Each time a company requests a temporary employee, TEC makes an entry in the Openings folder. That folder contains an opening number, a company name, required qualifications, a starting date, an anticipated ending date, and hourly pay.

- Each opening requires only one specific or main qualification.

- When a candidate matches the qualification, the job is assigned, and an entry is made in the Placement Record folder. The folder contains such information as an opening number, candidate number, and total hours worked. In addition, an entry is made in the job history for the candidate.

- An opening can be filled by many candidates, and a candidate can fill many openings.

- TEC uses special codes to describe a candidate's qualifications for an opening. The list of codes is shown in Table P4.12.

TABLE P4.12

CODE	DESCRIPTION
SEC-45	Secretarial work; candidate must type at least 45 words per minute
SEC-60	Secretarial work; candidate must type at least 60 words per minute
CLERK	General clerking work
PRG-VB	Programmer, Visual Basic
PRG-C++	Programmer, C++
DBA-ORA	Database Administrator, Oracle
DBA-DB2	Database Administrator, IBM DB2
DBA-SQLSERV	Database Administrator, MS SQL Server
SYS-1	Systems Analyst, level 1
SYS-2	Systems Analyst, level 2
NW-NOV	Network Administrator, Novell experience
WD-CF	Web Developer, ColdFusion

TEC's management wants to keep track of the following entities:

COMPANY, OPENING, QUALIFICATION, CANDIDATE, JOB_HISTORY, PLACEMENT, COURSE, and SESSION. Given that information, do the following:

a. Draw the Crow's Foot ERDs for this enterprise.

b. Identify all necessary relationships.

c. Identify the connectivity for each relationship.

d. Identify the mandatory and optional dependencies for the relationships.

e. Resolve all M:N relationships.

13. Use the following description of the operations of the RC_Charter2 Company to complete this exercise.

   • The RC_Charter2 Company operates a fleet of aircraft under the Federal Air Regulations (FAR) Part 135 (air taxi or charter) certificate, enforced by the FAA. The aircraft are available for air taxi (charter) operations within the United States and Canada.

   • Charter companies provide so-called unscheduled operations—that is, charter flights take place only after a customer reserves the use of an aircraft at a designated date and time to fly to one or more designated destinations; the aircraft transports passengers, cargo, or some combination of passengers and cargo. Of course, a customer can reserve many different charter trips during any time frame. However, for billing purposes, each charter trip is reserved by one and only one customer. Some of RC_Charter2's customers do not use the company's charter operations; instead, they purchase fuel, use maintenance services, or use other RC_Charter2 services. However, this database design will focus on the charter operations only.

   • Each charter trip yields revenue for the RC_Charter2 Company. This revenue is generated by the charges a customer pays upon the completion of a flight. The charter flight charges are a function of aircraft model used, distance flown, waiting time, special customer requirements, and crew expenses. The distance flown charges are computed by multiplying the round-trip miles by the model's charge per mile. Round-trip miles are based on the actual navigational path flown. The sample route traced in Figure P4.13 illustrates the procedure. Note that the number of round-trip miles is calculated to be 130 + 200 + 180 + 390 = 900.

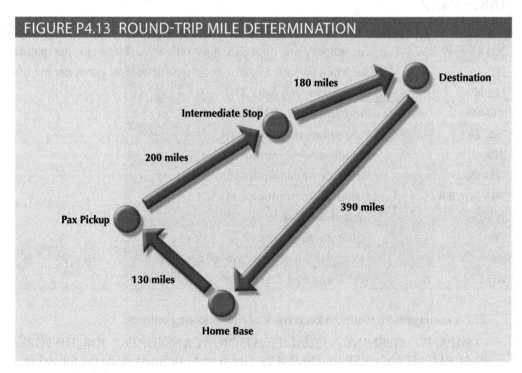

FIGURE P4.13 ROUND-TRIP MILE DETERMINATION

   • Depending on whether a customer has RC_Charter2 credit authorization, the customer may do the following:

   a. Pay the entire charter bill upon the completion of the charter flight.

   b. Pay a part of the charter bill and charge the remainder to the account. The charge amount may not exceed the available credit.

c. Charge the entire charter bill to the account. The charge amount may not exceed the available credit.

d. Customers may pay all or part of the existing balance for previous charter trips. Such payments may be made at any time and are not necessarily tied to a specific charter trip. The charter mileage charge includes the expense of the pilot(s) and other crew required by FAR 135. However, if customers request *additional* crew *not* required by FAR 135, those customers are charged for the crew members on an hourly basis. The hourly crew-member charge is based on each crew member's qualifications.

e. The database must be able to handle crew assignments. Each charter trip requires the use of an aircraft, and a crew flies each aircraft. The smaller, piston-engine charter aircraft require a crew consisting of only a single pilot. All jets and other aircraft that have a gross takeoff weight of at least 12,500 pounds require a pilot and a copilot, while some of the larger aircraft used to transport passengers may require flight attendants as part of the crew. Some of the older aircraft require the assignment of a flight engineer, and larger cargo-carrying aircraft require the assignment of a loadmaster. In short, a crew can consist of more than one person, and not all crew members are pilots.

f. The charter flight's aircraft waiting charges are computed by multiplying the hours waited by the model's hourly waiting charge. Crew expenses are limited to meals, lodging, and ground transportation.

The RC_Charter2 database must be designed to generate a monthly summary of all charter trips, expenses, and revenues derived from the charter records. Such records are based on the data that each pilot in command is required to record for each charter trip: trip date(s) and time(s), destination(s), aircraft number, pilot data and other crew data, distance flown, fuel usage, and other data pertinent to the charter flight. Such charter data is then used to generate monthly reports that detail revenue and operating cost information for customers, aircraft, and pilots. All pilots and other crew members are RC_Charter2 Company employees; that is, the company does not use contract pilots and crew.

FAR Part 135 operations are conducted under a strict set of requirements that govern the licensing and training of crew members. For example, pilots must have earned either a commercial license or an Airline Transport Pilot (ATP) license. Both licenses require appropriate ratings, which are specific competency requirements. For example, consider the following:

- To operate a multiengine aircraft designed for takeoffs and landings on land only, the appropriate rating is MEL, or Multiengine Landplane. When a multiengine aircraft can take off and land on water, the appropriate rating is MES, or Multiengine Seaplane.

- The instrument rating is based on a demonstrated ability to conduct all flight operations with sole reference to cockpit instrumentation. The instrument rating is required to operate an aircraft under Instrument Meteorological Conditions (IMC), and all such operations are governed under FAR-specified Instrument Flight Rules (IFR). In contrast, operations conducted under "good weather" or *visual* flight conditions are based on the FAR Visual Flight Rules (VFR).

- The type rating is required for all aircraft with a takeoff weight of more than 12,500 pounds or for aircraft that are purely jet-powered. If an aircraft uses jet engines to drive propellers, that aircraft is said to be turboprop-powered. A turboprop—that is, a turbo-propeller-powered aircraft—does not require a type rating unless it meets the 12,500-pound weight limitation.

- Although pilot licenses and ratings are not time limited, exercising the privilege of the license and ratings under Part 135 requires both *a current medical certificate and a current Part 135 checkride*. The following distinctions are important:

    a. The medical certificate may be Class I or Class II. The Class I medical is more stringent than the Class II, and it must be renewed every six months. The Class II medical must be renewed yearly. If the Class I medical is not renewed during the six-month period, it automatically reverts to a Class II certificate. If the Class II medical is not renewed within the specified period, it automatically reverts to a Class III medical, which is not valid for commercial flight operations.

    b. A Part 135 checkride is a practical flight examination that must be successfully completed every six months. The checkride includes all flight maneuvers and procedures specified in Part 135.

Nonpilot crew members must also have the proper certificates to meet specific job requirements. For example, loadmasters need an appropriate certificate, as do flight attendants. Crew members such as loadmasters and flight attendants may be required in operations that involve large aircraft with a takeoff weight of more than 12,500 pounds and more than 19 passengers; these crew members are also required to pass a written and practical exam periodically. The RC_Charter2 Company is required to keep a complete record of all test types, dates, and results for each crew member, as well as examination dates for pilot medical certificates.

In addition, all flight crew members are required to submit to periodic drug testing; the results must be tracked as well. Note that nonpilot crew members are not required to take pilot-specific tests such as Part 135 checkrides, nor are pilots required to take crew tests such as loadmaster and flight attendant practical exams. However, many crew members have licenses and certifications in several areas. For example, a pilot may have an ATP and a loadmaster certificate. If that pilot is assigned to be a loadmaster on a given charter flight, the loadmaster certificate is required. Similarly, a flight attendant may have earned a commercial pilot's license. Sample data formats are shown in Table P4.13.

Pilots and other crew members must receive recurrency training appropriate to their work assignments. Recurrency training is based on an FAA-approved curriculum that is job specific. For example, pilot recurrency training includes a review of all applicable Part 135 flight rules and regulations, weather data interpretation, company flight operations requirements, and specified flight procedures. The RC_Charter2 Company is required to keep a complete record of all recurrency training for each crew member subject to the training.

The RC_Charter2 Company is required to maintain a detailed record of all crew credentials and all training mandated by Part 135. The company must keep a complete record of each requirement and of all compliance data.

To conduct a charter flight, the company must have a properly maintained aircraft available. A pilot who meets all of the FAA's licensing and currency requirements must fly the aircraft as Pilot in Command (PIC). For aircraft that are powered by piston engines or turboprops and have a gross takeoff weight under 12,500 pounds, single-pilot operations are permitted under Part 135 as long as a properly maintained autopilot is available. However, even if FAR Part 135 permits single-pilot operations, many customers require the presence of a copilot who is capable of conducting the flight operations under Part 135.

TABLE P4.13

PART A TESTS

TEST CODE	TEST DESCRIPTION	TEST FREQUENCY
1	Part 135 Flight Check	6 months
2	Medical, Class I	6 months
3	Medical, Class II	12 months
4	Loadmaster Practical	12 months
5	Flight Attendant Practical	12 months
6	Drug test	Random
7	Operations, written exam	6 months

PART B RESULTS

EMPLOYEE	TEST CODE	TEST DATE	TEST RESULT
101	1	12-Nov-15	Pass-1
103	6	23-Dec-15	Pass-1
112	4	23-Dec-15	Pass-2
103	7	11-Jan-16	Pass-1
112	7	16-Jan-16	Pass-1
101	7	16-Jan-16	Pass-1
101	6	11-Feb-16	Pass-2
125	2	15-Feb-16	Pass-1

PART C LICENSES AND CERTIFICATIONS

LICENSE OR CERTIFICATE	LICENSE OR CERTIFICATE DESCRIPTION
ATP	Airline Transport Pilot
Comm	Commercial license
Med-1	Medical certificate, Class I
Med-2	Medical certificate, Class II
Instr	Instrument rating
MEL	Multiengine Land aircraft rating
LM	Loadmaster
FA	Flight Attendant

EMPLOYEE	LICENSE OR CERTIFICATE	DATE EARNED
101	Comm	12-Nov-93
101	Instr	28-Jun-94
101	MEL	9-Aug-94
103	Comm	21-Dec-95
112	FA	23-Jun-02
103	Instr	18-Jan-96
112	LM	27-Nov-05

The RC_Charter2 operations manager anticipates the lease of turbojet-powered aircraft, which are required to have a crew consisting of a pilot and copilot. Both the pilot and copilot must meet the same Part 135 licensing, ratings, and training requirements.

The company also leases larger aircraft that exceed the 12,500-pound gross takeoff weight. Those aircraft might carry enough passengers to require the presence of one or more flight attendants. If those aircraft carry cargo that weighs more than 12,500 pounds, a loadmaster must be assigned as a crew member to supervise the loading and securing of the cargo. *The database must be designed to meet the anticipated capability for additional charter crew assignments.*

a. Given this incomplete description of operations, write all applicable business rules to establish entities, relationships, optionalities, connectivities, and cardinalities. (*Hint:* Use the following five business rules as examples, and write the remaining business rules in the same format.) A customer may request many charter trips.

- Each charter trip is requested by only one customer.

- Some customers have not yet requested a charter trip.

- An employee may be assigned to serve as a crew member on many charter trips.

- Each charter trip may have many employees assigned to serve as crew members.

b. Draw the fully labeled and implementable Crow's Foot ERD based on the business rules you wrote in Part a. of this problem. Include all entities, relationships, optionalities, connectivities, and cardinalities.

MODULE

Building a Database and Defining Table Relationships

Creating the Billing, Owner, and Animal Tables

OBJECTIVES

Session 2.1
- Learn the guidelines for designing databases and setting field properties
- Create a table in Design view
- Define fields, set field properties, and specify a table's primary key
- Modify the structure of a table
- Change the order of fields in Design view
- Add new fields in Design view
- Change the Format property for a field in Datasheet view
- Modify field properties in Design view

Session 2.2
- Import data from Excel
- Import an existing table structure
- Add fields to a table with the Data Type gallery
- Delete and rename fields
- Change the data type for a field in Design view
- Set the Default Value property for a field
- Import a text file
- Define a relationship between two tables

Case | *Riverview Veterinary Care Center*

The Riverview database currently contains one table, the Visit table. Kimberly Johnson also wants to track information about the clinic's animals, their owners, and the invoices sent to them for services provided by Riverview Veterinary Care Center. This information includes such items as each owner's name and address, animal information, and the amount and billing date for each invoice.

In this module, you'll create three new tables in the Riverview database—named Billing, Owner, and Animal—to contain the additional data Kimberly wants to track. You will use two different methods for creating the tables, and learn how to modify the fields. After adding records to the tables, you will define the necessary relationships between the tables in the Riverview database to relate the tables, enabling Kimberly and her staff to work with the data more efficiently.

STARTING DATA FILES

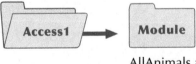

Access1 → **Module**

AllAnimals.accdb
Invoices.xlsx
Kelly.accdb
Owner.txt
Riverview.accdb (*cont.*)

Review

Supplies.xlsx
Vendor.accdb (*cont.*)

Case1

Beauty.accdb (*cont.*)
Customers.txt

Case2

Agreements.xlsx
Client.accdb
Programming.accdb (*cont.*)
Students.txt

Case3

Auctions.txt
Center.accdb (*cont.*)
Donations.xlsx

Case4

Appalachia.accdb (*cont.*)
Bookings.txt
Travel.accdb

AC 51

Session 2.1 Visual Overview:

Design view allows you to define or modify a table structure or the properties of the fields in a table.

The default name for a new table you create in Design view is Table1. This name appears on the tab for the new table.

The top portion of the Table window in Design view is called the **Table Design grid**. Here, you enter values for the Field Name, Data type, and Description field properties.

In the Field Name column, you enter the name for each new field in the table. When you first open a new Table window in Design view, Field Name is the current property.

In the Data Type column, you select the appropriate data type for each new field in the table. The data type determines what field values you can enter for a new field and what other properties the field will have. The default data type for a new field is Short Text.

After you assign a data type to a field, the General tab displays additional field properties for that data type. Initially, most field properties are assigned default values.

When defining the fields in a table, you can move from the Table Design grid to the Field Properties pane by pressing the **F6** key.

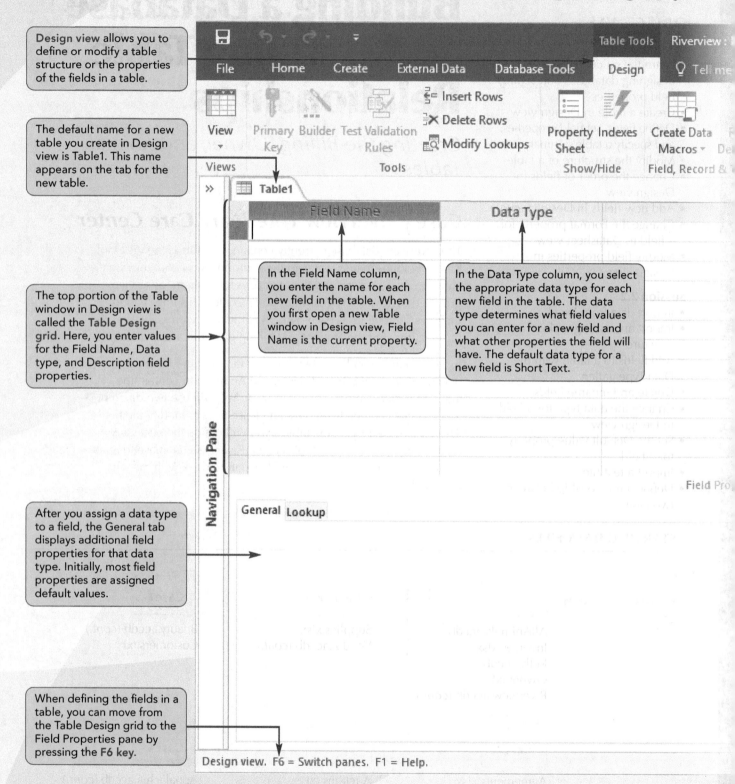

File   Home   Create   External Data   Database Tools   Design   Tell me

Table Tools   Riverview :

View

Primary Key

Builder   Test Validation Rules

Insert Rows
Delete Rows
Modify Lookups

Property Sheet   Indexes   Create Data Macros   De

Views   Tools   Show/Hide   Field, Record &

Navigation Pane

Table1

Field Name   Data Type

General   Lookup

Field Pro

Design view. F6 = Switch panes. F1 = Help.

Table Window in Design View

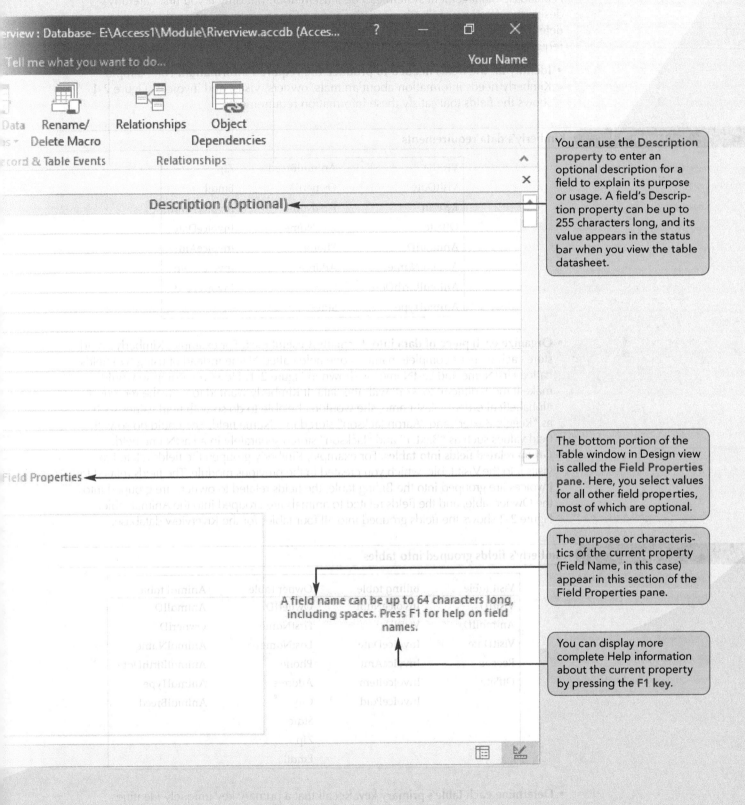

Riverview : Database- E:\Access1\Module\Riverview.accdb (Acces... ? — □ ×

Tell me what you want to do...   Your Name

Data   Rename/   Relationships   Object
        Delete Macro   Dependencies

cord & Table Events   Relationships

Description (Optional)

You can use the **Description property** to enter an optional description for a field to explain its purpose or usage. A field's Description property can be up to 255 characters long, and its value appears in the status bar when you view the table datasheet.

Field Properties

The bottom portion of the Table window in Design view is called the **Field Properties pane.** Here, you select values for all other field properties, most of which are optional.

The purpose or characteristics of the current property (Field Name, in this case) appear in this section of the Field Properties pane.

A field name can be up to 64 characters long, including spaces. Press F1 for help on field names.

You can display more complete Help information about the current property by pressing the **F1 key.**

Guidelines for Designing Databases

A database management system can be a useful tool, but only if you first carefully design the database so that it meets the needs of its users. In database design, you determine the fields, tables, and relationships needed to satisfy the data and processing requirements. When you design a database, you should follow these guidelines:

- **Identify all the fields needed to produce the required information.** For example, Kimberly needs information about animals, owners, visits, and invoices. Figure 2-1 shows the fields that satisfy these information requirements.

Figure 2-1	Kimberly's data requirements

VisitID	AnimalBreed	Zip
VisitDate	OwnerID	Email
Reason	FirstName	InvoiceNum
OffSite	LastName	InvoiceDate
AnimalID	Phone	InvoiceAmt
AnimalName	Address	InvoiceItem
AnimalBirthDate	City	InvoicePaid
AnimalType	State	

- **Organize each piece of data into its smallest useful part.** For example, Kimberly could store each owner's complete name in one field called Name instead of using two fields called FirstName and LastName, as shown in Figure 2-1. However, doing so would make it more difficult to work with the data. If Kimberly wanted to view the records in alphabetical order by last name, she wouldn't be able to do so with field values such as "Reggie Baxter" and "Aaron Jackson" stored in a Name field. She could do so with field values such as "Baxter" and "Jackson" stored separately in a LastName field.
- **Group related fields into tables.** For example, Kimberly grouped the fields related to visits into the Visit table, which you created in the previous module. The fields related to invoices are grouped into the Billing table, the fields related to owners are grouped into the Owner table, and the fields related to animals are grouped into the Animal table. Figure 2-2 shows the fields grouped into all four tables for the Riverview database.

Figure 2-2	Kimberly's fields grouped into tables

Visit table	Billing table	Owner table	Animal table
VisitID	InvoiceNum	OwnerID	AnimalID
AnimalID	VisitID	FirstName	OwnerID
VisitDate	InvoiceDate	LastName	AnimalName
Reason	InvoiceAmt	Phone	AnimalBirthDate
OffSite	InvoiceItem	Address	AnimalType
	InvoicePaid	City	AnimalBreed
		State	
		Zip	
		Email	

- **Determine each table's primary key.** Recall that a primary key uniquely identifies each record in a table. For some tables, one of the fields, such as a credit card number, naturally serves the function of a primary key. For other tables, two or more fields might be needed to function as the primary key. In these cases, the primary key is called a **composite key**. For example, a school grade table would use a combination of student number, term, and course code to serve as the primary key. For a third category of tables, no single field or combination of fields can uniquely identify a record in a table. In these cases, you need to add a field whose sole purpose is to serve as the table's primary key. For Kimberly's tables, VisitID is the primary key for the Visit table, InvoiceNum is the primary key for the Billing table, OwnerID is the primary key for the Owner table, and AnimalID is the primary key for the Animal table.

- **Include a common field in related tables.** You use the common field to connect one table logically with another table. For example, Kimberly's Visit and Animal tables include the AnimalID field as a common field. Recall that when you include the primary key from one table as a field in a second table to form a relationship, the field in the second table is called a foreign key; therefore, the AnimalID field is a foreign key in the Visit table. With this common field, Kimberly can find all visits to the clinic made by a particular animal; she can use the AnimalID value for an animal and search the Visit table for all records with that AnimalID value. Likewise, she can determine which animal made a particular visit by searching the Animal table to find the one record with the same AnimalID value as the corresponding value in the Visit table. Similarly, the VisitID field is a common field, serving as the primary key in the Visit table and a foreign key in the Billing table. Since animals have owners responsible for their bills, there must be a relationship between the animals and owners for the clinic to contact; therefore, the OwnerID field is a foreign key in the Animal table.

- **Avoid data redundancy.** When you store the same data in more than one place, **data redundancy** occurs. With the exception of common fields to connect tables, you should avoid data redundancy because it wastes storage space and can cause inconsistencies. An inconsistency would exist, for example, if you type a field value one way in one table and a different way in the same table or in a second table. Figure 2-3, which contains portions of potential data stored in the Animal and Visit tables, shows an example of incorrect database design that has data redundancy in the Visit table. In Figure 2-3, the AnimalName field in the Visit table is redundant, and one value for this field was entered incorrectly, in three different ways.

Figure 2-3	Incorrect database design with data redundancy

AnimalID	AnimalName	AnimalBirthDate	AnimalType
12286	Lady	8/12/2015	Dog
12304	Tweets	11/12/2010	Bird
12332	Smittie	5/19/2014	Cat
12345	Herford5	4/28/2015	Cattle
12359	Merino4	8/2/2014	Sheep

data redundancy

VisitID	AnimalID	AnimalName	VisitDate	OffSite
1202	12500	Bonkers	12/11/2016	No
1250	12332	Smitty	12/19/2016	No
1276	12492	Bessie	1/10/2017	Yes
1308	12332	Smity	1/23/2017	No
1325	12612	Tweets	2/6/2017	No
1342	12595	Angus	2/27/2017	Yes
1367	12332	Smittee	3/7/2017	No

Inconsistent data

- **Determine the properties of each field.** You need to identify the **properties**, or characteristics, of each field so that the DBMS knows how to store, display, and process the field values. These properties include the field's name, data type, maximum number of characters or digits, description, valid values, and other field characteristics. You will learn more about field properties later in this module.

The Billing, Owner, and Animal tables you need to create will contain the fields shown in Figure 2-2. Before creating these new tables in the Riverview database, you first need to learn some guidelines for setting field properties.

Guidelines for Setting Field Properties

As just noted, the last step of database design is to determine which values to assign to the properties, such as the name and data type, of each field. When you select or enter a value for a property, you **set** the property. Access has rules for naming fields and objects, assigning data types, and setting other field properties.

Naming Fields and Objects

You must name each field, table, and other object in an Access database. Access stores these items in the database, using the names you supply. It's best to choose a field or object name that describes the purpose or contents of the field or object so that later you can easily remember what the name represents. For example, the four tables in the Riverview database are named Visit, Billing, Owner, and Animal because these names suggest their contents. Note that a table or query name must be unique within a database. A field name must be unique within a table, but it can be used again in another table.

Assigning Field Data Types

Each field must have a data type, which is either assigned automatically by Access or specifically by the table designer. The data type determines what field values you can enter for the field and what other properties the field will have. For example, the Billing table will include an InvoiceDate field, which will store date values, so you will assign the Date/Time data type to this field. Then Access will allow you to enter and manipulate only dates or times as values in the InvoiceDate field.

Figure 2-4 lists the most commonly used data types in Access, describes the field values allowed for each data type, explains when you should use each data type, and indicates the field size of each data type. You can find more complete information about all available data types in Access Help.

| Figure 2-4 | Common data types |

Data Type	Description	Field Size
Short Text	Allows field values containing letters, digits, spaces, and special characters. Use for names, addresses, descriptions, and fields containing digits that are *not used in calculations*.	0 to 255 characters; default is 255
Long Text	Allows field values containing letters, digits, spaces, and special characters. Use for long comments and explanations.	1 to 65,535 characters; exact size is determined by entry
Number	Allows positive and negative numbers as field values. A number can contain digits, a decimal point, commas, a plus sign, and a minus sign. Use for fields that will be used in calculations, except those involving money.	1 to 15 digits
Date/Time	Allows field values containing valid dates and times from January 1, 100 to December 31, 9999. Dates can be entered in month/day/year format, several other date formats, or a variety of time formats, such as 10:35 PM. You can perform calculations on dates and times, and you can sort them. For example, you can determine the number of days between two dates.	8 bytes
Currency	Allows field values similar to those for the Number data type, but is used for storing monetary values. Unlike calculations with Number data type decimal values, calculations performed with the Currency data type are not subject to round-off error.	Accurate to 15 digits on the left side of the decimal point and to 4 digits on the right side
AutoNumber	Consists of integer values created automatically by Access each time you create a new record. You can specify sequential numbering or random numbering, which guarantees a unique field value, so that such a field can serve as a table's primary key.	9 digits
Yes/No	Limits field values to yes and no, on and off, or true and false. Use for fields that indicate the presence or absence of a condition, such as whether an order has been filled or whether an invoice has been paid.	1 character
Hyperlink	Consists of text used as a hyperlink address, which can have up to four parts: the text that appears in a field or control; the path to a file or page; a location within the file or page; and text displayed as a ScreenTip.	Up to 65,535 characters total for the four parts of the hyperlink

Setting Field Sizes

The **Field Size property** defines a field value's maximum storage size for Short Text, Number, and AutoNumber fields only. The other data types have no Field Size property because their storage size is either a fixed, predetermined amount or is determined automatically by the field value itself, as shown in Figure 2-4. A Short Text field has a default field size of 255 characters; you can also set its field size by entering a number from 0 to 255. For example, the FirstName and LastName fields in the Owner table will be Short Text fields with sizes of 20 characters and 25 characters, respectively. These field sizes will accommodate the values that will be entered in each of these fields.

Decision Making: Specifying the Field Size Property for Number Fields

When you use the Number data type to define a field, you need to decide what the Field Size setting should be for the field. You should set the Field Size property based on the largest value that you expect to store in that field. Access processes smaller data sizes faster, using less memory, so you can optimize your database's performance and its storage space by selecting the correct field size for each field. Field Size property settings for Number fields are as follows:

- **Byte**: Stores whole numbers (numbers with no fractions) from 0 to 255 in one byte
- **Integer**: Stores whole numbers from –32,768 to 32,767 in two bytes
- **Long Integer** (default): Stores whole numbers from –2,147,483,648 to 2,147,483,647 in four bytes
- **Single**: Stores positive and negative numbers to precisely seven decimal places in four bytes
- **Double**: Stores positive and negative numbers to precisely 15 decimal places in eight bytes
- **Replication ID**: Establishes a unique identifier for replication of tables, records, and other objects in databases created using Access 2003 and earlier versions in 16 bytes
- **Decimal**: Stores positive and negative numbers to precisely 28 decimal places in 12 bytes

Choosing an appropriate field size is important to optimize efficiency. For example, it would be wasteful to use the Long Integer field size for a Number field that will store only whole numbers ranging from 0 to 255 because the Long Integer field size uses four bytes of storage space. A better choice would be the Byte field size, which uses one byte of storage space to store the same values. By first gathering and analyzing information about the number values that will be stored in a Number field, you can make the best decision for the field's Field Size property and ensure the most efficient user experience for the database.

Setting the Caption Property for Fields

The **Caption property** for a field specifies how the field name is displayed in database objects, including table and query datasheets, forms, and reports. If you don't set the Caption property, Access displays the field name as the column heading or label for a field. For example, field names such as InvoiceAmt and InvoiceDate in the Billing table can be difficult to read. Setting the Caption property for these fields to "Invoice Amt" and "Invoice Date" would make it easier for users to read the field names and work with the database.

Setting the Caption Property vs. Naming Fields

Although Access allows you to include spaces in field names, this practice is not recommended because the spaces cause problems when you try to perform more complex tasks with the data in your database. Setting the Caption property allows you to follow best practices for naming fields, such as not including spaces in field names, while still providing users with more readable field names in datasheets, forms, and reports.

In the previous module, you created the Riverview database file and, within that file, you created the Visit table working in Datasheet view. According to her plan for the Riverview database, Kimberly also wants to track information about the invoices the care center sends to the owners of the animals. Next, you'll create the Billing table for Kimberly—this time, working in Design view.

Creating a Table in Design View

Creating a table in Design view involves entering the field names and defining the properties for the fields, specifying a primary key for the table, and then saving the table structure. Kimberly documented the design for the new Billing table by listing each field's name and data type; each field's size and description (if applicable); and any other properties to be set for each field. See Figure 2-5.

| Figure 2-5 | Design for the Billing table |

Field Name	Data Type	Field Size	Description	Other
InvoiceNum	Short Text	5	Primary key	Caption = Invoice Num
VisitID	Short Text	4	Foreign key	Caption = Visit ID
InvoiceAmt	Currency			Format = Currency
				Decimal Places = 2
				Caption = Invoice Amt
InvoiceDate	Date/Time			Format = mm/dd/yyyy
				Caption = Invoice Date
InvoicePaid	Yes/No			Caption = Invoice Paid

You'll use Kimberly's design as a guide for creating the Billing table in the Riverview database.

To begin creating the Billing table:

▶ **1.** Start Access and open the **Riverview** database you created in the previous module.

Trouble? If the security warning is displayed below the ribbon, click the **Enable Content** button.

▶ **2.** If the Navigation Pane is open, click the **Shutter Bar Open/Close Button** ⟨⟨ to close it.

▶ **3.** On the ribbon, click the **Create** tab.

▶ **4.** In the Tables group, click the **Table Design** button. A new table named Table1 opens in Design view. Refer to the Session 2.1 Visual Overview for a complete description of the Table window in Design view.

Defining Fields

When you first create a table in Design view, the insertion point is located in the first row's Field Name box, ready for you to begin defining the first field in the table. You enter values for the Field Name, Data Type, and Description field properties, and then select values for all other field properties in the Field Properties pane. These other properties will appear when you move to the first row's Data Type box.

REFERENCE

Defining a Field in Design View

- In the Field Name box, type the name for the field, and then press the Tab key.
- Accept the default Short Text data type, or click the arrow and select a different data type for the field. Press the Tab key.
- Enter an optional description for the field, if necessary.
- Use the Field Properties pane to type or select other field properties, as appropriate.

The first field you need to define is the InvoiceNum field. This field will be the primary key for the Billing table. Each invoice at Riverview Veterinary Care Center is assigned a specific five-digit number. Although the InvoiceNum field will contain these number values, the numbers will never be used in calculations; therefore, you'll assign the Short Text data type to this field. Any time a field contains number values that will not be used in calculations—such as phone numbers, zip codes, and so on—you should use the Short Text data type instead of the Number data type.

To define the InvoiceNum field:

TIP

You can also press the Enter key to move from one property to the next in the Table Design grid.

1. Type **InvoiceNum** in the first row's Field Name box, and then press the **Tab** key to advance to the Data Type box. The default data type, Short Text, is selected in the Data Type box, which now also contains an arrow, and the field properties for a Short Text field appear in the Field Properties pane. See Figure 2-6.

Figure 2-6   Table window after entering the first field name

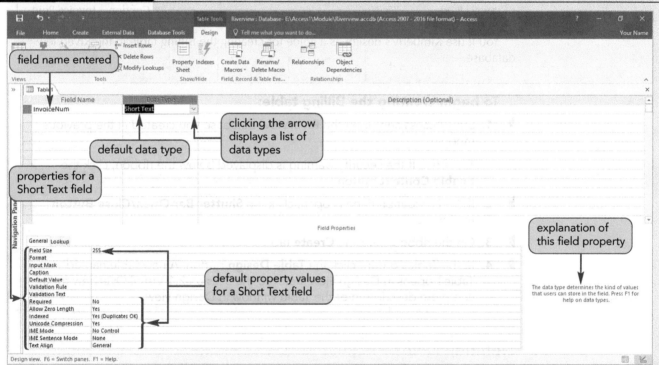

Notice that the right side of the Field Properties pane now provides an explanation for the current property, Data Type.

Trouble? If you make a typing error, you can correct it by clicking to position the insertion point, and then using either the Backspace key to delete characters to the left of the insertion point or the Delete key to delete characters to the right of the insertion point. Then type the correct text.

Because the InvoiceNum field values will not be used in calculations, you will accept the default Short Text data type for the field.

2. Press the **Tab** key to accept Short Text as the data type and to advance to the Description (Optional) box.

> **3.** Next you'll enter the Description property value as "Primary key." The value you enter for the Description property will appear in the status bar when you view the table datasheet. Note that specifying "Primary key" for the Description property does *not* establish the current field as the primary key; you use a button on the ribbon to specify the primary key in Design view, which you will do later in this session.

> **4.** Type **Primary key** in the Description (Optional) box.

> Notice the Field Size property for the field. The default setting of 255 for Short Text fields is displayed. You need to change this number to 5 because all invoice numbers at Riverview Veterinary Care Center contain only five digits.

> **5.** Double-click the number **255** in the Field Size property box to select it, and then type **5**.

> Finally, you need to set the Caption property for the field so that its name appears with a space, as "Invoice Num."

> **6.** Click the **Caption** property box, and then type **Invoice Num**. The definition of the first field is complete. See Figure 2-7.

Figure 2-7 **InvoiceNum field defined**

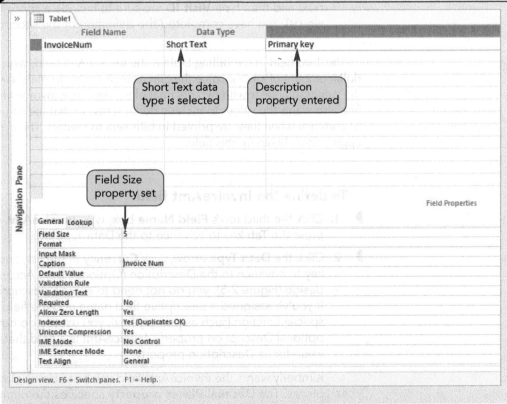

Kimberly's Billing table design (Figure 2-5) shows VisitID as the second field. Because Kimberly and other staff members need to relate information about invoices to the visit data in the Visit table, the Billing table must include the VisitID field, which is the Visit table's primary key. Recall that when you include the primary key from one table as a field in a second table to connect the two tables, the field is a foreign key in the second table. The field must be defined in the same way in both tables—that is, the field properties, including field size and data type, must match exactly.

Next, you will define VisitID as a Short Text field with a field size of 4. Later in this session, you'll change the Field Size property for the VisitID field in the Visit table to 4 so that the field definition is the same in both tables.

To define the VisitID field:

▶ **1.** In the Table Design grid, click the second row's **Field Name** box, type **VisitID**, and then press the **Tab** key to advance to the Data Type box.

▶ **2.** Press the **Tab** key to accept Short Text as the field's data type. Because the VisitID field is a foreign key to the Visit table, you'll enter "Foreign key" in the Description (Optional) box to help users of the database understand the purpose of this field.

▶ **3.** Type **Foreign key** in the Description (Optional) box. Next, you'll change the Field Size property.

▶ **4.** Press the **F6** key to move to the Field Properties pane. The current entry for the Field Size property, 255, is selected.

▶ **5.** Type **4** to set the Field Size property. Finally, you need to set the Caption property for this field.

▶ **6.** Press the **Tab** key three times to position the insertion point in the Caption box, and then type **Visit ID** (be sure to include a space between the two words). You have completed the definition of the second field.

The third field in the Billing table is the InvoiceAmt field, which will display the dollar amount of each invoice the clinic sends to the animals' owners. Kimberly wants the values to appear with two decimal places because invoice amounts include cents. She also wants the values to include dollar signs, so that the values will be formatted as currency when they are printed in bills sent to owners. The Currency data type is the appropriate choice for this field.

To define the InvoiceAmt field:

▶ **1.** Click the third row's **Field Name** box, type **InvoiceAmt** in the box, and then press the **Tab** key to advance to the Data Type box.

▶ **2.** Click the **Data Type** arrow, click **Currency** in the list, and then press the **Tab** key to advance to the Description (Optional) box. According to Kimberly's design (Figure 2-5), you do not need to enter a description for this field. If you've assigned a descriptive field name and the field does not fulfill a special function (such as primary key), you usually do not enter a value for the optional Description property. InvoiceAmt is a field that does not require a value for its Description property.

Kimberly wants the InvoiceAmt field values to be displayed with two decimal places. The **Decimal Places property** specifies the number of decimal places that are displayed to the right of the decimal point.

TIP

You can display the arrow and the list simultaneously by clicking the right side of a box.

3. In the Field Properties pane, click the **Decimal Places** box to position the insertion point there. An arrow appears on the right side of the Decimal Places box, which you can click to display a list of options.

4. Click the **Decimal Places** arrow, and then click **2** in the list to specify two decimal places for the InvoiceAmt field values.

5. Press the **Tab** key twice to position the insertion point in the Caption box, and then type **Invoice Amt**. The definition of the third field is now complete. Notice that the Format property is set to "Currency," which formats the values with dollar signs. See Figure 2-8.

| Figure 2-8 | Table window after defining the first three fields |

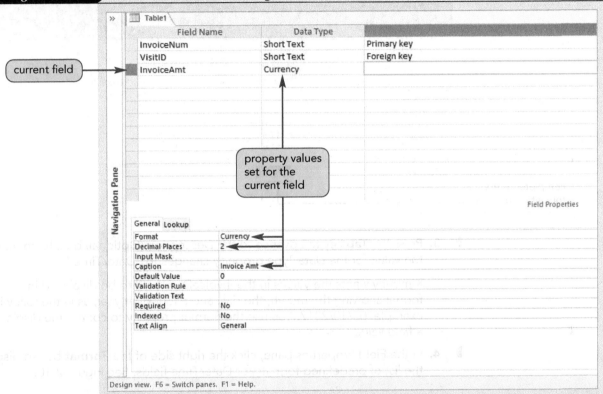

The fourth field in the Billing table is the InvoiceDate field. This field will contain the dates on which invoices are generated for the animals in the care center. You'll define the InvoiceDate field using the Date/Time data type. Also, according to Kimberly's design (Figure 2-5), the date values should be displayed in the format mm/dd/yyyy, which is a two-digit month, a two-digit day, and a four-digit year.

To define the InvoiceDate field:

1. Click the fourth row's **Field Name** box, type **InvoiceDate**, and then press the **Tab** key to advance to the Data Type box.

   You can select a value from the Data Type list as you did for the InvoiceAmt field. Alternately, you can type the property value in the box or type just the first character of the property value.

2. Type **d**. Access completes the entry for the fourth row's Data Type box to "date/Time," with the letters "ate/Time" selected. See Figure 2-9.

Figure 2-9 **Selecting a value for the Data Type property**

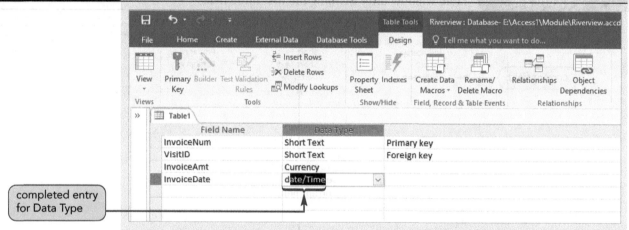

completed entry for Data Type

3. Press the **Tab** key to advance to the Description (Optional) box. Note that the value for the Data Type property changes to "Date/Time."

   Kimberly wants the values in the InvoiceDate field to be displayed in a format showing the month, the day, and a four-digit year, as in the following example: 03/10/2017. You use the Format property to control the display of a field value.

4. In the Field Properties pane, click the right side of the **Format** box to display the list of predefined formats for Date/Time fields. See Figure 2-10.

Figure 2-10 **Displaying available formats for Date/Time fields**

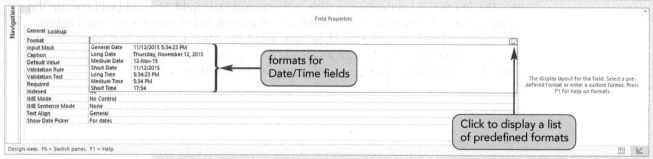

formats for Date/Time fields

Click to display a list of predefined formats

Trouble? If you see an arrow instead of a list of predefined formats, click the arrow to display the list.

As noted in the right side of the Field Properties pane, you can either choose a predefined format or enter a custom format. Even though the Short Date format seems to match the format Kimberly wants, it displays only one digit for months that contain only one digit. For example, it would display the month of March with only the digit "3"—as in 3/10/2017—instead of displaying the month with two digits, as in 03/10/2017.

Because none of the predefined formats matches the exact layout Kimberly wants for the InvoiceDate values, you need to create a custom date format. Figure 2-11 shows some of the symbols available for custom date and time formats.

| Figure 2-11 | Symbols for some custom date formats |

Symbol	Description
/	date separator
d	day of the month in one or two numeric digits, as needed (1 to 31)
dd	day of the month in two numeric digits (01 to 31)
ddd	first three letters of the weekday (Sun to Sat)
dddd	full name of the weekday (Sunday to Saturday)
w	day of the week (1 to 7)
ww	week of the year (1 to 53)
m	month of the year in one or two numeric digits, as needed (1 to 12)
mm	month of the year in two numeric digits (01 to 12)
mmm	first three letters of the month (Jan to Dec)
mmmm	full name of the month (January to December)
yy	last two digits of the year (01 to 99)
yyyy	full year (0100 to 9999)

Kimberly wants the dates to be displayed with a two-digit month (mm), a two-digit day (dd), and a four-digit year (yyyy).

5. Click the **Format** arrow to close the list of predefined formats, and then type **mm/dd/yyyy** in the Format box.

6. Press the **Tab** key twice to position the insertion point in the Caption box, and then type **Invoice Date**. See Figure 2-12.

Figure 2-12   Specifying the custom date format

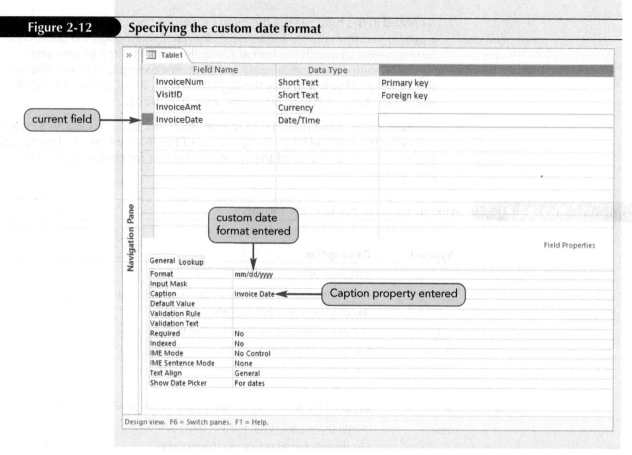

The fifth and final field to be defined in the Billing table is InvoicePaid. This field will be a Yes/No field to indicate the payment status of each invoice record stored in the Billing table. Recall that the Yes/No data type is used to define fields that store true/false, yes/no, and on/off field values. When you create a Yes/No field in a table, the default Format property is set to Yes/No.

To define the InvoicePaid field:

1. Click the fifth row's **Field Name** box, type **InvoicePaid**, and then press the **Tab** key to advance to the Data Type box.

2. Type **y**. Access completes the data type as "yes/No".

3. Press the **Tab** key to select the Yes/No data type and move to the Description (Optional) box. In the Field Properties pane, note that the default format of "Yes/No" is selected, so you do not have to change this property.

4. In the Field Properties pane, click the **Caption** box, and then type **Invoice Paid**.

You've finished defining the fields for the Billing table. Next, you need to specify the primary key for the table.

Specifying the Primary Key

As you learned earlier, the primary key for a table uniquely identifies each record in the table.

Specifying a Primary Key in Design View

- Display the table in Design view.
- Click in the row for the field you've chosen to be the primary key to make it the active field. If the primary key will consist of two or more fields, click the row selector for the first field, press and hold the Ctrl key, and then click the row selector for each additional primary key field.
- In the Tools group on the Table Tools Design tab, click the Primary Key button.

According to Kimberly's design, you need to specify InvoiceNum as the primary key for the Billing table. You can do so while the table is in Design view.

To specify InvoiceNum as the primary key:

1. Click in the row for the InvoiceNum field to make it the current field.

TIP

This button is a toggle; you can click it to remove the key symbol.

2. On the Table Tools Design tab, in the Tools group, click the **Primary Key** button. The Primary Key button in the Tools group is now selected, and a key symbol appears in the row selector for the first row, indicating that the InvoiceNum field is the table's primary key. See Figure 2-13.

Figure 2-13	InvoiceNum field selected as the primary key

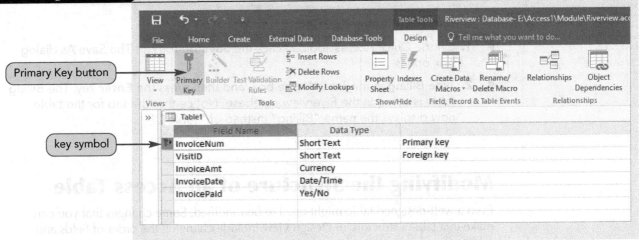

Primary Key button

key symbol

Understanding the Importance of the Primary Key

Although Access does not require a table to have a primary key, including a primary key offers several advantages:

- A primary key uniquely identifies each record in a table.
- Access does not allow duplicate values in the primary key field. For example, if a record already exists in the Visit table with a VisitID value of 1550, Access prevents you from adding another record with this same value in the VisitID field. Preventing duplicate values ensures the uniqueness of the primary key field.
- When a primary key has been specified, Access forces you to enter a value for the primary key field in every record in the table. This is known as **entity integrity**. If you do not enter a value for a field, you have actually given the field a **null value**. You cannot give a null value to the primary key field because entity integrity prevents Access from accepting and processing that record.
- You can enter records in any order, but Access displays them by default in order of the primary key's field values. If you enter records in no specific order, you are ensured that you will later be able to work with them in a more meaningful, primary key sequence.
- Access responds faster to your requests for specific records based on the primary key.

Saving the Table Structure

The last step in creating a table is to name the table and save the table's structure. When you save a table structure, the table is stored in the database file (in this case, the Riverview database file). Once the table is saved, you can enter data into it. According to Kimberly's plan, you need to save the table you've defined as "Billing."

To name and save the Billing table:

▶ 1. On the Quick Access Toolbar, click the **Save** button 🔛. The Save As dialog box opens.

▶ 2. Type **Billing** in the Table Name box, and then press the **Enter** key. The Billing table is saved in the Riverview database. Notice that the tab for the table now displays the name "Billing" instead of "Table1."

Modifying the Structure of an Access Table

Even a well-designed table might need to be modified. Some changes that you can make to a table's structure in Design view include changing the order of fields and adding new fields.

After meeting with her assistant, Kelly Flannagan, and reviewing the structure of the Billing table, Kimberly has changes she wants you to make to the table. First, she wants the InvoiceAmt field to be moved so that it appears right before the InvoicePaid field. Then, she wants you to add a new Short Text field named InvoiceItem to the table to include information about what the invoice is for, such as office visits, lab work, and so on. Kimberly would like the InvoiceItem field to be inserted between the InvoiceAmt and InvoicePaid fields.

Moving a Field in Design View

To move a field, you use the mouse to drag it to a new location in the Table Design grid. Although you can move a field in Datasheet view by dragging its column heading to a new location, doing so rearranges only the *display* of the table's fields; the table structure is not changed. To move a field permanently, you must move the field in Design view.

Next, you'll move the InvoiceAmt field so that it is before the InvoicePaid field in the Billing table.

To move the InvoiceAmt field:

▶ **1.** Position the pointer on the row selector for the InvoiceAmt field until the pointer changes to ➡.

▶ **2.** Click the **row selector** to select the entire InvoiceAmt row.

▶ **3.** Place the pointer on the row selector for the InvoiceAmt field until the pointer changes to ⬚, press and hold the mouse button and then drag to the row selector for the InvoicePaid field. Notice that as you drag, the pointer changes to ⬚. See Figure 2-14.

Figure 2-14	Moving the InvoiceAmt field in the table structure

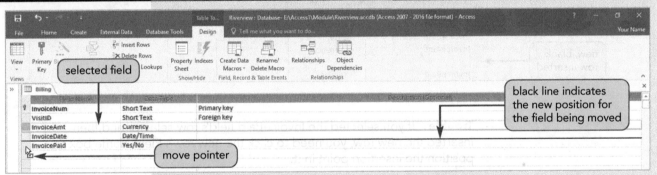

▶ **4.** Release the mouse button. The InvoiceAmt field now appears between the InvoiceDate and InvoicePaid fields in the table structure.

Trouble? If the InvoiceAmt field did not move, repeat Steps 1 through 4, making sure you hold down the mouse button during the drag operation.

Adding a Field in Design View

To add a new field between existing fields, you must insert a row. You begin by selecting the row below where you want the new field to be inserted.

REFERENCE

Adding a Field Between Two Existing Fields

- In the Table window in Design view, select the row below where you want the new field to be inserted.
- In the Tools group on the Table Tools Design tab, click the Insert Rows button.
- Define the new field by entering the field name, data type, optional description, and any property specifications.

Next, you need to add the InvoiceItem field to the Billing table structure between the InvoiceAmt and InvoicePaid fields.

To add the InvoiceItem field to the Billing table:

1. Click the **InvoicePaid Field Name** box. You need to establish this field as the current field so that the row for the new record will be inserted above this field.

2. On the Table Tools Design tab, in the Tools group, click the **Insert Rows** button. A new, blank row is added between the InvoiceAmt and InvoicePaid fields. The insertion point is positioned in the Field Name box for the new row, ready for you to type the name for the new field. See Figure 2-15.

Figure 2-15	Table structure after inserting a row

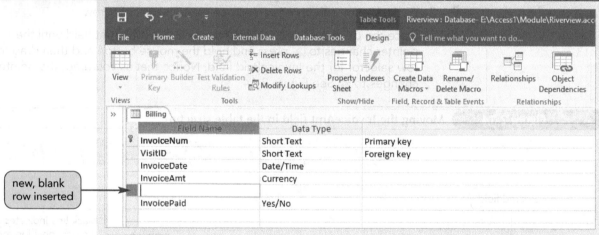

new, blank row inserted

Trouble? If you selected the InvoicePaid field's row selector and then inserted the new row, you need to click the new row's Field Name box to position the insertion point in it.

You'll define the InvoiceItem field in the new row of the Billing table. This field will be a Short Text field with a field size of 40, and you need to set the Caption property to include a space between the words in the field name.

3. Type **InvoiceItem**, press the **Tab** key to move to the Data Type property, and then press the **Tab** key again to accept the default Short Text data type.

4. Press the **F6** key to select the default field size in the Field Size box, and then type **40**.

5. Press the **Tab** key three times to position the insertion point in the Caption box, and then type **Invoice Item**. The definition of the new field is complete. See Figure 2-16.

Figure 2-16	InvoiceItem field added to the Billing table

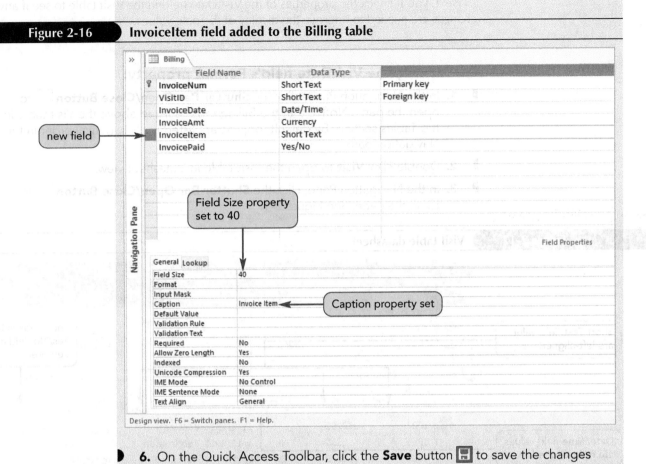

6. On the Quick Access Toolbar, click the **Save** button 🖫 to save the changes to the Billing table structure.

7. Click the **Close 'Billing'** button ⊠ on the object tab to close the Billing table.

Modifying Field Properties

With the Billing table design complete, you can now go back and modify the properties of the fields in the Visit table you created in the previous module, as necessary. You can make some changes to properties in Datasheet view; for others, you'll work in Design view.

Changing the Format Property in Datasheet View

The Formatting group on the Table Tools Fields tab in Datasheet view allows you to modify some formatting for certain field types. When you format a field, you change the way data is displayed, but not the actual values stored in the table.

Next, you'll check the properties of the VisitDate field in the Visit table to see if any changes are needed to improve the display of the date values.

To modify the VisitDate field's Format property:

1. In the Navigation Pane, click the **Shutter Bar Open/Close Button** >> to open the pane. Notice that the Billing table is listed above the Visit table in the Tables section. By default, objects are listed in alphabetical order in the Navigation pane.

2. Double-click **Visit** to open the Visit table in Datasheet view.

3. In the Navigation Pane, click the **Shutter Bar Open/Close Button** << to close the pane. See Figure 2-17.

Figure 2-17	Visit table datasheet

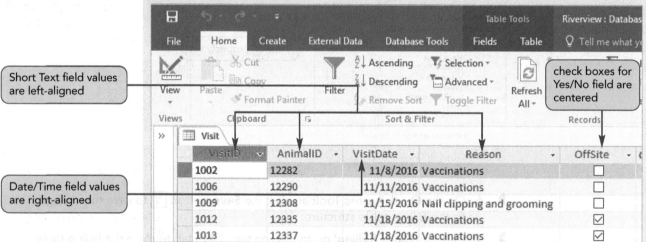

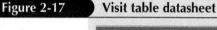

Notice that the values in the three Short Text fields—VisitID, AnimalID, and Reason—appear left-aligned within their boxes, and the values in the Date/Time field (VisitDate) appear right-aligned. In Access, values for Short Text fields are left-aligned, and values for Number, Date/Time, and Currency fields are right-aligned. The Offsite field is a Yes/No field, so its values appear in check boxes that are centered within the column.

4. On the ribbon, click the **Table Tools Fields** tab.

5. Click the **first field value** in the VisitDate column. The Data Type option shows that this field is a Date/Time field.

By default, Access assigns the General Date format to Date/Time fields. Note the Format box in the Formatting group, which you use to set the Format property (similar to how you set the Format property in the Field Properties pane in Design view.) Even though the Format box is empty, the VisitDate field has the General Date format applied to it. The General Date format includes settings for date or time values, or a combination of date and time values. However, Kimberly wants *only date values* to be displayed in the VisitDate field, so she asks you to specify the Short Date format for the field.

6. In the Formatting group, click the **Format** arrow, and then click **Short Date**. See Figure 2-18.

Figure 2-18	VisitDate field after modifying the format

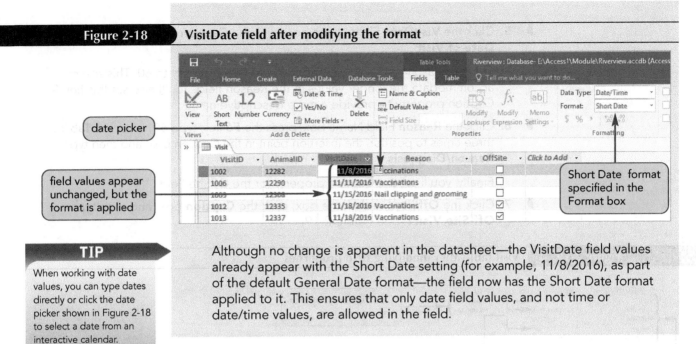

Although no change is apparent in the datasheet—the VisitDate field values already appear with the Short Date setting (for example, 11/8/2016), as part of the default General Date format—the field now has the Short Date format applied to it. This ensures that only date field values, and not time or date/time values, are allowed in the field.

Changing Properties in Design View

Recall that each of the Short Text fields in the Visit table—VisitID, AnimalID, and Reason—still has the default field size of 255, which is too large for the data contained in these fields. Also, the VisitID and AnimalID fields need descriptions to identify them as the primary and foreign keys, respectively, in the table. Finally, each of these fields needs a caption either to include a space between the words in the field name or to make the name more descriptive. You can make all of these property changes more easily in Design view.

To modify the Field Size, Description, and Caption field properties:

1. On the Table Tools Fields tab, in the Views group, click the **View** button. The table is displayed in Design view with the VisitID field selected. You need to enter a Description property value for this field, the primary key in the table, and change its Field Size property to 4 because each visit number at Riverview Veterinary Care Center consists of four digits.

2. Press the **Tab** key twice to position the insertion point in the Description (Optional) box, and then type **Primary key**.

3. Press the **F6** key to move to and select the default setting of 255 in the Field Size box in the Fields Properties pane, and then type **4**. Next you need to set the Caption property for this field.

4. Press the **Tab** key three times to position the insertion point in the Caption box, and then type **Visit ID**.

Next you need to enter a Description property value for the AnimalID field, a foreign key in the table, and set its Field Size property to 5 because each AnimalID number at Riverview Veterinary Care Center consists of five digits. You also need to set this field's Caption property.

5. Click the **VisitDate** Field Name box, click the **Caption** box, and then type **Date of Visit**.

For the Reason field, you will set the Field Size property to 60. This size can accommodate the longer values in the Reason field. You'll also set this field's Caption property to provide a more descriptive name.

6. Click the **Reason** Field Name box, press the **F6** key, type **60**, press the **Tab** key three times to position the insertion point in the Caption box, and then type **Reason/Diagnosis**.

Finally, you'll set the Caption property for the OffSite field.

7. Click the **OffSite** Field Name box, click the **Caption** box, and then type **Off-Site Visit?**. See Figure 2-19.

| Figure 2-19 | Visit table after modifying field properties |

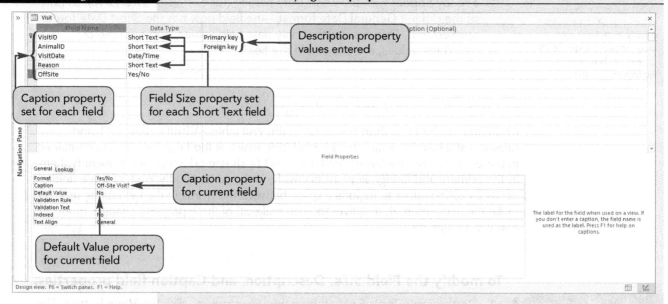

Notice that the OffSite field's Default Value property is automatically set to "No," which means the check box for this field will be empty for each new record. This is the default for this property for any Yes/No field. You can set the Default Value property for other types of fields to make data entry easier. You'll learn more about setting this property in the next session.

The changes to the Visit table's properties are now complete, so you can save the table and view the results of your changes in Datasheet view.

To save and view the modified Visit table:

1. On the Quick Access Toolbar, click the **Save** button to save the modified table. A dialog box opens informing you that some data may be lost because you decreased the field sizes. Because all of the values in the VisitID, AnimalID, and Reason fields contain the same number of or fewer characters than the new Field Size properties you set for each field, you can ignore this message.

2. Click the **Yes** button.

3. On the Table Tools Design tab, in the Views group, click the **View** button to display the Visit table in Datasheet view. Notice that each column (field) heading now displays the text you specified in the Caption property for that field. However, now the Off-Site Visit? field caption doesn't fully display.

4. Place the pointer on the column border to the right of the Off-Site Visit? field name until the pointer changes to ↔, and then double-click the column border to fully display this field name. See Figure 2-20.

Figure 2-20	Modified Visit table in Datasheet view

column headings display Caption property values

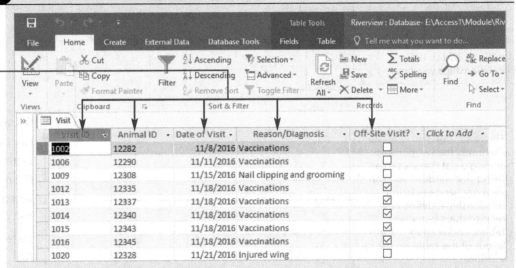

5. Click the **Close 'Visit'** button ✕ on the object tab to close the Visit table, and click **Yes** to save the changes to the Visit table.

6. If you are not continuing to Session 2.2, click the **File** tab, and then click **Close** in the navigation bar of Backstage view to close the Riverview database.

You have created the Billing table and made modifications to its design. In the next session, you'll add records to the Billing table and create the Animal and Owner tables in the Riverview database.

Session 2.1 Quick Check

REVIEW

1. What guidelines should you follow when designing a database?

2. What is the purpose of the Data Type property for a field?

3. The _____ property specifies how a field's name is displayed in database objects, including table and query datasheets, forms, and reports.

4. For which three types of fields can you assign a field size?

5. The default Field Size property setting for a Short Text field is _____.

6. In Design view, which key do you press to move from the Table Design grid to the Field Properties pane?

7. List three reasons why you should specify a primary key for an Access table.

Session 2.2 Visual Overview:

Click the Close button to close the Relationships window.

You click the **Show Table** button to open the Show Table dialog box. From there, you can choose a table to add to the Relationships window.

The Relationships window illustrates the relationships among a database's tables. Using this window, you can view or change existing relationships, define new relationships between tables, and rearrange the layout of the tables in the window.

The key symbol next to a field name indicates that the field is the table's primary key. For example, OwnerID is the primary key for the Owner table.

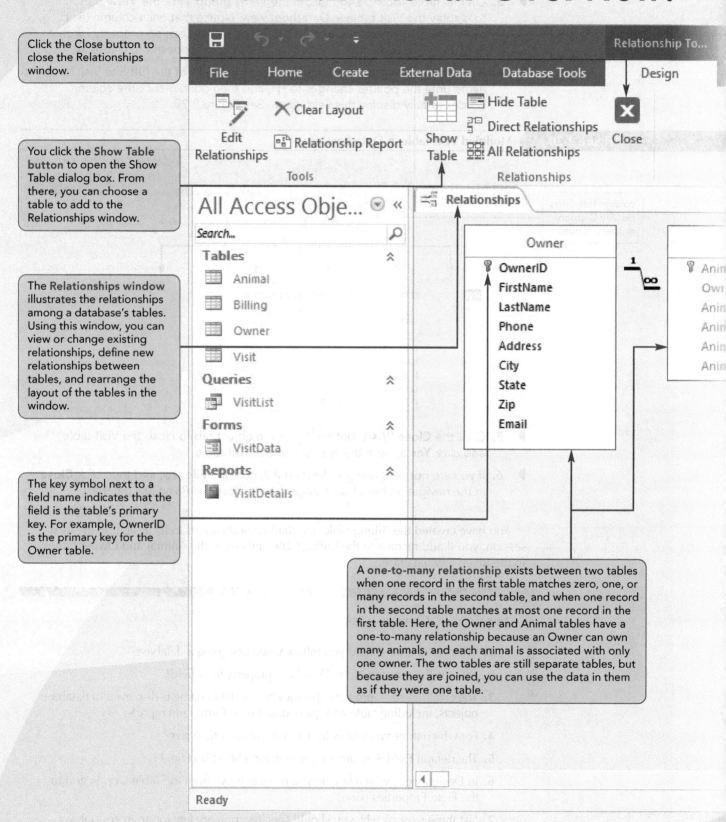

A **one-to-many relationship** exists between two tables when one record in the first table matches zero, one, or many records in the second table, and when one record in the second table matches at most one record in the first table. Here, the Owner and Animal tables have a one-to-many relationship because an Owner can own many animals, and each animal is associated with only one owner. The two tables are still separate tables, but because they are joined, you can use the data in them as if they were one table.

Modified Visit table in Datasheet view

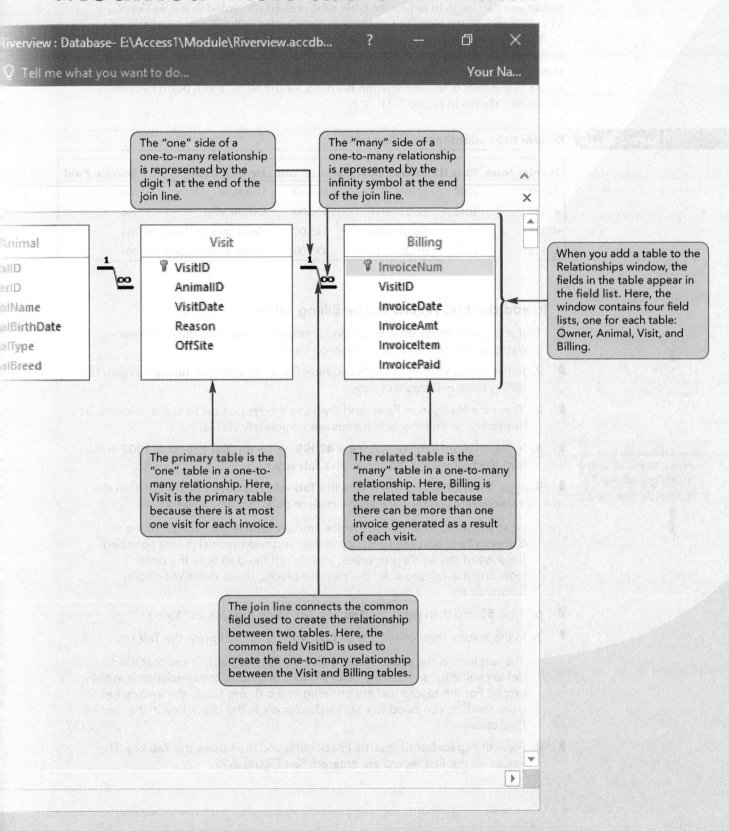

Riverview : Database- E:\Access1\Module\Riverview.accdb...   ?   —   ☐   ✕

💡 Tell me what you want to do...   Your Na...

The "one" side of a one-to-many relationship is represented by the digit 1 at the end of the join line.

The "many" side of a one-to-many relationship is represented by the infinity symbol at the end of the join line.

When you add a table to the Relationships window, the fields in the table appear in the field list. Here, the window contains four field lists, one for each table: Owner, Animal, Visit, and Billing.

Animal
- allD
- erID
- alName
- alBirthDate
- alType
- alBreed

Visit
- 🔑 VisitID
- AnimalID
- VisitDate
- Reason
- OffSite

Billing
- 🔑 InvoiceNum
- VisitID
- InvoiceDate
- InvoiceAmt
- InvoiceItem
- InvoicePaid

The **primary table** is the "one" table in a one-to-many relationship. Here, Visit is the primary table because there is at most one visit for each invoice.

The **related table** is the "many" table in a one-to-many relationship. Here, Billing is the related table because there can be more than one invoice generated as a result of each visit.

The **join line** connects the common field used to create the relationship between two tables. Here, the common field VisitID is used to create the one-to-many relationship between the Visit and Billing tables.

Adding Records to a New Table

Before you can begin to define the table relationships illustrated in the Session 2.2 Visual Overview, you need to finish creating the tables in the Riverview database.

The Billing table design is complete. Now, Kimberly would like you to add records to the table so it will contain the invoice data for Riverview Veterinary Care Center. As you learned earlier, you add records to a table in Datasheet view by typing the field values in the rows below the column headings for the fields. You'll begin by entering the records shown in Figure 2-21.

Figure 2-21   **Records to be added to the Billing table**

Invoice Num	Visit ID	Invoice Date	Invoice Amt	Invoice Item	Invoice Paid
42098	1002	11/09/2016	$50.00	Lab work	Yes
42125	1012	11/21/2016	$50.00	Off-site visit	No
42271	1077	12/15/2016	$45.00	Flea & tick medications	Yes
42518	1181	01/26/2017	$35.00	Heartworm medication	No

To add the first record to the Billing table:

1. If you took a break after the previous session, make sure the Riverview database is open and the Navigation Pane is open.

2. In the Tables section of the Navigation Pane, double-click **Billing** to open the Billing table in Datasheet view.

3. Close the Navigation Pane, and then use the ✛ pointer to resize columns, as necessary, so that the field names are completely visible.

4. In the Invoice Num column, type **42098**, press the **Tab** key, type **1002** in the Visit ID column, and then press the **Tab** key.

5. Type **11/9/2016** and then press the **Tab** key. The date "11/09/2016" in the Invoice Date column reflects the custom date format you set.

   Next you need to enter the invoice amount for the first record. This is a Currency field with the Currency format and two decimal places specified. Because of the field's properties, you do not need to type the dollar sign, comma, or zeroes for the decimal places; these items will display automatically.

6. Type **50** and then press the **Tab** key. The value displays as "$50.00."

7. In the Invoice Item column, type **Lab work**, and then press the **Tab** key.

   The last field in the table, InvoicePaid, is a Yes/No field. Recall that the default value for any Yes/No field is "No"; therefore, the check box is initially empty. For the record you are entering in the Billing table, the invoice has been paid, so you need to insert a checkmark in the check box in the Invoice Paid column.

8. Press the **spacebar** to insert a checkmark, and then press the **Tab** key. The values for the first record are entered. See Figure 2-22.

> Be sure to type the numbers "0" and "1" and *not* the letters "O" and "I" in the field values.

Figure 2-22	First record entered in the Billing table

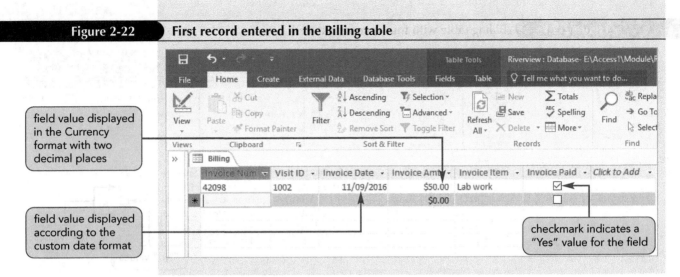

field value displayed in the Currency format with two decimal places

field value displayed according to the custom date format

checkmark indicates a "Yes" value for the field

Now you can add the remaining three records. As you do, you'll learn a keyboard shortcut for inserting the value from the same field in the previous record. A **keyboard shortcut** is a key or combination of keys you press to complete an action more efficiently.

To add the next three records to the Billing table:

1. Refer to Figure 2-21 and enter the values in the second record's Invoice Num, Visit ID, and Invoice Date columns.

   Notice that the value in the second record's Invoice Amt column is $50.00. This value is the exact same value as in the first record. You can quickly insert the value from the same column in the previous record using the Ctrl + ' (apostrophe) keyboard shortcut. To use this shortcut, you press and hold the Ctrl key, press the ' key once, and then release both keys. (The plus sign in the keyboard shortcut indicates you're pressing two keys at once; you do not press the + key.)

2. With the insertion point in the Invoice Amt column, press the **Ctrl + ' keys**. The value "$50.00" is inserted in the Invoice Amt column for the second record.

3. Press the **Tab** key to move to the Invoice Item column, and then type **Off-site visit**.

4. Press the **Tab** key to move to the Invoice Paid column, and then press the **Tab** key to leave the Invoice Paid check box unchecked to indicate the invoice has not been paid. The second record is entered in the Billing table.

5. Refer to Figure 2-21 to enter the values for the third and fourth records. Your table should look like the one in Figure 2-23.

Figure 2-23 **Billing table with four records entered**

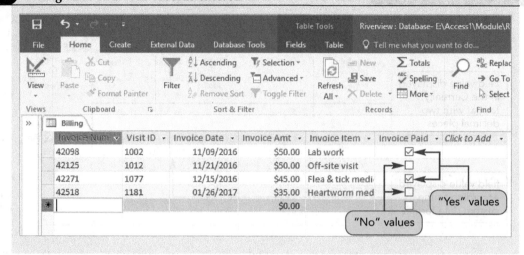

To finish entering records in the Billing table, you'll use a method that allows you to import the data.

Importing Data from an Excel Worksheet

Often, the data you want to add to an Access table exists in another file, such as a Word document or an Excel workbook. You can bring the data from other files into Access in different ways. For example, you can copy and paste the data from an open file, or you can **import** the data, which is a process that allows you to copy the data from a source without having to open the source file.

Kimberly had been using Excel to track invoice data for Riverview Veterinary Care Center and already created a worksheet, named "Invoices," containing this data. You'll import this Excel worksheet into your Billing table to complete the entry of data in the table. To use the import method, the columns in the Excel worksheet must match the names and data types of the fields in the Access table.

The Invoices worksheet contains the following columns: InvoiceNum, VisitID, InvoiceDate, InvoiceAmt, InvoiceItem, and InvoicePaid. These column headings match the field names in the Billing table exactly, so you can import the data. Before you import data into a table, you need to close the table.

TIP

Caption property values set for fields are not considered in the import process. Therefore make sure that the field names match the Excel worksheet column headings. If there are differences, change the column headings in the Excel worksheet to match the Access table field names.

To import the Invoices worksheet into the Billing table:

1. Click the **Close 'Billing'** button ⊠ on the object tab to close the Billing table, and then click the **Yes** button in the dialog box asking if you want to save the changes to the table layout.

2. On the ribbon, click the **External Data** tab.

3. In the Import & Link group, click the **Excel** button. The Get External Data - Excel Spreadsheet dialog box opens. See Figure 2-24.

| Figure 2-24 | Get External Data – Excel Spreadsheet dialog box |

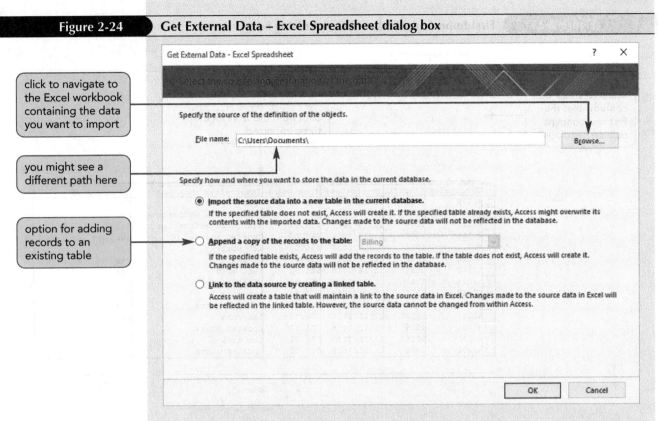

click to navigate to the Excel workbook containing the data you want to import

you might see a different path here

option for adding records to an existing table

The dialog box provides options for importing the entire worksheet as a new table in the current database, adding the data from the worksheet to an existing table, or linking the data in the worksheet to the table. You need to add, or append, the worksheet data to the Billing table.

4. Click the **Browse** button. The File Open dialog box opens. The Excel workbook file is named "Invoices" and is located in the Access1 > Module folder provided with your Data Files.

5. Navigate to the **Access1 > Module** folder, where your Data Files are stored, and then double-click the **Invoices** Excel file. You return to the dialog box.

6. Click the **Append a copy of the records to the table** option button. The box to the right of this option becomes active and displays the Billing table name, because it is the first table listed in the Navigation Pane.

7. Click the **OK** button. The first Import Spreadsheet Wizard dialog box opens. The dialog box confirms that the first row of the worksheet you are importing contains column headings. The bottom section of the dialog box displays some of the data contained in the worksheet. See Figure 2-25.

Figure 2-25

Figure 2-25   **First Import Spreadsheet Wizard dialog box**

selected check box confirms that the first row contains column headings

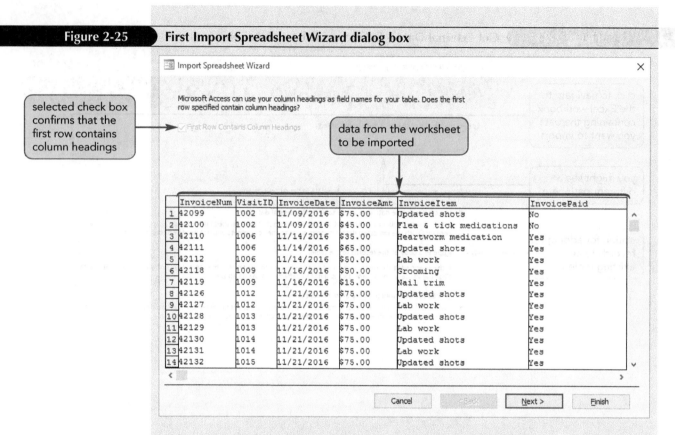

data from the worksheet to be imported

8. Click the **Next** button. The second, and final, Import Spreadsheet Wizard dialog box opens. Notice that the Import to Table box shows that the data from the spreadsheet will be imported into the Billing table.

9. Click the **Finish** button. A dialog box opens asking if you want to save the import steps. If you needed to repeat this same import procedure many times, it would be a good idea to save the steps for the procedure. However, you don't need to save these steps because you'll be importing the data only one time. Once the data is in the Billing table, Kimberly will no longer use Excel to track invoice data.

10. Click the **Close** button in the dialog box to close it without saving the steps.

The data from the Invoices worksheet has been added to the Billing table. Next, you'll open the table to view the new records.

To open the Billing table and view the imported data:

1. Open the Navigation Pane, and then double-click **Billing** in the Tables section to open the table in Datasheet view.

2. Resize the Invoice Item column to its best fit, scrolling the worksheet and resizing, as necessary.

3. Press the **Ctrl + Home** keys to scroll to the top of the datasheet. Notice that the table now contains a total of 204 records—the four records you entered plus 200 records imported from the Invoices worksheet. The records are displayed in primary key order by the values in the Invoice Num column. See Figure 2-26.

Figure 2-26	Billing table after importing data from Excel

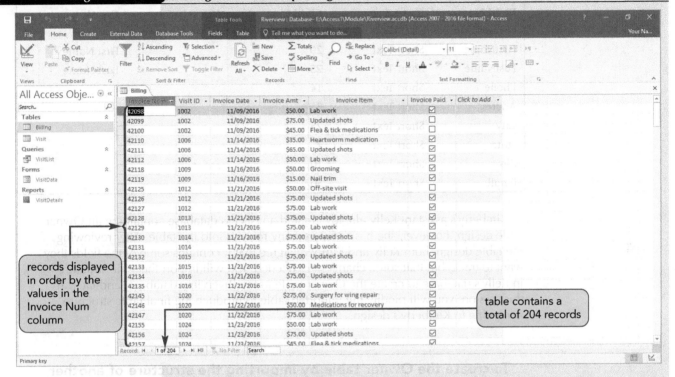

records displayed in order by the values in the Invoice Num column

table contains a total of 204 records

4. Save and close the Billing table, and then close the Navigation Pane.

Two of the tables—Visit and Billing—are now complete. According to Kimberly's plan for the Riverview database, you still need to create the Owner and Animal tables. You'll use a different method to create these tables.

Creating a Table by Importing an Existing Table or Table Structure

If another Access database contains a table—or even just the design, or structure, of a table—that you want to include in your database, you can import the table and any records it contains or import only the table structure into your database. To create the new Owner and Animal tables per Kimberly's plan shown in Figure 2-2, you will import a table structure from a different Access database to create the Owner table and an existing table structure and records from another database to create the Animal table.

Importing an Existing Table Structure

Kimberly documented the design for the new Owner table by listing each field's name and data type, as well as any applicable field size, description, and caption property values, as shown in Figure 2-27. Note that each field in the Owner table will be a Short Text field, and the OwnerID field will be the table's primary key.

Figure 2-27 **Design for the Owner table**

Field Name	Data Type	Field Size	Description	Caption
OwnerID	Short Text	4	Primary key	Owner ID
FirstName	Short Text	20		First Name
LastName	Short Text	25		Last Name
Phone	Short Text	14		
Address	Short Text	35		
City	Short Text	25		
State	Short Text	2		
Zip	Short Text	10		
Email	Short Text	50		

Kimberly's assistant Kelly already created an Access database containing an Owner table design, however, she hasn't entered any records into the table. After reviewing the table design, both Kelly and Kimberly agree that it contains some of the fields they want to track, but that some changes are needed. You will import the table structure in Kelly's database to create the Owner table in the Riverview database, and later in this session, you will modify the imported table to produce the final table structure according to Kimberly's design.

To create the Owner table by importing the structure of another table:

1. Make sure the External Data tab is the active tab on the ribbon.

2. In the Import & Link group, click the **Access** button. The Get External Data - Access Database dialog box opens. This dialog box is similar to the one you used earlier when importing the Excel spreadsheet.

3. Click the **Browse** button. The File Open dialog box opens. The Access database file from which you need to import the table structure is named "Kelly" and is located in the Access1 > Module folder provided with your Data Files.

4. Navigate to the **Access1 > Module** folder, where your Data Files are stored, and then double-click the **Kelly** database file. You return to the dialog box.

5. Make sure the **Import tables, queries, forms, reports, macros, and modules into the current database** option button is selected, and then click the **OK** button. The Import Objects dialog box opens. The dialog box contains tabs for importing all the different types of Access database objects—tables, queries, forms, and so on. The Tables tab is the current tab.

6. Click the **Options** button in the dialog box to see all the options for importing tables. See Figure 2-28.

| Figure 2-28 | Import Objects dialog box |

tabs for importing other
types of database objects

table object to be
imported

this option imports
the table structure
and the table

this option imports the
table structure only

Import Objects   ? ✕

Tables Queries Forms Reports Macros Modules

Owner

OK
Cancel
Select All
Deselect All
Options >>

Import
☑ Relationships
☐ Menus and Toolbars
☐ Import/Export Specs
☐ Nav Pane Groups
☐ All Images and Themes

Import Tables
◉ Definition and Data
○ Definition Only

Import Queries
◉ As Queries
○ As Tables

▶ **7.** On the Tables tab, click **Owner** to select this table.

▶ **8.** In the Import Tables section of the dialog box, click the **Definition Only** option button, and then click the **OK** button. Access creates the Owner table in the Riverview database using the structure of the Owner table in the Kelly database, and opens a dialog box asking if you want to save the import steps.

▶ **9.** Click the **Close** button to close the dialog box without saving the import steps.

▶ **10.** Open the Navigation Pane, double-click **Owner** in the Tables section to open the table, and then close the Navigation Pane. The Owner table opens in Datasheet view. The table contains no records. See Figure 2-29.

| Figure 2-29 | Imported Owner table in Datasheet view |

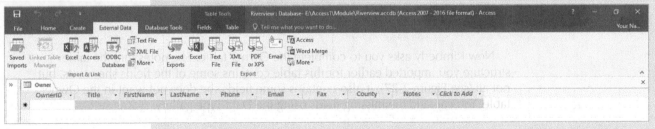

Before you add records to the Owner table and fine-tune its design, you need to first add the Animal table to the Riverview database. You will do this by importing a table and its data from another database.

Importing an Existing Table

Kelly has already created a database called "AllAnimals" that contains a table called "Animal." To import this Animal table into the Riverview database, you will follow the same process you used to import the table structure from the Kelly database to create the Owner table; however, this time you will choose the Definition and Data option, instead of the Definition only option in the Import Objects dialog box. This will import the structure and the data that Kelly has created and verified in the Animal table in the AllAnimals database.

To create the Animal table by importing the structure and data of another table:

1. Close the Owner table, make sure the External Data tab is the active tab on the ribbon, and then in the Import & Link group, click the **Access** button. The Get External Data - Access Database dialog box opens.

2. Click the **Browse** button. The File Open dialog box opens. The Access database file from which you need to import the table is named "AllAnimals" and is located in the Access1 > Module folder provided with your Data Files.

3. Navigate to the **Access1 > Module** folder, where your Data Files are stored, and then double-click the **AllAnimals** database file. You return to the dialog box.

4. Make sure the **Import tables, queries, forms, reports, macros, and modules into the current database** option button is selected, and then click the **OK** button to open the Import Objects dialog box opens. The Tables tab is the current tab.

5. Click **Animal** to select this table, click the **Options** button to display the options for importing tables, and then, in the Import Tables section, make sure the **Definition and Data** option button is selected.

6. Click the **OK** button, and then click the **Close** button to close the dialog box without saving the import steps. Access creates the Animal table in the Riverview database using the records and structure of the Animal table in the AllAnimals database.

7. Open the Navigation Pane, double-click **Animal** in the Tables section to open the table, and then close the Navigation Pane. The Animal table opens in Datasheet view. Kimberly reviews the new Animal table and is satisfied with its structure and the records it contains, so you can close this table.

8. Close the Animal table.

Now Kimberly asks you to complete the Owner table. She notes that the table structure you imported earlier for this table contains some of the fields she wants, but not all (see Figure 2-27); it also contains some fields she does not want in the Owner table. You can add the missing fields using the Data Type gallery.

Adding Fields to a Table Using the Data Type Gallery

The **Data Type gallery**, available from the More Fields button located on the Add & Delete group on the Table Tools Fields tab, allows you to add a group of related fields to a table at the same time, rather than adding each field to the table individually.

The group of fields you add is called a **Quick Start selection**. For example, the **Address Quick Start selection** adds a collection of fields related to an address, such as Address, City, State, and so on, to the table at one time. When you use a Quick Start selection, the fields added already have properties set. However, you need to review and possibly modify the properties to ensure the fields match your design needs for the database.

Next, you'll use the Data Type gallery to add the missing fields to the Owner table.

To add fields to the Owner table using the Data Type gallery:

1. Open the **Owner** table, and then on the ribbon, click the **Table Tools Fields** tab. Before inserting fields from the Data Type gallery, you need to place the insertion point in the field to the right of where you want to insert the new fields. According to Kimberly's design, the Address field should come after the Phone field, so you need to make the next field, Email, the active field.

2. Click the **first row** in the Email field to make it the active field.

3. In the Add & Delete group, click the **More Fields** button. The Data Type gallery opens and displays options for different types of fields you can add to your table.

4. Scroll down the gallery until the Quick Start section is visible. See Figure 2-30.

> Make sure the correct field is active before adding new fields.

| Figure 2-30 | Owner table with the Data Type gallery displayed |

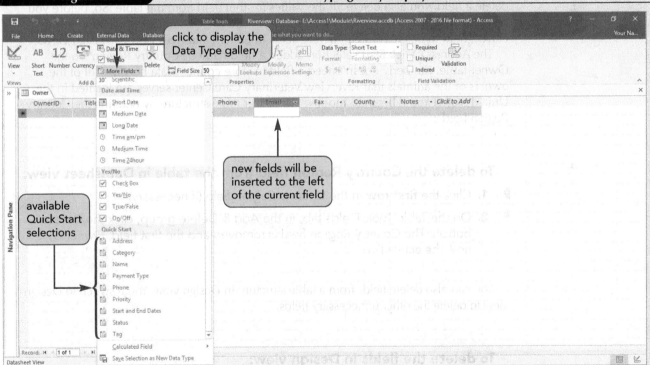

The Quick Start section provides options that will add multiple, related fields to the table at one time. The new fields will be inserted to the left of the current field.

5. In the Quick Start section, click **Address**. Five fields are added to the table: Address, City, State Province, ZIP Postal, and Country Region. See Figure 2-31.

Figure 2-31

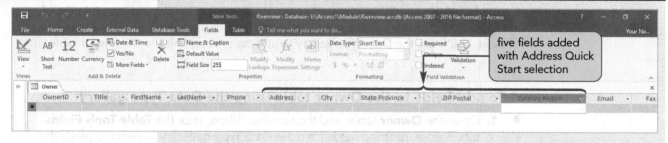

Figure 2-31   Owner table after adding fields from the Data Type gallery

Modifying the Structure of an Imported Table

Refer back to Kimberly's design for the Owner table (Figure 2-27). To finalize the table design, you need to modify the imported table by deleting fields, renaming fields, and changing field data types. You'll begin by deleting fields.

Deleting Fields from a Table Structure

After you've created a table, you might need to delete one or more fields. When you delete a field, you also delete all the values for that field from the table. So, before you delete a field, you should make sure that you want to do so and that you choose the correct field to delete. You can delete fields in either Datasheet view or Design view.

The Address Quick Start selection added a field named "Country Region" to the Owner table. Kimberly doesn't need a field to store country data because all of the owners of the animals that Riverview Veterinary Care Center serves are located in the United States. You'll begin to modify the Owner table structure by deleting the Country Region field.

To delete the Country Region field from the table in Datasheet view:

1. Click the **first row** in the Country Region field (if necessary).

2. On the Table Tools Fields tab, in the Add & Delete group, click the **Delete** button. The Country Region field is removed and the first field, OwnerID, is now the active field.

You can also delete fields from a table structure in Design view. You'll switch to Design view to delete the other unnecessary fields.

To delete the fields in Design view:

1. On the Table Tools Fields tab, in the Views group, click the **View** button. The Owner table opens in Design view. See Figure 2-32.

Figure 2-32   Owner table in Design view

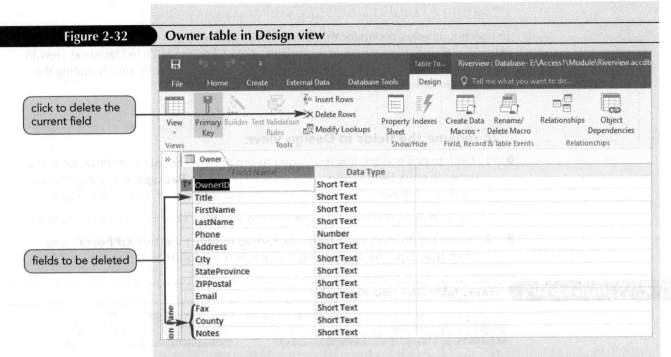

click to delete the current field

fields to be deleted

> **2.** Click the **Title** Field Name box to make it the current field.

> **3.** On the Table Tools Design tab, in the Tools group, click the **Delete Rows** button. The Title field is removed from the Owner table structure. You'll delete the Fax, County, and Notes fields next. Instead of deleting these fields individually, you'll select and delete them at the same time.

> **4.** On the row selector for the **Fax** field, press and hold the mouse button and then drag the mouse to select the **County** and **Notes** fields.

> **5.** Release the mouse button. The rows for the three fields are outlined in red, indicating all three fields are selected.

> **6.** In the Tools group, click the **Delete Rows** button. See Figure 2-33.

Figure 2-33   Owner table after deleting fields

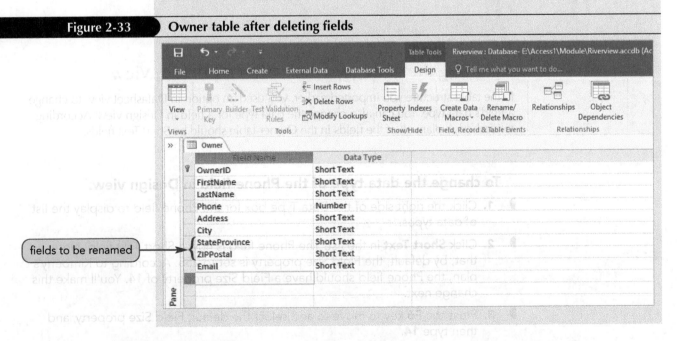

fields to be renamed

Renaming Fields in Design View

To match Kimberly's design for the Owner table, you need to rename some of the fields. You already have renamed the default primary key field (ID) in Datasheet view in the previous module. You can also rename fields in Design view by simply editing the names in the Table Design grid.

To rename the fields in Design view:

1. Click to position the insertion point to the right of the text StateProvince in the seventh row's Field Name box, and then press the **Backspace** key eight times to delete the word "Province." The name of the seventh field is now State.

   You can also select an entire field name and then type new text to replace it.

2. In the eighth row's Field Name box, drag to select the text **ZIPPostal**, and then type **Zip**. The text you type replaces the original text. See Figure 2-34.

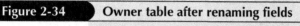

| Figure 2-34 | Owner table after renaming fields |

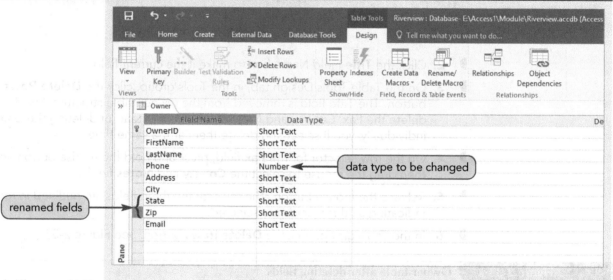

Changing the Data Type for a Field in Design View

In the table structure you imported earlier, you used an option in Datasheet view to change a field's data type. You can also change the data type for a field in Design view. According to Kimberly's plan, all of the fields in the Owner table should be Short Text fields.

To change the data type of the Phone field in Design view:

1. Click the right side of the Data Type box for the Phone field to display the list of data types.

2. Click **Short Text** in the list. The Phone field is now a Short Text field. Note that, by default, the Field Size property is set to 255. According to Kimberly's plan, the Phone field should have a Field Size property of 14. You'll make this change next.

3. Press the **F6** key to move to and select the default Field Size property, and then type **14**.

Each of the remaining fields you added using the Address Quick Start selection—Address, City, State, and Zip—also has the default field size of 255. You need to change the Field Size property for these fields to match Kimberly's design. You'll also delete any Caption property values for these fields because the field names match how Kimberly wants them displayed, so captions are unnecessary.

To change the Field Size and Caption properties for the fields:

▶ **1.** Click the **Address Field Name** box to make it the current field.

▶ **2.** Press the **F6** key to move to and select the default Field Size property, and then type **35**. Note that the Caption property setting for this field is the same as the field name. This field doesn't need a caption, so you can delete this value.

▶ **3.** Press the **Tab** key three times to select Address in the Caption box, and then press the **Delete** key. The Caption property value is removed.

▶ **4.** Repeat Steps 1 through 3 for the City field to change the Field Size property to **25** and delete its Caption property value.

▶ **5.** Change the Field Size property for the State field to **2**, and then delete its Caption property value.

▶ **6.** Change the Field Size property for the Zip field to **10**, and then delete its Caption property value.

▶ **7.** On the Quick Access Toolbar, click the **Save** button 🖫 to save your changes to the Owner table.

Finally, Kimberly would like you to set the Description property for the OwnerID field and the Caption property for the OwnerID, FirstName, and LastName fields. You'll make these changes now.

To enter the Description and Caption property values:

▶ **1.** Click the **Description (Optional)** box for the OwnerID field, and then type **Primary key**.

▶ **2.** In the Field Properties pane, click the **Caption** box.

After you leave the Description (Optional) box, the Property Update Options button 🖅 appears below this box for the OwnerID field. When you change a field's property in Design view, you can use this button to update the corresponding property on forms and reports that include the modified field. For example, if the Riverview database included a form that contained the OwnerID field, you could choose to propagate, or update, the modified Description property in the form by clicking the Property Update Options button, and then choosing the option to make the update everywhere the field is used. The ScreenTip on the Property Update Options button and the options it lists vary depending on the task; in this case, if you click the button, the option is "Update Status Bar Text everywhere OwnerID is used." Because the Riverview database does not include any forms or reports that are based on the Owner table, you do not need to update the properties, so you can ignore the button for now. In most cases, however, it is a good idea to perform the update.

▶ **3.** In the Caption box for the OwnerID field, type **Owner ID**.

▶ **4.** Click the **FirstName** Field Name box to make it the current field, click the **Caption** box, and then type **First Name**.

5. Click the **LastName** Field Name box to make it the current field, click the **Caption** box, and then type **Last Name**. See Figure 2-35.

Figure 2-35 Owner table after entering descriptions and captions

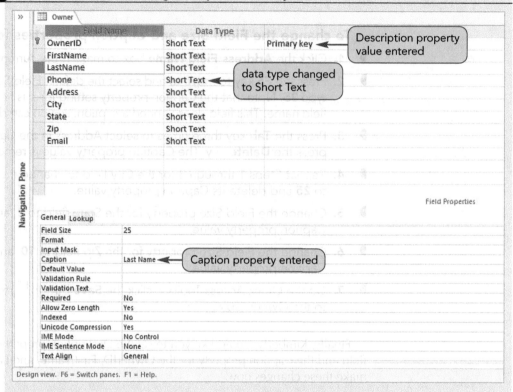

6. On the Quick Access Toolbar, click the **Save** button 💾 to save your changes to the Owner table.

7. On the Table Tools Design tab, in the Views group, click the **View** button to display the table in Datasheet view.

8. Resize each column to its best fit, and then click in the first row for the **Owner ID** column. See Figure 2-36.

Figure 2-36 Modified Owner table in Datasheet view

Kimberly feels that data entry would be made easier if the State field value of "WY" was automatically filled in for each new record added to the table, because all of the owners live in Wyoming. You can accomplish this by setting the Default Value property for the field.

Setting the Default Value Property for a Field

The **Default Value property** for a field specifies what value will appear, by default, for the field in each new record you add to a table.

Because all of the owners at Riverview Veterinary Care Center live in Wyoming, you'll specify a default value of "WY" for the State field in the Owner table. With this setting, each new record in the Owner table will have the correct State field value entered automatically.

To set the Default Value property for the State field:

1. On the Home tab, in the Views group, click the **View** button to display the Owner table in Design view.

2. Click the **State** Field Name box to make it the current field.

3. In the Field Properties pane, click the **Default Value** box, type **WY**, and then press the **Tab** key. See Figure 2-37.

Figure 2-37	Specifying the Default Value property for the State field

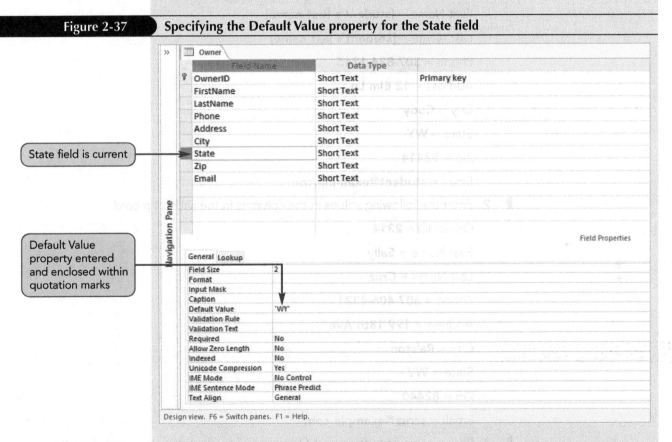

State field is current

Default Value property entered and enclosed within quotation marks

Note that a text entry in the Default Value property must be enclosed within quotation marks. If you do not type the quotation marks, Access adds them for you. However, for some entries, you would receive an error message indicating invalid syntax if you omitted the quotation marks. In such cases, you have to enter the quotation marks yourself.

4. On the Quick Access Toolbar, click the **Save** button to save your changes to the Owner table.

TIP

You can change the value in a record from the default value to another value, if necessary.

5. Display the table in Datasheet view. Note that the State field for the first row now displays the default value "WY" as specified by the Default Value property. Each new record entered in the table will automatically have this State field value entered.

With the Owner table design set, you can now enter records in it. You'll begin by entering two records, and then you'll use a different method to add the remaining records.

Note: Be sure to enter your last name and first name where indicated.

To add two records to the Owner table:

1. Enter the following values in the columns in the first record; note that you can press **Tab** to move past the default State field value:

Owner ID = **2310**

First Name = **[student's first name]**

Last Name = **[student's last name]**

Phone = **307-824-1245**

Address = **12 Elm Ln**

City = **Cody**

State = **WY**

Zip = **82414**

Email = **student@example.com**

2. Enter the following values in the columns in the second record:

Owner ID = **2314**

First Name = **Sally**

Last Name = **Cruz**

Phone = **307-406-4321**

Address = **199 18th Ave**

City = **Ralston**

State = **WY**

Zip = **82440**

Email = **scruz@example.com**

3. Resize columns to their best fit, as necessary, and then save and close the Owner table.

Before Kimberly decided to store data using Access, Kelly managed the owner data for the care center in a different system. She exported that data into a text file and now asks you to import it into the new Owner table. You can import the data contained in this text file to add the remaining records to the Owner table.

Adding Data to a Table by Importing a Text File

There are many ways to import data into an Access database. So far, you've learned how to add data to an Access table by importing an Excel spreadsheet, and you've created a new table by importing the structure of an existing table. You can also import data contained in text files.

To complete the entry of records in the Owner table, you'll import the data contained in Kelly's text file. The file is named "Owner" and is located in the Access1 > Module folder provided with your Data Files.

To import the data contained in the Owner text file:

▶ **1.** On the ribbon, click the **External Data** tab.

▶ **2.** In the Import & Link group, click the **Text File** button. The Get External Data - Text File dialog box opens. This dialog box is similar to the one you used earlier when importing the Excel spreadsheet and the Access table structure.

▶ **3.** Click the **Browse** button. The File Open dialog box opens.

▶ **4.** Navigate to the **Access1 > Module** folder, where your Data Files are stored, and then double-click the **Owner** file. You return to the dialog box.

▶ **5.** Click the **Append a copy of the records to the table** option button. The box to the right of this option becomes active. Next, you need to select the table to which you want to add the data.

▶ **6.** Click the arrow on the box, and then click **Owner**.

▶ **7.** Click the **OK** button. The first Import Text Wizard dialog box opens. The dialog box indicates that the data to be imported is in a delimited format. A **delimited text file** is one in which fields of data are separated by a character such as a comma or a tab. In this case, the dialog box shows that data is separated by the comma character in the text file.

▶ **8.** Make sure the **Delimited** option button is selected in the dialog box, and then click the **Next** button. The second Import Text Wizard dialog box opens. See Figure 2-38.

Figure 2-38	Second Import Wizard dialog box

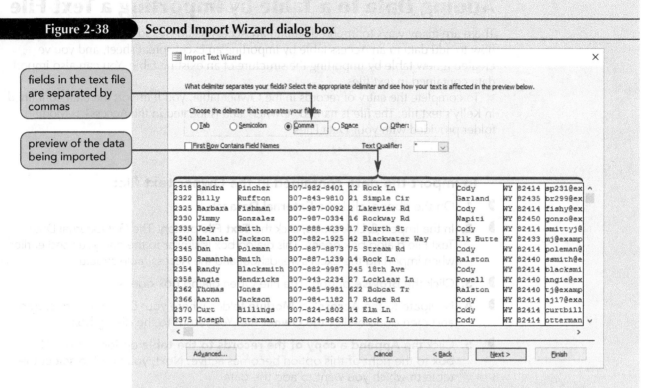

fields in the text file are separated by commas

preview of the data being imported

This dialog box asks you to confirm the delimiter character that separates the fields in the text file you're importing. Access detects that the comma character is used in the Owner text file and selects this option. The bottom area of the dialog box provides a preview of the data you're importing.

9. Make sure the **Comma** option button is selected, and then click the **Next** button. The third and final Import Text Wizard dialog box opens. Notice that the Import to Table box shows that the data will be imported into the Owner table.

10. Click the **Finish** button, and then click the **Close** button in the dialog box that opens to close it without saving the import steps.

Kimberly asks you to open the Owner table in Datasheet view so she can see the results of importing the text file.

To view the Owner table datasheet:

1. Open the Navigation Pane, and then double-click **Owner** to open the Owner table in Datasheet view. The Owner table contains a total of 25 records.

2. Close the Navigation Pane, and then resize columns to their best fit, scrolling the table datasheet as necessary, so that all field values are displayed. When finished, scroll back to display the first fields in the table, and then click the first row's **Owner ID** field, if necessary. See Figure 2-39.

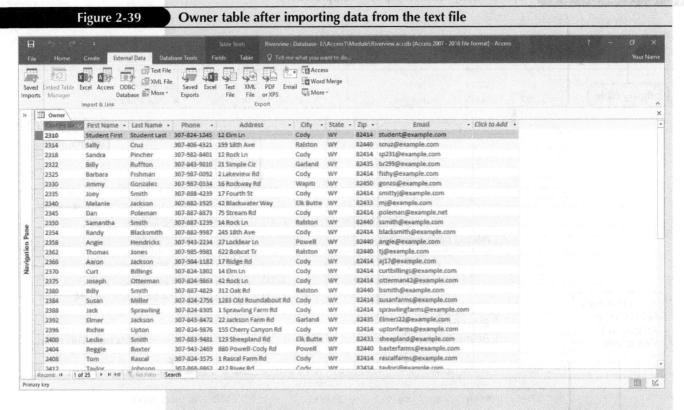

| Figure 2-39 | Owner table after importing data from the text file |

> **3.** Save and close the Owner table, and then open the Navigation Pane.

The Riverview database now contains four tables—Visit, Billing, Owner, and Animal—and the tables contain all the necessary records. Your final task is to complete the database design by defining the necessary relationship between its tables.

Defining Table Relationships

One of the most powerful features of a relational database management system is its ability to define relationships between tables. You use a common field to relate one table to another. The process of relating tables is often called performing a **join**. When you join tables that have a common field, you can extract data from them as if they were one larger table. For example, you can join the Animal and Visit tables by using the AnimalID field in both tables as the common field. Then you can use a query, form, or report to extract selected data from each table, even though the data is contained in two separate tables, as shown in Figure 2-40. The AnimalVisits query shown in Figure 2-40 includes the AnimalID, AnimalName, AnimalType, and AnimalBreed fields from the Animal table, and the VisitDate and Reason fields from the Visit table. The joining of records is based on the common field of AnimalID. The Animal and Visit tables have a type of relationship called a one-to-many relationship.

Figure 2-40   **One-to-many relationship and sample query**

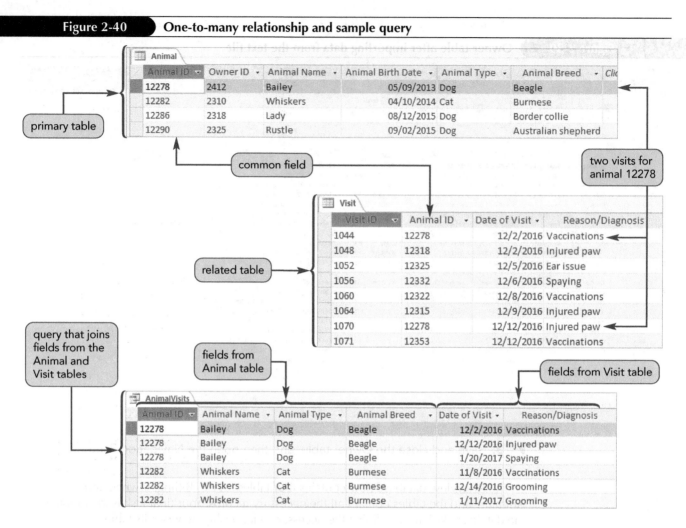

One-to-Many Relationships

As shown earlier in the Session 2.2 Visual Overview, a one-to-many relationship exists between two tables when one record in the first table matches zero, one, or many records in the second table, and when one record in the second table matches at most one record in the first table. For example, as shown in Figure 2-40, Animal 12278 has two visits in the Visit table. Other animals have one or more visits. Every visit has a single matching animal.

In Access, the two tables that form a relationship are referred to as the primary table and the related table. The primary table is the "one" table in a one-to-many relationship; in Figure 2-40, the Animal table is the primary table because there is only one animal for each visit. The related table is the "many" table; in Figure 2-40, the Visit table is the related table because an animal can have zero, one, or many visits.

Because related data is stored in two tables, inconsistencies between the tables can occur. Referring to Figure 2-40, consider the following three scenarios:

- Kimberly adds a record to the Visit table for a new animal, Fluffy (a Siberian cat), using Animal ID 12500. She did not first add the new animal's information to the animal table, so this visit does not have a matching record in the animal table. The data is inconsistent, and the visit record is considered to be an **orphaned record**.
- In another situation, Kimberly changes the AnimalID in the Animal table for Bailey the beagle from 12278 to 12510. Because there is no longer an animal with the AnimalID 12278 in the Animal table, this change creates two orphaned records in the Visit table, and the database is inconsistent.

- In a third scenario, Kimberly deletes the record for Bailey the beagle, Animal 12278, from the Animal table because this animal and its owner have moved and so the animal no longer receives care from Riverview. The database is again inconsistent; two records for Animal 12278 in the Visit table have no matching record in the Animal table.

You can avoid these types of problems and avoid having inconsistent data in your database by specifying referential integrity between tables when you define their relationships.

Referential Integrity

Referential integrity is a set of rules that Access enforces to maintain consistency between related tables when you update data in a database. Specifically, the referential integrity rules are as follows:

- When you add a record to a related table, a matching record must already exist in the primary table, thereby preventing the possibility of orphaned records.
- If you attempt to change the value of the primary key in the primary table, Access prevents this change if matching records exist in a related table. However, if you choose the **Cascade Update Related Fields option**, Access permits the change in value to the primary key and changes the appropriate foreign key values in the related table, thereby eliminating the possibility of inconsistent data.
- When you attempt to delete a record in the primary table, Access prevents the deletion if matching records exist in a related table. However, if you choose the **Cascade Delete Related Records option**, Access deletes the record in the primary table and also deletes all records in related tables that have matching foreign key values. However, you should rarely select the Cascade Delete Related Records option because doing so might cause you to inadvertently delete records you did not intend to delete. It is best to use other methods for deleting records that give you more control over the deletion process.

Defining a Relationship Between Two Tables

At the Riverview Veterinary Care Center, the owners own animals, the animals visit the clinic, and the owner receives the bill for the visits. It is important to understand these relationships in order to determine which owner to send the bill to for the visit each animal makes. Understanding these relationships also allows you to establish relationships between the tables of records in the Riverview database. When two tables have a common field, you can define a relationship between them in the Relationships window, as shown in the Session 2.2 Visual Overview.

Next, you need to define a series of relationships in the Riverview database. First, you will define a one-to-many relationship between the Owner and Animal tables, with Owner as the primary table and Animal as the related table and with OwnerID as the common field (primary key in the Owner table and a foreign key in the Animal table). Second, you will define a one-to-many relationship between the Animal and Visit tables, with Animal as the primary table and Visit as the related table and with AnimalID as the common field (the primary key in the Animal table and a foreign key in the Visit table). Finally, you will define a one-to-many relationship between the Visit and Billing tables, with Visit as the primary table and Billing as the related table and with VisitID as the common field (the primary key in the Visit table and a foreign key in the Billing table).

To define the one-to-many relationship between the Owner and Animal tables:

1. On the ribbon, click the **Database Tools** tab.

2. In the Relationships group, click the **Relationships** button to display the Relationship window and open the Show Table dialog box. See Figure 2-41.

Figure 2-41	Show Table dialog box

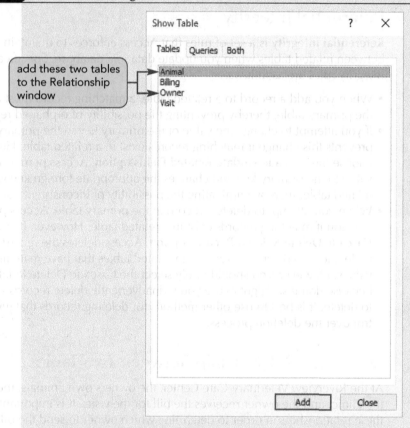

You must add each table participating in a relationship to the Relationships window. Because the Owner table is the primary table in the relationship, you'll add it first.

TIP

You can also double-click a table in the Show Table dialog box to add it to the Relationships window.

3. Click **Owner**, and then click the **Add** button. The Owner table's field list is added to the Relationships window.

4. Click **Animal**, and then click the **Add** button. The Animal table's field list is added to the Relationships window.

5. Click the **Close** button in the Show Table dialog box to close it.

So that you can view all the fields and complete field names, you'll resize the Owner table field list.

6. Position the mouse pointer on the bottom border of the Owner table field list until it changes to $\updownarrow$, and then drag the bottom of the Owner table field list to lengthen it until the vertical scroll bar disappears and all the fields are visible.

To form the relationship between the two tables, you drag the common field of OwnerID from the primary table to the related table. Then Access opens the Edit Relationships dialog box, in which you select the relationship options for the two tables.

7. Click **OwnerID** in the Owner field list, and then drag it to **OwnerID** in the Animal field list. When you release the mouse button, the Edit Relationships dialog box opens. See Figure 2-42.

Figure 2-42   **Edit Relationships dialog box**

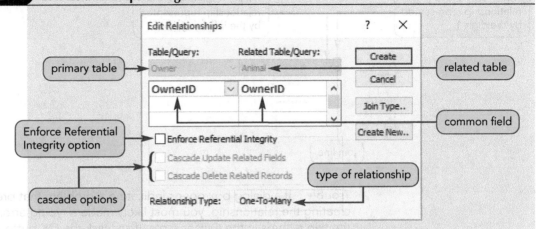

The primary table, related table, common field, and relationship type (One-To-Many) appear in the dialog box. Note that Access correctly identifies the "One" side of the relationship and places the primary table Owner in the Table/Query section of the dialog box; similarly, Access correctly identifies the "Many" side of the relationship and places the related table Animal in the Related Table/Query section of the dialog box.

8. Click the **Enforce Referential Integrity** check box. After you click the Enforce Referential Integrity check box, the two cascade options become available. If you select the Cascade Update Related Fields option, Access will update the appropriate foreign key values in the related table when you change a primary key value in the primary table. You will *not* select the Cascade Delete Related Records option because doing so could cause you to delete records that you do not want to delete; this option is rarely selected.

9. Click the **Cascade Update Related Fields** check box.

10. Click the **Create** button to define the one-to-many relationship between the two tables and to close the dialog box. The completed relationship appears in the Relationships window, with the join line connecting the common field of OwnerID in each table. See Figure 2-43.

Figure 2-43 | **Defined relationship in the Relationship window**

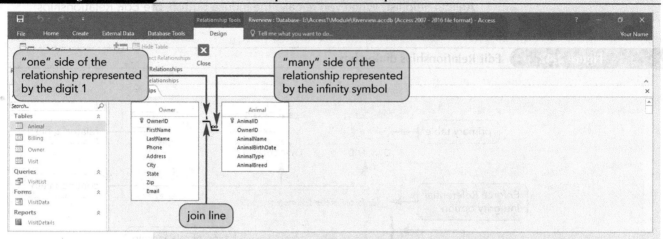

Trouble? If a dialog box opens indicating a problem that prevents you from creating the relationship, you most likely made a typing error when entering the two records in the Owner table. If so, click the OK button in the dialog box and then click the Cancel button in the Edit Relationships dialog box. Refer back to the earlier steps instructing you to enter the two records in the Owner table and carefully compare your entries with those shown in the text, especially the OwnerID field values. Make any necessary corrections to the data in the Owner table, and then repeat Steps 7 through 10. If you still receive an error message, ask your instructor for assistance.

The next step is to define the one-to-many relationship between the Animal and Visit tables. In this relationship, Animal is the primary ("one") table because there is at most one animal for each visit. Visit is the related ("many") table because there are zero, one, or many visits that are generated for each animal. Similarly, you need to define the one-to-many relationship between the Visit and Billing tables. In this relationship, Visit is the primary ("one") table because there is at most one visit for each invoice. Billing is the related ("many") table because there are zero, one, or many invoices that are generated for each animal visit. For example, some visits require lab work, which is invoiced separately.

To define the relationship between the Animal and Visit tables and to define the relationship between the Visit and billing tables:

1. On the Relationship Tools Design tab, in the Relationships group, click the **Show Table** button to open the Show Table dialog box.

2. Click **Visit** on the Tables tab, click the **Add** button, and then click the **Close** button to close the Show Table dialog box. The Visit table's field list appears in the Relationships window to the right of the Animal table's field list.

   Because the Animal table is the primary table in this relationship, you need to drag the AnimalID field from the Animal field list to the Visit field list.

3. Drag the **AnimalID** field in the Animal field list to the **AnimalID** field in the Visit field list. When you release the mouse button, the Edit Relationships dialog box opens.

TIP

You can also use the mouse to drag a table from the Navigation Pane to add it to the Relationships window.

4. Click the **Enforce Referential Integrity** check box, click the **Cascade Update Related Fields** check box, and then click the **Create** button. The Edit Relationships dialog box closes and the completed relationship appears in the Relationships window.

   Finally, you will define the relationship between the Visit and Billing tables.

5. On the Relationship Tools Design tab, in the Relationships group, click the **Show Table** button to open the Show Table dialog box.

6. Click **Billing** on the Tables tab, click the **Add** button, and then click the **Close** button to close the Show Table dialog box. The Billing table's field list appears in the Relationships window to the right of the Visit table's field list.

7. Click and drag the **VisitID** field in the Visit field list to the **VisitID** field in the Billing field list. The Edit Relationships dialog box opens.

8. In the Edit Relationships dialog box, click the **Enforce Referential Integrity** check box, click the **Cascade Update Related Fields** check box, and then click the **Create** button to define the one-to-many relationship between the two tables and to close the dialog box. The completed relationships for the Riverview database appear in the Relationships window. See Figure 2-44.

Figure 2-44	All three relationships now defined

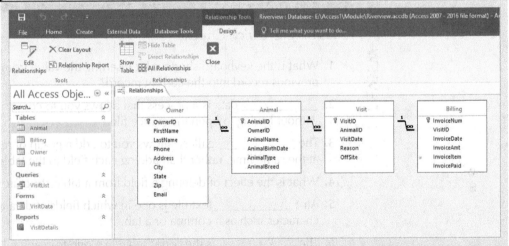

9. On the Quick Access Toolbar, click the **Save** button 🖫 to save the layout in the Relationships window.

10. On the Relationship Tools Design tab, in the Relationships group, click the **Close** button to close the Relationships window.

11. Compact and repair the Riverview database, and then close the database.

PROSKILLS

Problem Solving: Creating a Larger Database

The Riverview database is a relatively small database containing only a few tables, and the data and the reports you will generate from it will be fairly simple. A larger database would most likely have many more tables and different types of relationships that can be quite complex. When creating a large database, follow this standard process:

- Consult people who will be using the data to gain an understanding of how it will be used. Gather sample reports and representative data if possible.
- Plan the tables, fields, data types, other properties, and the relationships between the tables.
- Create the tables and define the relationships between them.
- Populate the tables with sample data.
- Design some queries, forms, and reports that will be needed, and then test them.
- Modify the database structure, if necessary, based on the results of your tests.
- Enter the actual data into the database tables.

Testing is critical at every stage of creating a database. Once the database is finalized and implemented, it's not actually finished. The design of a database evolves as new functionality is required and as the data that is gathered changes.

REVIEW

Session 2.2 Quick Check

1. What is the keyboard shortcut for inserting the value from the same field in the previous record into the current record?

2. _____ data is a process that allows you to copy the data from a source without having to open the source file.

3. The _____ gallery allows you to add a group of related fields to a table at the same time, rather than adding each field to the table individually.

4. What is the effect of deleting a field from a table structure?

5. A(n) _____ text file is one in which fields of data are separated by a character such as a comma or a tab.

6. The _____ is the "one" table in a one-to-many relationship, and the _____ is the "many" table in the relationship.

7. _____ is a set of rules that Access enforces to maintain consistency between related tables when you update data in a database.

Review Assignments

PRACTICE

Data File needed for the Review Assignments: Vendor.accdb (*cont. from Module 1*) and Supplies.xlsx

In addition to tracking information about the vendors Riverview Veterinary Care Center works with, Kimberly also wants to track information about their products and services. First, Kimberly asks you to modify the necessary properties in the existing Supplier table in the Vendor database; then she wants you to create a new table in the Vendor database to contain product data. Complete the following:

1. Open the **Vendor** database you created in the previous module.
2. Open the **Supplier** table in Design view, and set the field properties as shown in Figure 2-45.

Figure 2-45	Field properties for the Supplier table

Field Name	Data Type	Description	Field Size	Other
SupplierID	Short Text	Primary key	6	Caption = Supplier ID
Company	Short Text		50	
Category	Short Text		15	
Address	Short Text		35	
City	Short Text		25	
State	Short Text		2	
Zip	Short Text		10	
Phone	Short Text		14	Caption = Contact Phone
ContactFirst	Short Text		20	Caption = Contact First Name
ContactLast	Short Text		25	Caption = Contact Last Name
InitialContact	Date/Time			Format = Short Date
				Caption = Initial Contact

3. Save the Supplier table. Click the **Yes** button when a message appears, indicating some data might be lost. Switch to Datasheet view and resize columns, as necessary, to their best fit. Then save and close the Supplier table.
4. Create a new table in Design view, using the table design shown in Figure 2-46.

Figure 2-46	Design for the Product table

Field Name	Data Type	Description	Field Size	Other
ProductID	Short Text	Primary key	5	Caption = Product ID
SupplierID	Short Text	Foreign key	6	Caption = Supplier ID
ProductName	Short Text		75	Caption = Product Name
Price	Currency			Format = Standard
				Decimal Places = 2
TempControl	Yes/No			Caption = Temp Controlled?
Sterile	Yes/No			Caption = Sterile?
Units	Number		Integer	Decimal Places = 0
				Caption = Units/Case
				Default Value = [no entry]

5. Specify ProductID as the primary key, and then save the table as **Product**.

6. Modify the table structure by adding a new field between the Price and TempControl fields. Name the new field **Weight** (data type: **Number**; field size: **Single**; Decimal Places: **2**; Caption: **Weight in Lbs**; Default Value: [no entry]). Then move the **Units** field so that it is positioned between the Price and Weight fields.

7. Enter the records shown in Figure 2-47 in the Product table. Resize all datasheet columns to their best fit. When finished, save and close the Product table.

Figure 2-47   **Records for the Product table**

Product ID	Supplier ID	Product Name	Price	Units/Case	Weight in Lbs	Temp Controlled?	Sterile?
PT100	KLS321	Paper tape roll	20.00	12	3	No	No
TC050	QLS002	Thermometer covers	27.00	50	1	No	Yes

8. Use the Import Spreadsheet Wizard to add data to the Product table. The data you need to import is contained in the Supplies workbook, which is an Excel file located in the Access1 > Review folder provided with your Data Files.

   a. Specify the Supplies workbook as the source of the data.

   b. Select the option for appending the data.

   c. Select Product as the table.

   d. In the Import Spreadsheet Wizard dialog boxes, make sure Access confirms that the first row contains column headings, and import to the Product table. Do not save the import steps.

9. Open the **Product** table in Datasheet view, and resize columns to their best fit, as necessary. Then save and close the Product table.

10. Define a one-to-many relationship between the primary Supplier table and the related Product table. Resize the table field lists so that all field names are visible. Select the referential integrity option and the cascade updates option for the relationship.

11. Save the changes to the Relationships window and close it, compact and repair the Vendor database, and then close the database.

Case Problem 1

APPLY

Data Files needed for this Case Problem: Beauty.accdb *(cont. from Module 1)* **and Customers.txt**

Beauty To Go   Sue Miller wants to use the Beauty database to track information about customers who subscribe to her business, which provides a variety of salon services on a subscription basis, and the plans in which customers are enrolled. She asks you to help maintain this database. Complete the following:

1. Open the **Beauty** database you created in the previous module, open the **Option** table in Design view, and then change the following field properties:

   a. OptionID: Enter **Primary key** for the description, change the field size to **3**, and enter **Option ID** for the caption.

   b. OptionDescription: Change the field size to **45** and enter **Option Description** for the caption.

   c. OptionCost: Change the format to **Standard**, specify **0** decimal places, enter **Option Cost** for the caption, no default value.

   d. FeeWaived: Enter **Fee Waived** for the caption.

2. Save and close the Option table. Click the Yes button when a message appears, indicating some data might be lost.

3. Create a new table in Design view, using the table design shown in Figure 2-48.

| Figure 2-48 | Design for the Member table |

Field Name	Data Type	Description	Field Size	Other
MemberID	Short Text	Primary key	4	Caption = Member ID
OptionID	Short Text	Foreign key	3	Caption = Option ID
FirstName	Short Text		20	Caption = First Name
LastName	Short Text		25	Caption = Last Name
Phone	Short Text		14	
OptionEnd	Date/Time	Date Option Ends		Format = Short Date
				Caption = Option Ends

4. Specify **MemberID** as the primary key, and then save the table as **Member**.

5. Use the Address Quick Start selection in the Data Type gallery to add five fields between the LastName and Phone fields.

6. Switch to Design view, and then make the following changes to the Member table design:

   a. Address field: Change the name of this field to **Street**, change the field size to **40**, and delete the entry for the caption.

   b. City field: Change the field size to **25**, and delete the entry for the caption.

   c. StateProvince field: Change the name of this field to **State**, change the field size to **2**, delete the entry for the caption, and enter **FL** for the default value.

   d. ZIPPostal field: Change the name of this field to **Zip**, change the field size to **10**, and delete the entry for the caption.

   e. Delete the **CountryRegion** field from the Member table structure.

   f. Between the Phone and OptionEnd fields, add a new field named **OptionBegin** (data type: **Date/Time**; format: **Short Date**; Caption: **Option Begins**).

7. Enter the records shown in Figure 2-49 in the Member table. Resize all datasheet columns to their best fit. When finished, save and close the Member table. Be sure to enter your first and last name in the appropriate fields in the first record.

| Figure 2-49 | Records for the Member table |

Member ID	Option ID	First Name	Last Name	Street	City	State	Zip	Phone	Option Begins	Option Ends
2103	123	Student First	Student Last	22 Oak St	Orlando	FL	32801	407-832-3944	2/1/17	3/1/17
2118	120	Susan	Reyes	3 Balboa St	Orlando	FL	32804	407-216-0091	11/2/16	2/2/17

8. Use the Import Text File Wizard to add data to the Member table. The data you need to import is contained in the Customers text file, which is located in the Access1 > Case1 folder provided with your Data Files.

   a. Specify the Customers text file as the source of the data.

   b. Select the option for appending the data.

   c. Select Member as the table.

   d. In the Import Text File Wizard dialog boxes, choose the options to import delimited data, to use a comma delimiter, and to import the data into the Member table. Do not save the import steps.

9. Open the **Member** table in Datasheet view and resize columns to their best fit, as necessary. Then save and close the Member table.

10. Define a one-to-many relationship between the primary Option table and the related Member table. Resize the Member table field list so that all field names are visible. Select the referential integrity option and the cascade updates option for this relationship.

11. Save the changes to the Relationships window and close it, compact and repair the Beauty database, and then close the database.

Case Problem 2

APPLY

Data Files needed for this Case Problem: Programming.accdb *(cont. from Module 1)*, **Client.accdb, Students.txt, and Agreements.xlsx**

Programming Pros   Brent Hovis plans to use the Programming database to maintain information about the students, tutors, and contracts for his tutoring services company. Brent asks you to help him build the database by updating one table and creating two new tables in the database. Complete the following:

1. Open the **Programming** database you created in the previous module, open the **Tutor** table in Design view, and then set the field properties as shown in Figure 2-50.

Figure 2-50 **Field properties for the Tutor table**

Field Name	Data Type	Description	Field Size	Other
TutorID	Short Text	Primary key	4	Caption = Tutor ID
FirstName	Short Text		20	Caption = First Name
LastName	Short Text		25	Caption = Last Name
Major	Short Text		25	
YearInSchool	Short Text		12	Caption = Year In School
School	Short Text		30	
HireDate	Date/Time			Format = Short Date
				Caption = Hire Date

2. Add a new field as the last field in the Tutor table with the field name **Groups**, the **Yes/No** data type, and the caption **Groups Only**.

3. Save the Tutor table. Click the **Yes** button when a message appears, indicating some data might be lost.

4. In the table datasheet, specify that the following tutors conduct group tutoring sessions only: Carey Billings, Fredrik Karlsson, Ellen Desoto, and Donald Gallager. Close the Tutor table.

5. Brent created a table named Student in the Client database that is located in the Access1 > Case2 folder provided with your Data Files. Import the structure of the Student table in the Client database into a new table named Student in the Programming database. Do not save the import steps.

6. Open the **Student** table in Datasheet view, and then add the following two fields to the end of the table: **BirthDate** (Date/Time field) and **Gender** (Short Text field).

7. Use the Phone Quick Start selection in the Data Type gallery to add four fields related to phone numbers between the Zip and BirthDate fields. (*Hint:* Be sure to make the BirthDate field the active field before adding the new fields.)

8. Display the Student table in Design view, delete the BusinessPhone and FaxNumber fields, and then save and close the Student table.

9. Reopen the Student table and modify its design so that it matches the design in Figure 2-51, *including the revised field names and data types.*

Figure 2-51	Field properties for the Student table

Field Name	Data Type	Description	Field Size	Other
StudentID	Short Text	Primary key	7	Caption = Student ID
LastName	Short Text		25	Caption = Last Name
FirstName	Short Text		20	Caption = First Name
Address	Short Text		35	
City	Short Text		25	
State	Short Text		2	Default Value = NC
Zip	Short Text		10	
HomePhone	Short Text		14	Caption = Home Phone
CellPhone	Short Text		14	Caption = Cell Phone
BirthDate	Date/Time			Format = Short Date
				Caption = Birth Date
Gender	Short Text		1	

10. Move the LastName field so it follows the FirstName field.
11. Save your changes to the table design, and then add the records shown in Figure 2-52 to the Student table.

Figure 2-52	Records for the Student table

Student ID	First Name	Last Name	Address	City	State	Zip	Home Phone	Cell Phone	Date of Birth	Gender
LOP4015	Henry	Lopez	19 8th St	Raleigh	NC	27601	919-264-9981	919-665-8110	2/19/1998	M
PER4055	Rosalyn	Perez	421 Pine Ln	Cary	NC	27511	984-662-4761	919-678-0012	4/12/1996	F

12. Resize the fields to their best fit, and then save and close the Student table.
13. Use the Import Text File Wizard to add data to the Student table. The data you need to import is contained in the Students text file, which is located in the Access1 > Case2 folder provided with your Data Files.
   a. Specify the Students text file as the source of the data.
   b. Select the option for appending the data.
   c. Select Student as the table.
   d. In the Import Text File Wizard dialog boxes, choose the options to import delimited data, to use a comma delimiter, and to import the data into the Student table. Do not save the import steps.
14. Open the **Student** table in Datasheet view, resize columns in the datasheet to their best fit (as necessary), and then save and close the table.
15. Create a new table in Design view, using the table design shown in Figure 2-53.

Figure 2-53 **Design for the Contract table**

Field Name	Data Type	Description	Field Size	Other
ContractID	Short Text	Primary key	4	Caption = Contract ID
StudentID	Short Text	Foreign key	7	Caption = Student ID
TutorID	Short Text	Foreign key	4	Caption = Tutor ID
SessionType	Short Text		15	Caption = Session Type
Length	Number		Integer	Decimal Places = 0
				Caption = Length (Hrs)
				Default Value = [no entry]
NumSessions	Number		Integer	Decimal Places = 0
				Caption = Number of Sessions
				Default Value = [no entry]
Cost	Currency			Format = Currency
				Decimal Places = 0
				Default Value = [no entry]
Assessment	Yes/No	Pre-assessment exam complete		Caption = Assessment Complete

16. Specify ContractID as the primary key, and then save the table using the name **Contract**.

17. Add a new field to the Contract table, between the TutorID and SessionType fields, with the field name **ContractDate**, the **Date/Time** data type, the description **Date contract is signed**, the **Short Date** format, and the caption **Contract Date**. Save and close the Contract table.

18. Use the Import Spreadsheet Wizard to add data to the Contract table. The data you need to import is contained in the Agreements workbook, which is an Excel file located in the Access1 > Case2 folder provided with your Data Files.

    a. Specify the Agreements workbook as the source of the data.

    b. Select the option for appending the data to the table.

    c. Select Contract as the table.

    d. In the Import Spreadsheet Wizard dialog boxes, choose the Agreements worksheet, make sure Access confirms that the first row contains column headings, and import to the Contract table. Do not save the import steps.

19. Open the **Contract** table, and add the records shown in Figure 2-54. (*Hint:* Use the New (blank) record button in the navigation buttons to add a new record.)

Figure 2-54 **Records for the Contract table**

Contract ID	Student ID	Tutor ID	Contract Date	Session Type	Length (Hrs)	Number of Sessions	Cost	Assessment Complete
6215	PER4055	1018	7/6/2017	Group	2	5	$400	Yes
6350	LOP4015	1010	10/12/2017	Private	3	4	$720	Yes

20. Resize columns in the datasheet to their best fit (as necessary), and then save and close the Contract table.

21. Define the one-to-many relationships between the database tables as follows: between the primary Student table and the related Contract table, and between the primary Tutor table and the related Contract table. Resize the table field lists so that all field names are visible. Select the referential integrity option and the cascade updates option for each relationship.

22. Save the changes to the Relationships window and close it, compact and repair the Programming database, and then close the database.

Case Problem 3

Data Files needed for this Case Problem: Center.accdb *(cont. from Module 1)*, **Donations.xlsx, and Auctions.txt**

Diane's Community Center   Diane Coleman wants to use the Center database to maintain information about the patrons and donations for her not-for-profit community center. Diane asks you to help her maintain the database by updating one table and creating two new ones. Complete the following:

1. Open the **Center** database you created in the previous module, open the **Patron** table in Design view, and then change the following field properties:
   a. PatronID: Enter **Primary key** for the description, change the field size to **5**, and enter **Patron ID** for the caption.
   b. Title: Change the field size to **4**.
   c. FirstName: Change the field size to **20**, and enter **First Name** for the caption.
   d. LastName: Change the field size to **25**, and enter **Last Name** for the caption.
   e. Phone: Change the field size to **14**.
   f. Email: Change field size to **35**.

2. Save and close the Patron table. Click the Yes button when a message appears, indicating some data might be lost.

⊕ **Explore** 3. Use the Import Spreadsheet Wizard to create a table in the Center database. As the source of the data, specify the Donations workbook, which is located in the Access1 > Case3 folder provided with your Data Files. Select the option to import the source data into a new table in the database.

⊕ **Explore** 4. Complete the Import Spreadsheet Wizard dialog boxes as follows:
   a. Select Donation as the worksheet you want to import.
   b. Specify that the first row contains column headings.
   c. Accept the field options suggested by the wizard, and do not skip any fields.
   d. Choose DonationID as your own primary key.
   e. Import the data to a table named **Donation**, and do not save the import steps.

⊕ **Explore** 5. Open the Donation table in Datasheet view. Left-justify the DonationDescription field by clicking the column heading, and then on the Home tab, clicking the Align Left button in the Text Formatting group.

6. Open the Donation table in Design view, and then modify the table so it matches the design shown in Figure 2-55, including changes to data types, field name, and field position. For the Short Text fields, delete any formats specified in the Format property boxes.

Figure 2-55 **Design for the Donation table**

Field Name	Data Type	Description	Field Size	Other
DonationID	Short Text	Primary key	4	Caption = Donation ID
PatronID	Short Text	Foreign key	5	Caption = Patron ID
DonationDate	Date/Time			Format = mm/dd/yyyy
				Caption = Donation Date
Description	Short Text		30	
DonationValue	Currency	Dollar amount or estimated value		Format = Currency
				Decimal Places = 2
				Caption = Donation Value
				Default Value = [no entry]
CashDonation	Yes/No			Caption = Cash Donation?
AuctionItem	Yes/No			Caption = Possible Auction Item?

7. Save your changes to the table design, click Yes for the message about lost data, and then switch to Datasheet view.

8. Resize the columns in the Donation datasheet to their best fit.

⟳ **Explore** 9. Diane decides that the values in the Donation Value column would look better without the two decimal places. Make this field the current field in the datasheet. Then, on the Table Tools Fields tab, in the Formatting group, use the Decrease Decimals button to remove the two decimal places and the period from these values. Switch back to Design view, and note that the Decimal Places property for the DonationValue field is now set to 0.

10. Save and close the Donation table.

11. Use Design view to create a table using the table design shown in Figure 2-56.

Figure 2-56 **Design for the Auction table**

Field Name	Data Type	Description	Field Size	Other
AuctionID	Short Text	Primary key	3	Caption = Auction ID
AuctionDate	Date/Time			Format = mm/dd/yyyy
				Caption = Date of Auction
DonationID	Short Text		4	Caption = Donation ID
MinPrice	Currency			Format = Currency
				Decimal Places = 0
				Caption = Minimum Sale Price
ItemSold	Yes/No			Caption = Item Sold at Auction?

12. Specify **AuctionID** as the primary key, save the table as **Auction**, and then close the table.

13. Use the Import Text File Wizard to add data to the Auction table. The data you need to import is contained in the Auctions text file, which is located in the Access1 > Case3 folder provided with your Data Files.

   a. Specify the Auctions text file as the source of the data.

   b. Select the option for appending the data.

   c. Select Auction as the table.

   d. In the Import Text File Wizard dialog boxes, choose the options to import delimited data, to use a comma delimiter, and to import the data into the Auction table. Do not save the import steps.

14. Open the Auction table in Datasheet view, and resize all columns to their best fit.

15. Display the Auction table in Design view. Move the DonationID field to make it the second field in the table, and enter the description **Foreign key** for the DonationID field. Save the modified Auction table design.

16. Switch to Datasheet view, and then add the records shown in Figure 2-57 to the Auction table. (*Hint:* Use the New (blank) record button in the navigation buttons to add a new record.) Close the table when finished.

Figure 2-57   **Records for the Auction table**

AuctionID	DonationID	AuctionDate	MinPrice	ItemSold
205	5132	8/12/2017	200	No
235	5217	10/14/2017	150	No

17. Define the one-to-many relationships between the database tables as follows: between the primary Patron table and the related Donation table, and between the primary Donation table and the related Auction table. Resize any field lists so that all field names are visible. Select the referential integrity option and the cascade updates option for each relationship.

18. Save the changes to the Relationships window and close it, compact and repair the Center database, and then close the database.

Case Problem 4

Data Files needed for this Case Problem: Appalachia.accdb *(cont. from Module 1)*, **Travel.accdb, and Bookings.txt**

Hike Appalachia   Molly and Bailey Johnson use the Appalachia database to track the data about the hikers and tours offered through their business. They ask you to help them maintain this database. Complete the following:

1. Open the **Appalachia** database you created in the previous module, open the **Hiker** table in Design view, and then change the following field properties:

   a. HikerID: Enter **Primary key** for the description, change the field size to **3**, and enter **Hiker ID** for the caption.

   b. HikerFirst: Change the field size to **20**, and enter **Hiker First Name** for the caption.

   c. HikerLast: Change the field size to **25**, and enter **Hiker Last Name** for the caption.

   d. Address: Change the field size to **35**.

   e. City: Change the field size to **25**.

   f. State: Change the field size to **2**.

   g. Zip: Change the field size to **10**.

   h. Phone: Change the field size to **14**.

2. Save the Hiker table, click the Yes button when a message appears, indicating some data might be lost, resize the Hiker First Name and Hiker Last Name columns in Datasheet view to their best fit, and then save and close the table.

   a. Import the **Trip** table structure and data from the **Travel** database into a new table in the **Appalachia** database. As the source of the data, specify the Travel database, which is located in the Access1 > Case4 folder provided with your Data Files; select the option button to import tables, queries, forms, reports, macros, and modules into the current database; and in the Import Objects dialog box, select the **Trip** table, click the **Options** button, and then make sure that the correct option is selected to import the table's data and structure (definition).

   b. Do not save your import steps.

⊕ **Explore** 3. Using a shortcut menu in the Navigation Pane, rename the Trip table as **Tour** to give this name to the new table in the Appalachia database.

4. Open the **Tour** table in Design view, and then delete the VIPDiscount field.

5. Change the following properties:

   a. TourID: Enter the description **Primary key**, change the field size to **3**, and enter **Tour ID** for the caption.

   b. TourName: Enter **Tour Name** for the caption, and change the field size to **35**.

   c. TourType: Enter **Tour Type** for the caption, and change the field size to **15**.

   d. PricePerPerson: Enter **Price Per Person** for the caption.

6. Save the modified table, click the Yes button when a message appears, indicating some data might be lost, and then display the table in Datasheet view. Resize all datasheet columns to their best fit, and then save and close the table.

7. In Design view, create a table using the table design shown in Figure 2-58.

Figure 2-58   **Design for the Reservation table**

Field Name	Data Type	Description	Field Size	Other
ReservationID	Short Text	Primary key	4	Caption = Reservation ID
HikerID	Short Text	Foreign key	3	Caption = Hiker ID
TourID	Short Text	Foreign key	3	Caption = Tour ID
TourDate	Date/Time			Caption = Tour Date
People	Number		Integer	Decimal Places = 0
				Default Value = [no entry]

8. Specify **ReservationID** as the primary key, and then save the table as **Reservation**.

⊕ **Explore** 9. Refer back to Figure 2-11 to review the custom date formats. Change the Format property of the TourDate field to a custom format that displays dates in a format similar to 02/15/17. Save and close the Reservation table.

10. Use the Import Text File Wizard to add data to the Reservation table. The data you need to import is contained in the Bookings text file, which is located in the Access1 > Case4 folder provided with your Data Files.

    a. Specify the Bookings text file as the source of the data.

    b. Select the option for appending the data.

    c. Select Reservation as the table.

    d. In the Import Text File Wizard dialog boxes, choose the options to import delimited data, to use a comma delimiter, and to import the data into the Reservation table. Do not save the import steps.

11. Open the **Reservation** table, and then resize columns in the table datasheet to their best fit (as necessary), verify that the date values in the StartDate field are displayed correctly according to the custom format, and then save and close the table.

12. Define the one-to-many relationships between the database tables as follows: between the primary Hiker table and the related Reservation table, and between the primary Tour table and the related Reservation table. (*Hint:* Place the Reservation table as the middle table in the Relationships window to make it easier to join the tables.) Resize the Hiker field list so that all field names are visible. Select the referential integrity option and the cascade updates option for each relationship.

13. Save the changes to the Relationships window and close it, compact and repair the Appalachia database, and then close the database.

Managing Files and Directories

After reading this chapter and completing the exercises, you will be able to:

- Describe the Linux file system and the Filesystem Hierarchy Standard
- Navigate the Linux directory structure
- Manage files and directories in Linux

Now that you've installed openSUSE, it's time to open a terminal window and gain some command-line skills. Most major Linux distributions include a GUI desktop environment, such as GNOME or KDE, but learning the command line is important, especially for server administrators. In business environments, most Linux servers are in a locked room for security reasons and are administered from a remote terminal via the command line.

This chapter begins with the Linux directory structure and describes its major differences from the Windows directory structure. You're introduced to the Filesystem Hierarchy Standard, which specifies requirements and guidelines for file and directory placement. With this standard, software developers can create software that runs on all major Linux distributions.

Next, you learn commands for navigating the Linux directory structure and arguments for adding information to commands. You also learn how to find Linux documentation by using man pages and how to use wildcards to move around the directory structure quickly. You then learn how to manage files and directories and create hard and symbolic links, which are often compared with shortcuts in Windows. Finally, you see why using the root user account judiciously is important.

An Overview of the Linux Directory Structure

A **file system** is the way files are stored and organized to simplify access to data. Learning the Linux file system can be difficult because of its differences from Windows. For example, in Windows (see Figure 3-1), each partition is assigned a drive letter, such as assigning C to the first partition of the hard drive, and is separate from the others. In addition, each partition in

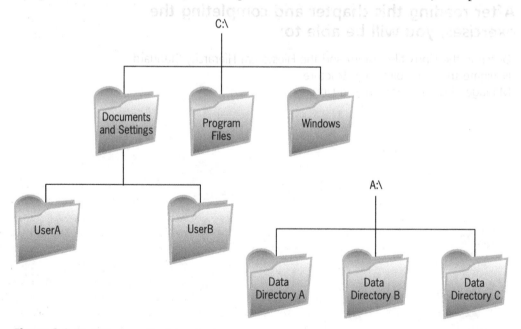

Figure 3-1 The Windows directory structure
© Cengage Learning 2013

Windows has its own root directory. In Linux, however, there's only one root directory, and all files and subdirectories are placed under the root directory in a treelike structure, as shown in Figure 3-2.

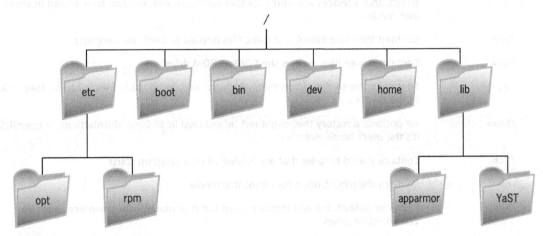

Figure 3-2 The Linux directory structure
© Cengage Learning 2013

As mentioned, Linux distributions vary in their interfaces and features. However, these distributions have nearly identical directory structures because of the **Filesystem Hierarchy Standard (FHS)**. This standard specifies requirements and guidelines for file and directory placement in UNIX-like operating systems (see *www.pathname.com/fhs/pub/fhs-2.3.html*). One benefit of FHS is that users are able to find the correct configuration files regardless of the Linux distribution. For instance, a Red Hat user can find the /etc/hosts file in openSUSE easily because it's in the same location as it is in Red Hat. Another benefit of FHS is that it enables Linux software developers to create software that works in all major Linux distributions.

You can review the Filesystem Hierarchy Standard at
http://proton.pathname.com/fhs/.

A basic understanding of FHS is a valuable tool for Linux administrators and users. Linux distributions closely follow the FHS and place their configuration files accordingly. Being able to find critical configuration files quickly cuts down on troubleshooting time. File systems based on the FHS have two distinctions: shareable versus unshareable files and variable versus static files. These distinctions are important because they indicate the kind of files in each directory. A **shareable file**, such as a user's home directory, can be stored on one machine and used by multiple users on other machines. An **unshareable file**, such as a configuration file in the /etc directory, can't be accessed by multiple users. **Static files**, such as those in the /boot directory, don't change on their own, but **variable files**, which are usually found in the /var directory, can. Table 3-1 lists some Linux directories defined by the FHS.

Table 3-1 Directories defined by the FHS

Directory	Description
/bin	Contains binary commands that can be used by system administrators, users, and scripts; this directory shouldn't contain subdirectories and can be accessed in single user mode
/boot	Contains the Linux kernel and static files needed to boot the computer
/dev	Contains device files, such as the CD/DVD-ROM drive
/etc	Contains static configuration files, which are also unshareable files, meaning they're local to the machine
/home	An optional directory that might not be included in all Linux distributions; in openSUSE, it's the user's home directory
/lib	Contains shared libraries that are loaded when a program starts
/media	Contains the mount point for removable media
/mnt	Empty by default, but administrators can use it to mount other resources, such as CD/DVD-ROM drives
/opt	Contains static shareable add-on software packages
/root	Contains the recommended home directory for the root user; not all Linux distributions use it, but it's used in openSUSE
/sbin	Contains system binaries used by the system administrator
/srv	Contains data files for services
/tmp	Contains temporary files that system administrators should delete whenever the system is booted
/usr	Contains shareable, read-only applications and files
/var	Contains variable data files, such as log files

Navigating the Linux Directory Structure

Imagine getting on a plane and flying to Rome for the first time. A taxi picks you up from the airport and drops you off in front of the Coliseum. Would you know what to do or where to go? How would you navigate the city? This feeling of unfamiliarity with a new setting is similar to what many new Linux users experience. Fortunately, many commands are available to help you navigate the Linux file system. The first commands you learn in this chapter are used to determine your current directory and move in and out of this directory.

When you first log in to a Linux system, you'll probably be in a GUI desktop environment. You can open the file manager and click your way around the Linux directory structure until you find the file or directory you want. The problem is that most Linux servers are installed without a graphical environment, which means you need to learn how to navigate without a GUI.

Here's how to open a terminal window in the KDE and GNOME desktop environments:

- *KDE*—Click the K menu button (the green circle) at the lower left and click Terminal.
- *GNOME*—Click Computer, More Applications to open the Application Browser, and then click the GNOME Terminal icon in the System Groups category.

 You can create a desktop shortcut for the terminal window in both environments by dragging the terminal icon to the desktop.

Changing Directories

Learning the pwd (print working directory) command is essential because it displays the directory you're currently working in. It's like looking at a map with an X and the message "You are here!" That's what the pwd command does, as shown in this example:

```
~> pwd
/home/dustin
```

 Linux is case sensitive, and commands in Linux are lowercase. For example, if you enter PWD, you get an error because the shell doesn't recognize the uppercase PWD as a command.

The **command-line prompt** in the preceding example is ~>. It simply indicates where to enter commands and varies depending on the shell. For instance, the previous example shows the prompt in the BASH shell, but in the Korn shell, it looks like this:

```
/home/dustin> pwd
/home/dustin
```

To navigate the directory structure, you use the cd (change directory) command to switch to other directories. You can add a **command-line argument**, which is information entered after a command to include specific instructions. For instance, you can add a command-line argument specifying which directory to change to, as shown in this example:

```
~> cd /bin
/bin> pwd
/bin
```

If you use the cd command without an argument, you return to your home directory, as shown in this example:

The ~ (tilde) symbol represents the user's **home directory**, which is the default directory on the file system where the user has full permission to store files. In the following example, the user's **current directory** is /bin, and the ~ symbol is used to change to the user's home directory:

```
/bin> cd ~
~> pwd
/home/isaiah
```

You can also use the ~ symbol to specify another user's home directory, as in this example:

```
~> cd ~jasmine
```

At this point, you haven't created any users other than the one you created during the openSUSE installation. You create more users in Chapter 7.

Pathnames in Linux So far, the arguments you've used with the cd command have specified the directory by using the **absolute path** method, which states the full pathname starting from root (/), as shown in this example:

```
~> cd /home/jake/Desktop
~/Desktop> cd /etc
~/etc> cd /home
```

You can also use the **relative path** method, which specifies the pathname starting from the current directory, as in this example:

```
~/Desktop> cd ../../../etc
~/etc> cd ..
~> cd home/jake
```

Remember that the absolute method always starts with a / symbol (root), so the command cd/home/jake/Desktop uses the absolute method. The relative method starts with the current directory, as shown in the command cd Desktop. To navigate to a directory above your current directory with the relative method, you use two dots, as shown in this example:

```
~/Desktop> cd ..
/jake> pwd
/home/jake
```

Two dots represent the parent directory, and one dot represents the current directory. The parent directory is one directory above your current directory in the directory structure. The only directory that doesn't have a parent directory is root (/).

The BASH Command Completion Feature You can use the **command completion** feature in the BASH shell to finish commands for you. To enable this feature, press the Tab key. For example, if you're in the /home/daniel directory and want to change to /home/daniel/Desktop, simply type cd De and press Tab. BASH completes the command for you and displays cd Desktop/ at the prompt. Remember to enter enough characters for this feature to work, particularly if you have more than one subdirectory beginning with the same letter. If you're in /home/daniel, and then type cd D and press Tab, you hear a beep: BASH is letting you know that it can't read your mind. If you press Tab again, BASH lists all possible choices, as shown:

```
Desktop/  Documents/  Download/
```

For all activities in this chapter, you can start in the KDE or GNOME desktop environment.

Activity 3-1: Using the pwd and cd Commands

Time Required: 10 minutes

Objective: Practice navigating the Linux directory structure.

Description: In this activity, you open a terminal window and use the pwd command to display your current directory and the cd command to change your current directory. You also get practice using the BASH command-completion feature.

1. Use the skills you learned in Chapter 2 to start VMware Player and start an openSUSE virtual machine.

2. Log in to openSUSE as a user other than root, and open a terminal window, using the instructions given earlier in this chapter.

3. Type **pwd** and press **Enter** to view your current directory. What is your current directory?

   _____

4. Type **cd /etc** and press **Enter**, and then type **pwd** and press **Enter**. Is your current directory the same? Why or why not? What method did you use to change to the /etc directory?

   _____

   _____

5. Use the relative method to change to your parent directory by typing **cd ..** and pressing **Enter**. What directory are you in now?

   _____

6. Type **cd** and press **Enter**. What happens when you use the cd command without arguments?

   _____

7. Type **cd D** and press **Tab** two times. What's displayed onscreen, and why?

   _____

8. Leave the terminal window open and the virtual machine running for the next activity.

Viewing Files and Directories

So far, you have learned how to determine your current position in the directory structure with the pwd command and navigate the directory structure with the cd command. To list files and subdirectories in the Linux directory structure, you use the ls command. The following example lists the contents of the user's home directory:

```
~> ls
bin Download
Desktop Documents
```

The `ls` command lists files and subdirectories in the current directory, and you can use arguments to specify other directories. For instance, if you're in your home directory and want a list of all files and directories in the parent directory, you can use an argument to specify this information:

```
~> ls ..
david jasmine lost+found
```

File types are indicated in different colors onscreen. For instance, directories might be blue, and regular files might be green or black. Linux distributions vary in the colors used to represent file types, however, so relying on this method to determine the file type isn't wise.

You can also use **options** to modify the way a command is carried out. Almost all Linux commands follow this syntax:

command -options argument

Notice the hyphen before *options*; you must include it before the first option you use. To view the contents of your current directory in a long list rather than a column format, you use the −1 option, as shown:

Make sure you use a lowercase L for the -l option, not the number 1. The hyphen used before an option is called different names, such as a dash or a minus sign.

```
~> ls -l
total 548
drwxr-xr-x 2 sarah users 4096 2012-03-06 20:01 bin
drwxr-xr-x 2 sarah users 4096 2012-03-09 09:42 Desktop
drwxr-xr-x 2 sarah users 4096 2012-03-09 12:34 Documents
drwxr-xr-x 2 sarah users 4096 2012-03-07 19:08 Download
-rw-r--r-- 1 sarah users 0 2012-04-15 20:00 file1
```

Another option used often with the `ls` command is `-a`, which displays all files, including hidden files. The following example shows using this option to find files in the current directory:

```
~> ls -a
. .cache .local bin Desktop Documents Download .. file1
```

Hidden files in Linux are usually system files that users rarely need. Their names always start with a period, such as `.cache` and `.local` in the preceding example, so they're often called "dot files."

You can string options together, too, as shown in this example of specifying a long list of all files and directories in your current directory:

```
~> ls -al
total 9466
drwxr-xr-x 42 alex users 4096 2012-04-15 20:00 .
drwxr-xr-x 5 root root 4096 2012-04-14 13:54 ..
drwxr-xr-x 7 alex users 4096 2012-03-13 11:19 .cache
drwxr-xr-x 3 alex users 4096 2012-03-06 20:02 .local
-rw-r--r-- 1 alex users 0 2012-04-15 20:00 file1
drwxr-xr-x 2 alex users 4096 2012-03-09 09:42 Desktop
drwxr-xr-x 2 alex users 4096 2012-03-09 12:34 Documents
drwxr-xr-x 2 alex users 4096 2012-03-07 19:08 Download
```

The order of options doesn't matter, as long as you add a hyphen in front of the first option, so `ls -1a` is the same as `ls -al`.

You can use many options with the `ls` command. Table 3-2 describes some of the most common.

Table 3-2 Options with the `ls` command

Option	Description
-a	Lists all files, including hidden files
-F	Appends a special character to each filename to represent the file type, such as * for an executable file and / for a subdirectory
-h	Stands for "human-readable" format, which shows file sizes in megabytes or gigabytes, for example, instead of in bytes
-i	Displays the inode number (discussed later in "Creating Links") for each file
-l	Changes the display from a column format to a long list
-R	Stands for recursive, meaning the `ls` command is repeated for all subdirectories
--help	Lists all options available with a command

Examining the `ls -1` Command The output of the `ls -1` command contains important information in eight separate columns, discussed in detail in the following list. Figure 3-3 gives you an overview of this output.

Here's an example of information the `ls -1` command returns; refer to this example as you read the explanations in the following list:

```
drwxr-xr-x 2 natalie users 4096 2012-02-06 20:01 Desktop
```

- *File type*—In this example, the file type column displays "d," which stands for a directory. Notice that there's no space after this first column.

- *File permissions*—The second column specifies file permissions. In the previous example, the file permissions are `rwxr-xr-x`. You learn about file permissions in Chapter 5, but for now, just be aware that file permissions are displayed for three categories: user, group, and other. Each category is assigned a combination of read (r), write (w), and execute (x) permissions.

- *Hard links*—The third column displays the number of hard links associated with the file. You learn more about hard links later in "Creating Links."
- *Owner*—The fourth column shows the user owner of the file (explained in Chapter 7).
- *Group*—The fifth column shows the file's group owner (explained in Chapter 7).
- *File size*—The sixth column displays the file size, which is in bytes by default. You can use the -h option to view file size in a format that's easier to read (such as kilobytes, megabytes, or gigabytes).
- *Modification time*—The seventh column displays a timestamp showing when the file was last modified.
- *Filename*—The eighth column shows the name of the file.

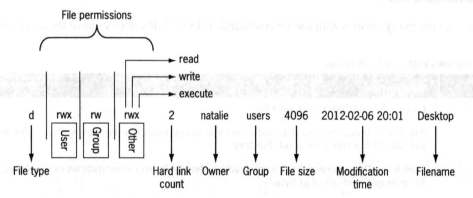

Figure 3-3 A guide to the `ls -l` command's output
© Cengage Learning 2013

Activity 3-2: Using the `ls` Command

Time Required: 10 minutes

Objective: Use commands for viewing Linux files and directories.

Description: In this activity, you use the `ls` command to view files and directories in your current directory and practice using options, including two you choose from Table 3-2.

1. If necessary, start VMware Player and start an openSUSE virtual machine. Log in to openSUSE as a user other than root, and open a terminal window.
2. Type **ls** and press **Enter**, and then type **ls -l** and press **Enter**.
3. Display a long list of the /etc directory by typing **ls -l /etc** and pressing **Enter**.
4. Display a long list of the /etc/hosts file by typing **ls -l /etc/hosts** and pressing **Enter**. What's the timestamp of this file?

   _____

5. Display all files in your home directory, including hidden files, by typing **ls -a ~** and pressing **Enter**.

6. Review Table 3-2 and choose two options to use in your current directory. List the options you chose and briefly describe the results of using them:

_____

_____

7. Leave the terminal window open and the virtual machine running for the next activity.

Getting Help

Few administrators, no matter how long they've been working with Linux, have every command memorized. There are thousands of Linux commands, and most have multiple options. The good news is that Linux stores documentation files on all commands. **Man (manual) pages** are documentation files that describe Linux shell commands, executable programs, system calls, special files, and so forth. The following example shows opening the man pages for the ls command:

```
man ls
Man: find all matching manual pages
 * ls (1)
   ls (1p)
Man: What manual page do you want?
```

An asterisk to the left of the first entry indicates the default selection. To select the man page for the ls command, type 1 (the numeral, in this case) and press Enter, or type 1p and press Enter to select the POSIX Programmer's Manual page for the ls command. Your screen should be similar to Figure 3-4.

```
LS(1)                    User Commands                    LS(1)


NAME
       ls - list directory contents

SYNOPSIS
       ls [OPTION]... [FILE]...

DESCRIPTION
       List  information  about  the FILEs (the current directory by default).
       Sort entries alphabetically if none of -cftuvSUX nor --sort.

       Mandatory arguments to long options are  mandatory  for  short  options
       too.

       -a, --all
              do not ignore entries starting with .

       -A, --almost-all
              do not list implied . and ..

       --author
              with -l, print the author of each file

       -b, --escape
              print octal escapes for nongraphic characters

       --block-size=SIZE
              use SIZE-byte blocks

       -B, --ignore-backups
              do not list implied entries ending with ~

       -c     with -lt: sort by, and show, ctime (time of last modification of
              file status information) with -l: show ctime and  sort  by  name
              otherwise: sort by ctime
Manual page ls(1) line 1
```

Figure 3-4 Excerpt from the man page for the ls command

Source: openSUSE

POSIX (an abbreviation for Portable Operating System Interface) is a set of standards based on UNIX. Many Linux commands have both a Linux man page and a POSIX Programmer's Manual page associated with them.

Man pages are organized into eight sections, described in Table 3-3.

Some UNIX systems offer man pages for section 0 (header files) and section 9 (kernel routines).

Table 3-3 Man page sections

Section	Description	Examples
1	Executable programs or shell commands	man ls, man pwd
2	System calls, which are system requests that programs make to the kernel	man kill, man read
3	Library calls (to access functions in program libraries)	man xcrypt, man stdin
4	Special files, such as the floppy disk, that are usually found in /dev	man fd, man tty
5	File formats and conventions	man passwd, man hosts
6	Games	man tetravex, man AisleRiot
7	Macro packages and conventions	man man (7), man gruff (7)
8	System administration commands	man yast, man suseconfig

You can also find man pages for the man command to get more information on man page sections and other features of this command.

Navigating Man Pages Notice the message at the bottom left in Figure 3-4: "Manual page ls(1) line 1." This message tells you the name of the command (ls), the man page section (1), and the first line number that can be read (line 1), so you're looking at the man page for the ls command, and line 1 is the first line shown onscreen. Table 3-4 lists ways to navigate man pages.

Table 3-4 Methods of navigating man pages

Action	Function
Press f or the spacebar	Move forward one window at a time.
Press b or backspace	Move backward one window at a time.
Press h	Open the help page.
Press / (forward slash)	Enter a string of text to search for in the man page.
Press n	Repeat the previous search.
Press N	Repeat the previous search in the reverse direction.

Activity 3-3: Working with Man Pages

Time Required: 10 minutes

Objective: Find and navigate man pages for any Linux command.

Description: In this activity, you use the man command to open help files on the pwd, cd, and ls commands. You also use the man command to find documentation on another command of your choice and refer to Table 3-4 to navigate the man page.

1. If necessary, start VMware Player and start an openSUSE virtual machine. Log in to openSUSE as a user other than root, and open a terminal window.

2. Display the man page for the pwd command by typing **man pwd** and pressing **Enter**. Press **q** to quit, and then try typing **man 1 pwd** and pressing **Enter**. What's the difference in the output of these two commands?

   _____

3. Display the man page for the cd command by typing **man cd** and pressing **Enter**. Read the information, as time permits.

4. Display the man page for the ls command by typing **man ls** and pressing **Enter**. Read the information, as time permits.

5. Display the man page for a command of your choice. Refer to Table 3-4 to practice navigating it.

6. Leave the terminal window open and the virtual machine running for the next activity.

Using Wildcards

In a card game, a wildcard represents any card the cardholder wants. In Linux, a **wildcard** represents letters and characters used to specify a filename for searches. For instance, you can use a wildcard to get a long list of all files in the current directory starting with "new." Linux administrators use wildcards to navigate to directories faster, move or delete a group of files, and locate files based on a portion of their filenames. You can use them, too, to help you navigate the Linux directory structure and manage files. Table 3-5 describes wildcards used in Linux. The two used most often are * and ?, explained in more detail in the following paragraphs.

Table 3-5 Wildcards

Wildcard	Description
*	Matches zero or more characters in a filename
?	Matches any one character in a filename
[acf]	Matches one of multiple characters in a filename; in this example, a, c, or f
[a-f]	Matches one of a range of characters in a filename; in this example, any character from a through f
[!a-f]	Matches filenames that don't contain a specified range of characters; in this example, filenames that don't contain a through f

The * wildcard is used to represent zero or more characters. Say your current directory contains five files: file1, file2, newfile1, newfile2, and notefile. You want a list of files starting with the letters "fi." You can use this wildcard as shown:

```
ls fi*
file1 file2
```

Note that because this wildcard represents zero or more characters, entering ls file1* would display only file1. You can also specify files ending with a certain character, as in this example:

```
ls *2
file2 newfile2
```

You can use the * wildcard with any command that needs an argument. For example, if you need to switch to a certain directory, but all you remember is that the directory name starts with "new," you can use the following command to list all directories starting with those characters:

```
cd new*
```

The ? wildcard is used to represent only one character, as shown in the following example:

```
~/newdirectory> ls -l
total 20
-rw-r--r-- 1 maria users 0 2012-03-18 22:31 file1
-rw-r--r-- 1 maria users 0 2012-03-18 22:31 file2
-rw-r--r-- 1 maria users 0 2012-03-18 22:31 newfile1
-rw-r--r-- 1 maria users 0 2012-03-18 22:31 newfile2
-rw-r--r-- 1 maria users 0 2012-03-18 22:31 notefile
~/newdirectory> ls file?
file1 file2
```

Activity 3-4: Using Wildcards

Time Required: 10 minutes

Objective: Use wildcards to search for files and directories.

Description: In this activity, you use the common wildcards * and ?. You also see the results of more uncommon wildcards.

1. If necessary, start VMware Player and start an openSUSE virtual machine. Log in to openSUSE as a user other than root, and open a terminal window.

2. Use the absolute method to change to the /etc directory by typing **cd /etc** and pressing **Enter**.

3. Display a long list of files and directories in the /etc directory by typing **ls -l** and pressing **Enter**.

4. Display a long list of files and directories in the /etc directory starting with the letter "h" by typing **ls -l h*** and pressing **Enter**. How are the results different from Step 3?

   _____

5. Display a long list of files and directories in the /etc directory and use two wildcards by typing **ls -l *.?** and pressing **Enter**. How are the results different from Step 3?

   _____

6. Display a long list of files and directories in the /etc directory starting with a, c, or k by typing **ls -l [ack]*** and pressing **Enter**.

7. Display a long list of files and directories in the /etc directory starting with a, b, or c by typing **ls -l [a-c]*** and pressing **Enter**.

8. Display a long list of files and directories in the /etc directory that don't start with the letters a through s by typing **ls -l [!a-s]*** and pressing **Enter**.

9. Change the current directory by typing **cd /h*** and pressing **Enter**. What happened, and why?

   _____

10. Leave the terminal window open and the virtual machine running for the next activity.

Managing Files and Directories

Now that you have explored the Linux directory structure, it's time to learn some important file management tasks. As a Linux administrator, you should know how to use the command line to create files and directories, move files in and out of directories, delete and copy files and directories, and view file and directory contents. The following sections explain how to perform these tasks.

Creating and Deleting Directories and Files

Directories are essential for keeping files organized in the Linux file system. Each directory has its own permissions assigned (as explained in Chapter 5). Remember that your home directory is created to give you full permission to create subdirectories, files, scripts, and so forth; as an administrator, you have the root password, which gives you full access to create directories and files throughout the file system. The commands you learn in this section are mkdir, touch, rm, and rmdir.

Creating Directories The mkdir (make directory) command is used to create directories. The following example shows creating a directory called Studynotes in the home directory:

```
~> mkdir Studynotes
~> ls
bin Documents Music Public Studynotes Videos
Desktop Download Pictures public_html Templates
```

Over time, a home directory usually increases to hundreds of files, which can make managing it difficult. Creating and using subdirectories help you organize files. For instance, in this example, the Studynotes subdirectory was created to contain all the user's study notes. Later, the user might decide to create a subdirectory of Studynotes for each class.

Creating Files There are several ways to create a file in Linux. The simplest is the touch command, used to create a new empty file or update the timestamp of an existing file. The following example shows creating an empty file with this command:

```
~/Studynotes> touch chapter1
~/Studynotes> ls -l
total 4
-rw-r--r-- 1 keith users 0 2012-03-19 13:29 chapter1
```

The timestamp for the new file, chapter1, is 2012-03-19 13:29, which is March 19, 2012 at 1:29 pm. If you use the touch command with this file again, it simply updates the file's date and time to match the current system date and time.

On a Linux file system that's shared across a network, you should update (touch) important files and scripts you have created. Some system administrators create scripts to delete files that haven't been modified in 90 days. This measure clears space in the file system but could delete a file you need. Make sure you use the touch command with important files periodically.

Wildcards are handy when you're updating multiple files at the same time, as shown in the following example with the touch command:

```
~/Studynotes> ls -l
total 16
-rw-r--r-- 1 david users 0 2009-11-03 13:00 chapter1
-rw-r--r-- 1 david users 0 2009-12-19 15:43 chapter2
-rw-r--r-- 1 david users 0 2012-01-12 18:02 chapter3
-rw-r--r-- 1 david users 0 2012-02-10 08:30 chapter4
~/Studynotes> touch *
~/Studynotes> ls -l
total 16
```

```
-rw-r--r-- 1 david users 0 2012-03-19 13:45 chapter1
-rw-r--r-- 1 david users 0 2012-03-19 13:45 chapter2
-rw-r--r-- 1 david users 0 2012-03-19 13:45 chapter3
-rw-r--r-- 1 david users 0 2012-03-19 13:45 chapter4
```

Remember the * represents zero or more characters. In this example, the * used alone instructs the touch command to update every file in the current directory.

Deleting Directories and Files Depending on the permissions your user account has, deleting directories can be dangerous. If you try to delete a folder in Windows, a message box opens, asking for confirmation that you want to delete it. Typically, there's no confirmation message in Linux. To avoid deleting files accidentally, most Linux users log in with an account that has limited permissions; they switch to the root user only when they need to do administrative tasks. The rm command is used to remove files and directories, and the rmdir command is used to remove empty directories.

You use the su (switch user) command later in "Switching Users and Becoming Root."

The following example shows deleting an empty subdirectory in the current directory:

```
1. ~/Studynotes> cd Math
2. ~/Studynotes/Math> ls
3. ~/Studynotes/Math> cd ..
4. ~/Studynotes> pwd
5. /home/andrea/Studynotes
6. ~/Studynotes> rmdir Math
7. ~/Studynotes> ls -l
8. total 24
drwxr-xr-x 2 andrea users 4096 2012-03-20 09:27 English
drwxr-xr-x 2 andrea users 4096 2012-03-20 09:27 Week1
drwxr-xr-x 2 andrea users 4096 2012-03-20 09:27 Week2
```

The current directory, Studynotes, contains four subdirectories: English, Math, Week1, and Week2. You change to the Math directory (line 1) and use the ls command (line 2) to determine whether this directory is empty. Next, you use the relative method (line 3) to change back to the parent directory and use the pwd command (line 4) to confirm the location. Finally, you use the rmdir command (line 6) to delete the empty directory. If the Math directory had contained files, an error would have been displayed because the rmdir command doesn't remove directories containing content.

If you try to remove a directory that isn't empty, you get an error message similar to the following:

```
rmdir: failed to remove 'Math': Directory not empty
```

Before removing a directory containing files, you must use the rm command to delete the files. Remember that there's no confirmation message in Linux, so be sure you're deleting the correct file. The following example shows using the `rm` command to delete files in the Math directory:

```
~/Studynotes/Math> ls -l
total 4
-rw-r--r-- 1 andrea users 0 2012-03-20 10:44 file1
~/Studynotes/Math> rm file1
```

You can also use the `-r` option with the `rm` command to delete directories and their contents recursively, meaning you don't need to delete files first. In other words, this option enables you to remove directories that aren't empty.

Activity 3-5: Creating and Deleting Directories and Files

Time Required: 15 minutes

Objective: Use Linux commands for creating and deleting directories and files.

Description: In this activity, you create a directory with the `mkdir` command, create files with the `touch` command, and update file timestamps by using the `touch` command with wildcards. Finally, you use the `rm` command to delete files and the `rmdir` command to delete a directory.

1. If necessary, start VMware Player and start an openSUSE virtual machine. Log in to openSUSE as a user other than root, and open a terminal window.

2. Change to your home directory by typing **cd** and pressing **Enter**.

3. Create and name a directory by typing **mkdir Activity3-5** and pressing **Enter**.

4. Change to the Activity3-5 directory by typing **cd Activity3-5** and pressing **Enter**.

5. Create three files in the Activity3-5 directory by typing **touch actfile1 actfile2 actfile3** and pressing **Enter**.

6. Display a long list of all files in the Activity3-5 directory by typing **ls -l** and pressing **Enter**.

7. Update the timestamps of these files by typing **touch *[2-3]** and pressing **Enter**. What files are updated?

_____

8. To return to your home directory, type **cd** and press **Enter**.

9. Try to delete the Activity3-5 directory by typing **rmdir Activity3-5** and pressing **Enter**. Were you able to delete the directory? Why or why not?

_____

10. Change to the Activity3-5 directory by typing **cd Activity3-5** and pressing **Enter**. Delete the three files (actfile1, actfile2, and actfile3) by typing **rm *** and pressing **Enter**.

11. Type **ls** and press **Enter**. Is the directory empty?

_____

12. Change to your home directory by typing **cd** and pressing **Enter**.

13. Now that the Activity3-5 directory is empty, delete it by typing **rmdir Activity3-5** and pressing **Enter**.

14. Leave the terminal window open and the virtual machine running for the next activity.

Moving, Renaming, and Copying Files

The command line makes moving or copying multiple files at once easy. Many Linux administrators actually find using the command line for this purpose simpler than using a GUI. In this section, you learn the mv and cp commands. The mv command has a dual purpose: renaming files and moving files from one directory to another. In fact, you can do both at the same time. The syntax for the mv command is as follows:

```
mv filename new location
```

The following example shows moving the week1notes file from the Math directory to the ~/Studynotes/Week1 directory. The ~ represents the user's home directory:

```
~/Studynotes/Math> mv week1notes ~/Studynotes/Week1
```

Here's an example of using the mv command to rename a file:

```
~/Studynotes/Week1> mv week1notes notes
```

The following example shows how to move the notes file to another directory and rename it Newnotes at the same time:

```
~/Studynotes/Week1> mv notes ~/Studynotes/Week2/newnotes
```

When you move a file to a new location, it no longer exists in the original directory. In other words, the mv command doesn't create new files. To have the same file in two locations, you use the cp (copy) command, which copies files and directories. It has the same syntax as the mv command:

```
cp filename new location
```

The following example shows creating a copy of the newnotes file in the Week1 directory:

```
~/Studynotes/Week2> cp newnotes ~/Studynotes/Week1
```

The main difference between the cp command and the mv command is that the cp command creates a new file, and the mv command is used with just one file.

Activity 3-6: Renaming, Moving, and Copying Files

Time Required: 15 minutes

Objective: Use Linux commands for renaming, moving, and copying files.

Description: In this activity, you create a directory called Activity3-6 and create a file in this directory. You use the mv command to rename the file and then move it to the parent directory. You also use the cp command to make a copy of the file in the Activity3-6 directory.

1. If necessary, start VMware Player and start an openSUSE virtual machine. Log in to openSUSE as a user other than root, and open a terminal window.

2. Type **mkdir Activity3-6** and press **Enter**, and then change to this new directory by typing **cd Activity3-6** and pressing **Enter**.

3. Type **touch actfile1** and press **Enter**. Type **ls** and press **Enter**.

4. Type **mv actfile1 actfile2** and press **Enter**, and then type **ls** and press **Enter**. What's the result of this mv command?

   _____

5. Type **mv actfile2 ..** and press **Enter**, and then type **ls** and press **Enter**. What's the result of this command?

   _____

6. Type **cd ..** and press **Enter**. What directory are you in?

   _____

7. Type **cp actfile2 actfile3** and press **Enter**. What's the result of this command?

   _____

8. Type **cp actfile2 Activity3-6** and press **Enter**. What happens? Change to the Activity3-6 directory, and then type **ls** and press **Enter**. What files are in this directory?

   _____

   _____

9. Leave the terminal window open and the virtual machine running for the next activity.

Creating Links

In the previous section, you learned how to create copies of files with the cp command. These copies are separate from the originals, so if you change the original file, the copied file doesn't reflect these changes. In this section, you learn how to create links with the ln command. To understand how links work, however, first you need to know what inodes are and how information is stored on a disk.

Inodes An **inode** is a data structure that stores all information (such as file permissions, ownership, and file type) about a file except the actual data and filename. Each inode is identified by an inode number, which can be thought of as an address. The **inode number** references an entry in the **inode table**, which is a list of inodes for all files on a Linux partition. This table entry points to the data's location on the disk. To view a file's inode number, use the `ls -il` command, as shown:

```
~/Math> ls -il
total 4
3327 -rw-r--r-- 1 dustin users 0 2012-03-21 15:46 algebra
```

The inode number for the algebra file in the preceding example is 3327. To display more inode information (such as file size, permissions, UID, and so forth), you use the stat (status) command. In the following example, it's used with the algebra file in the Math directory:

```
~/Math> stat algebra
  File: 'algebra'
  Size: 0 Blocks: 8 IO Block: 4096 regular empty file
Device: 803h/2051d Inode: 3327 Links: 1
Access: (0644/-rw-r--r--) Uid: ( 1000/ dustin) Gid: ( 100/ users)
Access: 2012-03-21 15:46:43.740447686 -0500
Modify: 2012-03-21 15:46:43.666449631 -0500
Change: 2012-03-21 15:46:43.761409157 -0500
```

 Each Linux partition has only one inode table. Every file (including directories) contains a unique inode number, unless you're dealing with hard links, discussed next.

Hard Links Hard links are files that point to data on the hard drive. When you create a file, it's automatically linked to the actual data stored on a partition and assigned an inode number referencing this data. You can then create hard links on the same partition to refer to this data. The following example shows creating a hard link:

```
~/Math/Week1/Calculus> ln notes ~/Math
```

In this example, a hard link is created in the Calculus directory to link the notes file to a file in the Math directory. You could then change to the Math directory and use the ls -il command to verify that the notes hard link was indeed created. The following example shows the results of using ls -il in the Math and Calculus directories. Notice that the link count is 2 and both have the same inode number (522815):

```
~/Math/Week1/Calculus> ls -il
522815 -rw-r--r-- 2 sasha users 0 2012-03-30 20:24 notes
dustin@linux-7cua:~/Math> ls -il
522815 -rw-r--r-- 2 sasha users 0 2012-03-30 20:24 notes
```

When the ls -il command is first used in the Calculus directory, the link count is 1 (shown in bold in the following line) because it's the only link to the actual data on the hard drive:

```
522815 -rw-r--r-- 1 sasha users 86 2012-03-21 16:29 notes
```

After a hard link to a file in the Math directory is created, the link count changes to 2. Notice that the inode number (522815) for the notes file in the Math directory is the same as for the notes file in the Calculus directory.

If a file contains three hard links and you delete one, the data isn't affected because two links still exist. For instance, if you delete the notes file in the Calculus directory in the previous example, the data still exists on the hard drive and can be accessed from the Math directory. The data isn't deleted until the last link is deleted.

Symbolic (Soft) Links Symbolic links (also called soft links) are special types of files that point to other files instead of pointing to data on the hard drive. They don't share the same inode number, as hard links do. The benefit of creating a symbolic link is you can link files that are on separate partitions or even different computers. To create a symbolic link, you use the -s option with the ln command, as shown in this example:

```
~/Sports> ln -s football baseball
~/Sports> ls -il
total 4
3935 lrwxrwxrwx 1 edward users 8 2012-03-22 10:11 baseball -> football
3934 -rw-r--r-- 1 edward users 0 2012-03-22 10:10 football
```

The inode number for the symbolic link (3935) is different from the inode number for the target file (3934). The symbolic link (baseball) points to the target file (football), and the target file's inode points to the actual data on the hard drive. If you modify the symbolic link, the target file is also modified. Likewise, if you modify the target file, the symbolic link is modified. If you delete the target file, the symbolic link no longer works.

An advantage of symbolic links is that you can create one to point to a file on a different partition, as shown in this example:

```
~> df -h
Filesystem Size Used Avail Use% Mounted on
/dev/sda2 7.7G 3.5G 3.9G 48% /
udev 372M 312K 371M 1% /dev
/dev/sda3 11G 393M 11G 4% /home
/dev/sda4 20G 10G 10G 50% /data
/data> ln -s cat /home/edward/dog
/data> ls -il
44543 -rw-r--r-- 1 edward users 0 2012-03-22 10:46 cat
/data> cd
~> ls -il
3934 lrwxrwxrwx 1 edward users 3 2012-03-22 10:47 dog -> cat
```

In this example, the df command shows disk space use so that you can see the available partitions. The -h option for output is in human-readable format. Notice that the cat file is on the /dev/sda4 partition, and the symbolic link dog is on the /dev/sda3 partition.

Activity 3-7: Working with Links

Time Required: 20 minutes

Objective: Identify inode numbers and create hard and symbolic links.

Description: In this activity, you identify a file's inode number, and then create a hard link and a symbolic link.

1. If necessary, start VMware Player and start an openSUSE virtual machine. Log in to openSUSE as a user other than root, and open a terminal window.

2. Type **mkdir Activity3-7** and press **Enter**. Change to this new directory by typing **cd Activity3-7** and pressing **Enter**.

3. Create a file in this directory by typing **touch actfile1** and pressing **Enter**. Type **ls -il** and press **Enter**. What's the inode number for `actfile1`?

   _____

4. Display additional inode information for `actfile1` by typing **stat actfile1** and pressing **Enter**.

5. Change to your home directory by typing **cd** and pressing **Enter**.

6. Type **mkdir Linkdir** and press **Enter**. Change to this new directory by typing **cd Linkdir** and pressing **Enter**.

7. Create a hard link by typing **ln ~/Activity3-7/actfile1 .** and pressing **Enter**. Type **ls -il** and press **Enter**. How many links are associated with `actfile1`? Has the number of hard links changed since Step 3?

   _____

8. Type **cd ~/Activity3-7** and press **Enter**. Try to remove `actfile1` by typing **rm actfile1** and pressing **Enter**, and then type **ls -il** and press **Enter**. Is the file removed? Is the data gone? Explain your answers:

   _____

   _____

9. Type **cd ~/Linkdir** and press **Enter**, and then type **ls -il** and press **Enter**. How many links does `actfile1` have, and why?

   _____

10. Type **cd ~/Activity3-7** and press **Enter**. Create a symbolic link by typing **ln -s ~/Linkdir/actfile1 .** and pressing **Enter**, and then type **ls -il** and press **Enter**. What's the link count for `actfile1`?

    _____

11. Type **cd ~/Linkdir** and press **Enter**, and then type **ls -il** and press **Enter**. Is the inode number the same as the inode number for `actfile1` in the `Linkdir` directory? Why or why not?

    _____

12. Leave the terminal window open and the virtual machine running for the next activity.

Switching Users and Becoming Root

You learn about creating users and groups in Chapter 7, but for now, you just need to know that in Linux, every user must have a username and password and belong to a primary group. A benefit of the Linux command line is being able to switch to a different user account while staying in the same terminal window. Remember that the root user has the highest level of permissions, so even if you're a Linux administrator, you should avoid logging in with this account unless you need to perform root administrative tasks, such as editing configuration files. The su (switch user) command enables one user to become another user temporarily. Here's an example of using the su command:

The exit command in lines 5 and 11 is used to switch back to the previous user. For instance, if you're logged in as user1, switch to user2, and then type exit, the command brings you back to user1.

```
1.  ~> su jasmine
2.  Password:
3.  jasmine@client:/home/dustin> pwd
4.  /home/dustin
5.  jasmine@client:/home/dustin> exit
6.  exit
7.  ~> su
8.  Password:
9.  client:/home/dustin # pwd
10. /home/dustin
11. client:/home/dustin # exit
12. exit
13. ~>
```

In this example, the user switches to the jasmine user account, but the current directory doesn't change; it's still the user's home directory. Note that you can't switch to another user if you don't know the account password (unless you're the root user). If you use the su command without an argument, it defaults to the root user, which changes the prompt to a # symbol (as shown in lines 9 and 11).

Another way to switch users is to add - after the su command, as in su - jasmine. This option loads the user's environment variables (discussed in Chapter 5).

Activity 3-8: Switching Users

Time Required: 10 minutes

Objective: Switch users without logging off the computer.

Description: In this activity, you use the su command to switch to the root user and use the - option to load this user's environment variables.

1. If necessary, start VMware Player and start an openSUSE virtual machine. Log in to openSUSE as a user other than root, and open a terminal window.

2. You should be in your home directory. (If necessary, use the pwd command to confirm.) Try to change to the /root directory by typing cd /root and then press **Enter**. Were you able to change to this directory? Why or why not?

_____

3. To switch to the root user, type su and press **Enter**. When prompted, type the root password you set during installation and press **Enter**.

4. Now that you have switched to the root user, change to the /root directory by typing cd /root and then press **Enter**.

5. Type **exit** and press **Enter**. Close the terminal window, and shut down your virtual machine.

Chapter Summary

- Learning to navigate the Linux directory structure at the command line is a useful skill for server administrators because most servers are installed without a GUI.

- In Linux, there's only one root directory, and all files and subdirectories are placed under it in a hierarchical structure.

- Nearly all major Linux distributions follow the Filesystem Hierarchy Standard (FHS), which defines the kind of files that should be in each subdirectory of root.

- The pwd command displays your current directory, and the cd command changes your current directory.

- To change the current directory, you can use the absolute method or the relative method. The absolute method always starts with root (/), and the relative method always starts with the current directory.

- The ls command lists the contents of a directory. The -l option is used with this command to display a long list of files and subdirectories in the directory.

- Linux includes man pages for finding information on commands and other Linux components.

- Wildcards are special characters used to help specify a filename or directory path. The two most common wildcards are * and ?. The * represents zero or more characters, and the ? represents only one character.

- The mkdir command is used to create directories, and the touch command is used to create empty files and update their timestamps.

- The rm command deletes files or directories, and the rmdir command deletes only empty directories.

- The mv command is used to move and rename files, and the cp command is used to create a copy of a file.

- The ln command is used to create hard and symbolic links. Hard links point to data on the hard drive, and soft links point to files that can span multiple partitions.

- The su command enables one user to become another user temporarily.

Key Terms

absolute path The full directory pathname starting from root (/).

command completion A BASH shell feature that finishes a command for you after you enter the first few characters; it's enabled by pressing the Tab key.

command-line argument Information entered after a command to include specific instructions.

command-line prompt An interface that enables users to interact with the OS by typing commands, options, and arguments.

current directory The directory a user is working in.

Filesystem Hierarchy Standard (FHS) A standard specifying requirements and guidelines for file and directory placement in UNIX-like operating systems.

file system The way files and directories are stored and organized to make access to data easier.

hard links Files that point to data on the hard disk and share the same inode number.

home directory A user's default directory on the file system.

inode A data structure that stores information about a file, such as the inode number, file permissions, file owner, and so on; the file's actual data and name aren't stored in the inode.

inode number A unique identification for an inode that references an entry in the inode table. *See also* inode.

inode table A list of inodes for all files on a Linux partition; entries in this table point to where files' actual data is stored. *See also* inode.

man (manual) pages Documentation files that describe Linux shell commands, executable programs, system calls, special files, and so forth.

options Information entered after a command to modify the way it's carried out.

relative path The directory pathname starting from the current directory.

shareable file A file that can be stored on one machine and used by multiple users on other machines.

static files Files that don't change on their own.

symbolic links Special types of files that point to other files (even on separate partitions or different computers) instead of pointing to data on the hard drive; they don't share the same inode number. *See also* hard links.

unshareable file A file that can be used only on the local machine.

variable files Files that can change on their own.

wildcard A character used in searches to specify certain conditions.

Review Questions

1. There can be multiple root directories in Linux. True or False?

2. Describe a benefit of the Filesystem Hierarchy Standard (FHS).

3. What command do you use to display your current directory?

   a. ln

   b. cd

   c. pwd

   d. ls

4. What command do you use to change to a different directory?

   a. ln

   b. cd

   c. pwd

   d. ls

5. What command is used to view the contents of your current directory?

    a. `ln`

    b. `cd`

    c. `pwd`

    d. `ls`

6. The `cd /home/user` command uses the relative method. True or False?

7. The `-l` option affects the `ls` command by:

    a. Changing the format to a long list

    b. Listing all files and directories

    c. Listing only files

    d. Listing inode numbers

8. After entering `ls -a`, how can you tell which files are hidden?

    a. Their names are displayed in a different color.

    b. Their names start with a . (dot).

    c. Their names start with an uppercase letter.

    d. Their names end with a . (dot).

9. Describe three options you can use with the `ls` command.

10. Which of the following is displayed after issuing the `ls -l` command? (Choose all that apply.)

    a. File permissions

    b. Parent directory

    c. File type

    d. Contents of subdirectories

11. Describe three man page sections.

12. After you use the `ls` command, the following files are displayed:
    `file1 file2 file3 file.a file.b file.c files`
    List the files displayed with each of the following options:

    a. `ls f*`

    b. `ls file?`

    c. `ls file[a-c]`

    d. `ls file[!1-3]`

13. What command creates an empty file?

    a. rm

    b. mkdir

    c. touch

    d. rmdir

14. What command deletes files and directories?

    a. rm

    b. mkdir

    c. touch

    d. rmdir

15. What command deletes empty directories?

    a. rm

    b. mkdir

    c. touch

    d. rmdir

16. What command creates directories?

    a. rm

    b. mkdir

    c. touch

    d. rmdir

17. Explain how the -r option affects the rm command.

18. What command is used to rename or move a file?

    a. rn

    b. cp

    c. mv

    d. Both b and c

19. What command is used to copy a file?

    a. rn

    b. cp

    c. mv

    d. Both b and c

20. Explain the difference between an inode table, an inode, and an inode number.

21. How does the `-i` option affect the `ls` command?

    a. Displays the inode table

    b. Displays the inode

    c. Displays the inode number

    d. None of the above

22. Explain the difference between hard links and symbolic links.

23. How does the `-s` option affect the `ln` command?

    a. Creates a symbolic link

    b. Creates a hard link

    c. Gives special permissions to the link

    d. Removes the link

24. What Linux command can you use to switch users without actually logging off your system?

Case Projects

CASE PROJECTS

Case Project 3-1: Working with Modified Files

You're the system administrator for a major automobile company, and you just found out that the chief financial officer (CFO) has resigned. Your boss asks you to find all files in the CFO's home directory that have been modified in the past 90 days, and then move them to your home directory for continuity purposes. What command should you use to find out which files have been modified in this timeframe, and what command should you use to copy these files to your home directory?

Case Project 3-2: Creating a Link

Four science instructors at East Coast Career College ask you whether they can access a particular log file from their home directories. They explain that they update a log file in the `/workgrp/project` directory weekly, and they don't want to change out of their home directories every time they want to view or edit the file. In addition, they want the log file in their home directories to be called `myjournal`. You need to create a link to the log file so that each instructor can access the file from his or her home directory, using the following criteria:

Scientist 1: Michio
Home directory: /home/michio
Scientist 2: Neil
Home directory: /home/neil
Scientist 3: Marty
Home directory: /home/marty
Scientist 4: Ellen
Home directory: /home/ellen
The log file is called sci.journal, and it's in the /workgrp/project directory.

Chapter

Introduction to Computer Networks and Data Communications

OBJECTIVES

After reading this chapter, you should be able to:

→ Define the basic terminology of computer networks

→ Recognize the individual components of the big picture of computer networks

→ Recognize the common examples of computer networks

→ Define the term "convergence" and describe how it applies to computer networks

→ Cite the reasons for using a network architecture and explain how they apply to current network systems

→ List the layers of the TCP/IP protocol suite and describe the duties of each layer

→ List the layers of the OSI model and describe the duties of each layer

→ Compare the TCP/IP protocol suite and OSI model, and list their differences and similarities

MAKING PREDICTIONS is a difficult task, and predicting the future of computing is no exception. History is filled with computer-related predictions that were so inaccurate that today they are amusing. For example, consider the following predictions:

"I think there is a world market for maybe five computers." *Thomas Watson, chairman of IBM, 1943*

"I have traveled the length and breadth of this country, and talked with the best people, and I can assure you that data processing is a fad that won't last out the year." *Editor in charge of business books for Prentice Hall, 1957*

"There is no reason anyone would want a computer in their home." *Ken Olsen, president and founder of Digital Equipment Corporation, 1977*

"640K ought to be enough for anybody." *Bill Gates, 1981*

"We believe the arrival of the PC's little brother [PCjr] is as significant and lasting a development in the history of computing as IBM's initial foray into microcomputing has proven to be." PC Magazine, *December 1983 (The PCjr lasted less than one year.)*

Apparently, no matter how famous you are or how influential your position, it is very easy to make very bad predictions. Nevertheless, it is hard to imagine that anyone can make a prediction worse than any of those above. Buoyed by this false sense of optimism, let us make a few forecasts of our own:

Someday before you head out the door, you will reach for your umbrella, and it will tell you what kind of weather to expect outside. A radio signal will connect the umbrella to a local weather service that will download the latest weather conditions for your convenience.

Someday you will be driving a car, and if you go faster than some predetermined speed, the car will send a text message to your parents informing them of your "driving habits."

Someday we will wear a computer—like a suit of clothes—and when we shake hands with a person, data will be transferred down our skin, across the shaking hands, and into the other person's "computer."

Sometime in the not too distant future, you will place some hot dogs and hamburgers on the grill and then go inside to watch the ball game. Suddenly, you will get a message on your cell phone: "Your food is done cooking."

Someday you will have a car battery that, when the power in the battery gets too weak to start the car, will call you on your cell phone to inform you that you need a replacement or a charge.

One day you will be in a big city and place a call on your cell phone to request a taxi. The voice on the other end will simply say, "Stay right where you are. Do you see the taxi coming down the street? When it stops in front of you, hop in."

Someday you will be driving in a big city and your phone or Global Positioning System (GPS) device will tell you where the nearest empty parking spot on the street is.

Do these predictions sound far-fetched and filled with mysterious technologies that only scientists and engineers can understand? They shouldn't, because they are not predictions. They are scenarios happening today with technologies that already exist. What's more, none of these advances would be possible today were it not for computer networks and data communications.

INTRODUCTION

The world of computer networks and data communications is a surprisingly vast and increasingly significant field of study. Once considered primarily the domain of network engineers and technicians, computer networks now involve business managers, computer programmers, system designers, office managers, home computer users, and everyday citizens. It is virtually impossible for the average person on the street to spend 24 hours without directly or indirectly using some form of computer network.

Ask any group, "Has anyone used a computer *network* today?" and more than one-half of the people might answer, "Yes." Then ask the others, "How did you get to work, school, or the store today if you did not use a computer network?" Most transportation systems use extensive communication networks to monitor the flow of vehicles and trains. Expressways and highways have computerized systems for controlling traffic signals and limiting access during peak traffic times. Some major cities are placing the appropriate hardware inside city buses and trains so that the precise location of each bus and train is known. This information enables the transportation systems to keep the buses evenly spaced and more punctual, and allows the riders to know when the next bus or train will arrive.

In addition, more and more people are using satellite-based GPS devices in their cars and on cell phones to provide driving directions and avoid traffic hotspots. Similar systems can unlock your car doors if you leave your keys in the ignition and can locate your car in a crowded parking lot—beeping the horn and flashing the headlights if you cannot remember where you parked.

But even if you didn't use mass transit or a GPS device in your car today, there are many other ways to use a computer network. Businesses can order parts and inventory on demand and build products to customer-designed specifications electronically, without the need for paper. Online retail outlets can track every item you look at or purchase. Using this data, they can make recommendations of similar products and inform you in the future when a new product becomes available. Twenty-four-hour banking machines can verify the user's identity by taking the user's thumbprint.

In addition, cable television continues to expand, offering extensive programming, pay-per-view options, video recording, digital television and music, and multi-megabit connectivity to the Internet. The telephone system, the oldest and most extensive network of communicating devices, continues to become more of a computer network every day. The most recent "telephone" networks can now deliver voice, Internet, and television over a single connection. Cellular telephone systems cover virtually the entire North American continent and include systems that allow users to upload and download data to and from the Internet, send and receive images, and download streaming video such as television programs. That handheld device you are holding can play music, make phone calls, take pictures, surf the Web, and let you play games while you wait for the next train.

Welcome to the amazing world of computer networks! Unless you have spent the last 24 hours in complete isolation, it is nearly impossible to *not* have used some form of computer networks and data communications. Because of this growing integration of computer networks and data communications into business and life, we cannot leave this area of study to technicians. All of us—particularly information systems, business, and computer science students—need to understand the basic concepts. Armed with this knowledge, we not only will be better at communicating with network specialists and engineers, but also will become better students, managers, and employees.

THE LANGUAGE OF COMPUTER NETWORKS

Over the years, numerous terms and definitions relating to computer networks and data communications have emerged. To gain insight into the many subfields of study, and to become familiar with the emphasis of this textbook, let us examine the more common terms and their definitions.

A **computer network** is an interconnected group of computers and computing equipment using either wires or radio waves that can share data and computing resources. Computer networks that use radio waves are termed **wireless** and can involve broadcast radio, microwaves, or satellite transmissions. Networks spanning an area of several meters around an individual are called **personal area networks (PANs)**. Personal area networks include devices such as laptop computers, smart cell phones, music players, and wireless connections. Networks that are a little larger in geographic size—spanning a room, a floor within a building, or an entire building—are **local area networks (LANs)**. Collections of local area networks that cover a campus (such as a college campus or a business campus) are often called **campus area networks (CANs)**. Networks that serve an area up to roughly 50 kilometers—approximately the area of a typical city—are called **metropolitan area networks (MANs)**. Metropolitan area networks are high-speed networks that interconnect businesses with other businesses and the Internet. Large networks encompassing parts of states, multiple states, countries, and the world are **wide area networks (WANs)**. Chapters 9 and 10 concentrate on wide area networks and metropolitan area networks, and Chapters 7 and 8 concentrate on local area networks and campus area networks.

A very common expression that we hear today is something like "we should store the data on the cloud" or "the application is in the cloud." The key concept here is **cloud** and the way we now use it. (Similar words or phrases that are commonly used today are **network cloud** and **cloud computing**.) Very often the cloud is simply the Internet. When a company places data or applications on some Web site on the Internet and allows people to access them, we often say the application we are using is cloud-based. One of the more visible examples of cloud computing is storing one's music and/or books at a remote location on the Internet rather than on a local device. Major corporations such as Amazon and Apple allow users to store personal data and recent purchases on their clouds. Companies such as Microsoft and Google (as well as many others) allow us to use cloud-based applications such as word processors and spreadsheets. The actual code that runs the word processor or spreadsheet does not exist on the user's computer but only exists on the Internet at some corporate Web site. This way, we don't have to take the time or expense to download the application to an individual machine. We will examine the cloud concept in more detail in a later chapter.

The study of computer networks would be missing a large component without the introduction of two important building blocks: data and signals. Data is information that has been translated into a form more conducive to storage, transmission, and calculation. As we shall see in Chapter 2, a signal is used to transmit data. We define **data communications** as the transfer of digital or analog data using digital or analog signals. Once created, these analog and digital signals then are transmitted over conducted media or wireless media (both of which are discussed in Chapter 3).

Connecting devices to a computer, or a computer to a network, requires **interfacing**, a topic covered in Chapter 4. Because sending only one signal over a medium at one time can be an inefficient way to use the transmission medium, many systems perform multiplexing. **Multiplexing** is the transmission of multiple signals on one medium. For a medium to transmit multiple signals simultaneously, the signals must be altered so that they do not interfere with one another. **Compression** is another technique that can maximize the amount of data sent over a medium. Compression involves squeezing data into a smaller package, thus reducing the amount of time (as well as storage space) needed to transmit the data. Multiplexing and compression are covered in detail in Chapter 5.

When the signals transmitted between computing devices are corrupted and errors result, error detection and error control are necessary. These topics are discussed in detail in Chapter 6.

Once upon a time, a **voice network** transmitted telephone signals, and a **data network** transmitted computer data. Eventually, however, the differences between voice networks and data networks disappeared. The merging of voice and data networks is one example of the term **convergence**, an important topic that will be presented later in this chapter and further developed in subsequent chapters.

Computer security (covered in Chapter 12) is a growing concern of both professional computer support personnel and home computer users with Internet connections. **Network management** is the design, installation, and support of a network and its hardware and software. Chapter 13 discusses many of the basic concepts necessary to support properly the design and improvement of network hardware and software, as well as the more common management techniques used to support a network.

THE BIG PICTURE OF NETWORKS

If you could create one picture that tries to give an overview of a typical computer network, what might this picture include? Figure 1-1 shows such a picture. Note that this picture shows two wide area networks (WAN 1 and WAN 2) and two local area networks (LAN 1 and LAN 2). Although a full description of the different components constituting wide area and local area networks is not necessary at this time, it is important to note that most LANs often include the following hardware:

- **Workstations,** which are personal computers (or microcomputers, desktops, laptops, or tablets, to name a few) or smart phones (or other handheld devices) where users reside
- **Servers,** which are the computers that store network software and shared or private user files
- **Switches,** which are the collection points for the wires that interconnect the workstations
- **Routers,** which are the connecting devices between local area networks and wide area networks such as the Internet

Figure 1-1 An overall view of the
interconnection between
different types of networks

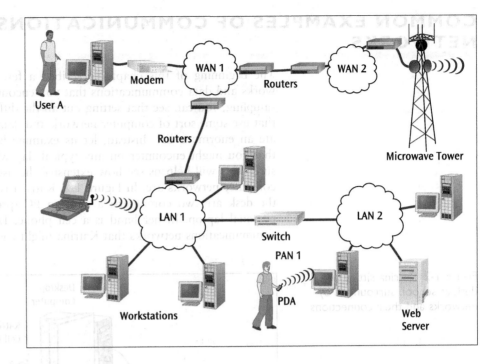

Figure I-I An overall view of the
interconnection between
different types of networks

There are also many types of wide area networks. Although many different technologies are used to support wide area networks, all wide area networks include the following components:

- **Nodes,** which are the computing devices that allow workstations to connect to the network and that make the decisions about where to route a piece of data
- Some type of high-speed transmission line, which runs from one node to another
- A **subnetwork,** which consists of the nodes and transmission lines, collected into a cohesive unit

To see how the local area networks and wide area networks work together, consider User A (in the upper-left corner of Figure 1-1), who wishes to retrieve a Web page from the Web server shown in the lower-right corner. To do this, User A's computer must have both the necessary hardware and software required to communicate with the first wide area network it encounters, WAN 1—User A's Internet service provider. Assuming that User A's computer is connected to this wide area network through a DSL telephone line, User A needs some type of modem. Furthermore, if this wide area network is part of the Internet, User A's computer requires software that talks the talk of the Internet: TCP/IP (Transmission Control Protocol/Internet Protocol).

Notice that no direct connection exists between WAN 1, where User A resides, and LAN 2, where the Web server resides. To ensure that User A's Web page request reaches its intended receiver (the Web server), User A's software attaches the appropriate address information that WAN 1 uses to route User A's request to the router that connects WAN 1 to LAN 1. Once the request is on LAN 1, the switch-like device connecting LAN 1 and LAN 2 uses address information to pass the request to LAN 2. Additional address information then routes User A's Webpage request to the Web server, whose software accepts the request.

Under normal traffic and conditions, this procedure might take only a fraction of a second. When you begin to understand all the steps involved and the great number of transformations that a simple Web page request must undergo, the fact that it takes *only* a fraction of a second to deliver is amazing.

COMMON EXAMPLES OF COMMUNICATIONS NETWORKS

The beginning of this chapter described a few applications of computer networks and data communications that you encounter in everyday life. From that sampling, you can see that setting out all the different types of jobs and services that use some sort of computer network and data communications would generate an enormous list. Instead, let us examine basic communications networks that you might encounter on any typical day while at school, work, or at leisure. This will help us see how extensive the uses of data communications and computer networks are. In Figure 1-2, Katrina is sitting at a desk at school. On the desk are two computers: a desktop PC (provided by the school) and her personal laptop. In her hand is a cell phone. Let's try to identify each of the communications networks that Katrina might encounter.

Figure 1-2 Katrina sitting at a desk at school, surrounded by networks and their connections

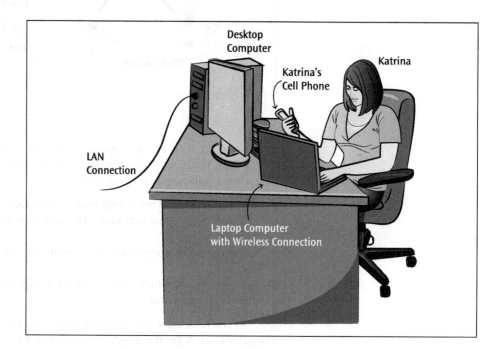

The desktop computer and the Internet

The desktop computer sitting on Katrina's desk is "connected" to the Internet via a cable at the back. ("Connected" was placed in quotations because as this book will hopefully demonstrate, it is a fairly involved process to connect a device to the Internet.) This is perhaps the most common network connection today and is found in virtually every business, every academic environment, and in many homes. The desktop computer—which also is commonly known as the personal computer, PC, microcomputer, laptop computer, notebook, netbook, or workstation—began to emerge in the late 1970s and early 1980s. (The term microcomputer is a good generic word for all these devices and we will use it often.)

In a business or education environment, the cable coming out the back of the desktop plugs into a wall jack and travels through the walls to some collection point, such as a network switch. This network switch, as we will see later, is part of a local area network. This local area network is possibly connected to other local area networks, but eventually connects to a router. From the router, we have some form of high-speed connection to a site which specializes in high-speed connections to the Internet.

The local area network, or LAN, as we shall see in Chapter 7, is an excellent tool for providing a connection to the Internet, as well as other networks, software, and peripherals. One way of stating the desktop-to-Internet example in the business/education world is the client/server system. In a **client/server system,** a user at a microcomputer, or client machine, issues a request for some form of data or service. This could be a request for a database record from a database server, a request for a Web page from a Web server, or a request to retrieve an e-mail message from an e-mail server. If the requested data is local, the request travels across the local system to a local server. If the requested data is not local, the request travels across the local system and then onto an external network, such as the Internet, to a remote server that contains a potentially large repository of data and/or programs. The remote server fills the request and returns the results to the client, displaying the results on the client's monitor. If users wish to print documents on a high-quality network printer, the LAN contains the network software necessary (a print server) to route their print requests to the appropriate printer. If users wish to access their e-mail from an e-mail server, the local area network provides a fast, stable connection between user workstations and the e-mail server. If a user wishes to access the Internet, the local area network provides an effective gateway to the outside world. Figure 1-3 shows a diagram of this type of desktop-to-Internet connection.

Figure 1-3 A desktop computer (or simply microcomputer) at work showing the connection between the user and the company's local area network.

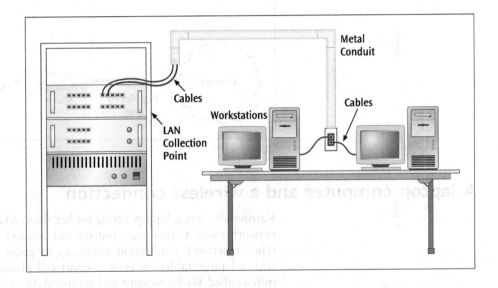

What about connecting a microcomputer to the Internet when the microcomputer is in your home? Once upon a time, most home users connected their microcomputer to the Internet via a dial-up telephone line and a modem. This arrangement allowed for a maximum data transfer rate of roughly 56,000 bits per second (56 kbps). (These dial-up connections do not actually achieve 56 kbps, but that is a discussion we will have in a later chapter.) No longer is the dial-up modem the most often used connecting device. Today, a majority of home users either connect to the Internet using digital subscriber line (DSL) or access the Internet through a cable modem service. DSL and cable modems are capable of achieving much higher connection speeds (or data transfer rates) than dial-up connections and thus continue to grow in popularity. (In comparing the various data transfer rates of services and devices, we will use the convention in which lowercase k equals 1000. Also as part of the convention, lowercase b will refer to bits, while uppercase B refers to bytes, which is a collection of 8 bits.)

To communicate with the Internet using a dial-up, DSL, or cable modem connection, a user's computer must connect to another computer already communicating with the Internet. The easiest way to establish this connection is through the services of an Internet service provider (ISP). In this case, the user's computer needs to have the necessary software to communicate with the Internet. The Internet "talks" only TCP/IP, so users must use software that supports the TCP and IP protocols. Once the user's computer is talking TCP/IP, a connection to the Internet can be established. Figure 1-4 shows a typical home microcomputer-to-Internet connection.

Figure 1-4 A microcomputer sending data over a DSL line to an Internet service provider and onto the Internet

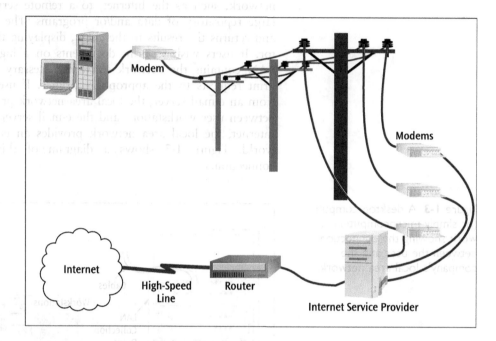

Modem

Modems

Internet

High-Speed Line

Router

Internet Service Provider

A laptop computer and a wireless connection

Katrina also has a laptop sitting on her desk. Many laptops do not connect to a network using a fixed wire but instead connect via a wireless connection. This type of network connection continues to grow in popularity. A user working with a laptop, tablet, or even a smart cell phone uses wireless communications (often called Wi-Fi) to send and receive data to and from a wireless access point (wireless router). This access point is usually connected to a wired local area network and basically serves as the "bridge" between the wireless user device and the wired network. As we shall see in later chapters, there are different data communication **protocols** (sets of rules used by communication devices) for wireless local area networks and wired local area networks. While the flexibility of not having to physically cable your device to a wall jack is nice, we shall see that there are also limitations as to how far the wireless signals will travel.

Because both wireless local area networks and wired local area networks are standard in business, academic, and even many home environments, it should come as no surprise that having just one local area network is not going to get the job done. Many organizations need the services of multiple local area networks, and it may be necessary for these networks to communicate with each other. For example, the school that Katrina attends may want the local area network that supports its chemistry department to share an expensive color laser printer with its biology department's local area network. Fortunately, it is possible to connect two local area networks so that they can share peripherals as well as software. The device that usually connects two or more LANs or segments of LANs is once again, the switch.

In some cases, it may be more important to *prevent* data from flowing between local area networks than to allow data to flow from one network to another. For instance, some businesses have political reasons for supporting multiple networks—each division may want its own network to run as it wishes. Additionally, there may be security reasons for limiting traffic flow between networks; or allowing data destined for a particular network to traverse other networks simply may generate too much network traffic. The switches that connect local area networks can help manage these types of services as well. For example, the switch can filter out traffic not intended for the neighboring network, thus minimizing the overall amount of traffic flow. Figure 1-5 provides an example of two LANs connected by a switch.

Figure **1-5** Two local area networks connected by a switch

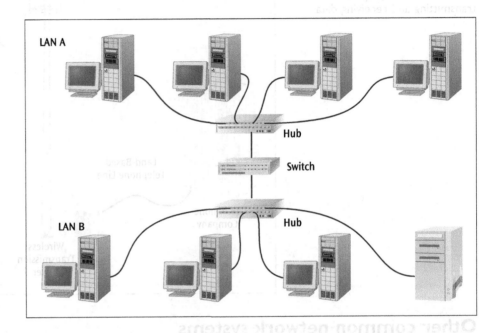

As mentioned above, it is common to connect to the Internet using a smart cell phone and Wi-Fi signals. But what if you find yourself in a place where there are no Wi-Fi signals? If you still want to connect to the Internet, you will have to use a cell phone network, or cell phone system. Let's examine cell phone systems in more detail.

Cell phone systems

One of the most explosive areas of growth in recent years has been cell phone systems. Once upon a time, cell phones could only perform voice calls. But then the cell phone providers got us hooked on text messages. Soon people were sending more text messages than they were making voice calls. It wasn't too long after we became comfortable with making voice calls and sending text messages that cell phones started including low-resolution cameras. Now we could take grainy pictures, and shortly after that, even grainier videos of everyday events. If that wasn't enough, cell phones started to offer the capability of storing and playing music. Today, we use our cell phones to send endless text messages, download Web pages and videos from the Internet, listen to music, and take high-resolution pictures and video. The processing power built within modern smart phones rivals the mainframe computers of generations ago. The network infrastructure that is needed to support modern smart phones has also increased in dramatic fashion. Large numbers of cell towers cover the face of

North America and elsewhere. All these cell towers are tied together into some form of network or networks, allowing us to send a text message all the way around the world. The data encoding technologies that support cell phones continue to increase in complexity so that users can access the networks at always-increasing speeds.

For a more precise view, let's examine Figure 1-6. When a user talks into his or her cell phone or sends a text message, the data is transmitted across the cell phone network to a telephone company building. The telephone company then transfers the cell phone's data over the public telephone network or through a connection onto the Internet.

Figure **1-6** An example of a user with a smart cell phone transmitting and receiving data

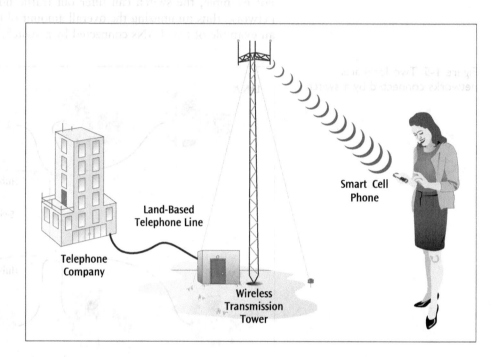

Other common network systems

The three sample networks we just viewed—a desktop computer connected to the Internet via a wired local area network, a laptop computer connected to the Internet via a wireless local area network, and a cell phone network—are only a few of the many examples of communication networks. Others that we should mention (and will examine in more detail in later chapters) include sensor networks, business mainframe systems, and satellite networks.

Sensor networks are often found in industrial and real-world settings. In this type of network, the action of a person or object triggers a sensor—for example, a left-turn light at a traffic intersection—that is connected to a network. In many left-turn lanes, a separate left-turn signal will appear if and only if one or more vehicles are in the left-turn lane. A sensor embedded in the roadway detects the movement of an automobile in the lane above and triggers the left-turn mechanism in the traffic signal control box at the side of the road. If this traffic signal control box is connected to a larger traffic control system, the sensor is connected to a local area network.

Another example of a sensor network is found within manufacturing environments. Assembly lines, robotic control devices, oven temperature controls, and chemical analysis equipment often use sensors connected to data-gathering computers that control movements and operations, sound alarms, and compute experimental or quality control results. These sensors are often interconnected via one or more local area networks. Figure 1-7 shows a diagram of a typical sensor network in a manufacturing environment.

Figure I-7 An automobile moves down an assembly line and triggers a sensor

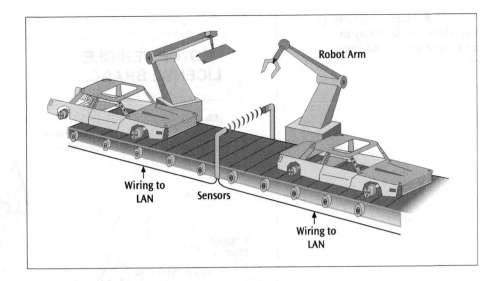

Finally, let's not forget all the sensor systems in our homes and garages. Home appliances, such as washing machines, dryers, and dish washers, include sensors to monitor water and air temperatures as well as water levels. Modern automobiles contain a myriad of sensors, monitoring fuel mixtures, oxygen levels, and wheel rotations (in order to trigger anti-locking brakes and anti-skid controls).

Another fairly common network system is the business mainframe network. A number of businesses still use mainframe computers to support their day-to-day operations. In order to "connect" to a mainframe, a user employs hardware and software that makes their microcomputer or workstation act as a computer terminal. A **computer terminal**, or simply terminal, was a device that was essentially a keyboard and screen with no large hard drives, no gigabytes of memory, and little, if any, processing power. Computer terminals were used for entering data into a system, such as a mainframe computer, and then displaying results from the mainframe. Because the terminal did not possess a lot of computing power, it was considered "dumb" and relied on the mainframe computer to control the sending and receiving of data to and from each terminal. This required special types of protocols and the data was usually transmitted at relatively slow speeds, such as 9600 or 19,200 bits per second (bps).

Although the number of these systems in use is not what it used to be during the 1960s and 1970s, the business mainframe network was in virtually every office, manufacturing, and academic environment. During this period, many of the same end users who had terminals on their desks also now found a microcomputer there (and thus had very little room for anything else). In time, terminal-emulation cards were developed, which allowed a microcomputer to imitate the abilities of a computer terminal. As terminal emulation cards were added to microcomputers, terminals were removed from end users' desks, and microcomputers began to serve both functions. Now, if users wished, they could download information from the mainframe computer to their microcomputers, perform operations on the data, and then upload the information to the mainframe. Today, one rarely sees dumb computer terminals. Instead, most users use microcomputers and access the mainframe using either a terminal emulation card, a Web browser and Web interface, Telnet software (more on this in Chapter 10), or a thin client. A thin client workstation is similar to a microcomputer but has no hard drive storage.

Business mainframe networks are still being used for inquiry/response applications, interactive applications, and data-entry applications, such as you might find when applying for a new driver's license at the Department of Motor Vehicles (Figure 1-8).

Figure 1-8 Using a terminal (or thin-client workstation) to perform a text-based input transaction

The last network example we will introduce is satellite and microwave networks. Satellite and microwave networks are continuously evolving technologies used in a variety of applications. If the distance between two networks is great and running a wire between them would be difficult (if not impossible), satellite and microwave transmission systems can be an extremely effective way to connect the two networks or computer systems. Examples of these applications include digital satellite TV, meteorology, intelligence operations, mobile maritime telephony, GPS navigation systems, wireless e-mail, worldwide mobile telephone systems, and video conferencing. Figure 1-9 shows a diagram of a typical satellite system. We will examine these networks in much more detail in Chapter 3.

Figure 1-9 Example of a television company using a satellite system to broadcast television services into homes and businesses

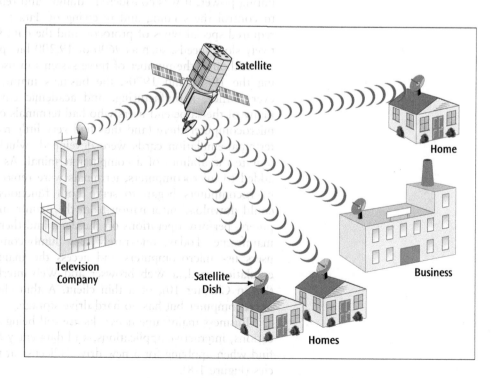

CONVERGENCE

A dictionary might define "convergence" as the process of coming together toward a single point. With respect to computer networks and communications systems, this definition is fairly relevant. Over the years, the communications industry has seen and continues to see different network applications and the technologies that support them converge into a single technology capable of supporting various applications. In particular, we can define three different types of convergence: technological convergence, protocol convergence, and industrial convergence. For example, one of the earliest and most common examples of technological convergence was the use of computers and modems to transmit data over the telephone system. This was an example of voice transmission systems converging with data transmission systems and yielding one system capable of supporting both data and voice. By the 1990s, telephone systems carried more computer data than voice. At about the same time, local area networks began to transfer telephone calls. Because local area networks originally were designed for data applications, this was another example of voice and data systems converging. Now we are seeing substantial growth in the Voice over Internet Protocol (VoIP) field. VoIP involves converting voice signals to packets and then sending those packets over packet-driven networks such as local area networks and the Internet.

Today we see many more examples of technological convergence, particularly in the wireless markets. For example, it is now quite common to snap a photo using a cell phone and then transfer the image over the cell phone network to another cell phone. Shortly after the introduction of photo-enabled cell phones, cell phones also became capable of sending and receiving instant messages. Then in 2005, cell phone providers started offering services that allow a user to transmit high-speed data over a cell phone connection. These all are examples of the convergence of two different applications (for example, digital photography and cell phones in the case of photo-enabled cell phones) into a single technology. As we will see in a later chapter, many of the telephone companies that provide local and long-distance telephone service have converged into fewer companies. These are examples of industrial convergence. Also in a later chapter, we will see how older network protocols have given way or merged with other protocols, thus demonstrating protocol convergence.

Throughout the rest of this book, we will examine other examples of convergence within the communications industry. In addition to introducing the technologies involved, we also will examine the effects a given convergence of technologies might have on individual users and businesses.

NETWORK ARCHITECTURES

Now that you know the different types of networks, we need a framework to understand how all the various components of a network interoperate. When someone uses a computer network to perform an application, many pieces come together to assist in the operation. A **network architecture**, or communications model, places the appropriate network pieces in layers. The layers define a *model* for the functions or services that need to be performed. Each layer in the model defines what services either the hardware or software (or both) provides. The two most common architectures known today are the **TCP/IP protocol suite** and the **Open Systems Interconnection (OSI) model**. The TCP/IP protocol suite is a working model (currently used on the Internet), while the OSI model (originally designed to be a working model) has been relegated to a theoretical model. We will discuss these two architectures in more detail in the following pages. But first you should know a bit more about the components of a network and how a network architecture helps organize those components.

Consider that a typical computer network within a business contains the following components that must interact in various ways:

- Wires
- Printed circuit boards

- Wiring connectors and jacks
- Computers
- Centrally located wiring concentrators
- Disk and tape drives
- Computer applications such as word processors, e-mail programs, and accounting, marketing, and electronic commerce software
- Computer programs that support the transfer of data, check for errors when the data is transferred, allow access to the network, and protect user transactions from unauthorized viewing

This large number of network components and their possible interactions inspires two questions. First, how do all of these pieces work together harmoniously? You do not want two pieces performing the same function, or no pieces performing a necessary function. Like the elements of a well-oiled machine, all components of a computer network must work together to produce a product.

Second, does the choice of one piece depend on the choice of another piece? To make the pieces as modular as possible, you do not want the selection of one piece to constrain the choice of another piece. For example, if you create a network and originally plan to use one type of wiring but later change your mind and use a different type of wiring, will that change affect your choice of word processor? Such an interaction would seem highly unlikely. Alternately, can the choice of wiring affect the choice of the software program that checks for errors in the data sent over the wires? The answer to this question is not as obvious.

To keep the pieces of a computer network working together harmoniously and to allow modularity between the pieces, national and international organizations developed network architectures, which are cohesive layers of protocols defining a set of communication services. Consider the following noncomputer example. Most organizations that produce some type of product or perform a service have a division of labor. Office assistants do the paperwork, accountants keep the books, laborers perform the manual duties, scientists design products, engineers test the products, and managers control operations. Rarely is one person capable of performing all these duties. Large software applications operate the same way. Different procedures perform different tasks, and the whole would not function without the proper operation of each of its parts. Computer network applications are no exception. As the size of the applications grows, the need for a division of labor becomes increasingly important. Computer network applications also have a similar delineation of job functions. This delineation is the network architecture. Let's examine our two network architectures or models: the TCP/IP protocol suite, followed by the OSI model.

The TCP/IP protocol suite

The TCP/IP protocol suite was created by a group of computer scientists in order to support a new type of network (the ARPANET) being installed across the United States in the 1960s and 1970s. The goal was to create an open architecture that would allow virtually all networks to inter-communicate. The design was based on a number of layers, in which the user would connect at the uppermost layer and would be isolated from the details of the electrical signals found at the lower layer.

The number of layers in the suite is not static. In fact, some books present the TCP/IP protocol suite as four layers, while others present it as five. Even then, different sources use different names for each of the layers. For this book, we will define five layers, as shown in Figure 1-10: application, transport, network, network access, and physical. Note that the layers do not specify precise protocols or exact services. In other words, the TCP/IP protocol suite does not tell us, for example, what kind of wire or what kind of connector to use to connect the pieces of a network. That choice is left to the designer or implementer of the system. Instead, the suite simply says that if you specify a type of wire or a specific connector, you do that in a particular layer. In addition, each layer of the TCP/IP protocol suite provides a service for the next layer. For example,

Figure 1-10 The five layers of the TCP/IP protocol suite

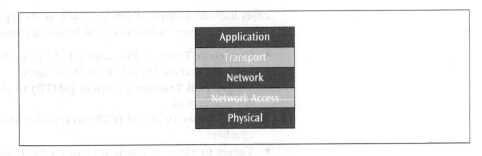

the transport layer makes sure the data received at the very end of a transmission is exactly the same as the data originally transmitted, but it relies upon the network layer to find the best path for the data to take from one point to the next within the network. With each layer performing its designated function, the layers work together to allow an application to send its data over a network of computers. Let us look at a simple e-mail application example (Figure 1-11) to understand how the layers of the TCP/IP protocol suite work together.

A common network application is e-mail. An e-mail program that accepts and sends the message, "Andy, how about lunch? Sharon," has many steps. Using the TCP/IP protocol suite, the steps might look like the following. To begin, the e-mail "application worker" prompts the user to enter a message and specify an intended receiver. The application worker would create the appropriate data package with message contents and addresses, and send it to a "transport worker," which is responsible for providing overall transport integrity. The transport worker might establish a connection with the intended receiver, monitor the flow between sender and receiver, and perform the necessary operations to recover lost data in case some data disappears or becomes unreadable.

The "network worker" would then take the data package from the transport worker and might add routing information so that the data package can find its way through the network. Next to get the data package would be the "network access worker," which would insert error-checking information and prepare the data package for transmission. The final worker would be the "physical worker," which would transmit the data package over some form of wire or through the air using radio waves.

Each worker has its own job function. Figure 1-11 shows how these workers work together to create a single package for transmission.

Figure 1-11 "Network workers" perform their job duties at each layer in the model

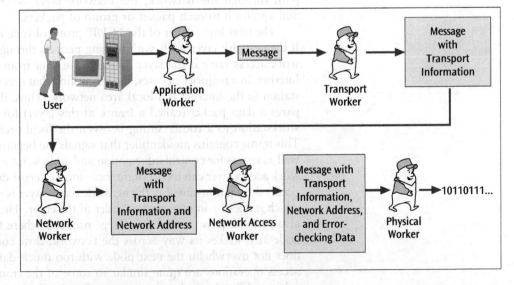

Let's examine each layer in more detail. The top layer of the TCP/IP protocol suite, the **application layer,** supports the network applications and might in some

cases include additional services such as encryption or compression. The TCP/IP application layer includes several frequently used applications:

- **Hypertext Transfer Protocol (HTTP)** to allow Web browsers and servers to send and receive World Wide Web pages
- **Simple Mail Transfer Protocol (SMTP)** to allow users to send and receive electronic mail
- **File Transfer Protocol (FTP)** to transfer files from one computer system to another
- **Telnet** to allow a remote user to log in to another computer system
- **Simple Network Management Protocol (SNMP)** to allow the numerous elements within a computer network to be managed from a single point

The next layer in the TCP/IP protocol suite is the transport layer. The TCP/IP **transport layer** commonly uses TCP to maintain an error-free end-to-end connection. To maintain this connection, TCP includes error control information in case one packet from a sequence of packets does not arrive at the final destination, and packet sequencing information so that all the packets stay in the proper order. We say that the transport layer performs *end-to-end* error control and *end-to-end* flow control. This means the transport layer is not in use while the data packet is hopping from point to point within the network—it is used *only* at the two endpoints of the connection. TCP is not the only possible protocol found at the TCP/IP transport layer. User Datagram Protocol (UDP) is an alternative also used, though less frequently, in the TCP/IP protocol suite.

The two layers described so far are called end-to-end layers. They are responsible for the data transmitted between the endpoints of a network connection. In other words, these layers perform their operations *only* at the beginning point and ending point of the network connection. The remaining three layers of the TCP/IP protocol suite—the network, network access, and physical layers—are not end-to-end layers. They perform their operations at each node (or device) along the network path, not just at the endpoints.

TCP/IP's **network layer**, sometimes called the Internet layer or IP layer, is used to transfer data within and between networks. The **Internet Protocol (IP)** is the software that prepares a packet of data so that it can move from one network to another on the Internet or within a set of corporate networks. As this layer sends the packet from node to node, it generates the network addressing necessary for the system to recognize the next intended receiver. To choose a path through the network, the network layer determines routing information and applies it to each packet or group of packets.

The next lower layer of the TCP/IP protocol suite is the **network access layer**. If the network layer deals with passing packets through the Internet, then the network access layer is the layer that gets the data from the user workstation to the Internet. In a majority of cases, the connection that gets the data from the user workstation to the Internet is a local area network. Thus, the network access layer prepares a data packet (called a **frame** at this layer) for transmission from the user workstation to a router sitting between the local area network and the Internet. This frame contains an identifier that signals the beginning and end of the frame, as well as spaces for control information and address information. In addition, the network access layer can incorporate some form of error detection software. If an error occurs during transmission, the network access layer is responsible for error control, which it does by informing the sender of the error. The network access layer might also perform flow control. In a large network where the data hops from node to node as it makes its way across the network, flow control ensures that one node does not overwhelm the next node with too much data. Note that these network access operations are quite similar to some of the transport layer operations. The primary difference is that the transport layer performs its operations only at the endpoints, while the network access layer performs its operations at every stop (node) along the path. This is also the last layer before the data is handed off for transmission across the medium. The network access layer is often called the data link layer.

The bottom-most layer in the TCP/IP protocol suite (or at least according to the way we are doing it) is the physical layer. The **physical layer** is the layer in which the actual transmission of data occurs. As noted earlier, this transmission can be over a physical wire, or it can be a radio signal transmitted through the air. To perform this transmission of bits, the physical layer handles voltage levels, plug and connector dimensions, pin configurations, and other electrical and mechanical issues. Furthermore, because the digital or analog data is encoded or modulated onto a digital or analog signal at this point in the process, the physical layer also determines the encoding or modulation technique to be used in the network. Note that some people combine the network access layer and physical layer into one layer.

Having distinctly defined layers enables you to "pull" out one layer and insert an equivalent layer without affecting the other layers. For example, let us assume a network was designed for copper-based wire. Later, the system owners decided to replace the copper-based wire with fiber-optic cable. Even though a change is being made at the physical layer, it should not be necessary to make any changes at any other layers. In reality, however, a few relationships exist between the layers of a communication system that cannot be ignored. For example, if the physical organization of a local area network is changed (say from a wired network to a wireless network), it is likely that the frame description at the network access layer also will need to be changed. (We will examine this phenomenon in Chapter 7.) The TCP/IP protocol suite recognizes these relationships and merges many of the services of the physical and data link layers into one layer.

The OSI model

Although the TCP/IP protocol suite is the model of choice for almost all installed networks, it is important to study both this architecture and the OSI model. Many books and articles, when describing a product or a protocol, often refer to the OSI model with a statement such as, "This product is compliant with OSI layer x." If you do not become familiar with the various layers of the OSI model and the TCP/IP protocol suite, this lack of important basic knowledge might impede your understanding of more advanced concepts in the future.

The OSI model was designed with seven layers, as shown in Figure 1-12. Note further the relationship between the five layers of the TCP/IP protocol suite and the seven layers of the OSI model. The top layer in the OSI model is the **application layer**, where the application using the network resides. This OSI layer is similar to the application layer in the TCP/IP protocol suite. The next layer in the OSI model, the **presentation layer**, performs a series of miscellaneous functions necessary for presenting the data package properly to the sender or receiver. For example, the presentation layer might perform ASCII-to-non-ASCII character conversions, encryption and decryption of secure documents, and the compression of data into smaller units. There is no separate presentation layer in the TCP/IP protocol suite.

Figure I-12 The seven layers of the OSI model compared to the five layers of the TCP/IP protocol suite

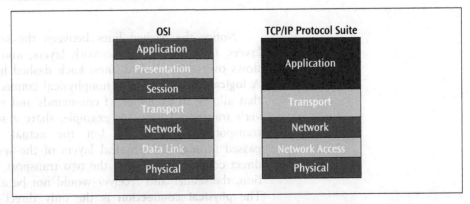

The **session layer** is another layer that does not exist in the TCP/IP protocol suite and is responsible for establishing sessions between users. It also can

support **token management**, a service that controls which user's computer talks during the current session by passing a software token back and forth. Additionally, the session layer establishes **synchronization points**, which are backup points used in case of errors or failures. For example, while transmitting a large document such as an electronic book, the session layer might insert a synchronization point at the end of each chapter. If an error occurs during transmission, both sender and receiver can back up to the last synchronization point (to the beginning of a previously transmitted chapter) and start retransmission from there. Many network applications do not include a specific session layer and do not use tokens to manage a conversation. If they do, the "token" is inserted by the application layer, or possibly the transport layer, instead of the session layer. Likewise, if network applications use synchronization points, these points often are inserted by the application layer.

The fourth layer in the OSI model, the **transport layer**, operates in the same way as the transport layer of the TCP/IP protocol suite. It ensures that the data packet that arrives at the final destination is identical to the data packet that left the originating station.

The **network layer** of the OSI model is similar to the network layer of the TCP/IP protocol suite and is responsible for getting the data packets from router to router through the network. The **data link layer**, similar to TCP/IP's network access layer, is responsible for taking data from the network layer and transforming it into a frame. The bottom layer in the OSI model—the **physical layer**—handles the transmission of bits over a communications channel. This layer is essentially identical to the physical layer of the TCP/IP protocol suite.

Logical and physical connections

An important concept to understand with regard to the layers of a communication model is the lines of communication between a sender and a receiver. Consider Figure 1-13, which shows the sender and receiver using a network application designed on the TCP/IP protocol suite.

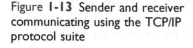

Figure 1-13 Sender and receiver communicating using the TCP/IP protocol suite

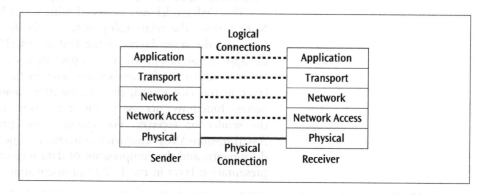

Notice the dashed lines between the sender's and receiver's application layers, transport layers, network layers, and network access layers. No data flows over these dashed lines. Each dashed line indicates a logical connection. A **logical connection** is a nonphysical connection between sender and receiver that allows an exchange of commands and responses. The sender's and receiver's transport layers, for example, share a set of commands used to perform transport-type functions, but the actual information or data must be passed through the physical layers of the sender and receiver, as there is no direct connection between the two transport layers. Without a logical connection, the sender and receiver would not be able to coordinate their functions. The **physical connection** is the only direct connection between sender and receiver, and is at the physical layer, where actual 1s and 0s—the digital content of the message—are transmitted over wires or airwaves.

For an example of logical and physical connections, consider an imaginary scenario in which the dean of arts and sciences wants to create a new joint degree with the school of business. In particular, the dean would like to create a degree that is a cross between computer science and marketing. The dean of arts and sciences could call the dean of business to create the degree, but deans are not necessarily experts at assembling all the details involved in a new degree. Instead, the dean of arts and sciences starts the process by issuing a request for a new degree from the dean of business. Before this request gets to the dean of business, however, the request must pass through several layers. First, the request goes to the chairperson of the computer science department. The chairperson examines the request for a new degree and adds the necessary information to staff the program. The chairperson then sends the request to the computer science curriculum committee, which designs several new courses. The curriculum committee sends the request to its department secretary, who types all the memos and creates a readable package. This package is then placed in the intercampus mail and sent to the marketing department in the school of business.

Once the request arrives at the marketing department, the secretary in the marketing department opens the envelope and gives all the materials to the marketing curriculum committee. The marketing curriculum committee looks at the proposed courses from the computer science curriculum committee and makes some changes and additions. Once these changes are made, the proposal is given to the chair of the marketing department, who looks at the staffing needs suggested by the chair of computer science, checks the request for accuracy, and makes some changes. The chair of marketing then hands the request to the dean of business, who examines the entire document and gives approval with a few small changes. The request then works its way back down to the secretary of the marketing department, who sends it back to the secretary of computer science. The computer science secretary then sends the reply to the request up the layers until it reaches the dean of arts and sciences. Figure 1-14 shows how this request for a degree might move up and down through the layers of a university's bureaucracy.

Figure **1-14** Flow of data through the layers of bureaucracy

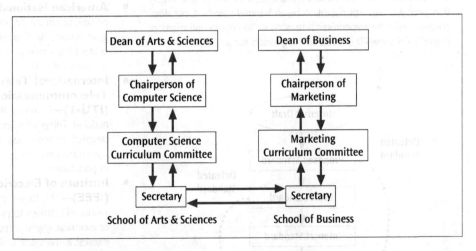

Note that the data did not flow directly between deans; nor did it flow directly between department chairpersons or curriculum committees. Instead, the data had to flow all the way down to the physical layer (in this case, the secretaries) and then back up the other side. At each layer in the process, information that might be useful to the "peer" layer on the other side was added. This example stretches the truth a little; college curriculums are not actually designed this way (the process is in fact much more complicated). Therefore, we will examine a more realistic example in which a person using a Web browser requests a Web page from somewhere on the Internet. But before we examine this more difficult scenario, let us take a look at an example of the connections that occur when a user connects his laptop to the company local area network.

DETAILS

The Internet's Request for Comment (RFC)

Network models, like communications protocols, computer hardware, and application software, continue to evolve daily. The TCP/IP protocol suite is a good example of a large set of protocols and standards constantly being revised and improved. An Internet standard is a tested specification that is both useful and adhered to by users who work with the Internet. Let us examine the path a proposal must follow on the way to becoming an Internet standard.

All Internet standards start as an Internet draft, which is a preliminary work in progress. One or more internal Internet committees work on a draft, improving it until it is in an acceptable form. When the Internet authorities feel the draft is ready for the public, it is published as a Request for Comment (RFC), a document open to all interested parties. The RFC is assigned a number, and it enters its first phase: proposed standard. A proposed standard is a proposal that is stable, of interest to the Internet community, and fairly well understood. The specification is tested and implemented by a number of different groups, and the results are published. If the proposal passes at least two independent and interoperable implementations, the proposed standard is elevated to draft standard. If, after feedback from test implementations is taken into account, the draft standard experiences no further problems, the proposal is finally elevated to Internet standard.

If, however, the proposed standard is deemed inappropriate at any point along the way, it becomes a historic RFC and is kept for historical perspective. (Internet standards that are replaced or superseded also become historic.) An RFC also can be categorized as experimental or informational. In these cases, the RFC in question probably was not meant to be an Internet standard, but was created either for experimental reasons or to provide information. Figure 1-15 shows the levels of progression for an RFC.

It is possible to obtain a printed listing of each RFC. See the Internet Engineering Task Force's Web page at *www.ietf.org/rfc.html* for the best way to access RFCs.

The Internet is managed by the work of several committees. The topmost committee is the Internet Society (ISOC). ISOC is a nonprofit, international committee that provides support for the entire Internet standards-making process. Associated with ISOC is the Internet Architecture Board (IAB), which is the technical advisor to ISOC. Under the IAB are two major committees: the Internet Engineering Task Force (IETF) and the Internet Research Task Force (IRTF). The IETF manages the working groups that create and support functions such as Internet protocols, security, user services, operations, routing, and network management. The IRTF manages the working groups that focus on the long-range goals of the Internet, such as architecture, technology, applications, and protocols.

Internet committees are not the only groups that create protocols or approve standards for computer networks, data communications, and telecommunications. Another organization that creates and approves network standards is the **International Organization for Standardization (ISO)**, which is a multinational group composed of volunteers from the standards-making committees of various governments throughout the world. ISO is involved in developing standards in the field of information technology and created the Open Systems Interconnection (OSI) model for a network architecture.

Other standards-making organizations include:

- **American National Standards Institute (ANSI)**—A private, nonprofit organization not associated with the U.S. government, ANSI strives to support the U.S. economy and protect the interests of the public by encouraging the adoption of various standards.

- **International Telecommunication Union-Telecommunication Standardization Sector (ITU-T)**—Formerly the Consultative Committee on International Telegraphy and Telephony (CCITT), ITU-T is devoted to the research and creation of standards for telecommunications in general, and telephone and data systems in particular.

- **Institute of Electrical and Electronics Engineers (IEEE)**—The largest professional engineering society in the world, IEEE strives to promote the standardization of the fields of electrical engineering, electronics, and radio. Of particular interest is the work IEEE has performed on standardizing local area networks.

- **Electronic Industries Association (EIA)**—Aligned with ANSI, EIA is a nonprofit organization devoted to the standardization of electronics products. Of particular interest is the work EIA has performed on standardizing the interfaces between computers and modems.

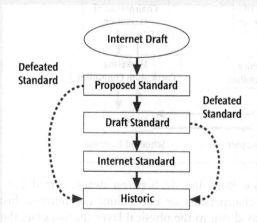

Figure 1-15 Levels of progression as an RFC moves toward becoming a standard

THE TCP/IP PROTOCOL SUITE IN ACTION

A more detailed and more challenging example of a request for a service moving through the layers of a communications model will help make the concepts involved clearer. Consider Figure 1-16, in which a user browsing the Internet on a personal computer requests a Web page to be downloaded and then displayed on his or her screen.

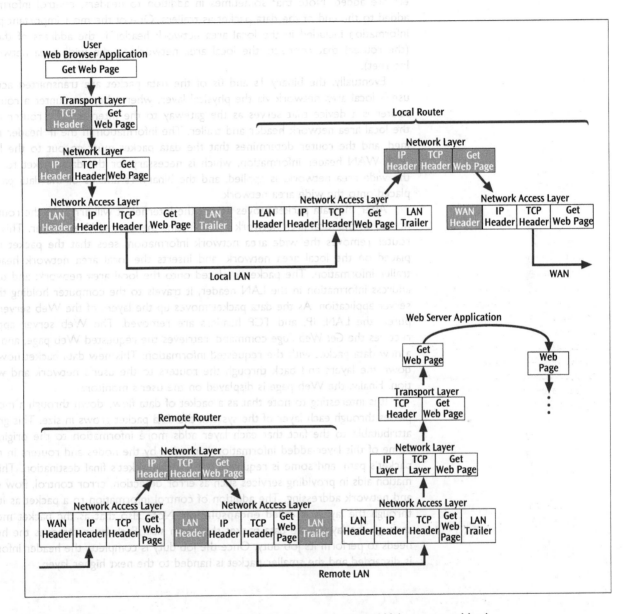

Figure 1-16 Path of a Web page request as it flows from browser to Internet Web server and back

Beginning in the upper-left corner of the figure, the process is initiated when the user clicks a link on the current Web page. In response, the browser software (the application) creates a *Get Web Page* command that is given to the browser's transport layer, TCP. TCP adds a variety of header information to be used by the TCP software on the receiving end. Added to the front of the packet, this information may be used to control the transfer of the data. This information assists with end-to-end error control and end-to-end flow control and provides the address of the receiving application (the Web server).

The enlarged packet is now sent to the network layer, where IP adds its header. The information contained within the IP header assists the IP software on the receiving end, and assists the IP software at each intermediate node (router) during the data's progress through the Internet. This assistance includes providing the Internet address of the workstation that contains the requested Web page.

The packet is now given to the network access layer. Because the user's computer is connected to a local area network, the appropriate local area network headers are added. Note that sometimes in addition to headers, control information is added to the end of the data packet as trailers. One of the most important pieces of information included in the local area network header is the address of the device (the router) that connects the local area network to the wide area network (the Internet).

Eventually, the binary 1s and 0s of the data packet are transmitted across the user's local area network via the physical layer, where they encounter a router. The router is a device that serves as the gateway to the Internet. The router removes the local area network header and trailer. The information in the IP header is examined, and the router determines that the data packet must go out to the Internet. New WAN header information, which is necessary for the data packet to traverse the wide area network, is applied, and the binary 1s and 0s of the data packet are placed onto the wide area network.

After the data packet moves across the Internet, it will arrive at the router connected to the local area network that contains the desired Web server. This remote router removes the wide area network information, sees that the packet must be placed on the local area network, and inserts the local area network header and trailer information. The packet is placed onto the local area network; and using the address information in the LAN header, it travels to the computer holding the Web server application. As the data packet moves up the layers of the Web server's computer, the LAN, IP, and TCP headers are removed. The Web server application receives the *Get Web Page* command, retrieves the requested Web page, and creates a new data packet with the requested information. This new data packet now moves down the layers and back through the routers to the user's network and workstation. Finally, the Web page is displayed on the user's monitor.

It is interesting to note that as a packet of data flows down through a model and passes through each layer of the system, the data packet grows in size. This growth is attributable to the fact that each layer adds more information to the original data. Some of this layer-added information is needed by the nodes and routers in the data packet's path, and some is required by the data packet's final destination. This information aids in providing services such as error detection, error control, flow control, and network addressing. The addition of control information to a packet as it moves through the layers is called **encapsulation**. Note also that as the packet moves up through the layers, the data packet shrinks in size. Each layer removes the header it needs to perform its job duty. Once the job duty is complete, the header information is discarded and the smaller packet is handed to the next higher layer.

SUMMARY

- Many services and products that we use every day employ computer networks and data communications in one way or another. Telephone systems, banking systems, cable television, audio and video systems, traffic control systems, and cell phones are a few examples.
- The field of data communications and computer networks includes data networks, voice networks, wireless networks, local area networks, campus area networks, metropolitan area networks, wide area networks, and personal area networks.

- The common examples of computer networks can be understood in terms of the way a user or device connects to the network:
  - Desktop computer connected to the Internet
  - Laptop computer and a wireless connection
  - Cell phone systems
  - Sensor networks
  - Business mainframe network
  - Satellite and microwave networks
- A key concept in networking these days is convergence, the phenomena in which network applications and the technologies that support them converge into a single technology that is capable of supporting various applications. In particular, we can define three different types of convergence: technological convergence, protocol convergence, and industrial convergence.
- A network architecture, or communications model, places network pieces in layers. The layers define a *model* for the functions or services that need to be performed. Each layer in the model defines the services that hardware, software, or both provide.
- The TCP/IP protocol suite is also known as the Internet model and is composed of five layers:
  - The application layer contains the network applications for which one uses a network and the presentation services that support that application.
  - The transport layer maintains an error-free end-to-end connection.
  - The network layer, or Internet layer, uses IP to transfer data between networks.
  - The network access layer defines both the physical medium that transmits the signal and the frame that incorporates flow and error control.
  - The physical layer handles the transmission of bits over a communications channel.
- To standardize the design of communications systems, the ISO created the OSI model. The OSI model is based on seven layers:
  - The application layer is the top layer of the OSI model, where the application using the network resides.
  - The presentation layer performs a series of miscellaneous functions necessary for presenting the data package properly to the sender or receiver.
  - The session layer is responsible for establishing sessions between users.
  - The transport layer is concerned with an error-free end-to-end flow of data.
  - The network layer is responsible for creating, maintaining, and ending network connections.
  - The data link layer is responsible for taking the raw data and transforming it into a cohesive unit called a frame.
  - The physical layer handles the transmission of bits over a communications channel.
- A logical connection is a flow of ideas that occurs, without a direct physical connection, between the sender and receiver at a particular layer.

KEY TERMS

American National Standards Institute (ANSI)	computer network	File Transfer Protocol (FTP)	International Organization for Standardization (ISO)
campus area network (CAN)	computer terminal	frame	International Telecommunication Union-Telecommunication
client/server system	convergence	Hypertext Transfer Protocol (HTTP)	
cloud	data communications		Standardization Sector (ITU-T)
cloud computing	data network	Institute of Electrical and Electronics Engineers (IEEE)	
compression	Electronic Industries Association (EIA)		Internet Protocol (IP)
	encapsulation	Interfacing	

local area network (LAN)	application layer	router	application layer
logical connection	presentation layer	server	transport layer
metropolitan area network (MAN)	session layer	Simple Mail Transfer Protocol (SMTP)	network layer
multiplexing	transport layer	Simple Network Management Protocol (SNMP)	network access layer
network cloud	network layer		physical layer
network architecture	data link layer		Telnet
network management	physical layer	subnetwork	token management
node	personal area network (PAN)	switch	voice network
Open Systems Interconnection (OSI) model	physical connection	synchronization point	wide area network (WAN)
	protocol	TCP/IP protocol suite	wireless
			workstation

REVIEW QUESTIONS

1. What is the definition of:
   a. a computer network?
   b. data communications?
   c. telecommunications?
   d. a local area network?
   e. a personal area network?
   f. a metropolitan area network?
   g. a wide area network?
   h. network management?
   i. convergence?
   j. campus area network?
2. What is the relationship between a subnetwork and a node?
3. What kind of applications might use a desktop computer to Internet network?
4. What kind of applications might use a business mainframe network?

5. What "language" must a home computer talk in order to interface with the Internet?
6. What kind of applications might use a sensor network?
7. Why is a network architecture useful?
8. List the five layers of the TCP/IP protocol suite.
9. List the seven layers of the OSI model.
10. How do the layers of the TCP/IP protocol suite compare with the layers of the OSI model?
11. What are some of the more common applications found in the TCP/IP protocol suite?
12. What is the difference between a logical connection and a physical connection?
13. How does convergence apply to the communications industry?

EXERCISES

1. Create a list of all the actions you perform in an average day that use data communications and computer networks.
2. If you could design your own home, what kinds of labor-saving computer network or data communications devices would you incorporate?
3. Two companies are considering pooling their resources to form a joint venture. The CEO of the first company meets with his legal team, and the legal team consults a number of middle managers in the proposed product area. Meanwhile, the CEO of the first company sends an e-mail to the CEO of the second company to offer a couple of suggestions concerning the joint venture. Does this scenario follow either the TCP/IP protocol suite or the OSI model? Explain your answer.
4. Using a laptop computer with a wireless connection to a company's local area network, you

download a Web page from the Internet. List all the different networks possibly involved in this operation.
5. You are working from home using a microcomputer, a DSL modem, and a telephone connection to the Internet. Your company is connected to the Internet and has both local area networks and a mainframe computer. List all the different networks possibly involved in this operation.
6. You are sitting at the local coffee shop, enjoying your favorite latte. You pull out your laptop and, using the wireless network available at the coffee shop, access your e-mail. List all the different networks possibly involved in this operation.
7. With your new cell phone, you have just taken a snapshot of your best friend. You decide to send this snapshot to the e-mail account of a mutual

friend across the country. List all the different networks possibly involved in this operation.

8. You are driving in a new city and have just gotten lost. Using your car's built-in navigational system, you submit a request for driving directions from a nearby intersection to your destination. List all the different networks possibly involved in this operation.

9. The layers of the TCP/IP protocol suite and OSI model are different. Which layers are "missing" from the TCP/IP protocol suite? Are they really missing?

10. If the data link layer provides error checking and the transport layer provides error checking, isn't this redundant? Explain your answer.

11. Similarly, the data link layer provides flow control, and the transport layer provides flow control. Are these different forms of flow control? Explain your answer.

12. You are watching a television show in which one character is suing another. The lawyers for both parties meet and try to work out a settlement. Is there a logical or physical connection between the lawyers? What about between the two parties?

13. You want to download a file from a remote site using FTP. To perform the file transfer, your computer issues a Get File command. Show the progression of messages as the Get File command moves from your computer, through routers, to the remote computer, and back.

14. What characteristics distinguish a personal area network from other types of networks?

15. Isn't a metropolitan area network just a big local area network? Explain your answer.

16. List the TCP/IP protocol suite layer that performs each of the following functions:
    a. data compression
    b. multiplexing
    c. routing
    d. definition of a signal's electrical characteristics
    e. e-mail
    f. error detection
    g. end-to-end flow control

17. For each function in the previous exercise, list the OSI layer that performs that function.

18. You are sending and receiving e-mail messages with a friend. Is this e-mail session a logical connection or a physical connection? Explain your answer.

THINKING OUTSIDE THE BOX

1. You have been asked to create a new network architecture model. Will it be layered, or will its components take some other form? Show your model's layers or its new form, and describe the functions performed by each of its components.

2. Take an example from your work or school in which a person requests a service and then diagram that request. Does the request pass through any layers before it reaches the intended recipient?

Do logical connections as well as physical connections exist? If so, show them in the diagram.

3. This chapter listed several different types of example networks. Do any other networks exist in the real world that are not listed in the chapter? If so, what are they?

4. Describe a real-life situation that uses at least three of the networks described in this chapter.

HANDS-ON PROJECTS

1. Recall a job you have had (or still have). Was a chain of command in place for getting tasks done? If so, draw that chain of command on paper or using a software program. How does this chain of command compare to either the OSI model or the TCP/IP protocol suite?

2. Because the TCP/IP protocol suite is not carved in stone, other books might discuss a slightly different layering. Find two other examples of the TCP/IP protocol suite that differ from this book's layering and cite the sources. How are those two suites alike, and how do they differ? How do they compare to the TCP/IP protocol suite discussed in this chapter? Write a short, concise report summarizing your findings.

3. What is the more precise form of the Get Web Page command shown in Figure 1-16? Show the form of

the command, and describe the responsibility of each field.

4. What types of network applications exist at your place of employment or your college? Are local area networks involved? Wide area networks? List the various types of networks. Draw a diagram or map of these applications and their layouts.

5. What other network models exist or have been in existence besides the OSI model and TCP/IP protocol suite? Research this topic and write a brief description of each network model you find.

6. What are the names of some of the routing protocols that currently are in use on the Internet? Can you describe each protocol with a sentence or two?

ndex

' (apostrophe), 307
* (asterisk), 149
/ (forward slash), 355
+ (plus sign), 149
\ (slash), 149
~ (tilde), 347

A
A class, 230, 249
a variable, 143, 149, 171, 177, 181
ABC, 158-159, 161
absolute paths, 348, 367
abstraction, 154-156, 177, 180, 182, 262
access, 7, 13, 21-24, 32, 51-52, 55, 61, 65-66, 69, 72, 76-77, 153, 156, 227, 233-234, 258, 260, 285-287, 292, 294, 296, 299-300, 302, 308, 312-314, 319-321, 323-324, 328-329, 331, 344, 354, 358, 363, 368, 371, 374-375, 379-380, 382-383, 386-390, 392, 394-396
   control, 24, 55, 69, 153, 156, 285, 292, 382-383, 386, 388, 390, 394-395
   rights, 23-24, 76, 153, 285, 292, 300, 323, 331, 374
Access button, 312, 314
access keys, 7
access point, 380
   wireless, 380
access time, 234, 258
accessing
   Internet, 23
accessories, 52
accomplishments, 12, 29, 31
Accountability, 25
accounting, 11, 21, 25-26, 32-33, 39, 240, 251, 253, 386
   problems, 21, 33
   software, 21, 25, 32, 386
accounts
   e-mail, 396
   user, 7, 57, 63-64, 70, 75, 344, 359, 365-366, 392
Accuracy, 391
active tab, 312, 314
adding
   Web pages, 84, 108
add-ons, 346
Address, 17-18, 20, 22, 24, 30, 56, 58, 73, 76-77, 128, 137, 144, 146-147, 149-150, 157, 160, 179-180, 195, 229, 231, 248, 265-266, 268-270, 282, 285, 312, 315-316, 319, 322, 333, 337, 362, 377, 387-388, 393-394
   letter, 144, 147, 179, 285
   return, 77, 128, 137, 157, 160, 180, 312
Address field, 315, 319
Addressing, 18, 21, 33, 388, 394
Administrator account, 64
Adobe, 6, 68
Adobe Flash, 68
advanced
   reports, 79, 272
advanced options, 74
advertising
   banners, 52
Adware, 50, 52, 69-70, 72
alarm, 51, 382
alert, 16, 63-64, 70, 78, 167, 175
algebra, 150, 362-363
Algorithms, 233
alias, 171
Alliances, 6, 28, 37
Amazon, 375
American National Standards Institute (ANSI), 392, 395
analog data, 376, 389
analog signals, 376, 389
Analysis, 8, 62-63, 77-78, 262, 382
Android, 21, 38, 55, 77
Android devices, 55
annotations

charts, 181
anomalies, 252, 258, 260
antispyware, 63, 70
antivirus software, 42, 57, 76
API, 145
app, 25, 39-40, 68, 75-76
Apple, 6, 9-10, 37-38, 44, 47, 114, 375
Apple iPhone, 9
Application layer, 387-390, 395-396
application programs, 49, 69
Application software, 61, 147, 235, 262, 271, 392
Applications, 1, 4, 15, 21, 24-25, 32, 34, 47-50, 55, 57, 60-62, 68-69, 73, 147, 155-156, 160, 163-164, 168, 172, 180-181, 190, 234-235, 262, 267, 271, 346-347, 375-376, 378, 383-390, 392-397
   remote, 47-50, 55, 68-69, 73, 375, 388, 394, 397
Appointments, 269
Argument, 21, 35-36, 344, 347-350, 356, 366-367
   command-line, 344, 347, 367
   default, 347, 366
arithmetic expressions, 146, 152
arithmetic operations, 140, 149, 153
arithmetic operators, 149, 151-153, 177, 180
ARPANET, 386
arranged, 124
ART, 251, 391
ASCII, 389
Aspect, 5, 17, 82, 122, 227, 243, 262
assembly language, 208
assigning
   tasks, 155, 178-179
Assignment, 7, 36, 146-151, 172, 179, 182, 184, 195, 243, 250, 268, 275-276, 278, 333
assignment operators, 146-147, 149-151, 179, 182
assignment statements, 146-147, 179
   variables, 146-147, 179
association, 15-16, 18, 20, 38, 171, 234, 244-245, 266, 392, 395
   defined, 20
Association for Computing Machinery (ACM), 15
associativity, 146, 151, 179-180, 182
attachments, 23, 44, 46
   sending, 44
attack, 42-43, 49, 55-58, 62, 65, 67, 69-70, 73
auctions, 339-341
Auditing, 21
audits, 16, 25-26, 28-29, 38-40, 190
Authorization, 52, 272, 274
AutoNumbers, 285
Averages, 43, 63, 131, 150, 186, 229, 233, 374, 396
avoiding, 48, 69, 173, 258

B
Back button, 77, 114
Background, 4, 12-13, 35, 56, 71, 83, 88, 101, 103, 112, 122-123, 127, 129-131, 134, 137-138, 271
Background checks, 13
background color
   controls, 101, 122
background images, 112
backing up, 57, 78
backpacks, 42, 57
BACKSPACE key, 288, 318
Backstage view, 303
backup, 41, 57, 65-68, 70, 72-73, 78-79, 390
   application, 57, 68, 73, 390
   data, 41, 57, 65-68, 70, 73, 78-79, 390
   database, 73
backup plans, 66
backup software, 66
Banking, 374, 394
banners, 52
Base, 32, 56, 186
baseline, 84
   using, 84
BASIC, 17, 44, 141, 145, 150, 152-153, 156, 188, 189, 192, 200-201, 209, 217-218, 220, 227-228, 251,

261-262, 268, 272-273, 345, 373, 375-376, 378, 389
Bay, 266
Behavior, 3, 10, 13-14, 21, 23, 25, 27, 29-30, 50, 52, 102, 146, 187
Benchmarks, 14, 17, 27
best fit, 310, 320, 322, 324, 342
Billing, 2, 160-161, 167-168, 274, 279, 282, 287, 296, 298-300, 305-311, 330-331
binary operators, 146, 149, 179, 182
binding, 11
Bit, 149, 379, 383, 385, 389-390, 395
bits per second, 379, 383
bits per second (bps), 383
block, 23, 56, 60-61, 63, 69, 124, 190, 193, 196, 219, 221, 363, 376
Blogging, 24
bold, 112-113, 117, 124, 128, 130, 132, 135-136, 363
Boolean data type, 172
Boolean variable, 172
border, 81-85, 88, 98, 100-101, 103-105, 108-110, 112-113, 116-117, 119, 122, 124, 127-129, 131-137, 303, 328
   custom, 112
   removing, 119
   table, 82-85, 98, 108-110, 116-117, 119, 122, 124, 127-129, 131-134, 136-137, 303, 328
bot, 55-56, 70
botnet, 35, 55-56, 69-72, 80
boxes, 64-65, 74-78, 81-86, 89, 91, 108, 127-128, 157, 167, 169, 181, 211, 229, 254, 287-294, 296, 298, 300-302, 304, 306-310, 312-314, 317-321, 323-324, 328-331, 342, 359, 382, 397
bps, 383
Breaks
   column, 173, 306
   page, 85, 160
   section, 306
Bribery, 10-11, 25, 28, 39
bridges, 227, 249, 380
broadband, 56
broadcast, 375, 384
Browse button, 309, 312, 314, 323
Browser, 50, 52, 55, 60, 63, 70, 76-78, 81-82, 84-89, 92-93, 98, 100-106, 108-110, 112, 114-116, 118-122, 124, 127-137, 347, 383, 388, 391, 393
Browser home page, 50
browser window, 52, 81, 84, 86-88, 92-93, 100, 102, 104-105
budget, 13
bugs, 187, 225
building, 10, 60, 81, 105, 190, 220, 250, 255-256, 279, 375-376, 382
building blocks, 190, 376
bullet characters, 110, 112, 127-128
Bulleted lists, 133
   document, 133
bullets, 110, 112, 127-128, 137
bus, 374
Business, 2, 4, 6-7, 10-11, 14, 18-21, 24-25, 28, 30, 32-33, 35, 37-38, 40, 43, 54, 155, 190, 220, 231, 236, 240, 242, 244-245, 250-251, 254, 256, 261-266, 269, 271-272, 278, 344, 373-375, 378-385, 391, 395-396
   cloud computing, 32-33, 375, 395
   personal data, 375
business applications, 190
Business cards, 30
business manager, 21, 374
Business plan, 6
business rules
   described, 240, 244, 265
business software, 6, 28
Business Software Alliance (BSA), 6, 28
Button tool, 295
buttons, 77, 114, 157, 287, 289, 295-304, 308-310, 312-317, 319-321, 323-324, 328-331, 342, 347
   macro, 312, 314
   overview, 287, 304

Byte, 141, 285-286, 351-352, 379

C

C#
  development, 208
C++, 141, 145, 152-153, 157, 188, 208, 273
cable, 374, 378-380, 389, 394
cable modem, 379-380
cable television, 374, 394
Cache, 350-351
Calculations, 121, 142, 144, 149, 163, 170, 173, 226, 234, 285, 288, 376
Calendar, 48, 252, 301
calling, 3, 153, 157, 166
  methods, 153
  procedures, 153
calls, 6-7, 19, 35-36, 52, 58, 88, 127, 146, 153-155, 157, 159-160, 163, 166-168, 177-178, 180, 182-183, 185-186, 188, 193-194, 216, 353-354, 368, 374-375, 381, 385, 391
camel casing, 144-145, 172, 179, 188
Cameras, 51, 381
Cancel button, 330
candidate key, 230
Capacity, 51, 187, 266
caption, 286-287, 289-291, 293-294, 298-299, 301-303, 308, 312, 319-320, 333, 335-338, 340, 342
Caption property, 286, 289-290, 294, 298-299, 301-303, 308, 319-320
cards, 16, 22, 30, 48, 51-53, 72, 225, 271, 355, 383
Cascade Update Related Fields, 327, 329, 331
Cascade Update Related Fields option, 327, 329
Case Problems, 334, 336, 339, 341
Casts, 56
Category, 55, 69, 124, 333, 347, 352
CBS, 84, 91
C&C, 55-56
CD (change directory) command, 347
cd command, 347-349, 355, 367
CDs, 346-349, 355-357, 359-360, 362, 364-369
Cell, 44, 116-122, 124-127, 129-132, 134, 137, 185, 337, 373-375, 378, 380-382, 385, 394-396
  worksheet, 44
cell padding, 130
Cell phone, 185, 337, 373-375, 378, 380-382, 385, 394-396
Cengage Learning, 5, 12, 16, 18, 24, 82-83, 85, 87, 89-95, 97, 99-100, 109-111, 115, 117, 121, 128, 130-138, 142-143, 158-159, 161, 163-167, 169-170, 173-176, 191, 193-194, 196-199, 202-206, 209-210, 213, 215, 222-223, 344-345, 352
Center, 16, 52, 103, 105, 122, 131, 271, 279, 289, 301, 339
centered, 87, 104, 117, 122, 128, 300
centering
  tables, 86
Central processing unit (CPU), 63
central processing units, 63
CEO, 12, 31, 38, 166, 396
Certificate, 274, 276-277
Certification, 3, 16-18, 28-29, 31-32, 35-36, 38, 232, 272, 276-277
certification programs, 17, 36
Change, 10, 34, 36, 43, 50, 58, 63-66, 74-75, 82, 84, 86, 101-105, 108, 110, 112, 114, 116, 118, 120, 122, 124, 127-138, 141-142, 146, 148, 167-168, 179, 204, 208-209, 217, 231-232, 234, 258, 260, 289-290, 292, 294, 297, 299, 301, 303-304, 308, 318-322, 328-329, 332, 342, 345, 347-349, 351, 357, 359-360, 362-368, 371, 386, 389, 391
Channel, 7, 390, 395
character code, 103, 105, 131
character conversions, 389
characters, 4, 29, 62, 73, 98, 103, 105, 110, 112, 122, 127-128, 131, 141, 144-145, 147, 172, 178-179, 281, 285, 288, 292, 302, 323-324, 348, 351, 355-356, 359, 367-368, 389, 397
  displaying, 292
  input, 141, 144, 178
  output, 4, 141, 351, 355
charts, 140, 166-168, 178, 181, 183, 185-187
  creating, 166, 168, 187
  line, 181, 187
chat, 22, 72
Chat rooms, 22
check boxes, 300, 302, 306-307, 310, 329, 331
China, 10-11, 15, 21, 25
Chips, 6-7
Chrome, 55, 60, 68, 85

CIO, 15, 35, 37
circuit board, 385
Cisco, 17-18, 32
Citations, 15
City field, 319
Class actions, 9
class diagrams, 228, 256, 258-259, 262, 267
Class table, 230, 235, 239-242, 244, 250
classes, 9, 14, 17, 42, 84-85, 87-88, 98-99, 101-105, 112, 114, 122, 124, 127, 130-134, 137-138, 228, 230, 234-235, 237-245, 249-250, 252-256, 258-259, 262, 264, 267, 271, 276-277, 358
  defined, 14, 17, 230, 237-238, 241, 243, 258
Classification, 43, 142, 178, 234-235, 262
Clause, 194, 196
Click, 55, 63-64, 74-78, 114, 120, 128, 132-133, 157, 287, 289-304, 306, 308-310, 312-321, 323-324, 328-331, 342, 346-347, 393
clicking, 52, 288, 291, 319
client/server systems, 379, 395
clipboard, 124, 128-130
Close button, 287, 300, 304, 310, 313-314, 324, 328, 330-331
closed, 30, 53, 62
closing
  Web page, 108, 110, 114, 122, 124, 130
closing tags, 108, 110, 112, 118, 124, 127-130, 132
cloud, 32-33, 39, 375-376, 395-396
cloud computing, 32-33, 375, 395
cloud-based applications, 375
CMSs, 38, 79
CNET, 37
CNN, 38
COBOL, 145, 153, 208
  development, 208
code
  testing, 5, 17
cohesion, 160, 180, 183
collecting, 50, 69
collections, 14, 16, 261, 375-376, 378-379
college degrees, 231
color, 53, 65, 82-83, 85, 88, 98, 101, 103, 105, 114, 122-123, 127, 129-131, 134, 137-138, 146, 154, 229, 231-233, 236, 265, 350, 369, 380
color scheme, 53
column, 107, 116-123, 125-126, 129-131, 134, 147, 165, 173, 232, 280, 300, 303, 306-311, 320, 322, 324, 342, 350-352
  datasheet, 300, 303, 306, 310-311, 320, 322, 324, 342
  table, 107, 116-123, 125-126, 129-131, 134, 232, 280, 300, 303, 306-311, 320, 322, 324, 342, 351-352
  worksheet, 308-311
column heading, 303, 308-310
com, 13, 35-40, 76-80, 81, 107, 109, 111, 113, 115, 117, 119, 121, 123, 125-126, 128, 130-136, 227-228, 231, 236, 263, 322, 345
command-line arguments, 347, 367
comment, 22, 84, 96, 101, 103-106, 108, 116, 124, 127, 129-138, 168-171, 173, 177-178, 181, 183-184, 187, 225, 242, 285, 392
commenting out, 118, 124
commercial software, 6, 25, 28
common, 12-14, 21, 31, 44, 55-56, 69, 84, 114, 127, 132, 145, 151, 153, 162, 194, 231, 245-246, 248, 283, 285, 305, 326, 328-329, 351, 357, 367, 373, 375-376, 378, 381-383, 385, 387, 395-396
  output, 246, 351
common field, 283, 305, 326, 328-329
Communication, 10, 15, 22, 35, 233, 373-376, 378, 380, 382, 385-386, 389-390, 392-396
communication protocols, 380
communications channels, 390, 395
communications device, 396
communications networks, 378
communications protocols, 392
comparing, 63, 379
  strings, 63
Compensation, 7, 9
Compiler, 144, 146, 172, 174
Compliance, 3, 24-26, 28, 40, 276
Component class, 238
Components, 82, 85, 126, 142, 146, 156-157, 164, 168, 172, 178, 187, 221, 227-228, 230-233, 236-238, 240, 242, 245, 251, 254, 256, 258, 262, 264, 267, 271, 367, 373, 376-377, 385-386, 397
composite
  attributes, 229-231, 248-249, 256, 262-265

composite key, 230, 241, 264, 283
composite primary key, 230
composition, 249, 265
  described, 265
compression
  data, 376, 388-389, 395, 397
  defined, 389
CompTIA, 18
computations, 173, 234, 260
Computer, 5-6, 12, 14-16, 18-19, 21-24, 30-32, 35, 38, 40, 41-55, 57-72, 74-79, 141-142, 144-147, 154, 157, 160, 162, 177-178, 180, 187, 190, 208, 217, 221, 226, 227, 251, 346-347, 364, 366, 368, 373-388, 390-397
computer engineer, 19
computer files, 44, 68
computer games, 22, 187
computer networks, 18, 22, 47, 55, 69, 373-376, 378, 385-386, 388, 392, 394-396
  definition, 375, 385, 396
  Internet, 22, 47, 374-376, 378, 385, 388, 392, 394-396
  LANs, 375-376, 394, 396
  WANs, 375-376, 394, 396
computer professionals, 146
computer programmers, 374
computer programming, 144, 177
Computer programs, 6, 54, 141, 154, 162, 178, 190, 217, 221, 226, 386
computer science
  definition, 375
Computer systems, 22, 43, 48, 55, 68, 384, 388
computer terminals, 383, 395
computer users, 6, 43, 374, 376
computer virus, 22-23, 35, 44, 47, 68, 70, 79
Computerworld, 35, 40
concentrators, 386
condition, 20, 30, 53, 163, 169, 193-194, 196-198, 201-204, 206-207, 211, 218-220, 224, 239-241, 243, 246, 252-253, 263, 267, 275, 285, 368, 373, 377
conducted media, 376
Confidentiality, 4, 6
Configuration, 43, 50, 59-60, 63, 71, 162, 164, 192, 345-346, 365, 389
configuration settings, 43, 60
Connect, 48, 61, 66, 200, 233, 305, 373, 377-381, 383-384, 386, 391, 394-395
connections, 25, 38, 47, 51, 59, 61, 375-380, 382, 385, 387-388, 390-391, 395-397
  creation, 25
Connectors
  drive, 72, 386
consistency, 108, 261
Consolidation, 39
Constants, 140-141, 146, 148-149, 152, 160-162, 171-172, 177-179, 182-183, 185-188, 234
constraints, 13, 234, 236, 243-244, 248, 254, 260, 262, 271
  cardinality, 236, 254, 262
  deletion, 260
  described, 244, 248
  foreign key, 236, 244, 248
  integrity, 244, 248, 260
  referential integrity, 248
  state, 271
Consultants, 2, 4, 7-8, 25, 30-31, 54
Contact information, 112, 124-125, 128, 130
  addresses, 128
  names, 112
Contacts
  online, 7, 53
  primary, 333
  Web, 124, 128, 130
Container class, 85, 87
containers, 84-88, 94-97, 101-105, 124, 130
content
  screens, 52, 84-85, 88, 119
contract workers, 30
contracts, 1-2, 8-10, 23, 28, 30-34, 40, 54, 253, 267, 275, 338
  errors, 33-34
contrast, 239, 275
Control, 2, 11, 14, 19, 24-26, 29, 33, 45, 50, 55, 57, 63-64, 69-71, 75, 81, 90, 96, 101-102, 122, 153, 156, 159, 180, 203, 206, 285, 292, 376-377, 382-383, 386, 388, 390, 393-395, 397
  form, 11, 376, 382, 388, 397
control operations, 386
Convergence, 373, 376, 385, 395-396
convert, 112, 114, 124, 132-134, 136-138, 185

Coordinates, 390
copying, 6-7, 40, 65, 70, 361
    files, 6-7, 65, 70, 361
    text, 70
Copyright, 24
Corners, 98, 103, 167, 209, 211, 377, 393
corporations, 6, 9, 11, 21, 236, 272, 373, 375
Cost, 2-3, 6-10, 16-17, 23, 31-34, 79, 137, 149, 174, 186, 192, 233, 260, 270, 275, 334, 338
    estimated, 3, 6, 33-34, 233
count, 66, 118, 363, 365
Coupling, 160
CPU, 63, 234
CR, 230, 237-238, 240-241
crashes, 46, 52, 71-72
Create button, 329, 331
creating, 23, 43, 55, 57, 65, 70, 78, 104, 110, 114, 119, 131, 133, 144, 149, 157, 160, 162, 166, 168, 171, 187, 214, 226, 232, 254, 267, 279, 287, 311, 330, 332, 351-352, 357-358, 360-365, 371, 395
    documents, 23, 65, 104, 133, 351, 358
    folders, 104, 131, 133
    forms, 332
    HTML templates, 358
    links, 114, 133, 351-352, 362-365, 371, 395
    unordered lists, 110, 114, 133
credentials, 15, 252, 276
Credit cards, 22, 48, 51-53, 72, 271
Crime, 8, 10-11, 29, 47
Crisis, 8
Crow's Foot notation, 228-229, 231, 233, 235, 237-238, 240-242, 249, 264, 266-267, 269, 271
css, 15-16, 27, 81-84, 86, 88, 90, 92-94, 96, 98-99, 101-106, 107-117, 119, 122-125, 127-138
CTRL, 295, 307, 311
CTRL + HOME, 311
CTRL + HOME keys, 311
CTRL key, 295, 307
Currency data type, 285
Currency format, 287, 306-307, 333, 338, 340
current, 9, 17, 30-31, 35, 59, 67, 90, 121, 156, 169, 171, 186, 229, 233-234, 253, 269, 276, 280-281, 288-291, 294-295, 298, 302, 309, 312, 314-315, 317, 319-321, 346-350, 352-353, 355-359, 366-369, 373, 390, 393
current date, 229, 233
custom bullets, 112
custom date formats, 293-294, 306-307, 342
Customer service, 30
Customers, 9-10, 13, 20, 22, 24, 30-32, 35, 55, 155, 157-159, 161, 175-176, 185-186, 234, 260, 266-267, 269-270, 274-276, 278, 334, 374
cutting, 31
Cycle, 234

D

Damballa, 80
data, 6-7, 16, 21-25, 32, 34-35, 41, 44, 48-50, 52, 54, 57, 59, 61, 65-71, 73, 78-79, 81, 101, 103-106, 107-108, 116-119, 122, 126-127, 129-131, 133-138, 141-145, 147-149, 152-153, 161-163, 171-172, 174-175, 177-181, 186, 188, 201-203, 205, 207-208, 219-220, 227-229, 231-232, 234, 236, 239, 244, 248-249, 252, 258-262, 265, 267, 269, 271, 275-276, 279-280, 282-290, 292, 294, 297-298, 300, 302, 304, 308-312, 314-316, 318, 320, 323-325, 330, 332-342, 344, 346, 362-365, 367-368, 373-383, 385-397
    corrupt, 25
    gathering, 286, 382
    grouping, 126
    importing, 308-312, 314, 323-325
    key, 7, 52, 67, 70, 178, 229, 231, 236, 239, 244, 248-249, 261, 265, 280, 282-283, 285, 287-290, 292, 294, 298, 302, 304, 311-312, 318, 333-342, 367, 374-375, 395
    markers, 108, 133, 137
    organizing, 107, 135
    points, 34-35, 44, 61, 141, 147, 152-153, 178-180, 207-208, 220, 229, 239, 249, 260, 285, 288, 290, 298, 302, 315, 318, 346, 362-364, 367-368, 376, 378, 380, 385, 387-390, 392, 396
    restore, 65, 67, 70, 78
data backup, 41, 57, 65-66, 68, 70, 73, 79
data communications, 373-376, 378, 380, 392, 394-396
data compression, 397
data dictionary, 172, 181, 229, 231

data duplication, 252
Data files
    document, 44, 54, 65, 103-105, 108, 133, 136
Data Link layer, 388-390, 395-397
data models
    described, 265
    logical, 228
data processing, 16, 373
data redundancy, 258, 283
data structures, 262, 362, 368
Data tables, 323
data transfer rate, 379
data transmission, 385
data type, 141-145, 147-149, 152, 172, 177-179, 181, 188, 280, 284-290, 292, 294, 297-298, 300, 312, 314-316, 318, 320, 332-333, 335-338, 340, 342
    overview, 280, 287
Data Type gallery, 314-316
Data Type property, 288, 292, 298
data variable, 147
Data worksheet, 309-310
database, 10, 13, 20, 23, 62-63, 69, 73, 131, 147, 155, 227-231, 233-236, 238-240, 242-243, 249-253, 256-262, 264-265, 267-269, 271, 273-275, 278, 279, 282-283, 286-287, 290, 296, 303-304, 306, 309, 312-314, 319, 328, 331-332, 342, 379
    fields, 282-283, 286-287, 290, 296, 303-304, 306, 312, 314, 319, 328, 331-332, 342
    objects, 227-228, 251, 256, 286, 303, 312-314
database administrator, 20, 229-230, 273
database design
    entities, 227-228, 235-236, 238, 242, 250, 252, 259-260, 264, 271
database designers, 231, 235-236, 238, 240, 251-252, 257, 260-262
database file, 312, 314
database models, 227-228
    relational database model, 228
database objects, 312-313
    table objects, 313
database programs, 147, 155
database tables, 234, 332, 342
    creating, 332
datagram, 388
datasheet, 281, 286, 289, 299-301, 303, 305-306, 310-311, 313-314, 316, 320, 322, 324, 342
    Datasheet view, 299-300, 303, 305-306, 310, 313-314, 316, 320, 322, 324, 342
Datasheet view, 299-300, 303, 305-306, 310, 313-314, 316, 320, 322, 324, 342
Date field, 301
date(s), 275
    reports, 275
dates, 13, 24, 55, 59, 63, 67-68, 101, 103-106, 108, 127, 131, 133-136, 138, 155, 160, 229, 233, 252, 261, 268-277, 285, 287, 292-294, 300-302, 306-307, 333, 335-338, 340, 342, 358
    comparing, 63
    storing, 252, 285
Date/Time fields, 292, 300
DB2, 273
DBAs, 20, 273
DBMS, 235, 244
Deception, 8, 29
Decimal places, 152, 178, 286-287, 290-291, 306-307, 333, 338, 340, 342
Decimal Places property, 290
decision symbol, 193-194
declarations, 84-88, 90-91, 96-98, 101, 103, 108, 110, 112, 114, 116, 122, 124, 130, 142-143, 158-163, 165, 169-170, 174-178, 181, 184, 202-207
declaring, 140-141, 143, 148-149, 160, 174
    variables, 140-141, 143, 148-149, 160, 174
declaring variables, 141, 160
decryption, 389
default
    arguments, 347, 366
default settings, 78, 289, 301
default value, 84-85, 143, 280, 302, 306, 321-322, 333, 337-338, 340, 342
Default value property, 302, 321-322
definition, 3-4, 43, 70, 79, 112, 132, 162, 227, 236, 240-241, 289-291, 298, 313-314, 375, 385, 396-397
definition lists, 112, 132
Delete button, 316
DELETE key, 288, 319
Delete row, 317
deleting, 45, 47, 54, 62, 68, 316-317, 357, 359-360
    tables, 316-317

delimited text files, 323
delimiter, 324, 342
Delivery, 34, 127
dependencies
    existence, 267
dependents, 19, 168, 236, 239-242, 249, 254, 263, 265
Derivation, 236
derived attributes, 233-234, 259-260, 263-264
Derives, 145
Description, 50, 56, 65, 75, 82-83, 85, 90, 92-94, 99, 104, 107, 110, 112-113, 116-117, 124, 126, 128, 130, 132, 135-137, 172, 181, 230, 236-238, 250, 266-274, 277-278, 280-281, 285, 287-290, 292-294, 297, 301-302, 312, 319-320, 333-338, 340, 342, 346, 349, 351-352, 354-357, 360-361, 364, 366, 376, 389, 397
Description field, 280, 285, 333, 335-338, 340, 342
Description property, 281, 289-290, 301-302, 319-320
design, 6-8, 14, 24-25, 36, 88, 115, 140, 155, 168-169, 171-172, 176-178, 186-187, 209, 227-228, 233-236, 238, 242-245, 250-252, 257-262, 264, 271, 274, 280-281, 283, 287-290, 295, 297-298, 300-301, 303, 312, 315-321, 330-333, 335, 338, 340, 342, 376, 386, 391, 395-396
Design button, 287
design grid, 280, 288, 290
DESIGN tab
    Insert Rows button, 297-298
Design View, 280-281, 287, 289, 295, 297, 300-301, 316-319, 321, 342
desk-checking, 168
Desktop
    defined, 346
desktop computer, 378-379, 382, 395-396
desktop shortcuts, 347
destination, 78, 135, 271, 274-275, 388, 390, 394, 397
detail loop tasks, 163, 178, 181
detailLoop() module, 163
determine, 20, 26, 29, 34, 47, 52, 63, 76, 82, 152, 171, 173, 185, 188, 195, 202, 212, 224, 226, 231, 239-241, 243, 246, 262, 267, 280, 282, 284-285, 346, 349-350, 359, 388-389, 394
devices, 21, 42-43, 46-48, 51-52, 55, 57, 59, 61, 66, 68-69, 71, 73-74, 84, 108, 269-270, 346, 363, 374-383, 388, 394-396
Diagrams, 168, 181, 192, 194, 196, 211, 217, 227-228, 233, 235-236, 250-251, 256, 258-259, 261-262, 267, 379, 382, 384, 397
Dialog box, 64-65, 74-78, 296, 302, 304, 308-310, 312-314, 323-324, 328-331, 342
    groups, 308, 312, 314, 323, 328, 330-331
dial-up connection, 379
dictionary, 172, 181, 224, 229, 231, 385
digital content, 390
Digital media, 65, 70
digital signals, 376
Digital Subscriber Line, 379
Digital Subscriber Line (DSL), 379
directory, 48, 343-353, 355-372
Directory structures, 343-349, 355, 357, 367
disable, 68
disk, 44, 46, 68, 71, 78, 354, 362, 364, 368, 386
    organization, 386
Disk drive, 46, 71
disk images, 78
Display, 46, 52-53, 69, 71-72, 75, 84, 88, 105, 112, 120, 122, 124-126, 130, 132, 134-136, 143, 146, 154, 157, 185-188, 200, 203, 207, 229, 239, 280-281, 288, 291-293, 295-297, 303, 306, 309, 314-315, 318, 320-322, 324, 328, 342, 347-352, 355-357, 360, 362, 365, 367-368, 371
display field, 292, 303
displaying, 125, 162-163, 183, 207, 292-293, 379, 383
    fields, 292-293
distribute, 25, 63
div tag, 130
division
    arithmetic operators, 149, 151-152, 177, 180
    integers, 152, 180, 188
divs, 84, 101, 103-104, 112, 124-125, 127, 130, 132, 138
document
    columns, 130, 134, 350-351
    creating, 23, 65, 104, 133, 351, 358
    effective, 23, 379
    headers, 84, 88, 92, 96, 102-105, 130, 134, 137
    navigating, 349
    saving, 103-105
    source, 16, 22, 54

documentation, 5, 25, 168-172, 181, 183, 262, 344, 353, 355, 368
classifications, 262
documenting
code, 171
docx, 44, 77
docx files, 44
Domain, 229, 374
Doors, 67, 373-374
DOs, 7, 20, 29-32, 35, 42, 48, 57-58, 65, 68, 76, 78, 141, 147-148, 150, 152, 154, 164, 191, 194, 198, 202, 204-205, 207, 210, 213, 219, 271, 342, 364, 374, 390, 397
(dot), 369
Double-click, 289, 300, 303, 306, 309-310, 312-314, 323-324, 328
download, 21, 48, 50, 56, 58-60, 65, 67-68, 76-78, 348-351, 358, 373, 375-376, 381, 383, 396-397
downloading, 52
Drag, 157, 297, 317-318, 328-331
drawings, 176, 196, 235, 241
drive, 43, 46-47, 49, 53, 57, 65-68, 70-72, 76, 78, 154, 275, 344, 346, 363-364, 367-368, 383, 386
DVD, 65-67, 346
inserting, 46
overview, 344
Drivers, 19, 383
DSL modem, 396
dual-alternative selection structures, 218
Duties, 4, 13-14, 20-21, 28, 373, 386-387, 394
DVD, 65-67, 153, 346
DVD-ROM, 346
DVD-ROM drive, 346

E

Eavesdropping, 24
eBay, 12
echo, 169, 175, 178, 184
edges
determining, 61, 88
Edit Relationships dialog box, 328-331
Editing, 365
editor, 35, 90, 92, 94, 96, 101-106, 108, 110, 112, 114, 116, 118, 120, 122, 124, 127-138, 146, 172, 373
edu, 16
Education, 4, 13-16, 18-20, 27-28, 251, 378-379
Effectiveness, 28, 261
electronic commerce, 386
electronic mail, 388
described, 388
electronic payments, 12
elements, 8, 34, 81-105, 107-134, 136-138, 140, 168, 171, 206, 386, 388
displaying, 125
index, 96-97, 101-105, 127-128, 130
missing, 118-119, 127, 129, 134
Else clause, 194
e-mail, 379, 384, 386-387, 396-397
addresses, 387
e-mail account, 396
email address, 30, 229
email attachments, 44, 46
e-mail program, 386-387
employee monitoring, 24
employee training, 35
Employees, 1-2, 4-7, 10-11, 13, 17, 20-25, 29-31, 34-35, 54, 71, 142, 155, 160, 163-164, 170, 194, 232-236, 239-242, 244-246, 248, 260-261, 263, 266, 270-271, 273, 275, 277-278, 375
employers, 2, 4-7, 10, 12, 17-18, 25, 27, 31, 35-36, 144
certification, 17-18, 31, 35-36
Employment, 5, 13, 54, 77, 272, 397
encapsulation, 180, 394-395
Encoding, 382, 389
Encryption, 388-389
End users, 6, 13, 21, 28, 228, 233, 251, 260, 262, 383
end-of-job tasks, 163-164, 178, 181
engineering, 15-16, 18-19, 21, 38, 267, 392
Enron, 39
ENTER key, 288, 296
Enterprise Resource Planning (ERP) systems, 19
Entities, 227-246, 248-252, 254-256, 259-265, 267-268, 271-273, 278, 296
entity integrity, 261, 296
entity relationship, 227-228, 235, 239, 241, 256
entity relationship diagrams (ERDs), 227
entity types, 245
Envelope, 391

environment
IDE, 172
interactive, 383
static, 63, 346
virtual, 63, 349, 366
work, 13, 22, 168, 231-232, 378
Equipment, 10, 32, 34, 43, 61, 373, 375, 382
erasing, 54
error checking, 397
error detection, 376, 388, 394, 397
Error messages, 207, 321, 330, 359
errors
reporting, 33
estimated cost, 3, 34
Ethernet, 75
ethical issues, 3, 13, 21, 23, 27
evaluation, 14, 27
event, 11, 43, 54, 64, 66-67, 69-70, 110, 138, 381
common, 69, 381
Evidence, 8, 48, 56
Excel, 44, 55, 308-312, 323
features, 55
worksheets, 44, 308-311
Excel button, 308
Excel, Microsoft, 55
Excel worksheet, 308
Exceptions, 14, 82, 373, 386
exchanges, 8, 10-11, 15, 25, 230-231, 390
executable files, 351
executable programs, 44, 48, 77, 353-354, 368
execute
described, 221, 235
macros, 44
executing, 160, 174, 180, 194
statements, 160, 174, 180, 194
exercise, 4, 27-28, 181, 184, 198, 219, 222-224, 274, 343, 396-397
Experience, 4, 8-9, 12, 15, 17-18, 20, 27-28, 31-32, 35, 52, 160, 208, 273, 286, 346, 392
exploit, 48, 58
Expressions, 146-147, 149-150, 152, 179-180, 185, 188, 375
extension, 71
list, 71
external data, 308-309, 312, 314, 323
EXTERNAL DATA tab
Access button, 312, 314
external documentation, 169, 181, 183
external hard drives, 66, 72

F

Facebook, 8-9, 37, 56
facility, 110
Fannie Mae, 79
Favorites, 225, 396
faxes, 317
Feedback, 72, 392
fiber-optic cable, 389
Field, 4, 7, 15, 18-19, 27, 35, 134, 254, 280-308, 312, 314-324, 326-333, 335-338, 340, 342, 374, 385, 392, 394, 397
field descriptions, 302
Field List, 305, 328-331, 342
field properties, 280-281, 284, 287-288, 290-294, 299-302, 319, 321, 333, 336-337
Field Properties pane, 280-281, 287-288, 290-294, 300, 319, 321
Field Size property, 285-286, 289-290, 299, 301-302, 318-319
File, 6-7, 37, 39, 44-49, 54-56, 62-63, 65-73, 75-78, 81, 92, 101, 103-106, 107-108, 112, 127, 131, 133, 135-136, 138, 155, 162-163, 171-172, 174, 183, 187, 203, 225, 227, 272, 279, 285, 303, 309, 312, 314, 323-325, 333-334, 336, 339, 341-342, 343-347, 349-365, 367-372, 376, 388, 395, 397
finding, 367, 397
inserting, 44, 46, 172
saving, 101, 103-106, 314, 324
file handling, 162
file management, 357
files, 357
file numbers, 171
file size, 351-352, 362
File system, 78, 343-347, 357-358, 368
File tab, 77, 303
File Transfer Protocol, 388, 395
File transfer protocol (FTP), 388, 395
file types, 44, 350-351, 362, 369
fill, 89, 93, 272-273, 379

Filter, 60, 69, 272, 381
filtering, 61
finding, 8, 25, 152, 367, 397
Fire, 22, 60, 66
firewalls, 18, 23-24, 28, 57, 60-62, 68-70, 73, 75
FIRST, 14, 16, 21, 27, 31, 44, 46-47, 56-59, 61-62, 64-66, 69, 76, 79, 85-86, 101, 103-106, 108-109, 114, 116, 118, 120, 123-124, 127, 129-131, 134, 138, 143, 145-146, 148, 150-151, 160, 162, 170-172, 175-176, 178-180, 182, 185, 187, 193-194, 196, 202, 205-206, 208, 212, 218-219, 224, 227-229, 233, 235-237, 239, 243, 246, 251, 260, 265, 273, 280, 286, 288-289, 291-293, 295, 300, 304, 306-307, 309-310, 312, 315-316, 319-320, 322-324, 328, 333, 335-337, 339, 341, 344, 346, 350-351, 353-354, 360, 362-363, 367, 377, 385-386, 391-392, 396
FirstName field, 319
fixed position, 102
flags, 26
Flash, 16, 43, 47, 67-68, 76
Flash, Adobe, 68
flash drive, 43, 47, 67, 76
Flashing, 374
float property, 89, 119
floating-point numbers, 141, 178
decimal digits, 141
sign, 141
floating-point values, 152
floating-point variables, 152
flood, 56
floppy disks, 44, 354
Flowcharts, 142-143, 146-147, 157, 159, 163, 166, 169-170, 174, 176, 181, 187-188, 190, 192-198, 202-206, 209, 211-212, 214-215, 217-218, 220, 222-226
flowlines, 163, 211
Fluids, 97
focus, 35, 49, 198, 233, 259, 274, 392
folder, 63, 67, 76, 81, 101, 103-106, 107-108, 112, 127, 131, 133, 135-138, 273, 309, 312, 314, 323, 342, 359
compressed, 76
creating, 104, 131, 133
deleting, 359
folder windows, 359
font, 108, 110, 112, 114, 116, 122, 124, 132-133, 136-137
changing, 132-133
effects, 122
size, 108, 110, 112, 114, 116, 124, 132-133
styles, 108, 110, 112, 114, 116, 122, 124, 132-133, 136-137
font family, 136
font size, 132-133
footer, 84, 86-88, 90-91, 94, 101-105, 108, 116-117, 124, 127-133, 135
for loop, 203, 219
flowchart, 203
nested, 203
output, 203
forecasting, 19
foreign key, 231, 235-237, 239, 241, 244, 248, 256, 261, 287, 290, 301, 329, 333, 335, 338, 340-342
overview, 287
referential integrity, 239, 248, 329, 342
form, 11, 31-32, 141, 145, 147, 154, 172-173, 177, 183, 208, 211, 228, 230, 251, 271-272, 286, 312, 314, 319, 328, 332, 374-376, 378-379, 382, 387-388, 392, 396-397
Format, 17, 58, 107, 122, 130, 136, 164, 212, 227, 229, 233, 235, 276, 278, 285, 287, 291-294, 299-301, 306-307, 323, 333, 335-338, 340, 342, 350-352, 354, 364, 369
Format property, 291-292, 299-300, 342
formatting, 96, 120, 130, 300
datasheets, 300
documents, 96, 130
text, 96, 120, 130, 300
Formula, 6, 22-23, 233
Fortune 500 companies, 15
forums, 15-16
frames
using, 7, 389-390, 395
frameworks, 263, 385
fraud, 1-3, 8-10, 26, 28, 34, 37-40, 50
FRED, 146
free, 11, 16, 67, 70, 77, 151, 173, 388, 395
frequency, 277
FST, 92, 334

TP, 388, 395, 397
unction, 8, 11, 19, 43-44, 49-50, 52, 54, 58, 61, 64,
9-70, 153, 155, 157, 177, 180, 233, 243, 251, 260,
264, 274, 290, 354-355, 383, 385-387, 389-390, 392,
895, 397
  calling, 153, 157
  declarations, 177
  defining, 386
  designing, 19
  error detection, 397
  naming, 177
  onto, 44, 70, 389
  parameters, 233
  range, 61, 392
  statements, 153, 155, 157, 177, 180, 243, 389
unctional components, 156
unctional decomposition, 154, 180
unctional requirements, 25

G

Gain, 22, 32, 155, 332, 344, 375
gallery, 314-316
Game, 7, 22, 55-56, 134, 187-188, 225, 267, 354-355,
373, 375
  computer, 22, 55, 187, 373, 375
Gap, 118-119, 129
Garbage, 45, 143, 178, 182, 207
Gates, 35, 373
Gates, Bill, 373
gateways, 379, 394
GB, 92, 94, 323
General Services Administration (GSA), 9
Gesture, 12
Get External Data - Excel Spreadsheet dialog box,
308-309
GIF, 112
gigabytes, 351-352, 383
global, 11, 35, 37-38, 103, 162, 178, 180, 183,
185-186, 374
global positioning system, 374
Global Positioning System (GPS), 374
global styles, 103
global variables, 162, 178, 185-186
  data types, 178
Gmail, 56
Google
  Google Chrome, 55, 60, 68
Google Chrome, 55, 60, 68
gov, 38
GPS, 82-84, 86, 88, 90, 92, 94, 96-98, 279, 282-288,
290-291, 294-296, 299, 301, 303, 306-308, 311-312,
314-316, 318-322, 326-327, 330, 332, 334-341, 374,
384
GPS devices, 374
graphic, 227
graphical user interfaces (GUIs), 57
grays, 128, 130
Greeks, 47
Grid, 116, 118-119, 124-125, 280, 288, 290
Gridlines, 116
Group, 6, 11, 14-16, 27, 29-32, 38, 42, 58, 116-117,
122, 130, 178, 196, 206, 219, 221, 267, 270, 282, 287,
295, 297-298, 300-301, 303, 308, 312, 314-317,
320-321, 323, 328, 330-331, 336, 347, 352, 355,
365, 374-375, 386, 388, 392
Grouping, 126
guest, 64
Guest account, 64
GUI, 57, 174, 294, 344, 346, 361, 367
guides, 14, 29, 38, 134, 188, 190, 258, 267, 270-271,
352

H

Handle, 31, 34, 49, 147, 200, 221, 231-232, 235, 267,
275, 389-390, 395
hard disk, 46, 71, 368
hard disk drives, 46, 71
Hard drive, 46, 49, 53, 57, 65-68, 70-72, 78, 344,
363-364, 367-368, 383
Hardware, 6-7, 10, 13, 23, 31-32, 38, 51, 61, 65, 69,
72-73, 155, 374, 376-377, 383, 385, 392, 395
hardware design, 6
hardware firewalls, 61
hash, 241
hash mark, 241
Head, 128-130, 373
header, 84, 88, 92-98, 101-105, 117, 120, 129-130,
134, 137-138, 156, 178, 180, 182, 354, 393-394

adding, 84, 120, 138
  functions, 180, 354
header files, 354
header row, 117, 120, 129
heading
  column, 120, 122, 129-131, 134, 165, 303, 308-310
  main, 92, 96, 98-99, 108, 122, 129-132, 134, 136,
    162
  Navigation pane, 309-310
  numbering, 108
  paragraph, 108
Heuristics, 63
Hidden files, 350-352
Hierarchy, 140, 166-168, 178, 181, 183, 185-187,
343-345, 367-368
high cohesion, 160
high-level programming languages, 154
highlights, 89, 118
high-resolution, 381
hits, 35, 186
Home page, 50, 77
Home tab, 321
horizontal space, 83
Hosts, 46-47, 60-62, 68-69, 345, 352, 354
Hosts file, 345, 352
housekeeping tasks, 162, 164, 166, 178, 180, 183,
206
HTML, 35-40, 76, 79, 83-84, 88-89, 92, 96, 99,
101-106, 108-118, 120, 122-125, 127-138, 345, 358,
392
HTML document, 88-89
HTML tags, 114
HTML5, 81, 107, 112
HTTP, 16, 36-40, 56, 79-80, 345, 388, 395
Hungarian notation, 145, 179
Hurricane, 43
Hyperlinks, 285
Hypertext, 56, 388, 395
Hypertext Transfer Protocol, 388, 395
Hypertext Transfer Protocol (HTTP), 388, 395
Hypertext Transport Protocol (HTTP), 56

I

IBM, 16-17, 33-35, 40, 273, 373
IBM DB2, 273
icons, 53, 65, 103, 347
ID field, 324
Id numbers, 265, 268-269
IDE, 146, 172
identifiers, 141-148, 156, 168, 171-173, 177-182, 188,
229-230, 256, 263, 286, 388
  scope, 180-181
IDSs, 24
IEEE, 15-16, 27, 38, 40, 392, 395
IEEE Computer Society, 38
If condition, 194, 201
if statement, 184
Ignore button, 319
illustrations, 85-86
images, 51, 67-68, 74, 77-79, 112, 119, 137, 375, 385
  digital, 385
  RGB, 137
implementation, 227-228, 231, 235-236, 240, 245,
247-248, 256, 259-262, 271, 392
  files, 227
import, 308-310, 312-314, 323-324, 342
Import & Link group, 308, 312, 314, 323
Import Spreadsheet Wizard, 309-310
importing data, 308, 310-311, 325
importing text, 323
incidents, 22, 44, 47, 54
Income tax, 7, 190
inconsistent data, 260-261, 283
indent levels, 127-128, 132
indentation, 188, 196-197
Index, 36-38, 58, 96-97, 101-106, 127-128, 130, 185,
260-261
index value, 97
Indexes, 36-38, 58, 96-97, 101-106, 127-128, 130,
185, 260-261
Indians, 37
Infinity symbol, 305, 330
information, 4, 6-11, 13, 15-16, 19, 21-28, 36, 38, 43,
48-53, 56, 60, 64-65, 67-69, 72, 76, 78-79, 92, 108,
112, 114, 116, 124-125, 128-136, 141, 156-157, 160,
166, 169, 171, 179-181, 226, 239, 251-252, 256-257,
259-260, 262, 267, 269-270, 273, 275, 281-282, 286,
344, 347, 350-351, 354-355, 362, 365, 367-368,
374-377, 383, 387-388, 390-394

described, 112, 116, 270, 354, 388
information security, 16, 38, 79
  malware, 79
information system, 11, 19, 21, 23, 28, 36, 251, 375
information technology, 15-16, 38, 392
initializing, 143, 148, 178
  named constants, 148
  variables, 143, 148, 178
input, 141-144, 157-161, 163, 165, 169-171, 173-178,
181, 184-185, 189, 201-208, 218-220, 384
  characters, 141, 144, 178
  designing, 160, 173
  strings, 141-144, 158-159, 161, 165, 170, 174-178,
    184, 219
Insert Rows button, 297-298
Insertion point, 112, 288, 290-291, 293, 298, 301-302,
307, 315, 318
installing
  software, 23, 42, 48, 50, 57, 62, 64-65, 68
instance
  diagrams, 228
instruction sets, 216
instructions, 4, 44-45, 49-50, 55-56, 142, 149,
154-155, 160, 162, 180, 183, 190, 196, 198, 208, 212,
216-217, 224, 347, 349, 367
Instruments, 72, 275, 277
Insurance, 25, 160, 239, 269
insurance companies, 269
Integer data type, 152
integer values, 233, 285
Integers, 141, 152, 178, 180, 188, 233, 285-286, 333,
338, 342
Integrity, 14, 25, 239, 244, 248, 260-261, 296, 327,
329, 331, 342, 387
Intel, 6
intelligence, 22, 54, 384
Interest, 7-8, 12, 15, 20, 28-30, 35, 145-146, 187, 228,
392
Interface, 6, 57, 65, 345, 354, 367, 383, 392, 396
Intermediate, 173, 181, 394
internal documentation, 169, 181
International Organization for Standardization (ISO),
392, 395
Internet, 16, 21-23, 32, 37, 47, 50-51, 56, 59-60, 66,
72, 75, 374-382, 385, 388, 391-397
  history, 75
  size, 375, 394
  structure, 60
Internet addresses, 394
Internet Architecture Board, 392
Internet Architecture Board (IAB), 392
Internet connections, 51, 376, 379-380
  types, 51, 379-380
Internet Engineering Task Force, 392
Internet Engineering Task Force (IETF), 392
Internet Protocol (IP), 56, 388, 395
Internet protocols, 56, 377, 385, 388, 392, 395
Internet service provider (ISP), 380
Internet Society, 392
Internet Society (ISOC), 392
Internet Storm Center, 16
Interpretation, 87, 276
Interpreter, 144
intersection, 116, 232, 382, 397
interviews, 31-32, 251
Inventory, 19, 267, 272, 374
inventory control, 19
investigation, 6, 25, 39
investment, 171
iOS, 363
IP, 56, 373, 377, 380, 385-390, 392-397
IP headers, 394
IP protocol, 373, 380, 385-390, 392-393, 395-397
IPad, 10
iPhone, 9-10
IPods, 10
ISO, 392, 395
isolate, 155
ISP, 380
ISs, 3-25, 27-36, 38-39, 42-79, 82-84, 86, 88-98,
101-106, 108, 110, 112, 114, 116-118, 120-122, 124,
126-128, 131-132, 141-157, 159-160, 162-188, 190,
192-215, 217-226, 227-256, 257-256, 278, 280-281,
285-291, 294-296, 298, 300-302, 304-307, 309-310,
312, 314-319, 321, 323-324, 328-330, 332, 338, 342,
344-354, 356-370, 372, 373-397
  italic, 132
items, 75, 100, 108-113, 116, 126-128, 133, 135-137,
141-142, 162, 171, 174-175, 177-178, 180, 211,

267-269, 272, 298, 306-307, 310, 340, 374
Iteration, 194, 219

J

Jacks, 378, 380, 386
Japan, 11
java, 68, 141, 144, 152-153, 157, 188, 208, 221
Jeopardy!, 225
Job interviews, 31
Job titles, 5, 13
Jobs, 5, 7, 12-13, 17-18, 20, 22-23, 30-31, 34-35, 42, 57, 160, 163-164, 170-172, 178, 181, 183, 185-187, 190, 204, 225, 236, 260-261, 272-273, 276, 378, 380, 386-387, 394, 397
join, 193, 270, 305, 325-326, 329-330, 342
join line, 305, 329-330
join tables, 342
joining, 2, 133
justified, 35

K

kernel, 346, 354
Key attributes, 229-230, 236, 249, 256
key fields, 295-296
key symbols, 295, 304
Keyboard, 51-52, 69, 72, 176, 307, 383
Keyboard shortcuts, 307
Keylogger, 51-52, 69-70, 72
keypunch, 144
keys, 3, 7-8, 11, 13, 27-28, 52, 55, 67, 70, 178, 187, 218, 229-231, 235-241, 244, 248-249, 251, 256, 261, 263-265, 280-283, 285, 287-296, 298, 301-302, 304, 306-307, 311-312, 318-319, 321, 329, 333-342, 348, 367, 374-375, 395
private, 13, 338
public, 7, 13, 27, 52
keyword, 144, 152, 178
kilobytes, 352
Knowledge, 3-4, 6, 15, 17, 19-21, 28, 31, 35-36, 38, 43, 48, 52, 68, 79, 176, 262, 375, 389
Korea, 10, 22

L

Labels, 112, 231, 241
Ladder, 13
Language
defined, 24
language translators, 144
LANs, 375-377, 379, 381, 394, 396
Laptop computers, 375, 378, 380, 382, 395-396
laptops, 42-43, 269, 375-376, 378, 380, 382, 391, 395-396
laser printer, 380
Lasers, 380
LastName field, 320
law, 3, 5-6, 8, 10-11, 13-14, 17, 19-20, 25-26, 29, 33, 37, 52-53, 69, 71, 168, 246
law enforcement, 25, 52-53, 69, 71
layers, 96, 100, 373, 385-391, 393-397
layout
CSS, 81-82, 84, 86, 93-94, 99, 103-106, 114, 119, 124-125
table, 82, 84, 86, 93-94, 99, 119, 124-125, 304, 308, 331
worksheet, 308
Lead times, 10
Leaders, 22
leading, 18, 109
left-align, 127, 129
left-aligned, 300
legacy systems, 10
Legends, 47
Length, 45, 82, 88, 120, 144, 270, 338, 373
length identifier, 144
length variable, 144
letter variable, 145
Letters, 108, 122, 134, 141, 144-145, 147-148, 156, 171-172, 179, 183, 228, 285, 292-293, 306, 344, 348, 355-357, 369
address, 144, 147, 179, 285
cover, 122
types, 108, 122, 141, 144-145, 147-148, 172, 179, 228, 285, 292-293, 306, 348, 369
level, 17-18, 22-23, 35, 38, 42, 49-50, 63-65, 73, 100, 108, 110, 122, 124, 127-128, 130, 132, 154, 162, 197, 228, 235, 248, 262, 266, 272-273, 365, 383, 389, 392
Library, 15, 52, 346, 354
described, 354

licenses
software, 6, 13, 19-21, 28, 32, 383
licensing, 3, 17-19, 25, 27-29, 275-277
licensing agreement, 25
Lightning, 66
Limitations, 36, 276, 380
line breaks, 85, 173
lines, 9, 12-13, 16, 18, 24, 54, 58, 61, 69, 82, 85-87, 108, 110, 112, 114, 116-118, 120, 122, 124, 127-130, 132-133, 135, 157, 161, 165, 169, 171, 173-174, 176, 181, 187, 197, 211, 214, 223, 225, 229, 231, 233, 237-238, 240-241, 249, 259-260, 267, 272, 297, 305, 329-330, 344, 347, 354, 357, 359, 361, 363, 365-367, 377, 379-380, 382-383, 390
Linking, 309
Links, 114-115, 128, 132-133, 308, 312, 314, 323, 344, 351-352, 362-365, 367-368, 371, 388-390, 393, 395-397
Linux, 343-350, 352-355, 357-363, 365, 367-368, 371
log files, 346, 371
operating systems, 345, 354, 368
liquid layout, 97
LISP, 145
list, 11-12, 14, 18, 27, 32, 41-42, 48, 50, 56, 71, 75, 77-79, 101-102, 107-114, 116, 124, 126-138, 144, 154, 172, 181, 188, 268, 273, 288, 290-293, 305, 318-319, 328-331, 342, 345, 348-357, 360, 362, 367-369, 373, 378, 396-397
Literal, 141, 148-149, 177-178
literal constants, 141, 149
loaders, 57
loading, 278
local area networks, 375-382, 385, 388-389, 391-392, 394, 396-397
local area networks (LANs), 375
local variables, 162, 182
log file, 346, 371-372
logging, 365-366, 371
levels, 365
options, 366, 371
Logic, 54-55, 69-71, 79, 145-146, 156-157, 159, 162-166, 168-169, 174, 176, 178, 180-181, 185-188, 189-192, 195-197, 201-209, 211-214, 217-219, 221, 223-225, 262
logic bombs, 54-55, 69-71, 79
logical
data types, 143
logical connections, 390, 395-397
logos, 17, 98-99, 232
logs, 48, 52, 56, 271-272, 346, 349, 352, 355, 357, 359-360, 362, 364, 366, 371-372, 388
managing, 357
long document, 92
Long Integer field, 286
long integers, 286
looking up, 224
Loop, 163-164, 178, 181, 183, 185-186, 189, 192, 194-201, 203-209, 211-221, 225
basic structures, 189, 192, 200-201, 209, 217-218, 220
while loops, 194, 197, 203, 217, 219
loop body, 194, 203, 206, 217-219, 221
looping, 194-195, 200, 208
loss, 9, 14, 32, 52, 260
Lowercase, 144-145, 172, 179, 347, 350, 379
lvalue, 147, 179

M

MAC, 47
machine language, 148
macro, 44, 312, 314, 354
reports, 312, 314
macro virus, 44
Mail server, 379
Main heading, 92, 96, 98-99
mainframe computers, 381, 383, 396
mainframes, 381-383, 395-396
mainline logic, 156-157, 162-163, 165, 178, 180
Maintenance, 18, 148, 187, 208, 225, 234, 271-272, 274
malicious code, 45, 48
malicious software, 43, 68
malware, 22, 41, 43-44, 47-50, 52-56, 60-64, 67-71, 73-74, 76-80
defined, 71
malware infection, 53
Management, 6-7, 16, 18, 21, 23-26, 29, 33, 35, 251-252, 269, 273, 357, 376, 388, 390, 392, 396
management team, 33

managers, 2-3, 7-8, 10, 16-17, 21, 23-24, 30-31, 35-36, 38, 104, 166, 185-186, 245-246, 272, 277, 346, 374-375, 386, 396
managing
tasks, 357
manuals, 1, 4-5, 353-354, 368, 386
Manufacturing, 6-7, 14, 19, 22, 30, 158-159, 161, 246, 382-383
margin, 81-88, 91, 100-105, 108-110, 112-113, 116-117, 124, 127-137
marketing, 4, 7, 35, 166, 251-252, 386, 391
information systems, 251
markups, 112, 133, 136-137
masks, 45
MasterCard, 188
masters, 71
Match, 43, 62-63, 69, 86, 100, 103, 105, 112, 114, 116, 118, 122, 126, 128, 130, 132-137, 148, 248, 273, 293, 304, 308, 356, 358
maximize, 376
maximum, 85, 92, 101-105, 235, 241, 251, 259, 266, 379
McAfee, 6
MCI, 1
mean, 11, 14, 17, 22, 24, 29, 35, 43, 47, 65, 69-70, 77, 119, 146, 151, 162, 171, 188, 192, 196, 235, 240-241, 245, 250, 258, 302, 346, 388
media players, 50
median, 32
Meetings, 2, 7, 11, 13, 15, 31
megabytes, 351-352
Members, 6, 11-16, 26-29, 40, 172, 271-272, 275-276, 278, 335
memory, 63, 141-142, 144, 146-147, 149-150, 157, 160, 177, 179-181, 286, 383
size, 181, 286
memory addresses, 144, 146-147, 149-150, 160, 179-180
memory locations, 142, 146, 177, 180
menus
using, 136-137, 342
merging, 376
Messages, 23, 31, 46, 52-53, 56, 64, 69, 71, 76-77, 154-155, 163, 174, 177, 181, 184-186, 207, 302, 321, 330, 342, 347, 354, 359, 373, 379, 381-382, 385, 387, 390, 397
Metropolitan area network (MAN), 396
metropolitan area networks (MANs), 375
Mouse, 52, 55, 89, 114, 184, 297, 317, 328-330
Microcomputers, 376, 378-380, 383, 396
Microsoft, 6, 17-18, 23, 35, 44, 54-55, 58-60, 64, 67, 70, 74, 77, 228, 233, 235, 242, 272, 375
certifications, 17-18, 35, 272
Microsoft Access, 233
Microsoft Excel, 55
Microsoft Office, 44
Microsoft Office documents, 44
Microsoft SQL Server, 233
Microsoft Windows, 44, 59, 64, 67, 70, 74
Microsoft Word, 23, 77
Microsoft Word documents, 23
Microwaves, 375, 384, 395
Minimum, 84, 131, 235, 241, 251, 266, 272, 340
(minus sign), 149
MIS, 30
mission, 6, 16, 28
mistakes, 38, 149
Mobile applications, 4, 25
mobile apps, 39
mobile devices, 59
mode, 64, 346
Model, 32, 42, 81-86, 187, 227-229, 231-232, 242, 249, 256, 262-267, 269, 271, 274-275, 373, 385-387, 389-390, 392-397
definition, 227, 385, 396-397
description, 82-83, 85, 266-267, 269, 271, 274, 389, 397
physical, 266, 386-387, 389-390, 394-397
Modeling, 168, 227-231, 235-236, 241, 248, 256, 260, 262
modems, 377, 379-380, 385, 392, 396
cable, 379-380
modular programs, 155, 180, 221
Modulation, 389
modules, 143, 153-157, 159-169, 171-172, 176-178, 180-183, 185-188, 208-209, 216, 221, 279, 287, 309, 312, 314, 323, 333-334, 336, 339, 341
modulus operator, 152
monetary values, 285

Monitor, 14, 16, 19, 50, 52, 62, 66-69, 148, 154, 174, 177, 181, 272, 374, 379, 383, 387, 394
Monitoring, 24, 50, 57, 63, 383
Mouse pointer, 89, 114, 328
move pointer, 297
moving, 91, 160, 297, 361, 393
moving files, 361
MP3, 269
MP3 players, 269
MS-DOS, 58
multiple windows, 59
multiplexing, 376, 396-397
    overview, 376
Multitasking, 55

N

name, 44, 60, 68, 71, 79, 89, 101, 103-106, 108, 112, 127, 131-133, 135-136, 138, 142, 144-146, 148-149, 151, 153, 156-162, 164-167, 171-172, 174-184, 186-188, 190, 192, 218-219, 228-229, 231, 234, 256, 265-266, 268-273, 280-281, 285-290, 292-294, 296-298, 302-304, 306, 308-309, 312, 317-322, 328, 333-342, 350, 352, 354, 356, 360, 368-369, 376, 386, 397
Name Box, 287-288, 290, 292, 294, 296, 298, 302, 317-321
Name field, 290
name variable, 146, 171
named constants, 141, 148-149, 152, 161, 177, 179, 185, 187-188
naming
    forms, 145, 172, 177, 183, 286
naming conventions, 144-145, 179, 255
NAS, 149, 153
Natural disasters, 65, 268
navigating, 344, 346, 349, 354-355
Navigation, 114, 128, 132-133, 136-137, 287, 300, 303, 306, 309-311, 313-314, 324-325, 330, 342, 384
Navigation bar, 114, 128, 132, 303
Navigation Pane, 287, 300, 306, 309-311, 313-314, 324-325, 330, 342
navigation systems, 384
Negative numbers, 285-286
NEST, 114, 197, 202-203, 220
nested, 101-102, 105, 108, 114-115, 123, 125, 137-138, 196-197, 200-201, 203, 206, 217
    blocks, 196
nested lists, 114
nesting, 114, 124, 196, 218-220
nesting structures, 196, 219
Net, 38-39, 164-165
Netbook, 378
Network, 4-5, 15-16, 18, 22-23, 32, 35, 37-38, 43, 47-48, 50, 55, 59-61, 68-71, 73, 75, 272-273, 358, 373-392, 394-397
network access layer, 388-390, 394-396
network administrator, 4, 16, 273
Network Connections, 378, 380, 388, 395
network devices, 61, 68-69
Network layer, 387-388, 390, 394-396
network models, 392, 397
network software, 376, 379
network switches, 378
Networking, 16, 56, 61, 395
    research, 16
networking services, 56
New York Times, 36-37
news
    about computers, 38
newsletter, 15
No option, 192, 218
Nodes, 377, 388, 394, 396
Nonprofit organizations, 268, 392
NOT function, 58, 386
note text, 321
notebook, 378
Novell, 273
null entries, 249
null value, 296
num variable, 152
number, 2, 6, 12, 14, 21-23, 31-34, 43-44, 48, 51-53, 56-57, 62, 72, 82, 87, 108-109, 116, 118-122, 127-128, 141-144, 146-149, 152, 157, 168, 171, 174, 177-179, 185-188, 190, 192, 195, 197, 200-209, 217-219, 224, 229-232, 235, 244, 251, 258-259, 262, 265-266, 268-275, 285-286, 289-290, 300-302, 306, 333-334, 338, 342, 350-352, 354, 362-365, 368-369, 371, 377, 381, 383, 386, 392, 396
    average, 43, 186, 229, 396

precision, 258
    storage, 51, 286, 383
number data, 285-286
    numbers, 285-286
Number data type, 285-286
Number fields, 286
Number-Doubling program, 142-143, 201-202, 208
numeric constants, 141, 178, 182
numeric data, 147, 152
numeric data types, 152
numeric values, 141, 147, 152, 178

O

oak, 335
object tabs, 299, 303, 308
Objectives, 20, 81, 107, 279, 349, 352, 355, 357, 360-361, 364, 366, 373
Objects
    database, 227-228, 251, 256, 286, 303, 312-314
    form, 228, 251, 286, 312, 314, 382
    picture, 168
    report, 251, 286, 312, 314
    table, 228, 256, 286, 299-300, 303, 308, 312-314
Office, 2, 11, 23, 25, 36-37, 44, 58, 74, 374, 383, 386
    Help, 23
Office documents, 44
OK button, 309, 312-314, 323, 330
one-to-many relationship, 236, 304-305, 326, 328-329, 331, 342
online, 7, 15, 25, 38-39, 50, 52-53, 56, 58, 65-70, 77, 79, 228, 236, 263, 271, 374
online backup, 67, 79
online education, 15
online storage, 66
open, 25, 29, 52, 75-78, 84, 92, 101, 103-106, 108, 114, 127-133, 135-138, 162-164, 224, 268, 280, 287, 296, 300, 302, 304, 306, 308-310, 312-316, 323-325, 328-331, 342, 344, 346-347, 349, 352-353, 355, 357, 359-362, 364-366, 385-386, 391-392, 396
open architecture, 386
Open dialog box, 309, 312, 314, 323
open systems, 385, 392, 396
opening
    files, 108, 112, 127, 162, 183, 353
opening tags, 120, 124, 128, 130
operands, 146-147, 149, 152, 179-180
operating environments, 254, 267
Operating system, 21, 46-49, 52, 54, 57-58, 60, 64-70, 78, 155, 345, 354, 368
Operations, 22, 32, 44, 56, 140, 142, 147, 149-153, 155, 166, 173, 177-181, 250-251, 266, 268-272, 274-278, 297, 382-388, 392, 396-397
operators, 25, 146-147, 149-153, 166, 177, 179-180, 182, 188
    binary, 146, 149, 179, 182
    precedence, 150-153, 177, 179-180, 182
    syntax, 182, 188
optimizing, 18
option buttons, 309, 312-314, 323-324
optional attributes, 229, 263
Options, 29, 58-60, 62-63, 66-67, 74, 101, 147, 155, 168, 172, 192, 218, 260, 291, 300, 309, 312-315, 319, 323-324, 327-329, 334-335, 341-342, 350-353, 360, 364, 366-371, 374
Options button, 312, 314, 319
Oracle, 9, 17, 20, 37, 68, 227, 233, 273
Oracle Database, 20
Oracle software, 20
Ordered lists, 107-110, 126-127, 135, 137
org, 6, 16, 36-40, 76, 79, 392
organizations
    customer relationships, 35
    knowledge, 3, 6, 15, 17, 28, 31, 35-36, 38, 389
orphaned records, 326
OSI Model, 373, 385-386, 389-390, 395-397
OSs, 367
Outlook, 37
output, 4, 141-143, 155, 157-161, 164-165, 170, 173, 175-176, 181, 185-186, 202-207, 246, 351-352, 355, 364
    characters, 4, 141, 351, 355
    designing, 160, 173
output statement, 157, 160
outsourcing, 7, 34, 37, 40
Overhead, 149, 160, 179, 182
Ownership, 362

P

p tag, 128, 132
packages, 7, 53, 58, 73, 268-269, 346, 354, 389, 391, 395
Packets, 60, 385, 388, 390, 393-394
padding, 81-88, 98, 100-105, 108-110, 112-1
116-117, 122, 124, 127-137
Page Footer, 130
Page Header, 93
page layout, 81
pages, 16, 37, 50, 77, 81-95, 97, 100-105, 108
116-119, 121-122, 124, 128, 130, 132-133, 16(
224, 285, 344, 353-355, 367-369, 377, 379, 381
388, 391-394, 396-397
    headers, 84, 88, 92-95, 97, 101-105, 117, 13(
        354, 393-394
    titles, 37
    URLs, 16, 77, 112
    views, 369, 377
Painting, 154
Panels, 271
panes, 74, 78, 280-281, 287-288, 290-294, 300-301
306, 309-311, 313-314, 319, 321, 324-325, 330, 342
PANs, 375, 396
Paper, 1, 42, 57, 154, 168, 176, 223, 225, 271, 334,
374, 397
Paragraph, 77, 84, 87, 108, 110, 133, 355
    heading, 108
Parameters, 202, 233
Parentheses, 112, 150-151, 153, 157, 177
parts, 2, 6-7, 11-12, 14, 24, 27, 30, 37, 45, 53, 61-62,
74, 121, 141, 144-146, 152, 157, 162-163, 169-172,
175, 178-179, 181, 193, 195-196, 208-209, 211-212,
214, 220, 231, 235-236, 240, 242, 245-247, 266,
270-272, 274-278, 282, 285, 301, 374-375, 377-379,
386
Pascal, 144-145, 179, 188
passing
    addresses, 195, 388
password, 24, 47-49, 51-52, 55-56, 64, 71-72, 79, 358,
365-366
    enable, 56, 365
patches, 57-60, 67-70, 73
patents, 24
path, 18, 112, 137, 187, 209, 214, 274, 285, 309, 348,
367-368, 387-388, 392-394
pathnames, 345, 348, 367-368
Payments, 10-12, 34, 52-53, 55, 69, 155, 269, 275
PayPal, 12
Payroll Report program, 164, 167
PC Magazine, 373
PCs, 21, 23, 59, 373, 378
people, 4, 6-8, 10, 13-14, 16-21, 28-29, 31-32, 35,
56-57, 63-64, 155, 171, 185, 193, 226, 231, 239, 241,
249, 268, 275, 332, 342, 373-375, 381-382, 386, 389,
391, 397
percent sign (%)
    modulus operator, 152
performance
    measures, 33
Period, 4, 32, 37, 46-47, 116, 120-121, 141, 145, 225,
253-254, 272, 276, 350, 383
peripherals, 379-380
Permissions
    folder, 359
    share, 368
Permutations, 260
Personal area network (PAN), 396
personal area networks, 375, 394, 396-397
personal area networks (PANs), 375
personal computers, 44, 74, 376, 378, 393
personal data, 375
Personal information, 50-51, 72
Phone field, 315, 318
phone numbers, 128, 229-231, 265-266, 269
phones, 11, 22, 24, 101-102, 128, 130, 185, 229-231,
265-266, 268-269, 282, 312, 315, 318, 322, 333, 335,
337, 373-376, 378, 380-382, 385, 394-396
photo, 22, 54, 65, 385
Photographs, 63
Photography, 385
Physical layer, 388-391, 394-396
picture, 154, 164-166, 168, 174, 209, 358, 373,
375-376, 381
    compression, 376
    digital, 373, 376
piracy, 6, 13, 21, 27-28, 37-38
pirated software, 24
Pixel, 82-83, 154
pixels (px), 82

376, 387,

3,   267, 269, 349, 352,
                                     75

          114,
          195,
          385,   6, 60-61, 82, 112, 141, 147,
                   80, 197, 199-200, 207-208,
                   239, 243, 249-250, 260, 285,
                   301-302, 307, 315, 318, 346,
                   376, 378, 380, 385, 387-390,

             303, 306, 328

          4, 368
          21, 23-29, 34, 39, 160, 231, 239
          9, 34, 231

          2, 52
          g, 68
          drives, 57

          22, 68
       operty, 92
     g, 81, 92-95, 98-100, 102-103, 105, 119, 374
     g tables, 99
     5, 56
     ence, 150-153, 177, 179-180, 182
     ion, 258
     rsor, 16
    efined formats, 292-293
    sentation layer, 389, 395-396
    esentations, 258, 273, 389, 395-396
    icing policies, 9
    rimary key, 229-231, 235-241, 248-249, 251, 256,
    265, 282, 285, 287, 289-290, 295-296, 301, 304,
    311-312, 319, 329, 333-342
        choosing, 319
Primary Key button, 295
primary key field, 295-296
primary table, 305, 326, 328-330
priming read, 205, 219
print server, 379
print styles, 130
Printer, 61, 379-380
    impact, 61
    laser, 380
printing, 183
Priorities, 27, 258
Privacy, 22, 24-25, 39
privacy policies, 25, 39
Problem solving, 332
problem(s), 269
problems, 7-8, 10, 12, 21, 23, 27, 33-35, 37, 53-54,
57, 153-156, 177, 187, 190, 194-195, 201, 203-207,
217, 225, 232, 242-245, 252, 260-262, 266, 269-271,
278, 286, 330, 332, 334, 336, 339, 341, 346, 392
    identifying, 156
    structured, 190, 194-195, 201, 203-207, 217, 225
    unstructured, 190, 205, 217
procedural programs, 162-163
Procedures, 5-6, 14, 23, 26, 36, 58, 76-77, 153, 162,
177, 180, 182, 250, 274, 276, 310, 377, 386
Process, 1, 6-7, 13-14, 16-17, 20, 22, 24, 29-34, 44,
59, 66, 68, 76, 154, 160, 163-164, 172, 180, 182,
190-192, 196, 198-200, 206, 210-213, 217, 219-220,
222, 224, 227, 248-251, 258, 260, 262-263, 267-268,
286, 308, 332, 378, 385, 389, 391-393
    sequential, 250
process symbols, 200
processing, 6, 11, 16, 33-34, 63, 155, 160, 188, 202,
220, 234, 257-258, 260, 262, 296, 373, 381, 383
processing speed, 257-258
processor, 65, 168, 375, 386
    installing, 65
production, 10, 19, 35, 170, 186, 188, 192, 252
    information systems, 19
    problems, 10, 35, 252
    sequences, 192
production plans, 10
productivity
    actions, 13, 22-23, 52
profiles, 54, 56
Program, 4, 6-7, 15-17, 19-20, 27-28, 35-36, 43-52,

54-55, 57, 60-65, 67-72, 77-78, 140-143, 145-164,
166-178, 180-181, 183, 185-188, 189-190, 192-193,
199-211, 214, 216-221, 225-226, 261, 267, 346,
353-354, 368, 375, 379, 386-387, 391, 397
    antimalware, 48, 51, 57, 62-63, 69-70
    backups, 57, 65, 67-68, 70, 72, 78
    bugs, 187, 225
    comments, 168-171, 173, 177-178, 181, 183, 187,
        225
    crash, 46, 52, 71-72
    documenting, 171, 181
    executable, 44, 48, 77, 353-354, 368
    extensions, 71
    indentation, 188
    input, 141-143, 157-161, 163, 169-171, 173-178,
        181, 185, 189, 201-208, 218-220
    iteration, 219
    maintenance, 148, 187, 208, 225
    modules, 143, 153-157, 159-164, 166-169,
        171-172, 176-178, 180-181, 183,
        185-188, 208-209, 216, 221
    outlines, 19, 27
    requirements, 7, 17, 19, 27, 157, 188, 261, 267,
        368
    selection, 155, 171, 189, 192-193, 199-201, 203,
        208-209, 211, 217-221, 353, 386
    sequence, 52, 62, 162, 189, 192-193, 199-203,
        205-206, 208-209, 211, 214, 216-221
    solution, 78, 205-207, 261
    stored, 43-44, 54, 65, 67-68, 70, 141-142, 146-147,
        149, 151-152, 169, 174, 178, 181, 267,
        368
    structured, 17, 190, 192, 199-211, 214, 217-219,
        221, 225-226
    testing, 17
    writing, 170, 174, 176
program code, 45, 63, 171, 176, 261
Program files, 44, 67
program libraries, 354
program maintenance, 148
programmers, 15, 19-20, 144, 146-147, 152-157, 160,
162, 165-166, 168-174, 177, 180, 182-183, 188, 194,
208-209, 218-219, 221, 273, 353-354, 374
    job, 20, 160, 170-172, 183, 273
programming, 5, 8, 20, 36, 72, 141-150, 152-154,
156-157, 162, 166, 168-174, 176-180, 182-184,
187-188, 191-192, 201, 208, 217-219, 221-222, 226,
336, 374
    bugs, 187
programming language, 5, 141-150, 152-154,
156-157, 162, 169, 171-174, 176-177, 179-180,
182-183, 187-188, 217, 221
    C++, 141, 145, 152, 157, 188
    machine language, 148
    Pascal, 144-145, 179, 188
    syntax, 144-145, 169, 182, 187-188
programming style, 188, 191
Project, 1-3, 5, 8-10, 18, 27, 33-36, 54, 62, 74, 76-79,
176, 208, 266, 271, 371-372, 397
project management, 18, 35
    need for, 35
Project Management Institute, 18, 35
project manager, 2, 8
promote, 3, 27, 218, 392
Prompt, 65, 68, 158, 169-170, 174-176, 178, 181,
184-187, 347-348, 366-367, 387
property, 8, 10-11, 29, 81-85, 87-94, 96, 99, 101-102,
104, 108-110, 112, 117, 119, 122, 124-125, 137, 154,
169, 180, 182, 235-237, 280-281, 284-294, 297-303,
306, 308, 318-322, 332-333, 336-337, 342
    values, 29, 82-85, 87-88, 90, 92-94, 99, 101-102,
        104, 108-110, 112, 122, 124-125, 137,
        182, 235, 280-281, 285-286, 288-293,
        300-303, 306, 308, 319-322, 333, 337,
        342
property controls, 122, 292
Property Update Options button, 319
protecting
    data, 21
    devices, 21, 43
Protocols
    TCP/IP, 373, 377, 380, 385-390, 393, 395-397
Pseudocode, 142-143, 146-147, 157, 159, 163, 166,
169-170, 173-174, 176, 183, 187-188, 193-198,
214-215, 217-218, 222-226
Purchasing, 19, 267-268
Puzzle, 263
px, 82-83, 105, 306-307, 314

Q

Qualifications, 12, 25, 270, 272-273, 275
qualify, 4
Quality, 1-2, 5, 25, 35, 140, 379, 382
quality assurance, 1, 5
quarantine, 75
Query, 231, 234, 252, 260, 312, 314, 326, 329, 332
Quick Access Toolbar, 296, 299, 302, 319-321, 331
Quick Reference, 144, 151, 199-200, 202
Quotas, 30
Quotations, 141, 176, 178, 321, 378

R

radio signals, 373, 389
Radio waves, 375, 387
Random numbers, 157, 188
range, 16, 61, 229, 235, 356, 392
Raw data, 395
RDBMS, 232
Readers, 35, 119, 149, 167, 169, 171
Real number, 141, 178
Receiver, 377, 387-390, 395
Receiving e-mail, 397
recipient, 10-12, 18, 34, 397
Record, 11, 13, 20, 22, 24-25, 37, 51, 56, 79, 155,
163, 260, 269-270, 272-273, 275-276, 285-286, 296,
298, 302, 304, 306-309, 311, 313-314, 322-324,
326-327, 329-330, 334-335, 337-338, 341, 379
    adding, 296, 306, 309, 314, 323
    computer, 22, 24, 51, 79, 379
    defined, 20, 24, 330
recover, 9, 57, 387
Recovery, 11, 67-68, 76
Rectangles, 118, 157, 224, 228-229, 240
recursive relationships, 245-248, 260-261, 263-264
Red Hat, 345
Redundancy, 258, 283
refactoring, 172
reference, 13, 36-37, 79, 82, 144, 148, 151, 169, 181,
199-200, 202, 236, 242, 269, 275, 287, 295, 297, 362,
368
    parameters, 202
Reference points, 82
referential integrity, 239, 248, 327, 329, 331, 342
Referrals, 6
Register, 243
Registry, 171
Regulations, 3-4, 25, 274, 276
related table, 283, 305, 326, 328-329
Relation, 4, 22, 81, 98, 256, 268
relational, 228-229, 232-233, 236, 249, 256, 261-263,
266
relational database, 228-229, 236, 262
relational database model, 228
Relationship diagrams, 227
relationships, 3-5, 7-8, 10, 12-15, 27, 35, 82, 119, 163,
168, 178, 181, 198, 227-228, 231-254, 256, 258-265,
267-268, 272-273, 278, 279, 304-305, 325-332, 342,
389, 396
    complex, 168, 233, 246, 259, 332
    defined, 14, 227, 231, 236-238, 241, 243, 258, 265,
        330-331, 389
relationships between tables, 304, 332
Relationships button, 328
Relationships group, 328, 330-331
Relationships window, 304-305, 328-331, 342
relative paths, 348, 368
relative positioning, 81, 94-95, 100, 102
Remainder, 132, 149, 152, 180, 188, 274
remainder operator, 152, 180, 188
removing, 119-120, 359
renaming fields, 318
renaming files, 361
rendering, 96, 108
Repetition, 194, 219, 250
Replace feature, 172
replacing
    fonts, 137
    text, 137
Replicating, 47
replication, 286
Reporting, 1, 7-8, 25, 32-33, 44, 252, 260
Requirements, 5, 7, 10, 17-19, 25, 27, 34, 157, 188,
228, 234, 239, 241, 252, 257, 259-262, 264, 267,
274-277, 282, 344-345, 368
research papers, 271
Resizing

columns, 310
tables, 310
Resolution, 381
resource, 5-8, 13, 16, 19, 22-24, 27, 31-32, 35, 47, 50, 73-74, 131-132, 160, 179, 346, 375, 396
networks, 5, 16, 22-23, 32, 35, 47, 50, 73, 375, 396
result cells, 120
retrieval, 259-260
return statement, 156-157, 178, 180, 182
RFCs, 392
Ribbon, 287, 289, 300, 308, 312, 314-315, 323, 328
right-aligned, 300
Right-click, 76
Risk, 13-16, 20-21, 23, 30, 40, 65
applications, 15, 21
data, 16, 21, 23, 65
hardware, 13, 23, 65
viruses, 23
robotics, 382
Robots, 55, 224
Root directory, 345, 366-368
rootkit, 48-49, 51, 69-70
round-OFF errors, 285
Router, 18, 68, 376-378, 380, 388, 390, 394, 396-397
routing, 387-388, 392, 397
routing protocol, 397
row selector, 124, 130, 295, 297-298, 317
Rows
table, 107, 116-127, 129-130, 132, 134, 137, 228, 232-233, 241-243, 288, 290, 295, 297-298, 309-310, 315-318, 320, 322, 324
worksheet, 309-310
RPG, 153, 208
RSS, 79
résumés, 12-13, 13, 27-29, 31-32, 38
Ruby, 145
rules
CSS, 16, 27, 82, 84, 86, 90, 92-93, 98-99, 101-105, 108-114, 116-117, 122-124, 127-137
Run, 12, 35, 60-61, 67-69, 78, 154, 175-176, 179-180, 185, 191, 204, 212-216, 252, 266, 269, 344, 375, 377, 381
running
apps, 76
Word, 361

S

safeguard, 13, 26
Salary, 5, 13, 17, 22
sales rep, 166
salespeople, 30, 33, 173
samples, 136, 164, 274, 276, 326, 332, 382
sampling, 378
SANs, 16, 27, 37-38, 136-137
SAP, 17, 32-33, 39
Sarbanes-Oxley Act, 25
SAS, 177
SAT, 42, 129, 293
satellite microwave transmission, 384
satellite transmission, 375
Save As dialog box, 296
Save button, 296, 299, 302, 319-321, 331
saving
selections, 208
scanner, 76
scans, 45, 48, 62, 67-69, 74-78
scenarios, 198, 236, 240, 242-244, 374, 391, 396
scenes, 22, 174
schema, 229, 263
Scope, 10, 15, 61, 162, 180-181, 183
Scratch, 192
screen, 31, 44, 51-52, 63-64, 84-85, 88, 119, 154, 157, 353, 383, 393
screen captures, 51
screen readers, 119
script, 44, 54, 346, 357-358
Scroll bar, 328
Scrolling, 102-103, 310, 324
Search box, 75-76
Search engine, 76-77, 79
searches
binary, 77
searching, 63
section, 4, 14-15, 21, 37, 84, 101, 103-106, 108-114, 116-117, 121-122, 124, 127-133, 135-138, 170, 206, 216, 230, 232-233, 236-241, 243, 245, 252-253, 281, 300, 306, 309-310, 313-315, 329, 354, 357-358, 361-362, 369

sectors, 78, 392, 395
security, 11, 16, 18, 24-25, 35-36, 38, 41-46, 49, 52-55, 57-58, 62-64, 67, 69-70, 72-75, 78-80, 171, 231, 260, 287, 344, 376, 381, 392
firewalls, 18, 24, 57, 62, 69-70, 73, 75
overview, 287, 344, 376
passwords, 24, 49, 52, 55, 64, 72, 79
policy, 11, 24-25, 231
security certifications, 36
security patches, 58, 67, 69
security software, 69
select, 58, 63, 67, 76-79, 84, 101, 124, 127, 129-130, 149, 233, 280-281, 287, 289, 292, 294, 297-298, 301, 313-314, 317-319, 323-324, 328-329, 342, 353
selecting
colors, 146
Selection, 112, 155, 171, 189, 192-201, 203, 208-209, 211-212, 217-221, 252, 315-316, 353, 386
selection structure, 193-194, 196, 203, 209, 211, 217-219, 221
conditions, 193-194, 196, 203, 211, 218-219
dual-alternative, 193, 218-219, 221
single-alternative, 194, 218
selectors, 84, 108-117, 122, 124, 127-133, 135-137, 295, 297-298, 317
Sender, 387-390, 395
sending
e-mail messages, 397
Sentence, 267, 397
sentinel values, 186
sentinels, 157, 186-187, 204
Sequence, 52, 62, 73, 162, 189, 192-203, 205-206, 208-209, 211-212, 214-221, 296, 388
sequential numbering, 285
series, 44, 153, 173, 192, 200, 218, 231, 389, 395
complex, 44
data, 44, 153, 231, 389, 395
Serif, 136-137
Server, 35, 54, 56, 60, 67, 233, 273, 344, 346, 367, 376-377, 379, 388, 393-396
file, 54, 56, 67, 344, 346, 367, 376, 388, 395
mail, 379, 388, 396
Web, 56, 60, 273, 376-377, 379, 388, 393-394, 396
Service packs, 58, 70, 73
service providers, 10, 16, 377, 380
services, 3, 7-11, 13, 16, 19, 23, 25, 29-34, 37, 55-56, 58, 66-70, 72-73, 77, 79, 155, 186, 269-272, 274, 346, 373, 377-381, 384-386, 388-390, 392-395, 397
restore, 67, 70
Windows, 58, 67, 70, 77
session layer, 389-390, 395-396
Set, 6, 14, 17, 19, 23-24, 27, 29, 33, 44, 48, 53, 55-58, 65, 67-69, 74, 81, 84-87, 89, 98, 101-105, 108, 110, 112, 116, 118, 122, 124, 127-137, 142-144, 146-147, 149-150, 154, 157, 160, 163, 168, 177-178, 181, 206, 212, 216-219, 228-229, 233, 246, 248, 252, 256, 262, 266, 271-272, 275, 284, 286, 289-291, 298-302, 306, 308, 318, 321, 354, 366, 380, 386, 388, 390, 392
settings, 6, 18, 21, 27-28, 43, 46, 49-50, 55, 60-62, 64, 68-69, 74-76, 78, 88, 92, 102-103, 122, 252, 260, 284-286, 289, 300-302, 319, 321, 346, 378, 382
keyboards, 69
projects, 18, 27, 62, 74, 76, 78
tasks, 55, 64, 286, 319
Shading, 161
share, 8, 11, 22, 32, 171, 220, 229, 364, 368, 375, 380, 390
sharing information, 13, 22, 27
Shipping, 67
Short Date format, 293, 300-301
Short Text data type, 287-289, 298
Short Text fields, 288-289, 298, 300, 302, 318
shortcut, 76, 307, 342, 344, 347
Shortcut menu, 76, 342
Show, 11, 34, 45, 52, 62, 64, 74, 84, 88, 90, 92, 94, 96, 108, 110, 112, 114, 116, 118, 120, 122, 124, 143, 163-164, 166-169, 173-175, 188, 193, 195-198, 201, 203, 206, 212, 214, 216, 225, 228, 234, 237, 242, 244, 256, 260, 262, 293, 300, 304, 310, 323-324, 328, 330-331, 347, 350-353, 358-361, 363-364, 376, 379-380, 382, 384, 387, 390-392, 397
Show Table button, 304, 330-331
Show Table dialog box, 304, 328, 330-331
showing, 35, 63, 93, 116, 196-197, 227, 292, 352, 379
Shutter Bar Open/Close button, 287, 300
SI, 149, 153, 156, 166, 168, 177
Sidebar, 84, 88, 137
Siebel, 35
signature, 62-63, 69-70, 73

signature files, 62-63, 69-70, 73
simple attributes, 230-231, 263-264
Simple Mail Transfer Protocol, 388, 396
Simple Mail Transfer Protocol (SMTP), 388, 396
Simple Network Management Protocol, 388, 396
Simple Network Management Protocol (SNMP), 388, 396
single-alternative selection structures, 194
single-valued attributes, 231, 263-264
Siri, 9, 37
sites
described, 378, 397
Size, 1, 78, 82, 108, 110, 112, 114, 116, 119, 124, 132-133, 172, 181, 183, 285-287, 289-290, 298-299, 301-302, 312, 318-319, 333, 335-338, 340, 342, 351-352, 362-364, 375, 386, 394
Size property
forms, 286, 319
Size setting, 286
Skills, 6, 12, 15, 17, 19-21, 29, 35-36, 72, 101-103, 127-130, 169, 178, 236, 344, 349, 367
people, 6, 17, 19-21, 29, 35
potential, 17
specific, 17, 20, 35, 178, 367
skins, 373
sleep, 66
slider, 75
smart phones, 376, 381
smartphone, 21, 103-106, 269
Social networking, 56
social networking services, 56
Social Security numbers, 171, 231
Software, 4, 6-7, 9-10, 13, 15-16, 19-21, 23-25, 27-28, 30, 32, 35, 37-38, 40, 41-43, 45, 48-51, 53, 55, 57-70, 72-74, 76-78, 147, 155, 188, 192, 229, 231, 235, 262, 271, 344-346, 376-377, 379-381, 383, 385-386, 388, 390, 392-395, 397
software development, 15
software engineering, 15-16, 21, 38
software firewalls, 61
Software license, 6
Software piracy, 6, 13, 21, 27-28, 37-38
software pirates, 6
software updates, 57
solutions, 18, 34, 42, 78, 205-207, 232, 252, 260-261
sort, 33, 157, 285, 378
Sound, 33, 57, 260, 262, 374, 382
source, 12-13, 16, 18, 22, 24, 35, 53-54, 56, 61, 155, 272, 342, 353, 386, 397
Spacebar, 120, 306, 355
spacing
line, 129, 173
spaghetti code, 189-192, 218
Spam, 35, 56, 71-72
Spamming, 56
Specifications, 24, 29, 187, 225, 297, 374, 392
Specificity, 122
spectrum, 40
Speed, 11, 17, 35, 66, 78, 233, 252, 257-260, 262, 373, 375, 377-379, 382-383, 385
processor, 375
wireless connection, 375
Spreads, 1, 32, 46-48, 56, 60-61, 69, 173
Spreadsheet, 44, 147, 155, 168, 230, 308-310, 312, 323, 375
Spyware, 35, 50-51, 62-63, 69-70, 72, 79
SQL, 227, 233, 235, 273
SQL Server, 233, 273
Square, 110, 173, 224
Stack, 96, 102, 136, 160, 180, 197, 202, 220
staffing, 22-23, 34, 391
Standard account, 64
standardization, 392, 395
standards, 11, 13-17, 19-21, 24, 27-29, 43, 56, 64, 100, 112, 117, 144, 149, 157, 170-171, 177, 188, 257-258, 262, 332-334, 343-345, 354, 367-368, 380, 392, 395
stars, 31
StartDate field, 342
State, 3-4, 6-7, 10-11, 14, 18-22, 27, 29, 33-35, 38, 52, 65, 68, 70, 171, 231, 245, 265, 268, 271, 274, 282, 312, 315, 318-319, 321-322, 333, 335, 337, 348, 375, 386
State field, 319, 321-322
statements, 9, 24-26, 30, 72, 100, 126, 142-143, 146-151, 153-157, 159-160, 163, 165, 169-170, 172-174, 176-180, 182-184, 188, 190, 192-194, 196-197, 201, 203, 205-209, 212, 217-221, 235, 243, 389

assignment, 146-151, 172, 179, 182, 184, 243
   block, 190, 193, 196, 219, 221
   decision, 24, 26, 30, 193-194, 196, 218-221, 236
   execution, 148, 173-174, 194, 203
   functions, 153, 155, 157, 177, 180, 243, 389
   null, 182, 194, 218, 236
   output, 142-143, 155, 157, 159-160, 165, 170, 173, 176, 203, 205-207
   priming read, 205, 219
station, 271, 390
Status bar, 281, 289, 301, 319
steering committees, 15
Stock, 11, 71, 266, 270
Storage, 51, 66, 234, 255, 286, 376, 383
storage capacity, 51
storing, 234, 252, 285, 375, 381
Strategies, 8, 68, 80
streaming
   video, 375
streaming video, 375
String, 62-63, 73, 141-144, 147-149, 158-159, 161-162, 165, 170, 172, 174-179, 182, 184, 219, 224, 231, 350, 355
   comparing, 63
   input, 141-144, 158-159, 161, 165, 170, 174-178, 184, 219
   length, 144
   output, 141-143, 158-159, 161, 165, 170, 175-176, 355
   processing, 63
string constants, 141, 178, 182
string variables, 147, 149, 172, 179, 182, 184
Structure, 55, 60, 107, 124, 130, 162, 166, 178, 183, 189, 192-203, 208-213, 215, 217-222, 226, 229-230, 232, 248, 258-259, 262, 280, 296-299, 311-314, 316-317, 323, 332, 343-349, 355, 357, 362, 367-368
   contents, 107, 124, 130, 230, 349, 357, 367
   data types, 178, 280, 297-298, 312, 314, 316, 332
   forms, 183, 208, 211, 230, 312, 314, 332
   global, 162, 178, 183
   local, 60, 162, 178, 346, 368
   ordered lists, 107
   pointers, 297
   single, 194, 196, 200-201, 208, 211, 218-220, 229, 232, 346
   usage, 211
   variables, 162, 178, 183, 345-346, 368
structure charts, 166
Structure statement, 193-194, 218
structured programming, 201, 208, 219, 226
structured programs, 190, 199-200, 206, 208-209, 218, 221
Student class, 249-250, 254-256
Style, 39, 82, 84-88, 90, 92-99, 101-106, 108-114, 116-117, 119, 122-124, 127-138, 145, 157, 179, 188, 191
style sheets, 84-87, 90, 92-93, 95-96, 108, 110, 124, 130, 138
Subdirectories, 345-346, 348-351, 357-359, 367, 369
subprocedures, 153
Subroutines, 153, 177, 180
subtotal, 259
suite, 373, 385-390, 392-393, 395-397
   described, 388, 397
sum variable, 149
summaries
   descriptions, 238, 272
summarizing
   data, 397
Sun, 36, 116, 121, 129, 293
Sun Microsystems, 36
suppliers, 4-5, 10-11, 13, 24, 27, 267, 333-334
Supply chain, 10
support
   activities, 14
Surveillance, 24
Surveys, 12, 22
switch, 2, 18, 64, 68, 137, 301, 347, 356, 359, 365-366, 371, 376-378, 381, 396
Symantec, 6, 52-53
Symantec Security Response, 53
synchronization, 390, 396
synchronization points, 390, 396
synonym, 182, 260
Syntax, 112, 137, 144-145, 169, 182, 187-188, 208, 225, 321, 350, 361
SysAdmin, Audit, Network, Security (SANS) Institute, 16, 38
system administrators, 346, 358, 371

System Monitor, 14
system requirements, 10
System software, 49, 69
Systems, 1, 4, 6, 8-11, 14-15, 19-23, 25-26, 28-29, 33-36, 43-44, 46-50, 52, 54-55, 57-58, 60, 64-70, 74-76, 78, 155, 168, 188, 244, 251, 262, 265-266, 268-271, 273, 343-347, 350, 353-354, 357-358, 368, 371, 373-376, 379, 381-386, 388-389, 392, 394-397
systems analysis, 262
systems analyst, 4, 14, 20, 273
systems integration, 35

T

tab, 75, 77, 280, 287-288, 290-303, 306-308, 312-317, 319-323, 328, 330-331, 348-349, 367
Tab key, 287-288, 290-294, 298, 301-302, 306-307, 319, 321, 348, 367
Table, 11-13, 16, 18, 23-25, 30, 48, 50, 56, 61, 79, 82-87, 90, 92-94, 98-99, 107-110, 116-134, 136-138, 150-151, 228-230, 232-237, 239-244, 246, 249-250, 252, 254, 256, 259-261, 267, 273, 276-277, 279-283, 285-291, 295-338, 340-342, 345-346, 351-356, 362-363, 368, 371
   building, 250, 256, 279
   check boxes, 300, 302, 306-307, 310, 329, 331
   creating, 23, 110, 119, 131, 133, 232, 254, 267, 279, 287, 311, 330, 332, 351-352, 362-363, 371
   formatting, 120, 130, 300
   linking, 309
Table button, 304, 330-331
table cell, 117, 121-122, 132
   closing, 122, 132
table data, 129, 134, 137
Table Datasheet View, 300, 303, 305-306, 310, 313, 316, 320, 322, 324, 342
Table Design button, 287
Table design grid, 280, 288, 290
Table Design View, 287, 295, 317, 321, 342
Table dialog box, 304, 328, 330-331
table headers, 117, 129-130, 134, 137-138
table layout, 308
Table objects, 313
table relationships, 279, 305, 325, 328, 330, 342
   one-to-many, 305, 328, 342
table row, 116, 118, 129, 132, 228, 233, 242
table tag, 116, 122, 130
TABLE TOOLS DESIGN tab, 295, 297-298, 303, 317, 320
table views, 310
   rows, 310
Table window, 280-281, 287-288, 291, 297
Tables group, 287
tablet, 21, 42-43, 269, 376, 380
tablet devices, 42
tags, 88, 103, 108, 110, 112, 114, 116, 118, 120, 122, 124, 127-130, 132
tape drives, 386
Target, 39, 364
Task
   assigning, 155, 178-179
   creating, 55, 70, 160, 162, 166, 168, 254, 357, 365
   managing, 357
   Object, 168, 286
   options, 155, 168, 192, 218, 319
   printing, 183
   removing, 359
TCP, 373, 377, 380, 385-390, 392-397
TCP headers, 394
TCP/IP, 373, 377, 380, 385-390, 393, 395-397
TCP/IP (Transmission Control Protocol/Internet Protocol), 377
Technical support, 9
Technology, 5, 12, 15-18, 24-25, 35, 38-40, 42-43, 50, 267, 374, 377, 382, 384-385, 392, 395
Telecommunications, 1, 392, 396
Telephone, 22, 52, 268, 270, 374-377, 379, 382, 384-385, 392, 394, 396
telephone numbers, 22, 268, 270
Television, 225, 374-375, 384, 394, 397
Telnet, 383, 388, 396
template, 358
   class, 358
   document, 358
Terminal, 344, 347, 349, 352-353, 355, 357, 360-362, 364-366, 383-384, 395
Test, 5, 18, 26, 28, 36, 61, 68, 76, 78, 93, 95, 97, 149-150, 156, 169, 194, 196, 202-203, 207, 211, 217-219, 224, 270, 276-277, 332, 386, 392

Test scores, 149-150
Testing, 5, 17, 276, 332
text, 51, 70, 84, 88, 92-93, 96, 98-101, 105, 112, 116, 119-122, 124, 127-137, 141, 147, 156-157, 172, 176, 179, 235, 254, 280, 285, 287-290, 298, 300, 302-303, 312, 318-321, 323-325, 330, 333, 335-338, 340, 342, 355, 373, 381-382, 384
   importing, 312, 323-325
   inserting, 172, 298
   overview, 280, 287
   setting properties, 302
Text box, 157, 254
   Word, 157
text data, 287-289, 298
Text data type, 287-289, 298
text editors, 92, 172
Text Fields, 288-289, 298, 300, 302, 318, 324
   properties, 288-289, 298, 300, 302, 318
text files, 323-325, 342
text flow, 92
text messages, 373, 381-382
text placeholders, 98
Theft, 35, 37, 50, 66
thin client workstations, 383
thin clients, 383
Thread, 262
threat, 35, 43, 79
three class, 242
time, 1-7, 10, 13, 22, 24, 30-32, 34-37, 43, 46-47, 51, 55-56, 59, 62-63, 67, 79-80, 134, 142-144, 149, 152-153, 155, 160, 164, 170, 172, 174, 177-178, 183, 187, 190, 192, 202-203, 207-208, 217, 220-221, 230, 233-235, 237-238, 240-241, 250, 252, 254, 256, 258, 260, 262, 266, 268-270, 272-276, 285, 287, 290, 292-293, 298, 300-302, 310, 315, 317-319, 333, 335-338, 340, 342, 344-346, 349, 352, 355, 357-358, 360-361, 364, 366, 371, 374, 376, 379, 381, 383, 385
   forms, 31-32, 172, 177, 183, 208, 230, 272, 319, 374, 376, 379
time(s), 275
timestamps, 352, 358, 360, 367
Title field, 317
token management, 390, 396
tokens, 11, 390, 396
Toolbar, 296, 299, 302, 319-321, 331
tools, 1, 8, 43, 48, 50, 58, 63, 69, 79, 84-86, 89, 118, 168, 170, 228, 235, 295, 297-298, 300-301, 303, 315-317, 320, 328, 330-331, 345, 379
   automatic, 50, 58, 69
   manual, 1
   systems, 1, 8, 43, 48, 50, 58, 69, 168, 345, 379
Tools group, 295, 297-298, 317
Tornado, 66
totals, 16, 23, 32, 77, 83, 121, 158-159, 161, 163, 173, 186, 233, 259, 268, 273, 285, 311, 324, 350-351, 356, 358-360, 362, 364
Touch screens, 52
Tracking, 50, 52, 246, 268, 271
tracks, 25, 50, 52, 160, 180, 234, 246, 262, 265, 267-268, 272-273, 310, 374
trade secrets, 6-7, 24, 27-28, 37
Trademarks, 24, 53
Traffic, 60-61, 69, 193, 374, 377, 381-382, 394
training, 4, 13, 15-17, 24-25, 27-28, 35, 38, 266-267, 273, 275-277
   general, 4, 17, 25, 27, 273
Translator, 144
Transport layer, 387-388, 390, 393, 395-397
Trends, 18, 60
trigonometric functions, 157
Trojan horses
   functions, 70
Trojan programs, 48
Troubleshooting, 18, 345
   networks, 18
true or false, 29, 172, 368-369
Trust, 8, 14, 27, 38, 49
Tweets, 283
Twitter, 56
type, 4-5, 10, 17-18, 24, 36, 41-45, 47-48, 50-52, 54-57, 60-64, 66, 68-71, 73, 77, 84, 86, 108-112, 114, 116, 118, 120, 122, 124, 127, 132-133, 135, 137, 141-145, 147-149, 152, 168-170, 172, 177-179, 181, 188, 194, 200, 203, 207, 217, 228, 231-232, 239, 243-245, 267-273, 275-276, 280, 284-294, 296-298, 300-302, 306-307, 312-316, 318-321, 329, 332-333, 335-338, 340, 342, 348-353, 360, 362, 364-366, 368-369, 377-383, 385-386, 390-391, 395, 397
type names, 144, 287, 298

U

UML, 228, 236, 256, 258-259, 262, 267
UML class diagrams, 228, 256, 258-259, 262, 267
Unary
    notation, 262
underlined, 229-230
Unified Modeling Language, 168, 228, 262
Unified Modeling Language (UML), 228, 262
Union, 1
unique fields, 285
unique identifier, 286
United Airlines, 25
units, 12, 60, 63, 81-84, 101, 103-106, 107-108, 127, 131, 133, 135-136, 138, 153, 155, 162, 177, 180, 192, 196, 218-219, 221, 233, 333-334, 377, 389, 395
UNIX, 345, 354, 368
unnamed constants, 141, 146, 148, 177-179
Unordered lists, 107, 110-112, 114, 126-128, 132-138
updates
    software, 57-60, 63, 66-67, 69-70, 73-74
    Windows, 58-60, 67, 70, 74, 329, 331, 342, 359-360
Updates, Windows, 58
Uppercase, 144-145, 148, 172, 179, 347, 369, 379
UPS, 5-6, 11, 17, 24-25, 34, 42, 44, 51-52, 56-59, 62, 65-69, 71, 73, 78, 82-84, 86, 88, 90-94, 96-99, 114, 132-133, 154, 163, 188, 193, 200, 211, 224, 226, 235, 249-250, 253-254, 262, 265-268, 270-271, 279, 281-291, 294-303, 306-308, 310-316, 318-327, 330, 332-341, 346, 375, 379-380, 390-391, 394
URL, 16, 76-78, 112, 137
USB, 43, 47, 51, 66-68, 72, 76, 78
USB flash drive, 43, 47, 67, 76
USB ports, 51, 66, 72
User, 1, 4-7, 9, 13, 16-17, 21-24, 26-28, 42-44, 46-55, 57-61, 63-73, 75, 78-79, 92, 96, 100, 108, 119, 122, 155, 157, 160, 162, 164, 168-169, 174-177, 181, 183-188, 204, 207, 228, 231, 233, 251, 260-262, 286, 290, 344-352, 355-369, 371, 374-377, 379-380, 382-383, 385-395
User Account Control (UAC), 63-64, 70
User accounts, 57, 63-64, 70, 75, 344, 359, 365-366
User Datagram Protocol, 388
User Datagram Protocol (UDP), 388
user documentation, 183
user ID, 24
User interface, 6, 57
User mode, 346
usernames, 56, 365
Users group, 365

V

Validation, 155
value box, 292, 321
value element, 83, 87
value variable, 179
Values, 6-7, 14, 17-18, 27, 29, 31-32, 82-88, 90, 92-94, 97-99, 101-105, 108-110, 112, 114, 121-122, 124-125, 127, 130-134, 137, 141-144, 146-150, 152, 155, 157, 160, 171, 173, 177-179, 181-182, 185-188, 202-207, 218, 229, 231-235, 248, 260, 268, 280-281, 285-286, 288-293, 296, 300-303, 306-308, 311, 319-322, 324, 329-330, 333, 337-338, 340, 342
Vandalism, 43
VANs, 135, 267
Variable
    addresses, 144, 146-147, 149-150, 157, 160, 179-180
    alias, 171
    assigning value, 146-147, 179
    Boolean, 172
    data types, 141-145, 147-149, 152, 172, 177-179, 181, 188
    declaring, 140-141, 143, 148-149, 160, 174
    functions, 153, 157, 177, 180
    globals, 162, 178, 180, 183, 185-186
    initialization, 143, 177
    integers, 141, 152, 178, 180, 188
    naming, 144-145, 156, 171-172, 177, 179, 183
    scope, 162, 180-181, 183
    start, 142-145, 156-157, 162, 169-171, 174, 176, 179-180, 346, 366
    value, 141-144, 146-150, 152, 157, 160, 171, 173, 177-179, 181-182, 185-186, 188
variable data, 346
variable declarations, 143, 177
variants, 82

vectors, 43
vendors, 8-10, 17-18, 25, 35-36, 43, 58, 60, 62-63, 67, 69-70, 77-78, 229, 236, 242, 267, 333
verbs, 157, 171-172, 177, 234, 250
vertical scroll bar, 328
Video, 22, 24, 141, 148, 152-153, 160, 201, 217, 358, 374-375, 381, 384, 394
    low-resolution, 381
Video conferencing, 384
View button, 301, 303, 316, 320-321
viewing, 22, 349, 352, 386
Views group, 301, 303, 316, 320-321
virtual environment, 63
virtual keyboard, 52
virtual machine, 349, 352-353, 355, 357, 360-362, 364-366
Virus, 22-23, 35, 42, 44-48, 51, 62-63, 68-71, 73, 76-77, 79
virus signature, 62-63, 69
visibility, 122
Visual Basic, 141, 145, 152-153, 188, 273
VMware, 349, 352, 355, 357, 360, 362, 364, 366
Voice over Internet Protocol (VoIP), 385
voltage, 389
Volumes
    creating, 267
Vulnerability, 16, 47-49, 58, 68-69, 73

W

WANs, 375-377, 394, 396
warehouses, 266
Watson, 373
Watson, Thomas, 373
Wave, 31, 375, 387
weak, 33, 236-242, 254, 263-265, 374
Web, 6, 8, 15, 21-24, 30, 38, 50-52, 55-56, 60, 76-78, 81-84, 93, 101, 104, 108-111, 113-114, 117, 119, 121-122, 124, 128, 130, 188, 273, 375-377, 379, 381, 383, 388, 391-394, 396-397
Web addresses, 76-77
Web browser, 50, 52, 55, 60, 76-78, 82, 128, 383, 388, 391
Web Page command, 393-394, 397
Web server, 56, 377, 379, 393-394
Web sites, 6, 8, 15, 21-23, 30, 375-376
    overview, 376
Website, 50, 52, 56, 65, 68, 81, 92, 103-105, 107, 131, 133, 135-136
weight, 38, 112, 124, 185, 266, 268, 275-276, 278, 334
    described, 112
while loop, 194, 197, 203, 217, 219
Whistleblowers, 7, 11, 39
whistleblowing, 7
Whole numbers, 141, 152, 178, 286
Wide area network (WAN), 396
wide area networks (WANs), 375
Width property, 82-83
Wi-Fi, 17, 59, 61, 380-381
Wi-Fi networks, 59
WikiLeaks, 22, 39
wildcards, 344, 355-358, 360, 367-368
Window
    defined, 330-331, 345
    open, 52, 75-78, 84, 92, 104-105, 280, 287, 304, 328-331, 342, 344, 347, 349, 352-353, 355, 357, 359-362, 364-366
Windows 7, 59
Windows 8, 60
Windows Defender, 74-75
Windows Firewall, 75
Windows, Microsoft, 44, 59, 64, 67, 70, 74
Windows Search, 76
Windows Server, 35
wireless, 68, 375-376, 380, 382, 384-385, 389, 394-396
wireless access point, 380
wireless communications, 380
wireless routers, 68, 380
wiretapping, 24
Wizards, 309-310, 323-324, 342
Word, 4, 23, 31, 44, 65, 77, 128, 144-148, 150, 155, 157, 160, 162-163, 168-169, 171-172, 177-179, 183, 196, 203, 224, 228-229, 238, 241, 250, 273, 290, 298, 318, 360-361, 375, 378, 386, 388
    formats, 229
    starting, 65, 145, 203, 273
    tables, 23, 128, 150, 228-229, 241, 250, 273, 290, 298, 318

Word processors, 65, 168, 375, 386
workbook, 309
Workers, 1, 3-8, 10, 12-17, 19-20, 22, 24, 27-28, 30, 32, 34-36, 38, 79, 272, 387
Worksheet, 44, 308-311
    functions, 44
    window, 44
Workstation, 376-379, 383-384, 388, 394, 396
World Wide Web, 388
worm, 44, 47-48, 62, 68, 70-71, 79
wrap, 225
writing
    programs, 170, 174, 176
WWW, 6, 13, 16, 35-40, 76-80, 228, 231, 236, 263, 345, 392

X

xlsx, 44, 333, 336, 339

Y

Yahoo!, 12
Yes button, 302, 308, 342
Yes/No data type, 294
Yes/No fields, 300, 302, 306

Z

zip codes, 147, 231, 265
ZIP field, 319
zombie, 55-56, 69-70, 72
zombie computers, 55, 69
Zuckerberg, Mark, 8